The Journey Ahead

Scan the QR code to see all the titles in this series.

EUROPE AND CENTRAL ASIA STUDIES

The Journey Ahead

Supporting Successful Migration in Europe and Central Asia

Laurent Bossavie
Daniel Garrote Sánchez
Mattia Makovec

WORLD BANK GROUP

ISBN (paper): 978-1-4648-2143-1
ISBN (electronic): 978-1-4648-2144-8
DOI: 10.1596/978-1-4648-2143-1

Cover, central illustration of people: Generated by Adobe Firefly, July 10, 2024, from the prompt "A diverse crowd of people walking in fast blurry motion and in different directions in a European city. Large buildings and trees on each side." Subsequent modifications made using traditional design tools.
Cover, village illustration: © DavorLovincic / iStock; modified using traditional design tools. *Compass:* © Oksana Kalashnykova / iStock. Also used on interior pages. *Additional graphic elements:* © iStock. All iStock images used with permission; further permission required for reuse.

Cover design: Jihane El Khoury Roederer / World Bank Creative Services, Global Corporate Solutions.

Library of Congress Control Number: 2024942699

Europe and Central Asia Studies

The Europe and Central Asia Studies series features analytical reports on main challenges and opportunities faced by countries in the region, with the aim to inform a broad policy debate. Titles in this series undergo extensive internal and external review prior to publication.

Previous Books in This Series

2018

Toward a New Social Contract: Taking on Distributional Tensions in Europe and Central Asia (2018), Maurizio Bussolo, Vito Peragine, Ramya Sundaram

Critical Connections: Promoting Economic Growth and Resilience in Europe and Central Asia (2018), David Michael Gould

2017

Reaping Digital Dividends: Leveraging the Internet for Development in Europe and Central Asia (2017), Tim Kelly, Shawn W. Tan, Hernan Winkler

Risks and Returns: Managing Financial Trade-Offs for Inclusive Growth in Europe and Central Asia (2017), David Michael Gould, Martin Melecky

2015

Golden Aging: Prospects for Healthy, Active, and Prosperous Aging in Europe and Central Asia (2015), Maurizio Bussolo, Johannes Koettl

2014

Shared Prosperity : Paving the Way in Europe and Central Asia (2014), Maurizio Bussolo, Luis F. Lopez-Calva

All books in the Europe and Central Asia Studies Series are available free at https://hdl.handle.net/10986/2155.

Contents

Boxes

Figures

Maps

Tables

Foreword

Migration has long been a feature of Europe and Central Asia (ECA). Now home to over 100 million immigrants, the region accounts for one-third of the world's migrant population. Intentions to emigrate are also high, with one in five adults in ECA currently wanting to leave their home permanently.

Driven by income gaps, demographic shifts, climate change, and conflict, migration is set to increase globally, including across ECA countries. As it does, long-term, coordinated, and evidence-based policies will be required to promote safe and orderly cross-border movements that help maximize the shared gains of migration for everyone—from building trade and investment links to boosting productivity, building and transferring skills, and reducing poverty.[1]

If managed well, migration can be a powerful force in addressing growing demographic and socioeconomic imbalances in the ECA region. Economic migrants—both low and high skilled—and refugees can help alleviate labor shortages in Western Europe, for example, where the working-age population is projected to decline by 14 percent between 2020 and 2050. Moreover, in countries of origin with bulging youth populations, migration offers employment opportunities that can ease the strain of limited domestic job creation.

For migrants, the wage gap between advanced and developing economies can be life changing. Despite the hardships of leaving family, familiarity, and social networks behind, migrants can make at least twice the salary they earned in their home country by moving abroad—income gains unmatched by any policy intervention.

Yet migration's full economic potential remains untapped. This World Bank Group report, *The Journey Ahead: Supporting Successful Migration in Europe and Central Asia*, identifies multiple challenges keeping migration from achieving its full potential and offers ways to address them.

---

[1] World Bank. 2023. *World Development Report 2023: Migrants, Refugees, and Societies*. Washington, DC: World Bank. doi:10.1596/978-1-4648-1941-4.

In destination countries, for example, including in Western Europe, integrating economic migrants and refugee populations remains a challenge, evidenced by persistent employment gaps between native-born and migrant populations. Immigration also has uneven distributional impacts among the native-born population, benefiting some groups while negatively impacting others. Early skill and language training for refugees and economic migrants can support their long-term integration, while active labor market policies and social protection programs may help prevent or mitigate adverse impacts on native-born workers.

Meanwhile, some origin countries—including in the Western Balkans and Eastern Europe—risk labor and skill shortages associated with the departure of part of their workforce. "Brain drain" challenges can be turned into "brain gain" opportunities by leveraging skill circulation and accumulation. One way to do that is through skills monitoring systems to anticipate labor shortages and respond to increased worker demands, together with education cost-sharing mechanisms between destination and origin countries, such as Global Skills Partnerships.

Finally, migrants themselves can face several barriers, inefficiencies, and vulnerabilities throughout their migration journey. Before departing, migrants often lack accurate information about employment abroad, are typically ill-prepared for work in receiving countries, and frequently experience occupational downgrade at destination. In addition, they are highly exposed to negative economic shocks while abroad and often lack protection to cope with those shocks. Strengthening formal migration systems in origin countries, establishing social protection systems for migrants, and implementing mechanisms for the recognition of foreign educational credentials all can support a more productive and resilient migration experience.

By identifying challenges and opportunities associated with migration in ECA, this work aims to inform a more tailored, evidence-based debate on the costs and benefits of cross-border mobility throughout the region. Crucially, the authors argue that the effects of migration are largely shaped by policies in place in both origin and destination countries. As such, policy reforms can greatly enhance the benefits of migration and help effectively manage the economic, social, and political costs. Coordination between countries will be key.

Drawing knowledge from the World Bank Group's extensive data- and policy-oriented activities around the world, this report offers a range of policy options to unlock the economic potential of migration for the benefit of all actors, including migrants, origin, and destination countries.

The report's recommendations have been tailored both to the type of migration considered—forced displacement, high-skilled and low-skilled economic migration—and the perspective of either sending or receiving countries. It is offered as a comprehensive resource for governments, development partners, and other stakeholders throughout Europe and Central Asia, where the richness and diversity of migration experiences offer valuable insights for policy makers in other regions in the world.

Antonella Bassani
Regional Vice President
Europe and Central Asia Region
World Bank

Acknowledgments

This regional flagship report has been prepared by a World Bank team under the guidance and supervision of Cem Mete (former Practice Manager, Social Protection and Jobs, Europe and Central Asia), Fadia Saadah (former Regional Director, Human Development, Europe and Central Asia), and Michal Rutkowski (former Global Director of Social Protection and Jobs) and has been finalized under the guidance and supervision of Paolo Belli (Practice Manager, Social Protection and Jobs, Europe and Central Asia) and Michal Rutkowski (Regional Director, Human Development, Europe and Central Asia). The team would like to acknowledge guidance, support, and comments provided at different stages by Aslı Demirgüç-Kunt (former Chief Economist of the Europe and Central Asia Region), Ivailo Izvorski (Chief Economist of the Europe and Central Asia Region), Carolina Sánchez-Páramo (Director for Strategy and Operations of the Europe and Central Asia region), and Iffath Sharif (Global Director of Social Protection and Jobs).

The report has been authored by a core team including Mattia Makovec (task team leader), Laurent Bossavie (co-task team leader), and Daniel Garrote Sánchez. The authors acknowledge inputs, comments, and contributions provided at different stages of the report preparation and finalization by Siddharth Hari, Maddalena Honorati, Mirey Ovadiya, Çağlar Özden, and Mauro Testaverde. The final version of the report benefited from suggestions and comments by Indhira Santos and guidance by Dhushyanth Raju. The authors wish to thank Stefanie Brodmann for her support for the dissemination phase. The authors acknowledge comments provided to earlier versions of the report by the following peer reviewers: Pablo Acosta, Syud Amer Ahmed, Manjula Luthria, Dilip Ratha, Maheshwor Shrestha, Erwin Tiongson, and Iván Torre.

The report benefited from background papers and notes prepared for different chapters by the following contributors:

- Chapter 1—Samir K.C. (University of Shanghai and International Institute for Applied Systems Analysis [IIASA], Vienna) and Nicholas Gailey (IIASA, Vienna)

- Chapter 2—Olof Åslund (Uppsala University), Francesco Campo (University of Padova), Sara Giunti (University of Milan), Linus Liljeberg (Institute for Evaluation of Labour Market and Education Policy [IFAU]), Mariapia Mendola (University of Milan–Bicocca), Jacquelyn Pavilon (Center for Migration Studies, New York), and Sara Roman (IFAU)

- Chapter 3—Michele Battisti (University of Glasgow), Andrea Bernini (University of Oxford), Francesco Bloise (University La Sapienza, Rome), Pietro Campa (University of Geneva), Giacomo De Giorgi (University of Geneva), Tommaso Frattini (University of Milan), Thomas Gautier (Kiel Institute for the World Economy), Isa Kuosmanen (formerly at the VATT Institute for Economic Research, Helsinki), Greta Morando (University of Sheffield), Costanza Naguib (University of Berne), Michele Pellizzari (University of Geneva), Hana Pesola (VATT Institute for Economic Research, Helsinki), Panu Poutvaara (University of Munich), Michele Prado (University of Copenhagen), Battista Severgnini (University of Copenhagen), and Irene Solmone (Bocconi University, Milan). The authors wish to thank Alicia Adsera (Princeton University), Tito Boeri (Bocconi University, Milan), Michael Landesmann (WIIW, Vienna), and Paolo Naticchioni (University La Sapienza, Rome) for comments and discussions at the inception phase of the report.

Specific chapters of the report also benefited from contributions by Marie Renée Andreescu, Andrea Cinque, Evelina Dahlgren, Erkan Duman, Michael Green, Florentin Kerschbaumer, Julia Kornelia Miskiewicz, Andrea Petrelli, Kirsten Schuettler, Ivan Tzintzun, and Ling Zu. Carson Rayhill provided support to the finalization of the full report. The authors also wish to thank the following World Bank colleagues for their comments, for their support during the preparation phase of the report, and for their help with the dissemination phase: Anna Akhalkatsi, Loli Arribas-Banos, Aaron Buchsbaum, Rafael De Hoyos, Sandor Karacsony, Alessandra Marini, Gonzalo Reyes Hartley, Jamele Rigolini, Manuel Salazar, Achim Schmillen, William Seitz, Ekaterina Ushakova, Paolo Verme, and Mitchell Wiener, among others. The authors additionally thank all the participants to the kick-off workshop in Vienna for their helpful contributions and suggestions, as well as participants and organizers of a seminar at the Italian Ministry of Finance in Rome.

The communication and engagement strategy was led by a team comprising Nicole Frost, Christine Lynch, and Ivelina Taushanova. Special thanks are extended to Caroline Polk, who coordinated and oversaw formal production of the report, and to the World Bank's Formal Publishing Program, including Cindy Fisher, Patricia Katayama, and Devika Seecharran Levy, for their support, professionalism, and patience throughout the publishing process.

The authors wish to thank the ECA Vice Presidency, including Silvia Malgioglio, Emily Rose Adeleke, and Wilza Samakoen, for the support and the coordination in the preparation of the report launch and of the subsequent phases of dissemination. The report benefited from several rounds of editing by Karen Brandon and Lauri Scherer. The executive summary and main messages benefited from editing by Paul McClure. Last, but certainly not least, the authors would like to thank Bernadine G. D'Souza, Mohammad Javed Karimullah, Agnes Nderakindo Mganga, Eva K. Ngegba, Helena Nejedla, Loan Thi Phuong Nguyen , and Ngoc-Dung Thi Tran for administrative support throughout the stages of the report preparation and dissemination.

About the Authors

Laurent Bossavie is a senior economist in the Social Protection and Jobs Global Practice, Europe and Central Asia unit, at the World Bank. His main areas of expertise are labor economics and the economics of migration. His work explores the role of labor and migration policies in shaping the labor market outcomes of workers in both high-income and developing countries. He has edited four books, and his research on these topics has been published in leading academic journals such as the *Journal of Human Resources* and the *Journal of Development Economics*. He holds a doctorate in economics from the European University Institute in Florence, Italy.

Daniel Garrote Sánchez is an economist in the Social Protection and Jobs Global Practice, Europe and Central Asia unit, at the World Bank. His areas of expertise include labor migration and forced displacement, the changing task content of jobs, and the impact of the green transition on the labor market. Prior to joining the World Bank, he worked for the Lebanese Center of Policy Studies, the Ministry of Labor of Saudi Arabia, and the Central Bank of Spain. He holds a master's degree in public administration and international development from the Harvard Kennedy School and a bachelor's degree in economics and law from Carlos III University.

Mattia Makovec is a senior economist in the Social Protection and Jobs Global Practice, Latin America and the Caribbean unit, at the World Bank. He has also been leading operations, analytic activities, and policy dialogue on jobs, social protection, and migration in the Europe and Central Asia region. Previously, he worked at the World Bank Office in Jakarta (Indonesia) and held positions at Essex University, at the University of Chile, and at the Ministry of Labor in Chile. Mattia has a doctorate in economics from Bocconi University in Milan and a master's degree in economics from University College London.

Key Findings and Main Messages

Migration is a powerful force to address socioeconomic and demographic imbalances in Europe and Central Asia (ECA). The region hosts more than 100 million migrants, one-third of the world's migrant population. Projections suggest that the population of ECA will age significantly, while some other world regions will struggle to provide jobs for a growing young population, increasing the need for international mobility (refer to figure MM.1). Economic migrants and refugees can help fill labor shortages, especially in places with a rapidly aging population (in Western Europe, the working-age population is aging and expected to drop 14 percent between 2020 and 2050). In countries of origin with a growing working-age population, migration can provide employment and earnings opportunities to supplement limited creation of domestic employment.

Migration is often the surest path to higher income and better quality of life. The earnings and welfare gains that migrants experience are unmatched by any other policy intervention. By moving abroad, many can earn at least twice the salary they earned in their country of origin. The annual gains from a best-practice poverty program are only about 2.5 percent of the wage gains that low-skilled workers see when they move from a low- or middle-income country to one of the most advanced economies. And remittances extend the gains to their home countries. This means migration is a key contributor to poverty reduction for households in low- and middle-income countries in the ECA region.

But migration has yet to realize its full economic potential. In ECA, inefficiencies and vulnerabilities prevent migrants and countries from benefiting fully. For example, low-skilled migrants are often ill prepared for work abroad and may lack skills needed in destination countries. There is also scope to distribute the costs and benefits of migration more equally. For example, home countries often bear the cost of educating their high-skilled migrants without reaping the benefits of their mobility. In destination countries, a large inflow of foreign workers may be challenging to integrate into the local society.

FIGURE MM.1

Demographic trends

a. All world regions

Legend: ECA, EAP, LAC, MENA, NA, SAR, SSA

b. Subregions within ECA

Legend: Western Europe, EU-NMS13, Western Balkans, Eastern Europe, Türkiye and Caucasus, Central Asia

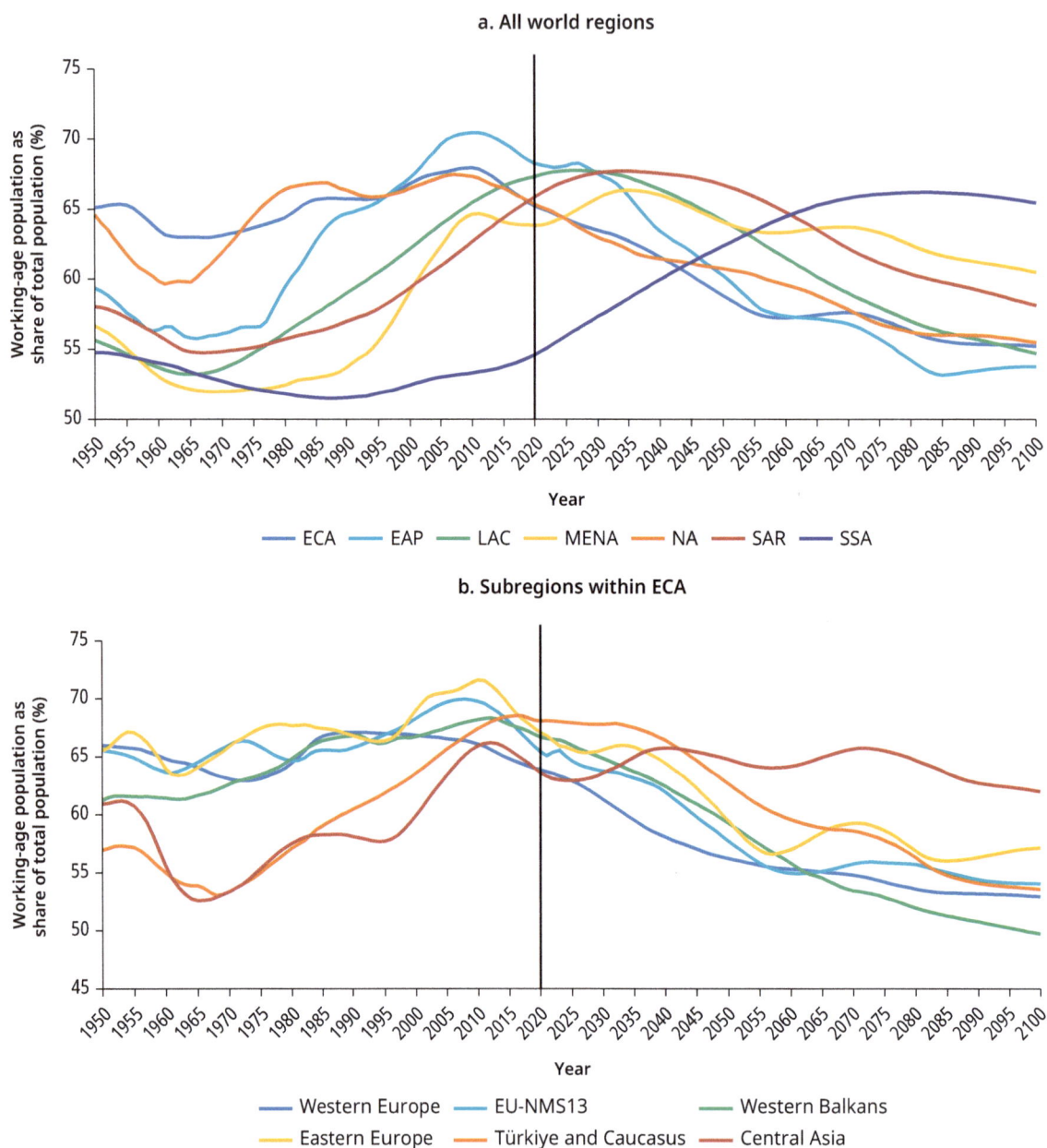

Source: UN World Population Prospects 2022.

Note: Data to the right of the vertical line are projected. EAP = East Asia and Pacific; ECA = Europe and Central Asia; LAC = Latin America and the Caribbean; MENA = Middle East and North Africa; NA = North America; SAR = South Asia; SSA = Sub-Saharan Africa; Western Europe = European Union members before 2004 + European Free Trade Association (Austria, Belgium, Denmark, Finland, France, Germany, Greece, Iceland, Ireland, Italy, Liechtenstein, Luxembourg, the Netherlands, Norway, Portugal, Spain, Sweden, Switzerland, and the United Kingdom); EU-NMS13 = new member states joining the European Union in 2004, 2007, and 2013 (Bulgaria, Croatia, Cyprus, Czechia, Estonia, Hungary, Latvia, Lithuania, Malta, Poland, Romania, Slovak Republic, and Slovenia); Western Balkans = Albania, Bosnia and Herzegovina, Kosovo, Montenegro, North Macedonia, and Serbia; Eastern Europe = Belarus, Moldova, the Russian Federation, and Ukraine; Türkiye and Caucasus = Armenia, Azerbaijan, Georgia, and Türkiye; Central Asia = Kazakhstan, Kyrgyz Republic, Tajikistan, Turkmenistan, and Uzbekistan.

Policies to better leverage migration should address varied challenges and experiences in ECA. Experiences here vary widely in terms of migrants' skills and reasons for migrating. To help frame solutions, the report distinguishes between types of migrants (high skilled or low skilled) and two main drivers of migration—to seek economic opportunity (economic migration) or to flee wars, conflicts, or persecution (forced migration; refer to figure MM.2). Policy responses needed to be tailored to these different types of migration. Some measures can be taken unilaterally; others require bilateral or regional coordination.

Early interventions in host countries can support integration and turn refugees into assets. A key lesson from recent experiences is that policies to unlock refugees' productive potential and self-reliance should be implemented very early. They should include developing and strengthening frameworks that support refugees; undertaking early skills and needs assessments; establishing rights and access to formal work; ensuring access to social protections, health care, and education; and applying language training and active labor market policies. Dispersal policies, which help connect refugees to local labor demand, lead to better outcomes. And making assistance available to local people in need can help mitigate the adverse impacts of refugee inflows while also improving social cohesion.

FIGURE MM.2

Typologies of migrants, drivers, challenges, and migration-regulating policies

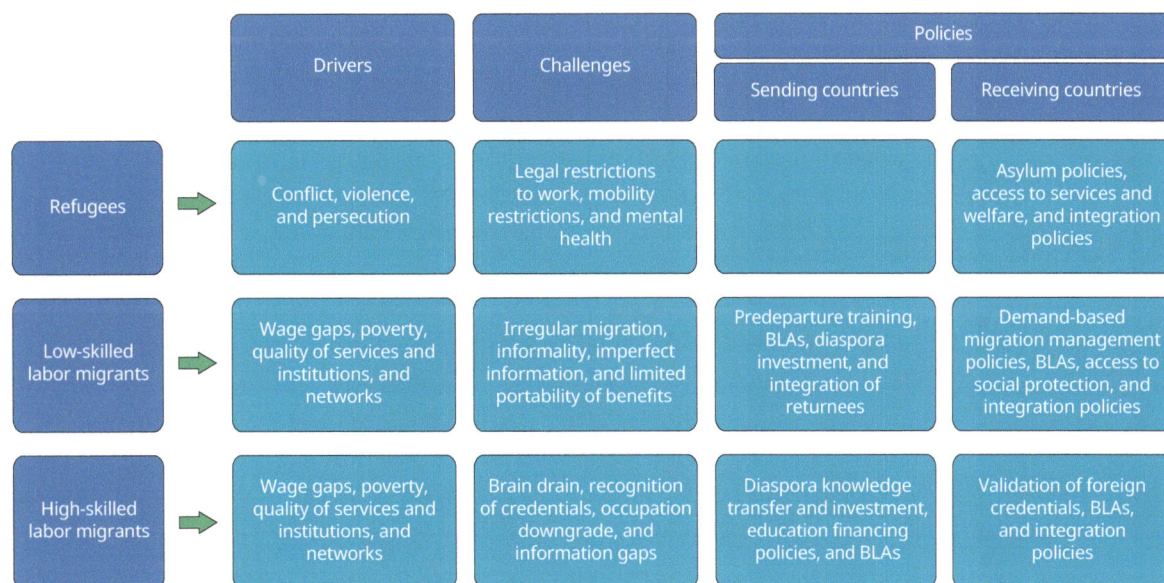

	Drivers	Challenges	Policies	
			Sending countries	Receiving countries
Refugees	Conflict, violence, and persecution	Legal restrictions to work, mobility restrictions, and mental health		Asylum policies, access to services and welfare, and integration policies
Low-skilled labor migrants	Wage gaps, poverty, quality of services and institutions, and networks	Irregular migration, informality, imperfect information, and limited portability of benefits	Predeparture training, BLAs, diaspora investment, and integration of returnees	Demand-based migration management policies, BLAs, access to social protection, and integration policies
High-skilled labor migrants	Wage gaps, poverty, quality of services and institutions, and networks	Brain drain, recognition of credentials, occupation downgrade, and information gaps	Diaspora knowledge transfer and investment, education financing policies, and BLAs	Validation of foreign credentials, BLAs, and integration policies

Source: Original figure for this publication.
Note: Bilateral labor agreements (BLAs) are international agreements signed between two countries to regulate the flow of migrant workers between them.

Destination countries can benefit from immigration and integration while managing costs. Immigration has brought economic gains in destination countries, but it comes with costs, both actual and perceived. There is scope for countries to increase the benefits of immigration, reduce its costs, and ensure that native-born residents share in the gains. Countries can implement needs-based immigration policies, invest in migrants' integration—for example, through access to training—and provide support to affected native-born individuals through social protection or access to active labor market programs. By improving how both migrant and native-born workers experience migration, such interventions may also help reduce negative perceptions about immigration.

In countries of origin, brain drain can become "brain gain." In some places, such as the Western Balkans, over a third of the high-skilled population works abroad, generating concerns about brain drain and potential labor shortages, especially with an aging population. But countries can implement policies to mitigate these risks. These include skills monitoring to anticipate labor shortages and flexible educational systems that can respond rapidly to increased demand for skilled workers, with cost-sharing mechanisms between destination and origin countries, such as Global Skill Partnerships. Diaspora programs can increase knowledge transfers and financial flows back home. Governments can incentivize the return of their high-skilled migrants through reforms to the labor market and business environment, fewer bureaucratic hurdles to returning, and monetary incentives to returnees.

Home countries can support more productive and resilient low-skilled migration, in coordination with destination countries. Countries of origin can develop and strengthen frameworks for safer, more productive formal migration. These include domestic registration systems for migrants as well as bilateral arrangements with destination countries. Mechanisms can ensure that prospective migrants receive accurate information about work opportunities and have access to orientation programs, skills training, and financial literacy courses. Countries can develop social protection programs for migrants and ensure the portability of social insurance and benefits while abroad, in coordination with destination countries. Social assistance and employment support programs to returnees can reduce their vulnerability and facilitate productive reintegration into home labor markets.

Overview

More people migrate to countries in Europe and Central Asia (ECA) than to any other region in the world. ECA hosts more than 100 million migrants, a third of the world's migrant population.[1] The patterns and experiences that characterize this migration are diverse in terms of reasons for migrating, migrants' skills, and the lengths of stay abroad. Migrants come both from within the region and from outside it. Their immigration is highly concentrated in Western European countries and the Russian Federation: half of all migrants in the region live in just five countries (France, Germany, Italy, Russia, and the United Kingdom). Some ECA countries, such as those in the Western Balkans, have high emigration rates; others, such as Poland, both send and receive many migrants. Economic migration is predominantly high skilled in some corridors, such as the European Union, but predominantly low skilled in others, including Central Asia. Some migrants move abroad permanently, others temporarily. Although migration largely driven by economic factors, the region is also the destination of more than a third of the world's refugees (refer to figure O.1).

Migration is a natural response to wide disparities in countries' income levels, living standards, and population trends across the region— disparities that are persistent and rising. Large differences in wages that workers earn in similar occupations across the region provide a strong incentive to migrate. Living standards and access to public services also vary widely. Some countries have an aging and shrinking labor force, whereas others face a bulge in the young adult population that they are struggling to absorb into the labor market (refer to figure O.2). At the global level, projections suggest that the ECA region's population will age significantly, while Sub-Saharan Africa will struggle to provide jobs for a growing, young population. These trends further increase the need for international mobility.

Cross-border labor mobility is an engine of economic prosperity in ECA. Migration is a powerful force in addressing the region's socioeconomic and demographic imbalances. It generates substantial benefits for migrants, countries of origin, and destination countries. By moving abroad, many

FIGURE O.1

Trends in the number of international migrants, by destination region

a. All migrants

b. Refugees

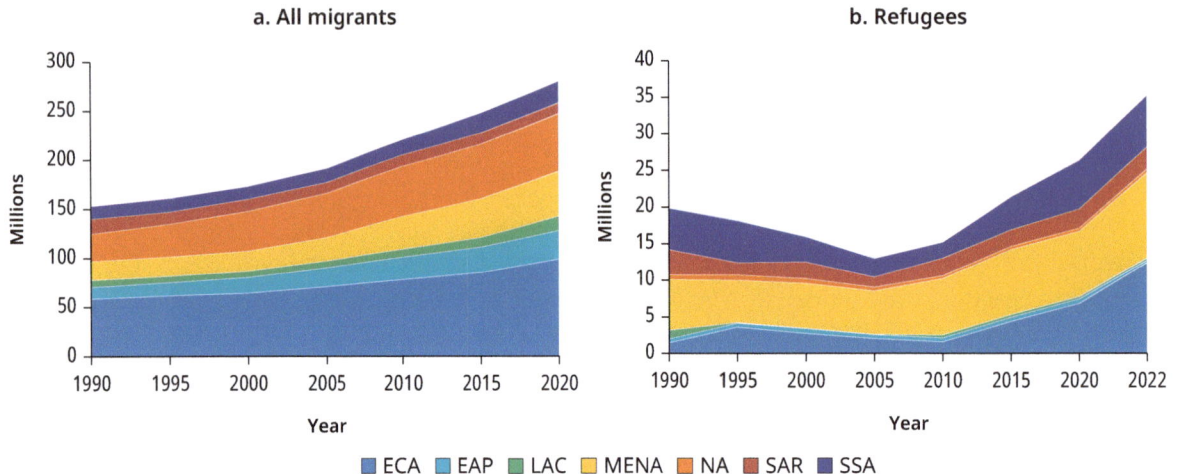

ECA   EAP   LAC   MENA   NA   SAR   SSA

Sources: UN DESA (https://www.un.org/development/desa/pd/data-landing-page) and World Development Indicators, World Bank (https://databank.worldbank.org/source/world-development-indicators).
Note: International migrants include both economic migrants and refugees. EAP = East Asia and Pacific; ECA = Europe and Central Asia; LAC = Latin America and the Caribbean; MENA = Middle East and North Africa; NA = North America; SAR = South Asia; SSA = Sub-Saharan Africa.

migrants can earn at least twice the salary they earned in their country of origin. These earnings gains are unmatched by any other policy intervention: the annual gains from a best-practice poverty program are only about 2.5 percent of the wage gains that low-skill workers see when they move from a low- or middle-income country to one of the most advanced economies (Pritchett 2018). In countries of origin, emigration generates large income flows through remittances, investments, and transfers of know-how. In the Kyrgyz Republic and Tajikistan, for example, remittances represent more than a third of the gross domestic product (GDP).

Migration also fosters broader human development gains. Emigration can enhance human capital in home countries over the longer term, providing greater incentives to invest in education and opportunities to capitalize on migrants' skills and experiences when they return. Emigration helps home countries with a demographic youth bulge absorb a growing labor force that local markets cannot accommodate. In destination countries, migration can produce net welfare gains by helping fill labor shortages, especially in places with a rapidly aging population (for example, Western Europe, where the working-age population is expected to fall by 14 percent between 2020 and 2050).

Migration in ECA, however, has yet to realize its full potential. Inefficiencies and risks prevent migrants and countries in the region from fully benefiting from cross-border mobility. For example, low-skilled

FIGURE O.2
Demographic trends

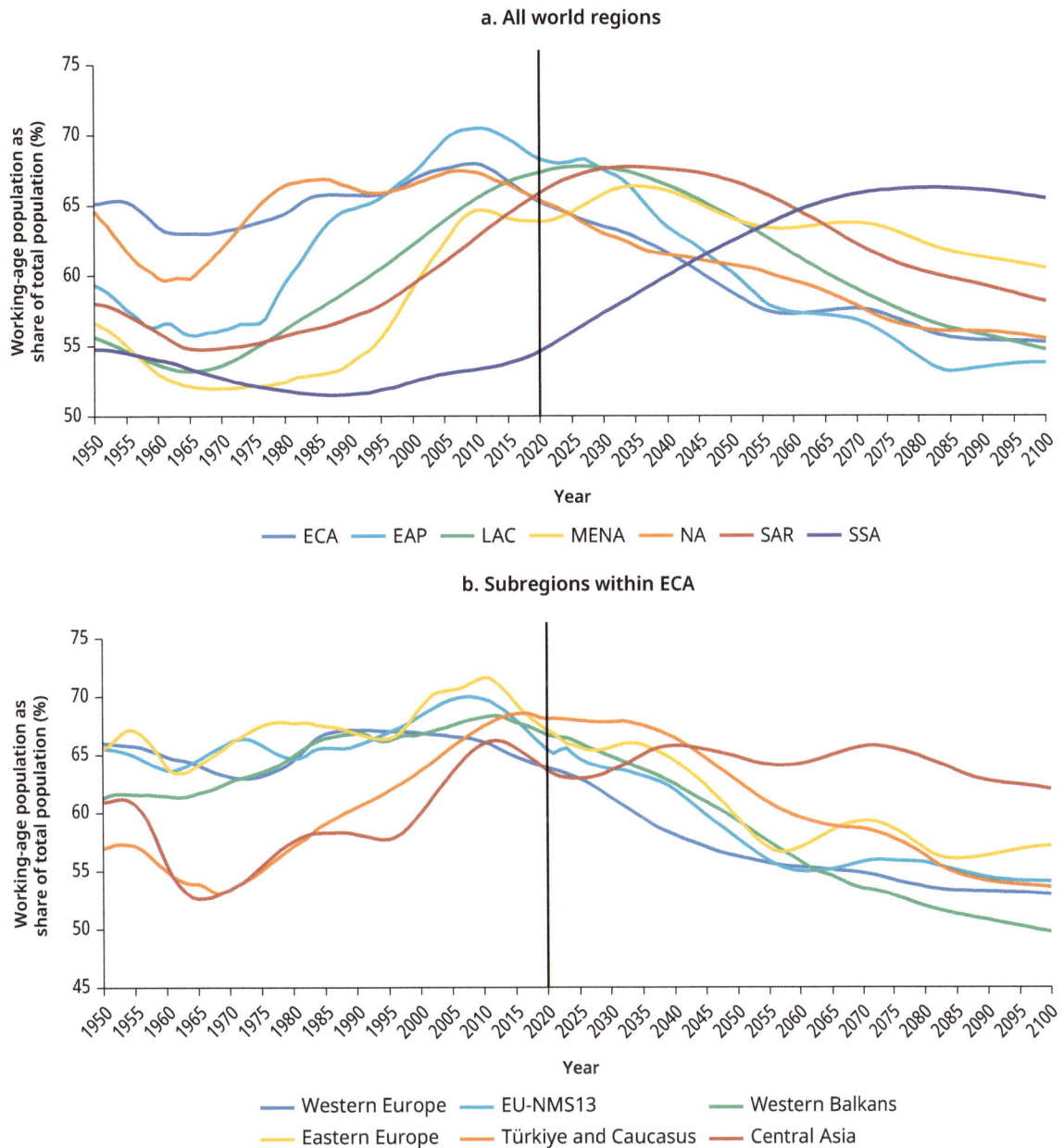

a. All world regions

Legend: ECA, EAP, LAC, MENA, NA, SAR, SSA

b. Subregions within ECA

Legend: Western Europe, EU-NMS13, Western Balkans, Eastern Europe, Türkiye and Caucasus, Central Asia

Source: UN World Population Prospects 2022.
Note: Data to the right of the vertical line are projected. EAP = East Asia and Pacific; ECA = Europe and Central Asia; LAC = Latin America and the Caribbean; MENA = Middle East and North Africa; NA = North America; SAR = South Asia; SSA = Sub-Saharan Africa; Western Europe = EU-15 + EFTA; EU NMS13 = new member states joining the European Union in 2004, 2007, and 2013.

migrants are sometimes ill-prepared for work abroad, which increases vulnerabilities and reduces the benefits of migration for workers and for origin and destination countries. There is also scope to distribute the costs and benefits of migration more equally. For example, home countries often bear the cost of educating their high-skilled migrants while not always being able to reap the benefits of their mobility. In destination countries, various skill groups of native-born workers are affected by immigration, though not all in the same way. A large inflow of foreign workers also poses challenges for their integration into host country society.

The policy focus should be on implementing the right policies to best benefit from migration. The experience in ECA shows that the costs and benefits of migration are shaped by policies both in origin and destination countries. Building on established as well as new evidence, this report provides a comprehensive set of policy recommendations to address the migration challenges in ECA. It formulates these recommendations to help enhance the net gains for the three main groups of actors: migrants themselves, countries of origin, and destination countries (refer to figure O.3). Some of these measures can be taken unilaterally by countries, such as developing registration systems for labor migrants. Others, for example Global Skill Partnerships (GSPs), require close collaboration between origin and destination countries, or even at the regional level. Some of the policies can be implemented rapidly in the short term. Others, such as building institutional frameworks for safer and more productive migration, require deeper reforms but can yield large returns over the long term.

The great variety of migration experiences within ECA offers policy lessons and insights for other regions. The ECA region's richness and diversity of migration provides an ideal ground to study multiple facets of the phenomenon, considering a range of perspectives, complex impacts, and policy ramifications. Although this report focuses on one region, the variety of migration experiences in ECA makes its policy recommendations relevant on a global scale—in the spirit of the *World Development Report 2023: Migrants, Refugees, and Societies* (World Bank 2023).

The report is organized according to typologies that reflect the range of migration experiences in the region. This approach is intended to improve understanding of the drivers, opportunities, and challenges of each type of migration and to help frame policy solutions and options. The report distinguishes between two main types of migrants (high skilled and low skilled) and between two main drivers of migration—either the search for economic opportunity (economic migration) or the need to flee war, conflict, or persecution (forced migration). Migrants, countries of origin, and destination countries face distinct challenges based on the nature of migration, and different contexts require distinct policy responses (refer to figure O.4). These typologies help target and coordinate policies to address challenges and enhance the benefits of migration for migrants, origin countries, and destination countries.

FIGURE O.3

Enhancing migration outcomes for all parties through policy

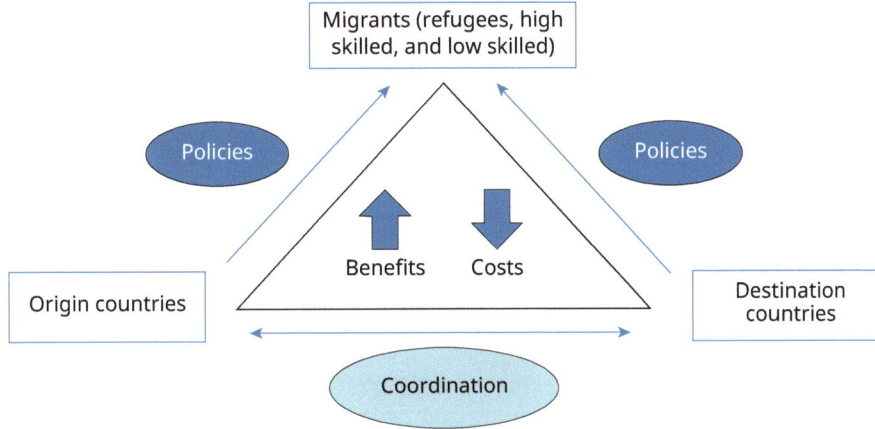

Source: Original figure for this publication.

FIGURE O.4

Broad typologies of migrants, drivers, challenges, and migration-regulating policies

	Drivers	Challenges	Policies	
			Sending countries	Receiving countries
Refugees	Conflict, violence, and persecution	Legal restrictions to work, mobility restrictions, and mental health		Asylum policies, access to services and welfare, and integration policies
Low-skilled labor migrants	Wage gaps, poverty, quality of services and institutions, and networks	Irregular migration, informality, imperfect information, and limited portability of benefits	Predeparture training, BLAs, diaspora investment, and integration of returnees	Demand-based migration management policies, BLAs, access to social protection, and integration policies
High-skilled labor migrants	Wage gaps, poverty, quality of services and institutions, and networks	Brain drain, recognition of credentials, occupation downgrade, and information gaps	Diaspora knowledge transfer and investment, education financing policies, and BLAs	Validation of foreign credentials, BLAs, and integration policies

Source: Original figure for this publication.
Note: Bilateral labor agreements (BLAs) are international agreements signed between two countries to regulate the flow of migrant workers between them.

Key Takeaways

Socioeconomic and Labor Impacts of Migration in Destination Countries

Since the mid-1990s, immigration has contributed significantly to population expansion and demographic change in the 15 countries that were EU member states before 2004 (the EU-15). Net migration inflows account for nearly 80 percent of population growth in these countries, providing a vital lift to stagnant or declining growth rates among native-born populations. In addition, because immigrants are typically younger than the native-born population, immigration also has significant effects on a country's demographic structure.

In Western European countries, migrants support employment in all sectors, particularly the key sectors of manufacturing, health care, and social care. In several European economies, shortages of workers in specific sectors and occupations present a threat to competitiveness and are increasing the demand for foreign workers. Foreign workers are employed to a greater degree in low-skilled occupations and in services catering to the needs of an aging population. Non-EU immigrants in the European Union, however, are less likely than EU-born persons to be employed, largely because of the additional barriers they face.

Migration is associated with net economic gains in receiving regions. Most empirical studies on immigration and economic growth in Europe's receiving countries reveal a positive connection. The empirical findings of studies of specific EU countries are in line with the international evidence, suggesting that immigration boosts growth. High-skilled immigration can particularly affect growth through labor input, human capital accumulation, and productivity. Human capital gains are typically larger in immigrant-receiving countries and regions: the larger and more diverse human capital contributed by immigration increases worker productivity. The diversification of skills and the concentration of migrants in tasks for which they are better suited increases economic productivity and stimulates innovation. This privileges native-born workers who specialize in occupations where they have a comparative advantage, such as those requiring extensive communication.

The overall impact of immigration on native-born individuals' employment outcomes has been small but asymmetric across groups, and net fiscal impacts tend to be positive. The prevailing view in receiving-country governments, and, to some degree, among the public, is that immigration lowers earnings and reduces job opportunities for native-born workers. However, evidence from ECA shows otherwise. The arrival of migrants may have short-term, negative effects on the wages of native-born workers with comparable skills (especially low-skilled workers), although these impacts are usually small. By contrast, the presence of migrants tends to have positive effects on the wages of native-born workers who have complementary skills. Over the long term, immigration has been shown to raise productivity, promote occupational advancement, and increase native-born workers' wages. In most Organisation for Economic Co-operation and Development (OECD) countries, the fiscal impact of immigration has been neutral or marginally positive, indicating that immigrants tend to be net contributors to taxes and social insurance. However, these fiscal effects tend to be greater for migrants who are high skilled or from the European Economic Area, versus those who are low skilled or from low- or middle-income countries.

Immigrants' labor market outcomes lag behind those of native-born workers, although the gaps diminish with time spent in the destination country. The gap in employment rates between native-born and immigrant workers in EU countries was around 4.5 percentage points in 2020. Immigrants are also considerably more likely to be employed in low-pay and low-status occupations. Accounting for differences in the profiles of migrants and native-born individuals does not reduce the gap, which indicates that immigrants face specific hurdles in labor market integration. However, employment gaps decrease over time. This indicates that some of the barriers that migrants face are eased the longer they stay in the host country. Two key barriers associated with immigrants' poorer labor market outcomes are a lack, or limited command, of the host country language as well as occupational downgrade.

Many migrants are employed in occupations that require a lower level of skills than their formal level of educational attainment would predict. This occupational downgrade limits the economic gains from migration. The phenomenon is most pronounced among non-EU migrants. Migrants from the newer EU member states (the EU-NMS13) have, on average, 1.3 more years of schooling than native-born people in the same occupation. Occupational downgrade among high-skilled women migrants to the European Union is striking, because the top two occupations of tertiary-educated women migrants from the EU-NMS13 are cleaners and personal care workers. The occupational downgrade of high-skilled migrants in ECA is linked to a lack of location-specific skills, including language; to training in occupations that do not match the demand in destination countries; and to imperfect recognition of qualifications obtained in the country of origin.

Policy Recommendations

In destination countries, enhancing the gains from migration starts by identifying needed skills that migrants can bring or acquire. The benefits of immigration for ECA countries tend to be the greatest if immigrants are high skilled, concentrated in occupations that are in demand, and complement the skills of the native-born population. Hence it is important to have policies in place that ensure immigration flows fulfill these criteria. This starts by establishing and strengthening skills monitoring systems and labor market observatories to identify skills needed that the native-born population cannot fill. Such systems could also be developed on a regional scale by building an EU-wide labor demand system. In addition, destination countries can develop consultative processes with employers, labor unions, and other stakeholders. In the United Kingdom, for example, the Migration Advisory Committee reviews labor needs with stakeholders in selected sectors and advises the government on how immigration could help respond to those needs.

Once needed skills are identified, managed migration policies and training programs can help guarantee that migrants address those needs. The first option is for destination countries to develop bilateral labor agreements (BLAs) that target occupations where they face shortages or rising demand. Such an approach can be implemented in the context of GSP programs, in which destination and origin countries agree on the quantity and skills profile of migrant labor required and then provide technical and financial resources to train migrants in their countries of origin. Another policy option is to select prospective migrants based on their potential for integration with market needs. In this spirit, Austria, Germany, Portugal, and Sweden have established job-search visas that allow entry for the purpose of finding employment to foreign workers who meet specific criteria. Another approach, followed by Spain, is for countries to streamline migration procedures for occupations or migrant profiles that are needed. Other countries, such as in Sweden and the United Kingdom, are trying to make immigration systems more selective to reduce migration flows that are less suited to their labor markets.

Ensuring that migrants work at their level of qualification, through mechanisms to recognize foreign credentials, is also key to enhancing gains for migrants and destination countries. Although migrants within EU countries are de jure granted the same rights to access jobs as native-born individuals, de facto limitations remain in recognizing qualifications and skills, especially for migrants from outside the European Union. To tackle this issue, destination countries must build or strengthen mechanisms to determine whether origin countries' standards for each skill are equivalent to their own (Nielson 2004). Regional cooperation to validate foreign educational credentials, as well as the development of regional qualification frameworks, such as the European Qualifications Framework for EU countries, are promising efforts in this direction. In June 2023, member states of the Eurasian Economic Union (EaEU) passed an agreement on mutual recognition of academic degrees, though it needs to be implemented and enforced.

Labor market and social protection policies can prevent or mitigate adverse effects of immigration for some native-born groups, such as low-skilled workers. A broader effort to support labor market flexibility in destination countries can allow native-born workers who have complementary skills and capital to move to the areas and sectors where migrants enter, while also helping workers with similar skills move to other regions, sectors, or occupations (World Bank 2023). This can support faster labor market adjustments and reduce adverse effects on wages or employment for some native-born, low-skilled workers. But even with the right labor market and migration policies in place *ex ante*, immigration may produce adverse impacts on some groups, at least in the short term. To mitigate such impacts, targeted social protection and active labor market policies (ALMPs) can be implemented. Effective public employment services can help individuals who lose their jobs and assist with mobility costs as they seek work in other regions or sectors. Retraining and upskilling programs can also help native-born workers with skills similar to those of migrants to move toward higher-paying jobs where they have a comparative advantage. And social protection systems and programs can support those who are temporarily affected by job losses, especially in destination countries, where immigration generates additional fiscal resources to finance such programs.

Integration policies and interventions that raise awareness of migrants' contributions can help reduce negative perceptions and improve how both immigrants and native-born workers experience migration. Recent evidence shows that inclusive integration policies have a positive impact on integration outcomes for migrants (Bilgili, Huddleston, and Joki 2015; Huddleston 2020; Kende et al. 2022; Pecoraro et al. 2022), including better employment and less reliance on social assistance. This, in turn, helps improve perceptions among the native-born population. Addressing misinformation and ensuring that people are aware of the role migrants play in receiving societies is also crucial to mitigate the risk of anti-immigration sentiments. But whereas providing counter-information only on the magnitude of migration has a limited impact on attitudes (Hopkins, Sides, and Citrin 2019), information on the characteristics of migrants and their impacts on the labor market or welfare system can significantly improve popular support for immigration (Grigorieff, Roth, and Ubfal 2020; Haaland and Roth 2020; Jørgensen and Osmundsen 2022).

Socioeconomic Integration of Refugee Populations

In the Nordic countries, compulsory language training, active labor market policies, and assignment of refugees to areas with high labor demand have helped improve refugees' employment outcomes. Language training is a vital part of the "activation package" offered to refugees in these countries, and it has produced substantial long-term effects. Language training tends to be compulsory, with participation and completion often being conditions to retain social benefits as well as access to on-the-job training or subsidized employment. Evidence shows that compulsory language training has been the most effective program to support refugees' employment outcomes. Other successful programs include (in order) assignment to areas with high labor demand and participation in programs that were part of the ALMP package.

Türkiye's experience of hosting Syrian refugees shows that better long-term outcomes can be achieved by rapidly shifting policies from an exclusive focus on emergency response to early support for longer-term integration. After providing vital income to the most vulnerable— the Syrians under temporary protection (SuTPs), through the Emergency Social Safety Net (ESSN) in 2016, Türkiye developed a framework for the inclusion of SuTPs into mainstream basic services. The government issued residency cards that allowed access to education, health care, and other public services. Housing policies also changed from an initial approach that focused on accommodating refugees in temporary shelters to providing housing support to live in urban centers near more job opportunities. Policies addressing labor market issues were adopted, with the government offering work permits, services (such as counseling), and financial support for entrepreneurship. Surveys in Türkiye show that a relatively high share of SuTPs are employed and that the integration of SuTPs has been positive overall, partly because of these government support interventions, which have supported social cohesion between refugees and host communities. In addition, the impacts of SuTPs on overall employment and wages for Turkish citizens were limited, although some vulnerable native-born groups were negatively affected.

The experiences in Türkiye also show the importance of sharing responsibility among receiving countries in the region. The costs imposed on Türkiye from the sudden inflow of refugees—with ramifications particularly in the capacity of its health care system—ushered in calls for a cost-sharing approach. This led to the EU–Türkiye agreement in 2016, under which the European Union provided €6 billion to support the humanitarian response.

In addition, the Turkish experience illustrates the need to streamline access to formal employment, reduce disincentives to refugee employment, and offer early skills assessments. Although estimates suggest that more than 1.5 million Syrians in Türkiye can work, fewer than 100,000 work permits are issued annually. Permits are difficult to obtain, costly for employers, and valid for only a year. Moreover, upon receiving a formal employment contract through a work permit, Syrian refugees lose their eligibility for social assistance cash transfers through the ESSN program, creating a disincentive to enter formal employment. Establishing more comprehensive assessments of refugees' skills and qualifications at the time of entry could also ensure more effective use of labor market services available to refugees.

Germany's experiences showed the value of expedited asylum procedures, rationalized dispersal policies, and comprehensive integration programs. The sudden increase in asylum seekers in Europe over the 2015–17 period focused on Germany, where half of the 3.1 million asylum applications were filed. In response, Germany suspended the Dublin II Regulation (Tjaden and Heidland, forthcoming), allowing refugees who had passed through other EU countries to apply for asylum. It grouped asylum cases by complexity to speed up processing times and provide integration services before adjudication in cases where asylum seekers were likely to receive protection. Germany also invested heavily in language training for Syrian refugees; provided job counseling and job search assistance; developed a public portal to assess and recognize foreign professional qualifications; and implemented a dispersal policy, assigning refugees to specific regions on the basis of local labor demand. Although the efforts significantly improved the labor market outcomes for refugees (Battisti, Giesing, and Laurentsyeva 2019), the success came at some cost, because nonprioritized asylum seekers faced longer wait times and worse access to public resources.

The more recent inflow of Ukrainian refugees into EU countries has highlighted the importance of a large-scale, rapid, and coordinated response to support refugees' outcomes. Several policies have likely helped secure better labor market outcomes than in past refugee waves. Shortly after the start of the Ukrainian refugee crisis, the European Union approved the Temporary Protection Directive, giving refugees the right to temporary protection for one year (renewable for up to three years), without the need for lengthy asylum procedures. Ukrainian refugees also received residence permits, while requirements for work visas were waived. Measures to ease work permit regulations and enhance labor market access had rapid, positive impacts on the labor market in host countries. Additional interventions aimed at improving the match between labor market supply and demand included dedicated employment platforms for recruitment of refugees; wage subsidies and other financial incentives for employers; and support, such as start-up loans, for entrepreneurship. The European Union also developed a refugee skills passport specifically for Ukrainians.

Policy Recommendations

Host countries can ensure sufficient humanitarian support and reception capacity through several key measures. First, the timely provision of temporary protection status has been fundamental in ensuring that humanitarian aid reaches asylum seekers quickly. Second, one-stop-shop reception centers have been effective in providing a rapid assessment of refugees' characteristics, needs, and vulnerabilities and directing them to services needed in the short term. Third, to weather the initial shock and cover basic needs, cash transfers have been effective in improving refugees' welfare, with few adverse effects on earnings opportunities, at least in the short term (Bahar, Brough, and Peri 2024). Fourth, physical and mental health support has also been essential. These efforts require significant resources and coordination among receiving countries. Cost-sharing agreements and corresponding financing mechanisms need to be in place, especially when refugee inflows focus on countries with limited reception capacity.

Early policy measures to support refugees' labor market integration can generate high payoffs for host countries. Measures to support integration include early skills and needs assessments, rapid access to labor markets and public services, language training, and ALMPs. Most successful interventions combine rapid and extensive humanitarian assistance upon arrival with policies that promote long-term integration. Experience shows that measures supporting integration should begin very early, in the emergency response phase. Because refugees often arrive without key documents to verify their skills and credentials, refugee skills passports can help validate their skills and enhance their employability. Ensuring that refugees can quickly access technical and language training programs is also key to integration.

Giving refugees rapid access to the labor market is particularly important. It can be facilitated by policy measures, including removing or relaxing restrictions that apply to third-country nationals entering the labor market, expediting or removing work permit procedures, and streamlining asylum processes. In addition, well-targeted active labor market programs have also been shown to support economic integration.

Refugees' geographical locations and mobility are fundamental to integration and can be supported by dispersal policies that address local labor market needs. A key takeaway from both research and experience is that refugees should not be isolated from the native-born population in receiving countries. Rigid housing policies that tie refugees to a physical location far from economic activity—limiting employment opportunities and preventing mobility—should be discouraged, because they are negatively associated with refugees' long-term employment outcomes. Instead, policies should facilitate movement to areas with high demand for labor and high absorptive capacity, which can avoid generating additional imbalances in local labor markets. Such policies should be underpinned by information on local market conditions and demand, as well as on refugees' sociodemographic characteristics, educational attainment, and employment aspirations.

High-Skilled Migration: Lessons for Origin Countries

High-skilled emigration from ECA countries is rising even more rapidly than overall migration. The number of high-skilled migrants in the European Union, the main destination of high-skilled migrants from ECA, more than tripled over 2004–18, from about 4 million to 13 million. In some countries of origin in ECA, particularly smaller ones such as those in the Western Balkans, the incidence of high-skilled emigration is very large compared with the size of the working-age population. For example, an estimated 30 percent of Albania's working-age population with a tertiary degree lives abroad. For Bosnia and Herzegovina, this figure is 45 percent.

This "brain drain" can have a negative effect on home economies in the short term by reducing the supply of skilled workers in essential occupations. Because emigrants from most ECA countries are more skilled than the population that does not emigrate, their departure decreases the stock of human capital available, at least in the short term. Without the right policies in place, this can result in domestic labor shortages, including in critical sectors and occupations, such as health care and information technology, especially in countries with an aging population. The loss of high-skilled workers can negatively affect firm productivity, total factor productivity, entrepreneurship, and innovation, as documented in some Eastern European countries (Giesing and Laurentsyeva 2018) and in Italy (Anelli et al. 2019). Because emigration mostly comes from less developed regions of origin countries, it can also widen the gap between prospering and lagging parts of a country. And beyond economic impacts, the departure of high-skilled workers raises concerns about the sustainability of pension systems. From a fiscal standpoint, outflows of high-skilled labor also shrink the fiscal base, especially when emigration is concentrated among higher-paid workers.

In the medium to long term, however, countries of origin can experience net gains in human capital ("brain gain"), as observed in some ECA countries. To experience brain gain, these countries must be able to increase their educational institutions' capacity to meet the demand for certain types of labor abroad. And the number of newly educated individuals who do not emigrate, or who ultimately return, must be large enough to add to the collective human capital within the home country. Overall, origin countries in ECA have experienced a net positive association between emigration and human capital accumulation, as long as emigration rates remain moderate (Beine, Docquier, and Oden-Defoort 2011; Beine, Docquier, and Rapoport 2008; Docquier, Lohest, and Marfouk 2007). For example, in some countries, the rapid rise in the number of graduates in medicine more than compensated for the doctors who emigrated. This was the case in the Czechia, Romania, and Slovenia, although not in Estonia, Hungary, and Latvia. The variation in experiences suggest that policies and local contexts are key in determining whether home countries can also increase their own supply of high-skilled workers as a secondary benefit of migration opportunities.

Origin countries can also benefit from their high-skilled diasporas through remittances, greater diffusion of knowledge and technology, and increased financial flows and trade. The most direct and tangible impact of these diasporas on origin countries is through remittances sent home, which boost income and can improve macroeconomic stability. The presence of highly skilled migrants overseas can also help diffuse knowledge and technology back to their home countries, as reported in the context of migration from former Yugoslav countries to Germany (Bahar, Brough, and Peri 2024). Diaspora networks can support trade and finance in their countries of origin by reducing transaction costs and information asymmetries. And beyond economic impacts, diasporas can positively affect institutions and governance in migrant-sending countries, as in Moldova (Barsbai et al. 2017).

The return of high-skilled migrants may also benefit their home countries, although countries in Eastern Europe and the Western Balkans struggle to attract these emigrants back. When migrants do return, countries of origin can benefit from the human and financial capital they have accumulated while abroad. Although nearly half of migrants to the European Union return to their home countries, overall just 12 percent of high-skilled migrants from Eastern European countries do. Likewise, there is little evidence of returns by high-skilled migrants from Albania,

Bosnia and Herzegovina, and Kosovo. Likely explanations include the persistence of economic challenges and the push-and-pull factors that lead skilled workers to emigrate. Hence the economies of Eastern Europe and the Western Balkans have been unable to reap many of the benefits associated with the return of high-skilled migrants.

Policy Recommendations

Countries that want to reduce emigration can address root causes, such as domestic labor market performance, governance, and the quality of public sector services. Home countries can increase their relative attractiveness by reducing bottlenecks to employment creation; improving the business environment; and strengthening institutions and public services. Overall, measures that make the domestic labor market more attractive and efficient—with a focus on youth, who have a higher propensity to emigrate—can reduce the strength of push-and-pull factors. Approaches include traditional labor market policies such as support to entrepreneurship, ALMPs (including wage subsidy programs), training, and labor market intermediation services, as well as changes in labor regulations that may discourage employment. Supply-side policies must be accompanied by broader demand-side policies that affect the labor market and employment creation, such as measures to improve the business and macroeconomic environment or the tax and benefits system. Beyond the labor market, the provision of quality public services, primarily through more investment in health and education, may also encourage workers and their families to stay. Such measures may also increase the likelihood of return among high-skilled workers who have already left.

Reforms to tertiary education financing in countries of origin, combined with bilateral agreements with destination countries, may help mitigate the financial losses when graduates of publicly funded universities emigrate. In addition to university funding, financing policies involve measures aimed directly at students and graduates, including student loans, time-based repayment loans, and income-contingent loans (ICLs). For example, ICL contracts could be designed to make loan repayments feasible and tax deductible in destination countries. Such measures, combined with bilateral agreements, could help ensure a more equitable distribution of educational costs between origin and destination countries (Poutvaara 2004).

GSPs can help address financial burdens and losses of human capital in countries of origin and ensure a better match between migrants and jobs in destination countries. Under these bilateral arrangements, the country of origin agrees to train people in skills needed both in home and destination countries. Evidence from ECA countries and beyond indicates that three core principles are essential for such partnerships to succeed. First, investing in human capital expansion in both origin and destination countries should be the paramount goal. Second, extensive cooperation between origin and destination countries is essential for the long-term investments in training and labor market access that such partnerships aim to promote. Third, well-managed and systematic international systems for social protection and labor market intermediation are needed to facilitate cross-border economic gains. Last, institutional capacity is needed for recruitment, training, and diaspora engagement.

Countries of origin can establish systems to monitor emigration flows and the supply and demand of workers with needed skills, so that they anticipate potential shortages, especially in critical occupations. For the educational system to respond rapidly, it needs timely and precise information on the demand for high-skilled professionals both from within the home country and from destination countries. Such monitoring of demand is available today in only a handful of countries. Data about emigrants' skills and educational profiles should be collected at the time of departure, and monitoring systems should also be put in place for specific skills.

Educational systems in countries of origin should also be flexible enough to address rapid changes in internal and external demand. Rigid training systems for certain occupations—such as highly regulated systems based on narrow entry criteria or a small, fixed number of places in medical education—may not align with the needs created by changes in demand for these occupations. Efforts to address changes in demand for specific skills can be made at both the intensive margin (by enhancing capacity at schools and universities) and the extensive margin (by establishing new education centers).

Countries of origin may encourage high-skilled migrants to return by removing or reducing regulatory, bureaucratic, and informational barriers; providing financial incentives; and ensuring greater portability of social benefits. Regulatory and bureaucratic barriers, such as restrictions and regulations on citizenship and residency rights, make it difficult and costly for migrants to return to their home countries. Informational barriers may also prevent them from returning: policies that make information more accessible about job opportunities and changes in conditions in the home country may help. Financial or fiscal incentives encouraging the permanent return of high-skilled migrants have also been effective in some contexts, provided they are large enough. Such incentives could include tax exemptions and benefits, interest-free or low-interest loans, temporary salary supplements to facilitate career entry, housing assistance, schooling for children, and employment opportunities for spouses. And greater portability of social benefits, particularly retirement benefits, can alleviate constraints to return migration and incentivize migrants to return home (Avato, Koettl, and Sabates-Wheeler 2010).

Regardless of whether migrants return, countries of origin can leverage high-skilled migration through diaspora programs. Emigrants can help transfer knowledge back to their origin country after their exposure to more productive and innovative environments in destination countries. The first step is to establish, strengthen, or make better use of diaspora platforms through registries, interactive portals, and fellowship programs. This can help build relationships with the diaspora and provide matching and network services that connect migrants in various destination countries with each other and with the private and public sectors in their home economies. For example, collaboration between researchers or institutions abroad and in countries of origin could be facilitated by establishing scientific networks and knowledge funds. Such initiatives have started in the Western Balkans and are in various stages of implementation (OECD 2022).

Low-Skilled Migration: Lessons for Origin Countries

Low-skilled migration generates large benefits for migrants, their families, and origin countries. The most direct impacts are large wage gains for workers and the subsequent increase in household income and welfare through remittances, which generate substantial income flows to home countries. For example, in the Kyrgyz Republic and Tajikistan, remittances represent up to 30 percent of GDP and more than 50 percent of migrant households' total income. Because low-skilled migration is concentrated among lower-income households, it can have a drastic effect on poverty reduction. In Uzbekistan, for example, it is estimated that the poverty rate would rise from 9.6 percent to 16.8 percent in the absence of remittances. Beyond these direct welfare impacts, low-skilled emigration can affect households and communities left behind by enabling large investments in human capital and entrepreneurial activities. In the home country, migration can affect labor market participation among household members, as well as improve financial literacy and women's empowerment.

However, if not well managed, low-skilled migration can involve inefficiencies and vulnerabilities, which are often borne by migrants and their households. Vulnerabilities manifest throughout the migration life cycle: before departure, while abroad, and after return. The COVID-19 pandemic and, more recently, the economic spillovers from Russia's invasion of Ukraine have exposed the limitations of current migration systems as well as low-skilled migrants' vulnerability to shocks. Although a few of the challenges migrants faced during these shocks were specific to those events, most vulnerabilities are more general and will persist in the absence of adequate policy measures.

Vulnerabilities and inefficiencies are evident before migrants depart, with many of them insufficiently prepared and reliant on inaccurate information and informal arrangements. Formal information channels for prospective low-skilled migrants in ECA are underdeveloped, likely contributing to insufficient understanding about the processes, costs, and benefits of emigration. Low-skilled migrants often lack prior experience and adequate skills for the jobs most in demand in destination countries. They are seldom prepared for the vulnerabilities they will likely face while abroad. Many of them depart without even securing an employment contract with an employer in the destination country.

Once at their destination, low-skilled migrants are highly exposed to shocks and have limited access to social protection. In many cases, low-skilled migrants concentrate in only one or two destination countries and in very few sectors of activity. As a result, low-skilled migration flows, countries of origin, and migrants are highly exposed to negative shocks, as evidenced by the COVID-19 pandemic. Low-skilled migrants often hold temporary or seasonal employment contracts, or work without contracts. Hence, they are typically the first to be laid off when a shock hits (Fasani and Mazza 2023), and they often lack access to social protections to cope with these shocks. Even within the European Union, where formal migration and employment arrangements are more common, migrants typically have more limited access to social protection programs than native-born individuals.

Vulnerabilities and inefficiencies can continue when low-skilled migrants return home, especially when they do so unexpectedly. Temporary migrants who return for reasons they had not anticipated are especially vulnerable. They have often paid for the journey upfront, sometimes by taking out loans. Unable to stay abroad long enough to earn as much as they expected, they return without set plans and face the risk of unemployment at home. This can have profound impacts on migrants and their families, as evidenced by harmful coping strategies seen in households with return migrants during the COVID-19 pandemic. Even when migrants return as planned, there are policy challenges for their home countries—but also opportunities. A key issue facing policy makers in these countries is finding more effective ways to boost the productive use of the financial and human capital that returning migrants have accumulated while abroad.

Policy Recommendations

Strengthening systems to support formal migration is a key step toward more productive and resilient low-skilled migration. Such efforts must begin before departure, with measures to strengthen the role of public institutions and regulatory frameworks in providing accurate information about the migration experience and work opportunities abroad. Creating and enhancing the use of formal migration routes also requires that countries develop or strengthen registration systems for low-skilled migration. This requires close cooperation with destination countries, which can be formalized through BLAs. In their various forms, these agreements have been effective tools to manage international labor flows and improve the migration experience for all parties involved. Implementing them at scale, however, requires administrative capacity in both origin and destination countries. Proper enforcement involves transparent negotiation processes and strong implementation, monitoring, and evaluation.

Programs to upgrade prospective migrants' skills, when combined with initiatives to diversify migration flows, can enhance the benefits of migration. To reduce exposure to shocks and increase gains from migration, origin countries need to broaden the range of migration destinations and work opportunities. Entering new markets requires building a more qualified workforce with verifiable credentials for jobs that are in demand in new places. Identifying the demand for specific types of workers requires more capacity in line agencies responsible for managing labor migration. Close cooperation with destination countries is also essential; this can be formalized through development of new BLAs. Once the demand from new markets is identified, origin countries need to reorient their skills development efforts, by training migrants for new occupations as well as providing language training. This requires expanding the capacity and resources of public training programs along with potential partnerships with private providers. Such efforts can be supported by destination countries, for example through GSPs, where the destination country provides technical and financial resources for the training of prospective migrants in their home country. Skills development needs to be complemented by certification to signal technical ability, accompanied by due recognition of qualifications in overseas markets.

Several policies can help migrants gain better access to social protection and reduce their vulnerability abroad. Host country governments can better integrate migrants into social safety nets, create social protection programs tailored to the needs of migrants, or use a combination of the two. Sending country governments could coordinate with destination countries to create systems in which migrant workers make contributions and have access to unemployment benefits and health care at the same levels offered to the destination country's citizens. Such a system, ensuring the portability of social rights, could be devised within existing institutional frameworks such as the EaEU. To mitigate unemployment risks for migrants, origin countries could work with the private sector to develop job-loss insurance. This could cover job losses— particularly those related to exogenous shocks. Social protection interventions (such as welfare funds) can also help migrants cope with shocks in the destination country.

Measures to improve migrants' financial literacy and inclusion and to formalize remittance flows can support more productive use of these funds. Remittances are a major source of income for lower-income migrant households and for home countries. They could contribute to more productive investments—enhancing their development impact. In many countries of origin, especially those at lower income levels, remittances are mainly used for immediate consumption. Formalizing remittance flows would support a more productive use of these funds for investment and self-employment activities. Measures can be taken to improve migrant households' access to, and inclusion in, the formal financial sector. This would expand their use of financial products and reduce transaction costs for sending remittances through formal channels. In addition, financial literacy programs can enhance households' understanding of the options for investments and savings. In contexts outside ECA, such programs have been effective in increasing migrants' financial knowledge, increasing their savings and productive usage of remittances.

After migrants return, key interventions may support more productive reintegration into home labor markets and reduce their vulnerabilities. The first step is establishing or strengthening registration systems for return migrants, which should be linked to national registries and a pool of support services. To gather information for such registries, systematic rapid needs assessments for returning migrants can be carried out at one-stop shops at main points of entry into the country. Referrals can then direct migrants to social protections and labor programs that address their needs. In parallel, support programs tailored to returnees' needs should be carefully designed, piloted, and evaluated before being scaled up—to help ensure their effectiveness. For returnees who intend to stay in the origin country, productive reintegration into home labor markets could be facilitated through better linkages with ALMPs and greater cooperation with receiving countries. Return migrants who have savings and entrepreneurial aspirations may benefit from one-stop-shop services that provide in-kind assistance, help with financial literacy, support to develop a business plan, and access to banking and microcredit. In situations where migrants return involuntarily or earlier than expected, short-term support can help alleviate temporary hardship.

Note

1. The definition of Europe and Central Asia used throughout this report also includes countries of the European Union. Refer to the "Classifications" section at the start of this volume.

References

Anelli, M., G. Basso, G. Ippedico, and G. Peri. 2019. "Youth Drain, Entrepreneurship and Innovation." Working Paper No. 26055, National Bureau of Economic Research, Cambridge, MA.

Avato, J., J. Koettl, and R. Sabates-Wheeler. 2010. "Social Security Regimes, Global Estimates, and Good Practices: The Status of Social Protection for International Migrants." *World Development* 38 (4): 455–66.

Bahar, D., R. J. Brough, and G. Peri. 2024. "Forced Migration and Refugees: Policies for Successful Economic and Social Integration." Working Paper 32266, National Bureau of Economic Research, Cambridge, MA.

Bahar, D., A. Hauptmann, C. Özgüzel, and H. Rapoport. 2024. "Migration and Knowledge Diffusion: The Effect of Returning Refugees on Export Performance in the Former Yugoslavia." *Review of Economics and Statistics* 106 (2): 287–304.

Barsbai, T., H. Rapoport, A. Steinmayr, and C. Trebesch. 2017. "The Effect of Labor Migration on the Diffusion of Democracy: Evidence from a Former Soviet Republic." *American Economic Journal: Applied Economics* 9 (3): 36–69.

Battisti, M., Y. Giesing, and N. Laurentsyeva. 2019. "Can Job Search Assistance Improve the Labour Market Integration of Refugees? Evidence from a Field Experiment." *Labour Economics* 61: 101745.

Beine, M., F. Docquier, and C. Oden-Defoort. 2011. "A Panel Data Analysis of the Brain Gain." *World Development* 39 (4): 523–32.

Beine, M., F. Docquier, and H. Rapoport. 2008. "Brain Drain and Human Capital Formation in Developing Countries: Winners and Losers." *Economic Journal* 118 (528): 631–52. https://doi.org/10.1111/j.1468-0297.2008.02135.x.

Bilgili, O., T. Huddleston, and A. Joki. 2015. *The Dynamics between Integration Policies and Outcomes: A Synthesis of the Literature.* Barcelona: Barcelona Centre for International Affairs.

Docquier, F., O. Lohest, and A. Marfouk. 2007. "Brain Drain in Developing Countries." *World Bank Economic Review* 21 (2): 193–218.

Fasani, F., and J. Mazza. 2023. "Being on the Frontline? Immigrant Workers in Europe and the COVID-19 Pandemic." *ILR Review* 76 (5): 890–918.

Giesing, Y., and N. Laurentsyeva. 2018. "Firms Left Behind: Emigration and Firm Productivity." Working Paper No. 6815, CESifo, Munich.

Grigorieff, A., C. Roth, and D. Ubfal 2020. "Does Information Change Attitudes toward Immigrants?" *Demography* 57 (3): 1117–43.

Haaland, I., and C. Roth. 2020. "Labor Market Concerns and Support for Immigration." *Journal of Public Economics* 191: 104256.

Hopkins, D. J., J. Sides, and J. Citrin. 2019. "The Muted Consequences of Correct Information about Immigration." *Journal of Politics* 81 (1): 315–20.

Huddleston, T. 2020. "Global Links between Indicators of Integration Policies and Outcomes: A Roadmap to Improve Integration Policies and Outcomes for Egyptian Immigrants." Research Paper no. 5, UCD Clinton Institute, Dublin.

Jørgensen, F. J., and M. Osmundsen. 2022. "Correcting Citizens' Misperceptions about Non-Western Immigrants: Corrective Information, Interpretations, and Policy Opinions." *Journal of Experimental Political Science* 9 (1): 64–73.

Kende, J., O. Sarrasin, A. Manatschal, K. Phalet, and E. G. T. Green. 2022. "Policies and Prejudice: Integration Policies Moderate the Link between Immigrant Presence and Anti-Immigrant Prejudice." *Journal of Personality and Social Psychology* 123 (2): 337–52. https://doi.org/10.1037/pspi0000376.

Nielson, J. 2004. "Trade Agreements and Recognition." In *Quality and Recognition in Higher Education: The Cross Border Challenge*, 155–203. Paris: Organisation for Economic Co-operation and Development.

OECD (Organisation for Economic Co-operation and Development. 2022. *Labour Migration in the Western Balkans: Mapping Patterns, Addressing Challenges and Reaping Benefits*. Paris: OECD. https://www.oecd.org/south-east-europe/programme/Labour-Migration-report.pdf.

Poutvaara, P. 2004. "Educating Europe: Should Public Education Be Financed with Graduate Taxes or Income-Contingent Loans?" *CESifo Economic Studies* 50 (4): 663–84.

Pritchett, L. 2018: "Alleviating Global Poverty: Labor Mobility, Direct Assistance, and Economic Growth." Working Paper 479, Center for Global Development, Washington, DC.

Tjaden, J., and T. Heidland. Forthcoming. "Did Merkel's 2015 Decision Attract More Migration to Germany?" *European Journal of Political Research*. https://doi.org/10.1111/1475-6765.12669.

World Bank. 2023. "*World Development Report 2023: Migrants, Refugees, and Societies.*" Washington, DC: World Bank. https://doi.org/10.1596/978-1-4648-1941-4.

Abbreviations

ALMPs	active labor market policies
BLA	bilateral labor agreement
CEAS	Common European Asylum System
CPIs	consumer price indices
DGMM	Directorate General for Migration Management
EaEU	Eurasian Economic Union
EAP	East Asia and Pacific
ECA	Europe and Central Asia
EFTA	European Free Trade Association
EQPR	European Qualifications Passport for Refugees
ESSN	Emergency Social Safety Net
EU	European Union (used as modifier; spelled out as noun, sim. to US and UK)
EU-15	European Union members before May 1, 2004
EU LFS	European Union Labour Force Survey
EU-NMS13	new member states joining the European Union on May 1, 2004; January 1, 2007; and July 1, 2013
FDI	foreign direct investment
G2G	government-to-government
GDP	gross domestic product
GSP	Global Skill Partnership
ICL	income-contingent loan
ICT	information and communications technology
ISEI	International Socio-Economic Index of Occupational Status
ISKUR	Turkish Employment Office
IT	information technology
IV	instrumental variable
KOSGEB	Small and Medium Enterprises Development Organization
LAC	Latin American and the Caribbean

MENA	Middle East and North Africa
MiRPAL	Migration and Remittance Peer-Assisted Learning Network
NA	North America
NEET	neither employment nor education or training
NGOs	nongovernmental organizations
NUTS	Nomenclature of Territorial Units for Statistics
NUTS-2	NUTS level 2
NUTS-3	NUTS level 3
PES	public employment services
PMM	Presidency of Migration Management
PPP	purchasing power parity
SAR	South Asia
SSA	Sub-Saharan Africa
SuTPs	Syrians under temporary protection
THLFS	Turkish Household Labor Force Surveys
TKYB	Development Investment Bank of Türkiye
TOBB	Union of Chambers and Commodity Exchanges of Türkiye
TPR	Temporary Protection Regulation
UN	United Nations
UN DESA	United Nations Department of Economic and Social Affairs
UNHCR	UN High Commissioner for Refugees

Regional Classifications Used in This Report

		European Union (EU)				
		Western EU	**Southern EU**	**Central EU**	**Northern EU**	**Western Balkans**
Europe and Central Asia	EU and Western Balkans	Austria Belgium France Germany Ireland Luxembourg Netherlands (Before January 31, 2020, Western EU included the United Kingdom.)	Cyprus Greece Italy Malta Portugal Spain	Bulgaria Croatia Czechia Hungary Poland Romania Slovak Republic Slovenia	Denmark Estonia Finland Latvia Lithuania Sweden	Albania Bosnia and Herzegovina Kosovo Montenegro North Macedonia Serbia
		Caucasus	**Central Asia**	**Russian Federation**	**Türkiye**	**Eastern Europe**
	Eastern Europe and Central Asia	Armenia Azerbaijan Georgia	Kazakhstan Kyrgyz Republic Tajikistan Turkmenistan Uzbekistan			Belarus Moldova Ukraine
	EFTA (Iceland, Liechtenstein, Norway, Switzerland) and United Kingdom					

Other country groups mentioned in this report:

EFTA: Iceland, Liechtenstein, Norway, Switzerland

EU (European Union): Austria, Belgium, Bulgaria, Croatia, Cyprus, Czechia, Denmark, Estonia, Finland, France, Germany, Greece, Hungary, Ireland, Italy, Latvia, Lithuania, Luxembourg, Malta, Netherlands, Poland, Portugal, Romania, Slovakia, Slovenia, Spain, Sweden. Before January 31, 2020 (Brexit), the EU member states included the United Kingdom.

EU-15: Austria, Belgium, Denmark, Finland, France, Germany, Greece, Ireland, Italy, Luxembourg, Netherlands, Portugal, Spain, Sweden, United Kingdom (EU member states before May 1, 2004)

Northern EU-15: Austria, Belgium, Denmark, Finland, France, Germany, Ireland, Luxembourg, Netherlands, Sweden, United Kingdom

Southern EU-15: Greece, Italy, Portugal, Spain

EU-28: Austria, Belgium, Bulgaria, Croatia, Cyprus, Czechia, Denmark, Estonia, Finland, France, Germany, Greece, Hungary, Ireland, Italy, Latvia, Lithuania, Luxembourg, Malta, Netherlands, Poland, Portugal, Romania, Slovak Republic, Slovenia, Spain, Sweden, United Kingdom (coincides with EU before January 31, 2020).

EU-NMS13: Bulgaria, Croatia, Cyprus, Czechia, Estonia, Hungary, Latvia, Lithuania, Malta, Poland, Romania, Slovak Republic, Slovenia

Western Europe: Before January 31, 2020, included EU-15 and EFTA. After January 31, 2020, included Austria, Belgium, Denmark, Finland, France, Germany, Greece, Ireland, Italy, Luxembourg, Netherlands, Portugal, Spain, Sweden, EFTA and the United Kingdom.

Introduction

The region of Europe and Central Asia (ECA), one of the most developed economic areas globally, has a rich history of migration that has shaped its economic and social structures. Today, the region hosts more than 100 million migrants—both from within the region and from non-ECA countries—driven by income and demographic disparities, increasing mobility within the region, and conflict.[1] Migration flows have changed over the years, both in terms of destination and origin countries and in terms of the characteristics of migrants and migration arrangements. After World War II, the economic rebuilding of Europe was supported partly by inflows of migrants—predominantly coming from former colonies of Western European nations (Van Mol and de Valk 2016). Later, the oil crisis of 1973–74, which reduced the demand for labor, led to restrictions to the entrance of foreign workers and the emergence of "stop policies" in the main traditional migrant destination countries of Northwest Europe (Boyle, Halfacree, and Robinson 1998). During this period, immigration policy centered around family reunification, and work visa permits were more limited.

In the 1990s, migration in ECA was shaped by the fall of the Berlin Wall, war in the former Yugoslavia, and migration across ethnic lines, together with the enhancement of freedom of movement brought about through the European Union. Toward the end of the 1980s, the fall of the Iron Curtain drastically redrew administrative boundaries in ECA, with the fragmentation of the Soviet Union and Yugoslavia into different new countries and the German reunification. These changes induced new migration flows across ECA, partly linked to ethnic ties. There was a sizable resettlement of Russian-speaking migrants living in other former Soviet

1

republics, which represented around 60 percent of arrivals to the Russian Federation during the 1990s (Chudinovskikh and Denisenko 2017). Migration in Germany, the country with the largest increase in the stock of immigrants in ECA during the 1990s (around 3 million migrants), was also strongly driven by the arrival of *Aussiedler* (ethnic Germans from different countries in Central and Eastern Europe, such as Poland, Romania, and Russia). The war in the former Yugoslavia during the 1990s led to outflows of forcibly displaced populations in the different Balkan countries, with Serbia and, to a lesser extent, Croatia hosting the bulk of the 1 million intraregion migrants. A spike in asylum seekers to Western European countries, such as Austria and Germany (Hatton 2004), and the Nordic countries also occurred. Migration in ECA in the 1990s also reflected the increasing prominence of the European Union in migration policy making and the management of flows from non-EU countries. The 1992 Maastricht Treaty established freedom of movement within the European Union, fueling intraregion movements. In 1995, this freedom of movement grew with the accession of Austria, Finland, and Sweden to the European Union.

During the 2000s, migration flows in ECA accelerated, fueled by buoyant economic activity in the Southern EU and the EU enlargement with Central and Eastern European countries. In the first decade of the 21st century, the stock of migrants in ECA increased by nearly 14 million. On the one hand, favorable conditions in the Southern EU diverted the main migration poles to two countries: Italy and Spain, which, combined, accounted for close to 60 percent of the total regional increase. Migration inflows in these countries were partly of an irregular nature, with different regularization episodes of informal migrants in the 1990s and 2000s. On the other hand, Germany tightened its migration policy and net inflows were cut to a third compared with the previous decade. Although quotas for ethnic Germans were significantly reduced, migration in Germany shifted more toward temporary labor programs (Oezcan 2004). During this decade, migration flows originated mainly from Central and Eastern Europe—particularly from countries that joined the European Union since 2004. The largest increases in bilateral corridors were seen from Romania to Italy and Spain and from Poland to Germany and the United Kingdom. After sizable migration flows between former Soviet countries, the stock of permanent migrants in this region remained largely constant, with new forms of temporary and seasonal migration gaining traction, particularly from Central Asia and the Caucasus to Russia and, to a smaller extent, Kazakhstan. Overall, migration policies paid increasing attention to linking migration flows to labor market needs, developing specific visa programs to attract high-skilled migrants (such as the EU Blue Card Scheme; Van Mol and de Valk 2016), and advancing integration policies to improve the economic outcomes of migrants (Doomernik and Bruquetas-Callejo 2016).

In the 2000s, while the European debt and COVID-19 crises temporarily slowed down migration in ECA, new waves of conflict and economic migration continued driving migration flows in the region. The global financial and European debt crises at the turn of the decade slowed down the flows of migration in ECA—especially in the Southern EU countries that experienced the largest increases in migration in the previous decade. During this time, only the United Kingdom sustained increases in migration, mostly from non-ECA countries (for example, India). However, the 2015 refugee crisis led to a sharp acceleration in asylum seeker petitions in Europe—particularly in Germany as well as in Türkiye, where more than 3.0 million refugees were hosted. Conflicts and insecurity in Afghanistan, Iraq, the Syrian Arab Republic, and some countries in Africa were push factors for this wave of migration. At the same time, intra-EU migration flows further strengthened, given the free mobility and continuous disparities in income opportunities. In recent years, some traditionally migrant-sending countries have started to attract more migration inflows to fill emerging labor shortages (for example, Poland). The COVID-19 pandemic, however, brought strong mobility restrictions, significantly reducing the inflows of migrants in ECA in 2020. In 2021, migration flows rapidly resumed before drastically increasing in 2022 because of the war in Ukraine—which led to the largest forced displacement in recent history. As a result, 5.5 million refugees and asylum seekers were hosted in ECA countries—mainly in Germany, Poland, and Russia and, when compared in proportion with the size of the domestic population, in Czechia, Moldova, and Romania.

Megatrends, such as demographic imbalances, technological change, and automation, are expected to continue being driving forces for both low- and high-skilled migration in the region. The population of Europe is aging rapidly, with an expected increase in the median age in EU countries of 4.5 years in the next three decades (Eurostat 2020). This megatrend has important implications for the European economies, because it will continue to reduce the share of the working-age population while increasing the number of elderly people—adding pressure to welfare systems. It will also continue to be a driving demand force, attracting migration flows to fill labor shortages, especially in the care economy. In 2022, the average EU vacancy rate reached a historic high of around 3 percent, and labor shortages were found across different occupations and skill levels (Eurofound 2023). Foreign-born workers are now significantly more likely to be employed in occupations with more structural labor shortages (European Commission 2023). Technological progress and automation will also continue to increase the demand in certain sectors, fueling inflows of skilled workers to more advanced economies in the coming years.

A Unified Typology to Analyze Migration in Europe and Central Asia

Migration is a complex phenomenon, with different push and pull factors—often intertwined—including a diverse set of impacts across countries of origin and destination and across different groups of the populations of these countries, depending on the type of migration and policies in place. Throughout the rest of this report, the analysis of migration is divided into different typologies of migrants and countries to help focus the analysis on the specific challenges of migration and provide tailored policy recommendations.

With respect to migrants, it is important to differentiate between refugees and economic migrants. Although the economic migrant-refugee dichotomy simplifies a more complex reality—one that includes a continuum of degrees of vulnerability, agency in the migration decision (forced vs. voluntary), drivers of migration, and barriers faced—it is commonly used to distinguish migrants from those two categories and leads to different legal pathways to entering host countries, which, in turn, has a significant impact on a migrant's integration into the destination labor markets. Within this framework, refugees not only differ from economic migrants in terms of their drivers for migration—being forced to flee their home because of war, violence, or persecution and having their capacity to return to their home country be contingent upon a change in safety—but also on how well they integrate and the barriers they face in host countries. In Europe, the labor market outcomes for refugees are systematically worse than those for other migrants with otherwise similar characteristics. These outcomes often persist for 10–15 years after their arrival in the destination country (Fasani, Frattini, and Minale 2022). Refugees face additional barriers, both in the form of mental health trauma after fleeing violence and in restrictive policies at destination. Such policies include spatial dispersal policies that limit their ability to select the place of residence and temporary employment bans (in most cases between two and 12 months) that have long-term negative implications for their integration into the labor market (Fasani, Frattini, and Minale 2021).

The report also distinguishes between high- and low-skilled migrants, which allows for a more detailed analysis of specific challenges they face and tailored policy recommendations to support the overall benefits of migration. High- and low-skilled migrants share most of the same push and pull factors—including income disparities and other gaps in welfare and quality of living—although low-skilled migrants, who tend to be from lower-income households in their countries of origin, face further barriers to migration such as credit constraints or wider information asymmetries.

Although they might come through similar legal pathways, complex immigration and visa systems in destination countries sometimes put high- and low-skilled migrants on different legal tracks. For example, low-skilled migrants are more likely to engage in short-term migration programs such as seasonal agricultural programs or to use more irregular pathways, which increase their vulnerabilities in destination countries. On the one hand, high-skilled migrants can access more selective visa entries such as the European Talent Passport residence permit, which provides longer-term legal stability in any European country. On the other hand, high-skilled migrants are more likely to experience other relevant challenges derived from the lack of recognition of foreign credentials and occupational downgrade in host labor markets. In terms of impacts in destination countries, both high- and low-skilled migrants tend to fill essential occupations, improving the conditions of workers with complementary skills while negatively affecting, at least in the short term, workers with substitute skills. However, high-skilled migrants who bring diverse talent and expertise are more likely to support productivity increases in host countries and have a stronger net positive welfare effect (Battisti et al. 2018). Low-skilled migrants tend to work more in manual, routine jobs, incentivizing the native-born population to move to more complex occupations that require more language and communication skills, for which they have an advantage (Jaumotte, Koloskova, and Saxena 2016). In sending countries, the extent of high- and low-skilled migration shapes the emergence of potential occupational gaps, creates different incentives to invest in human capital, and has asymmetric implications on the debate over brain drain or brain gain in the economy. In comparison with the "match-and-motive" framework proposed by the *World Development Report 2023* (World Bank 2023), the rows of figure I.1, with the different typologies of migrants, correspond to the "motive" axis, where migrants are pushed by different circumstances, aspirations, and vulnerabilities. Similarly, the columns of figure I.1 are more related to the "match" axis, because the elements considered are the factors that will determine migrants' destination, as well as the match of migrants in receiving countries with local demand and the outcomes of those matches depending on migration-regulating institutions. The rest of this report follows this framework, and the chapters are divided according to the typology of migrants and countries (figure I.2).

This report also uses the migration life cycle as a framework to analyze policy challenges and propose solutions related to migration. The migration life cycle can typically be divided into four phases: premigration decision, predeparture, in service (while migrants are abroad), and return (refer to figure I.3). During the predecision phase, a worker decides to migrate on the basis of their understanding of the costs and benefits of migrating.

FIGURE I.1

Broad typologies of migrants, drivers, challenges, and migration-regulating policies

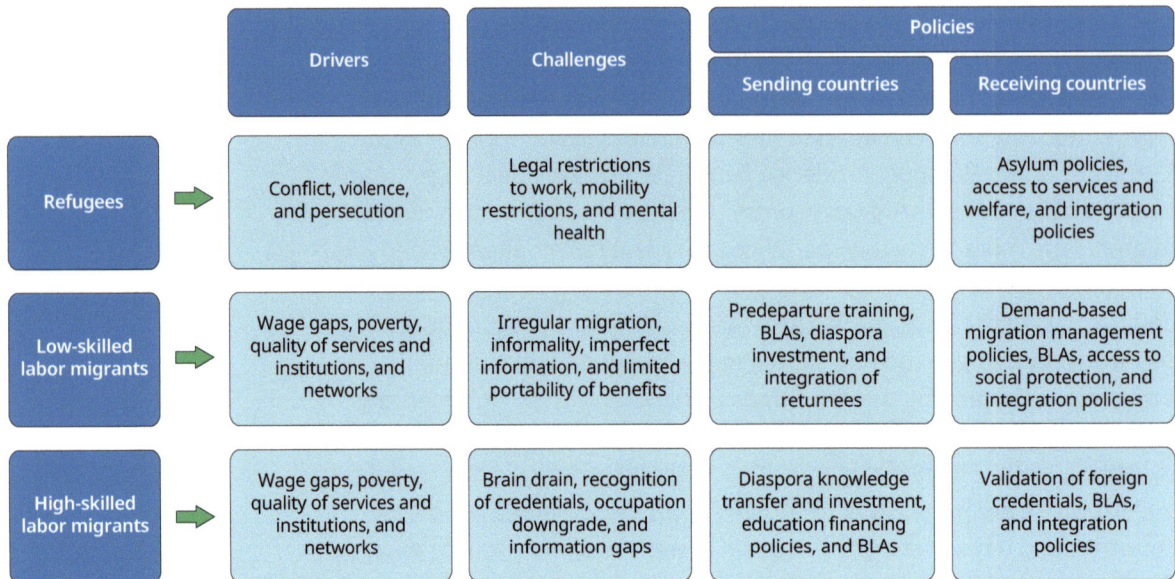

	Drivers	Challenges	Policies	
			Sending countries	Receiving countries
Refugees	Conflict, violence, and persecution	Legal restrictions to work, mobility restrictions, and mental health		Asylum policies, access to services and welfare, and integration policies
Low-skilled labor migrants	Wage gaps, poverty, quality of services and institutions, and networks	Irregular migration, informality, imperfect information, and limited portability of benefits	Predeparture training, BLAs, diaspora investment, and integration of returnees	Demand-based migration management policies, BLAs, access to social protection, and integration policies
High-skilled labor migrants	Wage gaps, poverty, quality of services and institutions, and networks	Brain drain, recognition of credentials, occupation downgrade, and information gaps	Diaspora knowledge transfer and investment, education financing policies, and BLAs	Validation of foreign credentials, BLAs, and integration policies

Source: Original figure for this publication.
Note: Bilateral labor agreements (BLAs) are international agreements signed between two countries to regulate the flow of migrant workers between them.

FIGURE I.2

Typologies of migrants and country contexts

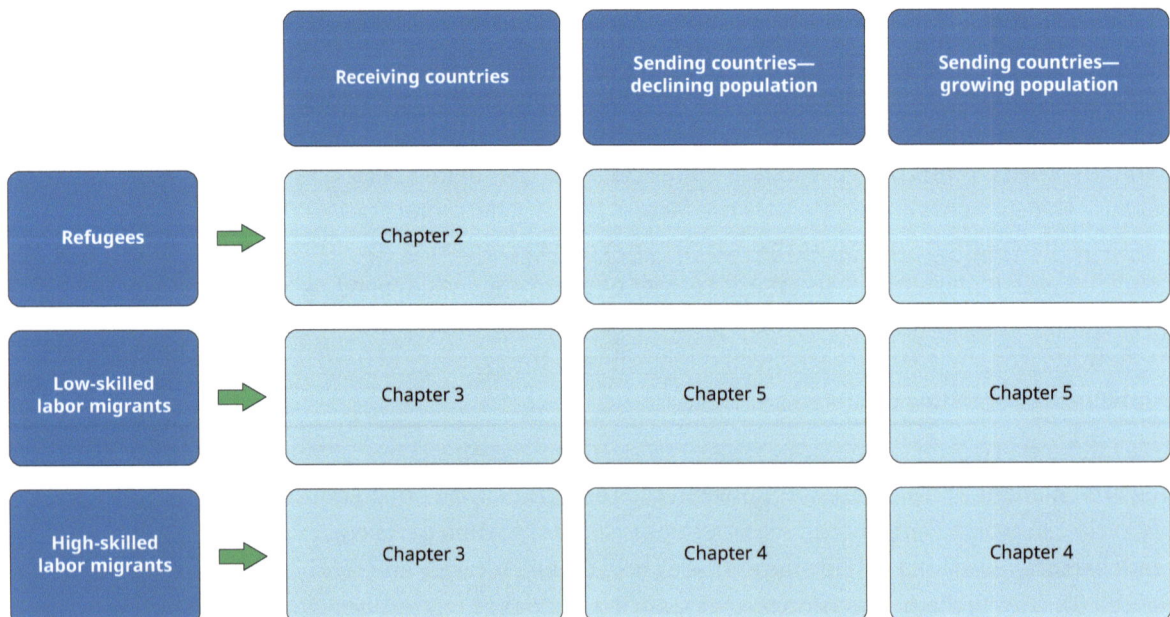

	Receiving countries	Sending countries— declining population	Sending countries— growing population
Refugees	Chapter 2		
Low-skilled labor migrants	Chapter 3	Chapter 5	Chapter 5
High-skilled labor migrants	Chapter 3	Chapter 4	Chapter 4

Source: Original figure for this publication.

FIGURE I.3

The four stages of the migration life cycle for economic migration policy

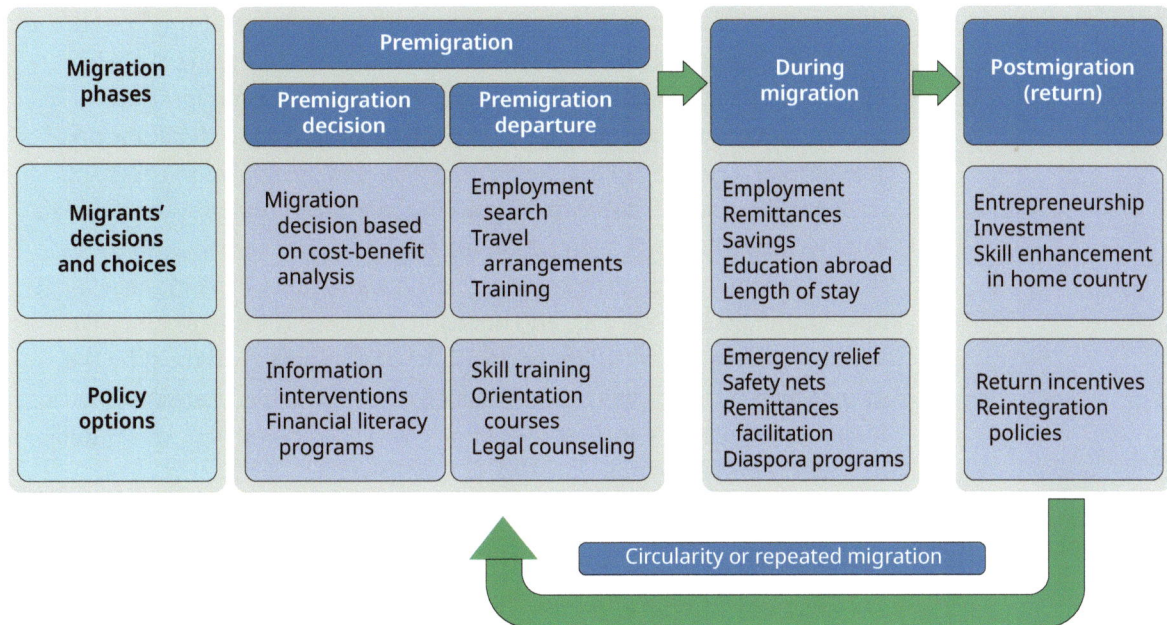

Migration phases	Premigration		During migration	Postmigration (return)
	Premigration decision	Premigration departure		
Migrants' decisions and choices	Migration decision based on cost-benefit analysis	Employment search Travel arrangements Training	Employment Remittances Savings Education abroad Length of stay	Entrepreneurship Investment Skill enhancement in home country
Policy options	Information interventions Financial literacy programs	Skill training Orientation courses Legal counseling	Emergency relief Safety nets Remittances facilitation Diaspora programs	Return incentives Reintegration policies

Circularity or repeated migration

Source: Original figure for this publication based on Ahmed and Bossavie 2022.

After the worker has decided to pursue a job abroad, they can take measures predeparture to improve their employability, find and obtain a job, and obtain the necessary legal documents to migrate. The third stage is during migration when the migrant is employed abroad; decisions at this stage include the selection of occupation, whether to invest in general or country-specific human capital, and whether to send remittances back home, and, if so, how much. The final stage is after migration (in the case of temporary migration), when a migrant leaves the destination to return home and, in most cases, starts an economic activity in their home labor market. Some migrants, such as seasonal workers, repeat this migration cycle several times over their lifetime, in what is called circular migration. Although the migration life cycle framework can be divided into stages, all stages are interconnected, and outcomes and policies at each life cycle stage have repercussions for the others. This report builds on this framework to identify inefficiencies and vulnerabilities at each stage of the migration life cycle and consider the interconnectedness among the different stages when formulating policy solutions.

Policies implemented by sending and receiving countries at each stage of the migration life cycle also affect the outcomes and vulnerabilities of migrants at other stages. At each stage of this process, migrants require information and support from the migration management systems of both their country of origin and the destination country. Because life cycle stages are part of the same lifetime decisions (Bossavie et al. 2021; Dustmann and Görlach 2016), they cannot be seen in isolation. They are all intertwined, and policies implemented at one stage of the life cycle have dynamic repercussions on other stages. For example, premigration employment outcomes and age at departure are linked to the duration of stay abroad. Duration of stay, in turn, is affected by migration costs and wages abroad, which determine how long migrants need to stay abroad to achieve a given savings target. Coming full circle, the ability to finance a self-employment activity after return will be affected by the monetary costs of migration, wages abroad, and duration of stay at the destination. Policies aiming to influence any of these decisions or outcomes will thus, by the very nature of these links, also influence the others. It is therefore critical for policy makers to consider these links when designing policies related to temporary migration.

The rest of the report is structured as follows: chapter 1 provides an overview of trends and drivers of the stock and flows of migrants from and to ECA, as well as the different types of migration and the main data gaps that limit the analysis of this phenomenon. Chapter 2 analyzes the different waves of refugees and asylum seekers in the region of ECA and their profiles, and it extracts lessons on how policies put in place across different host countries shape their integration and outcomes. Chapter 3 explores evidence regarding the impacts of both low- and high-skilled economic migrants in destination countries. In turn, chapter 4 focuses on the prevalence and impact of high-skilled economic migration in sending countries, including its effects on human capital accumulation and domestic labor markets. Finally, chapter 5 studies low-skilled emigration across ECA sending countries, the vulnerability of migrants to various shocks, the challenges they face to maximize the benefits of migration, the role of remittances, and potential return migration to the home country.

Note

1. The definition of Europe and Central Asia used throughout this report also includes countries of the European Union.

References

Ahmed, S. A., and L. Bossavie. 2022. *Toward Safer and More Productive Migration for South Asia*. Washington, DC: World Bank. http://documents.worldbank.org/curated/en/903161585816440273/Toward-Safer-and -More-Productive-Migration-for-South-Asia.

Battisti, M., G. Felbermayr, G. Peri, and P. Poutvaara. 2018. "Immigration, Search and Redistribution: A Quantitative Assessment of Native Welfare." *Journal of the European Economic Association* 16 (4): 1137–88. https://doi.org/10.1093/jeea/jvx035.

Bossavie, L., J. S. Görlach, Ç. Özden, and H. Wang. 2021. "Temporary Migration for Long-Term Investment." World Bank Policy Research Working Paper 9740, World Bank, Washington, DC. https://doi.org/10.1596 /1813-9450-9740.

Boyle, P., K. Halfacree, and V. Robinson. 1998. *Exploring Contemporary Migration*. New York: Routledge.

Chudinovskikh, O., and M. Denisenko. 2017. *Russia: A Migration System with Soviet Roots*. Washington, DC: Migration Policy Institute.

Doomernik, J., and M. Bruquetas-Callejo. 2016. "National Immigration and Integration Policies in Europe Since 1973." In *Integration Processes and Policies in Europe: Contexts, Levels and Actor*, edited by B. Garcés-Mascareñas and R. Penninx, 57–76. IMISCOE Research Series. Cham, Switzerland: Springer.

Dustmann, C., and J. S. Görlach. 2016. "The Economics of Temporary Migrations." *Journal of Economic Literature* 54 (1): 98–136. https://doi.org/10.1257/jel.54.1.98.

Eurofound. 2023. *Measures to Tackle Labour Shortages: Lessons for Future Policy*. Dublin: Eurofound.

European Commission, Directorate-General for Employment, Social Affairs and Inclusion. 2023. *Employment and Social Developments in Europe 2023: Addressing Labour Shortages and Skills Gaps in the EU*. Luxembourg: Publications Office of the European Union.

Eurostat, Statistics Explained. 2020. "Ageing Europe: Looking at the Lives of Older People in the EU." https:// ec.europa.eu/eurostat/statistics-explained/index.php?title=Ageing_Europe_-_statistics_on_population _developments.

Fasani, F., T. Frattini, and L. Minale. 2021. "Lift the Ban? Initial Employment Restrictions and Refugee Labour Market Outcomes." *Journal of the European Economic Association* 19 (5): 2803–54. https://doi.org/10.1093 /jeea/jvab021.

Fasani, F., T. Frattini, and L. Minale. 2022. "(The Struggle for) Refugee Integration into the Labour Market: Evidence from Europe." *Journal of Economic Geography* 22 (2): 351–93. https://doi.org/10.1093/jeg /lbab011.

Hatton, T. 2004. "Seeking Asylum in Europe." *Economic Policy* 19 (38): 5–62.

Jaumotte, F., K. Koloskova, and S. C. Saxena. 2016. "Impact of Migration on Income Levels in Advanced Economies." Spillover Note 2016/008, International Monetary Fund, Washington, DC.

Oezcan, V. 2004. "Germany: Immigration in Transition." *Migration Information Source*, July 1, 2004.

Van Mol, C., and H. de Valk. 2016. "Migration and Immigrants in Europe: A Historical and Demographic Perspective." In *Integration Processes and Policies in Europe: Contexts, Levels and Actors*, edited by B Garcés-Mascareñas and R. Penninx, 31–56. IMISCOE Research Series. Cham, Switzerland: Springer.

World Bank. 2023. *World Development Report 2023: Migrants, Refugees, and Societies*. Washington, DC: World Bank. https://www.worldbank.org/en/publication/wdr2023.

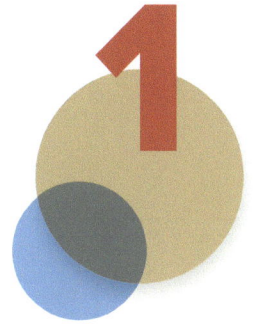

International Migration
in Europe and Central Asia
Trends, Corridors, Typologies, and Drivers

Chapter Highlights

- Europe and Central Asia (ECA) is the region with the largest number of migrants globally (100 million, one-third of the world total).

- Migration in ECA has drastically expanded in the past two years with the displacement of Ukrainian refugees (about 5 million in 2022 alone).

- Migration in ECA is highly concentrated in Western European countries and the Russian Federation, with the top five receiving countries hosting half of the total number of migrants in the region (France, Germany, Italy, Russia, and the United Kingdom).

- Close to 2 in 3 migrants in ECA come from other ECA countries.

- As a percentage of the population, emigration rates are the highest in Western Balkan countries, Armenia, and Moldova, whereas various European Union (EU) new member states have shown the largest increases since 2004.

- The largest migration corridors in ECA include that between Russia and the former USSR republics, as well as between EU countries, such as from Poland to Germany and from Romania to Italy. The concentration of bilateral migration corridors has decreased since 1990.

- Migration flows in ECA are diverse, with different drivers and outcomes, creating distinct opportunities and challenges for policy makers:

  - *Economic migrants versus refugees.* Most migrants move for economic reasons, although the share of refugees has been increasing, fueled by the Syrian war and Russia's invasion of Ukraine. Countries in ECA with lower levels of gross domestic product (GDP) per capita have a higher ratio of refugees over the total migrant population.

  - *Gender.* Migration tends to be gender-neutral, with close to 50 percent of migrants being female. However, forced displacement is associated with a larger share of women and children than is economic migration, whereas shorter-term economic migration is more male dominated.

  - *Temporary versus permanent.* After 15 years, fewer than half of migrants in the European Union remain in the destination country. Some return migrants stay in their home country, whereas others have multiple migration episodes (seasonal or circular).

  - *Formal versus informal.* Although the vast majority of migration in the region is formal, irregular migration also occurs, which takes place when migrants enter the country without adequate documents or when they overstay.

- The drivers of migration flows include conflict and violence, income differentials and searches for better economic opportunities, quality of services and rule of law, demographic changes and aging, social networks, and the expansion of economic unions that facilitate intraregion mobility.

- Data gaps limit the analysis of migration in the region, particularly from the sending countries' perspective. Few surveys and administrative data capture the full extent of emigration and return migration.

Patterns and Trends across Main Corridors and by Migration Type

The ECA region hosts the largest number of global migrants, and the share of migrants as a proportion of its population has dramatically increased over time. According to 2020 data from the United Nations Department of Economic and Social Affairs (UN DESA), ECA hosts close to 99 million migrants (refer to figure 1.1, panel a),[1] representing 35 percent of the total global migrant population. Taking into consideration the recent inflows of refugees from Ukraine, the number of migrants in the region reached around 104 million in 2022. In comparison, the other two regions with the largest share of immigrants are North America (around 60 million) and the

Middle East and North Africa (more than 40 million, a sizable number of them refugees). The number of migrants in the ECA region has rapidly increased over the past two decades, growing about 50 percent by the end of 2020, from slightly above 60 million in 2000. In ECA, migrants represent 11 percent of the total population (close to 12 percent when refugees from Ukraine are included). This percentage is similar to the Middle East and North Africa (10 percent) and significantly above the world average (3 percent), but it is lower than in North America (16 percent; refer to figure 1.1, panel b).

Migration from the Destination Countries' Perspective

Migration in ECA is highly concentrated in terms of destination countries, with five countries hosting half of the total stock of migrants. This concentration, however, has declined from 1990 to 2020. Migration flows are largely imbalanced in the region, with the vast majority of immigrants going to Western European countries and Russia (refer to figure 1.2, panel a). Migration to southern EU countries grew the fastest during the 2000s, whereas northern EU countries and Türkiye took the lead as the fastest growing after the 2008 financial crisis and the Syrian civil war that began in 2011, respectively. However, migration to other ECA regions has stayed roughly constant (for example, Russia, Western Balkans) or even declined (for example, Eastern European countries such as Belarus or Ukraine). The concentration of migration

FIGURE 1.1

Immigration by region of destination, 1990–2020

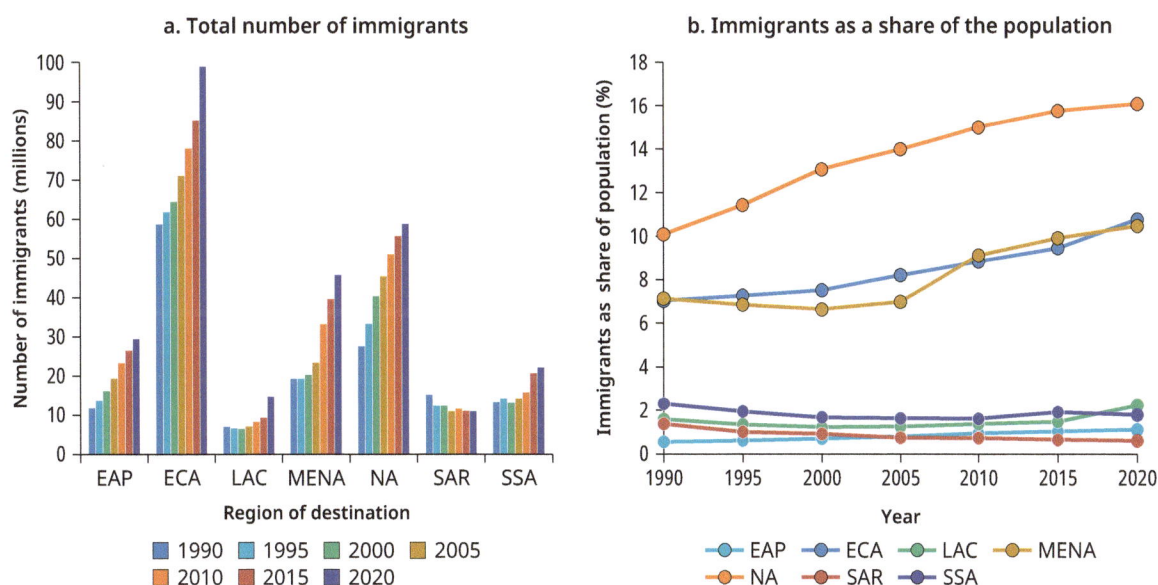

a. Total number of immigrants

b. Immigrants as a share of the population

Source: UN 2020.
Note: EAP = East Asia and Pacific; ECA = Europe and Central Asia; LAC = Latin American and the Caribbean; MENA = Middle East and North Africa; NA = North America; SAR = South Asia; SSA = Sub-Saharan Africa.

BOX 1.1 Defining International Migrants

When analyzing the topic of migration, its size, and its impact, it is fundamental to clarify who counts as a migrant. However, there is no single, universally accepted definition of a migrant. Most commonly, migrants can be defined in terms of place of birth—those who reside in a country different from the one in which they were born—or citizenship—those who reside in a place different from the country of their citizenship. Although there is no single, formal definition of an international migrant, the most prevalent one considers those who change their country of usual residence, regardless of the driver of migration (for example, fleeing violence or conflict, searching for economic opportunities, pursuing studies, or for family reasons) or their legal status (regular or irregular). This definition of migration is the one accepted by the International Organization for Migration and the *United Nations Recommendations on Statistics of International Migration* (UN 1998). However, definitions of migration based on place of birth or on citizenship have strengths and weaknesses, and the choice of definition largely depends on the focus and objective of study.

Throughout this report, international migrants are considered to be those who reside in a country different from their place of birth, irrespective of their citizenship. In EU countries, this definition of international migrants also includes populations born in other EU member states. This definition allows a broad analysis of the development challenges that emerge from moving to a different place irrespective of the legal status (e.g., citizen, EU national, third-country national with or without visa). In comparison, using the citizenship-based definition focuses on the specific challenges related to a lack of citizenship (United Nations 2020). Defining migration on the basis of citizenship can exclude groups who moved across countries but then naturalized in the destination country. Although naturalized or intra-EU migrants no longer face barriers in the host country based on their legal status and, thus, tend to be more integrated, they might still experience other barriers related to more limited networks, cultural or linguistic gaps, or discrimination. Furthermore, even if they are less likely to return to their country of origin, they might still have links to that country through diaspora groups. Therefore, this report considers it important to include this group in the analysis of migration from the perspective of both sending and receiving countries.

Another reason for the selection of the place-of-birth definition is that estimates of the stock of migrants are not shaped by citizenship policies—especially the residency requirements for naturalization—and this selection avoids estimate challenges in instances in which people have citizenship in more than one country. It also avoids counting, as international migrants, people who were born and raised in a country where citizenship is conferred based on *jus sanguinis* and whose parents did not have citizenship.

However, a definition based on place of birth also has some important limitations. A main one is that it includes people born in a previously unified country (for example, the former Soviet Union or Yugoslavia) who then left for another part of the country when it became independent—even if they did not cross any international borders. That is why migration corridors between former USSR countries register as some of the largest numbers in Europe and Central Asia (ECA) using the place-of-birth definition, whereas numbers are more modest when using the citizenship definition.

Continued

BOX 1.1 Defining International Migrants *(Continued)*

In ECA, although there were an estimated 99 million foreign-born migrants in 2020, the number of foreign citizens was estimated to be 57 million in the same year (United Nations 2020). That is, around 4 in 10 people who moved to another country in the region naturalized and received the nationality of the destination country. By region of destination, the stock of migrants based on the residency definition is always larger than that based on citizenship (refer to figure B1.1). Nevertheless, the cross-country correlation between the two measures of migration is very high (0.95). This suggests robustness of results, regardless of the definition of migrant used.

FIGURE B1.1

Share of migrants in destination countries, by citizenship or place of birth, 2020

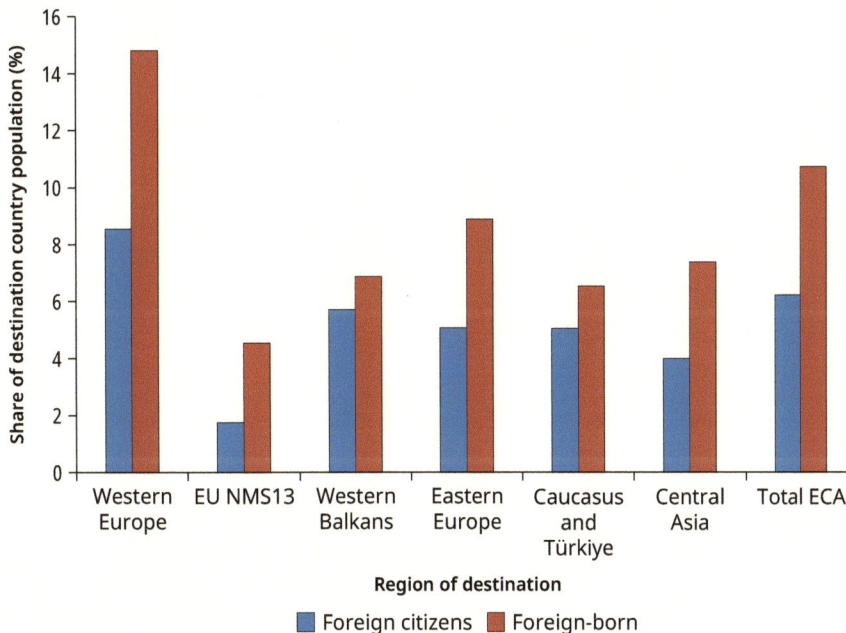

Sources: UN 2020; World Bank 2023.
Note: Foreign-born are defined as individuals who were born in a country different from their current country of residence. Foreign citizens are defined as individuals who have a citizenship different from their current country of residence. Eastern Europe = Belarus, Moldova, Russia and Ukraine; ECA = Europe and Central Asia. EU NMS13 = 13 new member states joining the European Union in 2004, 2007, and 2013 (Bulgaria, Croatia, Cyprus, Czechia, Estonia, Hungary, Latvia, Lithuania, Malta, Poland, Romania, Slovak Republic, and Slovenia); Western Europe = EU-15 + European Free Trade Association.

is also observed when looking at the stock of migrants by individual destination countries. Figure 1.2, panel b, shows the concentration of migrants in ECA as the cumulative distribution of migrants by destination countries ranked on the *x* axis from top receiving countries to bottom receiving countries. In 2020, only five of the 50 ECA countries hosted more than 50 percent of all migrants in

FIGURE 1.2

Immigration in Europe and Central Asia, by region of destination and country concentration, 1990–2020

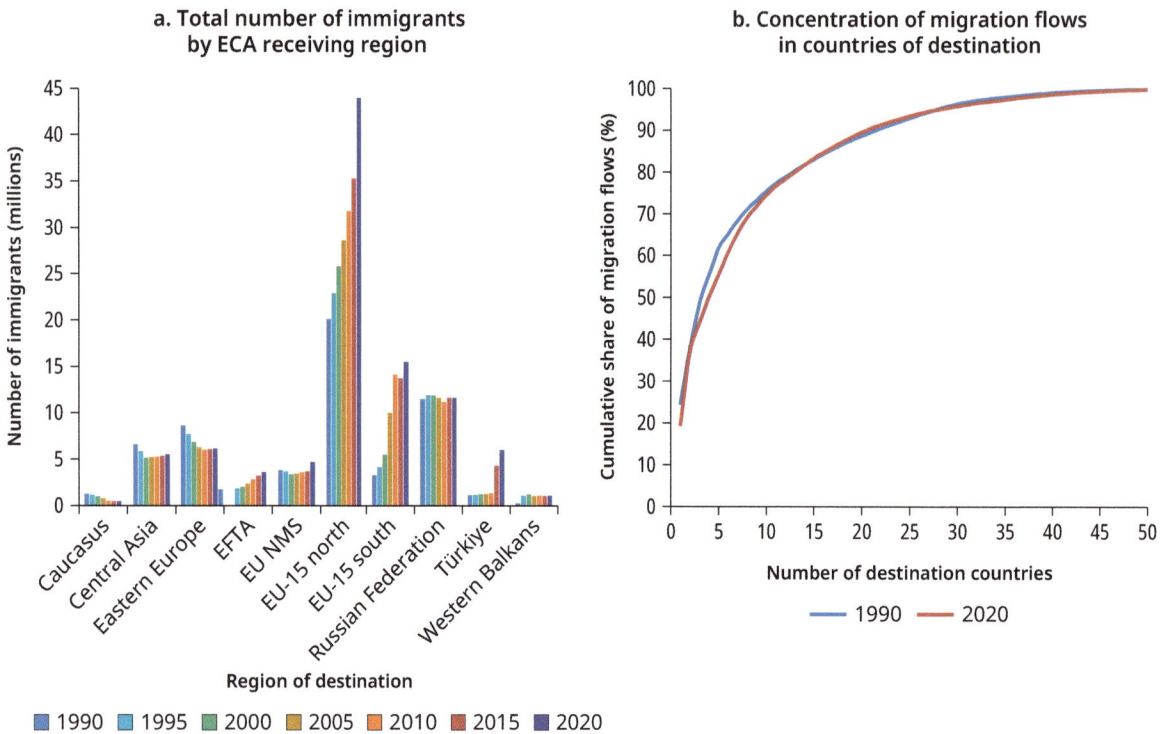

a. Total number of immigrants by ECA receiving region

b. Concentration of migration flows in countries of destination

Region of destination

Number of destination countries

■ 1990 ■ 1995 ■ 2000 ■ 2005 ■ 2010 ■ 2015 ■ 2020

— 1990 — 2020

Source: UN 2020.
Note: ECA = Europe and Central Asia; Eastern Europe = Belarus, Moldova, and Ukraine; EFTA = European Free Trade Association (Iceland, Liechtenstein, Norway, and Switzerland); EU-15 = European Union members before 2004; EU NMS13 = 13 new member states joining the European Union since 2004.

the region. Furthermore, the top 10 migrant-receiving countries received more than 75 percent of the total number of migrants to ECA. This concentration has slightly decreased between 1990 and 2020, as more countries in the Southern EU and Türkiye attracted more migrants, and migration in Russia, the second largest destination country, remained constant.

France, Germany, Russia, and the United Kingdom host the largest number of migrants in ECA. Most migrants in ECA are hosted by these countries and, more recently, Türkiye as well. Figure 1.3, panel a, provides the distribution of the total number of migrants within ECA by country for 1990–2020. On the one hand, Germany hosts the largest migrant population in absolute terms (above 15 million), which rose substantially between 2015 and 2020 due to a sizable inflow of asylum seekers—especially from the Syrian Arab Republic. On the other hand, the number of migrants hosted by Russia, the second largest receiving country, has remained constant over the same period. This is because migration to Russia mostly reflects pre-1990 migration within the Soviet Union. In the United Kingdom (third most migrants), the share of total

FIGURE 1.3

Top 15 migrant-receiving countries in Europe and Central Asia, 1990–2020

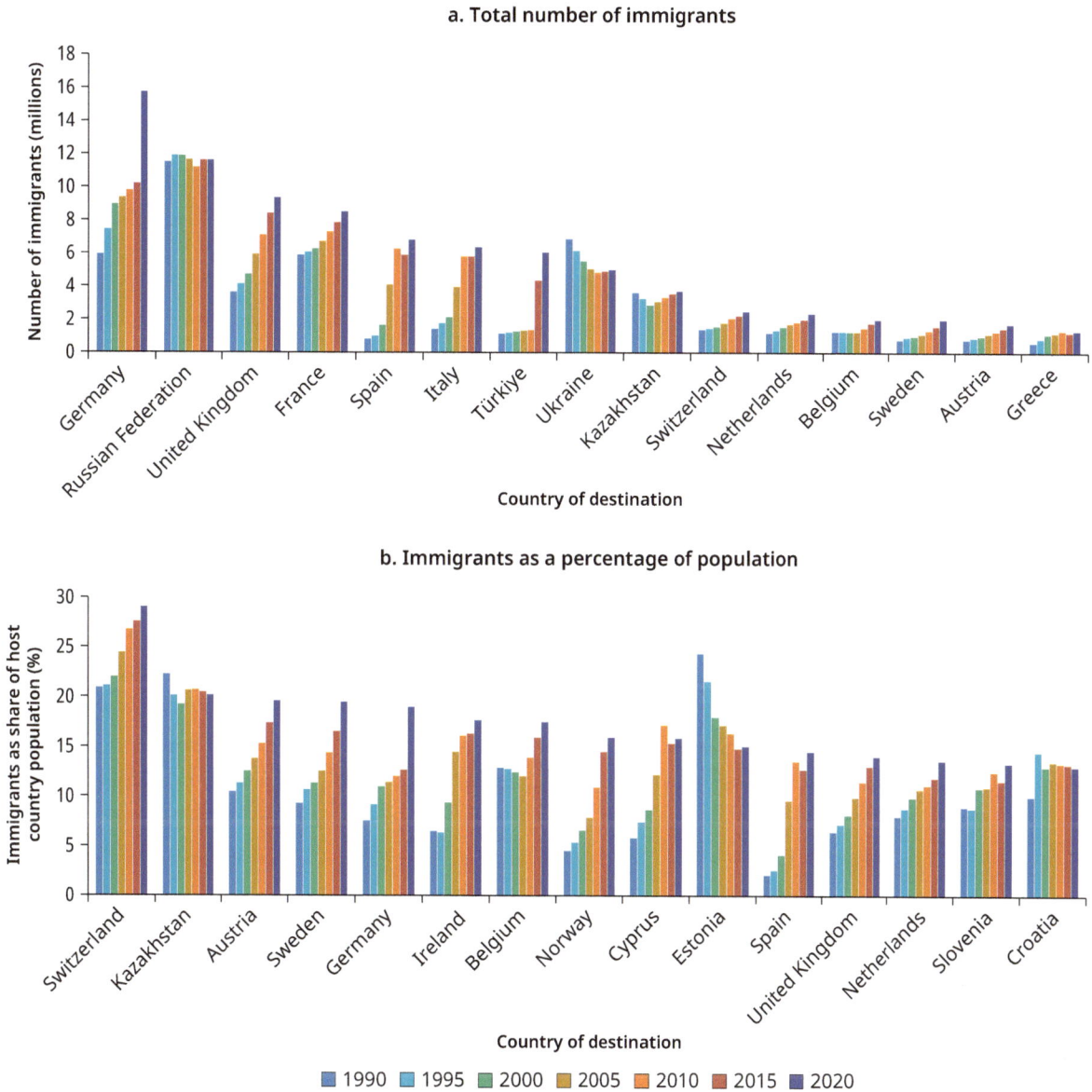

a. Total number of immigrants

b. Immigrants as a percentage of population

■ 1990 ■ 1995 ■ 2000 ■ 2005 ■ 2010 ■ 2015 ■ 2020

Source: UN 2020.
Note: Panel a reports statistics for the 15 countries in ECA with the highest absolute number of immigrants, ranked from the highest to the lowest number in 2020. Panel b reports statistics for the 15 countries with the highest share of immigrants as a percentage of their total population, ranked from the highest to the lowest share in 2020.

migrants has steadily increased over the period under consideration, especially after the eastward expansion of the European Union. In France (fourth most migrants), the total number of migrants increased less rapidly than in Germany, Spain, or the United Kingdom, likely because migration from its former colonies subsided. Spain and Italy host the fifth and sixth largest share of migrants, respectively. Through the early 2000s, until the 2008 financial crisis, both countries' share of overall migration increased substantially, driven by the inflow of generally low-skilled migrants from the new EU member states (particularly Romania). Finally, in Türkiye, the share of total migrants has increased substantially since 2011 because of a considerable number of Syrian refugees settling in the country (4 million).

Except for Kazakhstan, countries in ECA with the highest incidence of immigrants are typically smaller in population and located in Western Europe. The countries with the highest share of migrants are Switzerland (26 percent), Kazakhstan (20 percent), Austria (18 percent), Ireland (16 percent), and Sweden (15 percent; refer to figure 1.3, panel b). These countries, apart from Kazakhstan, are all small and wealthy Western European countries. They all saw their share of migrants increase steadily over time, with the increase becoming more pronounced from the 2000s onward. In contrast, Kazakhstan's share of migrants over the total population remained steady over time, strongly shaped by the dissolution of the Soviet Union in the early 1990s.

Migration from the Origin Countries' Perspective

Migration in ECA is largely an intraregional phenomenon, although conflict in the Middle East and North Africa has increased migration from that region. In absolute terms, intraregional migration in 2020 accounted for more than 60 million migrants in ECA (to which 5.5 million refugees from Ukraine were added by 2022). About 2 in 3 migrants in ECA come from other ECA countries (refer to figure 1.4), a share that increased mostly because of intra-EU migration boosts after the expansion of the European Union to 13 new member states from Eastern Europe in 2004, 2007, and 2013 (EU-NMS13). The number of migrants from outside ECA has also increased between 1990 and 2020, although at a slower pace. Migration from the Middle East and North Africa is perhaps an exception, because the population of migrants from that region doubled in the past decade, from 7 to 13 million in response to conflict in Syria and Iraq. Other regions, such as Latin America and the Caribbean, Sub-Saharan Africa, and East Asia and the Pacific, each sent about 4 million migrants to ECA, followed by South Asia (3.4 million) and North America (with only about a million migrants). Despite this geographical concentration, migration outflows from individual sending countries compared with inflows to receiving countries have been more diversified during the past 30 years, with the top five sending countries accounting for 45 percent of emigrants from ECA. In comparison, the top five receiving countries in ECA receive more than 50 percent of the total number of immigrants from ECA countries. The concentration declined from 1990 to 2020, mostly because of a smaller number of migrants coming from Russia, which is one of ECA's main sending countries.

FIGURE 1.4

Migration in Europe and Central Asia, by region of origin and country concentration, 1990–2020

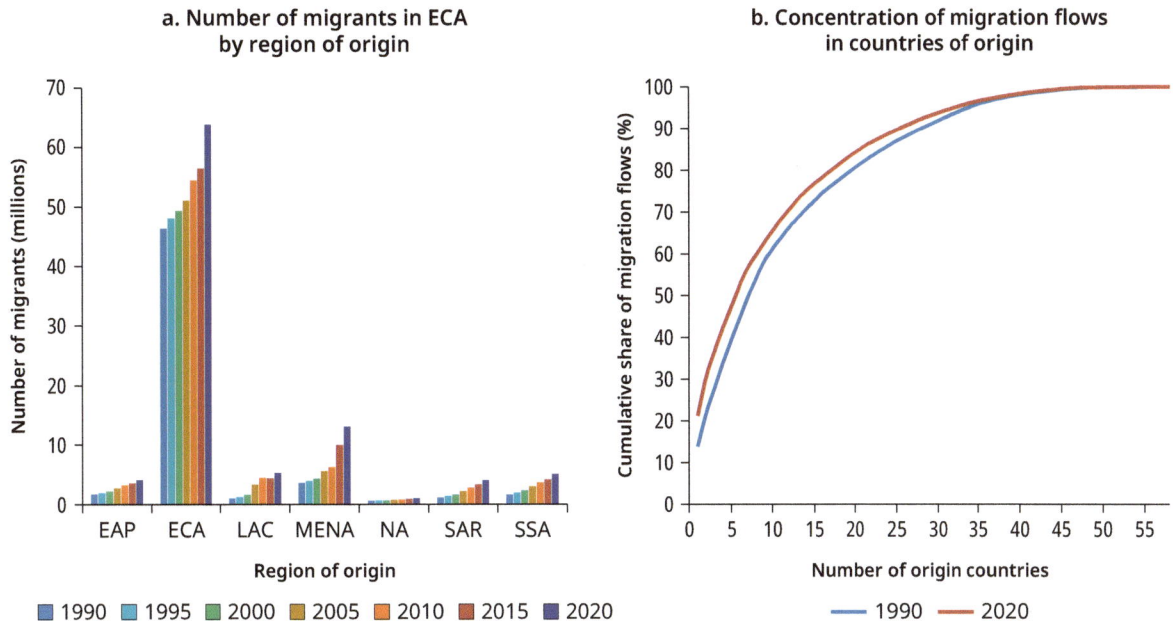

a. Number of migrants in ECA by region of origin

b. Concentration of migration flows in countries of origin

Source: UN 2020.

Note: EAP = East Asia and Pacific; ECA = Europe and Central Asia; LAC = Latin American and the Caribbean; MENA = Middle East and North Africa; NA = North America; SAR = South Asia; SSA = Sub-Saharan Africa.

During the past few years, emigration within ECA has increased more rapidly in new EU member states, driven by the free mobility of its citizens across its territory. In 2020, the biggest sending region was the EU-NMS13, with more than 15 million emigrants (refer to figure 1.5, panel a). This region is followed by northern EU-15 countries (i.e., Austria, Belgium, Denmark, Finland, France, Germany, Ireland, Luxembourg, the Netherlands, Sweden, and the United Kingdom) and Russia. There has been an especially sharp increase in emigration in Central and Eastern Europe since 2005, reflecting the EU enlargement that opened the EU's labor market to the new member states. Additionally, Russia's invasion of Ukraine has almost doubled the number of emigrants from that country, from 6.1 million to 11.6 million in 2022. This lifted the average emigration in Eastern Europe to 14.2 million. As a share of the population in sending countries, emigration rates are highest in the Western Balkans, reaching 30 percent, followed by the Caucasus (17 percent) and Eastern Europe and EU-NMS13 (around 15 percent; refer to figure 1.5, panel b).

The largest number of intra-ECA emigrants come from Kazakhstan, Russia, and Ukraine, partly linked to co-ethnic migration within the former USSR and Russia's invasion of Ukraine. In 2020, there were more Russian-born migrants in ECA than from any other country in the region by a significant

FIGURE 1.5

Emigration from Europe and Central Asia, sending regions, 1990–2020

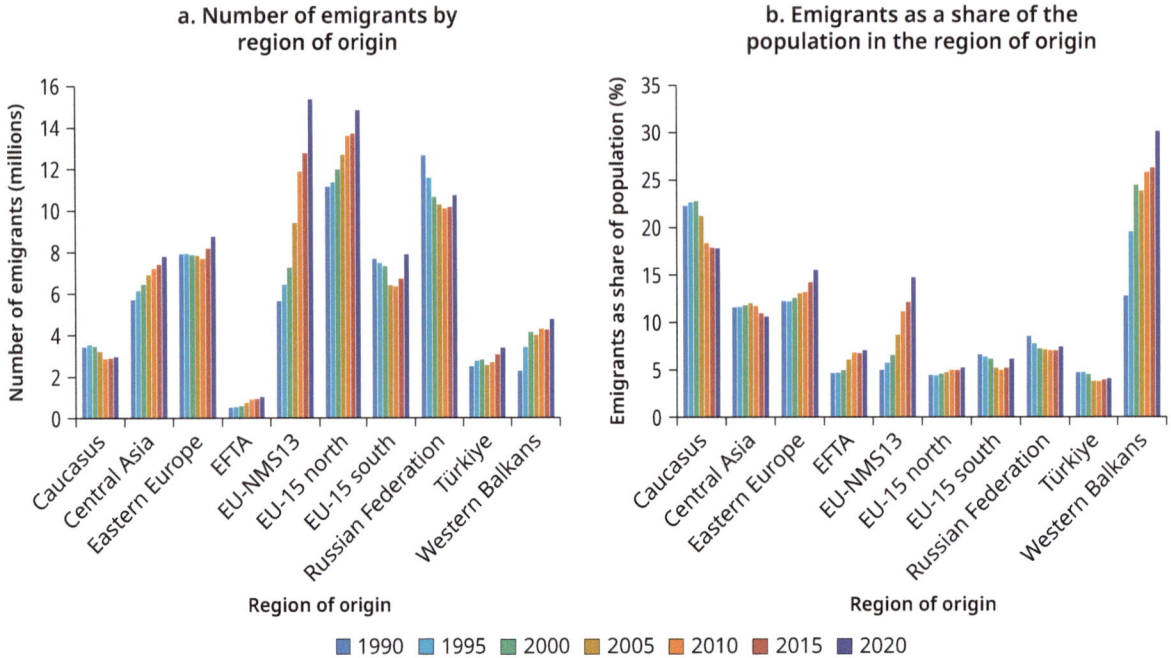

a. Number of emigrants by region of origin

b. Emigrants as a share of the population in the region of origin

■ 1990 ■ 1995 ■ 2000 ■ 2005 ■ 2010 ■ 2015 ■ 2020

Source: UN 2020.
Note: Eastern Europe = Belarus, Moldova, and Ukraine; EFTA = European Free Trade Association; EU-15 = European Union members before 2004; EU-NMS13 = new member states joining the EU in 2004, 2007, and 2013.

margin (10 million). However, by the end of 2022, Russia's invasion of Ukraine rapidly increased the number of Ukrainian emigrants to about 11.6 million, potentially surpassing Russia as the top emigrant country. After Russia and Ukraine, Poland, Kazakhstan, and Romania have about 5.0, 4.2, and 4.0 million people living abroad, respectively. Other countries with high sending numbers include Germany, Italy, and Türkiye.

Emigration rates as a percentage of the population are highest in several Western Balkan countries, Armenia, and Moldova, with rapid increases also observed in various EU-NMS13 countries. The top sending countries in ECA in relative terms are mostly Eastern European and Balkan countries, which have smaller total populations. The biggest sending country in the ECA region is Bosnia and Herzegovina, which has a staggering 46 percent of its total population living abroad (refer to figure 1.6). Moldova, Albania, and Armenia follow on the list with 41, 40, and 29 percent of their total population living abroad, respectively. Bulgaria, Croatia, Georgia, Kazakhstan, and Lithuania have comparable shares of their population living abroad, at around 22 percent. The only non–Eastern European country in the list of top 15 sending countries is Portugal, with about 14 percent of the population living abroad.

FIGURE 1.6

Top 15 migrant-sending countries in Europe and Central Asia

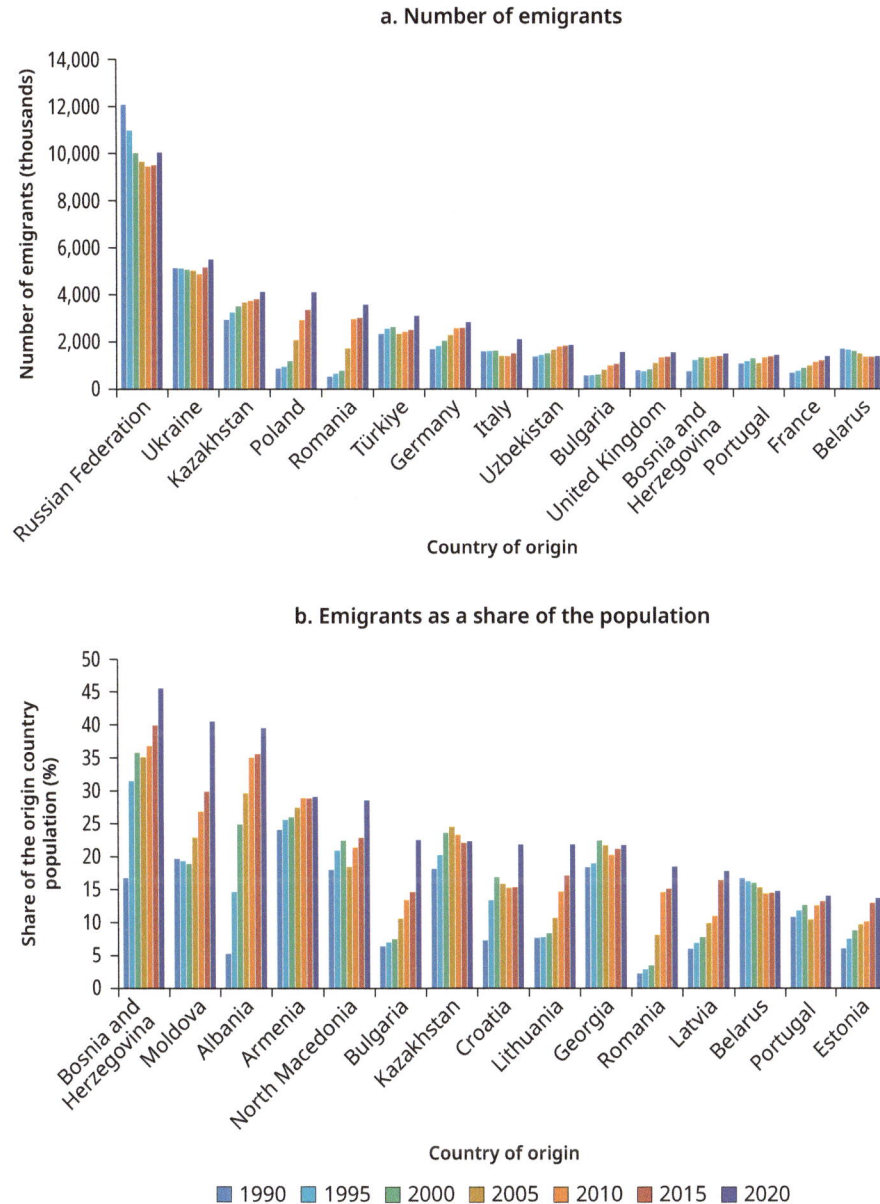

a. Number of emigrants

b. Emigrants as a share of the population

■ 1990 ■ 1995 ■ 2000 ■ 2005 ■ 2010 ■ 2015 ■ 2020

Source: UN 2020.
Note: Panel a reports statistics for the 15 countries in ECA with the highest absolute number of emigrants. Panel b reports statistics for the 15 countries with the highest share of emigrants as a percentage of their total population, ranked from the highest to the lowest share in 2020.

Although emigrants from ECA mostly reside within ECA, the profile of destination countries varies depending on the specific region of origin. Emigrants from Western European countries are perhaps the exception in ECA, because a significant number of them migrate to non-ECA countries (38 percent), mostly to other Organisation for Economic Co-operation and

Development (OECD) countries such as Australia, Canada, or the United States (refer to figure 1.7, panel a). About half of Western European emigrants live in other countries in the EU-15 or European Free Trade Association (EFTA). Overall, emigrants in this region tend to be more dispersed, although mostly in more developed economies. However, emigrants from EU-NMS13 mostly reside in EU-15 countries (70 percent).

Emigrants from the Western Balkans tend to reside either in EU-15 countries or other Balkan neighbors, with sizable differences across countries (figure 1.7, panel b). In Albania, emigration is mostly channeled to

FIGURE 1.7

Subregions or countries of destination of emigrants, by subregion or country of origin in Europe and Central Asia, 2020

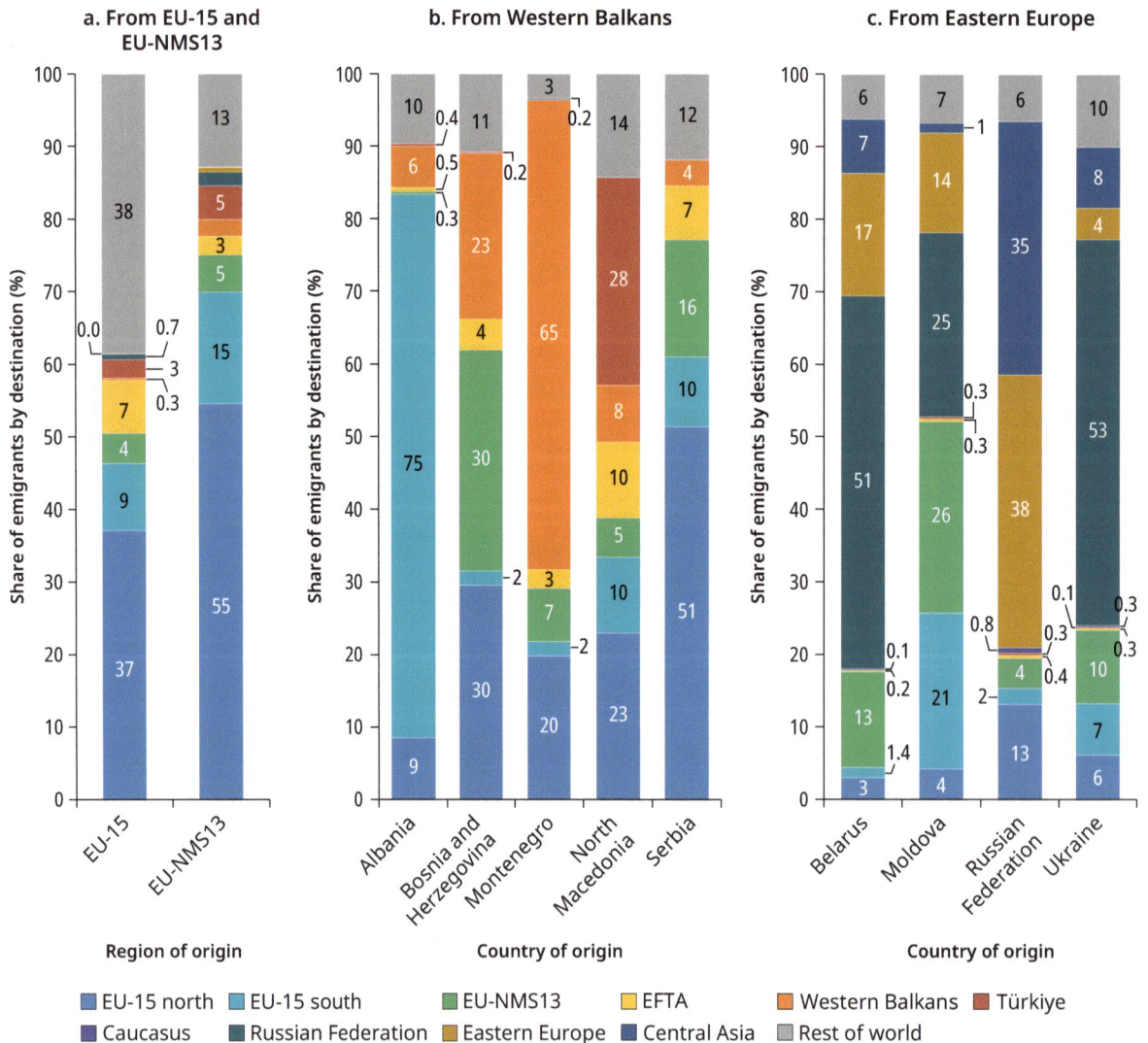

Continued

Figure 1.7

Subregions or countries of destination of emigrants, by subregion or country of origin in Europe and Central Asia, 2020 (Continued)

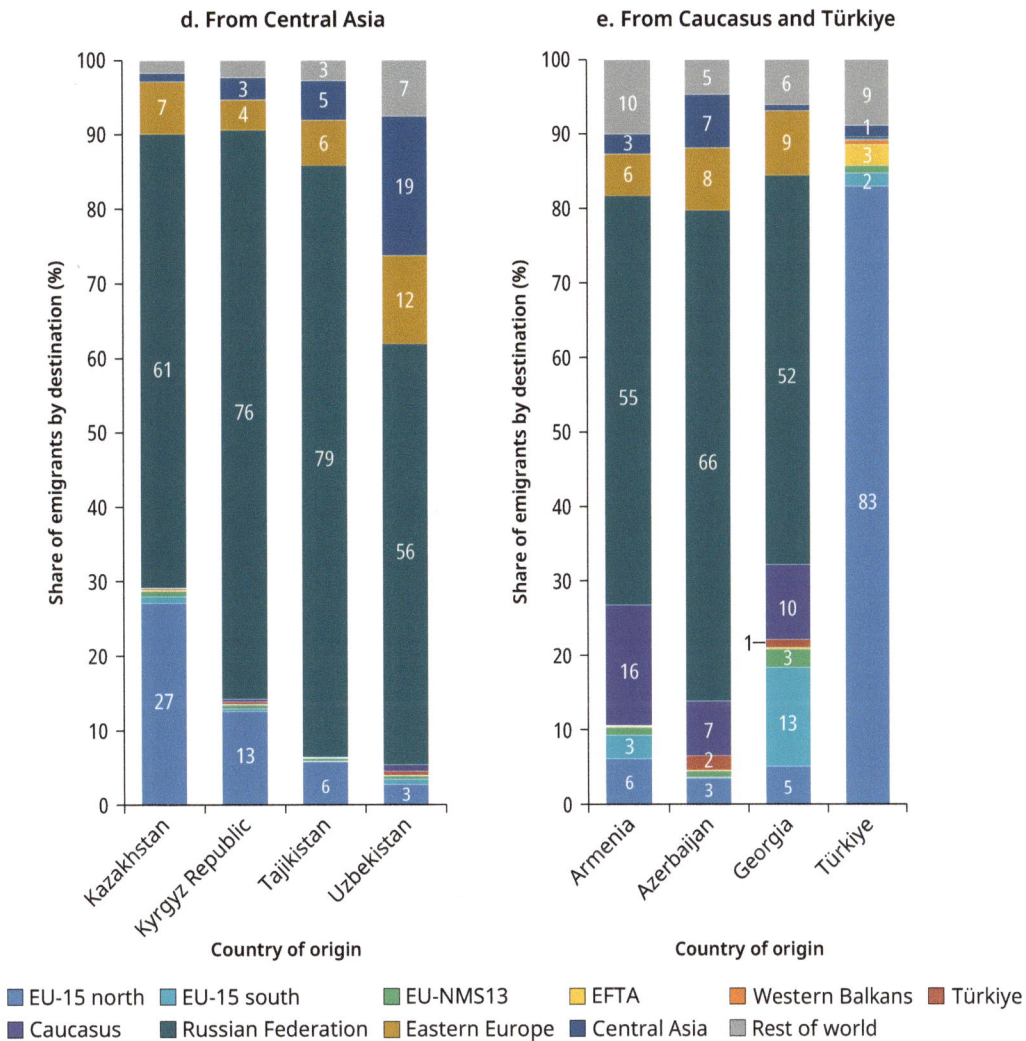

d. From Central Asia

e. From Caucasus and Türkiye

EU-15 north · EU-15 south · EU-NMS13 · EFTA · Western Balkans · Türkiye · Caucasus · Russian Federation · Eastern Europe · Central Asia · Rest of world

Source: UN 2020.
Note: EFTA = European Free Trade Association; EU-15 = European Union members before 2004; EU-NMS13 = new member states joining the European Union in 2004, 2007, and 2013.

Greece and Italy. The most prevalent destinations among Serbian migrants are northern EU-15 countries, mostly Austria and Germany. In Bosnia and Herzegovina, emigration destinations are more diversified, with main destination countries ranging from Austria and Germany to Croatia, Slovenia, and Serbia. However, Montenegrin migrants are concentrated in Serbia. The diaspora of North Macedonia is the most spread out across regions, with more than one-quarter residing in Türkiye because of ethnic ties (ethnic Turks).

Emigrants from non-EU Eastern Europe largely remain in the region, with Russia as the main destination country (figure 1.7, panel c). Emigration from Russia is partly linked to ethnic and historical ties after the disintegration of the USSR. Another 1 million live in Germany. In other Eastern European countries, such as Belarus and Ukraine, more than half of emigrants in 2020 were living in Russia. As previously mentioned, the recent wave of Ukrainian refugees has been concentrated in neighboring Poland and Russia, as well as in Germany. Emigration from Moldova is more split, with a balanced division between Eastern Europe and EU countries.

Migration flows from Central Asian countries are highly concentrated in Russia (figure 1.7, panel d). In 2020, close to two-thirds of the 4 million Kazakhstani emigrants resided in Russia, and more than one-quarter did so in Germany. The dependence on the Russian economy is even larger for emigrants from the Kyrgyz Republic and Tajikistan. Migration from Uzbekistan is slightly more diversified, with 57 percent of Uzbeks living in Russia, 15 percent in Kazakhstan, and 10 percent in Ukraine.

Emigration flows from the Caucasus are also concentrated in Russia, whereas Turkish emigrants are clustered in northern EU-15 countries (refer to figure 1.7, panel e). Two-thirds of Azerbaijani emigrants and more than half of migrants from Armenia and Georgia were living in Russia in 2020. There is also a sizable minority of the Armenian diaspora in other countries in the Caucasus, related to the ethnic conflict in the region. Of the 3.4 million Turkish emigrants, 5 in 6 live in northern EU-15 countries, mostly in Germany but also in Austria, France, and the Netherlands.

Main Bilateral Corridors of Migration

The largest migration corridors in the region involve Russia and its former USSR neighbors, as well as intra-EU country pairs such as Poland–Germany and Romania–Italy. The top migration corridors within the region are characterized by flows of people who began to move as a result of the demise of the Soviet Union. There has also been more recent migration to Germany, Italy, and the United Kingdom from eastern EU countries. Because of the fall of the Soviet Union, many of those born within its boundaries were characterized as migrants as they moved between the newly created countries. This development determines the region's top migration corridors, such as the corridors from Russia to Ukraine (3.3 million migrants), from Russia to Kazakhstan (2.4 million migrants), from Ukraine to Russia (3.2 million migrants), and from Kazakhstan to Russia (2.5 million migrants). The next largest migration corridors are from Poland to Germany (1.9 million migrants), from Türkiye to Germany (1.6 million migrants), from Romania to Italy, and from Poland to the United Kingdom. Except for the corridor between Portugal and France, all of the main bilateral corridors in the European Union are between a new (sending) and an old (receiving) member state. In contrast, the main migration corridors between current EU countries in 1990 were mainly between old member states because the future new member states had not yet entered the Common Market.

The top migration corridor from outside ECA to the region is from Syria to Türkiye, a flow that has surfaced because of conflict. The other dominant corridors represent more traditional migration routes, many of them determined by postcolonial patterns, exemplified by migrants from Morocco and Tunisia going to France, migrants from India and Pakistan going to the United Kingdom, and migrants from Indonesia going to the Netherlands. Most of the main corridors from outside ECA to ECA were similar in 1990, except those originating from recent conflicts. These corridors are mostly shaped by migration from former colonies to France, Italy, the Netherlands, Portugal, Spain, and the United Kingdom.

The concentration of bilateral migration corridors has decreased over the past three decades. This implies that migration, although more concentrated in the top receiving countries (refer to figure 1.8), is less concentrated in terms of bilateral migration corridors. The largest bilateral corridors accounted for slightly more than 30 percent of total migration in ECA in 2020, compared with more than 40 percent in 1990. As previously mentioned, more corridors have emerged, particularly within the European Union, and older corridors based on ethnic or colonial ties have slowly decreased in relative size.

Recent Migration Trends in the Context of COVID-19 and Russia's Invasion of Ukraine

The COVID-19 pandemic and the subsequent mobility restrictions affected migration in the short term, although the overall upward trend in migration has resumed. The lockdowns that most ECA countries put in place to curb the transmission of the COVID-19 virus had a negative impact on mobility within and across countries. The unprecedented restrictions and limited availability of transportation derailed many current and prospective migrants' plans.[2] According to Eurostat (2023), the number of immigrants who arrived in the European Union during 2020 was 26 percent lower than in the previous year (refer to figure 1.9, panel a). In Russia, the inflow of new immigrants fell to less than 50 percent in the same period. However, the COVID-19 pandemic affected not only the arrival of new immigrants but also the number of returns to the countries of origin. The stock of migrants in receiving countries remained relatively stable in 2020 and continued to grow in 2021 (refer to figure 1.9, panel b).

FIGURE 1.8

Bilateral migration corridors

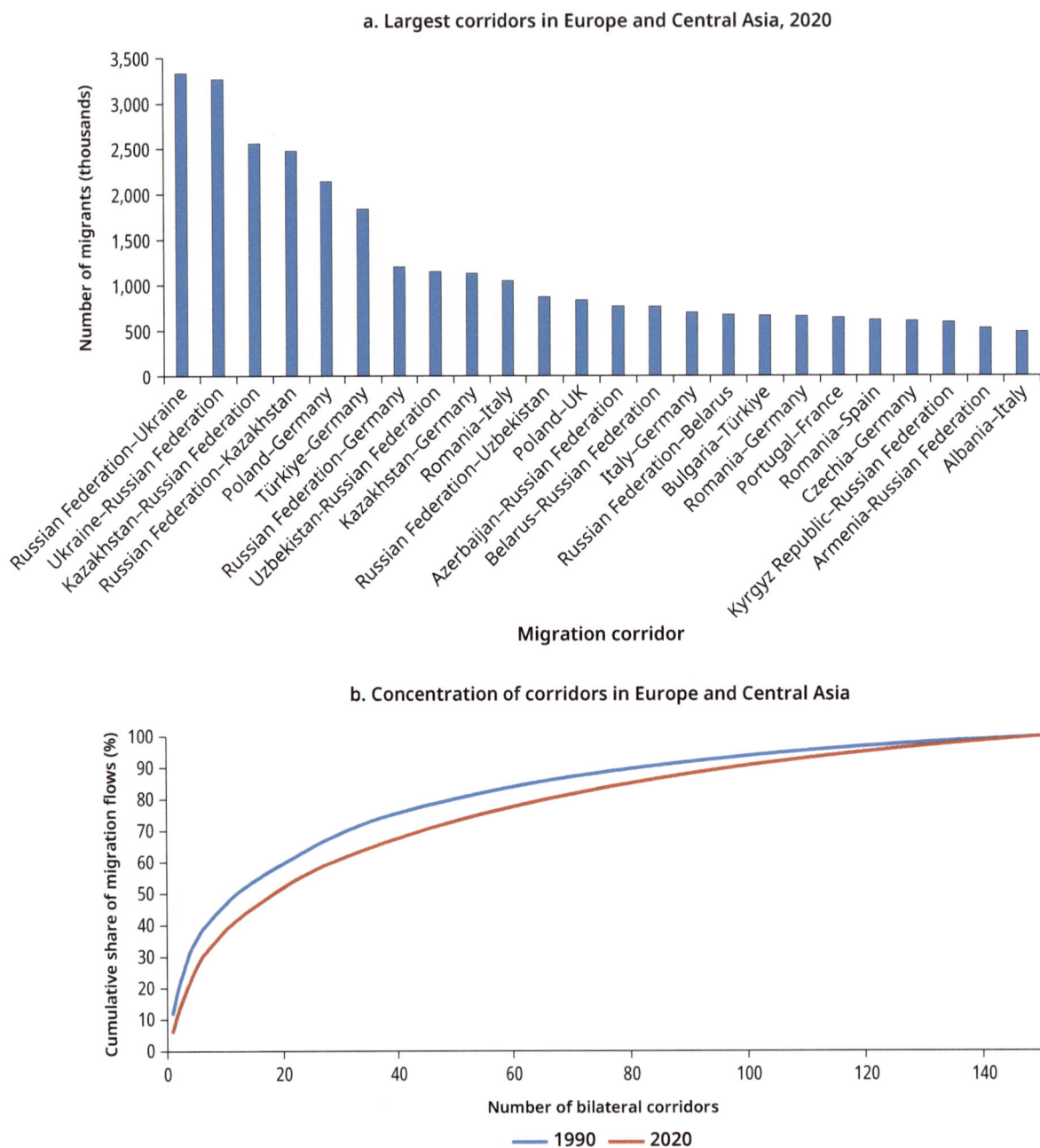

a. Largest corridors in Europe and Central Asia, 2020

b. Concentration of corridors in Europe and Central Asia

Source: UN 2020.
Note: ECA = Europe and Central Asia.

FIGURE 1.9

Migration trends in the European Union and Russian Federation during the COVID-19 pandemic

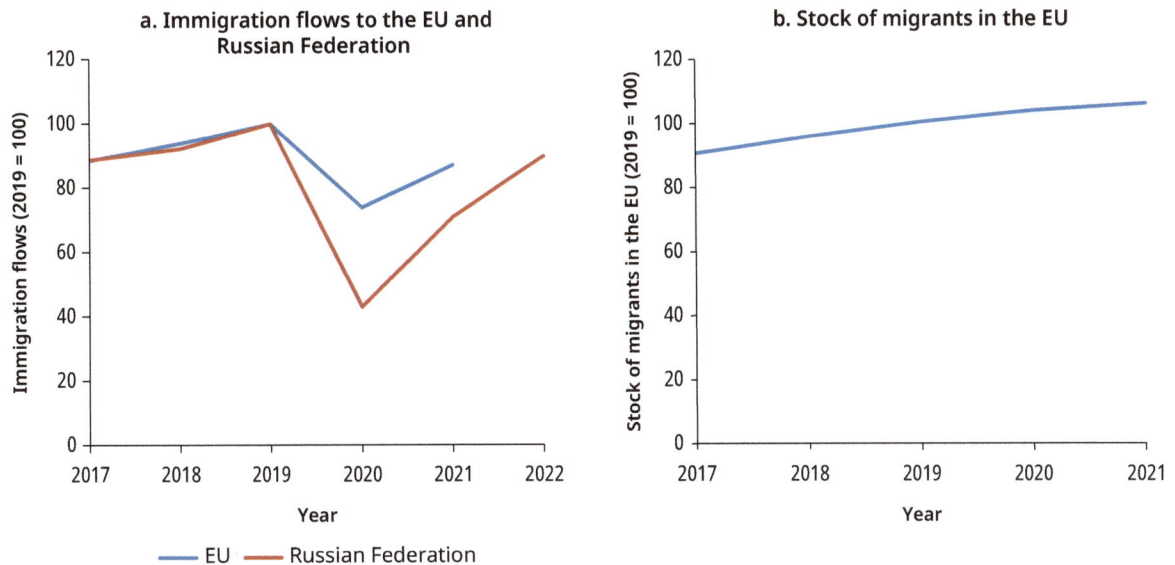

a. Immigration flows to the EU and Russian Federation

b. Stock of migrants in the EU

— EU — Russian Federation

Sources: Eurostat and Ministry of Internal Affairs of the Russian Federation.
Note: Statistics are normalized so that in every case the size of flows or stocks in 2019 was equal to 100. EU = European Union.

Migration in ECA has drastically expanded in the past two years with the displacement of Ukrainian refugees. Russia's invasion of Ukraine is having dramatic, direct effects in terms of deaths and injuries, disruption of economic activities, and massive increases in internally displaced populations and refugees. It has led to the largest and fastest forced displacements in recent history, with 5.5 million refugees and asylum seekers in 2022 alone. Almost all of these refugees sought refuge in ECA countries (99.7 percent). The countries with the largest inflows of refugees in 2022 were Russia (1.5 million), Poland (1.2 million), Germany (1 million), and Czechia (0.4 million; refer to map 1.1, panel a). France, Italy, Spain, and the United Kingdom received, in the same year, between 100,000 and 200,000 refugees, with other countries neighboring Ukraine, such as Bulgaria, Moldova, and Romania, also observing relevant inflow. The arrival of refugees in 2022 represented more than 3 percent of the total host population in Czechia, Moldova, and Poland; around 2 percent in the three Baltic countries, Estonia, Latvia, and Lithuania; and more than 1 percent in Austria, Germany, Montenegro, and Slovakia (refer to map 1.1, panel b).

In addition to the direct impacts on the Ukrainian population, the war will also have indirect human, social, and economic effects at regional and global levels that will shape migration corridors in the years to come.

MAP 1.1

Increase in immigration in 2022 because of the arrival of Ukrainian refugees

a. Increase in the number of immigrants

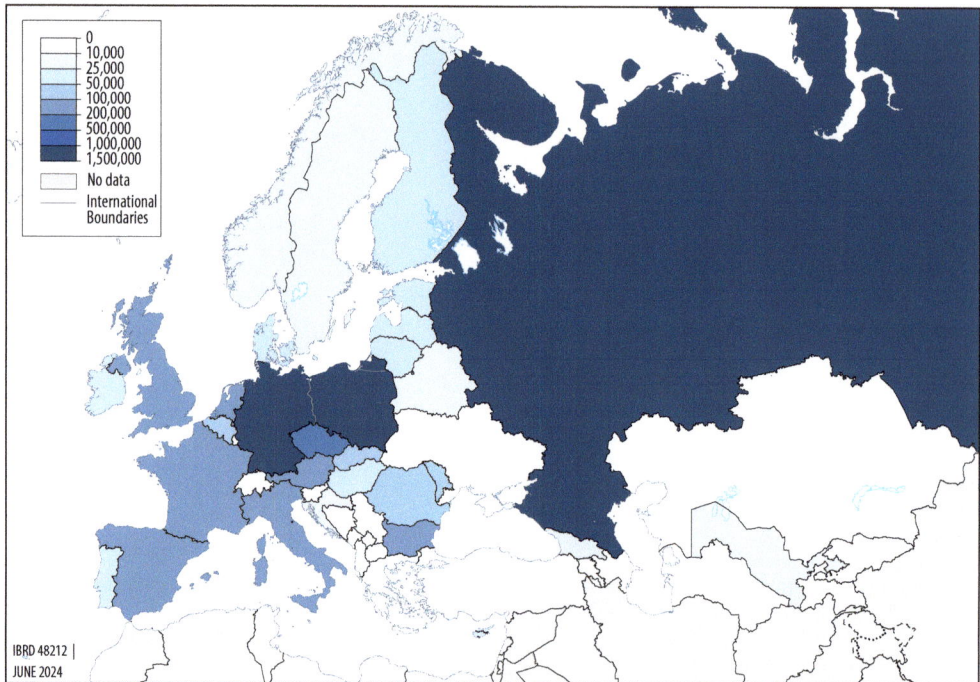

b. Increase as a percentage of the host population

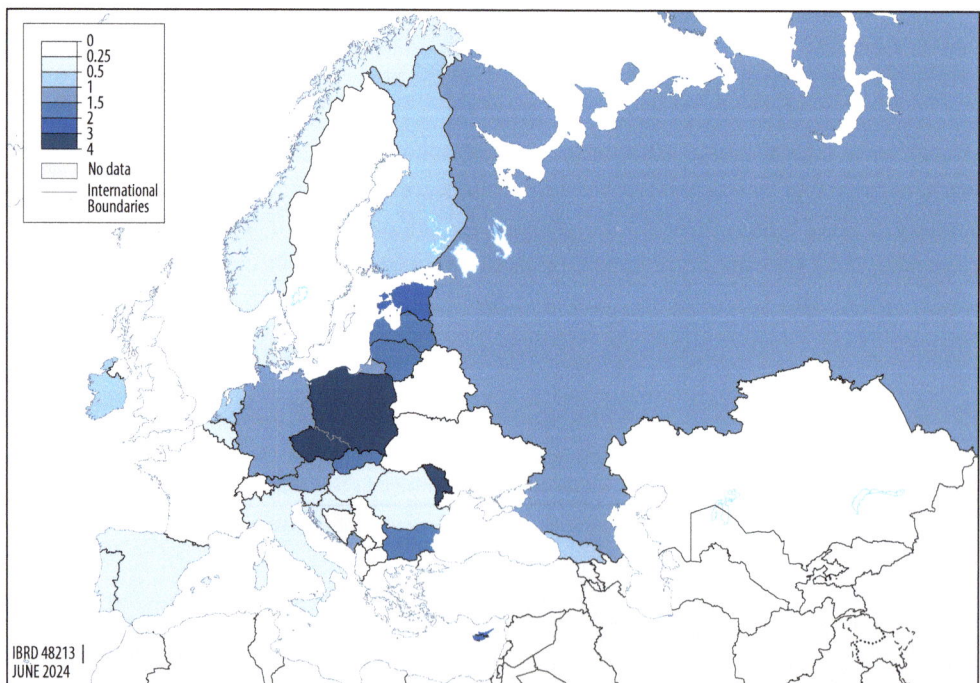

Source: Original calculations based on UN High Commissioner for Refugees Refugee Data Finder (https://www.unhcr
.org/refugee-statistics/) and UN Department of Economic and Social Affairs Population Statistics (https://population
.un.org/wpp/).
Note: The data include refugees and asylum seekers. UN = United Nations.

Russia's invasion of Ukraine has already had repercussions on currencies, energy, commodity and food prices, value chains, and trade linkages. It has particularly affected countries that are economically dependent on or connected to Ukraine and Russia, such as many Central Asian republics. Given the relevance of Russia as a main destination country of migration in Central Asia and the Caucasus, the shock is expected to have profound consequences on migration flows in several intra-ECA corridors, reducing overseas employment opportunities and disrupting inflows of remittances in these subregions. The uncertainties about the conflict's duration and possible resolution make it difficult to predict how the political and economic situation in the region will evolve. High-frequency data from the Kyrgyz Republic and Uzbekistan, two countries for which emigration is heavily concentrated in Russia, show that although the stock of migrants remained relatively stable in the first six months of the war, it started to fall significantly in September 2022 (refer to figure 1.10), right after the military draft decree was enacted in Russia and its economy deteriorated. In only one month, the number of emigrants from these two countries was reduced by 15 percent, and the number of emigrants from the Kyrgyz Republic fell by 36 percent during the last three months of 2022 alone.

FIGURE 1.10

Recent trends in the stock of the Kyrgyz Republic and Uzbek migrants abroad

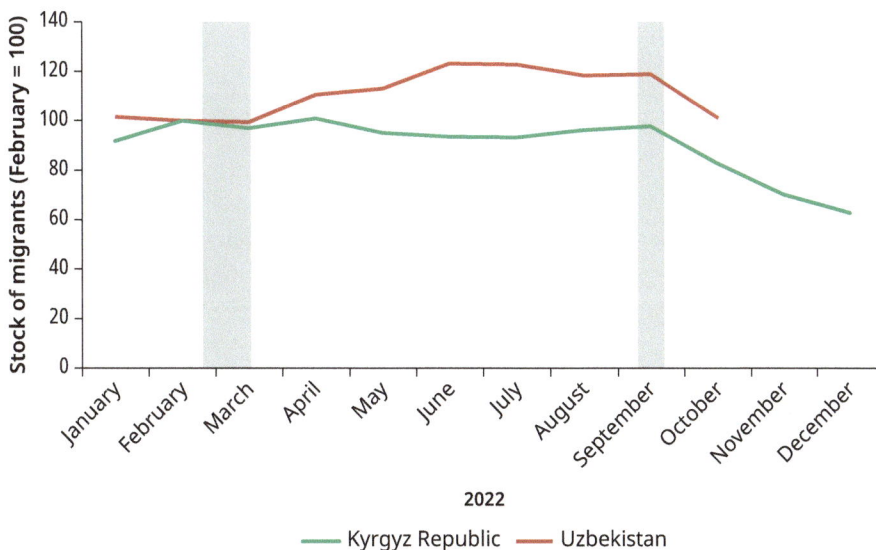

2022

Kyrgyz Republic — Uzbekistan

Sources: Listening to the Citizens of Uzbekistan survey (2022) and Listening to the Citizens of the Kyrgyz Republic survey (2022).
Note: The gray bars represent the start of Russia's invasion of Ukraine and the passing of the Russian decree on military conscription.

Diversity of Migration in Europe and Central Asia

Migration to and from the region is not a monolithic phenomenon; there is much diversity in the types of migrants and drivers. The migration experience in ECA is also diverse in many respects. First, the region experiences both labor migration driven by economic opportunities and forced displacement fueled by conflict. Second, it covers a wide array of skill profiles, including low-skilled and high-skilled migrants. Third, migration in the region can be permanent or temporary. Among temporary migrants, some migrate only once to the destination before returning home, and others migrate repeatedly to take advantage of seasonal employment opportunities (circular or seasonal migration). Among those who permanently return home, some return according to their premigration plans—for example, after finalizing their education or obtaining enough savings from working abroad—and others unexpectedly return because of issues with their legal status, losing employment, or a family issue. Finally, although a large share of migration to the region is formal, some of it is informal. These different categories of migration generate distinct opportunities and challenges for policy makers in both receiving and sending countries.

Forced versus Economic Migration

Although the vast majority of immigrants in ECA migrated for economic reasons between 1990 and 2020, there has been a rapid increase in forcibly displaced populations. Migration due to conflict has been on the rise in ECA during the past decade. Driven first by the Syrian war and, more recently, by Russia's invasion of Ukraine, the number of refugees and asylum seekers hosted in the region spiked from 2 million in 2013 to 14 million in 2022 (refer to figure 1.11). Conflict-driven migration represented about 13 percent of the total stock of migrants in the region in 2022, compared with only 2 percent in 2010. The ECA region has been the main recipient of forced migrants, and it currently hosts more than 40 percent of all refugees globally. The presence of refugees and asylum seekers is also the highest as a percentage of the total population: 1.5 percent, compared with 0.7 percent in the Middle East and North Africa and Sub-Saharan Africa or the world average of 0.4 percent. Within ECA, the inflow of refugees has been highly concentrated in Türkiye— mostly Syrian refugees and, to a lesser extent, Afghans—and EU countries, initially mostly northern EU countries such as Germany; however, more recently, EU-NMS13 states such as Poland have been the major receiving countries of Ukrainian refugees. Although forced migration shares some commonalities with economic migration, it also poses additional and distinct challenges to receiving countries. Refugees themselves confront different sources of risks and vulnerabilities compared with economic migrants.

FIGURE 1.11

Refugees and asylum seekers in Europe and Central Asia, by receiving country or region

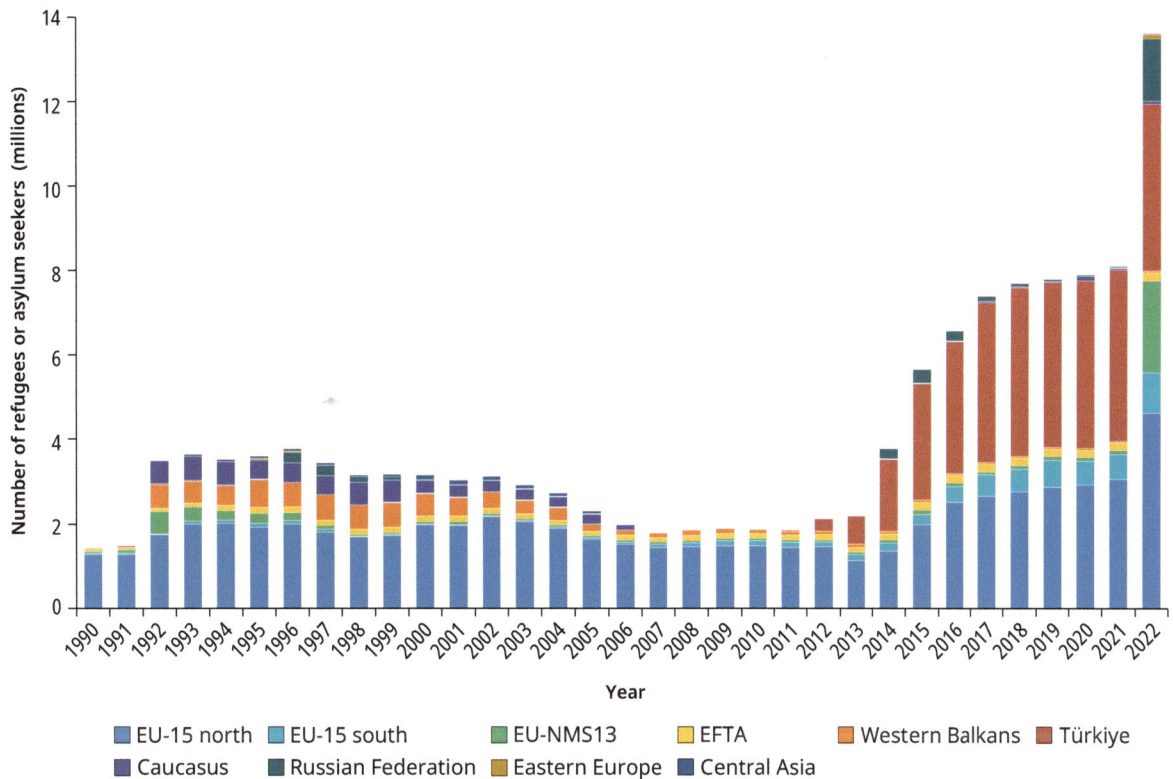

Sources: Refugee Data Finder (database), United Nations High Commissioner for Refugees, Geneva.
Note: Eastern Europe = Belarus, Moldova, and Ukraine; EFTA = European Free Trade Association; EU-15 = European Union members before 2004; EU-NMS13 = new member states joining the European Union in 2004, 2007, and 2013.

They also require different policies and interventions that help protect their well-being and the well-being of the communities in which they live.

Given the geopolitical situation, countries in ECA have very different mixes of economic migrants and refugees. Although labor migrants move in search of better economic opportunities, forcibly displaced migrants tend to remain in neighboring countries, although trends in recent decades suggest an increased spatial dispersion of refugees (Devictor, Do, and Levchenko 2021). Large wage differentials attract a higher number of economic migrants to Western European countries, particularly Germany, Sweden, and Switzerland. Meanwhile, Kazakhstan and Russia are a regional migration hub for emigrants from Central Asia and the Caucasus (refer to figure 1.13, panel a). Although wage differentials drive economic migration in ECA, geographical location and distance to conflict are key determinants of the size of refugee inflow and forcibly displaced migrants.

As a result of the two largest ongoing conflicts in Syria and Ukraine, their respective neighboring countries of Türkiye and Poland host the largest number and share of refugees across ECA (refer to map 1.2, panel b). In general, the combination of proximity to more fragile states and lower economic opportunities leads to higher ratios of refugees over economic migrants across less-developed ECA countries (refer to map 1.2, panel c).

High-Skilled versus Low-Skilled Migrants

There are also clear divergences in the education level of migrant populations across receiving countries in ECA. Although sharing important commonalities of push and pull factors and impacts, the migration of high-skilled and low-skilled workers has different implications for both sending and receiving countries in terms of its effects on human capital accumulation, productivity, job creation and relocation, and fiscal implications (Bossavie et al. 2022). Immigrants' skill composition is largely driven by relative wage differentials across education levels in receiving countries. Studies looking at individual ECA-sending countries such as Bulgaria also show a strong correlation between the relative returns to

MAP 1.2
Prevalence of economic migrants and refugees in ECA countries

a. Share of economic migrants in the total population

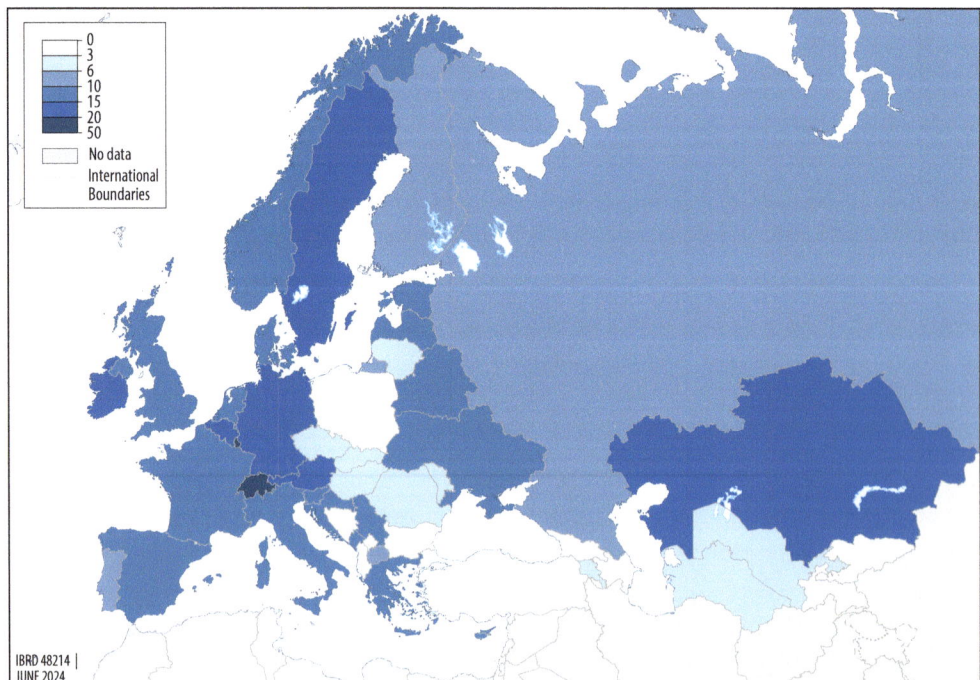

IBRD 48214 | JUNE 2024

Continued

MAP 1.2

Prevalence of economic migrants and refugees in ECA countries *(Continued)*

b. Share of refugees in the total population

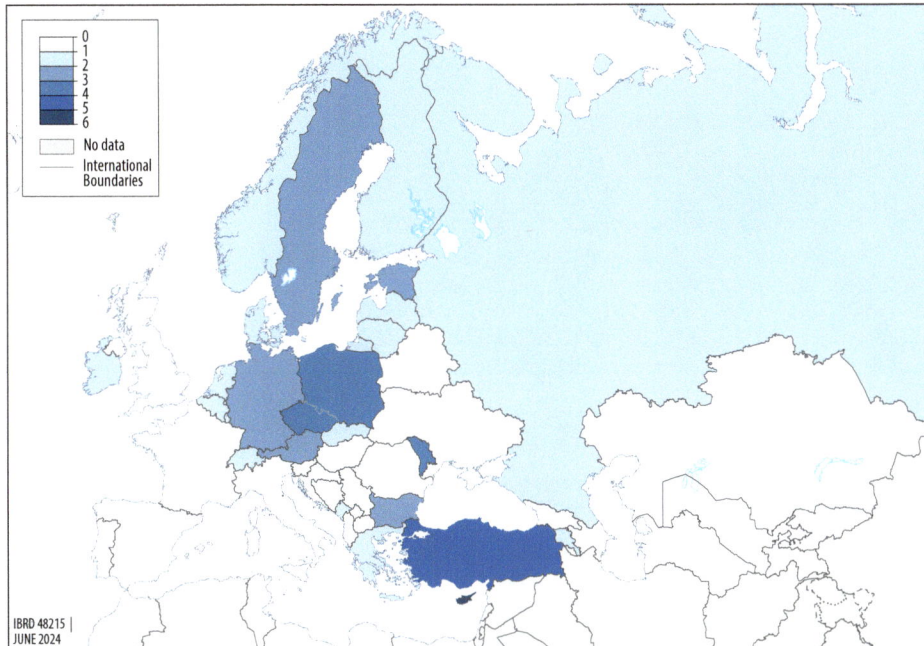

c. Share of refugees among all migrants

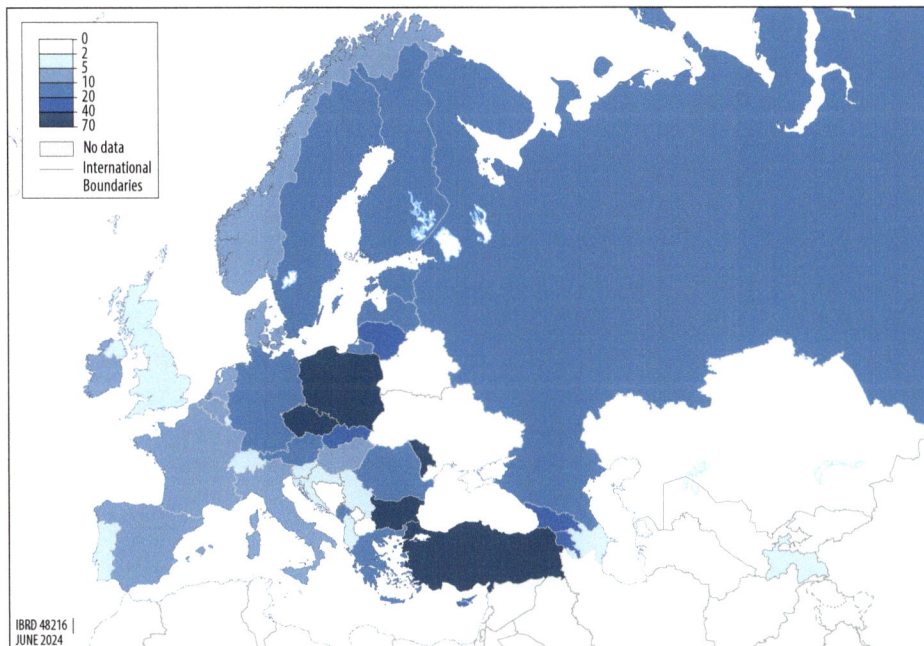

Sources: Original calculations based on UN High Commissioner for Refugees Refugee Data Finder (https://www.unhcr.org/refugee-statistics/) and UN Department of Economic and Social Affairs Population Statistics (https://population.un.org/wpp/).
Note: UN = United Nations.

MAP 1.3

Share of migrants with tertiary education in main receiving ECA countries

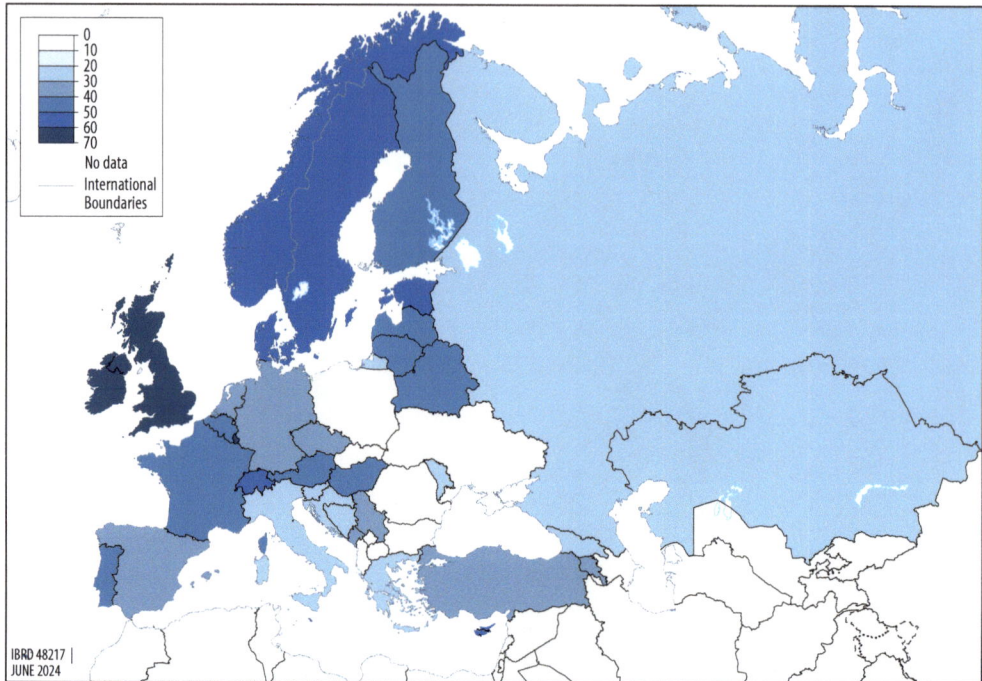

Sources: European Union Labour Force Survey and national labor force surveys, 2015–20.

education and the skill composition of migrants (Garrote-Sanchez, Kreuder, and Testaverde 2021). In ECA, Ireland and the United Kingdom are the countries that attract the highest share of skilled migrants relative to overall migrants, with more than 1 in 2 having tertiary education (refer to map 1.3). Other Northern European countries also have more than 40 percent of tertiary-educated migrants (Denmark, Estonia, Norway, Sweden, and Switzerland). However, the Southern EU and eastern ECA countries tend to have a pool of migrants with lower skill levels—with secondary education or less. Italy tops the list of countries with a lower share of tertiary-educated migrants (14 percent), followed by Kazakhstan (16 percent), Greece (17 percent), and Russia (slightly less than 20 percent).[3]

Male versus Female Migration

Although the share of female migrants in ECA is close to parity, the gender profile of the migrant population is uneven in some countries and varies depending on the type of migration. Statistics on migration from UN DESA based on censuses and other administrative data show that in 2020

51 percent of migrants in ECA were female. This ratio mimics that of the nonmigrant population in sending countries. However, this balanced migration masks important variations across countries. On the one hand, emigration from Eastern European and Nordic countries is more female-dominated, with the share of women at 60 percent in Finland and between 57 percent and 59 percent in Belarus, Bulgaria, Czechia, Norway, and Russia. On the other hand, men represent a majority of emigrants in most countries in Central Asia, Türkiye, and the Caucasus—that is, 57 percent in Tajikistan and 54 percent in Armenia and Azerbaijan. Censuses in destination countries collect information on migrants who are more established in the host country—those who have an official residence and move less often—and do not capture other forms of migration that are more irregular in nature (for example, short-term migrants who recently changed their place of residence or undocumented migrants). The share of female migrants depends on the type of migration. In general, forced displacement is associated with a larger share of women and children than is economic migration. However, there are cases, such as Syrian refugees in Türkiye or asylum seekers from Africa in Europe, in which there are more men than women. Shorter-term forms of migration, in particular temporary migration, are more heavily male dominated. For example, although statistics on Central Asian migrants in Russia using the Russian census report a close-to-parity gender split, surveys from sending countries that capture more temporary forms of migration show that migration is mostly a male-dominated phenomenon (with the percentage of men reaching about 80 percent in the Kyrgyz Republic and Tajikistan and 90 percent in Uzbekistan).[4]

Temporary versus Permanent Migration

Migration in ECA can be permanent or temporary. The most discussed type of migration in the policy literature is permanent migration, when a worker moves to a given destination and stays there without returning to the home country. Low-skilled international labor migration, however, is often temporary (Bossavie and Özden 2022; Dustmann and Görlach 2016). Figure 1.12 shows the number of migrants in Western Europe (including the European Union, Iceland, Norway, Switzerland, and the United Kingdom) from different cohorts (who arrived between 2000 and 2004, 2005 and 2009, or 2010 and 2014) and remained in the country after 5–9 years, 10–14 years, 15–19 years, or 20–24 years, respectively.[5] The number of immigrants from a given cohort decreases noticeably over time, in particular for those who arrived between 1995 and 1999. After 20–24 years of stay, the number of immigrants who moved to the European Union in 1995–99 was reduced by more than half compared with 15 years earlier.

FIGURE 1.12

Number of foreign-born residents who still live in Western Europe after 5, 10, 15, and 20 years

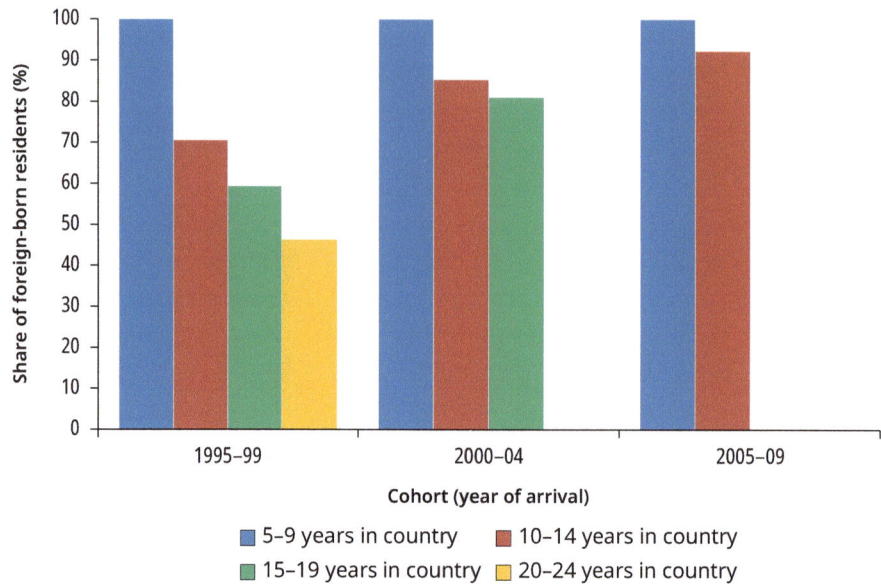

Sources: EU Labour Force Surveys of 2009, 2014, and 2019 (https://ec.europa.eu/eurostat/web/microdata/european-union-labour-force-survey).

There are several reasons for the prevalence of temporary migration.[6] First, migration may have been intended as temporary ex ante. This can be because it is legally imposed by regulations in destination countries, which prohibit permanent stays. Additionally, even when permanent stays are allowed, migration may have been planned by migrants as temporary because it is optimal for them to return home after some time in the host country, such as, for example, if migrants want to accumulate human and financial capital overseas to then utilize it in their home country. Within that category, seasonal or circular migration is a specific type of planned temporary migration in which migrants go back and forth between their home and destination countries for seasonal economic activities, such as agriculture or tourism (Constant, Nottmeyer, and Zimmermann 2013). In some other cases, temporary migration may not have been intended as such ex ante: migrants may originally have intended to migrate permanently or for a longer period of time but return because of a change in circumstances in the origin or destination countries, inaccurate information on outcomes at destination before departure (voluntary return, for example, after losing employment or not being able to find a job), or legal issues related to their stay at destination (forced return).

Formal versus Informal Migration

Migration modalities can also differ by legal status: although a large share of migration to the region is formal, some of it is informal. Irregular migration is defined as the entry into, stay in, or work in a country without the necessary authorization or documents required under immigration regulations. There are severe challenges when trying to capture the extent of irregular or informal migration. By definition, official statistics are not able to give an accurate picture of the extent of the phenomenon. More than 1 million people were detected staying illegally in the European Union or the United Kingdom in 2022, trending up from less than 0.5 million in 2020, but still way below the peak of 2.1 million irregular migrants detected in 2015 at the height of the Syrian crisis (Eurostat 2023). Of the 1 million irregular migrants in 2022, about 300,000 were caught illegally crossing a border of the European Union or the United Kingdom, and the rest were already in the country, and either their visa expired or their asylum application was rejected. However, the number of detected irregular migrants could reflect both a real evolution in the number of migrants and changes in national immigration and enforcement policies. Ad hoc studies have tried to estimate the broader extent of irregular migration. In Russia, about 2 million irregular migrants are estimated to be residing in the country (Chudinovskin 2021), whereas that number reached 4.1–5.3 million in the European Union and the United Kingdom in 2016 and then fell to 3.9–4.8 million in 2017 (Connor and Passel 2019). The largest number of irregular migrants in the region are seen in Germany (1–1.2 million), the United Kingdom (0.8–1.2 million), Italy (0.5–0.7 million), and France and Spain (0.3–0.4 million). In Western Europe, 30 percent of irregular migrants come from Asia and the Pacific, 23 percent from non-EU or EFTA Europe, 21 percent from the Middle East and North Africa, 17 percent from Sub-Saharan Africa, and 8 percent from the Americas. These groups of migrants tend to have short periods of residence in the destination country (56 percent for less than five years) and are more likely to be male (54 percent) and relatively young (15 percent minors and 50 percent ages 18–34). Although overall these figures might underestimate the extent of irregular migration, they show that irregular migration represents only a small fraction of migration in ECA.

Drivers of Migration to and from Europe and Central Asia

Migration in the region is fueled by a mix and often intertwined set of push and pull factors. People move to other countries because of both push factors from the country of origin and pull factors from the destination. In general, economic migrants move in search of better living conditions for themselves and their families, given the sizable differentials between sending and receiving countries in employment opportunities, wages, quality of services or governance, and corruption. In turn, forcibly displaced populations are primarily pushed from their countries because of violence, conflict, and persecution. However, most of the time the migration decision is made because of compounding factors that are hard to disentangle. For example, although refugees might leave their country of origin to escape war, their choice of country of settlement can be driven by other considerations, such as income opportunities and living standards.

Income and Wage Differentials and Other Labor Market Imbalances

Disparities across regions provide strong incentives to migrate, thus shaping migration patterns. The literature on labor migration has found very large wage and productivity gaps among workers with similar skill levels depending on where they reside (Clemens 2013; Clemens, Montenegro, and Pritchett 2019). Labor mobility between countries and regions is a rational response to these large differentials in economic opportunities (wage gaps and job prospects) and, to some extent, to the variations in the public services individuals can expect to receive, such as the quality of schooling, health care, and respect for the rule of law. Some ECA countries with poorer domestic employment opportunities (such as the Western Balkans and Central Asia) exhibit dramatically high emigration rates, whereas those with dynamic labor markets, such as Germany and the United Kingdom, are primarily receivers of international migrants. Meanwhile, other countries are both senders and receivers (for example, Italy, Spain, and, more recently, Poland). These disparities may have been reinforced by the COVID-19 pandemic, which disproportionately affected populations of workers who were already at a disadvantage before the crisis (del Rio-Chanona et al. 2020; Garrote Sanchez et al. 2020; Mongey, Pilossoph, and Weinberg 2021; Papanikolaou and Schmidt 2022; Yasenov 2020). Income gaps between lagging and leading regions are also driving migration, with emigration rates in ECA closely mapping to lagging regions (Farole, Goga, and Ionescu-Heroiu 2018). For example, the top 10 emigration areas in Romania showed a 15.8 percent net outflow between 2002 and 2017, compared with the slightly positive net inflows (1.9 percent) in the top 10 immigration counties.

Despite progress in convergence, income differentials have remained very large across ECA countries and regions. During the past two decades,

FIGURE 1.13

Gross domestic product convergence between 2000 and 2020 in Europe and Central Asia

a. GDP per capita levels and economic growth

b. Within- and between-country variation in GDP per capita

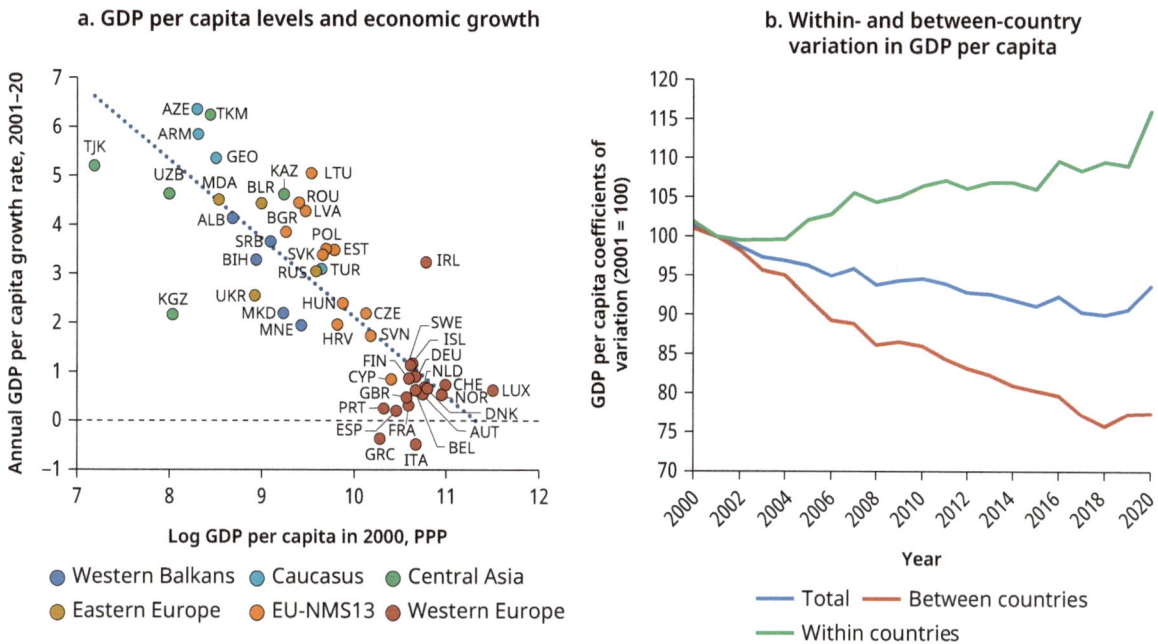

Western Balkans ● Caucasus ● Central Asia
● Eastern Europe ● EU-NMS13 ● Western Europe

Total — Between countries — Within countries

Sources: World Bank World Development Indicators database (https://databank.worldbank.org/source/world-development-indicators); Organisation for Economic Co-operation and Development Regional Statistics database (https://doi.org/10.1787/region-data-en). *Note:* The within- and between-country variations are calculated on the basis of the CoV, which is the standard deviation in the GDP per capita (using PPP in constant 2015 US dollars) divided by the mean. The CoV each year is then divided by the CoV in 2001 to show the cumulative changes in the CoV with 2001 as the baseline period. For a list of country codes, go to https://www.iso.org/obp/ui/#search. CoV = coefficient of variation; Eastern Europe = Belarus, Moldova, Russian Federation, and Ukraine; EU-NMS13 = new member states joining the European Union in 2004, 2007, and 2013; GDP = gross domestic product; PPP = purchasing power parity; Western Europe = EU-15 + European Free Trade Association.

a robust process of economic convergence has occurred in ECA by which poorer countries grew at a faster rate than more advanced economies (refer to figure 1.13, panel a). However, the region is still characterized by sizable income disparities. In 2020, the GDP per capita of the poorest country (Tajikistan) was only 3 percent that of the richest one (Luxembourg), adjusted for purchasing power standards. When considering subregions, gaps remain extremely large: in Europe, Moldova's GDP was about 12 percent that of Luxembourg, and Tajikistan's was likewise 12 percent that of Russia, the region's main economic center. Furthermore, although income convergence is observed between countries, there has been further divergence across lagging and leading regions within countries (refer to figure 1.13, panel b), limiting the overall reduction in disparities across regions in ECA. These persistent gaps in opportunities continue to be driving forces behind labor migration flows.

Emigration rates increase with the level of development until a certain point at which they start to decrease. This nonlinear relationship has been observed in different contexts (Clemens 2014; Dao et al. 2018; World Bank 2023). Similar findings emerge in ECA, where middle-income countries have the highest share of emigration (Albania, Armenia, Bosnia and Herzegovina, North Macedonia; refer to figure 1.14, panel a). In general, regions with higher income-generating opportunities attract more migration inflows, whereas the opposite is true in areas with the least income-generating opportunities (outmigration). However, constraints in financing migration costs might limit mobility in poorer countries and regions (Faini and Venturini 2010; Vanderkamp 1971), creating the inverted U-shaped correlation. The tipping point when economic development starts being associated with lower emigration has increased over the years in ECA countries (refer to figure 1.14, panel b) from a GDP per capita of US$4,100 (constant purchasing power parity [PPP]) in 2000, to US$9,300 in 2010, and US$13,800 in 2020.

FIGURE 1.14

Economic development and migration

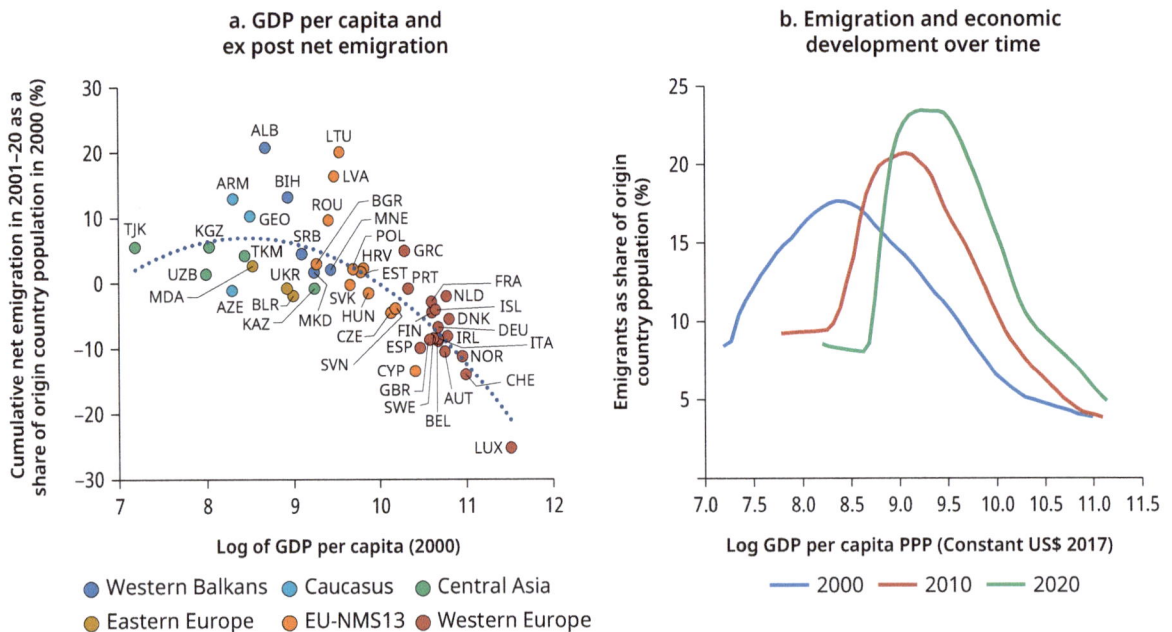

a. GDP per capita and ex post net emigration

b. Emigration and economic development over time

Western Balkans ● Caucasus ● Central Asia
Eastern Europe ● EU-NMS13 ● Western Europe

2000 — 2010 — 2020

Sources: World Bank World Development Indicators database (https://databank.worldbank.org/source/world-development-indicators); United Nations 2020.
Note: Net emigration is calculated as cumulative emigration flows minus cumulative immigration flows over the corresponding period. For a list of country codes, go to https://www.iso.org/obp/ui/#search. Eastern Europe = Belarus, Moldova, Russian Federation, and Ukraine; EU-NMS13 = 13 new member states joining the European Union in 2004, 2007, and 2013; GDP = gross domestic product; PPP = purchasing power parity; Western Europe = EU-15 + European Free Trade Association.

Therefore, because the correlation between migration and development does not mean, per se, that at some point a country's economic development emigration slows down, the relationship might not be causal but rather a reflection of other underlying factors (Berthiaume et al. 2021). These factors include changes in countries' demographic structures and population aging, which both correlate with economic development and migration. Nevertheless, studies looking at emigration trends of countries over time instead of static cross-sections show that emigration in middle-income countries continues to increase while those countries develop until they reach upper-middle-income levels (approximately US$13,000 PPP), and this effect is stronger for small countries compared with larger ones (World Bank 2023).

In the labor market, wage and employment disparities, which are associated with migration flows, remain large. Similar to overall economic activity, gaps in employment and unemployment rates have been reduced in ECA during the past two decades, led by increasing employment opportunities in ECA countries that started with weak conditions in 2000 (that is, Bosnia and Herzegovina, Montenegro, and North Macedonia). Availability of job opportunities in poorer ECA countries, however, remains lower than in more advanced Western European economies. Furthermore, as panels a and b in figure 1.15 show, wage differentials are still strikingly large across ECA. Luxembourg and Belgium both have average net earnings above US$6,000 (PPP), and Austria, Germany, the Netherlands, and Switzerland have average earnings of more than US$5,000 (PPP). At the other extreme, wages adjusted for PPP remain at around US$800 in the Kyrgyz Republic, US$700 in Armenia, and US$600 in Tajikistan. Studies have found that part of those wage gaps are due not to differences in workers' skills but to where they reside. Therefore, individuals could earn more for the same work in other places, which is known as the "place premium" (Clemens, Montenegro, and Pritchett 2019), incentivizing them to migrate. Figure 1.15, panel b, shows the strong association between initial wage levels and posterior migration flows. In particular, countries with the lowest average wages in ECA in 2014 saw the largest net migration outflows as a percentage of their population. In the same vein, there is a strong correlation between migration flows and both the presence and the quality of job opportunities. Lower unemployment rates and higher shares of nonroutine cognitive jobs (for example, public relations and analytical, medical, and technical positions—which tend to be better quality, higher skilled, and higher pay—attract more migrants [refer to figure 1.15, panels c and d]). Surveys of migrants across different ECA countries show that searching for better employment opportunities is the main reason behind migrants' decision to migrate.[7]

Demographic Imbalances

Population aging in Western Europe and the subsequent need to sustain labor supply are a strong pull force for migration in the region, regardless of sending countries' demographic profile. Demographic trends vary substantially, and differences in aging have widened even further in the

FIGURE 1.15

Wage disparities and migration flows

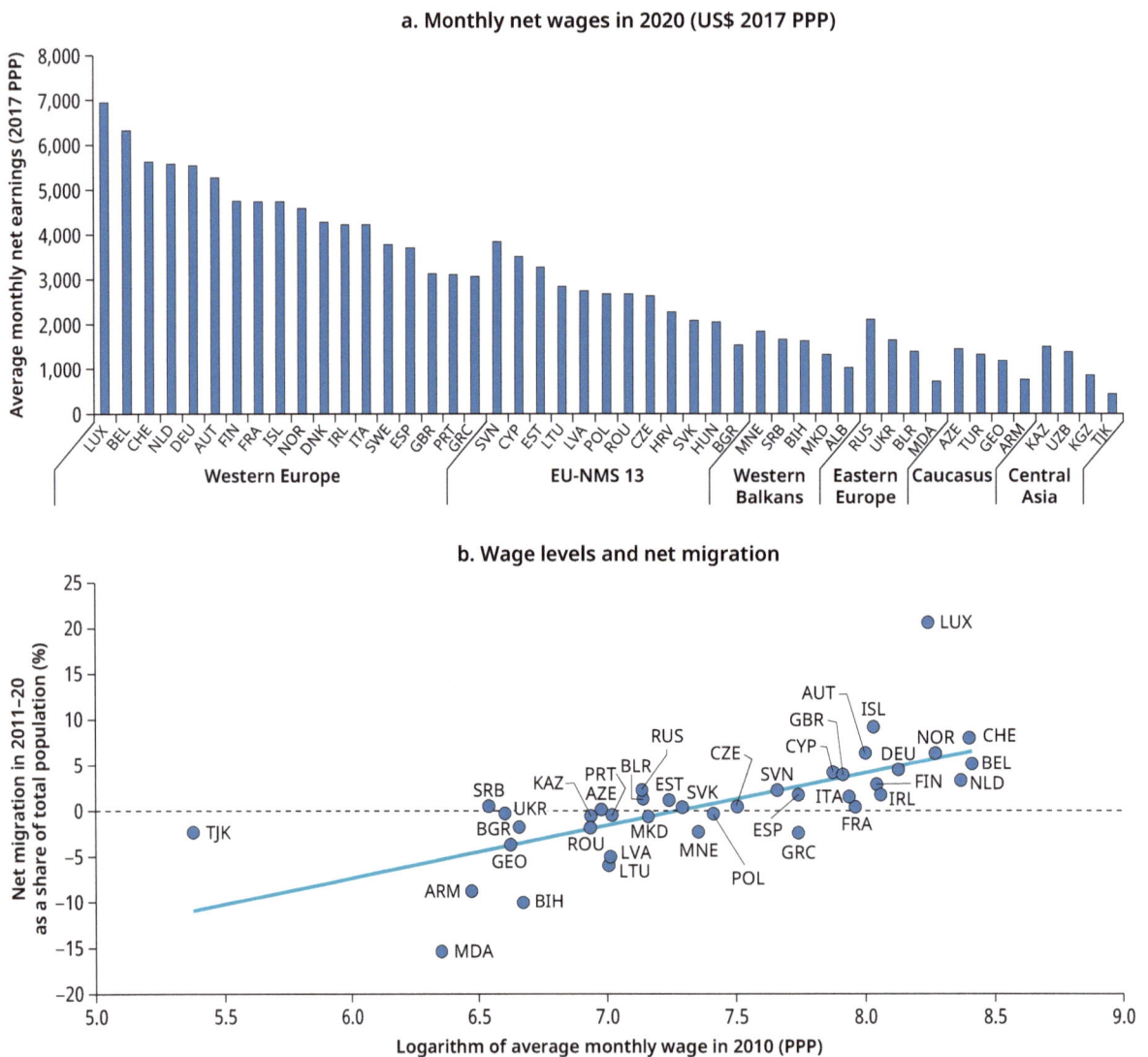

a. Monthly net wages in 2020 (US$ 2017 PPP)

b. Wage levels and net migration

Continued

Figure 1.15
Wage disparities and migration flows *(Continued)*

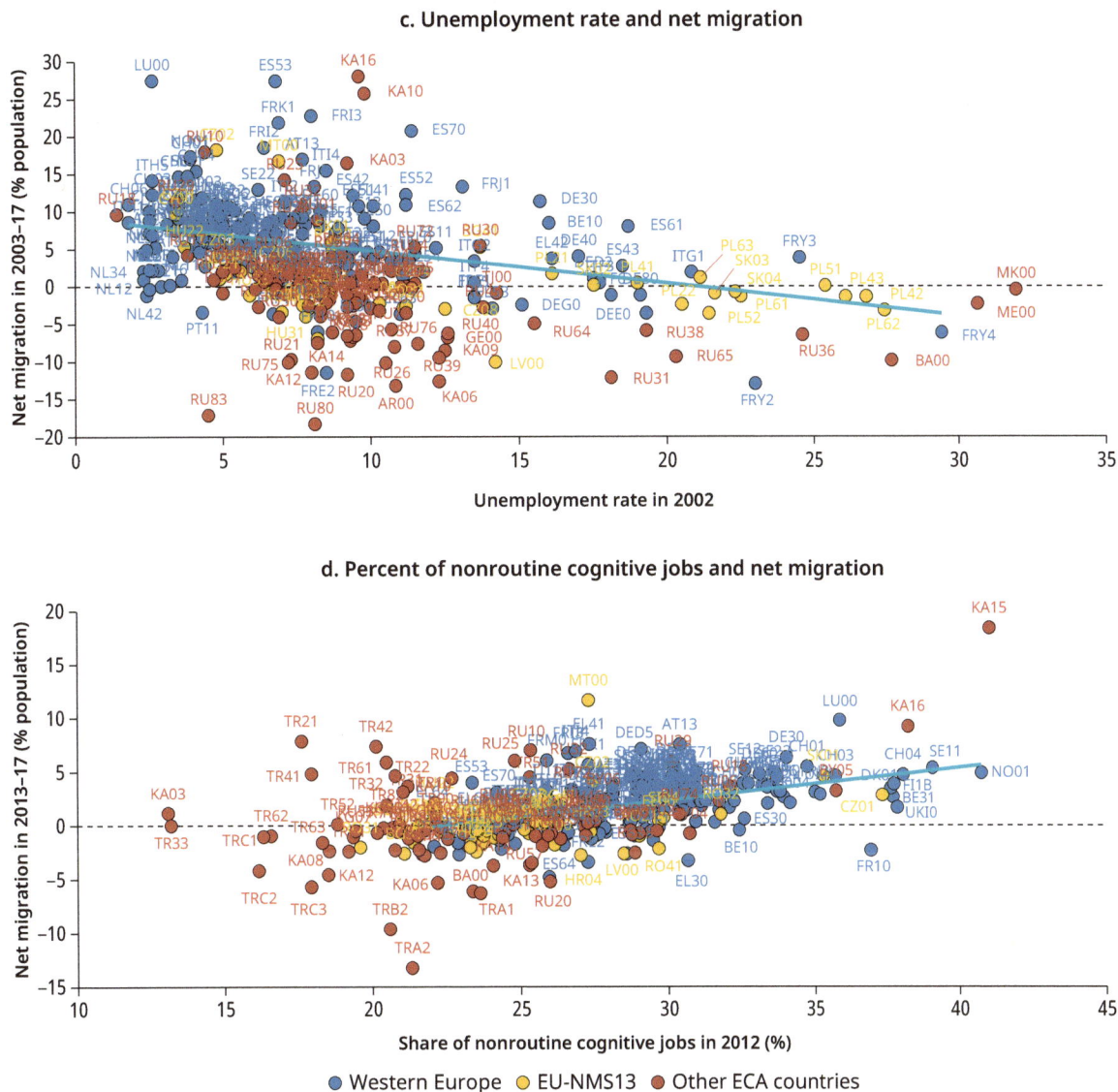

c. Unemployment rate and net migration

d. Percent of nonroutine cognitive jobs and net migration

● Western Europe   ○ EU-NMS13   ● Other ECA countries

Sources: International Labour Organization ILOSTAT database (https://ilostat.ilo.org/); European Commission Eurostat database (https://ec.europa.eu/eurostat/data/database); European Union Labour Force Survey; national labor force surveys; Organisation for Economic Co-operation and Development Regional Statistics database (https://doi.org/10.1787/region-data-en).
Note: Net migration is defined as total immigration flows minus total emigration flows over a given period. Annual net earnings (in purchasing power) are based on a full-time single worker without children earning an average wage. Nonroutine jobs are those that involve activities that are not repetitive or based on rules and may require flexibility and task switching. Cognitive jobs are those that involve problem solving and analysis and are associated with higher educational attainment. Nonroutine cognitive jobs include public relations and analytical, medical, and technical positions. The blue line in panels b, c, and d refers to the linear fitted line of all observations. The labels in panels c and d show the NUTS-2 regional code, which includes the alpha-2 country code and the two-digit principal subdivision code. For a list of NUTS-2 regional codes, go to https://ec.europa.eu/eurostat/web/nuts. The labels in panel b show 3-digit country codes. For a list of country codes, go to https://www.iso.org/obp/ui/#search. Western Europe = EU-15 + European Free Trade Association; EU-NMS13 = new member states joining the European Union in 2004, 2007, and 2013; other ECA countries = European and Central Asian countries not part of the European Union or EFTA countries (Albania, Armenia, Azerbaijan, Belarus, Bosnia and Herzegovina, Georgia, Kazakhstan, Kosovo, Kyrgyz Republic, Moldova, Montenegro, North Macedonia, Serbia, Tajikistan, Turkmenistan, Ukraine, and Uzbekistan); PPP = purchasing power parity.

past 20 years (refer to figure 1.16). Because of declines in fertility rates and gains in longevity, Western European countries that had the highest shares of elderly population in 2000 have since experienced further aging of their population. This has led to a reduction in the working-age population. This trend is expected to intensify in the coming decades with potential negative effects on labor force participation and skills availability for firms and ensuing fiscal pressures on support systems for older people with pensions. For example, Eurostat (2023) estimates an increase of 20 percentage points in the dependency ratio in Western Europe, potentially rising to 76.6 percent by 2060. On the one hand, aging in Western Europe and other key migrant-recipient countries such as Russia is a pull factor for migration. It creates labor supply shortages across different occupations, which puts pressure on wages, further increasing wage differentials that attract immigration. On the other hand, countries in Central Asia, which had the lowest shares of elderly

FIGURE 1.16

Share of the ECA population age 65 and older

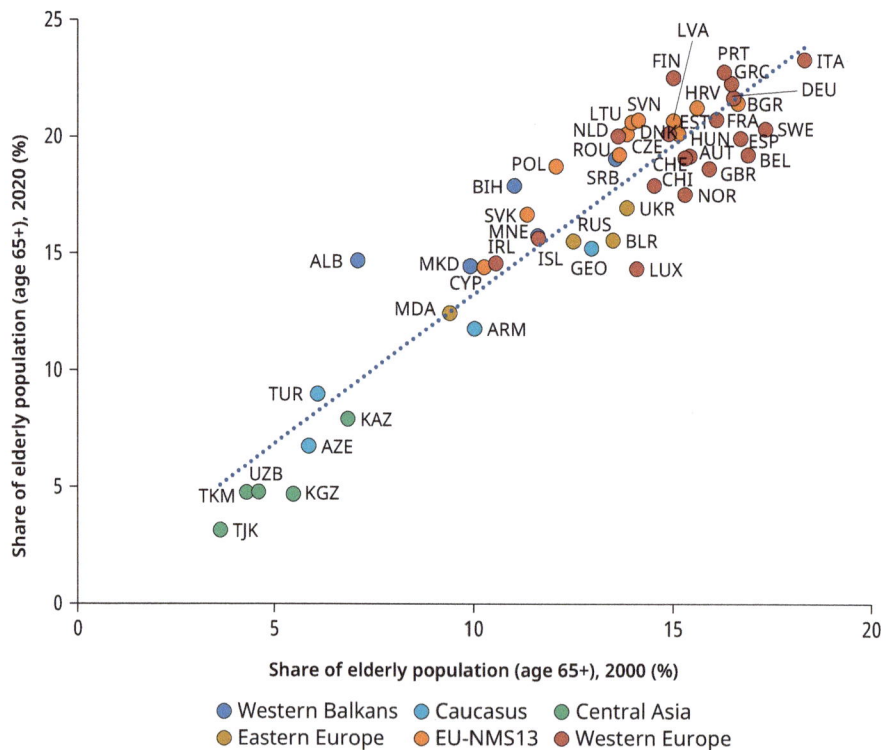

Source: World Bank World Development Indicators database (https://databank.worldbank.org/source /world-development-indicators).
Note: For a list of country codes, go to https://www.iso.org/obp/ui/#search. Eastern Europe = Belarus, Moldova, Russian Federation, and Ukraine; EU-NMS13 = new member states joining the European Union in 2004, 2007, and 2013; Western Europe = EU-15 + European Free Trade Association.

population and can still count on a large pool of youth, are not expected to experience any severe increase in the dependency ratio. These countries, as well as Türkiye and the Caucasus (although to a lesser extent), have more favorable demographics, with some even showing increases in their share of the working-age population because of what is called the "demographic dividend" of declining fertility rates, which lowers the youth dependency ratio. However, the increase in the working-age population has put further pressure on many economies that are not able to create enough jobs for the new workforce. Because of this labor surplus, there are pressures to emigrate in search of more economic opportunities.

Migration in ECA counterbalances population decline in certain receiving countries while exacerbating it in some sending countries. The main destination countries in ECA (Western Europe and Russia) are facing stagnating fertility rates that contribute to a weak or even negative population growth and a rapid aging of their population (refer to figure 1.17, panels a and b). Given that migrants are disproportionately of working age—because the majority migrate in search of employment opportunities—they increase the share of the working-age population in receiving countries. As is discussed in chapter 3, despite integration challenges resulting in lower employment rates and occupational downgrades, migrants tend to be net contributors to local economies, supporting public finances and pension systems. In the labor market in destination countries, migrants fill labor demand shortages, which is particularly important in key sectors such as agriculture, health care, and social services, for which demand has grown in parallel with the aging population. In countries of origin with a youth bulge and rapid population growth (for example, in most countries in the Caucasus and Central Asia), emigration of a part of the population alleviates population pressures and provides further employment opportunities abroad when the domestic labor demand does not grow fast enough to accommodate the increase in the labor supply as new cohorts of young workers enter the labor force. However, in other sending countries, particularly the new member states of the European Union, those in the Western Balkans, or those in Eastern Europe, emigration—which tends to feature younger cohorts—exacerbates the natural drop in population and aging, given the low fertility rates. Therefore, intra-ECA migration flows can amplify unequal population trends in certain corridors while supporting a more balanced demographic profile between sending and receiving countries in others.

Beyond population declines, emigration exacerbates aging itself among high migrant-sending regions. Because younger people show a greater tendency to migrate, emigration increases the share of older workers among the populations of migrant-sending countries. Between 1995 and 2021,

FIGURE 1.17

Contribution of migration to population change across ECA regions

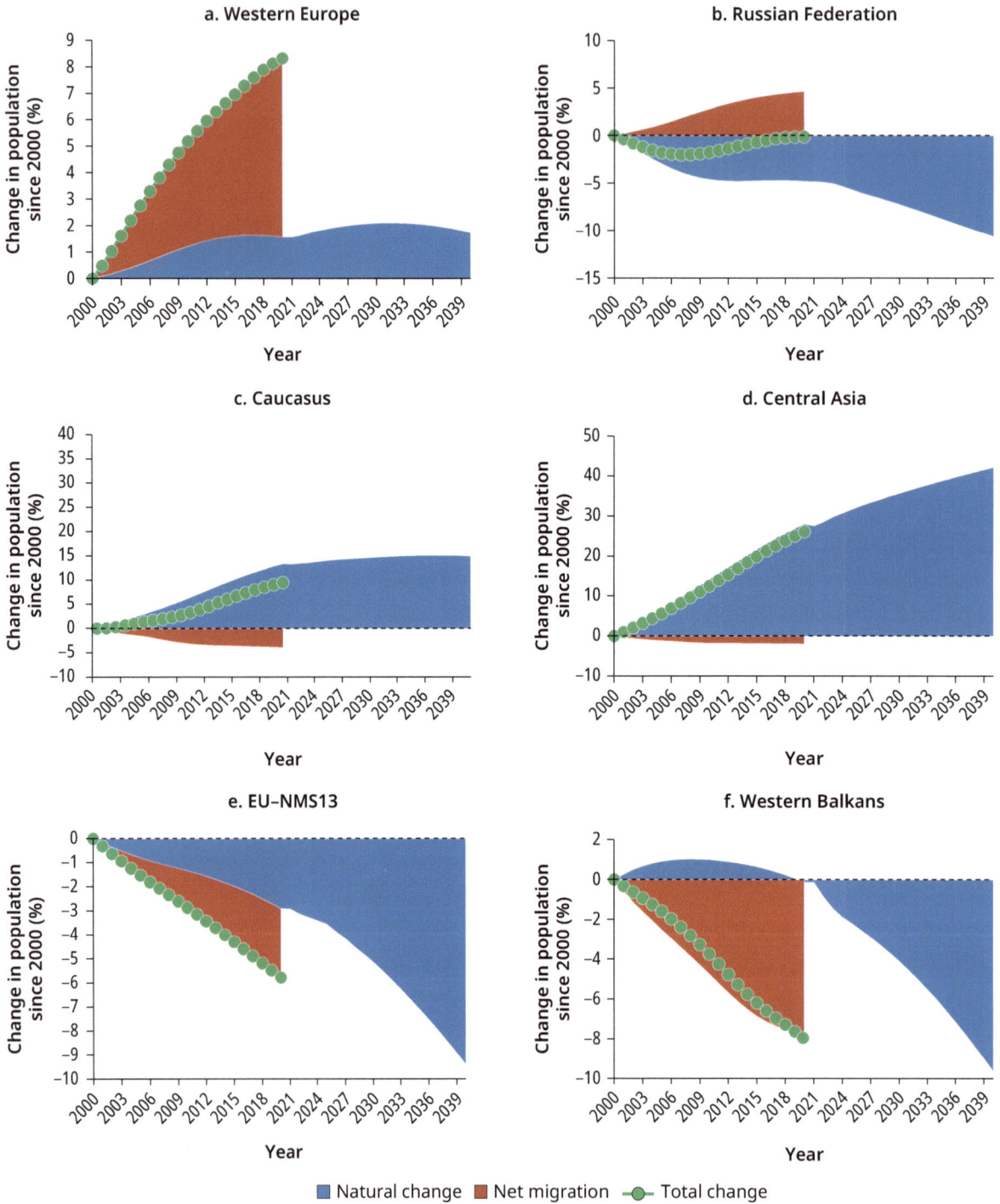

Source: UN Department of Economic and Social Affairs, Population Statistics (https://population.un.org/wpp/).
Note: Net migration is defined as cumulative immigration flows minus cumulative emigration flows over the corresponding period. Eastern Europe = Belarus, Moldova, and Ukraine; EU-15 = European Union members before 2004; EU-NMS13 = 13 new member states joining the European Union in 2004, 2007, and 2013; Western Europe = EU-15 + European Free Trade Association.

ECA countries with the largest net outflows of migrants saw a more rapid increase in the old-age dependency ratio compared with the 10 countries with the strongest net migration inflows (refer to figure 1.18, panel a). Similar patterns are observed when looking at subregions within countries, where the top 30 net emigration regions are rapidly catching up with the top receiving regions in terms of aging and old-age dependency (figure 1.18, panel b). These emigration trends are especially concerning for countries of origin with public pension systems that are already under stress and where there is cross-subsidization from high contributors to low contributors.

War and Conflict

Conflict, violence, and persecution are the fundamental catalysts of forced migration among refugees and asylum seekers. The main trigger of displacement among refugees is the insecurity created by conflict and humanitarian crises such as civil wars and genocides in their place of residence (Ibáñez 2014; Schmeidl 1997). The number of conflicts, civil wars, and their associated fatalities has been on the rise in the past two decades. In the context of an increasingly interconnected world, conflict

FIGURE 1.18
Trends in old-age dependency in migrant-sending and -receiving areas

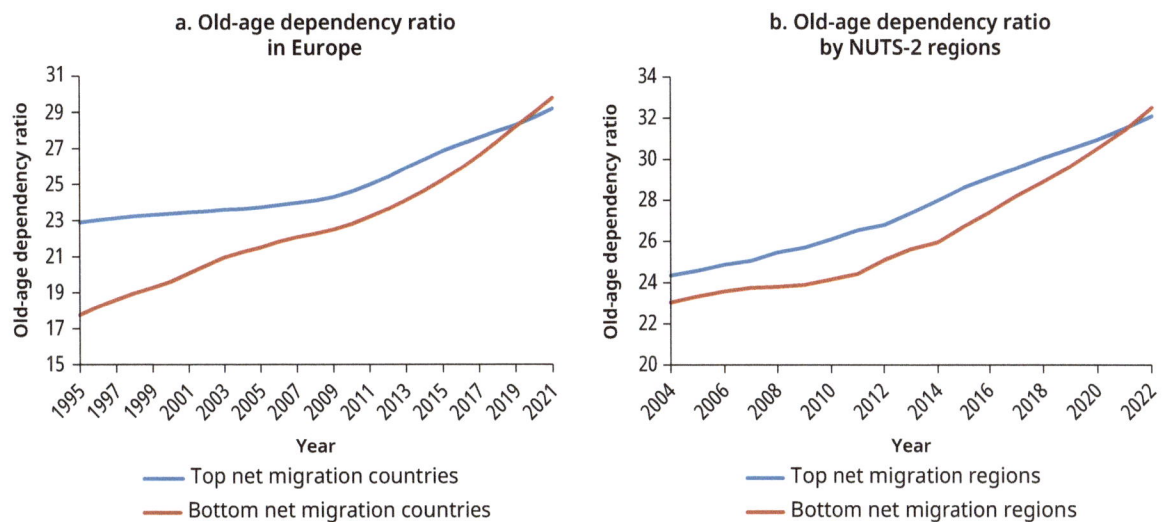

a. Old-age dependency ratio in Europe
b. Old-age dependency ratio by NUTS-2 regions

Top net migration countries
Bottom net migration countries
Top net migration regions
Bottom net migration regions

Source: Original figure based on Eurostat 2023.
Note: The old-age dependency ratio is the number of people 65 years old and older divided by the number of people ages 15–64. Net migration is defined as cumulative immigration flow minus cumulative emigration flows over the corresponding time period. Top net-migration regions are the 10 European countries with larger net inflows: Austria, Belgium, Ireland, Italy, Luxembourg, Norway, Spain, Sweden, Switzerland, and United Kingdom. Bottom net-migration regions are the 10 European countries with larger net outflows: Albania, Bosnia and Herzegovina, Bulgaria, Estonia, Greece, Latvia, Lithuania, Moldova, Romania, and Serbia. Top and bottom net-migration regions are the 30 percent of total Europe administrative regions (according to the NUTS-2) with larger net inflows and outflows, respectively. NUTS-2 = Nomenclature of Territorial Units for Statistics level 2.

has become more internationalized (World Bank 2020). The elasticity of refugees to conflict—that is, the number of refugees that conflict creates (measured by conflict-related deaths)—and the distance that refugees travel from their home countries has also progressively increased (World Bank 2020). The increasing capacity of refugees to travel further distances has resulted in more inflows of refugees to Western Europe even if most conflicts take place in places that are farther away. This happens because refugees, despite having different push factors for migration, have cost–benefit considerations similar to those of economic migrants when deciding where to migrate (World Bank 2018).

Other Drivers of Migration

Welfare and Social Services
The quality of public services is another driving force behind migration flows in both origin and destination countries. In destination countries, investments in robust education and health systems are associated with higher levels of immigration (Geis, Uebelmesser, and Werding 2013). Social safety nets are also correlated with migration flows, although the evidence is more mixed. Welfare-recipient immigrants in the United States are clustered in high-benefit states (Borjas 1999), although the impact of welfare benefits becomes insignificant once controlling for region and networks (Zavodny 1997). The hypothesis of welfare magnets is more likely to hold for migrants from the least-developed countries for which income differentials are larger (Pedersen, Pytlikova, and Smith 2008). Local amenities in sending countries, in particular security and public services, also serve as a push factor for migration, shaping intentions to emigrate (Dustmann and Okatenko 2014).

In ECA, gaps in social protection and health care systems are still substantial. Governments in high-income ECA countries such as Denmark, Germany, Norway, and Sweden spend more than US$5,000 per capita annually on the public health care system (refer to figure 1.19, panel a). On the other side of the spectrum, annual public health care spending per capita averages less than US$200 in Azerbaijan, the Kyrgyz Republic, Tajikistan, and Uzbekistan. These differentials, which consider different living standards (adjusted for purchasing power), result in higher availability and quality of services in more developed countries. Social assistance benefits also vary by country, in terms of both generosity of the system— amounts received as a share of the minimum wage or as a share of consumption—and coverage of the population, particularly those who are poor and more vulnerable, to whom they are often targeted. For example,

FIGURE 1.19

Public services and social protection programs across Europe and Central Asia

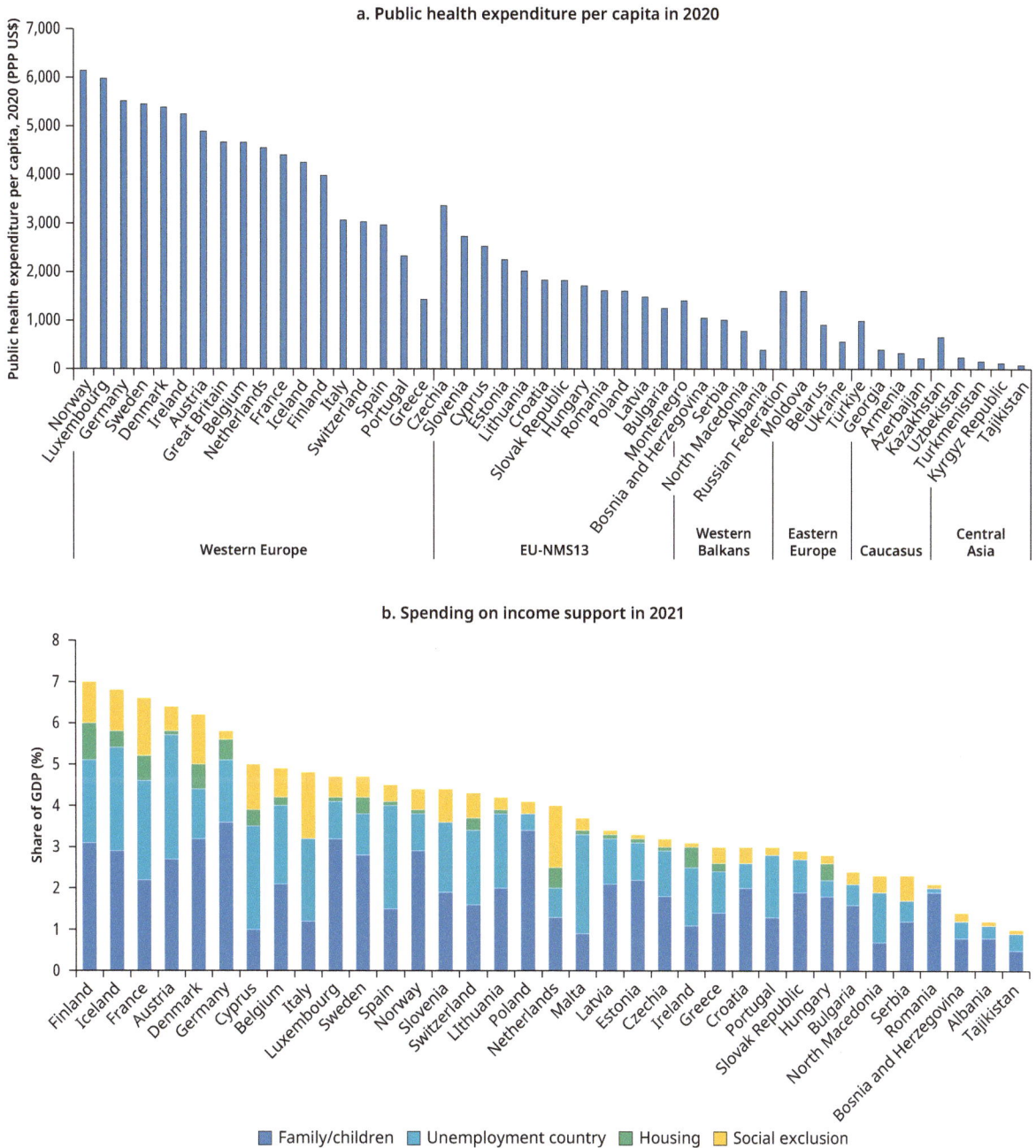

a. Public health expenditure per capita in 2020

b. Spending on income support in 2021

■ Family/children ■ Unemployment country ■ Housing ■ Social exclusion

Sources: World Bank World Development Indicators database (https://databank.worldbank.org/source/world-development-indicators); Eurostat (https://ec.europa.eu/eurostat/data/database).

Note: GDP = gross domestic product. For a list of country codes, go to https://www.iso.org/obp/ui/#search. Eastern Europe = Belarus, Moldova, and Ukraine; EU-NMS13 = new member states joining the European Union in 2004, 2007, and 2013; Western Europe = EU-15 + European Free Trade Association.

social assistance programs almost universally cover the poor population in Slovakia (98 percent), whereas fewer than half of the poor population in Belarus (45 percent) receive this type of assistance (refer to figure 1.19, panel b).

Quality of Institutions and Governance

Levels of corruption also shape migration flows from the perspective of both sending and receiving countries. Recent evidence in Europe shows that corruption levels in countries of origin are associated with sizable increases in outmigration, whereas corruption in destination countries deters immigration (Bernini et al. 2024). Corruption in a country disincentivizes immigration because it has negative impacts on economic conditions and job opportunities (Poprawe 2015). In sending countries, higher levels of corruption push part of the population away, increasing emigration rates (Ahmad and Arjumand 2015; Clausen, Kraay, and Nyiri 2011; Morano Foadi 2006) and limiting the return of those who migrated overseas (Auer, Römer, and Tjaden 2020). A key channel through which corruption affects emigration is the deterioration of local institutions, which results in lower citizen trust in institutions and weaker economic security. Furthermore, corruption affects emigration differently depending on education level, with high-skilled workers being particularly sensitive to it because it promotes favoritism in the labor market and reduces income and wage gains from educational investments (Ariu and Squicciarini 2013; Cooray and Schneider 2016; Dimant, Krieger, and Meierrieks 2013). As a result, corruption can aggravate the "brain drain" of the most educated individuals from origin countries and hinder their return.

Gaps in corruption and governance remain high in ECA countries, with slow improvements from 2000 to 2020 among those with lower-quality institutions. According to statistics from the World Bank's World Governance Indicators, progress in ECA in the overall levels of governance effectiveness and control of corruption during the past two decades has been limited. Although some convergence between countries has been observed, the disparities in the quality of institutions are still very large across countries in the region (refer to figure 1.20). Between 2000 and 2020, there was a somewhat stronger convergence in governance effectiveness, which captures perceptions of the quality of public services, the quality of the civil service and its independence from political pressures, and overall government policies. The dispersion across countries was reduced by 30 percent, led by strong improvements in countries such as Azerbaijan, Georgia, and Lithuania. However, improvements in control of corruption among the worst-performing countries in 2000 have been quite limited with few exceptions

FIGURE 1.20

Changes in institutional quality across ECA countries

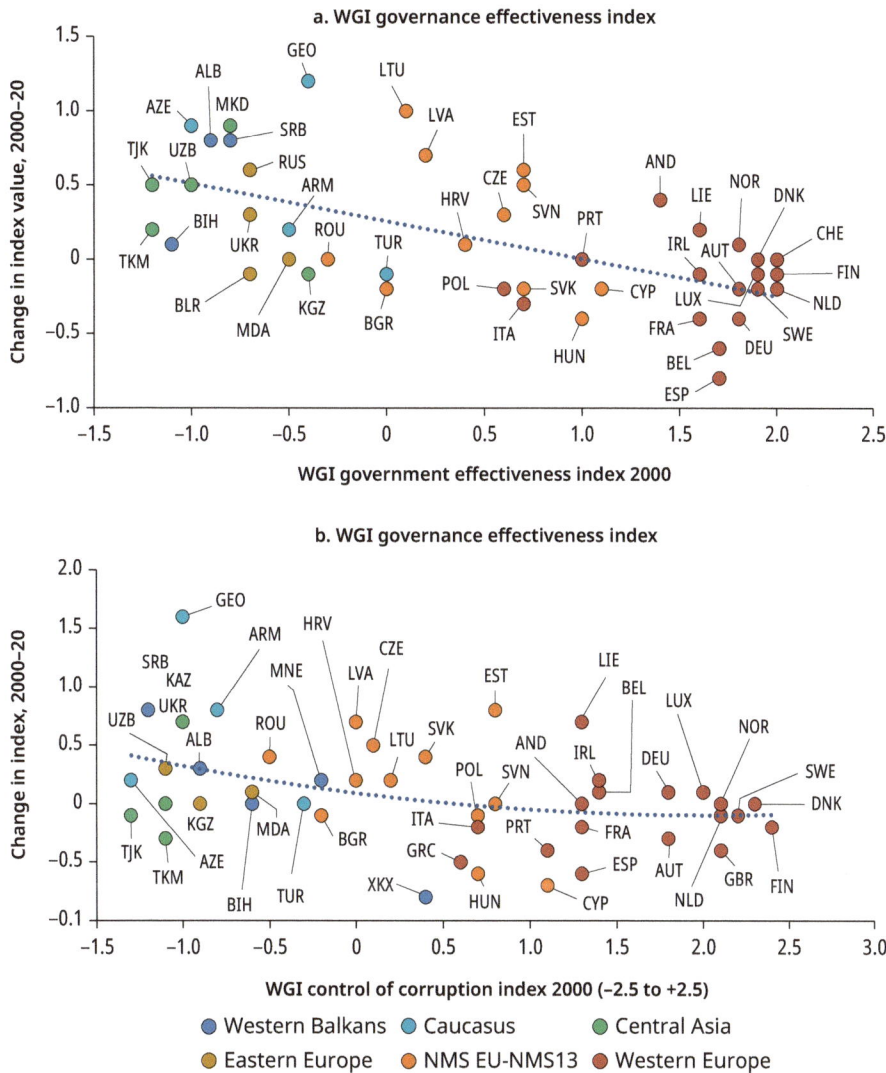

a. WGI governance effectiveness index

b. WGI governance effectiveness index

● Western Balkans ● Caucasus ● Central Asia
● Eastern Europe ● NMS EU-NMS13 ● Western Europe

Source: World Development Indicators (database).
Note: EU-NMS13 = 13 new member states joining the European Union in 2004, 2007, and 2013; WGI = World Governance Indicators. The Government Effectiveness Index captures perceptions of the quality of public services, the quality of the civil service, the quality of policy formulation and implementation, and the credibility of the government's commitment to such policies. The Control of Corruption Index captures perceptions of the extent to which public power is exercised for private gain as well as "capture" of the state by elites and private interests. Both indexes are based on more than 30 underlying data sources, which are combined and rescaled to have an average of zero and a range from –2.5 (worst) to 2.5 (best).

(for example, Georgia) and in some cases have even deteriorated (for example, Bulgaria, the Kyrgyz Republic, Turkmenistan). Sending countries thus have a wide scope to improve the country's institutional system to reduce emigration pressures and enhance return migration.

Networks

Social networks are another key driver of migration, reducing information asymmetries and the cost of migration but limiting the efficient allocation of labor to regions or occupations. Social networks are a fundamental driving force of international migration (Haug 2008; Manchin and Orazbayev 2018). For instance, having a relative in a destination country increases both intentions to migrate and actualized migration flows to that country. More broadly, the literature has found that the presence of migrant networks of the same nationality in each location attracts newer cohorts of migrants (Clark, Hatton, and Williamson 2007). These patterns perpetuate the relative predominance of certain bilateral corridors over others. Social networks help address barriers to international migration, such as financial constraints and asymmetric and limited information about prospective migrants. Migrant networks compensate for the lack of social capital in the host country, helping migrants navigate cultural norms and bureaucratic processes while also providing information on jobs and social services. Therefore, they play a key role in supporting their integration into the host communities. Although networks can be welfare enhancing at the beginning, they can generate a dynamically inefficient system if they persist over generations (Munshi 2020). This is because they can restrict the location and occupational choices of new waves of immigrants (Beaman 2012; Munshi and Rosenzweig 2006; Patel and Vella 2013). In the European Union, the migrants' use of networks to find employment pushes them more toward jobs with working conditions that increase their health risks (Bossavie, Garrote Sánchez, et al. 2021).

Physical, Cultural or Ethnic, and Linguistic Distance

The proximity of the host country in terms of distance, language, or culture reduces the fixed costs of migration; migrants are thus more likely to select destination countries on the basis of these similarities. Migrants tend to choose the destination country on the basis of the expected costs and benefits of migration. Although the benefits come in the form of income premiums (as discussed in previous paragraphs), costs arise not only from the living expenses at the destination but also from the initial costs, such as travel (which increases with distance) or the need to invest in learning another language or culture to be able to participate in host-country labor markets and reap the potential benefits from income differentials. When trying to integrate into and settle in a new country, these costs are not only monetary but also psychosocial (Lu 2012; Thapa et al. 2018). Low-skilled migrants who tend to be more credit constrained on average travel shorter distances than higher-skilled ones. Globally, more than 50 percent of migrants without tertiary education migrate to a neighboring country, compared with only 20 percent of highly educated migrants (World Bank 2018). The distance traveled tends to be even shorter for refugees. More than 80 percent remain in a neighboring country, because their primary motivation is to flee conflict and arrive at a safe place that accepts them, not to find where the highest income gains are. Cultural and linguistic distance are important drivers of bilateral migration corridors, perpetuating the creation of networks (Pedersen, Pytlikova, and Smith 2008). Because fluency in the language of the destination country strongly affects immigrants' success in the host labor market, the size of a bilateral migration corridor between two countries with linguistic similarities is strongly positively correlated (Bleakley and Chin 2004; Dustmann and Fabri 2003).

Economic Unions (European Union or Eurasian Economic Union)

During the past two decades, different institutional reforms in ECA have expanded free mobility of people within certain countries. In Europe, the European Union expanded to 13 new Central and Eastern European countries in 2004, 2007, and 2013. This process boosted migration flows from eastern to western EU members (World Bank 2019). The lifting of work restrictions between two countries in the European Union is associated with a 120 percent increase in bilateral migration flows (Bossavie et al. 2022). The process of political and economic integration into the Eurasian Economic Union (EaEU), which includes Armenia, Belarus, Kazakhstan, the Kyrgyz Republic, and Russia, has also facilitated the mobility of workers between its member countries, in particular to Kazakhstan and Russia as main destination countries. The treaty came into force on January 1, 2015. Survey data from Russia show that although the number of migrants from the Caucasus and Central Asian countries that did not join the EaEU decreased from 2.2 percent to 1.8 percent of the total labor force in Russia in the years after the treaty was signed (2016–17), the number of migrants from EaEU countries marginally increased from 2.5 percent to 2.6 percent (refer to figure 1.21). Difference-in-differences estimates show a 20 percent increase in migration flows resulting from accession to the EaEU. The impact seems to be smaller than that of the European Union on migration, which could be due to the lower levels of integration and mobility, as well as smaller wage differentials and the higher nature of short-term, seasonal migration that is harder to capture in survey data.

FIGURE 1.21

Number of immigrants in the Russian Federation, before and after the Eurasian Economic Union Treaty came into force

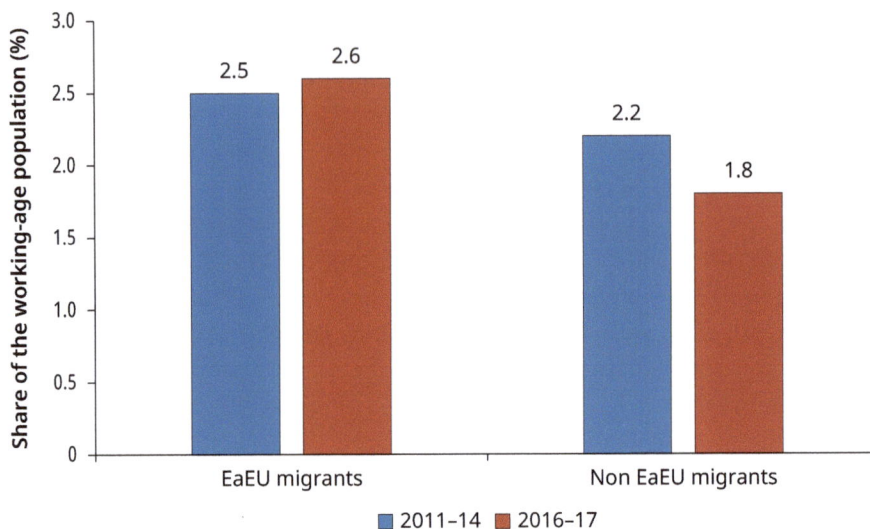

Source: Russia Longitudinal Monitoring Survey (https://rlms-hse.cpc.unc.edu/data/).
Note: The EaEU came into force in 2015 and provides free mobility of the population for the member countries. EaEU migrants are those from Armenia, Belarus, and Kazakhstan. Non-EaEU migrants are those from Azerbaijan, Georgia, Tajikistan, and Uzbekistan. EaEU = Eurasian Economic Union.

Data Gaps on Migration across ECA Countries

Data Gaps from the Destination Country Perspective

National population censuses are the main source of data on the stock of international migrants in recipient countries, but the low frequency of data collection limits real-time analysis. Given their universal coverage, they offer precise information on different socioeconomic outcomes of the migrant population in a given country. As such, censuses can better characterize the integration of international migrants of specific demographic or socioeconomic and geographic characteristics (GMG 2017). The relative similarity of questionnaires also facilitates cross-country comparability. The main limitation of censuses in capturing international migration is their reduced frequency, because they are generally conducted once every 10 years. Most ECA countries have not finished the 2020s round of the census, so the latest available information tends to be outdated (that is, early 2010s). Moreover, censuses cover a limited set of questions on labor market outcomes and the international migration trajectory compared with other surveys, such as the EU Labour Force Survey (LFS), a large quarterly household survey established in 1983 in all EU countries, as well as in Iceland, Norway, and Switzerland.

Survey data are another commonly used source of information on immigrants' labor market outcomes in destination countries, but these data tend to underreport the number of migrants, particularly those who are more mobile and have less formal status. These surveys tend to capture immigration by including questions on country of birth and nationality. Their main advantage is the richness and diversity of data they collect on labor market outcomes compared with other sources. One limitation, however, is that these household surveys are not particularly designed to measure migrants' outcomes but rather the outcomes of the total population or the working-age population in each country. On top of that, migrants are often harder to reach than the general population, given their higher mobility, sensitivity of their status, or prior perceptions of exclusion (Font and Méndez 2013). By design, sampling frames of standard household or labor force surveys at destination are not well suited to capture temporary migrants, because they are based on permanent addresses. As a result, surveys in destination countries may underestimate the number of migrants and capture a biased pool of more permanent migrants. A study comparing how migrants are sampled in different European surveys with official statistics on migration revealed that, although there is representativeness of migrants' aggregative outcomes, results for different breakdowns, such as age or gender, tend to be inaccurate because of small sample size (OECD 2017).

One of the main surveys to analyze labor migration in Europe is the EU LFS. Other national LFSs are not harmonized and are less comparable than the EU LFS. Overall, migrants tend to be slightly underrepresented in these surveys, and the problem is more acute in surveys in small countries (such as Luxembourg or Malta) or for those with a smaller sample size (Norway, Sweden; refer to table 1A.1 in annex 1A). The small sample size of migrants for certain countries limits the ability to provide an accurate characterization of their socioeconomic profile. Another drawback is that many LFSs (for example, the EU LFS) provide not migrants' country of origin but rather their region of origin. This prevents analysis of bilateral corridors.[8]

Data Gaps from the Sending Country Perspective

Data gaps are more salient in sending countries. From the perspective of the sending countries, two key concepts are related to migration: emigration and return migration. Emigrants are considered those who left their country of birth to reside abroad, and return migrants are part of the emigrant diaspora who return to their home country. In general, there are more identification problems in capturing the extent of emigration through data sources from the sending country than through data from destination countries. This is particularly true if entire households leave the country, which is more likely to happen among those fleeing violence and conflict. The main sources of information on migration in Europe in sending countries are survey and census data. However, the information on emigration and return migration is more limited, often requiring proxy variables to estimate the prevalence of this phenomenon.

The public availability of census data in Eastern European and Central Asian countries is limited and, in most cases, ill suited to capturing both emigration and return migration. When available, census questions on migration are limited to whether an individual's previous residence was abroad. This does not capture all of those who migrated abroad but then had more residency changes within the country or those residing abroad one year before the survey. Return migration estimates based on these metrics are very low (for example, 0.1 percent in Romania in 2011) and unable to fully capture the extent of the phenomenon. Furthermore, almost no census provides information on current emigrants, with few exceptions, such as the Kyrgyz Republic, which provides data on household members living abroad.

Survey data vary widely by country in terms of each country's ability to capture the extent of emigration and return migration. The EU LFS and national LFSs are the main surveys in migrant-sending countries in ECA. The most detailed surveys better approximate the returnee population by asking respondents questions about their migration history or whether they ever left the country. However, most labor surveys do not incorporate these questions, and returnees can only be observed through a narrower question on whether respondents were abroad one year before the survey or not. This restrictive approximation captures only emigrants who recently returned to their country of origin. Table 1A.1 summarizes all periodic labor surveys available in eastern ECA and highlights what questions they incorporate to capture immigration, emigration, and return migration. Only about one-half of the surveys have broad approximations of return migration (either asking whether the last place of residence was overseas or whether they had lived or worked abroad during the past 10 years), with the rest including only very restrictive proxies (residence one year ago).

Household surveys in sending countries face even more difficulties in capturing the extent of current emigration because, by definition, current emigrants cannot be directly surveyed. The most common question regarding present emigration is whether surveyed residents are currently working abroad while residing in their home country. However, this form of migration only happens in fewer cases, such as when individuals close to borders commute to work abroad or in the case of seasonal migrants. Only a few surveys in sending countries can capture current migrants (for example,

Albania, Armenia, the Kyrgyz Republic, Tajikistan, and Uzbekistan) through questions on whether household members are temporarily or permanently living overseas. However, those would be captured only if some members of the household have gone abroad while other members remained in the country of origin, but not if the entire household moved abroad.

Annex 1A. Availability of Migration Indicators in Surveys

TABLE 1A.1 **Information on migrants and returnees in nationally representative surveys in countries of origin**

Country	Region	Survey name	Last year	Returnee	Emigrant	Immigrant
Bulgaria	EU NMS	EU LFS	2021	Residence 1 year ago	Work abroad and residing at home	Place of birth
Croatia	EU NMS	EU LFS	2021	Residence 1 year ago	Work abroad and residing at home	Place of birth
Czechia	EU NMS	EU LFS	2021	Residence 1 year ago	Work abroad and residing at home	Place of birth
Estonia	EU NMS	EU LFS	2021	Residence 1 year ago	Work abroad and residing at home	Place of birth
Hungary	EU NMS	EU LFS	2021	Residence 1 year ago	Work abroad and residing at home	Place of birth
Latvia	EU NMS	EU LFS	2021	Residence 1 year ago	Work abroad and residing at home	Place of birth
Lithuania	EU NMS	EU LFS	2021	Residence 1 year ago	Work abroad and residing at home	Place of birth
Poland	EU NMS	EU LFS	2021	Residence 1 year ago	Work abroad and residing at home	Place of birth
Romania	EU NMS	EU LFS	2021	Residence 1 year ago	Work abroad and residing at home	Place of birth
Slovakia	EU NMS	EU LFS	2021	Residence 1 year ago	Work abroad and residing at home	Place of birth
Slovenia	EU NMS	EU LFS	2021	Residence 1 year ago	Work abroad and residing at home	Place of birth
Poland	EU NMS	EU LFS	2021	Residence 1 year ago	Work abroad and residing at home	Citizenship
Albania	Western Balkans	LSMS	2012	Ever lived abroad >3 months	HH member currently living abroad	Place of birth
Albania	Western Balkans	LFS	2013	Ever worked abroad	Work abroad and residing at home	Place of birth
Albania	Western Balkans	LFS	2017	Residence 1 year ago	Work abroad and residing at home	Place of birth
Bosnia	Western Balkans	LFS	2017	Residence 1 year ago	Work abroad and residing at home	Place of birth
Kosovo	Western Balkans	LFS	2017	Residence 1 year ago	Work abroad and residing at home	Place of birth
North Macedonia	Western Balkans	LFS	2017	Residence 1 year ago	HH member currently living abroad	Place of birth
Montenegro	Western Balkans	LFS	2018	Residence 1 year ago	Work abroad and residing at home	Place of birth
Serbia	Western Balkans	LFS	2018	Ever lived abroad > 1 year	Work abroad and residing at home	Place of birth

Continued

TABLE 1A.1 Information on migrants and returnees in nationally representative surveys in countries of origin *(Continued)*

Country	Region	Survey name	Last year	Returnee	Emigrant	Immigrant
Armenia	CIS	LFS	2020	—	HH member currently living abroad	Place of birth
Armenia	CIS	ILCS	2021	Previous residence abroad	—	Place of birth
Belarus	CIS	LFS	2017	Previous residence abroad	Work abroad and residing at home	Nationality
Georgia	CIS	LFS	2018	Previous residence abroad	Member temporary absent	Nationality
Kazakhstan	CIS	LFS	2013	Lived abroad in the past 10 years	Work abroad and residing at home	Nationality
Kyrgyz Republic	CIS	L2CK	2023	Lived abroad in the past 10 years for >3 months	Member temporary or permanently abroad	Nationality
Moldova	CIS	LFS	2016	—	—	—
Russian Federation	CIS	RLMS	2017	—	—	Place of birth
Tajikistan	CIS	L2CT	2023	Returned from abroad in past 10 days	HH member currently living abroad	—
Ukraine	CIS	HLCS / LFS	2016	—	—	—
Uzbekistan	CIS	L2CU	2023	Previous residence abroad	HH member currently living abroad	Place of birth

Source: World Bank, based on EU LFS, LFS, HLCS, ILCS, LSMS, L2CK, L2CT, L2CU, and RLMS. Data available at World Bank Datalibweb, https://datalibweb2.worldbank.org/.
Note: CIS = Commonwealth of Independent States; EU NMS = European Union new member state; EU LFS = European Union Labour Force Survey; LFS = labor force survey; HH = household; HLCS = Household Living Condition Survey; ILCS = Income and Living Condition Survey; LSMS = Living Standards Measurement Study; L2CK = Listening to the Citizens of Kyrgyzstan; L2CT = Listening to the Citizens of Tajikistan; L2CU = Listening to the Citizens of Uzbekistan; RLMS = Russian Longitudinal Monitoring Survey. — = not available.

Notes

1. See box 1.1 for a definition of migrant used in this report.
2. Chapter 5 looks in more detail at the impact of the pandemic on low-skilled migrants.
3. Some countries (mostly in Eastern Europe and Central Asia) have such a small share of migrants in the overall population (less than 2 percent) that statistics on skills from national surveys cannot be used because of the limited sample size (refer to map 1.2).
4. These statistics are from the Kyrgyz Integrated Household Survey (2018), Listening to the Citizens of Tajikistan (2019), and Listening to the Citizens of Uzbekistan (2020).
5. The European Union Labour Force Survey (LFS) reports brackets of five years instead of a more precise duration of stay.
6. For the purposes of this report, temporary migration is defined as instances in which migrants migrate for a period of time and then return to their home country. This is different from other definitions, such as that used by the European Union, which defines temporary migration as migration episodes in which migrants ex ante planned to migrate for a specific period of time, regardless of the final migration outcome (European Commission n.d.).
7. That is the case, for example, in Armenia (LFS 2020), the Kyrgyz Republic (Listening to the Citizens of Kyrgyzstan 2022), Tajikistan (Listening to the Citizens of Tajikistan 2022), and Uzbekistan (Listening to the Citizens of Uzbekistan 2022).

8.   The regions are divided among European Union members before 2004, EU accession countries in
      2004, EU member states joining after 2004, European Free Trade Association, other Europe,
      North Africa, other Africa, Near and Middle East, South Asia, North America, Central America,
      South America, and Oceania.

References

Ahmad, N., and S. Arjumand. 2015. "Impact of Corruption on GDP Per Capita through International
    Migration: An Empirical Investigation." *Quality and Quantity* 50 (4): 1633–43.

Ariu, A., and M. P. Squicciarini. 2013. "The Balance of Brains: Corruption and Migration." *EMBO Reports*
    14 (6): 502–4. https://doi.org/10.1038%2Fembor.2013.59.

Auer, D., F. Römer, and J. Tjaden. 2020. "Corruption and the Desire to Leave: Quasi-Experimental Evidence
    on Corruption as a Driver of Emigration Intentions." *IZA Journal of Development and Migration* 11 (1).
    https://doi.org/10.2478/izajodm-2020-0007.

Beaman, L. A. 2012. "Social Networks and the Dynamics of Labour Market Outcomes: Evidence from
    Refugees Resettled in the U.S." *Review of Economic Studies* 79 (1): 128–61. https://doi.org/10.1093
    /restud/rdr017.

Bernini, A., L. Bossavie, D. Garrote-Sánchez, and M. Makovec. 2024. "Corruption as a Push and Pull Factor of
    Migration Flows: Evidence from European Countries." *Empirica* 51: 263–81.

Berthiaume, N., N. Leefmans, N. Oomes, H. Rojas-Romagosa, and T. Vervliet. 2021. "A Reappraisal of the
    Migration-Development Nexus: Testing the Robustness of the Migration Transition Hypothesis." Policy
    Research Working Paper 9518, World Bank, Washington, DC. https://doi.org/10.1596/1813-9450-9518.

Bleakley, H., and A. Chin. 2004. "Language Skills and Earnings: Evidence from Childhood Immigrants."
    Review of Economics and Statistics 86 (2): 481–96.

Borjas, G. J. 1999. "Immigration and Welfare Magnets." *Journal of Labor Economics* 17 (4): 607–37.

Bossavie, L., D. Garrote Sánchez, M. Makovec, and Ç. Özden. 2021. "Occupational Hazards: Migrants and the
    Economic and Health Risks of COVID-19 in Western Europe." Policy Research Working Paper 9873, World
    Bank, Washington, DC. https://documents1.worldbank.org/curated/en/692831638797417505/pdf
    /Occupational-Hazards-Migrants-and-the-Economic-and-Health-Risks-of-COVID-19-in-Western-Europe.pdf.

Bossavie, L., D. Garrote Sánchez, M. Makovec, and Ç. Özden. 2022. *Skilled Migration: A Sign of Europe's Divide
    or Integration?* Washington, DC: World Bank. https://doi.org/10.1596/978-1-4648-1732-8.

Bossavie, L., and Ç. Özden. 2022. "Impacts of Temporary Migration on Development in Origin Countries."
    Policy Research Working Paper 9996, World Bank, Washington, DC. https://openknowledge.worldbank.
    org/server/api/core/bitstreams/f1cffa48-1040-5563-88e6-c684a39a6ffe/content.

Chudinovskin, O. 2021. "Estimating Irregular Migration in the Russian Federation." Paper presented at the
    International Organization for Migration Second International Forum on Migration Statistics, Cairo,
    January 19–21.

Clark, X., T. J. Hatton, and J. G. Williamson. 2007. "Explaining U.S. Immigration, 1971–1998." *Review of
    Economics and Statistics* 89 (2): 359–73. https://www.jstor.org/stable/40043066.

Clausen, B., A. Kraay, and Z. Nyiri. 2011. "Corruption and Confidence in Public Institutions: Evidence from a
    Global Survey." *World Bank Economic Review* 25 (2): 212–49.

Clemens, M. A. 2013. "Why Do Programmers Earn More in Houston than Hyderabad? Evidence from
    Randomized Processing of US Visas." *American Economic Review* 103 (3): 198–202. https://doi.org/10.1257
    /aer.103.3.198.

Clemens, M. A. 2014. "Does Development Reduce Migration?" Discussion Paper 8592, Institute for the Study
    of Labor, Bonn. https://docs.iza.org/dp8592.pdf.

Clemens, M. A., C. E. Montenegro, and L. Pritchett. 2019. "The Place Premium: Bounding the Price
    Equivalent of Migration Barriers." *Review of Economics and Statistics* 101 (2): 201–13. https://doi.org
    /10.1162/rest_a_00776.

Connor, P., and J. S. Passel. 2019. *Europe's Unauthorized Immigrant Population Peaks in 2016, Then Levels Off.* Washington, DC: Pew Research Center. https://www.pewresearch.org/global/2019/11/13/europes -unauthorized-immigrant-population-peaks-in-2016-then-levels-off/#:~:text=The%20total%20is%20 up%20from,to%205.3%25million%20in%202016.

Constant, A. F., O. Nottmeyer, and K. F. Zimmermann. 2013. "The Economics of Circular Migration." In *International Handbook on the Economics of Migration*, edited by A. F. Constant and K. F. Zimmermann, 55–74. Cheltenham, UK: Edward Elgar.

Cooray, A., and F. Schneider. 2016. "Does Corruption Promote Emigration? An Empirical Examination." *Journal of Population Economics* 29: 293–310. https://doi.org/10.1007/s00148-015-0563-y.

Dao, T. H., F. Docquier, C. Parsons, and G. Peri. 2018. "Migration and Development: Dissecting the Anatomy of the Mobility Transition." *Journal of Development Economics* 132: 88–101. https://doi.org/10.1016/j .jdeveco.2017.12.003.

del Rio-Chanona, R. M., P. Mealy, A. Pichler, F. Lafond, and J. D. Farmer. 2020. "Supply and Demand Shocks in the COVID-19 Pandemic: An Industry and Occupation Perspective." *Oxford Review of Economic Policy* 36 (Supplement 1): S94–137. https://doi.org/10.1093/oxrep/graa033.

Devictor, X., Q.-T. Do, and A. A. Levchenko. 2021. "The Globalization of Refugee Flows." *Journal of Development Economics* 150: 102605. https://doi.org/10.1016/j.jdeveco.2020.102605.

Dimant, E., T. Krieger, and D. Meierrieks. 2013. "The Effect of Corruption on Migration, 1985–2000." *Applied Economics Letters* 20 (13): 1270–4. https://doi.org/10.1080/13504851.2013.806776.

Dustmann, C., and F. Fabri. 2003. "Language Proficiency and Labour Market Performance of Immigrants in the UK." *Economic Journal* 113 (489): 695–717.

Dustmann, C., and J. S. Görlach. 2016. "The Economics of Temporary Migrations." *Journal of Economic Literature* 54 (1): 98–136. https://doi.org/10.1257/jel.54.1.98.

Dustmann, C., and A. Okatenko. 2014. "Out-Migration, Wealth Constraints, and the Quality of Local Amenities." *Journal of Development Economics* 110: 52–63. https://doi.org/10.1016/j.jdeveco .2014.05.008.

European Commission. n.d. "Temporary Migration." https://home-affairs.ec.europa.eu/networks/european -migration-network-emn/emn-asylum-and-migration-glossary/glossary/temporary-migration _en#:~:text=Definition(s),of%20origin%20or%20onward%20movement.

Eurostat. 2023. "EUROPOP2023: Population Projections at National Level (2022–2100)." Eurostat, May 25, 2023. https://ec.europa.eu/eurostat/cache/metadata/en/proj_23n_esms.htm.

Faini, R., and A. Venturini. 2010. "Development and Migration: Lessons from Southern Europe." In *Migration and Culture*, edited by G. S. Epstein and I. N. Gang, 105–36. Leeds, UK: Emerald Group. https://doi .org/10.1108/S1574-8715(2010)0000008011.

Farole T., S. Goga, and M. Ionescu-Heroiu. 2018. "Rethinking Lagging Regions: Using Cohesion Policy to Deliver on the Potential of Europe's Regions." World Bank Report on the European Union. Washington, DC: World Bank.

Font, J., and M. Méndez, eds. 2013. *Surveying Ethnic Minorities and Immigrant Populations: Methodological Challenges and Research Strategies.* Amsterdam: Amsterdam University Press.

Garrote Sanchez, D., N. Gomez Parra, C. Ozden, and B. Rijkers. 2020. "Which Jobs Are Most Vulnerable to COVID-19? What an Analysis of the European Union Reveals." Research and Policy Brief 148384, World Bank, Washington, DC. https://documents.worldbank.org/curated/en/820351589209840894 /Which-Jobs-Are-Most-Vulnerable-to-COVID-19-What-an-Analysis-of-the-European-Union-Reveals.

Garrote-Sanchez, D., J. Kreuder, and M. Testaverde. 2021. "Migration in Bulgaria: Current Challenges and Opportunities." Social Protection and Jobs Discussion Paper 2109, World Bank, Washington, DC. http://documents.worldbank.org/curated/en/914401640249485571/Migration-in-Bulgaria-Current -Challenges-and-Opportunities.

Geis, W., S. Uebelmesser, and M. Werding. 2013. "How Do Migrants Choose Their Destination Country? An Analysis of Institutional Determinants." *Review of International Economics* 21 (5): 825–40. https://doi .org/10.1111/roie.12073.

GMG (Global Migration Group). 2017. *Handbook for Improving the Production and Use of Migration Data for Development.* Washington, DC: World Bank, Global Knowledge Partnership for Migration and Development. https://www.knomad.org/sites/default/files/2017-11/Handbook%20for%20Improving%20the%20 Production%20and%20Use%20of%20Migration%20Data%20for%20Development.pdf.

Haug, S. 2008. "Migration Networks and Migration Decision-Making." *Journal of Ethnic and Migration Studies* 34 (4): 585–605. https://doi.org/10.1080/13691830801961605.

Ibáñez, A. M. 2014. "The Growth of Forced Displacement: Cross-Country, Subnational and Household Evidence on Potential Determinants." In *International Handbook on Migration and Economic Development,* edited by R. Lucas Jr., 350–87. Cheltenham, UK: Edward Elgar.

Lu, Y. 2012. "Household Migration, Social Support, and Psychosocial Health: The Perspective from Migrant-Sending Areas." *Social Science and Medicine* 74 (2): 135–42.

Manchin, M., and S. Orazbayev. 2018. "Social Networks and the Intention to Migrate." *World Development* 109: 360–74. https://doi.org/10.1016/j.worlddev.2018.05.011.

Mongey, S., L. Pilossoph, and A. Weinberg. 2021. "Which Workers Bear the Burden of Social Distancing Policies?" *Journal of Economic Inequality* 19: 509–26. https://doi.org/10.1007/s10888-021-09487-6.

Morano Foadi, S. 2006. "Key Issues and Causes of the Italian Brain Drain." *Innovation* 19 (2): 209–23.

Munshi, K. 2020. "Social Networks and Migration." *Annual Review of Economics* 12: 503–24. https://doi .org/10.1146/annurev-economics-082019-031419.

Munshi, K., and M. Rosenzweig. 2006. "Traditional Institutions Meet the Modern World: Caste, Gender, and Schooling Choice in a Globalizing Economy." *American Economic Review* 96 (4): 1225–52. https://doi .org/10.1257/aer.96.4.1225.

OECD (Organisation for Economic Co-operation and Development). 2017. "Migrants' Well-Being: Moving to a Better Life?" In *How's Life? 2017 Measuring Well-Being,* 119–56. Paris: OECD. https://www.oecd-ilibrary .org/sites/how_life-2017-7-en/index.html?itemId=/content/component/ how_life-2017-7-en#back-note-e-000041.

Papanikolaou, D., and L. D. W. Schmidt. 2022. "Working Remotely and the Supply-Side Impact of COVID-19." *Review of Asset Pricing Studies* 12 (1): 53–111. https://doi.org/10.1093/rapstu/raab026.

Patel, K., and F. Vella. 2013. "Immigrant Networks and Their Implications for Occupational Choice and Wages." *Review of Economics and Statistics* 95 (4): 1249–77. https://doi.org/10.1162/REST_a_00327.

Pedersen, P. J., M. Pytlikova, and N. Smith. 2008. "Selection and Network Effects—Migration Flows into OECD Countries 1990–2000." *European Economic Review* 52 (7): 1160–86. https://doi.org/10.1016/j .euroecorev.2007.12.002.

Poprawe, M. 2015. "On the Relationship between Corruption and Migration: Empirical Evidence from a Gravity Model of Migration." *Public Choice* 163: 337–54. https://doi.org/10.1007/s11127-015-0255-x.

Schmeidl, S. 1997. "Exploring the Causes of Forced Migration: A Pooled Time Series Analysis, 1971–1990." *Social Science Quarterly* 78 (2): 284–308.

Thapa, D. K., D. Visentin, R. Kornhaber, and M. Cleary. 2018. "Migration of Adult Children and Mental Health of Older Parents 'Left Behind': An Integrative Review." *PLoS One* 13 (10): e0205665.

UN (United Nations). 1998. *UN Recommendations on Statistics of International Migration.* Rev. 1. New York: UN.

UN (United Nations), Department of Economic and Social Affairs. 2020. *Methodology Report: International Migrant Stock 2020.* New York: UN. https://www.un.org/development/desa/pd/sites/www.un.org .development.desa.pd/files/undesa_pd_2020_international_migrant_stock_documentation.pdf.

Vanderkamp, J. 1971. "Migration Flows, Their Determinants and the Effects of Return Migration." *Journal of Political Economy* 79 (5): 1012–31. https://doi.org/10.1086/259812.

World Bank. 2018. *Moving for Prosperity: Global Migration and Labor Markets.* Washington, DC: World Bank. https://doi.org/10.1596/978-1-4648-1281-1.

World Bank. 2019. "Migration and Brain Drain." Europe and Central Asia Economic Update. Washington, DC: World Bank. https://doi.org/10.1596/978-1-4648-1506-5.

World Bank. 2020. *Violence without Borders: The Internationalization of Crime and Conflict.* Washington, DC. https://doi.org/10.1596/978-1-4648-1452-5.

World Bank. 2023. *World Development Report 2023: Migrants, Refugees, and Societies.* Washington, DC: World Bank.

Yasenov, V. 2020. "Who Can Work from Home?" Discussion Paper 13197, Institute of Labor Economics, Bonn.

Zavodny, M. 1997. "Welfare and the Locational Choices of New Immigrants." *Economic Review* Second Quarter: 2–10. https://www.dallasfed.org/~/media/documents/research/er/1997/er9702a.pdf.

Supporting Refugees' Socioeconomic Integration
Lessons from Current and Past Crises

Chapter Highlights

- Measures to address the inflow of refugees and facilitate their integration have varied across host countries in Europe and Central Asia and over time.

- Although until the 1980s responses to the inflow of refugees mostly focused on managing emergency situations, host countries have gradually been placing more emphasis on refugees' socioeconomic integration.

- Compulsory language training was one of the most meaningful interventions to improve refugees' employment outcomes in Nordic countries during the 1990s, together with demand-based dispersal policies and massive refugee enrollment in active labor market policies (ALMPs).

- Ensuring universal access to basic education and health services and establishing a large Emergency Social Safety Net cash transfer for refugees have been among the main success factors of Türkiye's response.

- Türkiye's response to the Syrian refugee crisis, however, illustrates the challenges associated with rapidly addressing refugees' immediate needs while also supporting longer-term integration.

- Restrictions on refugees' geographic mobility and disincentives created by the ESSN program, together with supply and demand challenges, have limited the effectiveness of policies implemented by Türkiye to facilitate refugees' access to the labor market.

- The impacts of refugees' inflow on employment levels and wages of native-born residents in Türkiye have been limited, except for low-skilled workers with skills similar to those of the refugee population.

- In Germany, a dispersal policy assigning refugees to regions based on labor demand, early employability, and vulnerability assessments and enrollment in language and on-the-job training were key to supporting Syrians' socioeconomic integration.

- A "cluster" procedure grouping asylum seekers on the basis of their vulnerabilities and employability allowed fast-tracking of labor market access and integration for some refugee groups in Germany, although challenges persisted for more vulnerable groups.

- Mentorship programs and the active involvement of local communities through volunteering and nongovernmental organizations also facilitated Syrian refugees' social integration and helped moderate antirefugee sentiments in Germany.

- One of the key factors behind the effectiveness of the response of European Union (EU) countries to the inflow of Ukrainian refugees has been granting refugees immediate access to the domestic labor market via visa waiver.

- Despite the progress achieved in the European Union over time toward a common EU policy for asylum seekers and refugees, challenges persist in sharing the costs and responsibilities of managing the inflow of refugees and in harmonizing integration policies across countries.

Key Policy Recommendations

- To effectively respond to an immediate crisis, governments of receiving countries must ensure sufficient humanitarian support and reception capacity to host refugees.

- When refugee crises involve multiple host countries, a timely and coordinated response is required, and they must consider their different response capacities, resources, and absorption potential depending on local labor market conditions.

- Measures to ensure de jure and de facto rapid access to education, health, and housing services, as well as to the national social protection system, are key features of a successful coordinated response to the refugee inflow.

- Providing asylum seekers with temporary protection status in a timely manner has proved to be fundamental to guaranteeing that they will quickly receive humanitarian aid.

- Investing in refugees' socioeconomic integration can generate high payoffs for host countries. It should be planned at the very early stages by ensuring that measures taken during the emergency response phase are also supportive of refugees' longer-term productive integration.

- The early assessment of refugees' qualifications, skills, and educational attainment is crucial to integration and can be facilitated by adopting harmonized and standardized procedures for rapid skills assessment at the regional level.

- The sooner refugees can formally participate in the labor market, the better they integrate. To ensure refugees' rapid labor market access, host countries can remove or relax restrictions applied to the hiring of third-country nationals (those who are not citizens of an EU member state), streamline asylum procedures, remove or expedite work permit procedures, and introduce visa waivers.

- Compulsory language training and ALMPs can support refugees' labor market integration, especially at the early stages.

- Policies that separate refugees from economic activities and employment opportunities have severe consequences for their long-term employment outcomes; housing policies that tie refugees to a physical place and prevent geographic mobility should thus be avoided.

- Dispersal policies assigning refugees to regions should consider labor demand and absorptive capacity of local labor markets to support refugees' labor market outcomes.

Introduction

Although migration in Europe and Central Asia (ECA) is still largely driven by the quest for economic opportunity, the share of forcibly displaced people in the region has grown dramatically. The number of refugees in ECA rose sharply from 2 million in 2013 to 14 million in 2022, representing 13 percent of the total stock of migrants compared with only 2 percent in 2010 (refer to figure 2.1, panel a). This increase resulted from the escalating flows of people fleeing the war in the Syrian Arab Republic and then Russia's invasion of Ukraine, which has generated the largest humanitarian crisis the region has faced since World War II. As a result, the number of refugees hosted in the region almost doubled; ECA is now the host to close to half of the total population of refugees worldwide (refer to figure 2.1, panel b). The vast majority of refugees come from either the Middle East and North Africa or ECA regions and mostly concentrate in Türkiye, the EU-15 (European Union [EU] members before 2004), and Eastern Europe as destination regions (refer to figure 2.2, panels a and b).

Over the past decades, host countries in ECA have offered different policy responses to the inflow of refugees, to both address emergency needs and foster long-term integration. The Nordic countries have been at the forefront of refugees' integration policies since the 1990s after the Balkan wars. The long-term horizon and availability of data on long-term outcomes of refugees in those countries, combined with differences in the policy approach they follow, allows the identification of policy interventions that are effective in fostering refugees' long-term integration. The experience of Türkiye, which has received more than 3.6 million Syrian refugees since 2011, highlights the challenges and opportunities associated with shifting

FIGURE 2.1

Trends in the number and share of refugees in Europe and Central Asia

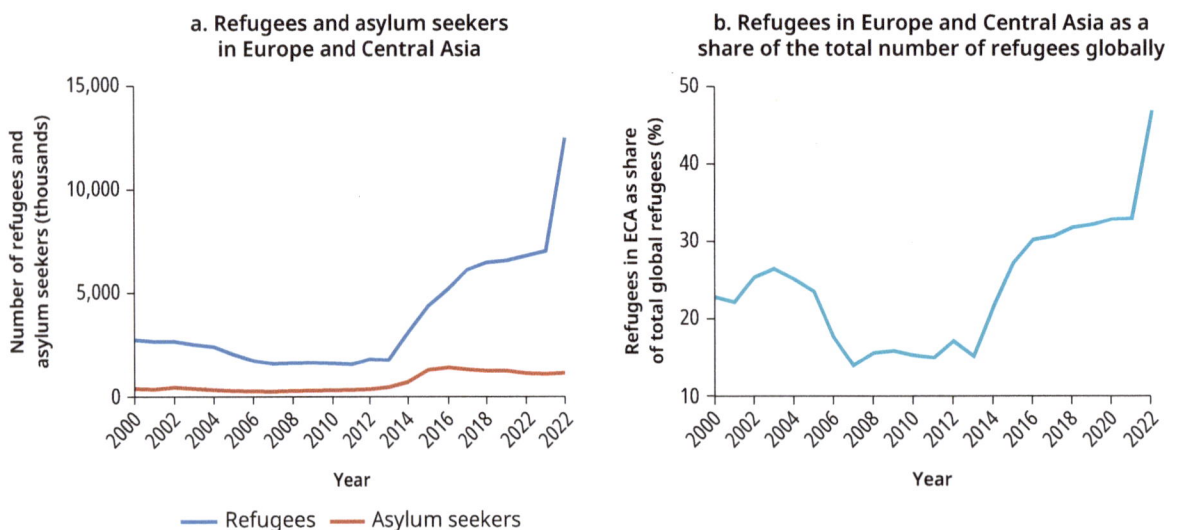

a. Refugees and asylum seekers in Europe and Central Asia

b. Refugees in Europe and Central Asia as a share of the total number of refugees globally

Refugees — Asylum seekers

Source: Original calculations based on data from the UN High Commissioner for Refugees (https://www.unhcr.org/refugee-statistics/download/?url=IAr67y).
Note: Refugees are defined as individuals who have been compelled to leave their country and cannot return because of a serious threat to their life, physical integrity, or freedom as a result of persecution, armed conflict, violence, or serious public disorder. *Asylum seekers* are defined as individuals who intend to seek or are waiting for a decision on their request for international protection.

FIGURE 2.2

Trends in the number of refugees in Europe and Central Asia, by region of origin and destination

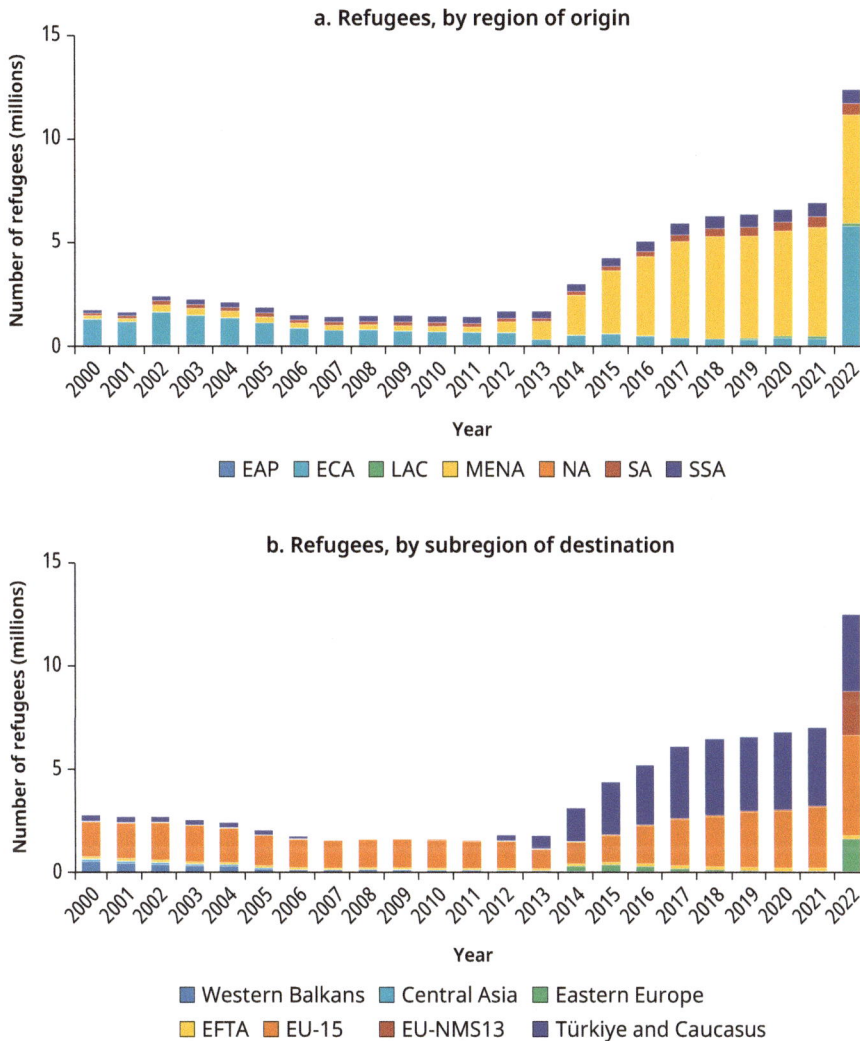

a. Refugees, by region of origin

Legend: EAP ■ ECA ■ LAC ■ MENA ■ NA ■ SA ■ SSA

b. Refugees, by subregion of destination

Legend: ■ Western Balkans ■ Central Asia ■ Eastern Europe ■ EFTA ■ EU-15 ■ EU-NMS13 ■ Türkiye and Caucasus

Source: Original calculations based on data from the UN High Commissioner for Refugees (https://www.unhcr.org/refugee-statistics/download/?url=IAr67y).
Note: Eastern Europe here includes the Russian Federation. EAP = East Asia and Pacific; ECA = Europe and Central Asia; EFTA = European Free Trade; EU-15 = European Union members before 2004; EU-NMS13 = new member states joining the European Union in 2004, 2007, and 2013; LAC = Latin American and the Caribbean; MENA = Middle East and North Africa; NA = North America; SAR = South Asia; SSA = Sub-Saharan Africa.

from exclusively emergency response to longer-term integration and the necessity for taking measures supporting integration at the very early stages. It also offers a detailed account of the impacts of a large, sudden inflow of low-skilled refugees on the native-born population. The experience of Germany, the main recipient of Syrian refugees in Europe during the

Syrian refugee crisis, also generated important lessons regarding asylum and dispersal policies that can support refugees' labor market integration. Finally, the rapid and unprecedented response of EU countries to the recent inflow of Ukrainian refugees has generated policy lessons for emergency response and integration support while highlighting remaining challenges in those responses.

This chapter extracts policy lessons from these experiences that can help host countries turn the "burden" of a refugee crisis into an asset. Evidence from different waves of refugee crises shows that the long-term integration outcomes of refugees and the welfare of refugees and native-born residents in destination countries vary dramatically in the wake of such events. These outcomes depend on the socioeconomic characteristics of refugees and on the policies of governments. This chapter shows that although refugee support must focus, first and foremost, on saving lives, policies to unlock refugees' productive potential and self-reliance in host countries are crucial and should be implemented very early on. The evidence from both the Syrian crisis and the 1990s Balkan wars has shown that there are high payoffs for actions facilitating the long-term integration of refugees, including undertaking early skills and needs assessments; establishing the right to work; ensuring access to social protections, health care, and education; and incentivizing participation in language training and active labor market policies (ALMPs). Furthermore, dispersal policies that allocate refugees on the basis of local labor demand without discouraging geographic mobility are conducive to better labor market outcomes. The sooner refugees can formally participate in the labor market, the sooner they can become assets, not only for their host country but also for their country of origin.

The remainder of the chapter is organized as follows. The "Policy Framework: Responses to Refugee Crises from Reception to Economic Integration" section introduces a framework to analyze and organize policy responses to refugee inflow in ECA, from emergency response to long-term integration. The "Nordic Countries' Policy Responses to Refugee Inflows" section then examines the experience of Nordic countries in integrating refugees from the former Yugoslavia. The "Syrian Refugee Inflow in Türkiye" and "Syrian Refugee Inflow in Germany" sections assess the responses of Türkiye and Germany, respectively, to the inflow of Syrian refugees and analyze their effectiveness. The "Ukraine's Refugee Response and Integration" section discusses the responses to the most recent inflow of Ukrainian refugees. On the basis of these past and ongoing refugee waves, the "Policy Recommendations" section extracts key policy recommendations for refugees' reception and socioeconomic integration in ECA moving forward.

Policy Framework: Responses to Refugee Crises from Reception to Economic Integration

Recent experiences have highlighted the importance of socioeconomic integration beyond humanitarian responses. Responses to the Ukrainian refugee crisis and international experiences with other recent crises have highlighted the importance of dealing with refugees not only in terms of offering humanitarian and emergency assistance, but also in terms of fostering human development and socioeconomic integration. The *World Development Report 2023* (World Bank 2023) makes a case for shifting the prevailing narrative on refugees—moving from considering them as a "burden" to recognizing them as valuable resources for host countries. When host countries invest in the right combination of policies, refugees have the potential to integrate and contribute to the economic development of those countries, and public policies can make a difference in the speed of their socioeconomic and labor market integration. Host countries clearly face costs in the short run, but with the right policy mix, refugees have the chance to become productive contributors to their host country's economy.

This section introduces a framework to analyze host countries' responses to refugee inflows. The framework (refer to figure 2.3) shows that host countries' responses to refugee inflows can be broken down into three main phases:

1. Initial humanitarian and emergency response,

2. Socioeconomic integration, and

3. Refugees' self-sufficiency and self-reliance.

The first phase consists of the immediate response countries put in place after a sudden inflow of refugees. In this phase, the refugee population experiences a high level of physical and emotional distress. Refugees have been forced to flee their homes and have undertaken dangerous, even life-threatening journeys; they are often unable to bring documents and valuables with them. In this initial phase, the priority for hosting countries is to offer refugees support for immediate needs, such as shelter, cash, food, clothes, health care, and psychological assistance, and to provide access to basic social services. Identity verification is typically an important step of the humanitarian response because asylum seekers often lack identity documents, such as passports, or documents that certify credentials—for example, for professional expertise and educational attainment. During this reception phase, those who are displaced are often given status as asylum seekers when entering the country for the first time; refugee status is formally granted after an application process and decision by the host country's authorities.

FIGURE 2.3

A framework for host countries' refugee response

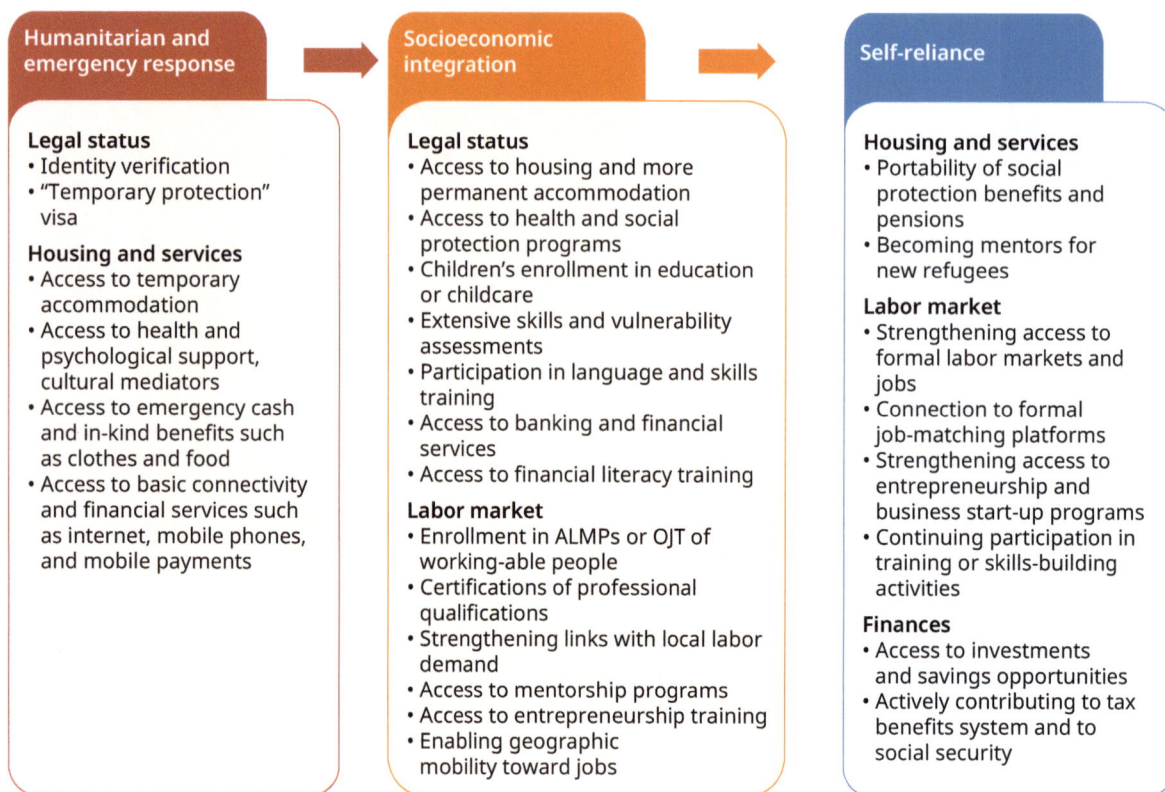

Humanitarian and emergency response	Socioeconomic integration	Self-reliance
Legal status • Identity verification • "Temporary protection" visa **Housing and services** • Access to temporary accommodation • Access to health and psychological support, cultural mediators • Access to emergency cash and in-kind benefits such as clothes and food • Access to basic connectivity and financial services such as internet, mobile phones, and mobile payments	**Legal status** • Access to housing and more permanent accommodation • Access to health and social protection programs • Children's enrollment in education or childcare • Extensive skills and vulnerability assessments • Participation in language and skills training • Access to banking and financial services • Access to financial literacy training **Labor market** • Enrollment in ALMPs or OJT of working-able people • Certifications of professional qualifications • Strengthening links with local labor demand • Access to mentorship programs • Access to entrepreneurship training • Enabling geographic mobility toward jobs	**Housing and services** • Portability of social protection benefits and pensions • Becoming mentors for new refugees **Labor market** • Strengthening access to formal labor markets and jobs • Connection to formal job-matching platforms • Strengthening access to entrepreneurship and business start-up programs • Continuing participation in training or skills-building activities **Finances** • Access to investments and savings opportunities • Actively contributing to tax benefits system and to social security

Source: Original figure for this publication.
Note: ALMPs = active labor market policies; OJT = on-the-job-training.

The length of this phase of reception and humanitarian assistance varies, depending on the time needed to process the request for refugee status. The processing time varies from country to country and depends on the displaced person's country of origin. Until a decision on refugee status is made, asylum seekers typically live under temporary protection in temporary accommodations or camps, with limited or no access to social services or social protection benefits. Often, asylum seekers are also banned from access to work and given few opportunities for training (including language training). In some cases, they are not allowed to move freely in different parts of the host country.

Under the framework, a second phase—an integration phase—begins with the recognition of refugee status, which involves access to a different set of rights and services than those initially offered to asylum seekers. One of the first relevant policy decisions of the integration phase concerns dispersal policies, which are the set of rules and regulations that determine the geographic distribution of refugees in the national territory.

Another fundamental aspect of the integration phase is access to schooling. Ensuring that school-age children have access to education in the host country is essential for integration and for avoiding the erosion of human capital associated with the displacement experience. Furthermore, parents whose children attend school have more opportunities to engage in economic activities and find work. Another important aspect of the integration phase concerns access to language instruction, entrepreneurship opportunities, training (especially on-the-job training), and ALMPs. In this phase, work permit regulations are also important because such regulations affect the possibility of refugees starting their own enterprises and their access to formal employment opportunities across the host country.

During the framework's third phase, refugees transition to self-reliance. Refugee status is typically granted for a limited number of years. At the end of this period, refugees can apply for permanent residency. At this point, at least in theory, refugees should be able to achieve self-reliance and have access to a broader set of rights and opportunities that are comparable with those of nationals and economic migrants.

The analysis in this chapter focuses largely on the integration phase and on the reception-stage policy decisions that affect integration. The chapter provides an overview of responses to refugee crises, analyzing the policies adopted by Nordic countries after the 1990s wars in the former Yugoslavia, the responses undertaken by Türkiye and Germany to the Syrian refugee crisis that began in 2011, and the ongoing responses to the Ukrainian refugee crisis.

Nordic Countries' Policy Responses to Refugee Inflows

In Nordic countries, municipalities have been responsible for providing programs for refugees' integration since the 1990s. Integration programs for refugees in Denmark, Norway, and Sweden were initially voluntary. With the inflow of refugees in the 1980s and 1990s, however, government provisions changed, requiring municipalities (which had previously been made responsible for integration efforts) to offer such programs and requiring refugee participation. Failure to participate in these programs was tied to penalties: the loss of financial assistance and access to social protection benefits and services (Hernes and Trondstad 2014).

The integration programs for refugees in the Nordic countries can be classified into two main types: educational programs and ALMPs. Educational programs are based on national curricula, whereas ALMPs consist of unpaid job training, subsidized employment, job search assistance, and counseling services. The duration of integration programs, in general, is three years, although this varies by country and has changed over time (Calmfors et al. 2019).

Whereas Denmark has prioritized boosting short-term employment outcomes for refugees, Norway's and Sweden's integration approach focused more on long-term integration. Denmark has prioritized rapid employment outcomes for refugees through the rapid enrollment of refugees into job-related measures for short-term employment. In contrast, Norway and Sweden have focused to a greater degree on the long term, placing a greater emphasis on upskilling, training, educational programs, and labor market participation to achieve more sustainable employment results and greater labor market integration in the long run.

For this reason, the educational programs implemented in the three countries differ, with Sweden placing the greatest emphasis on tertiary education upon arrival. Although longer amounts of time in intensive training and education programs help accumulate human capital, they also lower the amount of time participants can search for regular employment. This may result in weak employment outcomes in the short term but overall improvements in long-term employment outcomes, including job placements and earnings. When comparing the use of different integration measures before and after the 2015 refugee inflows, participation in education programs increased in all countries, although at different levels. Sweden has placed the greatest emphasis on tertiary education for refugees upon arrival. It has the highest rate of attainment of tertiary education within the first year of being granted a residence permit and a higher share of participants in integration programs having secondary and tertiary education at arrival.[1] Furthermore, the share of refugees with tertiary education on arrival who pursue further education within the first three years of obtaining a residence permit in Sweden is two to three times the share in Denmark and Norway. In contrast, in Denmark the post-2015 increase in enrollment was in primary education, and very few refugees participate in education above the lower-secondary level. Similarly, Norway has the highest share of participants in education at the elementary level (Calmfors et al. 2019).

ALMPs' use to support refugees' integration has also varied among the three countries; Denmark prioritized the rapid enrollment of refugees into job-related programs compared with Sweden, where the focus was on education enrollment. Efforts to incorporate job-related measures into integration programs also have significant effects on employment probability in the short run, although the effects tend to decline in the long run. Over time, Denmark has increasingly been enrolling refugees in job-related measures. As a result, many refugees participate in employment programs, especially in unpaid job training, but very few participate in education above the lower-secondary level. Denmark also made large increases in unpaid job training and subsidized employment programs, and Norway increased the use of unpaid job training. In Denmark and Norway, the share of refugees who obtain subsidized employment in the initial years is higher than in Sweden. In contrast, Sweden's approach has put more emphasis on training programs at the upper-secondary or higher levels and on public employment services (PES). The latter primarily consist of personalized counseling, job search assistance, and workplace introduction, which have been shown to enhance migrants' employment opportunities and employment rates (Åslund and Johansson 2011; Joona and Nekby 2012; Svantesson and Aranki 2006).

Language training is a very important component of the activation package offered to refugees in Nordic countries, with substantial long-term positive effects. Language training tends to be compulsory, and participation and completion are often conditions to retain both social benefits and the possibility of participating in on-the-job training or subsidized employment. Evidence shows that mandatory language training in Denmark substantially increased employment probabilities and that dropping out or not participating in the training was associated with worse labor market outcomes (Arendt, Dustmann, and Ku 2022). The 1999 reform that introduced mandatory language training courses for refugees arriving in Denmark was found to be the most effective of the policy interventions used, as measured in terms of ensuring higher employment probability and better earnings (Foged, Hasager, and Peri 2024); in terms of effectiveness, compulsory language training was followed by assignment to areas with high labor demand, then by participation in ALMPs, and then by a reduction in social assistance benefits. Furthermore, language training seemed to unlock better opportunities and higher lifetime earnings, especially for women and refugees from linguistically different countries.

Despite these encouraging findings related to education and training, a persistent long-run gap remains between the labor market outcomes of refugees and those of native-born individuals. More than a decade after obtaining a residence permit, only 35–40 percent of male refugees and 15–20 percent of female refugees reach the national median income level in the destination country (Calmfors et al. 2019). Therefore, the focus on short-term employment outcomes does not seem to lead to meaningful labor market results in the long term. Instead, investing in the validation of previously attained education, skills, and other human capital, which can temporarily delay labor market integration and self-sufficiency, may still offer better payoffs in terms of better labor market outcomes in the long run.

In the 1970s, Sweden's migration landscape shifted from being labor-based to humanitarian and family-oriented. During the 1970s and early 1980s, refugees' inflows from Chile, Lebanon, Poland, Türkiye, and Viet Nam resulted in high geographical concentration and poor labor market outcomes. This prompted political debates about the refugee reception system. By 1985, the responsibility for refugee integration shifted from the National Labour Market Board to local municipalities (Åslund, Liljeberg, and Roman 2023). The "Whole of Sweden" strategy emerged in response, aiming to distribute refugees more evenly across smaller towns and communities (Andersson 1998; Edin, Fredriksson, and Åslund 2003). Although this helped alleviate pressure on urban centers, it negatively affected economic integration, as initial placements were often mismatched with refugees' needs. Subsequent relocations partially addressed these issues, but challenges remained (Edin, Fredriksson, and Åslund 2004).

In the early 1990s, Sweden saw a massive and unprecedented inflow of refugees from the former Yugoslavia because of the Balkans wars, with nearly 70,000 arriving in 1992 alone. The Swedish government rapidly adopted a policy of granting permanent residency to this group (refer to figure 2.4), a more inclusive approach than that of other countries (Barslund et al. 2016). However, the economic integration of these refugees faced significant hurdles due to the concurrent economic recession and high unemployment rates. Despite these challenges, comparative studies have found that once refugees' background factors are accounted for, their long-term integration outcomes in Sweden are similar to those in other countries (Bevelander and Pendakur 2014).

As participation in language training and labor market programs rose, the employment rate for immigrants from the former Yugoslavia in Sweden increased significantly (refer to figures 2.5 and 2.6). In the 2000s, most had participated in language training, with 90 percent having taken part in such programs. About 50 percent of the group participated in adult education at

FIGURE 2.4

Migration to Sweden (1980–2017) and percentage of first-time migrants from the former Yugoslavia, by year of arrival

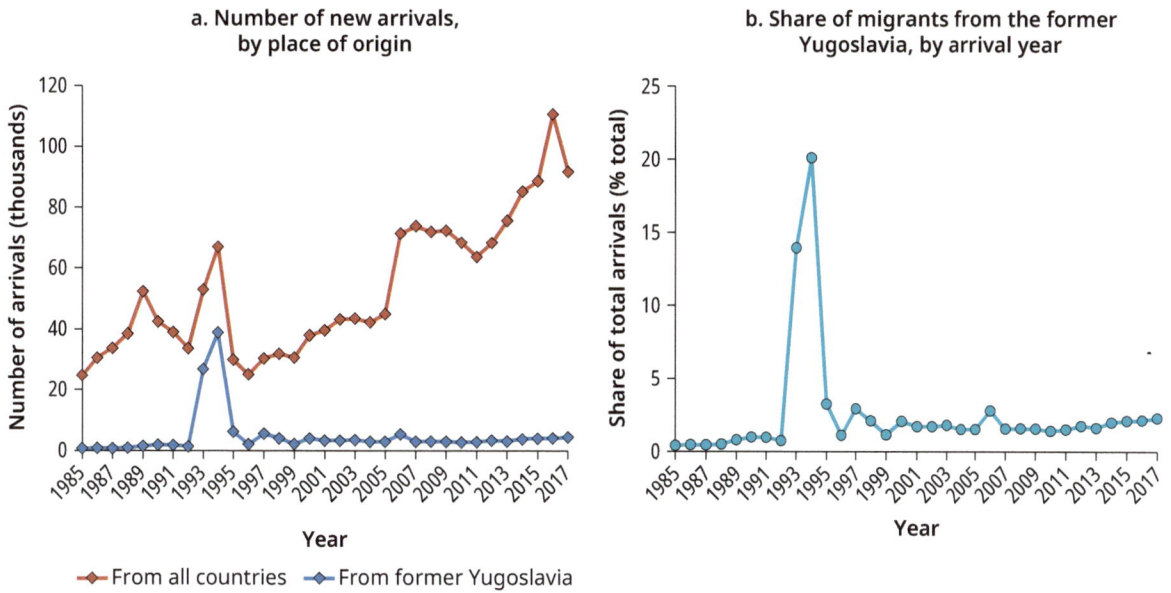

a. Number of new arrivals, by place of origin

b. Share of migrants from the former Yugoslavia, by arrival year

Legend: From all countries — From former Yugoslavia

Source: Åslund, Liljeberg, and Roman 2023.

FIGURE 2.5

Participation in active labor market programs and adult education in Sweden, by migrant status and country or region of origin

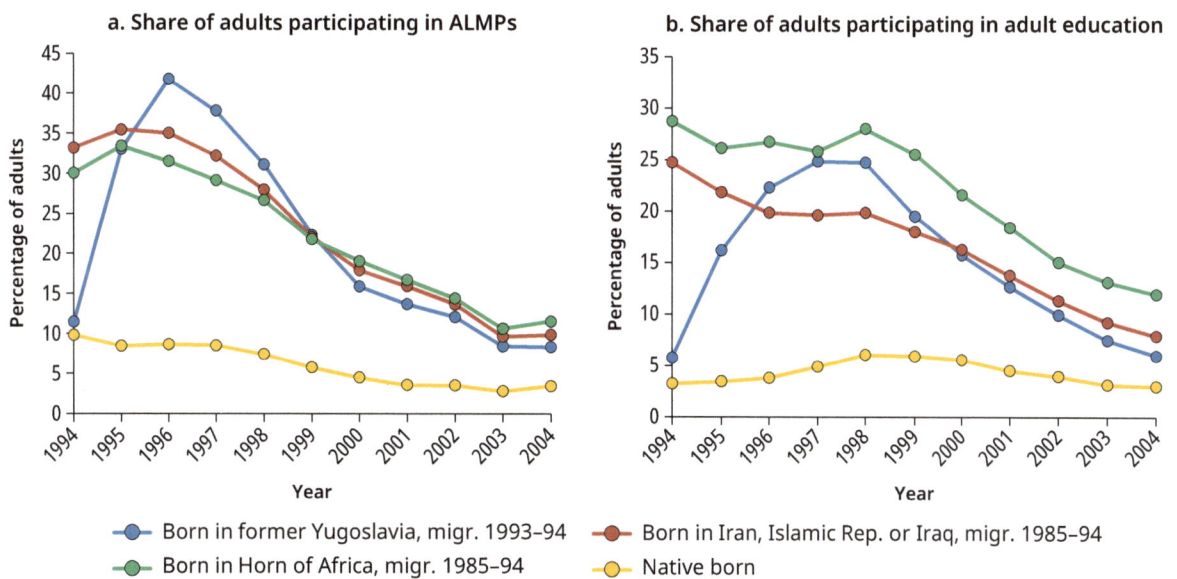

a. Share of adults participating in ALMPs

b. Share of adults participating in adult education

Legend: Born in former Yugoslavia, migr. 1993–94 — Born in Iran, Islamic Rep. or Iraq, migr. 1985–94 — Born in Horn of Africa, migr. 1985–94 — Native born

Source: Åslund, Liljeberg, and Roman 2023.
Note: ALMPs = active labor market policies; migr. = migrated.

FIGURE 2.6

Employment rates of adult refugees in Sweden relative to same-age native-born individuals, by country or region of origin

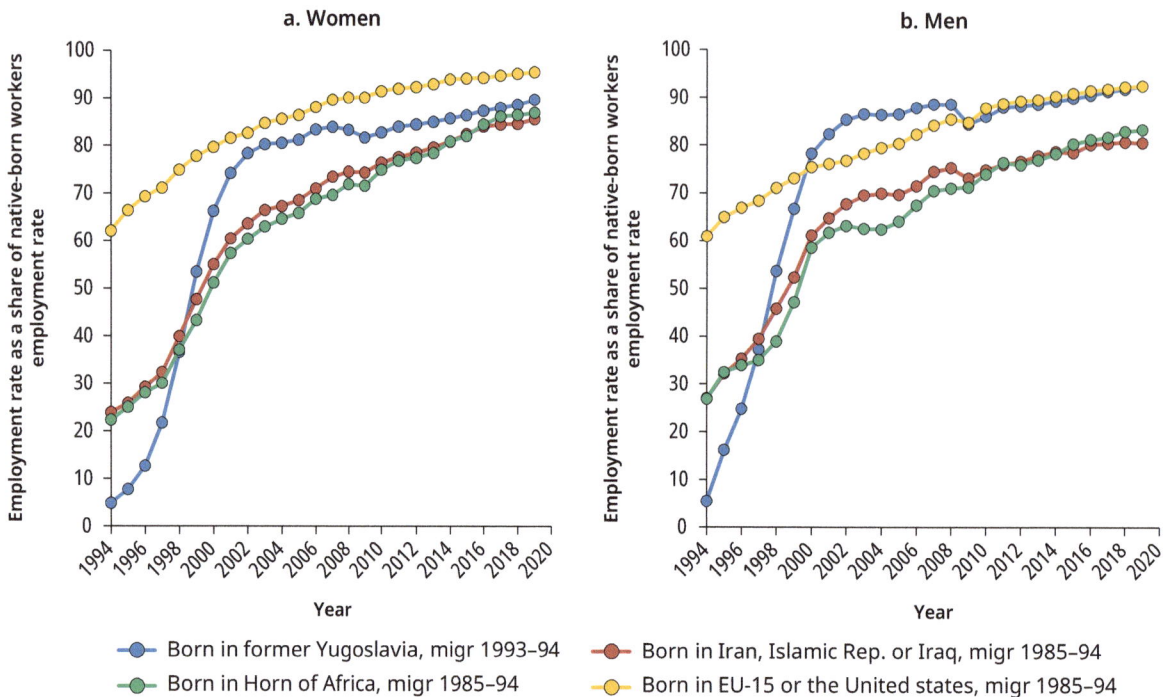

a. Women

b. Men

Born in former Yugoslavia, migr 1993–94

Born in Iran, Islamic Rep. or Iraq, migr 1985–94

Born in Horn of Africa, migr 1985–94

Born in EU-15 or the United states, migr 1985–94

Source: Åslund, Liljeberg, and Roman 2023.
Note: EU-15 = European Union members before 2004; migr = migrated.

the primary or upper-secondary level, and 7 percent participated in higher education. Almost 75 percent had been enrolled in a labor market program through PES, with participation peaking two to three years after immigration (Åslund, Liljeberg, and Roman 2023). In parallel, the employment rate of migrants from the former Yugoslavia increased from less than 5 percent in 1994 to almost 70 percent in 2000. Comparisons with other migrant groups from the Islamic Republic of Iran, Iraq, and the African Horn between 1985 and 1994 show that the integration process occurred more quickly among those from the former Yugoslavia; the other groups narrowed the employment gap more gradually (refer to figure 2.6). Exposure to immigrant networks—other foreign-born individuals, particularly those born in the former Yugoslavia, regardless of the year of immigration—was important for the integration of immigrants from this region. Employment levels, however, leveled off after this point, indicating that full assimilation had not been achieved. A similar pattern is observed when looking at the earnings of both adult men and women from the former Yugoslavia (refer to figure 2.7).

FIGURE 2.7

Earnings of refugees in Sweden relative to same-age native-born individuals, by country of origin

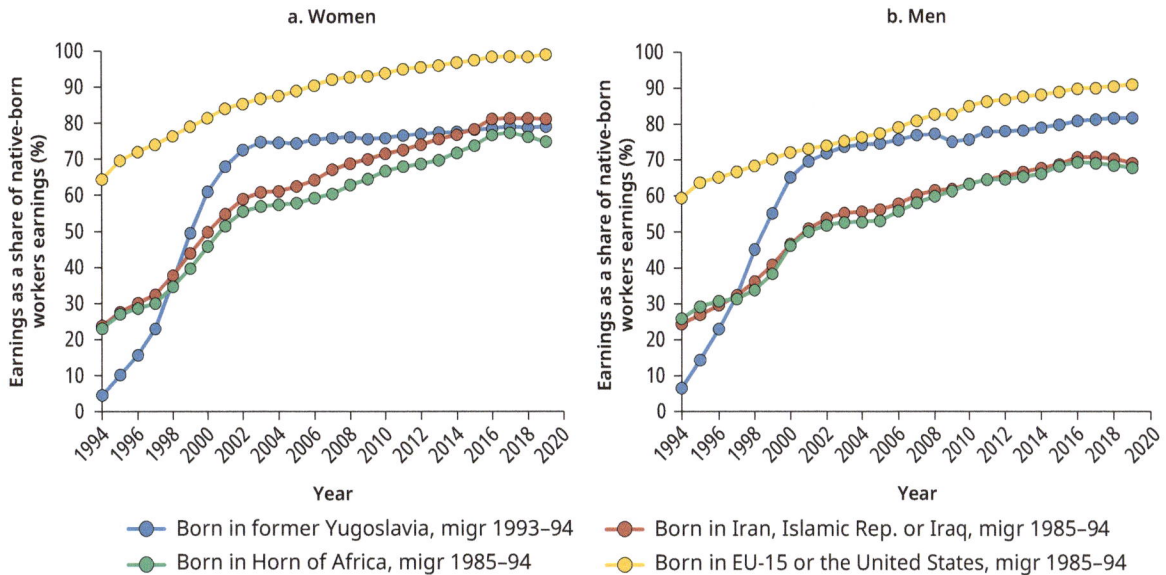

Source: Åslund, Liljeberg, and Roman 2023.
Note: EU-15 = European Union members before 2004; migr = migrated.

Syrian Refugee Inflow in Türkiye

Türkiye's refugee response has evolved from a short-term, focused emergency response to a more strategic and reintegration-oriented response. With the onset of the Syrian conflict in 2011 and the inflow of millions of refugees in a short period of time, Türkiye started to become more than a transit stop for refugees. For many refugees, Türkiye instead became a long-term home. Faced with this sudden inflow of refugees, the government reassessed the regulatory and institutional framework of its refugee response and developed a longer-term approach. Initially, Syrian refugees had been expected to stay for only a short period, but as the conflict in Syria continued, the government started to develop longer-term policies granting individuals legal status and access to basic services and benefits.

In 2013, the Law on Foreigners and International Protection was adopted establishing the Presidency of Migration Management (PMM). The Temporary Protection Regulation (TPR) in 2014 established a national strategy to support forcibly displaced Syrians in Türkiye (Türkiye 2013).[2] The TPR established rules on registration and documentation procedures, introduced a clear right to stay in Türkiye in line with the non-refoulement principle,[3] and clarified the set of rights and entitlements for temporary protection beneficiaries (Ineli-Ciger 2014). This set of regulations established the framework for the inclusion of Syrians under temporary protection (SuTPs) into Türkiye's mainstream basic services, including the health and education systems, labor market, social assistance, access to translation, and other public services (Özçürümez and İçduygu 2022). Therefore, although the PMM is the institution responsible for registering and monitoring refugees (including issuing identity and residence cards), services are provided through different central- and local-level public institutions and nongovernmental organizations (NGOs).

After 2015, relevant authorities registered displaced Syrians and gave them temporary protection status, allowing them to access basic health care and educational services. Syrian refugees with temporary protection status (SuTPs) became eligible for all education and health services available to Turkish nationals. Public health service centers of the Ministry of Health, with support from NGOs and local authorities, deliver primary and preventive care, including diagnosis and treatment, immunization, environmental health services, women's and reproductive health services, and health services for children and teenagers. They also provide support to fight the spread of communicable diseases, epidemics, and tuberculosis (Ministry of Health 2014). Similarly, with the 2016 opening of the Immigration and Emergency Education Department, affiliated with the General Directorate of Lifelong Learning of the Ministry of National Education, efforts to integrate SuTPs and other refugees by providing Turkish language education increased. Conditional cash transfer programs were also accelerated to encourage increased school enrollment. Special support was provided to SuTPs and other refugees completing high school to facilitate access to higher education through a special exam assessing their knowledge of the Turkish language and their readiness to enter tertiary education. This approach replaced the initial approach, which had provided education in special centers and in the Arabic language.

Although refugees were initially housed in temporary accommodation centers, the PMM was progressively given a broader mandate to refer individuals to live in urban centers and local communities and to support housing schemes. The PMM has the mandate to regulate and control settlement in and out of urban centers; however, housing access is not subsidized, and most refugees need to find and pay for their own accommodation.[4] This soon became a challenge because the inflow of refugees put upward pressure on housing prices in lower-income communities where large numbers of refugees moved, raising tensions between refugees and local community members.

As the number of refugees increased, the government facilitated legal pathways for refugee employment. Legislation passed in January 2016 provided SuTPs with access to employment six months after they received refugee status. The work permits are sponsored by employers and are workplace specific. They must also be submitted through an online portal in the city in which the individual has registered their residence, either by the prospective employer or, in the case of self-employment, by the individual. The regulations and policies on work permits are implemented under the supervision of the Ministry of Labor and Social Security (ILO n.d.). Although the work permit system provides opportunities for formal employment, take-up has remained low.[5] There are multiple reasons for the low take-up, ranging from inadequate information on the application process, the inability of interested employers to access the online registry, and informal work agreements used by refugees and employers to avoid associated labor tax payments (for employers) and to remain eligible for social assistance payments (for refugees). Nevertheless, about 65 percent of Syrian refugees who are of working age (roughly 2 million people) are estimated to be working, with about 30–35 percent of them working formally (Republic of Türkiye 2024).[6]

To support access to formal employment, SuTP job seekers and potential employers are offered a set of employment services and programs implemented by the Turkish Employment Agency (ISKUR), in collaboration with local authorities and NGOs. In conjunction with legislation allowing access to work permits, ISKUR began offering a suite of programs and counseling services to help SuTPs and other refugees with residence status gain access to the formal labor market. These programs offered language education, skills and on-the-job training, job search assistance, and payment of work permit application fees for employers willing to hire refugees. Provincial ISKUR offices in cities with large Syrian refugee communities also developed separate service windows and often assigned dedicated counselors and translators to serve Arabic-speaking job seekers. The financing of these programs (through daily wages and short-term health and occupational safety insurance) provided benefits and incentives for both job seekers and employers.

Financing and advisory support mechanisms to promote entrepreneurship among refugees and to support the expansion of refugee-owned businesses were also established. Such schemes were implemented by the government in partnership with the Small and Medium Enterprises Development Organization (KOSGEB) and the Development Investment Bank of Türkiye (TKYB). KOSGEB and TKYB provide financing and advisory support to Syrian- and other refugee-owned small businesses and entrepreneurial ventures, with a goal of helping to expand their businesses and promote the employment of more Turkish native-born workers and refugees in the formal labor market.

To help refugee households manage their livelihoods, attend to their basic needs, and reduce vulnerabilities, Türkiye implemented an Emergency Social Safety Net (ESSN) program. The program, which started in 2016, provides monthly cash assistance to registered families living in Türkiye under international or temporary protection. The ESSN is designed for the most vulnerable groups, including families with numerous dependents, elderly individuals, women-headed households, and people with disabilities (WFP 2017). At the peak of its caseload, the program supported more than 1.8 million vulnerable Syrian refugees with monthly cash assistance.[7] As of April 2023, more than 1.5 million people were receiving support.[8] The program is anchored in the Turkish safety net system. As such, its design and eligibility and assessment criteria mimic the social safety net schemes for which Turkish citizens are eligible. The program is delivered through a combination of local service centers affiliated with the Ministry of Family and Social Affairs and a large quasi-public organization, the Turkish Red Crescent, which has an extensive field presence. In 2021, part of the ESSN caseload was transferred to a new Complementary ESSN program, with 363,000 of the most vulnerable households receiving cash assistance from the Ministry of Family and Social Services (KIZILAYKART Programmes 2022). The government has also developed an exit strategy from ESSN intending to encourage refugees to enter the labor market while being supported with work readiness counseling and skills training.

Recent evidence indicates that the government's policies of providing access to services and the labor market, combined with a progressive approach to out-of-camp settlement, allowed refugees to rapidly integrate into socioeconomic life. A 2022 survey of Syrian refugees offers insights on their views about the successes and challenges of the government's refugee response and integration policies (UDA Consulting 2022). Two-thirds of respondents reported that they are employed and earning an income and that they have found the training and counseling services received from public institutions critical in finding formal employment and obtaining work permits. Similarly, active labor market programs and language training appear to have helped bring the native-born and refugee communities closer and to reduce prejudices by enabling people from both to coexist in workplaces, classrooms, and other spaces. Both employers and those hired through on-the-job training schemes report satisfaction with the program, which allowed employers to test beneficiaries and beneficiaries to become acquainted with Turkish work culture. Such programs have also brought many Syrian refugees in contact with Turkish public institutions and helped them to better understand the administration. Access to the education system for younger cohorts and opportunities for language and skills training for adults appear to have also contributed to this process.

Nevertheless, some challenges remain, especially in access to formal employment opportunities among refugees. Respondents reported difficulties in obtaining work permits and highlighted that employer-based hiring quotas for refugees make the transition from informal to formal employment difficult. Although the ESSN program helped vulnerable refugee families weather shocks (such as the COVID-19 pandemic–related economic downturn) and cover their basic needs, it is also a deterrent to accepting formal and more sustainable employment because eligibility for ESSN benefits is lost once a family member obtains formal employment. To have a greater impact on self-reliance, the ESSN exit strategy must thus be better articulated and implemented with wider coverage.

Regarding impacts on the native-born population, the arrival of refugees in Türkiye had a very limited impact on the overall employment and wages of Turkish citizens. Most studies find null or very limited effects of refugee inflows on the employment prospects of native-born individuals (Akgündüz, Van Den Berg, and Hassink 2015; Aksu, Erzen, and Kırdar 2018; Bagır 2018; Cengiz and Tekgüç 2022) and wages (Aksu, Erzen, and Kırdar 2018; Cengiz and Tekgüç 2022; Ceritoglu et al. 2017). Since 2015, the literature on the effects of Syrian refugees on the Turkish labor market and several socioeconomic outcomes has grown rapidly (refer to annex 2A for more details). Part of the explanation behind the limited overall effects on employment is that the arrival of refugees also boosts demand, fueling new firm creation and business sales.

These aggregate effects, however, mask disparities in the way distinct groups of native-born workers have been affected. There is evidence of sizable employment loss in the informal sector, which particularly affects lower-skilled workers (Aksu, Erzen, and Kırdar 2018; Ceritoglu et al. 2017; Del Carpio et al. 2016). The increased competition in the supply of labor in the informal economy is only partly compensated for by an increase in the creation of informal firms (Altındağ, Bakış, and Rozo 2020). At the same time, the refugee inflows caused an equally significant increase in formal employment and wages, particularly among native-born men, because of the complementarity between low-skilled immigrants and native-born formal workers (Aksu, Erzen, and Kırdar 2018; Del Carpio et al. 2016). In response to Syrian refugees' engagement in jobs involving routine and manual-intensive tasks, highly educated native-born workers move to jobs that require more abstract tasks (Akgündüz and Torun 2020). Therefore, refugees tend to displace low-skilled locals working in the informal sector in the short term while simultaneously upgrading the labor market status of local, high-skilled workers. Net employment losses are concentrated among women and low-skilled and young native-born individuals (Bagır 2018; Del Carpio et al. 2016). Furthermore, overall effects on domestic labor markets tend to be more positive as the development level of the region rises (Aracı, Demirci, and Kırdar 2022). The labor market outcomes in Türkiye seem to be in line with those reported in a summary of 56 case studies conducted in middle-income countries (Verme and Schuettler 2021).

The findings of the few studies on the impact of refugee inflows on prices are mixed; impacts vary depending on the type of item considered, such as food or housing. Few studies have assessed the impact of the refugee inflows on prices in Türkiye, and results so far are mixed. Some find that a higher refugee-to-native-born ratio was associated with an increase in prices at the regional level (Aksu, Erzen, and Kırdar 2018), and others report that the refugee inflows were strongly associated with reduced prices, especially for food items (Balkan and Tumen 2016). Balkan and Tumen (2016) find that the reduction in prices is mostly concentrated in informal labor-intensive sectors in hosting regions, arguably because the low cost of refugees' labor helps reduce prices. Regarding housing prices, significant increases resulting from the refugee inflows have been reported (Akgündüz, Van Den Berg, and Hassink 2015), likely because the supply in this market is less responsive to increased demand.

The refugee inflows led to greater investment in education among native-born individuals. High school enrollment of teenage Turks ages 15–18 significantly increased in regions with a higher inflow of refugees; this increase was concentrated among males, however, with no effect on female enrollment (Tumen 2018). It is argued that the effect stems from greater competition between refugees and native-born individuals in low-wage, informal sectors, crowding out native-born male youth. Given the overwhelming concentration of Syrian refugee youth in public schools, native-born children switch from public to private schools in response to the refugee shock (Tumen 2019). Not only are enrollments of Turkish youth higher, but test scores in math, science, and reading increased in areas with a heavier concentration of refugees, particularly among men and those who had lower test scores before the refugee crisis (Tumen 2021). The arrival of Syrian refugees also reduced child labor among Turkish families because they crowded out informal employment (Çakır, Erbay, and Kırdar 2023).

The arrival of refugees is associated with a more crowded health care system. The large and sudden increase in demand for health care associated with refugees' arrival puts additional pressure on health care resources. It has been shown in the Turkish context that a 10-percentage-point increase in the refugee-to-native-born ratio decreases the number of doctors per person between 6 and 9 percent, depending on estimations (Aygün, Kırdar, and Tuncay 2021). No effects on neonatal, infant, or adult mortality rates were found, however.

Crime has been reported to either fall or remain the same with increased refugee presence. Only a limited number of studies have analyzed the impact of refugees on crime. Depending on the methodology, some studies find that crime rates either do not change or slightly decrease in response to refugees' presence (Kayaoglu, Şahin-Mencütek, and Erdoğan 2022). Another study reports suggestive evidence for a significant decrease in crime rates in response to the refugee inflow, especially in rates of assaults, sexual crimes, kidnapping, and defamation (Kırdar, Lopez Cruz, and Türküm 2022). The latter study also shows that the decrease in crime rates is not simultaneously determined by an increase in armed forces in the refugee-hosting regions.

Syrian Refugee Inflow in Germany

Between 2015 and 2017, Germany became the top destination for asylum seekers and refugees in the European Union while putting in place more accommodative asylum policies. In this period, the country received around half of the 3.1 million first-time asylum applications submitted across the European Union; an estimated 1.1 million asylum seekers arrived in Germany alone. As of December 2018, there were 1.8 million people with a refugee background in the country, compared with 744,000 at the end of 2014. In 2015, in response to the large inflow of migrants and asylum seekers into Europe, German Chancellor Angela Merkel suspended the Dublin II Regulation (Tjaden and Heidland forthcoming; refer to box 2.1 for a brief overview of the evolution of the asylum policy framework in the European Union). The action permitted refugees and asylum seekers who had already landed in other EU countries to enter and apply for asylum or settle in Germany. This policy became known as Merkel's open-door policy to accommodate refugees, which led to a large inflow of migrants, refugees, and asylum seekers into Germany, as shown in figure 2.8. At the time, the vast majority of refugees and asylum seekers in Germany came from just a few countries; Syrians comprised the largest group of refugees, and Afghans comprised the largest group of asylum seekers.

Upon their case's decision, asylum seekers may receive different forms of protection with different residence durations. After a refugee applies for asylum, the Federal Office for Migration and Refugees (BAMF) conducts an

BOX 2.1 Evolution of European Union Asylum Policy

The European Union (EU) recognizes the 1951 Geneva convention on the status of refugees and the 1967 Protocol related to the status of refugees, and it shares responsibilities for asylum policies with its Member States. The first major turning point toward creating an integrated EU asylum policy was the Maastricht Treaty, which introduced the Common European Asylum System (CEAS) and aimed to harmonize the asylum policies of EU member states. Before the adoption of the Maastricht Treaty in 1993, asylum policy within the European Union was primarily the responsibility of the individual member states. Because each country relied on its own laws and procedures for processing asylum applications and managing the reception of refugees, limited coordination and harmonization existed between European countries, and no coherent and unified system for addressing asylum-related challenges existed at the EU level. The aim of creating the CEAS, which became effective in 1999, was to establish common standards and procedures for the treatment of asylum seekers across the European Union. The Maastricht Treaty incorporated the principles established by the 1990 Dublin Convention, mainly that the first EU member state an asylum seeker enters is responsible for processing their asylum application (European Commission n.d.; Tsourdi and Costello 2021). This principle, commonly referred to as the principle of first-entry responsibility, was supposed to spread the responsibility for processing asylum applications more fairly among member states.

The Amsterdam Treaty was adopted in 1999 alongside further efforts to improve cooperation on asylum and migration issues within the European Union. The Amsterdam Treaty improved coordination and cooperation between member states on asylum issues. The Dublin Regulation (Dublin II), adopted in 2003, strengthened the principle of first-entry responsibility, underlining that the member state of first entry is responsible for processing asylum applications.

The Lisbon Treaty entered into force in 2009, further expanding efforts to create a more harmonized system to address asylum and migration matters in the European Union. Changes were made to create a fair and more harmonized system for asylum seekers across the European Union. To further support member states in processing asylum applications and to improve cooperation, the European Union set up the European Asylum Support Office in 2010. The office's role is to provide support, guidance, and expertise to member states in implementing the CEAS and to ensure a consistent approach to asylum issues across the European Union.

To address criticisms and challenges related to the Dublin system, the Dublin Regulation was revised (Dublin III) in 2013. The updated regulation aims to improve the sharing of responsibilities among member states, particularly in cases of secondary migration and family reunification. In 2013, the Asylum Procedures Directive was introduced, which lays down common rules for asylum procedures to ensure that asylum applications are processed fairly and efficiently. In the same year, the Reception Conditions Directive was implemented to strengthen the rights and treatment of asylum seekers and to include aspects such as access to health care and education.

The 2015 refugee crisis triggered by the war in Syria highlighted the challenges of the existing framework and the problems of coordination and responsibility sharing

Continued

BOX 2.1 Evolution of European Union Asylum Policy *(Continued)*

among member states. As a result, the European Commission proposed in 2016 a package of reforms to the CEAS with the objective to achieve a more efficient, fair, and humane asylum policy able to withstand episodes of high migratory pressure. To promote cooperation with neighboring countries, the EU-Türkiye Statement was also adopted in 2016. The aim of this agreement was to manage migration flows (including establishing processes for Greece to send irregular migrants back to Türkiye) and to provide assistance to refugees in Türkiye. In addition, the European Union concluded migration pacts with several African countries, such as the Karthoum and Valletta processes, to address migration challenges and promote cooperation on various aspects of migration management.

One of the outcomes of the reform process has been the entering into force of the European Union Asylum Agency, which became effective in 2022 and replaced the European Asylum Support Office, with a strengthened mandate to address migration crisis, and greater operational and coordination capacity. Further, in 2020, the European Commission proposed the EU Pact on Migration and Asylum, aiming to include a broader set of reforms in the following areas: enforcement of stronger border protection and swift asylum management at entry; solidarity and fair responsibility sharing, to replace the Dublin principle of "first country of entry responsibility" with a more flexible system and introducing mandatory solidarity contributions; more efficient return procedures; stronger partnerships with third countries of origin and transit; and expansion of legal migration pathways.

As of September 2024, however, the 2020 EU Pact has not become effective yet, and despite the progress made toward greater harmonization and integration of EU asylum policy over time, challenges remain. Some of the proposed reforms, in fact, remain contentious among member states. One of the main concerns is fair responsibility sharing among member states. The continuous inflow of asylum seekers, determined by conflicts and economic crises in neighboring regions, poses ongoing difficulties. Further efforts are needed to improve the efficiency, fairness, and effectiveness of the EU asylum system. For example, because of their geographic location, Greece, Italy, and Spain are often under significant pressure as major entry points for asylum seekers arriving by sea. These countries are struggling to cope with the large number of arrivals and to ensure adequate reception and processing facilities. At the same time, countries in Eastern Europe, such as Hungary and Poland, have been criticized for their restrictive asylum policies and limited capacity to process asylum applications. Western European countries with robust social protection and integration systems, such as Germany and Sweden, may face challenges related to social cohesion. Member states with limited economic resources may struggle to provide adequate support and resources to asylum seekers. These countries may face challenges in meeting the minimum standards for the recognition of refugees and for the granting of subsidiary protections set out in the 2004 and 2011 EU Directives on subsidiary protection and refugee status.

FIGURE 2.8

Stock of refugees and asylum seekers in Germany, 2013–23

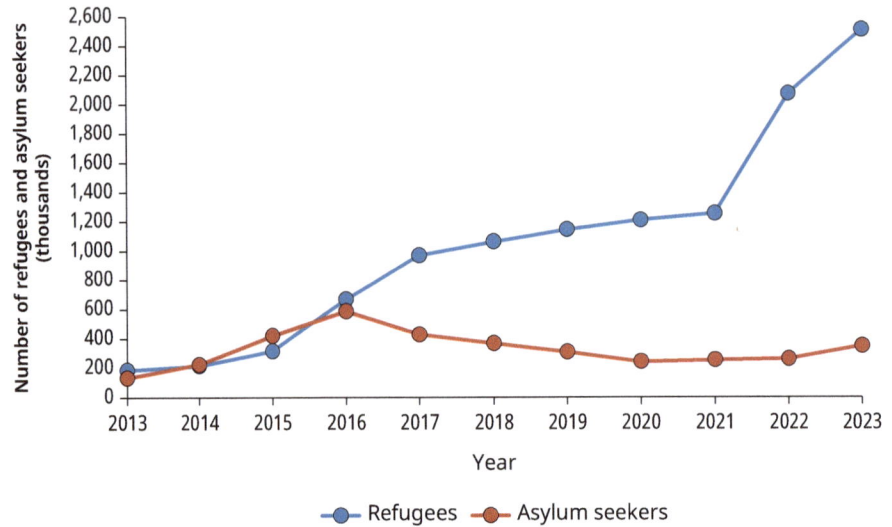

Source: UN High Commissioner for Refugees Population Statistics Database 2024 (https://www.unhcr
.org/refugee-statistics/download/?url=IAr67y).
Note: Refugees are defined as individuals who have been compelled to leave their country and cannot
return because of a serious threat to their life, physical integrity, or freedom as a result of persecution,
armed conflict, violence, or serious public disorder. *Asylum seekers* are defined as individuals who intend
to seek or are waiting for a decision on their request for international protection.

interview with the refugee and determines an outcome for the case.
In theory, the type of legal protection given should be based on the reasons
for fleeing and seeking protection, as outlined in the 2004 and the 2011
Directives of the Council of the European Union on subsidiary protection
and refugee status (Council Directive 2004/83/EC and Council Directive
2011/95/EU). An asylum seeker may receive a three-year guaranteed
permission to stay if the outcome of their case is one of the following forms
of full refugee protection: refugee status, entitlement to asylum, admission
on other humanitarian grounds, or family reunification. Other asylum
seekers may receive permission to stay for one year if subsidiary protection
is granted. These initial legal statuses and corresponding residence titles
are temporary and require renewal (with a contingency that their reasons
for fleeing still apply) until the refugee receives permanent settlement (for
which they are eligible after five years). Refugees whose cases are rejected
may receive a temporary suspension of deportation status if immediate
deportation is infeasible. Those who are granted full refugee protection or
subsidiary protection have full labor market and benefits access and may
move within their federal state (in 10 of the 16 states) but not between
states. Those with temporary suspension of deportation are granted three-
to six-month residence permits and receive limited labor market access.

The use of subsidiary protection in Germany in the context of the 2015 Syrian refugee crisis has been discretionary. Although the criteria (reasons for flight) used to determine the outcome of an asylum case are rooted in the 2004 and 2011 EU Directives, individual governments have interpreted the law in different ways and at different times. Asylum seekers were granted subsidiary protection very rarely, both in the period before 2015 when the open-door policy began and in the initial period afterward, during which a very large inflow of migrants and refugees arrived. Subsidiary protection had rarely been granted, mostly because many asylum seekers were fleeing from conflicts (such as those in Afghanistan, Eritrea, Iraq, and Syria) that provided clear-cut cases for granting full refugee protection. Political tensions surrounding migration in Germany and the open-door policy were very high, and in March 2016, 15 months after the implementation of that policy, a court in Germany ruled that asylum seekers from Syria should only be eligible to receive subsidiary protection (Pavilon 2021). According to the Eurostat database, whereas 96 percent of Syrians had been granted refugee status in 2015, this rate dropped to 58 percent in 2016 (refer to figure 2.9). Conversely, the rate of Syrians granted subsidiary protection rose from 0.1 percent in 2015 to 41 percent in 2016 (refer to figure 2.9).

FIGURE 2.9

Share of Syrian asylum seekers in Germany, by type of decision, 2013–18

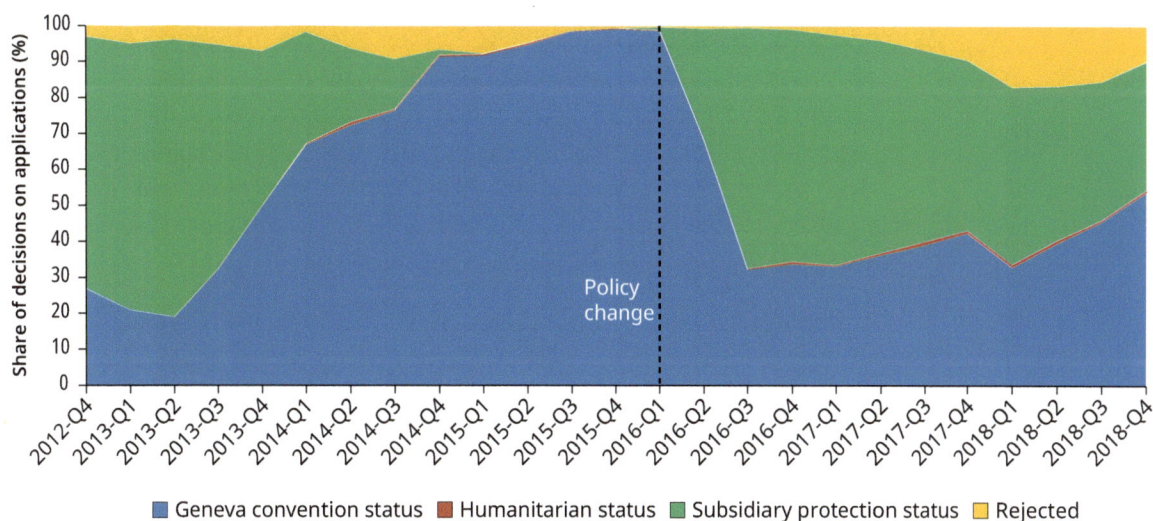

Source: Eurostat 2024 (https://ec.europa.eu/eurostat/databrowser/view/migr_asydcfstq/default/table?lang=en).
Note: Geneva Convention status is granted to non-EU citizens who, owing to a well-founded fear of being persecuted for reasons of race, religion, nationality, political opinion, or membership in a particular social group, are unable or unwilling to return to their country of nationality. Subsidiary protection status is granted to those who do not qualify as refugees but who have substantial grounds for believing that if they returned to their home country, they would face a real risk of suffering serious harm. Humanitarian status is granted to those who are not eligible for international protection in the EU context but who are nonetheless protected against removal under the obligations imposed on EU member states by international refugee and human rights instruments. Rejected applications are all those who did not receive one of the preceding statuses. EU = European Union; Q = quarter.

One unique aspect of the approach adopted by Germany for processing asylum applications was the so-called cluster procedure, which sought to speed up average processing times by grouping asylum seekers on the basis of the potential complexity of their cases. Asylum seekers from countries with a high probability of receiving protection status (cluster A) were entitled to begin accessing integration services before their applications were adjudicated. Meanwhile, groups with a lower chance of receiving protection status were excluded from these programs until after adjudication. This was done both to efficiently target resources to those with the best prospects of staying in Germany and to reduce incentives for prospective migrants to misuse the asylum route.

In a relatively short time, the cluster procedure approach led to marked improvements in refugees' language skills, personal networks, participation in education and training, access to job opportunities, and earnings capacity. For instance, refugees in the cluster A group obtained work permits relatively quickly, typically within three months of their application. This substantially reduced barriers to labor market access. As a result, almost 50 percent of working-age refugees able to work reported obtaining employment within five years of arrival. In their first year of work, asylum seekers' and refugees' earnings equaled roughly 66 percent of the average wage for German nationals, and this figure increased to 76 percent after five years (the figures for other migrants are 86 percent in the first year and 93 percent in the fifth year). Rates of enrollment in and completion of language training programs are very high. Within five years of arrival, around 90 percent of Syrians reported having completed language training. Furthermore, the share of refugees with self-reported "good" or "very good" German-language skills increased from 12 percent in the first year after arrival in Germany to 41 percent within three years of arrival (Brücker, Kosyakova, and Vallizadeh 2019). Empirical evidence has shown that counseling and job search assistance programs have significantly contributed to the improvement of refugees' labor market outcomes (Battisti, Giesing, and Laurentsyeva 2019).

An important element of the refugee integration strategy in Germany has been a detailed assessment of refugees' backgrounds, qualifications, and skills. A public portal was set up explicitly for the recognition of foreign professional qualifications (https://www.bq-portal.de/en; see also BQ Portal 2024) and skills recognition and assessment. The public portal also provided links to job vacancies, targeted at employing Syrian refugees.

A dispersal policy that assigned refugees to regions depending on labor demand and the absorptive capacity of local labor markets was also a factor of success in the labor market integration of Syrians (refer to box 2.5). Refugees were also allowed early access to social protection benefits, supporting their livelihoods and their economic subsistence. Access to existing programs that supported entrepreneurship and business start-ups was also facilitated. After the initial phases of reception and internal resettlement, local communities were significantly involved in the integration of Syrian refugees through volunteer households and NGOs in mentorship programs. This approach, together with successful labor market outcomes, helped change the perception of Syrian refugees over time. In 2015, according to public opinion surveys, refugees represented the main concern of the German population; by 2019, the refugee crisis had fallen considerably behind other priorities and concerns of the public at large (Brücker et al. 2019).

The elements of the German strategy that helped integrate Syrian refugees may have come at the expense of nonprioritized groups who experienced prolonged wait times and a lack of access to resources. The exclusion of certain groups from integration support measures such as language courses may have come at high economic and social costs—especially in the long term—by, for example, allowing refugees' human capital to decline in the meantime or by pushing people into the informal economy.

Ukrainian Refugee Response and Integration

Background on Ukrainian Refugees in Europe and Central Asia

Data on the sociodemographic characteristics of Ukrainian refugees come from different, complementary sources. This section relies on the following data sources: statistical updates from the UN High Commissioner for Refugees (UNHCR; https://www.unhcr.org/refugee-statistics/download/); a survey conducted by the Organisation for Economic Co-operation and Development (OECD 2023) with a sample of Ukrainian refugees across receiving countries between April and August 2022; and, when possible, national administrative data sources. However, these sources have different sampling frameworks and depend on data collected at different times. Therefore, the data may not be fully comparable and may not yield results that are fully representative of the total population of Ukrainian refugees. Finally, given the relatively small sample size, results may be affected by the survey participation of some subgroups (such as younger people and those with higher education).

The invasion of Ukraine in February 2022 led to a rapid displacement of the population, both internally and internationally. In a few months, more than 6 million Ukrainians sought refuge in Europe. Refugee outflows were concentrated in two main recipient countries, Germany and Poland, and, to a lesser extent, in Czechia (refer to figure 2.10).

The population of Ukrainian refugees consists predominantly of women and children (refer to figure 2.11). This mostly results from the obligation of

FIGURE 2.10

Ukrainian refugees under temporary protection, by host countries

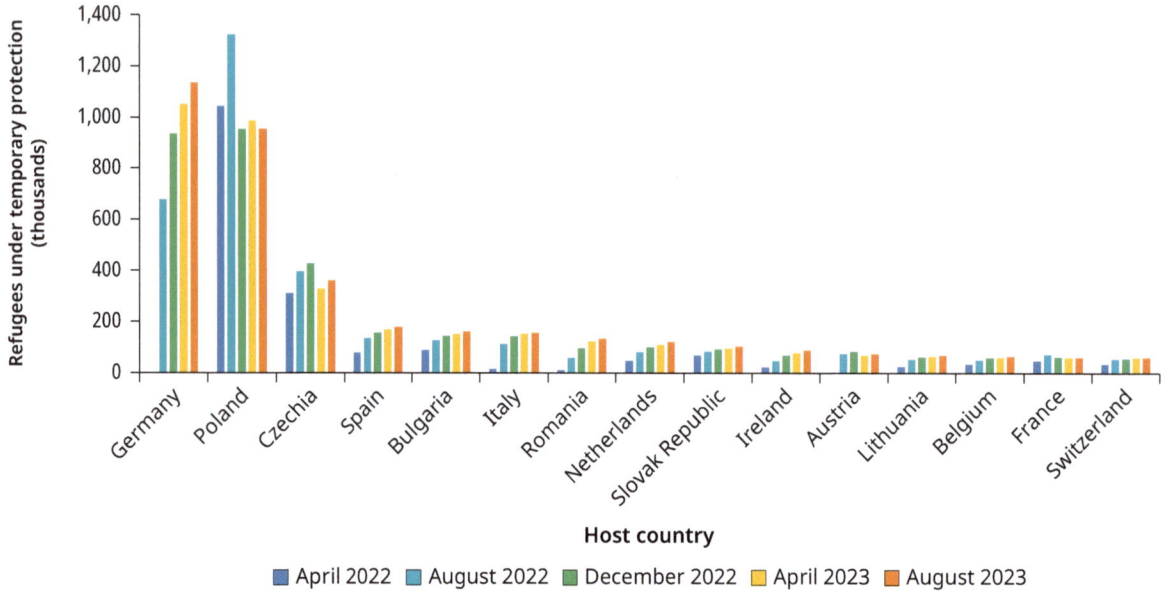

Source: Eurostat, European Commission, EACEA, and Eurydice 2022.

FIGURE 2.11

Age and gender composition of Ukrainian refugees

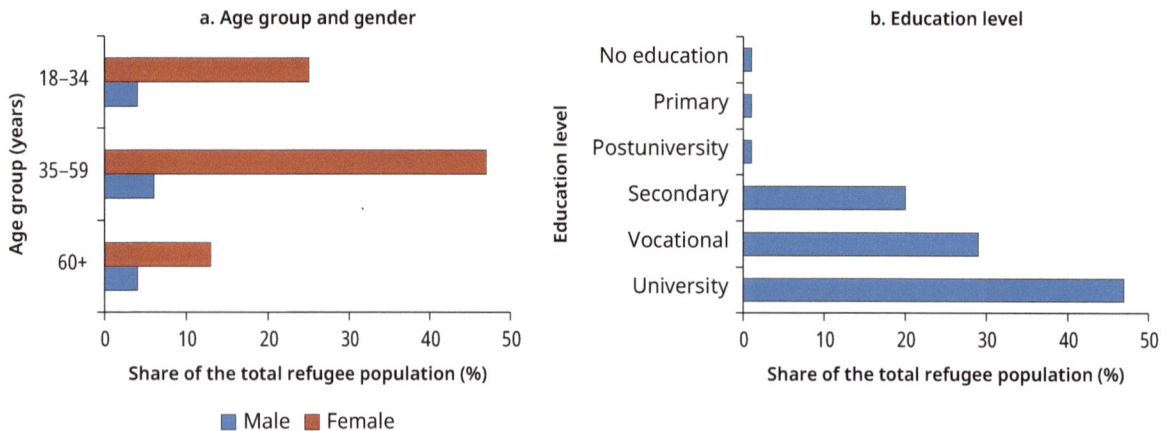

Source: UN High Commissioner for Refugees 2022c.

working-age men to join the military forces. According to the UNHCR profiling survey of December 2022, 85 percent of Ukrainian ages 18 and older are women. There is, however, variation across receiving countries in the prevalence of women among the refugee population; Estonia, Italy,

Poland, and the United Kingdom have highest shares of women (OECD 2022). The incidence of children (defined as individuals younger than age 18) in the refugee population varies between 30 percent and 40 percent across receiving countries. The survey shows that elderly individuals, those older than age 60, represent 17 percent of the adult refugee population.

Almost half of the Ukrainian refugee working-age population is highly skilled. According to the UNHCR update of December 2022, 47 percent of the adult population of Ukrainian refugees have tertiary education, 29 percent have vocational education, and 20 percent have secondary education (refer to figure 2.11). The percentages vary across countries, with different country sources indicating that more than 66 percent of refugees have tertiary education (OECD 2023). Selectivity among respondents, sampling issues, and different survey periods might explain the variations. Nevertheless, the Ukrainian refugee population is better educated than refugees of previous waves that arrived, for example, in the European Union from Syria, in Türkiye from Syria, and in Nordic countries from the Balkans. As a result of their higher educational attainment, Ukrainian refugees have better employment and integration opportunities, but, at the same time, they face potential skill mismatch; that is, jobs available for refugees, at least in the short run, may not require a university education and may result in an occupational downgrade for job seekers.

Before leaving Ukraine, refugees had a high employment rate. According to the UNHCR December 2022 survey, 73 percent of the adult population interviewed were employed before fleeing from Ukraine, 14 percent were retired, 8 percent were employed in housekeeping and domestic work, and 4 percent were unemployed. Furthermore, around 30 percent of those in work before fleeing the country were employed in medium- to high-skilled service sectors, mostly in wholesale and retail (11 percent), education (11 percent), and health care (6 percent).

As an immediate response to the crisis, the European Union granted Ukrainian refugees temporary protection for one year, renewable for up to three years. This entails the acquisition of a residence permit, access to the labor market, housing, medical assistance, education, and a basic bank account; as of June 2023, it benefits more than 4.7 million people, more than half of the total population of Ukrainian refugees (refer to figure 2.12).

At the beginning of the war, the European Union enacted the temporary protection directive that facilitates social security assimilation. The implementation of the EU directive with Ukrainian refugees and the resulting possibility of engaging in work created the conditions for strong labor market participation. Many countries have enacted legislation to facilitate easier access to the labor market for Ukrainian refugees. Various laws—such as the

FIGURE 2.12

Ukrainian refugees with temporary protection relative to the total number of Ukrainian refugees, over time

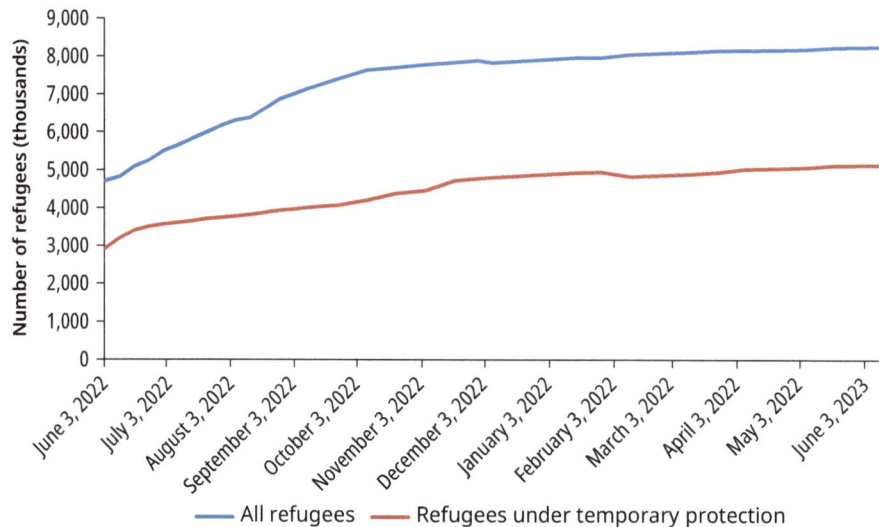

Source: UN High Commissioner for Refugees (2022–23). Original elaborations.

Polish Labor Law of March 12, 2022—allow for expedited procedures to obtain a work permit and to recognize one's qualifications, which is particularly important for those with a high level of education. After the initial emergency phase, the increase in the employment rates among refugees has been sustained in all receiving countries.

In 2023, the percentage of Ukrainian refugees employed was particularly high in Czechia, Estonia, Germany, and Poland. In Poland at that time, 900,000 (56 percent) of 1.6 million refugees had registered for temporary protection and were employed, 70 percent of whom were women. According to a declaration by Marlena Malag, the Minister of Family, Labour and Social Policy for the Polish government, the largest share of refugees are primarily working in low-skilled sectors, such as the hotel industry (29 percent). Furthermore, the distribution of refugees across occupations reflects the employment distribution of the Ukrainian population by occupation in their home country before the war (refer to figure 2.13). Important territorial differences exist, however. A survey implemented in Krakow showed that 65 percent of working-age refugees were not employed (Pędziwiatr, Brzozowski, and Nahorniuk 2022). In Czechia, of the 390,000 refugees settled in the country as of February 2023, 100,000 (26 percent) were reported as employed. In Estonia, of the 20,000 registered as searching for work, 8,200 working-age Ukrainians were employed (41 percent).

In contrast, the share of refugees employed in Romania and Moldova is low. In Romania, as of February 2023, 80 percent of Ukrainian refugees were

FIGURE 2.13

Occupational status of Ukrainian refugees in Poland, compared with the prewar Ukrainian population

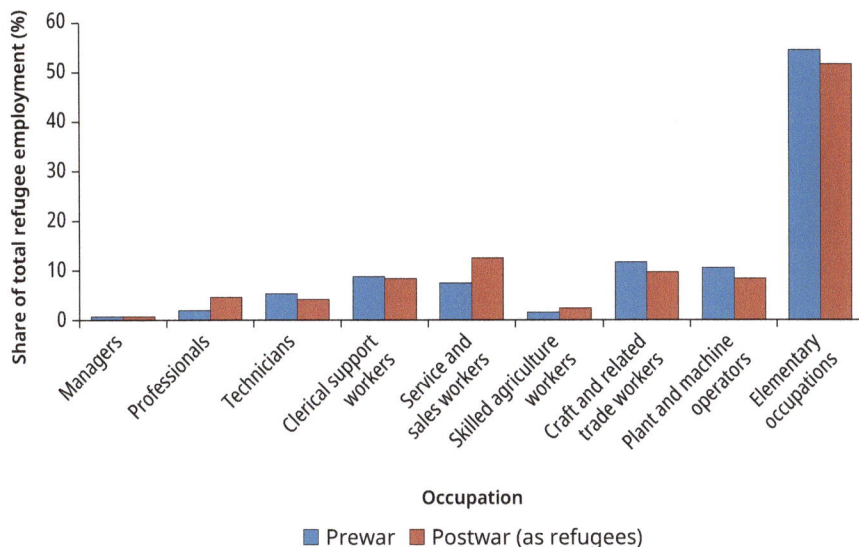

Source: Gromadzki and Lewandowski 2022.

women and 40 percent were children. At that time, of the 105,000 refugees registered for temporary protection, only 5,800 refugees had found work, and 1,362 were registered as looking for work. Of the 5,800 employed refugees, more than one-third were in Bucharest and one-third were working in low-skilled jobs (ANOFM 2023). In Moldova, the share of employed refugees is extremely low, slightly above 1 percent. As of January 2023, only 1,000 refugees of the 80,000 settled in the country were registered as employed. In Germany, 350,000 of the 900,000 working-age Ukrainian refugees (39 percent) were recorded as job seekers under temporary protection. However, estimating the exact number of employed refugees remains challenging because work permit regulatory information may not include data on refugees working part time, those engaged in short-term contracts, or those employed informally.

Refugees' intentions to stay vary across host countries, with the highest share of refugees expressing such intentions in Poland. In Poland, nearly 80 percent of the 4,900 Ukrainian refugees surveyed in the UNHCR (2022a) "Lives on Hold" survey of July declared they would be willing to stay in the country after the conflict ends. This was the highest percentage observed, followed by nearly 60 percent of refugees in the Slovak Republic. Among other countries, the percentage of refugees with intentions to stay drops to below 50 percent in Hungary, Moldova, and Romania and to 27 percent in Czechia. In the case of Poland, a strong presence of Ukrainian immigrants before the war, family ties and networks, and favorable employment opportunities may explain the high share of those expressing a preference to remain in the host country. In

Czechia, Hungary, and Romania, around 30 percent of refugees plan to return to Ukraine in the immediate future. Furthermore, in Hungary, Moldova, and Romania, a significant share of refugees plan to move to other host countries in the immediate future; such views were expressed by roughly 25 percent of those in Moldova, 19 percent of those in Hungary, and 16 percent of those in Romania. Such plans likely stem from the limited employment opportunities in these host countries. Among the most desired destinations mentioned, Germany is by far the most preferred (by 27 percent), followed by Canada (10 percent), Czechia (6 percent), the United Kingdom (6 percent), France (4 percent), and Austria (4 percent).

Reception and Emergency Response

In March 2022, the Council of the European Union unanimously voted in favor of the European Commission's proposal to activate the Temporary Protection Directive. This directive is designed to give guidance to member states on managing the mass arrival of refugees in the European Union. Through this directive, refugees have the right to temporary protection for one year, which can be extended for up to three years, without the need to go through lengthy asylum procedures. Refugees from Ukraine also have access to social protections, health care, education, banking services, and the labor market. The directive also enables families to reunite in their host country and allows refugees to move freely to other member states under specific circumstances.

One of the first emergency measures taken by host countries was to improve the reception capacity for refugees. Italy added 3,000 spots to existing reception facilities, and Spain opened four additional reception centers. Luxembourg opened its first reception center, offering temporary accommodation accessible 24 hours a day, seven days a week. Greece opened the new Sintiki/Kleidi reception center and facilitated the relocation of refugees from Ukraine to accommodation in existing facilities such as the Serres II site in northern Greece and the Elefsina site in the Attica region. Greece also allows refugees from Ukraine to freely access public health care services (public hospitals and medical centers, including mental health and physical rehabilitation facilities), even before obtaining a social security number (AMKA).

Early on, host countries provided immediate cash assistance, usually lump-sum payments, as an emergency measure (Aumayr-Pintar and Cantero Guerrero 2022; Eurofound, n.d.). In Bulgaria, cash assistance amounted to Lev 375 (€192) per household, Czechia offered CZK 5,000 (€203) per household, and Croatia provided a one-time payment of HRK 2,500 (€332) to refugees at the individual level. Slovenia offered individuals monthly payments of €120 or more, depending on household size and composition. Lithuania and Poland offered food vouchers, and Estonia offered free transportation. Furthermore, in all EU member states, governments rapidly set up websites providing Ukrainian refugees with information on their rights and the procedures necessary to access basic services and temporary protection and, if needed, national ID card or social security identification. Estimates show that 57 cash transfer measures across 25 host countries in the region were implemented in support of Ukrainian refugees (Gentilini et al. 2022). Around 60 percent of measures were new, ad hoc interventions implemented for the crisis, and around 40 percent of the measures were adaptations of existing programs. In-kind transfers (for example, clothes, medical supplies, and food and basic subsistence goods) accounted for 61 measures. Measures include the following: labor market–related interventions (73 measures across 31 countries), education (89 measures across 30 countries), health (84 measures across 31 countries), housing (84 measures across 33 countries), transport (41 measures across 20 countries), and social services interventions (91 measures across 24 countries); social insurance registration measures were undertaken by only three countries (Gentilini et al. 2022).

Labor Market Access

Special legislation in EU member states allows Ukrainian refugees the immediate right to work through exemptions from work permit requirements. For example, data from the Polish Ministry of Family and Social Policy show that the labor market responded quickly to the wave of refugees after the introduction of simplified legislation for hiring procedures, enabling about 425,000 Ukrainian citizens—around half of the total working-age refugee population (as of September 2022)—to find formal employment. Ukrainian refugees, therefore, have an advantage over other refugee groups because they can access a work permit immediately after entering their host country.

The easing of work permit regulations and labor market access had an immediate, positive impact on the labor markets in hosting countries. Estimates of the potential impact of Ukrainian refugees on European labor markets as of July 2022 suggest that the Ukrainian refugee crisis and the 2015 Syrian refugee crisis affected different countries and different labor market segments (OECD 2022). Although the latter crisis initially affected southern EU countries such as Greece, the former resulted in larger inflows to Eastern European economies. The OECD (2022) estimates suggest that the Ukrainian refugee crisis increased the European labor force by 0.5 percent, roughly double the growth in the total labor force that took place in 2015, with heterogeneous effects across countries. The OECD report does not anticipate that national workers will be displaced because of the inflow of Ukrainian refugees.

Additional interventions aimed at improving the match between labor supply and demand included job search support, dedicated employment platforms targeted to recruit refugees, and financial incentives for employers. In the Slovak Republic, PES offices provide comprehensive job search support to refugees. Under this scheme, a social worker who is a specialist in career guidance helps refugees identify professional goals, matches them to jobs, supports them in outreach to employers, fills out forms, provides information about active measures and education opportunities, and helps to address other barriers and challenges. The guidance process includes three meetings, each three hours in duration. Initiatives such as ad hoc employment platforms have been developed by private companies (for example, Adecco Jobs for Ukraine) and by government initiatives, as in the case of Austria (https://austrianjobs-for -ukraine.at/), Poland (https://www.pracawpolsce.gov.pl), and Portugal (https://portugalforukraine.gov.pt/). Language training has been provided by NGOs, PES, and government unemployment offices. Furthermore, tax allowances and financial incentives have been offered to firms willing to hire qualified Ukrainian refugees, often by adapting existing programs and instruments. In the case of Portugal, for instance, the ATIVAR scheme that provides financial help to companies recruiting young workers (originally created for the pandemic) was extended in June 2022 to benefit Ukrainian refugees (providing around €2,500 per recruited worker) (Aumayr-Pintar and Cantero Guerrero 2022; Eurofound n.d.).

Several EU member states have also set up new online job-matching platforms dedicated to helping Ukrainian refugees find work. In Czechia, the Jobs for Ukraine (https://jobs4ukr.com/) website is an initiative of the Czech Business and Investment Development Agency in cooperation with the Ministry of Industry and Trade, the Chamber of Commerce, and employer organizations. In Denmark, a newly established partnership, Partnerskab om ukrainere I job, brings together government, social partners, the National Association of Municipalities, and Danish regions to help Ukrainian refugees access the labor market by providing guidance material and information about available job opportunities. In Bulgaria, where 70 percent of refugees surveyed said they would be ready to accept a job, a job dashboard was established by the national employment agency, which also organizes face-to-face recruitment events. In Estonia, the Unemployment Insurance Fund set up a website with job vacancies for Ukrainians.

In Poland, the private sector has undertaken initiatives to facilitate refugee integration and access to labor markets. For instance, some firms are providing free training for refugees to boost their digital skills. Examples include AWS Academy Cloud Foundations, an initiative of Amazon Web Services; the Warsaw School of Computer Science; WSB University in Dabrowa Gornicza; and Accenture, which adapted some existing programs to provide cybersecurity training to female refugees. A survey by the human resources company Randstadt shows that private firms are willing to create job opportunities for refugees. Around one-fourth of all interviewed firms reported plans to hire refugees, with the willingness to hire greater among larger firms and becoming smaller as firm size decreases.

Advertisements for jobs also reflect firms' hiring intentions. In February 2022, only around 1 percent of the vacancy announcements in one of the main job portals in Poland (https://www.pracuj.pl/) targeted Ukrainian nationals, yet by April 2022, this number increased to 19 percent. The sectors that are most willing to hire Ukrainian refugees are the catering and hotel (47 percent), construction (33 percent), and manufacturing (30 percent) sectors. In Poland, 60 percent of vacant positions for refugees are supposed to be for unqualified manual workers. For the information technology and wholesale and trade sectors, the willingness to hire refugee workers drops to 15 percent and 16 percent, respectively. Additionally, language differences continue to present an important barrier for refugees seeking employment.

To ensure rapid labor market access, EU host countries removed several labor market restrictions and regulations that would usually have applied to third-country nationals. For instance, these restrictions required job seekers to obtain a work permit or employers interested in hiring a third-country national to adhere to a special set of rules and regulations. Countries removed many such requirements. For example, in Latvia, employers are no longer obliged to register vacancies filled with Ukrainian refugees with the state employment agency; as a result, Ukrainian refugees can be hired on flexible terms—at a wage lower than the national average wage, for example. In Austria, employers have been exempted from the obligation to undertake labor market assessments and tests and to prove before hiring refugees that there is no other national readily available to work who will be apt to take the job. Finally, Poland also passed a law to simplify foreign worker hiring procedures, allowing Ukrainian refugees to start work as soon as they arrive (refer to box 2.2 for more details).

Poland and Latvia have adopted measures to simplify the access of Ukrainian refugees to specific occupations, including health care professions. Health care professionals from Ukraine are allowed to practice their profession, albeit only in medical institutions, after notifying the Ministry of Health in Poland. In Latvia, medical practitioners or nurses with at least five years of work experience can work under the supervision of someone in the same specialization. Further simplifications have been added in Latvia to ease labor market access in health care professions, but also in the education, childcare, and transportation sectors; for example, for taxi drivers, language requirements and laws requiring the possession of a Latvian driver's license have been lifted (Aumayr-Pintar and Cantero Guerrero 2022; Eurofound, n.d).

Several host countries also adopted wage subsidies aimed at improving job opportunities for refugees. These subsidies take the form of a one-off allowance, a discount on the monthly labor cost, or other types of cash and

BOX 2.2 **Polish Labor Law of March 12, 2022**

Poland offers an example of how the simplification of labor laws can be used during emergency situations involving large refugee inflows. After the adoption of the temporary protection directive by the European Union, Poland adopted a law simplifying its foreign worker hiring procedures for Ukrainians only.[a] Refugees can start working as soon as they arrive, without having a PESEL number (the unique Polish personal identifier issued to residents), as long as their employer informs the labor office within two weeks of their start date. Between March and June 2022, about 225,000 refugees (representing roughly 20 percent of the refugees entering Poland) had found work under this scheme. The law also created new forms of support and assistance, such as a one-time allowance for subsistence equal to Zl 300. Furthermore, it opens the possibility for Ukrainian children to attend school on the same basis as Polish nationals and allows refugees to benefit from the same social benefits. The evidence so far has shown that the demand from employers exceeds the supply. For example, as of November 2022, there had been 11,000 such notifications by employers in Katowice since the start of the war; by contrast, there were 722 refugees registered with the public labor offices in Silesia, the wider province of which Katowice is the capital.

a. According to the act, employers do not need to apply for a foreigner's work permit but can simply notify the local labor office that they have hired a Ukrainian citizen within 14 days of the beginning of the employment.

noncash contributions. Latvia, for example, provides a lump-sum allowance corresponding to the existing minimum wage level (€500) for employers willing to hire refugees. In the Slovak Republic, both employers and refugees receive a monthly contribution for employers to hire refugees to perform volunteer activities, such as working in community centers, teaching languages, undertaking social work, cleaning public spaces, caring for dependent people (for example, elderly individuals and children), or working as domestic workers. In these cases, employers receive a maximum contribution of €110 monthly from the Office of Labour and Social Affairs, and refugees receive a flat rate of €218. In Hungary, the government finances 50 percent of accommodation and commuting costs of refugees hired by companies for at least one year, with the possibility to renew.

To facilitate labor market participation, start-up loan subsidies are targeted at refugees interested in entrepreneurship. Such subsidies have typically been devised through existing support programs. For example, Lithuania provides job creation support for small Ukrainian businesses through a version of the existing Startuok (start-up) financing program, supported by the European Regional Development Fund. This program allows refugees to obtain soft loans for business start-ups or working capital with lower interest rates (for example, at one-third the normal rate). Poland provides office spaces for Ukrainian refugees planning to start their own businesses and supports artists with a combination of in-kind and cash support in the form of scholarships (Aumayr-Pintar and Cantero Guerrero 2022; Eurofound, n.d).

Skill Training and Qualifications for Workers

As of June 2023, only three countries have opened training and qualification measures for Ukrainian refugees. Denmark offers an integration training program, which provides training and practical work experience. The program lasts two years and combines employment and a paid internship at a company with school-based education. Germany offers Ukrainian refugees with a temporary residency permit access to integration and language courses. The standard integration course, which usually includes 700 lessons and costs participants €1,540, is offered free to Ukrainian refugees. By the end of May 2022, more than 80,000 Ukrainian refugees had accessed such courses. The Slovak Republic gives refugees under temporary protection access to the education and training courses offered by labor offices under the Help to Refugees project. In Poland, training opportunities are provided directly by the private sector, particularly by selected large, multinational firms (refer to the "Education" section, next).

Education

Host countries responded strongly to the needs of Ukrainian refugees by enrolling children of compulsory schooling age in primary and secondary education programs. The approaches taken by host countries can be categorized into three main types. First, in many countries—including Croatia, Czechia, Estonia, France, Ireland, Italy, Latvia, Lithuania, Portugal, Romania, the Slovak Republic, and Slovenia—refugee children are enrolled in regular classes with additional language and learning support. A second group of countries—Austria, Belgium, Greece, Luxembourg, the Netherlands, and Sweden—adopted a different approach by enrolling refugee children in separate classes that include immersive language learning programs and allowing them to occasionally attend regular classes. A third group of countries—Germany, Poland, and Spain—adopted a hybrid approach that combines these two strategies. Furthermore, almost all EU hosting countries have recruited Ukrainian teachers to reduce language barriers and to facilitate the integration of Ukrainian pupils into national education systems. In Germany, refugees participating in tertiary education or other eligible education and training programs are eligible for subsidies under the Federal Training Assistance Act.

The results emerging from these different approaches are encouraging; nevertheless, challenges persist, with a significant share of refugee children still not enrolled in school. As of July 2022, the highest enrollment rates for children of compulsory education age were in Luxembourg (95 percent), Ireland (92 percent), and Belgium (85 percent), followed by Spain (75 percent), Lithuania (74 percent), Italy (71 percent), the Netherlands (66 percent), and Austria (64 percent). Countries that received a larger inflow of Ukrainian refugees had a lower proportion of children enrolled in school, likely because of congestion effects. For instance, in Czechia, Germany, Poland, and the Slovak Republic, enrollment rates are below 40 percent, whereas in Romania, enrollment rates are just 8 percent (as of July 2022; European Commission, EACEA, and Eurydice 2022). Overall, the United Nations Children's Fund estimated that, at the end of July 2022, approximately 650,000 Ukrainian children living as refugees across 12 different countries were still not enrolled in a national education system. More recent data for the start of the 2023–24 year shows improvements in enrollment rates in several countries (e.g., 83% in Romania), although rates remain generally low, particularly so in Moldova (8%), Slovenia (16%), Bulgaria (18%), Croatia (23%), and Belgium (23%) (UNHCR 2024).

The Act on Assistance to Citizens of Ukraine (Poland 2022) is an important example of bilateral recognition of specific degrees. Thanks to the Polish-Ukrainian bilateral agreement on the mutual recognition of university-level diplomas, most Ukrainian refugees can engage in higher-skilled jobs in Poland. However, there are professions for which additional certification is needed, such as for architects, veterinarians, and medical professionals. The Act on Assistance to Ukrainian Refugees allows doctors, nurses, dentists, and midwives to practice in Poland for a period of up to 18 months. It might still be necessary to enhance the skills of Ukrainian refugees, however, because not all medical procedures or equipment are the same.

Finally, an important step taken by EU countries in terms of education and skills has been the development of a version of the European Qualifications Passport for Refugees (EQPR). This document facilitates the self-assessment of socioemotional and technical skills that can be made known to employers willing to hire refugees. The EU Skills Profile Tool can support the assessment of refugees' skills and facilitate refugees' placement into jobs and training.[9]

Social Protection

Countries have introduced a variety of policy measures to enhance access to social services and social protection systems for Ukrainian refugees. For example, in Czechia, organizations and individuals providing support and services to refugees receive a subsidy. In Poland, refugees under temporary protection have access to a range of social benefits, most of which are targeted to families. In Belgium, the government gives providers of services to Ukrainian refugees a 35 percent top-up on reimbursements for such services for the first four months and a 25 percent top-up afterward. This promotes supporting Ukrainian refugees with extra resources to meet their needs. In Germany, the government offers refugees with residence permits the same open access available to citizens for social assistance (*Sozialgesetzbuch* [Social Code]; SGB XII) and job-seeker benefits (SGB II), and all refugees also have the right to join the national statutory health insurance. Additionally, those participating in training activities can receive support through the Federal Training Assistance Act.

The temporary protection directive has emphasized the protection of people, especially those who are most vulnerable. These people include children and unaccompanied minors who have been victims of violence, abuse, and rape and are currently experiencing disability or severe mental health issues or those who have been victims of sexual and psychological violence. Countries have implemented several measures to provide support to unaccompanied minors, people with disabilities, and elderly people with restricted mobility. For example, Croatia established special accommodations for these vulnerable groups, and Portugal created special support groups to help unaccompanied minors in foster care (Aumayr-Pintar and Cantero Guerrero 2022; Eurofound, n.d).

Housing

Countries have provided housing support to Ukrainian refugees by expanding existing accommodation opportunities and providing subsidies for hosting institutions and families. Countries have provided funds to build new accommodation centers and to expand and refurbish existing ones, and they have implemented other measures to provide housing support. For example, Norway and Sweden relaxed regulations to make housing available swiftly. In Czechia, municipalities and regional governments can receive funding to make needed changes to publicly owned buildings to host refugees. In Poland, some training facilities owned by the Social Insurance Institute have been made available to temporarily house refugees. In Greece, existing retention centers and private homes host refugees. In other countries, such as Cyprus, hotels house refugees. France simplified administrative procedures and requirements for Ukrainian refugees to use existing housing schemes. Some countries have opted to subsidize refugees directly. In Estonia, for example, refugees can benefit from a one-off, lump-sum transfer (€1,200 as of June 2022) to cover the initial costs of moving to a permanent accommodation. Latvia and the Netherlands provide housing benefits directly to refugees who decide to settle in the host country, under the condition that the refugees remain in the country for a given period (generally three months). Governments have also subsidized private households providing refugees with food and accommodation. In Lithuania, this subsidy is €150 per month for a single refugee, plus €50 for each additional person. In Romania, the 50/20 housing program provides subsidies to Romanians hosting Ukrainian refugees of €10 per day per person for accommodation, plus €4 per day per person for food (refer to box 2.3 for more details). In Poland, the subsidy is €8 per day per person (Aumayr-Pintar and Cantero Guerrero 2022; Eurofound, n.d).

Health Care

The Temporary Protection Directive set minimum standards for the health and medical support of Ukrainian refugees. Host countries should ensure access to medical care—at the very least for emergency care and essential treatment of illnesses. Many countries in the European Union provide refugees with health care and services that are comparable or equal to those provided to their citizens. This is the case, for instance, in Austria, Denmark, Estonia, Greece, Poland, Portugal, Romania, and Slovakia. In Denmark and Poland, access is conditional on applying for residency permits; in Austria and Romania, such access is free to all Ukrainians

BOX 2.3 The Romanian 50/20 Housing Program

The 50/20 program is a housing program initiated by Romania through Government Emergency Ordinance no. 15/2022 on February 27, 2022. The program aims to encourage Romanian citizens to host Ukrainian refugees by giving Romanian hosts leu 50 per refugee per day for accommodation and leu 20 per refugee per day for food. The program is funded by the Romanian government and European Commission emergency funds. Although data are not yet available on the number of recipients, a survey conducted by the UN High Commissioner for Refugees (2022b) with a sample of 262 respondents suggests that the vast majority (94 percent) of Ukrainian refugees settled in Romania have used the program. It showed that refugees found accommodation informally, through Facebook groups (36 percent), friends (33 percent), or Telegram groups (9 percent). In contrast, the government platform established to centralize refugee housing officers (Un Acoperiș) was used by only 1 percent of those who found accommodation through the 50/20 program.

Refugees report high levels of satisfaction with the program. Only 8 percent of respondents report having had problems with private landlords. Concerning food provision (of leu 20 per day), 57 percent say they receive cash directly; 36 percent say landlords retain the payment for either utilities or unspecified reasons, and 7 percent say they receive in-kind food from the landlord. The program faces some challenges. For example, an estimated 30 percent of refugees surveyed said landlords demanded deposit payments, and, in part because of the heavy reliance on informal interactions, 52 percent of refugees report not knowing where they can report abuse. Overall, the program is successful but could be improved with more supervision.

entering the country, independent of the refugee's status (in Romania, though, such access is limited up to 90 days after entry in the country).

Some countries provide additional medical services targeted specifically to Ukrainian refugees. For example, Estonia provides free health checks and vaccinations upon arrival in addition to treatment for chronic or preexisting medical conditions. It gives refugees a medical certificate that could be used if needed for work and allows refugees to use medical prescriptions issued in Ukraine to obtain medicines needed for treatment. Portugal offers medical consultations in Ukrainian languages for young people and children. Poland provides additional psychological support. The Slovak Republic offers to reimburse the costs of emergency medical services. Finally, Romania offers primary health care and emergency care, together with free treatment for severe or life-threatening conditions (Aumayr-Pintar and Cantero Guerrero 2022; Eurofound, n.d).

Remaining Challenges

Challenges remain in integrating refugees into host countries' labor markets. First, language remains a significant barrier to integration. Lack of sufficient language knowledge is reported to be an obstacle to finding a job in the host country for 63 percent of Ukrainian refugee job seekers, by far the main factor compared to other barriers, according to a cross-country survey in 10 EU host countries (Eurofound and the EU Agency for Fundamental Rights 2023). According to the EWL Migration Platform, 53 percent of refugees in Poland and 55 percent of those in Germany have no knowledge of the national language (Zymnin et al. 2022). A 2022 survey in Germany found that only 4 percent of refugees in the country rated their knowledge of German as good or very good, with 63 percent having no prior knowledge of the language before arriving in the country (INFO GmbH 2022). However, language acquisition is better in other host countries; according to the OECD (2023), 26 percent of refugees in the Slovak Republic and 38 percent of those in Poland have a good knowledge of the national language. Another challenge involves processes to establish and recognize refugees' skills. In Latvia and Poland, for example, almost 40 percent of refugees are classified as low skilled, even though 60–70 percent are estimated to have a university degree (OECD 2023). In Germany, around 22 percent of Ukrainian refugees reported being employed, but only less than half of them declared that their job matched their qualifications, according to an online survey by the Institute for Economic Research (IFO) between June and October 2022 (Panchenko and Poutvaara 2022). Other barriers include lack of childcare—a key issue for families with young children because many fathers remain in Ukraine to serve in the military. Transportation can also be an issue for refugees. Qualitative evidence from

Polish regional labor offices points to other challenges in labor market integration. Potential disincentives to work exist among refugees for a wide variety of reasons, including, for example, the uncertainty of the timing of their return. In addition, refugees risk working in poor conditions, working in the informal sector, and receiving pay below the minimum wage. Legal measures aiming to facilitate initial settlement and rapid labor market participation will also face important issues regarding renewals of residency and work permits, with permits typically expiring after nine months to a year. In fact, employers already raised concerns about the ability of refugees to engage in long-term employment because of the possibility of returning to their home country.

Policy Recommendations

Ensuring a coordinated response and fair sharing of responsibilities between countries is key to managing future refugee crises. Although progress has been made toward better coordinating the response to refugee inflow in ECA, as illustrated by the recent inflow of Ukrainian refugees, some challenges remain. Several measures can be implemented to ensure more coordinated policy responses and a more equal sharing of responsibilities. These measures include enabling the resettlement of refugees, financing assistance and international protection programs, investing in technical assistance and capacity building in host countries, and improving internal and regional migratory policies (World Bank 2023). Along these lines, the European Union is continuing negotiations to develop a solidarity mechanism that is predictable and flexible and that includes minimum annual thresholds and commitments guided by a fair-share principle (Del Monte and Orav 2023).

To effectively and rapidly respond to an immediate crisis, governments of receiving countries must ensure sufficient humanitarian support and reception capacity to host refugees. The provision of temporary protection status to refugees is a first step toward ensuring rapid humanitarian support and eligibility to protection programs and services. To weather the initial shock and cover basic needs, vulnerable refugee families need the early provision of social assistance benefits (for example, cash and in-kind support, such as food vouchers). Cash transfer programs have been shown to be effective interventions to improve the welfare of refugee populations, with few adverse effects on earnings opportunities, at least in the short run (Bahar, Brough, and Peri 2024). In the short run, those programs can be provided through externally funded systems in parallel with national systems to ensure a more rapid and flexible response tailored to refugees' immediate needs. Physical and mental health support are fundamental for a population that has faced severe trauma and war—as is the case for most refugees.

One-stop-shop reception centers have proven to be effective in undertaking a first, rapid assessment of refugees' characteristics, needs, and vulnerabilities and in directing them to the services they need in the short run.

During the emergency response phase, governments should be mindful of potential long-term impacts of policies implemented and already have taken some actions to improve refugees' productive integration. Most successful interventions combine fast and extensive use of humanitarian assistance when refugees initially arrive, with policies aimed at facilitating the integration of refugees into the labor market as soon as possible and for the long term. The ability to access some basic training, for example, especially language training, is important, even during this initial humanitarian support phase. Such training is essential for facilitating participation in the education system, the labor market, or ALMPs and on-the-job training down the line. Early integration of refugee children into the school system is fundamental to avoid longer-term disruptions in learning that can be more difficult to bridge later on and that can have detrimental, lasting implications for human development. Other programs tailored to refugees' needs—such as early childhood education programs—would also help integration. Regarding social assistance programs, cash transfer programs should be designed in a way that does not deter formal employment or does not promote dependence on welfare, which harms longer-term integration.

Beyond the emergency phase, investing in selected policies that support refugees' integration can generate high payoffs for host countries. Such efforts are needed to support refugees to make the transition from a heavy reliance on social assistance and welfare to self-reliance. Successfully integrating a large number of asylum seekers into local communities, including access to housing, education, and employment opportunities, requires significant resources and careful planning. However, these significant investments can pay off. Evidence from the refugee crises resulting from the wars in Syria and in the former Yugoslavia shows high payoffs from a few key measures for refugees' integration in the long run. These include conducting early skills and needs assessments; ensuring the right to work and offering workers' protection; providing access to social protections, health care, education, and language training; and facilitating participation in active labor market programs.

The early assessment of qualifications, skills, and educational attainment is crucial to the integration phase. Host countries do not always recognize educational attainment and professional qualifications from home countries, or refugees might not hold the documentation necessary to prove educational attainment. Validation procedures can be complicated, time consuming, and expensive. Sometimes receiving countries will establish ad hoc systems (such as using specific tests) to verify credentials and qualifications. The presence and use of standardized assessments of refugees' qualifications, skills, and educational attainment early in the experience have proven to be critical factors for labor market integration in the host country. Because many refugees lack documentation, the development of a refugee skills passport (such as the one introduced by the EU) that can be recognized by multiple countries can be a particularly effective tool for validating certain skills and testing employability. One example of a successful early assessment of skills and qualifications is the EQPR (Council of Europe n.d.; refer to box 2.4 for more details).

BOX 2.4 The European Qualifications Passport for Refugees: A Harmonized Early Assessment of Refugees' Skills and Qualifications

The European Qualifications Passport for Refugees (EQPR) aims to facilitate the integration of refugees into labor markets and societies by providing a standardized and transparent assessment of qualifications and skills. The EQPR is a pilot program introduced in Greece, Italy, and the Netherlands (2017–20). Sponsored by the Council of Europe with the support of the UN High Commissioner for Refugees, it follows the guidelines of the Lisbon Convention to facilitate recognition of refugees' qualifications, even in the absence of full documentation. It is intended to provide a reliable, transparent, and standardized assessment of refugees' qualifications and skills for employers, education institutions, and other relevant stakeholders. The EQPR is designed to be a flexible and adaptable tool that can be used in different contexts and countries. It aims to complement and not substitute for existing recognition procedures and systems by providing an additional option for refugees who face difficulties in gaining recognition of their qualifications. It can also be a practical tool to better match labor supply and demand and to better match refugees with appropriate providers of services, training, and education, including those that issue qualifications (Council of Europe n.d).

The program uses a four-step process: an initial assessment, documentation review, skills assessment, and final report. The first three steps are, in theory, intended to be completed in one hour, but the actual length may vary depending on the circumstances. The initial step consists of a self-assessment that refugees can complete online (or, alternatively, in person); using a questionnaire, refugees provide an overview of their qualifications and skills and a detailed description of their educational background. The second step consists of a review of the documentation of educational attainment and professional qualifications. Qualified assessors verify refugees' educational and professional documents and take steps to replace any missing documents. The third step consists of a practical and structured skills test during which credential evaluators assess refugees' skills in specific fields. In the final step, the evaluators create a report summarizing the results of the skills assessment and providing a clear, concise description of the refugees' educational attainment level, qualifications, and skills.

Registering refugees in databases that are compatible with other administrative databases (for example, for beneficiaries of social programs) is also crucial in helping to assess the vulnerabilities of refugee households and targeting appropriate interventions. Some countries have adopted more tailored assessments of refugees' needs and vulnerabilities and have developed case management systems through which refugee individuals and households are followed by social workers via customized plans to address specific vulnerabilities and then referred to social services, training, or job opportunities (this is the case, for instance, in Germany, the Netherlands, Norway and Sweden, and—outside the ECA region—in Canada and Australia). The available evidence has shown that the case management approach has yielded comprehensive access to settlement and support services for the beneficiary population, successful integration into the workforce for refugees, and positive community integration outcomes.

Rapid labor market access for refugees is key to supporting integration and can be facilitated by several policy measures. The sooner refugees can participate formally in the labor market, the sooner they can unlock the benefits of labor market access, and the sooner both host and origin countries can benefit as well. To achieve rapid access to the labor market, host countries can ease or remove restrictions and regulations that typically apply to third-country nationals entering the labor market. This includes simplifying, expediting, or removing work permit processes or granting visa waivers. Procedures for the hiring of foreign workers can also be simplified and expedited, for example, by removing requirements to adhere to a special set of rules and regulations for employers interested in hiring a third-country national. Furthermore, labor laws could be simplified during emergency situations involving large refugee inflows, such as Poland has done in response to the inflow of Ukrainian refugees. Finally, streamlined asylum procedures, such as the ones implemented in Germany, can support rapid access to the labor market.

Providing greater legal certainty to refugees in both the short and the longer run is also important. Refugees facing uncertainty regarding their legal status may be more reluctant to invest in activities that could support their socioeconomic integration in the host county. The EU Mass Immigration Directive and temporary residence permits are important steps toward ensuring greater legal certainty and preventing obstacles in the asylum procedure in the short term. To further support integration, such efforts could be complemented by offering prospects for long-term residency to refugees. Reducing legal uncertainty about longer-term prospects could incentivize refugees to invest in building skills valuable to host country labor markets: for example, through language or technical training, increasing their productive capacity and economic gains for host countries.

ALMPs can also support refugees' labor market integration, especially at the initial stages. Past experiences indicate that compulsory language training is a key element of a successful integration strategy that improves refugees' long-term labor market outcomes. Other ALMP programs for refugees include interventions aimed at improving the match between labor supply and demand, such as job search support and dedicated employment platforms targeted to the recruiting of refugees. For refugee workers who want to engage in formal wage work, wage subsidy programs may be a useful tool. Employers typically have quite limited information about the productivity of the refugee population and may thus be reluctant to hire refugee workers at the market price. By allowing employers to observe refugee workers' productivity by initially hiring them at a lower cost, wage subsidy programs may help increase the demand for refugee labor. For refugee workers interested in starting up a business, start-up loan subsidies combined with mechanisms to provide advisory services can help support aspiring entrepreneurs. The experience of past refugee waves indicates that facilitating social dialogue among key stakeholders—including NGOs, civil society organizations, chambers of commerce, and private sector employer associations—is key in designing and implementing interventions to support refugees' productive employment. To mitigate potential backlash associated with having specific programs supporting refugee populations, such programs could also cover native-born individuals in areas where refugees reside, as in Türkiye.

Another key determinant of refugees' integration is their geographical location, and a key takeaway from both research and experience is that refugees should not be isolated from the native-born population in receiving countries. A recent and growing body of work focuses on the medium-term implications of refugee exposure by analyzing the impacts on hosting societies that emerge from the relocation of refugees within a country.[10] In general, the empirical evidence shows that it is important to avoid constraining refugees and displaced populations in limited geographic areas—that is, creating what has been called a ghetto effect. For example, housing policies that tie refugees to a physical place and prevent geographic mobility should be discouraged.

Dispersal policies assigning refugees to regions should consider labor demand and absorptive capacity of local labor markets to improve the labor market outcomes of refugees. Experience from the inflow of refugees from Syria and the former Yugoslavia shows that dispersal policies that allocate refugees on the basis of local labor demand, without discouraging geographic mobility, are conducive to better labor market outcomes. Dispersal policies should, therefore, take local labor market demand conditions and absorptive capacity into account, as is done in Germany (refer to box 2.5 for more details). For example, such policies should be underpinned by information on regional and provincial gross domestic product, employment rates, youth unemployment rates, job vacancies, and skill and occupational shortages. Evidence suggests that dispersal policies based on algorithms that take local labor demand and refugees' sociodemographic characteristics and educational attainment into account can contribute to improving refugees' employment prospects. By using such methods rather than relying on traditional or existing assignment policies, refugees' likelihood of employment has been shown to improve by 40 percent in the United States and 70 percent in Switzerland (Bansak et al. 2018). On the other hand, the empirical evidence has also shown that in the presence of ad hoc or quasi-random dispersal policies—not supported by adequate integration services, reinforced management of refugees reception centers, and proper information campaigns or driven by political decisions or preferences—anti-immigration backlash can prevail among host communities, with high social and political costs (Campo, Giunti, and Mendola 2024).

Beyond labor markets, refugees' integration can be supported by facilitating access to national systems for health, education, and social protection services. Although supporting refugees through parallel externally funded systems can ensure a more rapid and tailored response to refugee needs in the short run, it can create tensions in the longer run if the quality of services provided is superior or inferior to those provided to nationals. It also raises concerns about sustainability, because separate systems are typically dependent on external financing. However, integrating refugees into functioning national systems can improve financial sustainability and fairness in access and quality in comparison with nationals. The first step toward integrating refugees in national systems is registering refugees in national databases that are interoperable with other administrative databases (such as those of social services). Governments also need access to financing arrangements that provide predictability and confidence that resources will be available beyond the short term. To limit additional pressure on national systems, sizable amounts of external financing are often needed to scale up and maintain national systems in refugee-hosting regions, especially in countries in which public services are already under pressure. Institutional arrangements also need to be in place to allow engagement of the relevant technical ministries—education, health, and social protection—in support of refugees. Finally, establishing platforms to coordinate the efforts of multiple agencies and ensure refugees' access to social services and jobs will also be an important factor in enhancing the effectiveness of integration measures.

BOX 2.5 Policy Insights from the Refugee Dispersal Policy in Germany

Germany follows a specific quota system for the geographic distribution of asylum seekers throughout the country. Upon arrival to Germany, asylum seekers are given a proof-of-arrival certificate at the point of entry and then assigned to a federal state on the basis of a quota system. This quota system, called the Königstein Key, considers both the size and the economic strength of each state when allocating assignments. It is designed to make more populous and economically stronger states accommodate more protection seekers. In this way, the number of asylum seekers is proportional to the state's population size and tax revenues (weighted by two-thirds and one-third, respectively). Generally, within the quota caps, asylum seekers are assigned to whatever state has space to accommodate them at the time, without consideration of the asylum seekers' characteristics or preferences. The allocation of asylum seekers to districts within a federal state is left to the discretion of the state officials. Asylum seekers do not have freedom of movement from their assigned district while their case is pending. The arrival of asylum seekers is often unpredictable, and the location and timing of places available to accommodate them vary. Thus, in practice, the number of asylum seekers living in each federal state often differs from the number of asylum seekers established by the government quota. Table B2.5.1 shows the distribution of asylum applications filed in 2019 across federal states and how the share of applications across districts differs from the quota (Pavilon 2021).

TABLE B2.5.1 Distribution of asylum seekers in Germany, 2019

Federal state	Quota (%)	First applications in 2019	Actual share in 2019 (%)
Baden-Württemberg	13.01	14,990	10.52
Bavaria	15.56	18,368	12.89
Berlin	5.14	8,221	5.77
Brandenburg	3.02	4,151	2.91
Bremen	0.96	1,683	1.18
Hamburg	2.56	3,551	2.49
Hesse	7.44	11,901	8.35
Lower Saxony	9.41	13,741	9.64
Mecklenburg-Vorpommern	1.98	2,548	1.79
North Rhine–Westphalia	21.09	33,879	23.77
Rhineland-Palatinate	4.82	7,406	5.17
Saarland	1.20	2,141	1.50
Saxony	4.99	6,310	4.43
Saxony-Anhalt	2.75	4,168	2.92
Schleswig-Holstein	3.40	5,729	4.02
Thuringia	2.65	3,558	2.47

Source: Federal Office for Migration and Refugees (BAMF) 2019, 2020.

Annex 2A: Impact of Syrian Refugee Inflow on the Turkish Economy

Labor Market Impact

Basic economic theory suggests that the massive labor supply shock to informal labor puts a downward pressure on employment and wages of native-born individuals in the informal sector. However, the effect of Syrian migrants on formal labor is ambiguous. As the cost of informal labor falls, employers will be tempted to substitute formal labor with informal labor. However, significant cost reductions brought by refugees may increase output and create more formal jobs. Therefore, if refugees complement native-born formal workers, then an increase in formal employment and wages of native-born individuals is expected to be observed.

The studies analyzing the impact of Syrian refugees on native-born employment and other labor market outcomes can be divided into two groups. The first group includes an initial set of studies that use labor force surveys to identify outcomes of interest and an instrumental variables (IV) approach to control for the endogeneity of the distribution of refugees across Turkish regions. A second group of studies looks at labor market impacts, combining various data sources, and tries to adopt a wider range of estimation and identification strategies to assess the causal effect of the presence of refugees on the outcomes of interest in the host communities.

Del Carpio et al. (2016) were among the first to study the labor market impacts of refugee inflows to Turkish regions. They investigate how private sector, paid employment of native-born workers (for example, self-employed and wage workers) is affected by the arrival of Syrian refugees using data from the Turkish Household Labour Force Surveys (THLFS). The employment measure is disaggregated into formal and informal employment, full and part time. They basically use an IV difference-in-differences strategy in which they exploit the distribution of refugees to the native-born, working-age population (ages 15–64 years) across 26 Nomenclature of Territorial Units for Statistics level 2 (NUTS-2) regions over the years 2011 and 2014. The location choice of refugees may be endogenous; thus, they use an IV for the refugee-to-native-born ratio based on the distance between 13 Syrian governorates and 26 Turkish subregions (the most populous city in each subregion). This instrument distributes the total number of refugees in a year in Türkiye across NUTS-2 regions, based on the prewar population shares of each Syrian governorate and the distance between each Syrian governorate and Turkish subregions. Therefore, regions closer to the Syrian border attract relatively more refugees than farther-away regions. However, closer regions may systematically vary from farther regions, which may invalidate the IV strategy. To address this concern, they include regional trade volumes of Turkish regions (for example, the Syrian war may have differentially affected trade with regions at the border) and a time-variant distance measure of each Turkish region to the Syrian border (distance to the border is interacted with year dummies) besides the usual year and subregion fixed effects.

They find significant and large adverse effects of refugees on the propensity of native-born workers' employment in the informal sector: for every 10 incoming refugees, around six Turkish workers are displaced. Displacement occurs among all types of native-born workers irrespective of their gender, age, and education. However, the displacement effect is more pronounced among native-born workers without a formal education (for example, less than primary education). Considering the formal sector, the IV estimates suggest that refugee inflow creates additional formal jobs for native-born workers: for every 10 refugees, around three native-born workers are formally employed. These increases in formal employment accrue to men without a completed high school education. Women and high-skilled populations do not benefit from the refugee inflow. The overall net impact on employment is negative; for every 10 refugees about two native-born workers are displaced from employment. Net employment losses are concentrated among women and low-skilled workers. The impact of refugees on unemployment is negative for men, but evidence shows that it is due to discouraged workers leaving the labor force rather than increases in employment. Considering wages, the IV estimates show significant increases in average wages, which are derived from the increase in male native-born workers' wages due to the inflow of refugees.

Ceritoglu et al. (2017) investigate the impacts of refugee flows on native-born workers' labor market outcomes. They differ from Del Carpio et al. (2016) and Aksu, Erzen, and Kırdar (2018) by focusing on a comparison of bordering regions with those neighboring the bordering regions but not subject to the refugee inflow. They take four NUTS-2 regions in southeastern Türkiye as treatment regions because they host between 2 percent and 30 percent of their native-born population as refugees and take five NUTS-2 regions in eastern Türkiye as control regions because these regions are quite similar to the treatment regions in terms of cultural traits, social norms and attitudes, level of economic development, and labor market characteristics but receive very few refugees. Unlike other studies, Ceritoglu et al. (2017) do not use the intensity of refugee inflows to regions (for example, refugee-to-native-born ratio) as the key variable of interest. They use a standard difference-in-differences methodology in which they compare the change in labor market outcomes (for example, informal and formal employment, unemployment).

As in Del Carpio et al. (2016), Ceritoglu et al. (2017) find that the impact of refugee inflow to treatment regions is to decrease informal employment propensity by 2.2 percentage points. Disadvantaged groups in the informal sector, women and those who are less educated, are affected the most. Male informal workers who are replaced by refugees stay in the labor force and search for jobs, which results in an increase in unemployment. Displaced female informal workers drop out of the labor force. There is a slight increase in formal employment in treatment regions, an effect of refugee inflow that is concentrated around males and those with less education (high school dropouts and below). Average wages are not affected by the refugee inflow. Akgündüz, Van Den Berg, and Hassink (2015) follow a similar difference-in-differences methodology and find that refugee inflow does not affect the employment prospects of native-born workers.

In another paper, Cengiz and Tekgüç (2022) look at the impacts of Syrian refugees on native-born workers' labor market outcomes. As do Ceritoglu et al. (2017), they choose three NUTS-2 regions with highest refugee-to-native-born population ratio as treatment regions and select 16 NUTS-2 regions as control units while excluding seven Turkish regions from the analysis. They use difference-in-differences and synthetic control methods to estimate the causal effect of refugee inflow using the THLFS from 2004 to 2015. Cengiz and Tekgüç (2022) use the parametric bootstrap method in a generalized synthetic control model, the wild cluster bootstrap method in an ordinary least squares model, and the wild restricted residual bootstrap method in a two-stage least squares model to produce *p* values that account for the overly narrow confidence intervals. They find null effects of refugee inflow on employment and wages.

The Aksu, Erzen, and Kırdar (2018) study is probably the most comprehensive among others that look at labor market impacts of refugees on native-born individuals. They similarly use pooled THLFS data from 2004 to 2015 to track changes in native-born workers' labor market indicators across 26 NUTS-2 regions. They use a rich set of labor market outcomes: employment (wage workers, self-employed workers, unpaid family workers, employers), unemployment, labor force participation, and wages disaggregated by informal or formal employment, gender, age, and education. They also look at changes in type and sector of employment in response to a refugee inflow. The sample consisted of 18- to 64-year-old native-born individuals. Aksu, Erzen, and Kırdar (2018) use an IV difference-in-differences methodology to reveal causal effects of refugee inflows. They treat location choices of refugees as endogenous and accordingly use a modified version of Del Carpio et al.'s (2016) IV.

Consistent with the canonical model, the outward shift in the labor supply in the informal sector—due to refugee inflows—causes significant decreases in native-born workers' employment—which is driven by the decrease in wage work—and wages in the informal sector, although the wage effect is only marginally significant. Because of complementarity between low-skilled immigrants and native-born formal workers, the refugee inflow causes an equally large increase in formal employment and wages of native-born men. Therefore, native-born men are overall not affected by the arrival of refugees with respect to employment and wages. The change is in the type of employment prevalent among native-born men: a shift from wage employment to self-employment and unpaid family work takes place during the study period. For women, total employment falls, and there is evidence that the decrease is partly due to a decrease in wage work in the formal sector. Nevertheless, the role of the decrease in part-time employment is more substantial in explaining the decrease in total employment of women. Those who lose their part-time jobs seem to exit the labor force. Overall, there is no effect of refugees on the wages of native-born women. Considering the sector of employment, native-born men in the construction sector (which tends to be dominated by informal employment) lose employment opportunities, whereas wages themselves are unaffected by refugee inflow. In the agricultural sector, women's employment and wages are both adversely affected, whereas men lose only on wages. In the manufacturing and services sectors, jobs created in the formal sector exceed those destroyed in the informal sector. Both men's and women's wages in the formal manufacturing sector and men's wages in the formal services sector increase. In terms of heterogeneity by age and education, the refugee inflow seems to most hurt less-educated and younger workers in the informal sector with respect to employment and wages. However, the same group of less-educated and younger workers seem to benefit from the arrival of refugees in both employment and wages in the formal sector.

Bagır (2018) differs from previous studies by analyzing the impacts of the refugee inflows on the basis of the characteristics of the moves. That is, he argues that the initial migration of Syrians to border regions in Türkiye is due to political reasons in the source country; therefore, it can be considered as exogenous. However, with the passage of time, those who reside in the border regions begin to consider return migration an impossibility; hence, they may move further into the country to seek better living conditions. This secondary migration, though, involves location choices that may coincide with regional shocks to labor markets. Thus, Bagır (2018) accounts for the endogeneity of this secondary migration by instrumenting the refugee-to-native-born population through ethnic and cultural ties between Syrian refugees and native-born individuals in the border regions. The instrument measures the share of native-born individuals from the border regions in the total number of immigrants to each NUTS-2 region. Metropolitan areas in Türkiye, such as Ankara, Istanbul, and Izmir, attract internal migrants because of their favorable labor market conditions, and they also take high values for the instrument. Therefore, for the IV method to achieve consistent estimates of refugee impacts on native-born individuals' labor market outcomes, it is crucial to condition on NUTS-2 region fixed effects. By implementing an IV difference-in-differences strategy for the secondary migration using THLFS with 2012 as the control period and 2015 as the treatment period, Bagır (2018) argues that an inflow of refugees generates causal impacts on native-born individuals' outcomes. The difference-in-differences results for the primary migration regions of Türkiye show a statistically significant decline in the probability of employment for males (3.4 percentage points) and females (4.2 percentage points). The refugee impact is concentrated, as in other studies, among low-educated and young native-born individuals. Wage effects follow a similar pattern: native-born men's wages decrease by 7.9 percentage points (statistically significant at 1 percent) and native women's wages decrease by 0.4 percentage points (insignificant). The impact was much larger among those who were unskilled and young. Considering the sectors, those native-born workers (male or female) who work in informally dominated construction and agriculture experience the largest wage declines. Workers in small firms are also vulnerable to the refugee inflow in terms of compensation. Analysis for the secondary migration regions did not yield a statistically significant refugee impact on employment. However, the IV difference-in-differences estimates suggest that a 1-percentage-point increase in the ratio of refugees to native-born individuals in a region decreases wages of native-born men and women by 1.4 percent and 0.8 percent, respectively. Again, the refugee impact is concentrated among young and less-educated individuals.

Akgündüz and Torun (2020) complement the ongoing debate on the impacts of Syrian refugees on native-born individuals' labor market outcomes by investigating how the rapid increase in the low-skilled labor supply affects the task inputs of native-born workers and the capital intensity of firms in Türkiye. Following Acemoglu and Autor (2011), they calculate task scores using the O*NET database and merge them with the two-digit International Standard Classification of Occupations occupation codes in THLFS. For per capita inputs and investment levels, they exploit variation in an administrative data set of the universe of registered Turkish firms known as the Entrepreneurship Information System (Turkish Ministry of Science and Industry). The results suggest that the tasks Syrian refugees perform are complementary to abstract tasks performed by native-born workers and substitutes for capital use and investment rates in firms.

There are heterogeneous effects by age and education. Young and highly educated native-born workers move to jobs with more abstract tasks in response to Syrian refugees' engagement in jobs with routine and manual-intensive tasks. In addition, the decline in capital use and investment rates is more concentrated among small firms. Their findings are important in suggesting rapid adjustment on both labor and capital margins. This swift adjustment in inputs can help explain the limited effect of Syrian refugees on the wages and employment of the native-born population found in previous studies (Ceritoglu et al. 2017; Del Carpio et al. 2016).

Aracı, Demirci, and Kırdar (2022) look at the issue of refugee impact on native-born workers' labor market outcomes from a different perspective. On the basis of the previous literature arguing that immigration is detrimental for native-born workers' employment prospects in middle-income countries rather than in high-income countries (Verme and Schuettler 2021), Aracı, Demirci, and Kırdar (2022) exploit the large variation in both level of development and refugee-to-native-born population share across 26 NUTS-2 regions to estimate whether refugee inflow to a region has differential effects on native-born workers' labor market outcomes with the development level of the region. This question has important policy implications, especially for the allocation of refugees across regions and countries to minimize their negative effects on native-born individuals. They focus on employment, labor force participation, unemployment, and wages as outcome variables measured using the THLFS from 2004 to 2015. Their estimation strategy is novel in creating synthetic control groups for each NUTS-2 region based on Abadie and Gardeazabal (2003).

Their findings show that the refugees' impact on both men's and women's labor market outcomes becomes more positive as the development level rises. For men, this is observed in employment, formal employment, nonwage employment, and wages among wage workers. For women, this is observed in employment, formal employment, labor force participation, and both employment and wages among wage workers. Moreover, for women, the negative effects of the refugee shock on employment and labor force participation observed at the mean level of development vanish at high levels of development. In addition, the transition from informal employment to formal employment—particularly in the manufacturing and service sectors, found at the mean level of development—becomes more pronounced for both men and women as the level of development rises.

Another set of papers looks at the impacts of the massive exodus of Syrian refugees into Türkiye on local businesses and firm creation. The set of outcomes investigated in this literature is more granular at a Nomenclature of Territorial Units for Statistics level 3. Altındağ, Bakış, and Rozo (2020) use the Annual Industry and Service Statistics survey (representative at the province level) produced by the Turkish Statistical Institute between 2006 and 2015 for measures of firms' input demand, production, and energy consumption. They use Company Establishment and Liquidation Statistics published by the Union of Chambers and Commodity Exchanges of Türkiye (TOBB, n.d.) for firm entry and exit behavior across provinces. They use province-level export and import figures made publicly available by the Turkish Statistical Institute (TUIK). Last, for labor market outcomes of native-born individuals, they use THLFS. Their estimation strategy is based on comparing firms in provinces with a larger share of refugees in total population with those in provinces with a smaller share of refugees in total population, before and after the onset of the Syrian civil war. They instrument the refugee-to-population ratio with the interaction of the share of the Arabic-speaking population in the province and the total number of individuals displaced outside Syria each year. The Arabic-speaking population information is from the 1965 census. The identification strategy is that through social capital and migrant networks, having the same mother tongue helps refugees with location choice but is uncorrelated with firm performance. Their IV estimates show no significant effect on firm sales or gross production; however, the production proxies, oil and electricity consumption, significantly increase in return to the refugee inflow (4.3 percent in response to a 1-percentage-point increase in the refugee-to-population ratio). Refugees significantly increase the number of firms, especially those with foreign partnerships. Provincial exports or imports are unaffected by the refugee inflow. However, firms decrease their capital use in regions with higher refugee density. As in previous literature (Aksu, Erzen, and Kırdar 2018; Ceritoglu et al. 2017; Del Carpio et al. 2016), the effects of refugees on native-born workers' employment show that low-skilled, native-born males in informal employment are replaced with their competitors, Syrian refugees. Altındağ, Bakış, and Rozo's (2020) results indicate that refugee inflows positively affect local businesses and firm creation, but this impact is concentrated in the informal economy.

The paper by Akgündüz et al. (2023) is another one that investigates the impacts of refugee inflow on firm performance and firm creation. The data on the number of new firms and their ownership status come from TOBB, as in Altındağ, Bakış, and Rozo (2020). The data on total sales and gross profits are obtained from the Ministry of Science and Technology. Akgündüz et al. (2023) use three different estimation strategies. The first one is their preferred IV estimation, which follows the exact same specification of Del Carpio and Wagner (2015)—they instrument the number of refugees in a province with Del Carpio and Wagner's (2015) distance-based instrument while controlling for a yearly varying measure of distance between each province and the nearest Syrian border. The control period in their IV difference-in-differences model is 2011, and the treatment period is 2014. The second strategy assumes that the initial migration of Syrian refugees to bordering regions is exogenous. So the standard difference-in-differences strategy in Ceritoglu et al. (2017) with control provinces in eastern Türkiye is enough to uncover the causal impact of refugee inflows. The third strategy extends the standard difference-in-differences strategy by creating synthetic control groups for treatment provinces from the rest of the 71 provinces in Türkiye.

Akgündüz et al.'s (2023) main finding is that the refugee inflow results in an increase in the number of new foreign firms. There is also a positive effect on the new firm entries, but it is statistically insignificant. In addition, there is a strong positive effect of refugee inflows on profits and net sales; however, the placebo regressions assume that the number of refugees in 2014 had arrived in 2011 and that use 2010 as the pretreatment period point to a differential time trend between provinces with a large number of refugees and those with a low number of refugees.

Using administrative data on the entirety of the firm population in Türkiye (the Entrepreneur Information System), Akgündüz and Torun (2020) investigate the impacts of refugee inflows on firm behavior and market structure. The set of firm outcomes includes sales, profits, labor costs, exports, export product variety, and export prices. In addition, they construct market structure variables, such as concentration and the total number of firms, at the sector-region level. They use the migrant supply shock across 81 provinces of Türkiye (refugee-to-native-born ratio) in a difference-in-differences estimation strategy. The control period is 2010–11, and the treatment period is 2014–15. They instrument the labor supply shock variable with the distance-based instrument defined in Aksu, Erzen, and Kırdar (2018) that accounts for the endogeneity in timing and size of the refugee shock as well as the location choice of refugees within Türkiye. They find that refugees increase firm sales in provinces where they constitute a relatively large portion of the population—a percentage point increase in the refugee-to-native-born ratio increases firm sales by 0.4 percent. These effects are concentrated in the construction and manufacturing sectors. The second set of results suggests that the number of active firms increases and the market concentration decreases in response to an increase in the refugee-to-native-born ratio in a province. The labor cost share among existing large firms in service and construction sectors decreases, which suggests switching to the cheap informal labor of refugees directly or outsourcing. Last, they find a higher probability of exporting for the firms in treatment regions. They further find that exporters increase their product variety and decrease the average price of their exports, which suggests a switch to lower-cost goods.

Cengiz and Tekgüç (2022) also investigate the change in new firm entries in response to refugee inflows to provinces. The data set comes from TOBB, and their analysis covers the 2009–15 period. They find a sizable positive effect of refugee inflows on new firm creation—a 10 percent increase in treated regions.

Impact on Prices

The impact of refugee inflows on prices is rather neglected in the literature. Among the few studies that look at the price effects, Akgündüz, Van Den Berg, and Hassink (2015), by focusing on the initial migration of refugees into camps in the bordering regions in 2012 and 2013, examine the change in food and housing prices and inflation in the hospitality sector (which is expected to be unaffected by the refugee shock because it encompasses luxury goods that vulnerable refugees would not demand) via a difference-in-differences methodology with the bordering six NUTS-2 regions as treatment regions and the remaining 20 NUTS-2 regions as control regions. Food and housing prices are regionally reported by TUIK. The study period covers 2004–13; 2012–2013 is the treatment period, and 2011 and earlier years correspond to the control period. They find a significant positive impact of refugees on housing prices in the treatment regions. However, employment is unaffected (regardless of the labor force's skill mix) by the refugee inflows. To explain this phenomenon, they look at migration patterns and find significant negative effects on entry rates to treatment regions while exit rates from those regions are unaffected by the refugees, resulting in significant decline in net migration rates. Hence, they argue that the labor supply shock to treatment regions is counteracted by the in-migration, translating to a null effect on employment rates of native-born workers.

Balkan and Tumen (2016) use a difference-in-differences strategy similar to that of Ceritoglu et al. (2017) in which they compare the changes in regional consumer price indices (CPIs) and the more than 400 items that make up the CPI in treatment regions with those in control regions before and after the Syrian refugee inflows. The treatment regions consist of the five NUTS-2 regions with a high concentration of immigrants, and the control regions consist of the four NUTS-2 regions that are in eastern Türkiye and contain no refugees. They construct 2010–11 as the preimmigration period and 2012–14 as the postimmigration period. They take settlement decisions of refugees in border regions as exogenous and driven by the conflict in Syria, which is unrelated to the economic conditions in Türkiye. The CPI data are provided by TUIK and are at the level of the 26 NUTS-2 regions. Contrary to Akgündüz, Van Den Berg, and Hassink (2015), they find a strong negative relationship between refugee inflows and prices, especially food prices. The overall prices in hosting regions declined by 2.5 percent because of refugee inflows, and food prices declined by 4.5 percent. The overall prices in hosting regions declined by 2.5 percent because of refugee inflows, and food prices declined by 4.5 percent. They further document that prices of goods and services declined by a similar amount.

Balkan and Tumen's (2016) difference-in-differences results show a strong decline in the prices of items produced in informal labor-intensive sectors in hosting regions of 4 percent, whereas the corresponding decrease in formal labor-intensive sector outputs is only a mere 0.4 percent. Therefore, they argue that the cheap labor of Syrian refugees produces cost advantages that help reduce prices in hosting regions. They argue that the controversy in price effects with Akgündüz, Van Den Berg, and Hassink (2015) is due to the more granular analysis that CPI data allow them.

Aksu, Erzen, and Kırdar (2018) also look at the change in the regional CPI that varies over 26 NUTS-2 regions between 2003 and 2015. Note that their estimation strategy accounts for the endogenous location choice of Syrian refugees and flexibly controls for differential regional time trends via inclusion of five region-by-year fixed effects. Their analysis suggests a positive effect of refugee inflows on consumer prices: a 10-percentage-point increase in the refugee-to-native-born ratio in a region is associated with an increase of 2.5 percent in prices. They postulate the increase in product prices as a channel for the increased demand in formal labor in regions with a high immigrant concentration.

Impact on Education

An important effect of the refugee inflows could be on the educational outcomes of native-born youth. Syrian refugees are younger and less educated than the native-born population (regardless of gender) and are predominantly informally employed. On the one hand, this labor channel may crowd out native-born youth into education because lowered wages in the informal sector may increase the future returns to education for native-born youth. On the other hand, adverse peer effects and crowded classrooms associated with Syrian refugee children may make it difficult for native-born children to get education.

Tumen (2018) investigates the impact of refugee inflows on high school enrollment of native-born youth ages 15–18. The data set they use is the THLFS, which includes detailed information on gender, age, enrollment status, labor market indicators, and parental background of the native-born noninstitutional population. He uses two different estimation strategies that vary by the characteristics of the refugees' migratory moves. The first is the standard difference-in-differences strategy of Ceritoglu et al. (2017), where Tumen (2018) defines the initial migration of refugees into camp areas as an exogenous migrant shock. The second method is the IV difference-in-differences strategy of Del Carpio and Wagner (2015), where Tumen instruments the location decisions of refugees with the distance-based IV and includes a distance measure between each NUTS-2 region's most populated province and the closest Syrian border that takes the value 0 before 2012 and the actual distance after 2012. The difference-in-differences and IV difference-in-differences results show that refugee inflow is associated with significant increases in high school enrollment in treatment regions. The effect, though, is completely due to increases in male high school enrollment rates. There is no effect on female high school enrollment. Male children with parents with less than a high school education seem to benefit in increasing their human capital. This effect is argued to be derived from the higher competition between refugees and native-born individuals in the low-wage, informal sector that crowds out native-born male youth. In terms of magnitude, the basic difference-in-differences strategy estimates that high school enrollment is 2.7–3.6 percentage points higher in regions with a high concentration of refugees. The IV estimates show that a 1-percentage-point increase in the refugee-to-native-born population increases high school enrollment rates by 0.4 percent. One possible drawback of Tumen's (2018) paper, though, is the handling of the 2012 national education reform, which may have affected the border regions differently because enrollment rates in southern and eastern Türkiye are traditionally lower than in the rest of Türkiye.

Çakır, Erbay, and Kırdar (2023) also examine the impact of the refugee inflow on native-born youths' (ages 15–17) employment and education outcomes. They use THLFS from 2004 to 2015, excluding 2012 data because provincial refugee numbers are not available for that year. They use an IV difference-in-differences methodology to estimate the causal effect of the refugees. The key variable of interest is the refugee-to-native-born ratio in NUTS-2 regions. The instrument is the distance-based IV of Aksu, Erzen, and Kırdar (2018). Their estimations show significant negative employment effects of refugee inflows on both boys and girls. However, refugees increase the likelihood of boys' school enrollment only. Quantitatively, a 1-percentage-point increase in the refugee-to-native-born ratio reduces boys' employment by 0.7 percentage points and increases their enrollment by 0.3 percentage points. A 1-percentage-point increase in the refugee-to-native-born ratio reduces girls' employment by about 0.5 percentage points. The informal sector completely drives the employment effects for both boys and girls. Çakır, Erbay, and Kırdar (2023) also estimate the heterogeneity in refugees' impacts by parents' education and find, in contrast to Tumen (2018), that boys' enrollment is stronger for those with more educated parents. This is in line with refugees increasing the formal employment and wages of native-born adult men (Aksu, Erzen, and Kırdar 2018; Del Carpio et al. 2016). With the increase in parental income, the marginal utility of child labor is reduced, which allows children of highly educated parents to spend more time in school. They further analyze the employment effects by looking at the change in those in neither employment nor education or training (NEET) and both study and work status of children. Every 10 refugees push three native-born boys from work to school only and an additional four from combining work and school to school only. There is no change in NEET status for boys overall. When Çakır, Erbay, and Kırdar (2023) separate the boys' sample into two on the basis of their parents' high school graduation, there is a decrease in NEET status of boys with highly educated parents. Among girls, for every 10 refugees, three girls are pushed from combining work and school to attending school only, and two are pushed from work only to NEET status. Moreover, the increase in NEET girls is due to girls with low-educated parents. In conclusion, the arrival of refugees helps boys to acquire more human capital, and the negative effects seem to concentrate on girls. An important caveat of this study is the handling of 2012 national education reform, as in Tumen (2018). Çakır, Erbay, and Kırdar's (2023) main findings rely on estimations that omit a control for the policy. Once they include a policy dummy interacted with the education category of the parent—the policy dummy takes the value 1 for children born in 1998 or after and takes the value 0 for older children—almost all of their estimates become statistically insignificant.

Tumen (2019) examines whether native-born primary school children switch to private schools as a response to the inflows of refugees to a province. He adopts the IV difference-in-differences strategy of Del Carpio and Wagner (2015) to compare the primary school enrollment rate of 5- to 14-year-old children in provinces with a high refugee-to-native-born ratio with that of those in provinces with a low refugee-to-native-born ratio before and after the arrival of Syrian refugees. He suggests that 96 percent of refugee children of primary school age (grades 1–8) are enrolled mostly in public schools. This constitutes a large demand factor, and the Turkish government acts accordingly by increasing schools, classrooms, and teachers, especially in provinces with high refugee density (Çakır, Erbay, and Kırdar 2023). Tumen (2019) finds that native-born children switch from public to private schools in response to an increase in the concentration of refugees in the province: a 10-percentage-point increase in the refugee-to-population ratio generates, on average, a 0.12-percentage-point increase in private primary school enrollment. The effect is slightly larger for boys.

Tumen (2021) looks at the impact of refugee inflows on Programme for International Student Assessment test scores of native-born adolescents, and his findings complement those of Tumen (2018), showing that refugee inflow to regions increases high school attendance of native-born youth—that is, refugee inflow has positive effects on the extensive margin. Hunt (2017) argues that there are two opposing channels through which forced migration may affect education outcomes of native-born individuals: the labor market mechanism and the educational experience mechanism. The labor market mechanism crowds native-born individuals into education as competition for low-skill jobs increases with the refugee inflows, and this puts downward pressure on wages in the low-skill labor market. Through adverse peer effects—knowledge barriers, cultural differences between native-born individuals and refugees, and so forth—the educational experience mechanism negatively affects native-born individuals' educational outcomes. Tumen (2021) makes use of the institutional setup that delays enrollment of refugee children in higher education in Türkiye until 2016 to net out the educational experience mechanism in explaining the refugee impact on native-born adolescents' test scores. He shows that math, science, and reading test scores of native-born adolescents increase after the arrival of the refugees, and the effect is more pronounced for boys than for girls. The increase in test scores comes mostly from the lower half of the test score distribution (the portion below the median) and from adolescents with low maternal education (less than high school). This implies that the refugee effect helps decrease test score inequality. Tumen (2021) concludes that, besides having positive effects on the extensive margin, refugees also benefit native-born adolescents in the intensive margin.

Aygün et al. (2024) take a different approach and investigate whether the largest unconditional cash transfer program—the Emergency Social Safety Net (ESSN), which addresses the most vulnerable refugees in Türkiye—affects the refugee children's labor inputs and educational outcomes. To answer that question, they use Comprehensive Vulnerability Monitoring Exercise surveys (numbers 3 and 4, respectively, conducted between March–August 2018 and September–December 2018). These surveys are representative of the refugee population in Türkiye and include ESSN beneficiary households, nonbeneficiary applicants, and households that did not apply to ESSN. The identifying variation comes from households that barely qualify for the ESSN benefits and those that miss by a small margin. That is, Aygün et al. (2024) use a regression discontinuity design. The eligibility criterion for a household is to have a dependency ratio of 1.5 or higher. This implies that for a household with parents of working age, at least three children, or a mix of children and elderly individuals, the ratio must sum up to at least 3.0 to benefit from ESSN cash transfers.

Some refugee households earn eligibility via other measures, and some with a dependency ratio higher than 1.5 do not benefit from ESSN. Therefore, Aygün et al. (2024) use a fuzzy regression discontinuity design approach and use the eligibility criterion as an IV for the treatment status of the household. Their results show significant large impacts of ESSN on labor and enrollment of refugee children. ESSN reduces the share of boys not in school by 64 percent, the share of girls not in school by 59 percent, the share of boys working by 86 percent, and the share of girls working by 95 percent. The effect on children ages 12–17 is larger than the effect on children ages 6–11 because the opportunity cost of schooling is larger for the former group. In terms of impact heterogeneity, the effect on child labor is more pronounced among households in the lowest consumption quintile (living in extreme poverty), and the effect on schooling is much more pronounced in the bottom two consumption quintiles. This implies that ESSN indeed benefits the most vulnerable refugee children.

Impact on Health

The impact of refugee inflows on health outcomes is still a neglected area of study in the Türkiye context. Aygün, Kırdar, and Tuncay (2021) examine, using administrative data on health care resources and mortality rates at the 81-province level, the impact of refugee inflow on native-born individuals' health outcomes. The most obvious effect of refugees is their impact on health care resources because their inflow is sudden and massive in size. Therefore, native-born people's access to health care may suffer from the refugee inflow. In addition, the previous literature on labor market impacts of refugees shows that low-skilled, native-born labor is displaced by refugees, and consumer prices increase (Akgündüz, Van Den Berg, and Hassink 2015; Aksu, Erzen, and Kırdar 2018). This channel might also negatively affect native-born adults' and their children's health conditions. Aygün, Kırdar, and Tuncay (2021) collect provincial data on the number of doctors, nurses, midwives, hospitals, hospital beds, pediatricians, and adult and neonatal intensive care beds. These outcomes constitute the dependent variables in their regressions of refugee impacts on health care resources. Their main findings show that refugee inflow causes the number of doctors, midwives, hospitals, and adult intensive care bed units per capita to worsen (per capita figures are calculated on the basis of the total population of provinces, including refugees). A 10-percentage-point increase in the refugee-to-native-born ratio decreases the number of doctors per person by 6–9 percent. This implies that the health care system cannot keep up with the preimmigration per capita resources, which, in turn, may imply an increase in mortality rates. In contrast to this evidence, Aygün, Kırdar, and Tuncay's (2021) IV difference-in-differences estimations could not find any effect on neonatal, infant, or adult mortality rates. However, the large increase in minimum wage in 2016 may contaminate their results for mortality rates. That is, the differential impact of the 2016 minimum wage hike may increase the means of native-born individuals with poor health to benefit from health care more effectively in treatment regions, which may help explain the null effects on mortality rates.

Impact on Crime

Kırdar, Lopez Cruz, and Türküm (2022) investigate the causal relationship between refugee shocks and crime rates using province-level crime rates published by TUIK—calculated as the share of incarcerated individuals in the total province population, including both native-born individuals and refugees—from 2008 to 2019. They use as a dependent variable the overall crime rate and offenses in 11 categories: assault, crimes involving firearms and knives, homicide, robbery, smuggling, theft, sexual crimes, kidnapping, defamation, use and purchase of drugs, and production of and commerce in drugs. The refugee-to-population ratio is instrumented with the distance-based cross-country IV of Aksu, Erzen, and Kırdar (2018). They find suggestive evidence for a decrease in the overall crime rate in response to the inflow of refugees. Quantitatively, the estimated effect is large: a 10-percentage-point increase in the refugee-to-population ratio decreases the crime rate by 8.1 percent. They find significant statistical evidence of a negative effect of the refugee shock on assaults, sexual crimes, kidnapping, and defamation. They show that the decrease in crime rates is not simultaneously determined with an increase in armed forces in the refugee-hosting regions. The judicial system in Türkiye is slow; a crime committed in a given year may not result in a conviction until a year or two later. Such a mechanism may put a downward bias in the refugee impacts if refugees' propensity to commit crime is higher than that of native-born individuals (the opposite of what the paper suggests).

The Kayaoglu, Şahin-Mencütek, and Erdoğan (2022) study is yet another that investigates the refugee shock–crime relationship. Kayaoglu, Şahin-Mencütek, and Erdoğan (2022) differ from Kırdar, Lopez Cruz, and Türküm (2022) by focusing on a different measure of crime rate and using three different estimation techniques to arrive at a robust conclusion about the direction of the relationship. Kayaoglu, Şahin-Mencütek, and Erdoğan (2022) use a number of new cases opened each year at the Basic and High Criminal Courts obtained from the Ministry of Justice. High Criminal Court cases include crimes such as homicide, rape, robbery, swindling, production and trading of drugs, embezzlement, and bribery that have the potential to invite a prison punishment of more than 10 years. Basic Criminal Court cases, however, are related to assault, kidnapping, defamation, theft, use and purchase of drugs, forgery, maltreatment, smuggling, traffic crimes, forestry crimes, crimes related to firearms and knives, threat, property damage, and so on. They are usually the cases for which convictions carry a sentence of less than 10 years in prison. These court cases proxy the total number of any reported crimes in each year in each province. The dependent variable is the crime rate, which is normalized by the total population of the province (migrant and native born). The key variable of interest is a treatment dummy (a province is considered a refugee-dense province if the share of refugees in the total population is 1 percent or higher) or treatment intensity, which is defined as the share of refugees in the total population of the province, as in Kırdar, Lopez Cruz, and Türküm (2022). Kayaoglu, Şahin-Mencütek, and Erdoğan (2022) estimate both the short-term effects using data from 2009 to 2014 and the long-term effects using data from 2009 to 2017. A standard difference-in-differences methodology is used to estimate the short-term effects, and the longer-term effects are estimated using staggered difference-in-differences and IV difference-in-differences methodologies. The staggered difference-in-differences methodology is appropriate in this context because the density of refugees across provinces increases over time, which switches the treatment status of different provinces in different years from control to treatment (recall that treated provinces are defined as those with a refugee-to-population ratio of 1 percent or higher). The IV approach is similar to that in Del Carpio et al. (2016). The difference-in-differences analyses yield a null effect of refugees on crimes per capita. However, the IV estimates find a negative effect on crime per capita. When the dependent variable is defined as crime per native-born resident, then the negative IV estimates vanish. Therefore, it is reasonable to argue like Kırdar, Lopez Cruz, and Türküm (2022) that refugees' propensity to commit crime is lower than those who are native born.

Notes

1. Although this difference in registered data may reflect a selection and composition issue, meaning that Sweden has a higher proportion of refugees who arrive with higher education levels, it could also be that Sweden has better systems for assessing and validating foreign education levels at an early stage in the integration process.
2. Law No. 6458 of 2013, Article 91 (Türkiye 2013).
3. This principle guarantees that no asylum seeker should be returned to a country where they would be at danger of persecution on the basis of race, religion, nationality, membership in a particular social group, or political opinion.
4. Article 37(1) of TPR, which was amended in 2018, provides authorization to the DGMM to build, and the Law on Foreigners and International Protection provides details on the financing schemes to be steered by the DGMM.

5. For instance, between 2019 and 2022, close to 23,000 Syrian refugees were supported with employment services by the Turkish Employment Agency (ISKUR); by contrast, at that time, only about 5,900 of them had obtained work permits and were formally working.

6. In a survey conducted among Syrian refugees who were beneficiaries of ISKUR active labor market policies in December 2021, about 66 percent of respondents reported being employed and earning an income, and 35 percent reported having a formal work contract.

7. The program is financed by the EU Directorate-General for European Civil Protection and Humanitarian Aid Operations and implemented in partnership with the International Federation of Red Cross and Red Crescent Societies, the Turkish Red Crescent, and the government.

8. See European Commission, ECHO (2022).

9. For information on the Skills Profile Tool, see https://ec.europa.eu/migrantskills/#/.

10. Such relocation programs, designed to reduce the concentration of asylum seekers and refugees in destination areas and share the costs of reception and hospitality across the national territory, are referred to as *dispersal policies*. The first dispersal programs were introduced during the 1980s and early 1990s to manage refugee flows from Eastern Europe and the Balkans. These interventions were reinforced and upgraded across Europe in response to the Syrian refugee crisis of 2014–17.

References

Abadie, A., and J. Gardeazabal. 2003. "The Economic Costs of Conflict: A Case Study of the Basque Country." *American Economic Review* 93 (1): 113–32.

Acemoglu, D., and D. Autor. 2011. "Skills, Tasks and Technologies: Implications for Employment and Earnings." In *Handbook of Labor Economics*, Vol. 4, Part B, edited by D. Card and O. Ashenfelter, 1043–171. Amsterdam: Elsevier.

Akgündüz, Y. E., K. Bağır, S. M. Cılasun, and M.G. Kırdar. 2023. "Consequences of a Massive Refugee Influx on Firm Performance and Market Structure." *Journal of Development Economics* 162: 103081.

Akgündüz, Y. E., and H. Torun. 2020. "Two and a Half Million Syrian Refugees, Tasks and Capital Intensity." *Journal of Development Economics* 145: 102470.

Akgündüz, Y. E., M. Van Den Berg, and W. H. Hassink. 2015. "The Impact of Refugee Crises on Host Labor Markets: The Case of the Syrian Refugee Crisis in Turkey." Discussion Paper No. 8841, Institute for the Study of Labor, Bonn.

Aksu, E., R. Erzan, and M. G. Kırdar. 2022. "The Impact of Mass Migration of Syrians on the Turkish Labor Market." *Labour Economics* 76: 102183.

Altındağ, O., O. Bakış, and S. V. Rozo. 2020. "Blessing or Burden? Impacts of Refugees on Businesses and the Informal Economy." *Journal of Development Economics* 146: 102490.

Andersson, R. 1998. "Socio-Spatial Dynamics: Ethnic Divisions of Mobility and Housing in Post-Palme Sweden." *Urban Studies* 35 (3): 397–428. https://doi.org/10.1080/0042098984835.

ANOFM (Agenţia Naţională pentru Ocuparea Forţei de Muncă). 2023. "The Employment Situation of Ukrainian Citizens on the Labor Market" [in Romanian]. Bucharest: ANOFM. https://www.anofm.ro/.

Aracı, D., M. Demirci, and M. G. Kırdar. 2022. "Development Level of Hosting Areas and the Impact of Refugees on Natives' Labor Market Outcomes in Turkey." *European Economic Review* 145: 104132.

Arendt, J. N., C. Dustmann, and H. Ku. 2022. "Refugee Migration and the Labour Market: Lessons from 40 Years of Post-Arrival Policies in Denmark." *Oxford Review of Economic Policy* 38 (3): 531–56.

Åslund, O., and P. Johansson. 2011. "Virtues of SIN: Can Intensified Public Efforts Help Disadvantaged Immigrants?" *Evaluation Review* 35 (4): 399–427.

Åslund, O., L. Liljeberg, and S. Roman. 2023. "The Long-Term Social Integration of Refugees: Swedish Experiences after the Yugoslav Wars." Working Paper No. 2023: 16, Institute for Evaluation of Labour Market Education Policy, Uppsala, Sweden.

Aumayr-Pintar, C., and M. Cantero Guerrero. 2022. "Policies to Support Refugees from Ukraine." Eurofound. https://www.eurofound.europa.eu/en/resources/article/2022/policies-support-refugees-ukraine.

Aygün, A. H., M. G. Kırdar, M. Koyuncu, and Q. Stoeffler. 2024. "Keeping Refugee Children in School and Out of Work: Evidence from the World's Largest Humanitarian Cash Transfer Program." *Journal of Development Economics* 168: 103266. https://doi.org/10.1016/j.jdeveco.2024.103266.

Aygün, A., M. G. Kırdar, and B. Tuncay. 2021. "The Effect of Hosting 3.4 Million Refugees on Native Population Mortality." *Journal of Health Economics* 80: 102534.

Bağır, Y. K. 2018. "Impact of the Syrian Refugee Influx on Turkish Native Workers: An Ethnic Enclave Approach." *Central Bank Review* 18 (4): 129–47.

Bahar, D., R. J. Brough, and G. Peri. 2024. "Forced Migration and Refugees: Policies for Successful Economic and Social Integration." Working Paper No. 32266, National Bureau of Economic Research, Cambridge, MA.

Balkan, B., and S. Tumen. 2016. "Immigration and Prices: Quasi-Experimental Evidence from Syrian Refugees in Turkey." *Journal of Population Economics* 29: 657–86.

BAMF (Federal Office for Migration and Refugees). 2019. *Das Bundesamt in Zahlen 2019* [The Federal Office in Figures 2019]. Nuremberg: BAMF. https://www.bamf.de/SharedDocs/Anlagen/DE/Statistik /BundesamtinZahlen/bundesamt-in-zahlen-2019.html?nn=284738.

BAMF (Federal Office for Migration and Refugees). 2020. *Das Bundesamt in Zahlen 2020* [*The Federal Office in Figures 2020*]. Nuremberg: BAMF. https://www.bamf.de/SharedDocs/Anlagen/DE/Statistik /BundesamtinZahlen/bundesamt-in-zahlen-2020.html?nn=284738.

Bansak, K., J. Ferwerda, J. Hainmueller, A. Dillon, D. Hangartner, D. Lawrence, and J. Weinstein. 2018. "Improving Refugee Integration through Data-Driven Algorithmic Assignment." *Science* 359 (6373): 325–9. https://doi .org/10.1126/science.aao4408.

Barslund, M., and M. Busse. 2016. "Labour Mobility in the EU: Addressing Challenges and Ensuring 'Fair Mobility'." Special Report No. 139, Centre for European Policy Studies, Brussels.

Battisti, M., Y. Giesing, and N. Laurentsyeva. 2019. "Can Job Search Assistance Improve the Labour Market Integration of Refugees? Evidence from a Field Experiment." *Labour Economics* 61: 101745.

Bevelander, P., and R. Pendakur. 2014. "The Labour Market Integration of Refugee and Family Reunion Immigrants: A Comparison of Outcomes in Canada and Sweden." *Journal of Ethnic and Migration Studies* 40 (5): 689–709.

BQ Portal. 2024. "About the Portal." https://www.bq-portal.de/en/About-the-portal.

Brücker, H., P. Jaschke, and Y. Kosyakova. 2019. *Integrating Refugees and Asylum Seekers into the German Economy and Society: Empirical Evidence and Policy Objectives*. Washington DC: Migration Policy Institute.

Brücker, H., Y. Kosyakova, and E. Vallizadeh. 2020. "Has There Been a 'Refugee Crisis'?" *Soziale Welt* 71 (1–2): 24–53.

Çakır, S., E. Erbay, and M. G. Kırdar. 2023. "Syrian Refugees and Human Capital Accumulation of Working-Age Native Children in Turkey." *Journal of Human Capital* 17 (4): 557–92.

Calmfors, L., N. Sánchez-Gassen, T. Pekkarinen, A. Böhlmark, P. A. Joona, V. Jakobsen, T. Tranaes, B. Bratsberg, O. Raaum, K. Røed. J. N. Arendt, M. L. Schultz-Nielsen. S. Ek, and P. Skedinger. 2019. *Integrating Immigrants into the Nordic Labour Markets*. Stockholm: Nordregio. https://nordregio.org/publications/integrating -immigrants-into-the-nordic-labour-markets/.

Campo, F., S. Giunti, and M. Mendola. 2024. "Refugee Crisis and Right-Wing Populism: Evidence from the Italian Dispersal Policy." *European Economic Review* 168: 104826. https://doi.org/10.1016/j.euroecorev.2024.104826.

Cengiz, D., and H. Tekgüç. 2022. "Is It Merely a Labor Supply Shock? Impacts of Syrian Migrants on Local Economies in Turkey." *ILR Review* 75 (3): 741–68.

Ceritoglu, E., H. B. G. Yunculer, H. Torun, and S. Tumen. 2017. "The Impact of Syrian Refugees on Natives' Labor Market Outcomes in Turkey: Evidence from a Quasi-Experimental Design." *IZA Journal of Labor Policy* 6: 1–28.

Council of Europe. n.d. "European Qualifications Passport for Refugees." Strasbourg: Council of Europe. https:// www.coe.int/en/web/education/recognition-of-refugees-qualifications.

Council of the European Community. Council Directive 2004/83/EC, of 29 April 2004. "On Minimum Standards for the Qualification and Status of Third Country Nationals or Stateless Persons as Refugees or as Persons Who Otherwise Need International Protection and the Content of the Protection Granted." *Official Journal L* 304, 30.9.2004, 12–23.

Council of the European Union. Council Directive 2011/95/EU, of 13 December 2011. "On Standards for the Qualification of Third-Country Nationals or Stateless Persons as Beneficiaries of International Protection, for a Uniform Status for Refugees or for Persons Eligible for Subsidiary Protection, and for the Content of the Protection Granted (recast)." Official Journal L 337, 20.12.2011, 9–26.

Del Carpio, X. V., C. Ozden, M. Testaverde, and M. Wagner. 2016. "Global Migration of Talent and Tax Incentives: Evidence from Malaysia's Returning Expert Program." Policy Research Working Paper No. 7875, World Bank, Washington, DC.

Del Carpio, X. V., and M. C. Wagner. 2015. "The Impact of Syrian Refugees on the Turkish Labor Market." Policy Research Working Paper No. 7402, World Bank, Washington, DC.

Del Monte, M., and A. Orav. 2023. *Solidarity in EU Asylum Policy.* Brussels: European Parliamentary Research Service.

Edin, P. A., P. Fredriksson, and O. Åslund. 2003. "Ethnic Enclaves and the Economic Success of Immigrants—Evidence from a Natural Experiment." *Quarterly Journal of Economics* 118 (1): 329–57.

Eurofound. n.d. "EU Policy Watch Database of National-Level Policy Measures: War in Ukraine." https://static.eurofound.europa.eu/covid19db/ukraine.html.

Eurofound and the European Union Agency for Fundamental Rights. 2023. "Barriers to Employment of Displaced Ukrainians." Eurofound research paper, Publications Office of the European Union, Luxembourg.

European Commission. n.d. "Common European Asylum System." Migration and Home Affairs. https://home-affairs.ec.europa.eu/policies/migration-and-asylum/common-european-asylum-system_en.

European Commission, EACEA (European Education and Culture Executive Agency), and Eurydice. 2022. *Supporting Refugee Learners from Ukraine in Schools in Europe.* Eurydice Report. Luxembourg: European Union. https://op.europa.eu/en/publication-detail/-/publication/51d16f1b-0c8f-11ed-b11c-01aa75ed71a1/language-en/format-PDF/source-262591763.

European Commission, ECHO (Directorate-General for European Civil Protection and Humanitarian Aid Operations). 2022. "Launch of Ambitious Partnership between IFRC and EU: A New Model for the Humanitarian Sector." News article, March 30, 2022. https://civil-protection-humanitarian-aid.ec.europa.eu/news-stories/news/launch-ambitious-partnership-between-ifrc-and-eu-new-model-humanitarian-sector-2022-03-30_en.

Foged, M., L. Hasager, and G. Peri. 2024. "Comparing the Effects of Policies for the Labor Market Integration of Refugees." *Journal of Labor Economics* 42 (S1): S335–77. https://doi.org/10.1086/728806.

Gentilini, U., M. B. A. Almenfi, H. T. M. M. Iyengar, Y. Okamura, E. R. Urteaga, G. Valleriani, J. Vulembera Muhindo, and S. Aziz. 2022. "Tracking Social Protection Responses to Displacement in Ukraine and Other Countries." Social Protection and Jobs Discussion Paper No. 2209, World Bank, Washington, DC. http://documents.worldbank.org/curated/en/099120006272232396/P1765850ac0a510f8087ab06e08c1cc016e.

Gromadzki, J., and P. Lewandowski. 2022. "Refugees from Ukraine on the Polish Labour Market." *Ubezpieczenia Społeczne. Teorla i praktyka,* 155 (4): 29–40. https://doi.org/10.5604/01.3001.0016.2353.

Hernes, V., and K. R. Tronstad. 2014. *Komparativ Analyse av Introduksjonsprogram i Norge, Sverige og Danmark.* Oslo: Norsk Institutt for by- og regionsorskning.

Hunt, J. 2017. "The Impact of Immigration on the Educational Attainment of Natives. *Journal of Human Resources* 52 (4): 1060–118.

ILO (International Labour Organization). n.d. *ILO's Support to Refugees and Host Communities in Turkey.* Geneva: ILO. https://www.ilo.org/projects-and-partnerships/projects/ilos-support-refugees-and-host-communities-turkey.

Ineli-Ciger, M. 2014. "Implications of the New Turkish Law on Foreigners and International Protection and Regulation No. 29153 on Temporary Protection for Syrians Seeking Protection in Turkey." *Oxford Monitor of Forced Displacement* 4 (2): 28. https://research-information.bris.ac.uk/en/publications/implications-of-the-new-turkish-law-on-foreigners-and-internation.

INFO GmbH. 2022. "Geflüchtete aus der Ukraine" ("Refugees from Ukraine"). Federal Ministry of the Interior and Home Affairs. https://www.bmi.bund.de/SharedDocs/downloads/DE/veroeffentlichungen /nachrichten/2022/umfrage-ukraine-fluechtlinge.pdf.

Joona, P. A., and L. Nekby. 2012. "Intensive Coaching of New Immigrants: An Evaluation Based on Random Program Assignment." *Scandinavian Journal of Economics* 114 (2): 575–600.

Kayaoglu, A., Z. Şahin-Mencütek, and M. M. Erdoğan. 2022. "Return Aspirations of Syrian Refugees in Turkey." *Journal of Immigrant & Refugee Studies* 20 (4): 561–83.

Kırdar, M. G., I. Lopez Cruz, and B. Türküm. 2022. "The Effect of 3.6 Million Refugees on Crime." *Journal of Economic Behavior & Organization*, 194: 568-582.

KIZILAYKART Programmes. 2022. "Monthly C-ESSN Project Infographics." https://platform.kizilaykart.org/en /Doc/rapor/C-ESSN_Infografik_March_2022_ENG.pdf.

Ministry of Health. 2014. *Gecici Koruma Altina Alinanlara verilecek Saglik Hizmetlerine Dair Esaslar Hakkinda Yonerge* [Fundamentals of Health Services to Be Delivered to Syrians under Temporary Protection]. Ankara: Ministry of Health, Government of Turkey. https://dosyasb.saglik.gov.tr/Eklenti/1376/0/saglik -bakanligi-gecici-koruma-yonergesi-25032015pdf.pdf?_tag1=284EBE67BBC860BBD5B18C4F81083 BD757AFFAB8.

OECD (Organisation for Economic Co-operation and Development). 2022. *The Potential Contribution of Ukrainian Refugees to the Labour Force in European Host Countries*. Paris: OECD. https://www.oecd.org /ukraine-hub/policy-responses/the-potential-contribution-of-ukrainian-refugees-to-the-labour-force-in -european-host-countries-e88a6a55/.

OECD (Organisation for Economic Co-operation and Development). 2023. *What We Know about the Skills and Early Labour Market Outcomes of Refugees from Ukraine*. Paris: OECD. https://www.oecd.org/ukraine-hub /policy-responses/what-we-know-about-the-skills-and-early-labour-market-outcomes-of -refugees-from-ukraine-c7e694aa/.

Özçürümez, S., and A. İçduygu. 2022. *Zorunlu Göç Deneyimi ve Toplumsal Bütünleşme: Kavramlar, Modeller ve Uygulamalar ile Türkiye*. Istanbul: İstanbul Bilgi Üniversitesi Yayınları.

Panchenko, T., and P. Poutvaara. 2022. "Intentions to Stay and Employment Prospects of Refugees from Ukraine." *EconPol Policy Brief* 6 (46). https://www.econpol.eu/publications/policy_brief_46.

Pavilon, J. 2021. "Immigration to Germany 2000–19." Background paper, World Bank, Washington, DC.

Pędziwiatr, K., J. Brzozowski, and O. Nahorniuk. 2022. *Refugees from Ukraine in Kraków*. Krakow: Krakow University of Economics, Centre for Advanced Studies of Population and Religion.

Poland. 2022. "Act of 2022: Law on Assistance to Citizens of Ukraine in Connection with Armed Conflict on the Territory of that Country," 12 March 2022. Warsaw: Government of Poland. https://www.gov.pl/web /udsc-en/the-law-on-assistance-to-ukrainian-citizens-in-connection-with-the-armed-conflict -on-the-territory-of-the-country-has-entered-into-force.

Romania. 2022. Emergency Ordinance No. 15/27 of 2022 Regarding the Provision of Humanitarian Support and Assistance by the Romanian State to Foreign Citizens or Stateless Persons in Special Situations, Coming from the Area of the Armed Conflict in Ukraine, 27 February 2022. https://legislatie.just.ro/Public /DetaliiDocumentAfis/251954.

Svantesson, E., and T. Aranki. 2006. "Do Introduction Programmes Affect the Probability of Immigrants Getting Work?" Working Paper No. 3/2006, Örebros Universitet, Örebro, Sweden. https://hdl.handle.net /10419/244422.

Tjaden, J., and T. Heidland. forthcoming. "Did Merkel's 2015 Decision Attract More Migration to Germany?" *European Journal of Political Research*. https://doi.org/10.1111/1475-6765.12669.

TOBB (Union of Chambers and Commodity Exchanges of Turkey). n.d. Company Establishment and Liquidation Statistics. Ankara: TOBB. https://www.tobb.org.tr/BilgiErisimMudurlugu/Sayfalar/Eng/KurulanKapanan Sirketistatistikleri.php.

Tsourdi, L., and C. Costello. 2021. "The Evolution of EU Law on Refugees and Asylum." In *The Evolution of EU Law* (3rd ed.), edited by P. Craig and G. de Búrca, 793–823. Oxford University Press. https://doi.org/10.1093 /oso/9780192846556.003.0025.

Tumen, S. 2018. "The Impact of Low-Skill Refugees on Youth Education." Discussion Paper No 11869, Institute of Labor Economics, Bonn. https://papers.ssrn.com/sol3/papers.cfm?abstract_id=3273708.

Tumen, S. 2019. "Refugees and 'Native Flight' from Public to Private Schools." *Economics Letters* 181: 154–59.

Tumen, S. 2021. "The Effect of Refugees on Native Adolescents & Apos; Test Scores: Quasi-Experimental Evidence from PISA." Discussion Paper No. 14039, Institute of Labor Economics, Bonn. https://docs.iza.org/dp14039.pdf.

Türkiye. 2013. Law No. 6458 of 2013, Law on Foreigners and International Protection [Amended], 4 April 2013. https://www.unhcr.org/tr/wp-content/uploads/sites/14/2017/04/LoFIP_ENG_DGMM_revised-2017.pdf.

Türkiye, Ministry of Interior, Presidency of Migration Management. n.d. "About Us." Accessed March 16, 2022. https://en.goc.gov.tr/.

Türkiye, Ministry of Interior, Presidency of Migration Management. 2024. "Distribution of Syrians under Temporary Protection by Year." https://en.goc.gov.tr/temporary-protection27.

UDA Consulting. 2022. "Türkiye Employment Support Program Assessment." Conducted as part of implementation support for the World Bank/EU-financed project.

UNHCR (United Nations High Commissioner for Refugees). 2020. *Refugee Population Statistics Database.* Geneva: UNHCR. https://www.unhcr.org/refugee-statistics/.

UNHCR (United Nations High Commissioner for Refugees). 2022a. *Lives on Hold: Profiles and Intentions of Refugees from Ukraine—Czech Republic, Hungary, Republic of Moldova, Poland, Romania & Slovakia.* Geneva: UNHCR.

UNHCR (United Nations High Commissioner for Refugees). 2022b. *Rapid Survey of the 50-20 Programme: UNHCR Romania Thematic Report.* Geneva: UNHCR. https://data.unhcr.org/en/documents/details/97974.

UNHCR (United Nations High Commissioner for Refugees). 2022c. *Ukraine Situation: Regional Protection Profiling and Monitoring Factsheet.* Geneva: UNHCR. https://data.unhcr.org/en/documents/details/97720.

UNHCR (United Nations High Commissioner for Refugees). 2022–23. *Flash Updates 1–39, March 2022–January 2023.* Geneva: UNHCR.

UNHCR (United Nations High Commissioner for Refugees). 2024. "Education of Refugee Children and Youth from Ukraine: An Analysis of Major Challenges and Trends Based on Multi-Sector Needs Assessment (MSNA) and Other Data." UNHCR, Geneva. https://migrant-integration.ec.europa.eu/system/files/2024-07/UNHCR%20Education%20of%20refugee%20children%20and%20youth%20from%20Ukraine%202024.pdf.

Verme, P., and K. Schuettler. 2021. "The Impact of Forced Displacement on Host Communities: A Review of the Empirical Literature in Economics." *Journal of Development Economics,* 150: 102606. https://doi.org/10.1016/j.jdeveco.2020.102606.

WFP (World Food Programme). 2017. *The Emergency Social Safety Net (ESSN): Helping Refugees in Turkey.* Rome: WFP. https://data2.unhcr.org/en/documents/download/62207.

World Bank. 2023. *World Development Report 2023: Migrants, Refugees, Societies.* Washington, DC: World Bank.

Zymnin, A., M. Kowalski, A. Karasińska, O. Lytvynenko, E. Dąbrowska, S. Bryzek, P. Gliński, and D. Koszykowska. 2022. "Uchodźcy z Ukrainy w Polsce" ("Refugees from Ukraine in Poland"). Special Report. EWL Migration Platform, the Foundation for the Support of Migrants in the Labor Market, and the Centre for East European Studies, University of Warsaw, Poland. https://migrant-integration.ec.europa.eu/library-document/special-report-refugees-ukraine-poland_en.

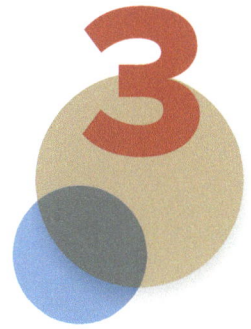

Toward Greater Gains from Economic Migration in Destination Countries

Chapter Highlights

- Migration is associated with overall net economic gains in receiving countries.

- Since the mid-1990s, immigration has significantly contributed to increases in the working-age population in high-income countries in Western Europe.

- In Western Europe, migrants supported employment in all economic sectors, and increasingly over time, particularly in manufacturing and health and social care.

- Despite overall economic gains, immigration can also involve socioeconomic costs, which can be actual or perceived.

- The aggregate impact of immigration on native-born workers' employment levels and wages has been mixed, ranging from moderately negative to moderately positive.

- Labor market impacts on native-born workers are heterogenous; although some skills groups benefit from immigration, others can be negatively affected, depending on immigrants' skills and educational attainment.

- In most Western European countries, the fiscal impact of immigration is neutral or marginally positive; positive effects tend to be larger in the case of high-skilled migration.

- The overall impacts of immigration on access and quality of the education and health care systems are mixed; native-born workers from lower socioeconomic backgrounds are more likely to experience small adverse effects, especially if resources are not adjusted in response to immigration.

- Overall perceptions of the impacts of immigration are more negative in ECA than in other regions, with some heterogeneity depending on the native-born and immigrant populations considered.

- Emerging evidence for Western Europe suggests that the potential negative impacts of immigration on crime are mostly perceived, rather than factual.

- The gap in labor market outcomes between native-born and immigrant workers in ECA remain substantial, especially for non–European Union (EU) migrants.

- The main reason why immigrants are disproportionately concentrated in the bottom part of the income distribution is the type of occupations in which they are employed.

- As highlighted by the COVID-19 pandemic, migrant workers are more exposed to employment shocks but are also less protected by social protection systems in the event of negative shocks.

- By taking up more risky and lower-level jobs, migrant workers may also protect native-born workers against negative employment shocks, as evidenced during the COVID-19 pandemic.

Key Policy Recommendations

- For countries in the region, especially those experiencing labor shortages due to high emigration rates, fast aging, or population decline, immigration can be a key policy tool not only to sustain population growth but also to spur economic activity.

- Both the real and the perceived costs of immigration are important to manage and mitigate to ensure that no population groups are disadvantaged and to increase the political buy-in.

- Integration policies, coupled with interventions addressing misinformation and raising awareness of migrants' contributions, can help improve outcomes and reduce negative perceptions of immigration.

- Policies and programs ensuring that migrants bring or acquire skills needed by destination countries are essential to enhancing economic gains and reducing potential costs.

- Investing in migrants' language training, recognition of foreign credentials, and ensuring access to formal employment can foster integration and contribute to greater economic gains for destination countries.

- Closing gaps in de jure and de facto access to basic social protection benefits and services between native-born individuals and migrants can further support integration.

- Labor market and social protection policies can help mitigate the potential adverse impacts of immigration on some groups.

- Building responsive, resilient, adaptive, and effective migration management systems in host countries can help mitigate the impacts of negative shocks on the welfare of both migrants and host communities.

Introduction

The impacts of immigration have been at the center of the policy debate in many countries in Europe and Central Asia (ECA). Despite the long-standing history of migration to ECA countries, immigration continues to be one of the topics subject to the most intense policy debates in many countries in the region. Its perceived impacts, which do not always align with the actual impacts, have shaped the political landscape in receiving countries. The public debate on immigration in Europe has often been fueled by beliefs and ideology rather than by facts. This often prevents an informed discussion of the costs and benefits of workers' cross-border mobility for destination countries and on suitable policy options to tackle them.

This chapter aims to inform an evidence-based debate on the benefits and costs of immigration and on the policies that can help shape successful migration. As shown in this chapter, the benefits and costs of immigration for destination countries are diverse, complex, and heterogeneous. The economic impacts include effects on growth, productivity, human capital, labor markets, and public finances. Beyond economic impacts, immigration has potential effects on other dimensions, such as education and health or social cohesion, which are partly shaped by perceptions of immigration among the native-born population. They are also highly heterogeneous, depending on the composition of the migrant population, native-born individuals' skill groups, and destination country context. It is therefore crucial to consider these multiple dimensions and heterogeneity when assessing the contribution of immigration to overall welfare in destination countries.

As the chapter shows, immigration generates overall net economic gains for destination countries by contributing to gross domestic product (GDP) per capita growth and native-born individuals' welfare. These positive impacts mainly take place through increased productivity and human capital, especially when migrant workers help fill labor shortages and hold skills complementary to those of the native-born population. In contrast with what is sometimes believed, the chapter also reports that the net fiscal contribution of immigrants has been positive in most European countries, and even more so when the migrant population is highly skilled. However, the chapter highlights that immigration can also generate costs. Some of them are factual, and others are mostly perceived by the native-born population and may not reflect actual impacts. Regardless, it is important to manage and mitigate these costs to ensure that no population groups are disadvantaged and no grievances are built up, enhancing the political buy-in.

The impacts of immigration, however, are heterogeneous, with benefits and costs varying across native-born population groups. Overall impacts mask important disparities in the effects of immigration. As the chapter shows, immigration can have redistributive effects and generate winners and losers among the native-born population, especially if the right policies are not in place. The chapter shows that both the skill composition of the migrant population and that of the native-born population are crucial in shaping its impacts. Specifically, native-born workers with skills that complement those of the migrant population have been shown to benefit the most from immigration in the labor market. In contrast, those with skills that are similar to those of migrants tend to benefit less. They can even be adversely affected, at least in the short run. Beyond the labor market, the overall effects of immigration on the educational and health care systems are mixed, although native-born workers from lower socioeconomic backgrounds seem more likely to be adversely affected if public resources are not adjusted in response to immigration.

The chapter also assesses the trajectory of migrants themselves by analyzing their degree of integration and socioeconomic outcomes over time in destination countries. Another key indicator of successful migration is the socioeconomic integration of migrant workers, particularly their labor market outcomes, because greater integration benefits both migrants and destination countries. The chapter examines the current state of migrants' integration in ECA destination countries. It finds that immigrants are overall lagging behind native-born workers in terms of both employment rates and wages and that these differences are largely explained by the type of occupations migrants take up rather than by systematic differences in immigrants' characteristics compared with native-born individuals. Here again, there is significant heterogeneity among the migrant population, because migrants from EU countries exhibit much more favorable employment outcomes compared with migrants from other regions. In addition to having poorer employment outcomes overall, migrant workers are more exposed to negative shocks, as evidenced by the COVID-19 pandemic. Furthermore, their access to services and programs to cope with these shocks is still limited.

The remainder of the chapter is organized as follows. The "Benefits and Costs of Migration for Receiving Countries" section examines the costs and benefits of immigration for destination countries along various dimensions, including the broader economy, the labor market, and beyond. It looks at both average impacts and heterogeneous effects, depending on the skill content of both immigrants and the native-born population considered. The "Migrants' Labor Market Integration in Destination Countries" section assesses migrants' current socioeconomic integration in destination countries and its drivers, primarily with respect to their labor market outcomes. The "Vulnerability of Migrants to Shocks and Access to Social Protection Systems in Destination Countries" section discusses the vulnerability of migrants to negative economic shocks and their access to services to mitigate the impacts of these shocks. The "Policy Recommendations" section discusses policies that can be implemented to enhance the gains and reduce the costs of migration for destination countries and migrants.

Benefits and Costs of Economic Migration for Receiving Countries

Aggregate Economic Impacts

Migration is associated with overall net economic gains in most receiving countries. Most empirical studies on immigration and economic growth in European receiving countries reveal a positive relationship. Results vary by approach, methodology, period considered, and sample of countries analyzed (Rutledge and Kane 2018). In general, in cross-country Organisation for Economic Co-operation and Development (OECD) studies, immigration has been found to boost growth in receiving countries (Aleksynska and Tritah 2015; Alesina, Harnoss, and Rapoport 2016; Boubtane, Dumont, and Rault 2016; Felbermayr, Hiller, and Sala 2010; Jaumotte, Koloskova, and Saxena 2016). Furthermore, additional studies show that high-skilled immigration improves growth in destination countries relatively more (Borjas 2019; Dolado, Goria, and Ichino 1994). A few studies of OECD countries find that immigration lowers GDP per capita in destination countries (Dolado, Goria, and Ichino 1994; Orefice 2010). However, these latter studies find that the negative effects on GDP per capita depend on the skill content of immigration: they mostly occur with low-skilled immigration while the effect is positive in the case of high-skilled immigration.

The empirical findings of studies on individual EU countries are in line with the international evidence that immigration boosts growth. Data from 1973 to 2009 show that immigration in the Netherlands reduces labor market challenges due to aging in the long run if migrants participate in the workforce at least as much as native-born individuals (Muysken and Ziesemer 2011). As in cross-country research, immigrants' growth contributions increase with education. In France, estimations using monthly data from 1994 to 2008 and measuring immigration by long-term residency permit issuance conclude that immigration, especially family immigration, enhanced France's GDP per capita (d'Albis, Boubtane, and Coulibaly 2015).

High-skilled immigration can support economic growth through higher labor inputs, capital accumulation, and productivity. Although cross-country macro-level studies reveal no or negative effects of immigration on productivity in destination countries (Ortega and Peri 2009, 2014), most single-country studies using firm-level data indicate positive benefits on firm productivity in, for example, France (Mitaritonna, Orefice, and Peri 2017) and the United Kingdom (Ottaviano, Peri, and Wright 2018) but no effect in Germany (Trax, Brunow, and Suedekum 2015). The effect of migration on productivity is stronger among high-skilled migrants, who have been demonstrated to encourage a country to adopt new technology

(Chander and Thangavelu 2004). A marginal increase in skilled human capital due to immigration boosts productivity growth the closer a country is to the technological frontier (Lodigiani 2008; Vandenbussche, Aghion, and Meghir 2006). Finally, the empirical evidence also shows that immigration increases innovation, as assessed by patents (Hunt and Gauthier-Loiselle 2010; Terry et al. 2020), and that high-educated immigrants increase capital accumulation (Ortega and Peri 2009).

Since the mid-1990s, immigration has significantly contributed to population expansion in EU-15 countries. From 1995 to 2017, the cumulative population growth in the EU-15 was 9.6 percent. This is lower than rates in most other developed nations, including Australia (36 percent), New Zealand (30 percent), Canada (25 percent), the United States (22 percent), and the Republic of Korea (14 percent). Nearly 80 percent of the growth was attributable to net migration inflows (refer to figure 3.1, panel a), providing a vital lift to an otherwise stagnant natural growth rate.

Although immigration helps rebalance the demographic structure in rapidly aging societies, significant changes would require much larger migration inflows than those observed over the past three decades. Migrants are disproportionately of working age, given that economic opportunity is their primary motivation for migration. In high-income EU destination countries with dwindling populations, migrants contribute to the growth and share of the

FIGURE 3.1

Contribution of migration to population growth in the EU-15

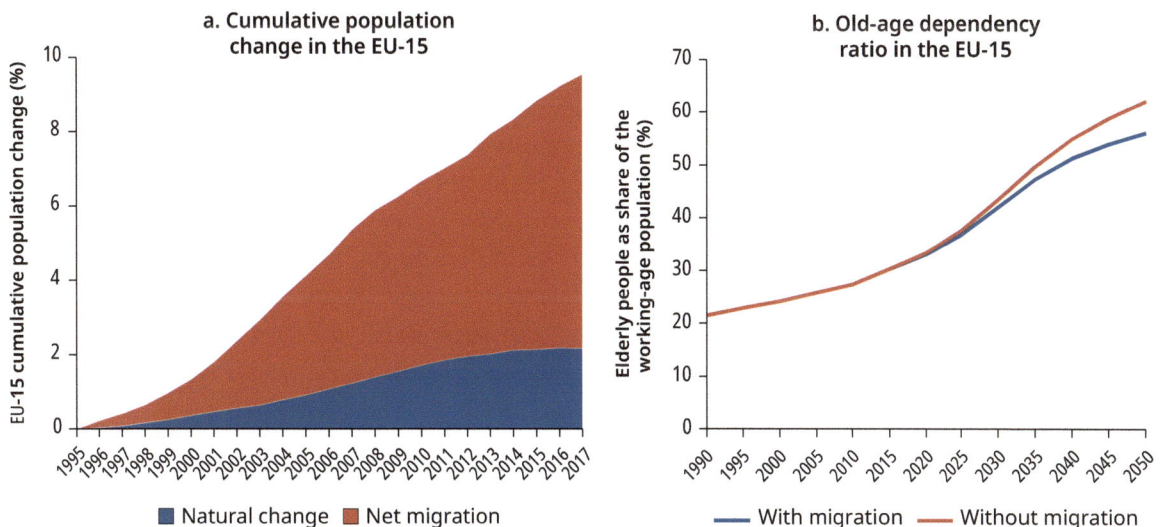

a. Cumulative population change in the EU-15

b. Old-age dependency ratio in the EU-15

Legend: Natural change ■ Net migration

With migration — Without migration

Source: Bossavie et al. 2022, based on Eurostat (https://ec.europa.eu/eurostat/web/main/data/database) and Wittgenstein Centre for Demography and Global Human Capital 2018, Wittgenstein Centre Data Explorer Version 2.0 (https://dataexplorer.wittgensteincentre.org/wcde-v2/).
Note: Net migration is calculated as immigration flows (arrivals) minus emigration flows (departures). Natural population change is defined as births minus deaths. The old-age dependency ratio is the population ages 65 and older divided by the population ages 16–64. EU-15 = European Union members before 2004.

working-age population (World Bank 2019). That said, at the present rate, immigration can contribute only marginally to a reduction in the average age of the population in recipient countries. In 2015, the old-age dependency ratio— the ratio between the population ages 65 and older and the population ages 15–64—was 30 percent in the EU-15. If recent migration trends persist, the rate is projected to reach 56 percent by 2050, which is only marginally lower than the rate estimated in the absence of immigration (refer to figure 3.1, panel b).

Skills beget skills, with migration supporting larger human capital advancements in more dynamic economic centers. Despite increases in educational attainment in the vast majority of regions (according to the Nomenclature of Territorial Units for Statistics level 2 [NUTS-2]) from 2011 to 2017, gains have been larger in regions with greater net migration flows (that is, more inflows than outflows) and smaller in migrant-sending regions (refer to figure 3.2, panel a). This pattern has been observed in both Western Europe and EU-NMS13 (countries joining the European Union in 2004, 2007, and 2013). It may be the result of several factors, including a higher overall demand for skills that incentivizes native-born individuals and migrants to accumulate more skills in those areas. Moreover, there is a positive correlation between educational attainment of the native-born population in host countries and the educational attainment of migrants: countries with a highly educated population attract more educated migrants. In several cases, migrants' educational attainment is even higher than in the local population (refer to figure 3.2, panel b).

The larger and more diverse human capital brought by immigration can lead to productivity gains through the reallocation of native-born workers to higher-productivity activities in which they have a comparative advantage. According to several studies, migrant workers specialize in occupations that require skills different from those of native-born workers, with the former being more likely to work in jobs that are intensive in manual or physical labor and the latter focusing on jobs more intensive in communication and language tasks (Peri and Sparber 2009). Migration thus promotes more efficient task specialization, pushing native-born workers toward occupations in which they have a comparative advantage (Peri 2012). This specialization of skills increases total factor productivity and stimulates innovation. At the same time, it minimizes competition between migrant and native-born workers, reducing any possible downward pressure on wages.

The fiscal impact of immigration is neutral or marginally positive in most Western European countries. Migrants to EU countries have, on average, been found to be net contributors in receiving countries (Sumption and Vargas-Silva 2019). As of 2006, it was estimated that migrant employees made a net contribution of approximately €42 billion to the national tax and benefit systems of a group of 13 EU countries (Barbone, Bontch-Osmolovsky, and Zaidi 2009). France (Chojnicki 2013), the United Kingdom (Dustmann and Frattini 2014; Vargas-Silva 2016), and the Scandinavian countries (Hansen,

FIGURE 3.2

International migration and human capital

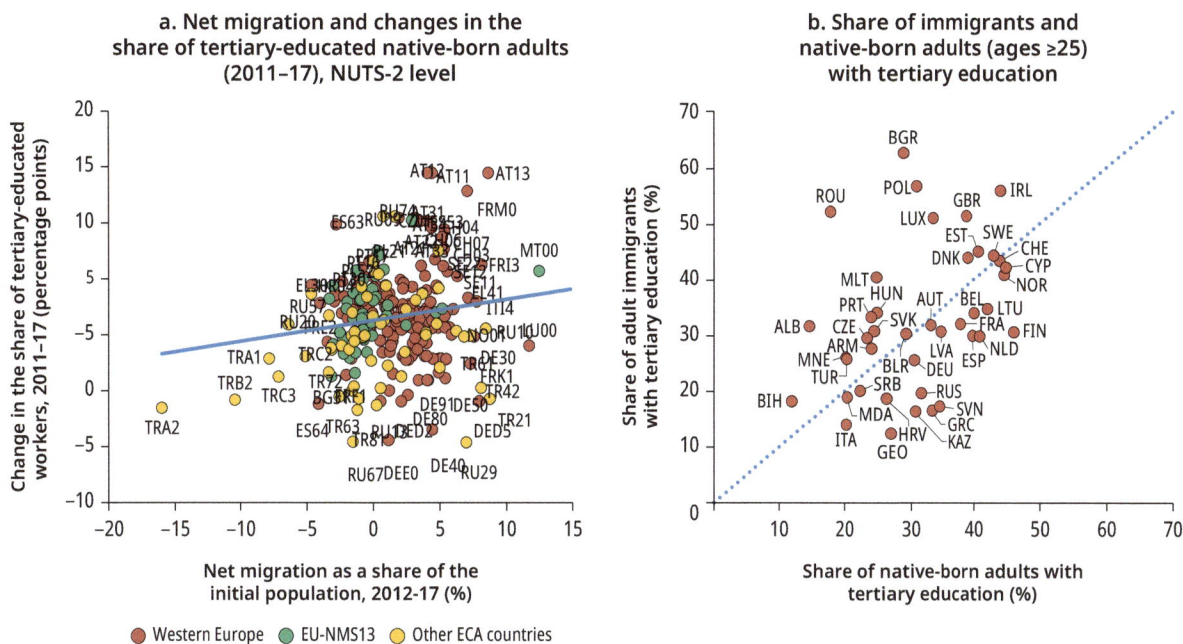

a. Net migration and changes in the share of tertiary-educated native-born adults (2011–17), NUTS-2 level

b. Share of immigrants and native-born adults (ages ≥25) with tertiary education

● Western Europe ● EU-NMS13 ○ Other ECA countries

Source: Eurostat (https://ec.europa.eu/eurostat/web/main/data/database).

Note: Net migration refers to the cumulative number of immigrants (arrivals) minus the number of emigrants (departures) between 2012 and 2017, as a percentage of the initial population in 2011. The line in panel a shows the linear fit estimated by regressing net migration flows over the change in the share of tertiary-educated adults. In panel b, the 45-degree line represents parity between the share of immigrants with tertiary education and the share of native-born adults with tertiary education. In countries located above or below the 45-degree line, the share of immigrants with tertiary education is higher or lower, respectively, than the share of native-born adults with tertiary education. The labels in panel a show the NUTS-2 regional code, which includes the alpha-2 country code and the two-digit principal subdivision code. For a list of NUTS-2 regional codes, go to https://ec.europa.eu/eurostat/web/nuts. The labels in panel a show 3-digit country codes. For a list of country codes, go to https://www.iso.org/obp/ui/#search. Western Europe = EU-15 + EFTA; EU15 = European Union members before 2004; EFTA = European Free Trade Association (CHE, ISL, LIE, NOR); EU-NMS13 = new member states joining the European Union in 2004, 2007, and 2013; other ECA countries = Albania, Belarus, Georgia, Kazakhstan, Kyrgyz Republic, Moldova, Montenegro, North Macedonia, Serbia, Russian Federation, Turkïye, Ukraine, and Uzbekistan; NUTS-2 = Nomenclature of Territorial Units for Statistics level 2.

Schultz-Nielsen, and Tranaes 2017) have all experienced similar positive net effects (Dustmann and Frattini 2014; Hansen, Schultz-Nielsen, and Tranaes 2017). This evidence is consistent with the broader (although earlier) evidence for advanced economies that the net fiscal contribution of immigration typically falls within a range of plus or minus 1 percent of GDP (Rowthorn 2008). A recent study based on microsimulation methods focusing on EU-15 countries with the exclusion of the UK, found that on average, migrants were net contributors to public finances over the period 2014–18 and, moreover, that they contributed approximately €1,500 more per capita each year than native-born residents (accounting for income taxes, social insurance and social security contributions paid, and cash transfers received, as well as value-added tax [VAT] paid and the receipt of in-kind benefits such as education, health care, and social housing). While this magnitude varies across specific countries, the net effect becomes negligible when controlling for self-selection and for the probability of migrants being net contributors to the tax-benefits system (Fiorio et al. 2024).

The fiscal effects of immigration, however, depend on the skill composition of migration and on whether it is temporary or permanent. Education and skill levels affect migrants' net fiscal contributions. Although individual government expenditures on migrants are similar across education levels, migrants' fiscal contributions vary across skill groups. As a result, the net fiscal impacts of immigration for ECA countries tend to be more positive for high-skilled migrants and migrants from the European Economic Area than for low-skilled migrants and migrants from low-income countries (OECD 2013). They also depend on whether immigration is temporary or permanent. Temporary workers typically return to their country of origin before needing the public expenditures associated with old age, health care and pensions. Many temporary workers migrate without their families and thus do not use the host country's education system. By contrast, permanent migrants need full access to health care, education, and pension systems and thus generate smaller fiscal gains (OECD 2013).

Labor Market Impacts

In EU countries, migrants increasingly support employment over time in all economic sectors, particularly in manufacturing and health and social care. The share of migrant workers in the European Union grew in the past decade in all sectors of the economy (refer to figure 3.3, panel a). Migrants' presence is highest in the personal care and services sectors, such as health care, hotels and restaurants, hospitality, and household services. Furthermore, migrants' incidence has also become more prevalent in the information technology sector and, to a lesser extent, in manufacturing. When considering employment growth, migrants' largest contributions to employment growth have been in both declining sectors (manufacturing, trade) and fast-growing ones (health and social care).

The average impact of immigration on native-born workers' wages in ECA destination countries has been mixed. Because labor market adjustments take time, an increase in labor supply associated with an inflow of immigrant workers can affect native-born workers' wages and employment, at least in the short run. Most studies of recipient countries in ECA find that immigration had either null or small aggregate effects on the wages of native-born workers (Barrett 2009; Blanchflower and Shadforth 2009; Docquier et al. 2014; Edo 2015; Glitz 2012). Insignificant average effects on native-born workers' wages have been found in France (Edo 2015), Germany (Glitz 2012), Spain (Carrasco, Jimeno, and Ortega 2008), and the United Kingdom (Dustmann, Fabbri, and Preston 2005). Small positive wage effects have been reported for Denmark (Foged and Peri 2016), Norway (Zorlu and Hartog 2005), and the United Kingdom

FIGURE 3.3

Migrants' contributions to employment in the European Union, by sector of activity

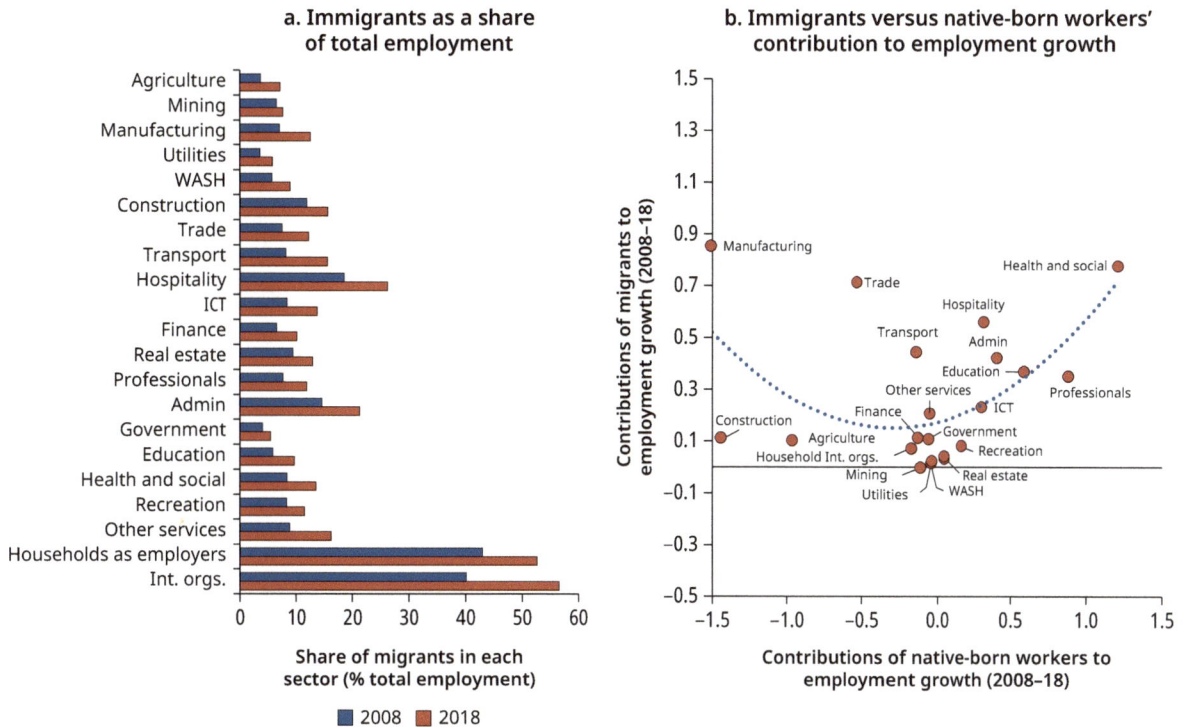

a. Immigrants as a share of total employment

b. Immigrants versus native-born workers' contribution to employment growth

Share of migrants in each sector (% total employment)

■ 2008 ■ 2018

Source: Eurostat (https://ec.europa.eu/eurostat/web/main/data/database).
Note: Contributions to total employment growth are calculated as the change in the number of employed individuals from a specific group (either native-born workers or migrants) in a particular sector between 2008 and 2018 divided by the total change in employment in that sector during the same period. ICT = information and communications technology; Int. orgs. = international organizations. WASH = water, sanitation, and hygiene.

(Dustmann, Frattini, and Preston 2013), although aggregate wage effects have been shown to be slightly negative in the Netherlands (Zorlu and Hartog 2005). Overall, the contribution of immigration to wage dynamics in Western European countries has been much lower than that of changes in the demographics and skill composition of the native-born workforce (Docquier et al. 2018).

The wage effects of immigration, however, critically depend on both the skill composition of immigrants and the skill level of the native-born population considered. Depending on its composition, immigration can create winners and losers among native-born individuals via changes in the wage structure (Borjas 2003a; Edo 2019; Ottaviano and Peri 2012). A key determinant of the impact of immigration on different groups of native-born individuals is the degree of substitutability or complementarity of their skills with those of migrant workers. Although negative wage effects can take place for groups of native-born individuals whose skills are similar to those of migrants (Dustmann, Glitz, and Frattini 2008), at least in the short run, the wages of native-born individuals with complementary skills may be positively affected. The available evidence for ECA is mostly consistent with this prediction. Lower-educated native-born workers have experienced small negative wage losses, and high-skilled workers have seen gains in destination countries where immigration has been mostly low skilled, such as in Germany (Brücker and Jahn 2011), the Netherlands, and the United Kingdom (Blanchflower and Shadforth 2009; Zorlu and Hartog 2005). In contrast, more recent high-skilled immigration to France has had small negative impacts on high-skilled native-born individuals while benefiting low-skilled workers' wages (Edo and Toubal 2015).

Likewise, the impacts on native-born individuals' employment are small and mixed, with heterogeneous effects across groups. If there are labor market rigidities in wage adjustments, immigration may also affect employment levels. The employment effects of immigration have been reported to be negative in the short term in France (Edo 2015) and Germany (Glitz 2012) and null in Spain (Carrasco, Jimeno, and Ortega 2008), the United Kingdom (Dustmann, Fabbri, and Preston 2005), and EU countries more broadly (Bossavie et al. 2022). As for wages, aggregate effects mask important heterogeneity across groups. Employment effects depend heavily on migrants' composition and the group of native-born workers considered. Employment effects are more often found to be negative for low- and medium-skilled native-born workers in France (Edo 2015) and the United Kingdom (Dustmann, Fabbri, and Preston 2005), whereas positive but small employment effects have been reported for high-skilled native-born workers in Denmark (Foged and Peri 2016). In France, an increase in high-skilled migration in select occupations had no impact on the employment levels of native-born workers (Signorelli 2024). Employment effects can also be gender specific. They can depend on the gender of both immigrants and native-born individuals, together with their education level. In Spain, an inflow of low-skilled female migrants into the domestic household service sector has been found to increase the economic participation and employment rates of tertiary-educated Spanish women by freeing up time from household activities (Farré, González, and Ortega 2011).

The impacts of immigration on native-born workers' wages and employment can dissipate in the long run, if labor markets are flexible enough, and through impacts from productivity growth. Although immigration may generate small negative impacts on some groups of the native-born population, markets may eventually adjust in the long run through a reallocation of capital and the movement of workers to other occupations, sectors, and regions. As a result, the impact of migration may decline. In France, immigration was estimated to decrease native-born workers' wages by 0.6 percent in the short run but had on average no impact on wages in the long run (Edo and Toubal 2015). These long-term adjustments, however, partly depend on labor market flexibility, because rigidities may prevent wage adjustments for some groups of native-born workers after labor supply shocks (World Bank 2023). Although generally quite scarce, evidence for Western European countries suggests that reduced market flexibility may protect native-born workers against potential adverse effects of immigration in the short run but at the cost of worsening their labor market outcomes in the longer run (Angrist and Kugler 2003). In France, the negative employment effects of immigration have been more pronounced among native-born workers with more rigid fixed-term employment contracts, although their wages have been less affected (Edo 2015, 2016).

Immigration can also induce native-born workers to relocate to higher-quality jobs, which are also less exposed to negative employment shocks. Immigrant workers often fill the difficult and dangerous jobs that locals are not willing to undertake, as shown in the ECA context and elsewhere (Orrenius and Zavodny 2009, 2013; Sparber and Zavodny 2022). By concentrating in these types of occupations, immigrant workers can induce native-born workers to relocate to higher-quality employment, as shown in Denmark (Foged and Peri 2016) and for EU countries as a whole (Bossavie et al. 2022). These high-quality jobs into which native-born workers relocate also turn out to be less exposed to negative employment shocks, such as those experienced during the COVID-19 pandemic. When the pandemic hit, native-born workers in the European Union were employed in jobs more amenable to working from home, less dependent on face-to-face interactions, and less sensitive to economic downturns, which ended up protecting them against the adverse impacts of the shock (Bossavie et al. 2022).

According to simulations, the welfare effects of an increase in immigration to Western Europe are mostly positive for nonimmigrants, although they are heterogeneous across countries and skill groups. A set of simulations for 24 European countries looked at the effects of an increase in immigration by 1 percentage point of the labor force on native-born individuals' welfare outcomes (Battisti and Poutvaara 2021). The simulations considered the newcomers' alternative skill structures, ranging from completely low skilled to completely high skilled (see annex 3A for more details). Although welfare effects are found to be heterogeneous across countries and skill groups, in most cases the effects of a marginal increase in the number of immigrants are positive for nonimmigrants. The results of the simulations indicate that the inflow of high-skilled immigrants has larger net benefits for host countries (refer to figure 3.4, panel a). The benefits are larger for low-skilled native-born workers through the complementarity channel and in almost all countries offset the negative impact on high-skilled native-born individuals because of substitution effects (that is, immigrant workers replacing native-born workers in some high-skilled jobs). Skill-balanced immigration tends to have either neutral or positive welfare effects, although it is asymmetric across skill levels of the native-born population (refer to figure 3.4, panel b). The net welfare impact of low-skilled migration is limited or neutral and, in some cases, negative for low-skilled native-born individuals (refer to figure 3.4, panel c).

FIGURE 3.4

Simulated welfare effects of an increase in immigration equal to 1 percentage point of the labor force, by country of destination

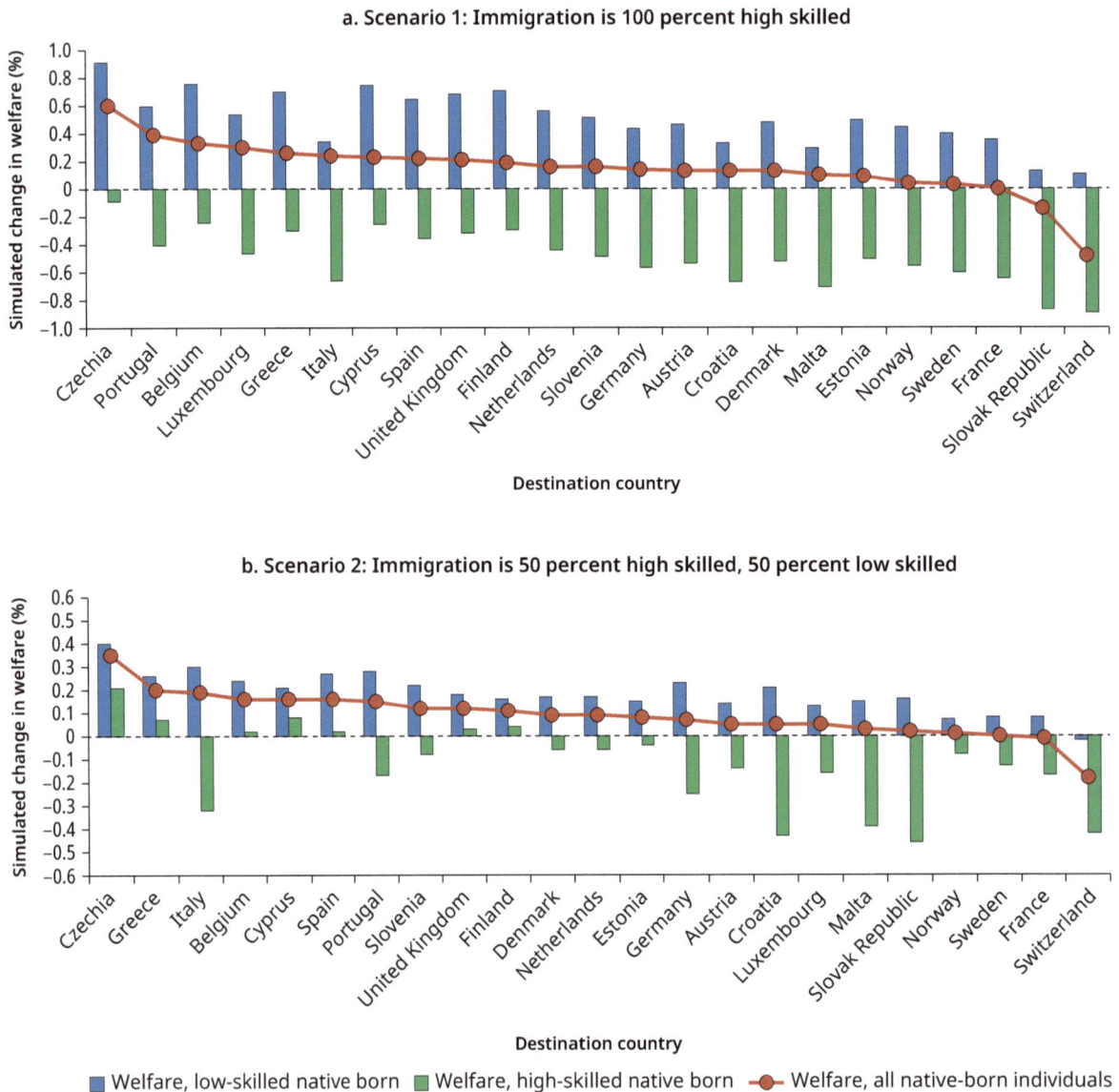

a. Scenario 1: Immigration is 100 percent high skilled

b. Scenario 2: Immigration is 50 percent high skilled, 50 percent low skilled

■ Welfare, low-skilled native born   ■ Welfare, high-skilled native born   ●— Welfare, all native-born individuals

Continued

Figure 3.4

Simulated welfare effects of an increase in immigration equal to 1 percentage point of the labor force, by country of destination *(Continued)*

c. Scenario 3: Immigration is 100 percent low skilled

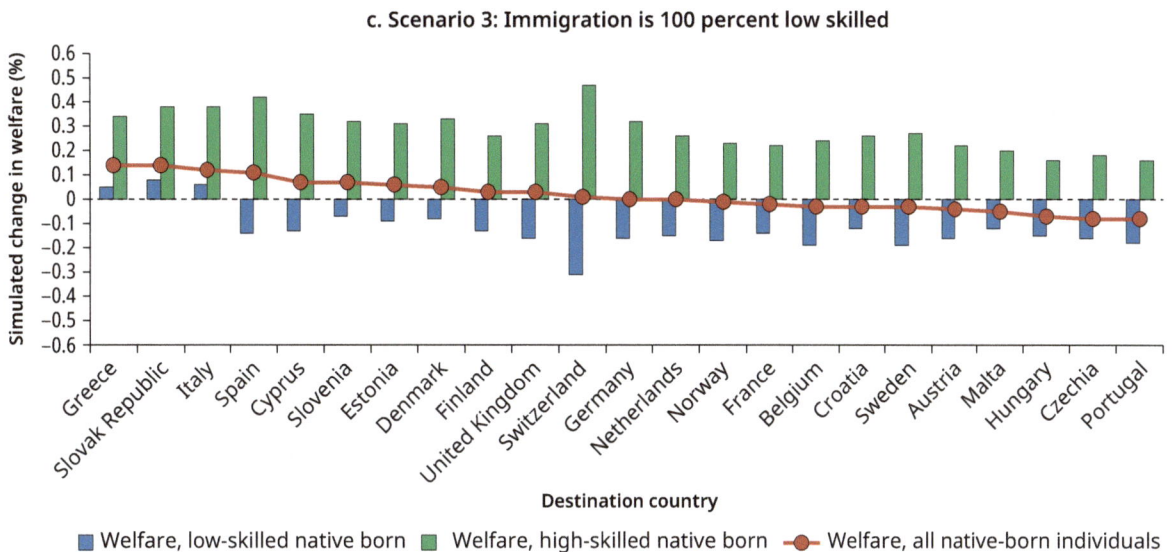

Legend: Welfare, low-skilled native born ■ Welfare, high-skilled native born ■ Welfare, all native-born individuals ●—

Source: Battisti and Poutvaara 2021.

Note: The welfare measure on the *y*-axes is a function of both employment level and wages of the native-born population derived from the model of Battisti and Poutvaara (2021). High-skilled individuals are defined as adults having a tertiary education degree. Low-skilled individuals are defined as adults without a tertiary education degree.

Other Socioeconomic Impacts

Immigration can also affect host countries' education systems and outcomes through several channels, depending on the context. The first channel is through its potential impact on the amount of educational resources available to native-born individuals. If educational resources, such as teachers, infrastructure, and financial resources, do not adjust to the presence of immigrant children, it can lead to a deterioration in the quality of education delivered. In Spain, for example, higher shares of immigrant children have been shown to be positively associated with higher student-teacher ratios (Tanaka, Farré, and Ortega 2018), which are known to have a negative impact on learning outcomes (Ballatore, Fort, and Ichino 2018). Second, the presence of immigrant children in schools and classrooms may directly affect native-born students' learning through learning peer effects. Available studies for ECA countries report mixed findings, ranging from null in Austria (Schneeweis 2015) and the Netherlands (Ohinata and Van Ours 2013) to small negative effects in Denmark (Jensen and Rasmussen 2011), Germany (Jürges et al. 2022), and Italy (Frattini and Meschi 2019; Tonello 2016). These impacts have also been shown to be heterogeneous and to depend on the share of migrant children in the classroom, whether their parents are highly or less educated, and whether they have a solid command of the local language.[1]

More negative impacts tend to be nonlinear and mostly observed when the shares of immigrant children are higher (Frattini and Meschi 2019). Finally, immigration may trigger native-born students to move out of schools with a high concentration of immigrant children, which further raises the ratio of migrants to nationals and can exacerbate negative impacts and perceptions. In Spain and Türkiye, the enrollment of native-born children in private education has been shown to increase in response to higher numbers of immigrant children in public schools, especially if the native-born students are from higher-income households (Farré, Ortega, and Tanaka 2018; Tumen 2019).

Immigration can affect the availability and quality of health services in host countries through several and sometimes conflicting channels, making its overall effects ambiguous. On the one hand, immigration can be expected to increase the demand for health care in a similar way as for education services, which can create pressure in accessing such services, especially in communities with limited public resources. In the United Kingdom, waiting times for health care have increased in disadvantaged areas with large inflows of immigrants (Giuntella, Nicodemo, and Vargas-Silva 2018). On the other hand, these effects may be mitigated by or even compensated for by several factors. First, migrants have a lower propensity to use health care services than nationals, in part because they tend to be younger and healthier. In addition, in many ECA countries, migrants account for a relatively large share of health care workers, thereby also providing the national population with additional human resources. Overall, the impact of migrants' consumption of health care services on nationals depends on multiple factors, including migrants' geographic concentration, their age profile and health status, and the share of patients who need specialized services (World Bank 2023).

Immigration affects housing prices in some host countries depending on the native-born population's mobility. An immigrant inflow in a specific country, city, or region resembles a positive housing demand shock. As a result, housing rents or values where there is a high immigrant presence would be expected to increase in response to immigration, given that housing supply is rather inelastic in the short run. Such impacts have been evidenced in Türkiye, where low-skilled migrant inflows have led to an increase in the rents of higher-quality housing units, although they had no effects on the rents of lower-quality ones. However, large immigrant inflows to specific areas may also induce native-born individuals to move out of these areas, which can ultimately contribute to reducing housing prices, as found in Italy (Accetturo et al. 2014) and the United Kingdom (Sá 2015). This initial evidence suggests that the overall effects of immigration on housing prices in ECA are context and country specific.

Although little association between actual crime and immigration has been reported so far, perceptions of crime may rise with immigration. Existing evidence for Western European countries indicates that an increase in immigration does not significantly affect actual crime victimization but is associated with an increase in the fear of crime, the latter being consistently and positively correlated with the native-born population's unfavorable attitude toward immigrants (Nunziata 2015). Likewise, in Italy, no significant effect on overall crime rates has been found (Bianchi, Buonanno, and Pinotti 2012). Immigrants' labor market outcomes, however, seem to matter. In the United Kingdom, immigration was shown to have either slightly positive or negative impacts on crime, depending on the labor market opportunities to which new entrants have access (Bell, Fasani, and Machin 2013). Emerging evidence also indicates that migrants' legal status matters: in Italy, irregular migrants have been shown to be less likely to commit crimes when they have a legal status that allows them to access the formal labor market (Fasani 2018; Mastrobuoni and Pinotti 2015; Pinotti 2017).

More broadly, perceptions of the impacts of immigration are more negative in ECA than in other regions. Despite the overall positive economic impacts of immigration, the average citizen in ECA has more negative views about migration in their country than do citizens of other regions (World Bank 2017). Nine of the 10 least-accepting countries in the world according to the Gallup Migrant Acceptance Index were in ECA (Esipova, Fleming, and Ray 2017).[2] This suggests that the perceived costs of migration in the region are high, because of either inaccurate perceptions of the economic benefits and costs of immigration among the native-born population or noneconomic costs that are hard to measure and can be missed by quantitative studies. Still, most Europeans are either neutral or positive about migration overall (Goubin, Ruelens, and Nicaise 2022).

The salience of migration as a main concern of the population fluctuates according to geopolitical and economic events, although perceptions are stable or even improving in the long run. Perceptions of labor mobility are shaped by the economic situation in the host country, with episodes of high unemployment rates and relevant strains on public finances leading to more concerns over immigration inflows. During the Syrian refugee crisis, the share of respondents in the Eurobarometer citing immigration as one of the two most pressing challenges in the European Union rapidly rose from below 10 percent in 2012 to close to 60 percent at its peak in November 2015 and then fell to below 40 percent in May 2017 and 28 percent in November 2023 (Schuettler 2017). This is in line with studies that show that short-term increases in immigration flows are associated with worsening perceptions of immigration (Dražanová and Gonnot 2023).

In Europe, regions highly exposed to the 2015 refugee crisis had higher antimigrant sentiment (Ajzenman, Giray Aksoy, and Guriev 2022). However, broader attitudes toward immigration and immigration policies have remained more stable and even trended upward in more recent years (Dražanová and Gonnot 2023).

Perceptions of migration vary depending on the characteristics of the native-born and immigrant populations. There are strong variations in perceptions of migrants across subregions and countries in ECA. In general, Western European countries tend to have more favorable views of immigration than Eastern European countries. In the long term, a higher prevalence of migration is correlated with more positive attitudes toward migrants (Dražanová and Gonnot 2023). This is because exposure to migrants increases knowledge and empathy and reduces prejudice (Bursztyn et al. 2024). At the individual level, citizens with a higher education level, who are younger, and who have more left-leaning political attitudes have on average more positive views of immigration and its fiscal and labor market implications (Boeri 2010; Goubin, Ruelens, and Nicaise 2022; World Bank 2017). Information also shapes perceptions, with those having more accurate knowledge about the magnitude and impact of immigration having a more pro-immigration stance (Sides and Citrin 2007). However, recent surveys show that more than two in three people in Europe overestimate the size of the migration phenomenon in their country (European Commission 2021), and there is a general underestimation of migrants' skills and education level (Alesina, Miano, and Stantcheva 2023). Beyond citizens' characteristics, there is a general preference for the migration of people with a similar background, because they are considered to assimilate more easily (Dražanová and Gonnot 2023). For example, in the Russian Federation, attitudes toward ethnic Russian migrants are significantly more positive than those toward migrants coming from the South Caucasus or Central Asia (Levada-Center 2017). Similarly, Europeans give broader support to the arrival of migrants from other EU countries or those having the same ethnic background (ESS Data Portal 2022).

Migrants' Labor Market Integration in Destination Countries

Immigrants in the European Union have lower employment rates than native-born individuals, even after accounting for differences in their age, gender, and education profiles. The gap in employment rate between native-born and immigrant workers in EU countries was around 4.5 percentage points in 2020. This variation could potentially stem from differences between the two populations in characteristics such as age structure, gender mix, and educational composition that affect labor market outcomes. However, estimates from European countries indicate that this is not the case. Accounting for differences in the age, gender, and education profiles of migrants and native-born individuals actually increases the employment gap, which is estimated to be 6.5 percentage points. Although lower education levels would explain part of migrants' lower employment rate, their higher concentration among prime-age workers, who are on average more likely to be employed, further exacerbates the employment gaps. These results indicate that differences in immigrant characteristics alone cannot explain their employment disadvantage. This job penalty might originate from immigrant-specific hurdles in labor market integration, such as discrimination from employers, difficulties in formal recognition of foreign qualifications, or a lack of fluency in the host country language, which would need to be addressed to close the gap.

This gap between native-born individuals and immigrants is driven by the relatively low levels of employment among non-EU immigrants. Across all European countries, EU immigrants have a slightly higher probability of employment than native-born individuals (3.6 percentage points), whereas immigrants from outside the European Union have employment rates that are 8.1 percentage points lower. The better employment performance of EU immigrants relative to their non-EU counterparts is barely driven by a different composition of the two groups in terms of age, gender, or education. In fact, when EU and non-EU immigrants are compared with native-born people with the same individual characteristics, the differences in employment probability gaps between the two groups are still substantial. The employment gap for EU immigrants becomes insignificant, whereas the gap for non-EU to native-born individuals increases slightly to 9.2 percentage points (Frattini and Ciampa 2020).

The persistence of large differences in the conditional employment gap between the two groups suggests that the better performance of EU immigrants may be due to the more favorable institutional setting they face. For instance, recognition of foreign qualifications and access to licensed occupations is easier for EU than non-EU citizens, which clearly facilitates the labor market integration of the former relative to the latter. Additionally, EU citizens can move freely across countries, and they are therefore able not only to settle in countries with higher labor demand but also to move out of their country of current residence and move back to their country of origin or to another EU country at a lower cost.

Employment gaps decrease over time, suggesting that some of the barriers migrants face are eased the longer they stay in the host country.

The average difference in employment probabilities between native-born individuals and immigrants who have been in the country for no more than five years (recent immigrants) is 15 percentage points, or 18 percentage points when comparing immigrants with native-born people with the same age–gender–education profile. For immigrants who arrived earlier, who have accumulated more than five years of residence in the host country, the gap instead decreases to just 6 percentage points, and it is essentially unchanged even when differences in individual characteristics are considered. This evidence is much stronger for non-EU immigrants. Their employment disadvantage decreases sizably with time spent in the destination country, from 27 percentage points among recent immigrants to 9 percentage points for those who have been in the host country longer. Recent EU migrants display a 1.5 times higher employment probability than native-born individuals, but this employment advantage is no longer present among earlier EU migrants, who have the same employment probability as native-born people (Frattini and Ciampa 2020).

Immigrants are considerably more likely than native-born people to be employed in low-pay and low-status occupations. To assess the occupational distribution of migrants versus native-born workers, occupational status is measured with the International Socio-Economic Index of Occupational Status (ISEI), a continuous index that scores occupations in relation to their average education and income levels, thus capturing the attributes of occupations that convert education into income.[3] Panel a of figure 3.5 shows that, across all EU countries, immigrants have on average lower occupational status than native-born workers, with a mean ISEI score 34 percent of a standard deviation lower than that of native-born workers. In particular, there are no Western European countries in which immigrants' average occupational status is higher than that of native-born workers, and the occupational gap is highest in Italy (75 percent of a standard deviation). Comparing the occupational distribution of immigrants and native-born workers in the same region, the immigrant–native-born differences in occupational status increase further (42 percent of a standard deviation lower than for native-born workers). This result indicates that immigrants are concentrated, within each country, in regions in which native-born workers have better occupations (Frattini and Ciampa 2020).

The patterns of occupational status distribution for EU and non-EU migrants are overall similar. Although this is generally true, EU migrants are slightly more similar to native-born workers, with a lower relative concentration in the bottom part of the distribution than non-EU migrants and a higher concentration in the middle. As the differences in the distribution of occupational status suggest, immigrants tend to be more disproportionately concentrated than native-born workers in the bottom part of the income distribution.

FIGURE 3.5

Migrant occupations and income relative to native-born workers in the European Union

a. Distribution of immigrants along the occupational status scale relative to native-born workers

b. Share of immigrants and native-born individuals, by national income deciles

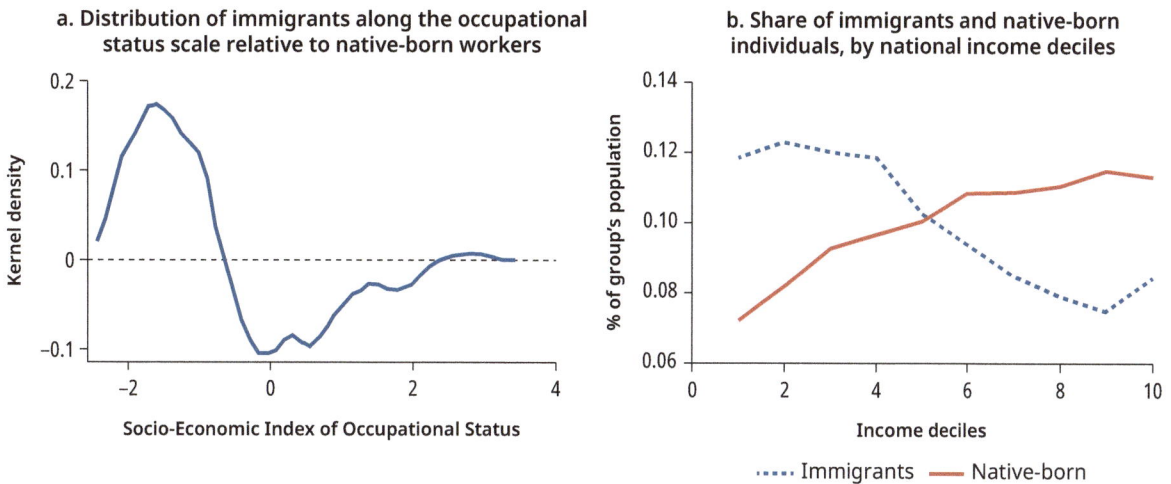

..... Immigrants   ⎯ Native-born

Source: Frattini and Ciampa 2020 based on the EU Labour Force Survey 2018.
Note: In panel a, the Socio-Economic Index of Occupational Status is a continuous index that scores occupations in relation to their average education and income levels, thus capturing the attributes of occupations that convert education into income. Higher values of the index correspond to occupations with a higher socioeconomic status. The measure is standardized so that it has a mean of zero and a standard deviation of 1; therefore, values above zero indicate occupations that are more prestigious than the national average and vice versa for values below zero. The y-axis refers to the relative distribution of migrants and native-born individuals, where values above or below zero indicate that migrants or native-born individuals, respectively, are more likely to work at a specific level of the occupational status scale. In panel b, income deciles are ranked from lowest to highest.

Differences in individual characteristics are unable to explain immigrants' income disadvantage. The portion of the difference in the probability of having a wage in the bottom decile explained by age, gender, and education profiles amounts to 0.6 percentage points, or 10.7 percent of the total difference, whereas differences in occupation account for a much larger share of the difference, namely 60.7 percent. When migrants and native-born workers in the same region are compared, gaps in the share of low-income workers increase further. This indicates a scenario in which immigrants are more concentrated in regions where native-born workers have better wages (Frattini and Ciampa 2020).

The main reason why immigrants are disproportionately concentrated in the bottom part of the income distribution is that they are overrepresented in low-quality occupations. In other words, it is the clustering of immigrants in low-paid occupations, not differences in the level of education, that explains more than half of the immigrant–native-born difference in the probability of being both in the bottom income decile and in the top income decile. The concentration of immigrants at the bottom of the income distribution is largely a consequence of immigrants' education not being rewarded as much as that of native-born individuals. This is often the result of the misallocation of immigrant skills between occupations, with highly formally educated immigrants being more likely to take up unskilled jobs than qualified native-born workers—for instance, foreign graduates working as deliverymen, cleaners, or caretakers.

Many migrant workers experience occupational downgrade in destination countries, especially non-EU migrants. Occupational downgrade refers to being employed in a lower-skilled occupation than one's formal level of educational attainment would predict. Migrants from the EU-NMS13 have, on average, 1.3 more years of schooling than do native-born people in the same occupation. Occupational downgrade among high-skilled female migrants to the European Union is striking; the top two occupations of tertiary-educated female migrants from the EU-NMS13 are cleaners or helpers and personal care workers. The occupational downgrade of high-skilled migrants has been linked to a lack of local-specific skills, including language skills, training in occupations that does not match the demand for high skills in destination countries, and the imperfect recognition of human capital obtained abroad.[4]

The concentration of migrants in low-quality occupations might help explain why the convergence in wages takes even longer than the convergence in employment, especially in high-income receiving countries. Wage gaps tend to build during the early years of working life and depend on the age at arrival. Estimation of lifetime wage equations for native-born workers and migrants based on administrative data that allow controlling for migrants' age at entry to destination countries shows that the later the age at arrival, the higher the wage penalty with respect to native-born workers. Migrants moving early in life exhibit wage profiles closer to those of native-born individuals (refer to figures 3.6 and 3.7 for Denmark, Finland, and Switzerland). These findings suggest that other factors can affect wage outcomes throughout the life cycle, such as language barriers, networks, geographic segregation, discrimination in the workplace, and lack of access to training and educational opportunities for migrants arriving at an early age.

One important factor associated with poorer labor market outcomes for immigrant workers is a lack of knowledge of or limited command of the host country language. Proficiency in the host country language can be viewed as part of immigrant workers' human capital. It has a positive effect on labor market outcomes and broader socioeconomic integration through several channels. First, language skills raise migrants' wages directly by affecting workers' productivity, but also indirectly by providing easier access to well-paid, communication-intensive jobs. Second, language skills play a key role in the transferability of skills and experience acquired before migration to the host country and ease the acquisition of additional human

FIGURE 3.6

Difference in annual wages of immigrants relative to native-born workers over the life cycle and across generations in Denmark

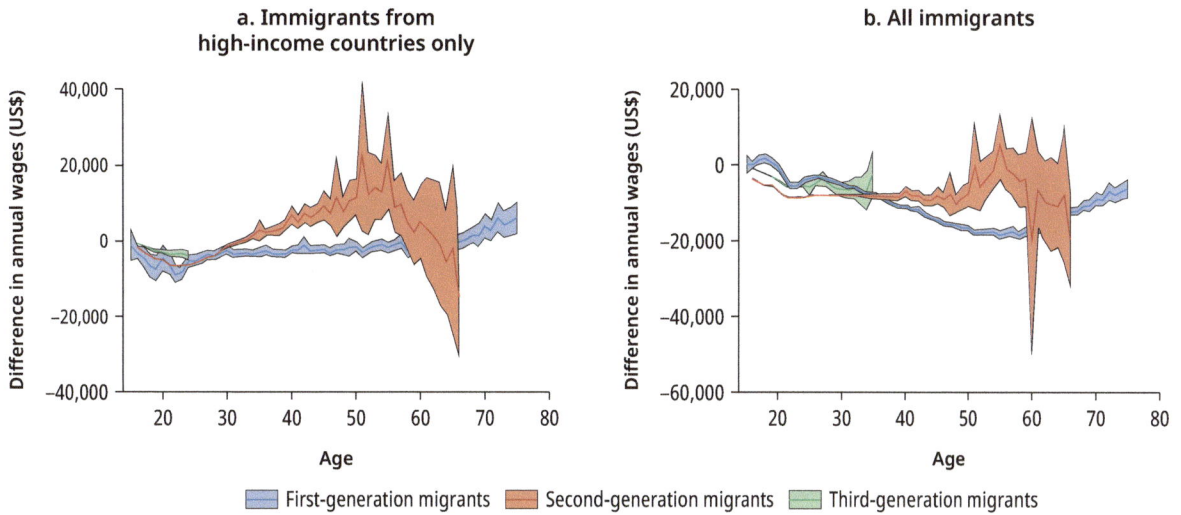

a. Immigrants from high-income countries only

b. All immigrants

First-generation migrants   Second-generation migrants   Third-generation migrants

Source: De Giorgi, Prado, and Severgnini 2022.
Note: Upper and lower bounds of the shading represent the standard errors of wage gaps' estimates.

FIGURE 3.7

Immigrants' age-wage profiles relative to native-born workers, by age at arrival and country of residence

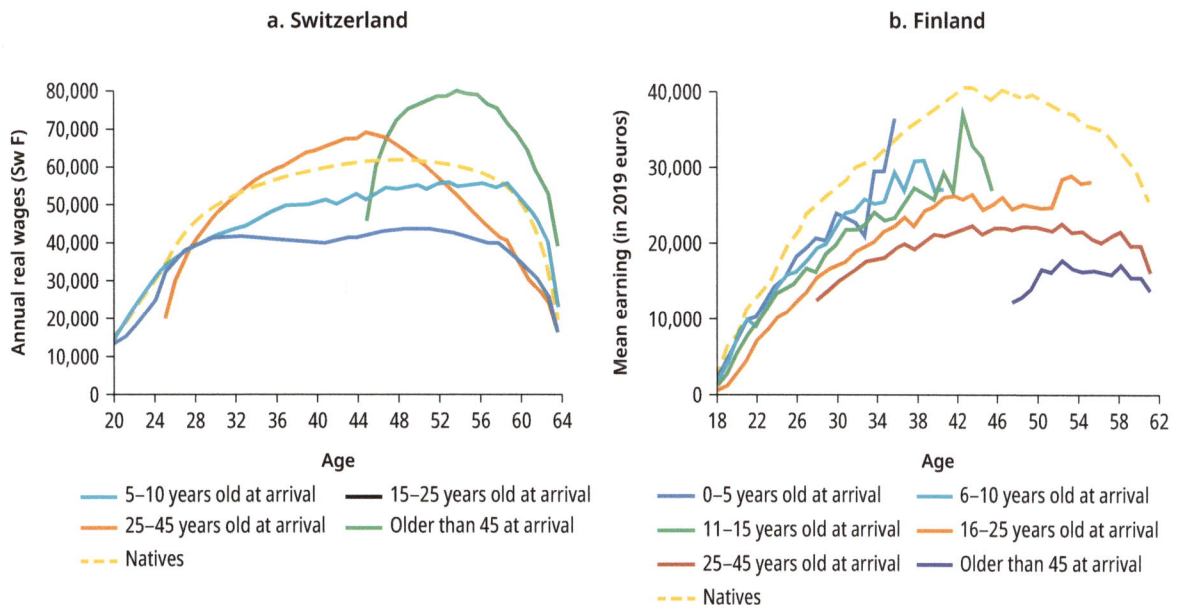

a. Switzerland

b. Finland

5–10 years old at arrival   15–25 years old at arrival
25–45 years old at arrival   Older than 45 at arrival
Natives

0–5 years old at arrival   6–10 years old at arrival
11–15 years old at arrival   16–25 years old at arrival
25–45 years old at arrival   Older than 45 at arrival
Natives

Source: De Giorgi, Pellizzari, and Naghib 2022; Kuosmanen and Pesola 2022.

capital in the host country. Finally, beyond labor market impacts, language skills also have an impact on immigrants' economic integration by affecting nonmarket outcomes such as education, health, marriage, social integration, and political participation.

Immigrants' proficiency in the host country language (or a lack thereof) has been shown to positively (or negatively) affect a range of migrant workers' outcomes in ECA host countries. First, language skills have been reported to have a positive effect on immigrants' wages in countries such as Germany (Dustmann and van Soest 2001), the Netherlands (Dustmann and van Soest 2001), and the United Kingdom (Dustmann and Fabbri 2003). Similarly, poor language proficiency has been shown to produce significant penalties for immigrants' labor force participation and employment in France (Lochmann, Rapoport, and Speciale 2019) and Italy (Ghio, Bratti, and Bignami 2023). In Spain, host language proficiency raises the probability of having a job by about 15 and 22 percentage points, respectively, among men and women (Budria, Colino, and de Ibarreta 2019). Beyond labor market outcomes, improved host country language proficiency increases immigrants' social integration in their communities in Denmark (Foged et al. 2022) and Germany (Bailey et al. 2022).

Despite the importance of host country language command for integration, many migrants in ECA lack proficiency, partly because of the costs associated with language acquisition. A sizable share of the immigrant population in the European Union struggles to master the host country's language: about one-third of immigrants in the European Union had at most an intermediate level in the host country language according to the EU Labour Force Survey. In Germany, fewer than half of immigrant workers report speaking German well or very well, according to the German Socio-Economic Panel for the period 1997–2010. Low levels of proficiency can be explained by the costs associated with immigrants' language acquisition, which are both monetary and nonmonetary. They include effort, time, the monetary cost of tuition and transportation, and the indirect costs of forgone earnings (opportunity costs) while learning the language. The magnitude of those costs is affected by several factors. The first is age at migration, which has been shown to be strongly negatively associated with the ability to learn the host country language. A second factor is linguistic distance—the degree of dissimilarity between two languages in vocabulary, grammar, pronunciation, and other elements of a language—which increases the costs associated with reaching a certain level of language proficiency (Isphording 2015). Furthermore, exposure to the host country language is key and is largely influenced by locational choice and residential segregation.[5] Finally, incentives for investing in language skills are also influenced by the expected length of stay.

Investments in language proficiency have been shown to be strongly positively associated with expected stay duration in the German context (Dustmann 1999).

Emerging evidence for ECA suggests that migrants' legal status is positively associated with labor market outcomes. Global evidence, mostly from the United States, indicates a strong positive relationship between immigrants' legal status and long-term labor market integration (World Bank 2018, 2023). Although evidence for ECA countries is currently quite sparse, in Italy just the prospect of being eligible for legal status among immigrants has been found to have a significant positive impact on the probability of being employed (Devillanova, Fasani, and Frattini 2018). The size of the estimated effect is equivalent to about half the increase in employment that undocumented immigrants in the sample normally experience during their first year in Italy. Migrants' legal status and formal employment are also key determinants of a migrant's net fiscal contribution because only documented migrants pay income or social security taxes. Having the right to work allows documented migrants to earn higher wages, which, in turn, can increase fiscal contributions (World Bank 2023).

Over the past 15 years, integration policies, which shape migrants' integration outcomes, have remained rather constant and heterogeneous across countries. An important gap persists between Western Europe and EU-NMS13, with the former showing a more favorable institutional environment for migrants' integration than the latter (refer to figure 3.8, panel a). Although this gap has slightly narrowed over time, the difference between Western Europe and EU-NMS13 remains close to 20 points, according to the Migrant Integration Policy Index.[6] When adding non-EU countries to the picture, the values for ECA remain lower than those for the European Union. The countries with more advanced integration policies, well above EU-15 averages (above 80 percent), are Finland, Portugal, and Sweden (refer to figure 3.8b). On the other side of the spectrum are Austria, Latvia, and Lithuania, which score below 40 percent, followed by Bulgaria, Croatia, Cyprus, Poland, and Slovakia, which score slightly above 40 percent but still quite below the overall EU-28 average (55 percent). There are also significant cross-country variations with respect to individual integration policies depending on the period. For instance, as far as labor market access is concerned, a slight but widespread improvement was registered across European countries (apart from the Netherlands) toward more conducive integration policies after the onset of the 2008–09 financial crisis (refer to figure 3.9, panel a). When considering the subperiod 2012–19, gains in labor market integration policies remained more subdued in most countries (refer to figure 3.9, panel b).[7]

FIGURE 3.8

Migrants' integration policy across host countries

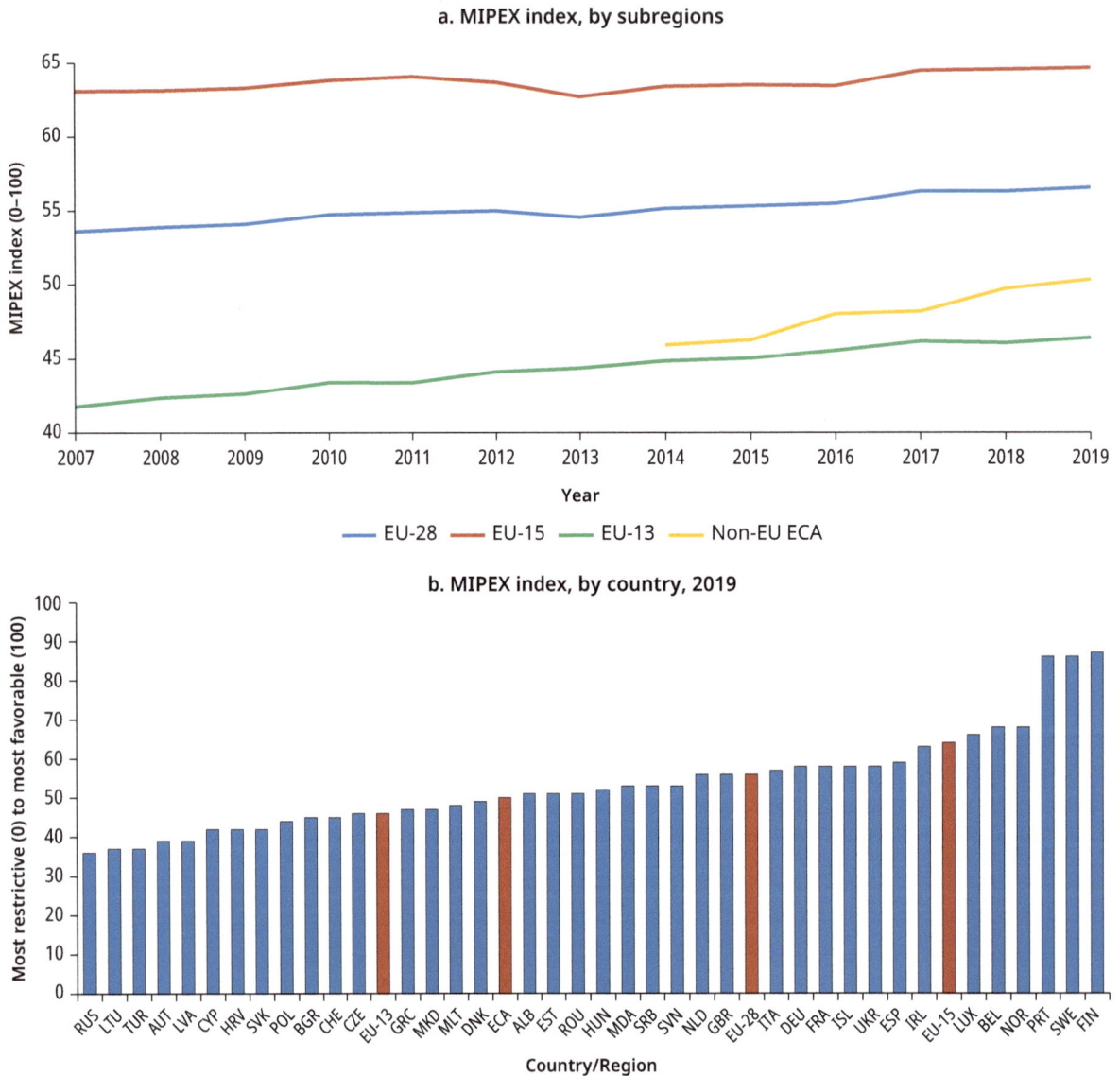

a. MIPEX index, by subregions

b. MIPEX index, by country, 2019

Source: Authors' elaboration based on MIPEX data (https://www.mipex.eu/).

Note: The MIPEX is an index between 0 and 100 that measures how conducive policies are to socioeconomic integration of migrants in destination countries. The composite index measures with equal weights policies in integration, including labor market participation, access to education and recognition of academic qualifications, access to social protection and social insurance benefits, family reunification, political participation, access to citizenship and permanent residency, and antidiscrimination. The blue bars indicate country level MIPEX, and the red bars indicate regional aggregates. For a list of country codes, go to https://www.iso.org/obp/ui/#search.

EU = European Union member states as of 2013; EU-15 = European Union members before 2004; EU-NMS13 = new member states joining the European Union in 2004, 2007, and 2013; EU-28 = EU-15 + EU-NMS13; MIPEX = Migrant Integration Policy Index.

FIGURE 3.9

Migrants' integration policies over time, as measured by the MIPEX index

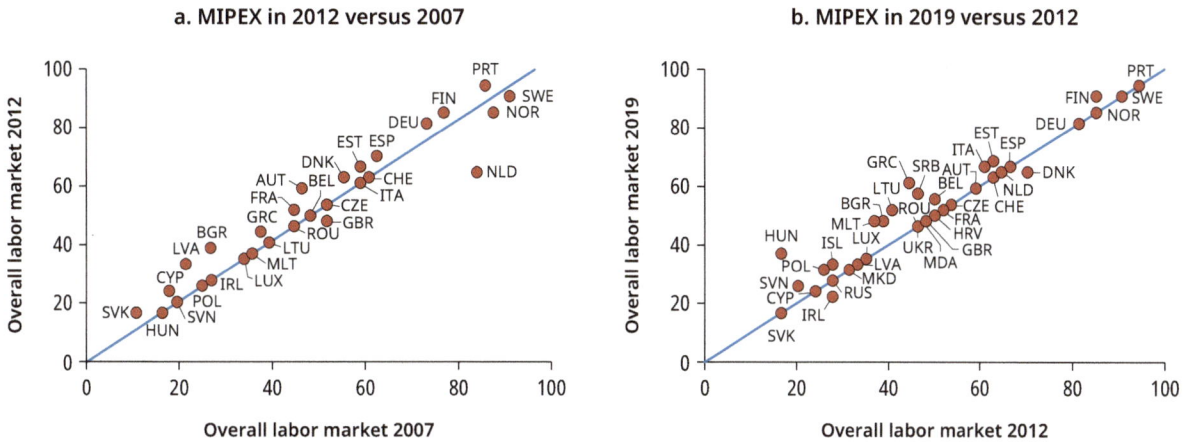

a. MIPEX in 2012 versus 2007

b. MIPEX in 2019 versus 2012

Source: Original figure for this publication based on MIPEX data (https://www.mipex.eu/).
Note: The MIPEX is an index between 0 and 100 that measures how conducive policies are to socioeconomic integration of migrants in destination countries. The composite index measures with equal weights policies in integration, including labor market participation, access to education and recognition of academic qualifications, access to social protection and social insurance benefits, family reunification, political participation, access to citizenship and permanent residency, and antidiscrimination. For a list of country codes, go to https://www.iso.org/obp/ui/#search. MIPEX = Migrant Integration Policy Index.

Vulnerability of Migrants to Shocks and Access to Social Protection Systems in Destination Countries

Migrant workers are employed in occupations that are more exposed to negative shocks in the economy. Immigrant workers tend to be concentrated in occupations that are highly sensitive to fluctuations in the business cycle and therefore more exposed to shocks (Dustmann, Glitz, and Vogel 2010; Orrenius and Zavodny 2010). Furthermore, migrants in the ECA region are more likely to work under nonstandard, informal, or short-term employment contracts, exhibiting shorter job tenures (Fasani and Mazza 2020a). Consequently, they face a higher likelihood of being laid off during downturns or in response to negative employment shocks, regardless of the source of the shock (Blanchard and Landier 2002).

The COVID-19 pandemic is a striking example of migrants' vulnerability to economic shocks and resulted in significant employment losses. A handful of studies in the European context have shown that immigrant workers were more exposed to the negative labor market consequences of the pandemic (Basso et al. 2020; Bossavie et al. 2021, 2022; Fasani and Mazza 2020a, 2020b). At the onset of the pandemic, employment dropped, and unemployment increased more strongly for migrants than for native-born individuals in most ECA countries. This pattern continued throughout 2020 as the pandemic unfolded. According to Eurostat data, employment of immigrants fell by 3.8 percent in the EU in 2020, higher than the 1 percent reduction among native-born workers (refer to figure 3.10, panel a). The employment contraction was larger for migrants in most EU countries. In some countries, though, total employment among foreign-born individuals increased (refer to figure 3.1, panel b), suggesting a possible increase in demand for essential workers during the pandemic. In Türkiye, where employment losses were larger, the year-on-year drop in employment among immigrants was twice as large as that of native-born individuals (−9 percent vs. −4.2 percent). Changes in total employment were not purely driven by population changes; when looking at employment rates, similar

FIGURE 3.10

Changes in employment by region of residence and migration status, 2019–20

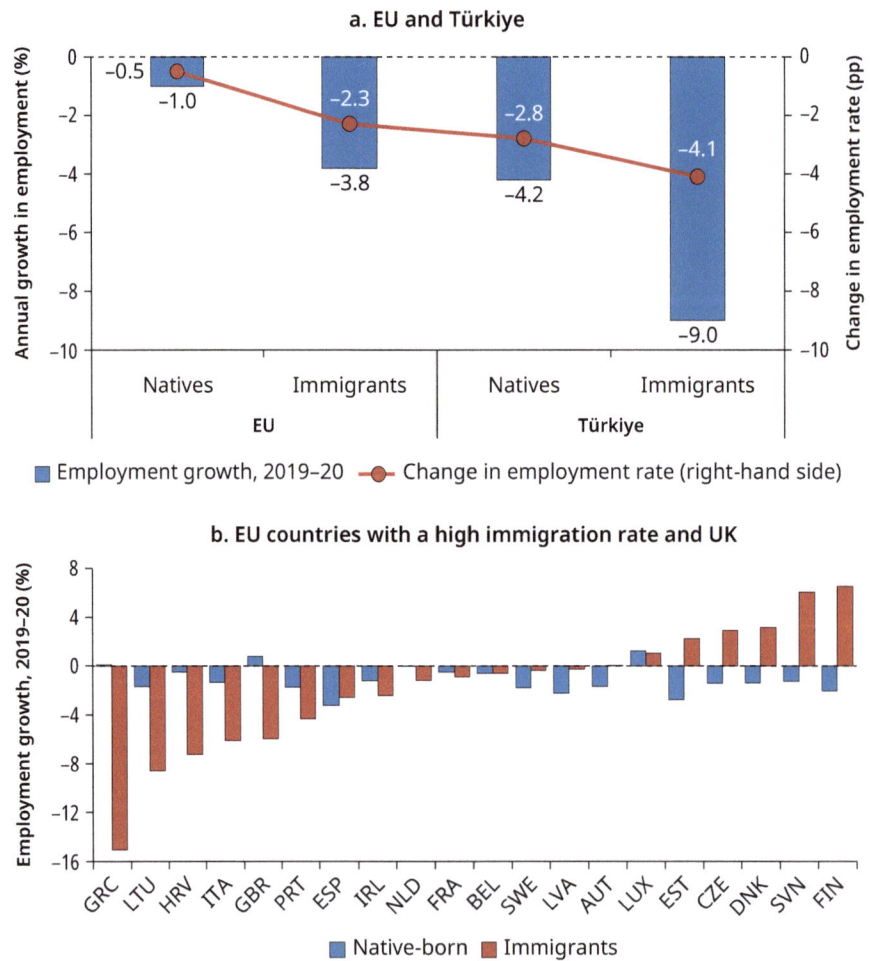

a. EU and Türkiye

■ Employment growth, 2019–20   ●— Change in employment rate (right-hand side)

b. EU countries with a high immigration rate and UK

■ Native-born ■ Immigrants

Source: Eurostat (https://ec.europa.eu/eurostat/web/main/data/database).
Note: EU countries with a high immigration rate are those whose immigration rate is higher than 3 percent. For a list of country codes, go to https://www.iso.org/obp/ui/#search.

findings emerge, with a larger reduction in the share of employed working-age immigrants in both the EU and Türkiye compared with the native-born population. In Russia, several surveys found that migrants from other countries in Central Asia and the Caucasus had larger employment losses in the first two months of the pandemic (Denisenko and Mukomel 2020; Varshaver, Ivanova, and Rocheva 2020).

The greater exposure of migrants to shocks in Europe primarily originates from the type of occupations in which migrants are employed compared with native-born individuals. As shown in the "Migrants' Labor Market Integration in Destination Countries" section, migrants and native-born workers concentrate in different occupations. In general, immigrant workers are more likely than native-born workers to work in occupations that are more manual and are less communication intensive (D'Amuri and Peri 2014; Foged and Peri 2016). These occupations also turned out to be more exposed to income and health risks in the context of the COVID-19 pandemic (Bossavie et al. 2022). Migrant workers in Europe were found to be significantly less likely to be employed in "teleworkable" jobs (Bossavie et al. 2021; Fasani and Mazza 2020a, 2020b), which were protected from the negative employment and income shocks associated with the pandemic (refer to figure 3.11). In addition, migrant workers were more likely to be

FIGURE 3.11

Trends in the share of vulnerable jobs in the European Union, by migration status

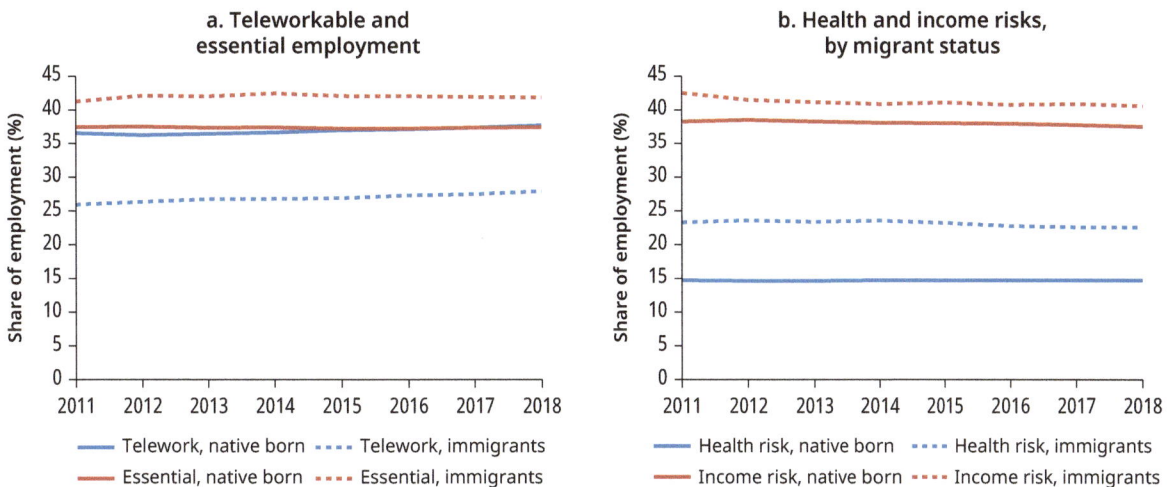

Source: EU Labour Force Survey data (https://ec.europa.eu/eurostat/web/microdata/european-union-labour-force-survey); Bossavie et al. 2021.
Note: "Teleworkable" jobs are those that can be done from home, involving the use of email or online platforms, and that do not require workers to (1) spend most time outdoors; (2) perform physical activity or handle moving objects, such as vehicles or machines; or (3) repair large mechanical or electronic equipment. Essential occupations are defined by lists of occupations that governments considered essential and that were thus exempt from mobility restrictions that were imposed during the COVID-19 pandemic. Jobs vulnerable to income risks are defined as those that are neither essential nor able to be undertaken via telework. Jobs vulnerable to health risks are defined as those with above-average face-to-face interaction levels, are considered essential, and cannot be performed from home, which increases exposure during a pandemic.

employed in face-to-face jobs, which exposed them to health risks associated with COVID-19.

Migrant workers are not only more vulnerable to shocks but are also less protected by social protection systems. Europe is typically characterized by advanced and generous welfare systems. The type of system in place affects the eligibility of the population for different programs, with important implications for the migrant population. Rules establishing migrants' participation in social protection and welfare schemes are far from harmonized at the EU level, and they are even less harmonized when the scope is broadened to include non-EU countries. Even when benefits can be accessed by nonnational residents, many welfare programs have strict conditionality requirements (Lafleur and Vintila 2020). This is, for instance, the case for social assistance benefits (for example, guaranteed minimum income schemes), child-related benefits for vulnerable households, or services (access to childcare or caregiving services). Minimum residency requirements for accessing social benefits across the EU might vary across countries and be more stringent for non-EU migrants (Avato, Koettl, and Sabates-Wheeler 2010). This means that while access to benefits might not be defined in terms of nationality, it might be limited de jure by program design features and eligibility conditions. Further, nonresident nationals across the European Union (especially non-EU migrants) might be excluded from the social benefits of their home country unless preestablished multilateral or bilateral social security agreements are in place. General exceptions include provisions in the EU coordination system that allow mobile EU citizens to access unemployment benefits from their home country while searching for another job in the European Union. Other legal requirements include specific periods of employment history for qualifying for the programs. Migrants with irregular legal status in the host country face more restrictions in accessing social protection systems and have heightened vulnerabilities that can lead to deportation.[8]

Beyond legal restrictions, migrants face other barriers in accessing health care and social protection services. These include financial constraints and a lack of access to social insurance (IOM 2020b), insufficient proficiency in the local language (Berntsen and Skowronek 2021), cultural disparities (IOM 2020b), transferability of credentials and qualifications, and a general lack of access to information and networks. Newly arrived migrants are in a particularly vulnerable position because they are away from their home community and have no access to important informal social networks and safety nets. In response to the COVID-19 pandemic, many destination countries expedited the digitalization of integration and language programs, resulting in enhanced efficiency and cost reduction.

However, this shift also carries the risk of excluding the most vulnerable migrant population subgroups with limited digital literacy and internet access (OECD 2021).

Recent economic crises in Europe, including the 2008 financial crisis, the sovereign debt crisis, and the COVID-19 pandemic, have unveiled the limitations of the current social protection schemes. These crises have been accompanied by increases in total migration to the region resulting from conflict in the Syrian Arab Republic and Iraq and, more recently, Russia's invasion of Ukraine. As a result, European countries have been increasingly concerned about the ability of welfare systems to meet the needs of their citizens as well as the unique needs of migrant communities. Despite this, many European countries (mainly Greece, Ireland, Portugal, and Spain) contained budgetary expenditures on welfare and pensions during the 2010s or limited the pool of potential beneficiaries of such programs.[9] Additionally, in the past two decades, several countries have moved away from passive income payments toward active employment measures to promote better activation policies and to facilitate the transition from social assistance to jobs for beneficiaries of the welfare system. Because many of the countries that have instituted such policies are also countries of entry or residence for migrants to the region, these policies have imposed a disproportionate challenge to already vulnerable migrant groups, because they have not been included in the new active labor market policies (ALMPs).

Policy Recommendations

Policy makers in host countries should consider immigration a major tool to sustain not only population growth but also economic growth and productivity. As shown in the "Benefits and Costs of Migration for Receiving Countries" section, international migration has contributed substantially to population growth in certain countries in ECA and has contained population decline in others over the past two decades. Addressing population decline and labor shortages through different migration policies is going to be a priority moving forward, particularly for small countries characterized by high emigration rates (for example, Eastern Europe, the Western Balkans) that have so far not developed comprehensive migration policies designed to attract foreign workers. These countries will need to consider more open migration policies designed to attract workers from non-EU middle-income or low-income countries while at the same time building up incentive systems and policies that can support the circulation and return of the emigrated workforce.

Policies to ensure that migrants bring or acquire skills needed by destination countries can enhance economic gains and reduce potential costs. The benefits of immigration for ECA countries tend to be the greatest if immigrants are highly skilled and concentrated in occupations that are in demand by the labor market and complement the skills of the native-born population. It is therefore key for destination countries to have policies in place that ensure immigration flows fulfill those criteria. This starts by establishing and strengthening skills monitoring systems and labor market observatories to identify skills in demand in home labor markets that the native-born population cannot fill. Such systems could even be developed on a regional scale by building an EU-wide labor demand system in the European Union. In addition to such systems, destination countries can develop consultative processes with employers, labor unions, and other stakeholders. In the United Kingdom, for example, the Migration Advisory Committee reviews labor needs with stakeholders in selected sectors to advise the government on the potential use of immigration as a response to those needs.

Once skills needs for foreign labor are identified, various managed migration policies can be implemented to ensure migrants fulfill those criteria. A first option is for destination countries to develop bilateral labor agreements tailored to their labor market needs and to target occupations in which the host countries face labor shortages or rising labor demand. Such an approach can be implemented in the context of Global Skill Partnerships in which the destination countries agree with countries of origin on the quantity and skill of migrant labor required and provide technical and financial resources for migrants' training in countries of origin. Another policy option is to select prospective migrants according to their potential for integration and their fit with identified labor market needs using a points system.[10] In this spirit, European countries such as Austria, Germany, Portugal, and Sweden have established job search visas that enable entry of foreign workers who meet specific criteria for the purpose of finding employment. Another approach followed by some countries is to streamline migration procedures for occupations or migrant profiles that are needed in destination countries' labor markets.

This is the case, for instance, of the recent immigration reform in Spain (Decree 629/2022), which introduced several improvements to the existing regulatory framework to enhance the migration application process and migrants' integration in the national labor market. Key aspects of the Spanish reform were enabling labor market access for foreign students resident in Spain under a student visa, streamlining criteria to define occupations in high demand through the Public Employment Service, extending temporary work-related visas from 2 years to 4 years, introducing more flexible possibilities of renewal, and introducing a new form of residence permit that allows migrants to work as self-employed and facilitates access to training opportunities provided by the Public Employment Service (Finotelli and Rinken 2023; Immigration Lawyers Spain, n.d.).

Other countries, however, have been trying to make their immigration system more selective to reduce migration flows that are considered less desirable in host countries' labor markets. The United Kingdom has recently followed this approach to reduce low-skilled immigration. Likewise, recent proposed reforms in Sweden have focused on implementing stricter conditions for low-skilled labor migrants and family reunification.

Integration policies, coupled with interventions addressing misinformation and raising awareness of migrants' contributions, can help reduce negative perceptions of immigration and improve buy-in from the native-born population. Recent evidence shows that inclusive integration policies can reduce anti-immigrant prejudice in high-immigration contexts (Kende et al. 2022). The mechanism through which this happens is integration policies that have a positive impact on different integration outcomes of migrants, including better employment and less reliance on social assistance, which in turn helps improve the native-born population's perceptions of them (Bilgili, Huddleston, and Joki 2015; Huddleston 2020; Pecoraro et al. 2022). Addressing misinformation and ensuring that people are aware of the key role played by migrants in receiving societies is also crucial to mitigate the potential rise of antimigration sentiments. Although providing information only about the magnitude of the migration phenomenon in a country has a limited impact on attitudes (Hopkins, Sides, and Citrin 2019), providing further information about the characteristics of migrants and their impacts on the labor market or welfare system can significantly improve support for immigration (Grigorieff, Roth, and Ubfal 2020; Haaland and Roth 2020; Jørgensen and Osmundsen 2022).

Targeted labor market and social protection policies in destination countries can help reduce and mitigate the potential costs of immigration for some groups. As discussed in the previous sections, the short-term adverse impacts of immigration on some groups can dissipate in the longer run, if the labor market is flexible enough. Therefore, a broader effort to support labor market flexibility in destination countries can also alleviate the potential adverse effects of immigration on wages or employment of some groups of native-born workers. This can allow complementary workers and capital to move to areas and sectors entered by migrants while facilitating workers with similar skills to move to other regions, sectors, or occupations (World Bank 2023). Even with the right labor market and migration policies ex ante in place, however, immigration may still produce some adverse impacts on specific groups in the labor market. To mitigate impacts and support adversely affected workers, social protection programs and ALMPs can be implemented. Here, effective public employment services can help individuals who face job losses and mobility costs as they search for employment in other regions or sectors. Retraining programs can also support native-born workers with skills similar to those of the migrant population to move toward higher-paying occupations where they have a greater comparative advantage. Finally, social protection systems and programs can support those who are temporarily affected by job losses, especially in destination countries in which immigration generates additional fiscal resources.

Investing in language programs can support migrants' labor market integration and economic gains for destination countries. Limited command of the host country's language among immigrant workers has been evidenced as an important barrier to successful integration in host labor markets. Because language acquisition is costly for migrants, receiving countries can further invest in language training programs for migrants as part of the broader introductory programs to enhance the integration of labor migrants and to improve the net fiscal balance of migration for the country. Government-led language training for immigrant workers with limited language proficiency has been shown to increase the labor force participation and employment rate of beneficiaries in France (Lochmann, Rapoport, and Speciale 2019) and Germany (Lang 2022). In the former case, positive impacts have been shown to be larger among more educated workers (Lochmann, Rapoport, and Speciale 2019).

Ensuring that migrants work at their level of qualification in destination countries is also essential. In destination countries, the untapped use of migrants' skills can reduce productivity and tax revenues (World Bank 2023). Recognition of degrees and skills certifications is, however, important to make the best of labor migration and avoid occupational downgrade.[11] Although migrants in EU countries are granted (at least on paper and based on the rule of law) the same rights to access jobs as native-born individuals, de facto limitations still exist in terms of recognition of qualifications and skills, especially for technical occupations and postsecondary, nontertiary education levels. Such limitations are stronger for migrants outside the European Union. To tackle this issue, destination countries must strengthen efforts in developing mechanisms to determine whether origin countries' standards for each skill are equivalent to their own (Nielson 2004). Regional cooperation to validate foreign education credentials and the development of regional qualification frameworks, such as the European Qualifications Framework in EU countries, are promising efforts in this direction. However, significant hurdles persist. According to the EU Labour Force Survey ad hoc migration module in 2014, about 10 percent of high-skilled migrants from the EU-NMS13 living in other EU countries had problems validating their education credentials. Eurasian Economic Union member states have recently passed an agreement on mutual recognition of academic degrees in June 2023, although it still needs to be implemented and enforced.[12] Strengthening ongoing efforts to certify foreign credentials across ECA countries, while highly technical and time consuming, is thus critical to maximizing the benefits of cross-border labor movements for migrants and destination economies alike.

Policies that improve migrants' legal status and formal labor market access can also support that objective. Providing migrants with formal employment rights and secure legal status—whether it involves having a valid employment visa, asylum or residency status, or citizenship—means predictable prospects of stay and greater protection. This increases migrants' incentives to invest in skills that are valuable to the destination country, including language skills, and gives them the ability to move more freely within the economy and society, increasing their income and personal ties, and to further integrate socially and economically (World Bank 2023). These can all facilitate their inclusion in the labor market. Against this backdrop, European countries have in the past decade been looking to reduce the number of undocumented residents and resorted to legalization programs. Several EU countries have intensified these efforts in recent years. Spain has been aiming to increase legal labor migration by facilitating obtaining work permits and simplifying processes for different migrant categories. It is also implementing a regularization program to allow residents living in Spain for at least two years to regularize their status and fill labor market shortages. Germany is also broadening eligibility for the work and residence permit for non-EU nationals and for labor immigration of skilled workers. In addition, a new law, effective as of January 2023, makes migrants with "tolerated status" eligible to obtain temporary residence permits for 18 months, providing an opportunity to meet requirements for longer-term residence. Finally, France introduced a new immigration bill to ease the legalization of undocumented workers in sectors with labor shortages.

To enhance migrants' rights and socioeconomic integration, further harmonization in the design of social protection and jobs programs in the region is needed. The European Union's common market has challenged traditional notions of citizenship and residency in relation to social protection. As such, the conventional relationship between welfare as a public good and its recipients has also been challenged. Traditionally, contributions and access to welfare programs have been based on residency and citizenship. Increased mobility among populations calls the issue of welfare coverage among nonnational residents and nonresident nationals into question. From the perspective of receiving countries, they must consider both the portability of social benefits and the inclusion of nonnational residents to reduce gaps in access to basic services and needs, promote social inclusion, and enhance migrants' overall integration, which results in higher societal welfare. These needs have been highlighted by recent shocks such as the COVID-19 pandemic, which pushed many countries to expand migrants' protection and access to social protection systems (see box 3.1 for a summary of main interventions in different European countries). Even when migrants have de jure access to services, the existence of various de facto barriers implies that migrants' use of health and other social welfare services remains limited. Such efforts must

BOX 3.1 Expanding Migrants' Access to Social Protection Systems and Jobs during the COVID-19 Pandemic

A number of migrant-receiving countries in Europe and Central Asia (ECA) put in place temporary measures to regularize migrants or prevent them from falling into irregular status. These measures featured automatic extension of residency permits (for example, Italy and the Russian Federation), simplified extension procedures (for example, Spain), or maintaining in-person immigration services as essential services (for example, Sweden; IOM 2020a; OECD 2021) to ensure migrants' continuous access to health care and social security throughout the pandemic. Several countries also carried out regularization programs for irregular migrants with different degrees of restrictiveness, given the vulnerabilities of undocumented migrants. Italy provided a two-track approach in which either employers or undocumented workers could apply for the regularization. This regularization, however, was targeted only to workers in the agriculture and domestic work sectors, and the administrative requirements related to workers' experience were quite stringent. Of the estimated 690,000 undocumented migrants in the country, only around 230,000 applied (Palumbo 2020). The Portuguese government granted temporary legal residence to immigrants who had started regularization applications before March 2020, and it allowed an estimated 223,000 immigrants access to health care and other state services (Mazzilli 2021). In Ireland, the government approved a program to regularize up to 17,000 undocumented migrants in the first quarter of 2022 (Citizens Information 2021).

Several ECA countries also eased the obstacles facing different groups of immigrants already residing in the country to work in some key sectors. In Poland, all immigrants who had access to the Polish labor market by March 13, 2020, were authorized for seasonal work without requiring new permits (Matusz and Aivaliotou 2020). Belgium and Germany temporarily allowed asylum seekers without work permits to work in agriculture during the harvest season, and France and Spain also eased their work restrictions for this group (OECD 2021). In Spain, immigrants age 18 years or older without work permits who arrived in the country as unaccompanied minors were

Continued

BOX 3.1 Expanding Migrants' Access to Social Protection Systems and Jobs during the COVID-19 Pandemic *(Continued)*

granted work permits (Moroz, Shrestha, and Testaverde 2020). In the health care sector, the United Kingdom automatically extended visas for foreign doctors for one year, and Spain sped up the process of recognizing foreign credentials of health care professionals residing in the country (Open Society Foundation 2020).

Access to health care for different vulnerable groups, including undocumented migrants and those without health insurance, became a concern among ECA countries because of equity and public health motivations. Beyond policies to enhance the legality of different groups of migrants, several countries temporarily expanded access to health care. Migrants were granted access to free medical care for COVID-19 through special regulations in both Kazakhstan and the Russian Federation, and in the latter, access to free health care support related to COVID-19 was granted even to irregular, undocumented migrants (Moroz, Shrestha, and Testaverde 2020). In the city of Moscow, the mayor approved medical assistance to all migrants. In Austria, even if immigrants were ineligible for health insurance because of residency requirements, they were still granted assistance for COVID-19 care (Freier 2020). In Poland, eligibility for COVID-19–related services and treatment was extended to all residents, including uninsured people and migrants, which was also made free of charge in the United Kingdom (Baptista et al. 2021).

Although there were no social protection programs in ECA countries specifically targeted to immigrants, several supported vulnerable families, including migrants. The Minimum Living Income passed by the Spanish government is open to any person who can prove at least one year of residence in the country (Open Society Foundation 2020). In Italy, all migrants with residence permits were allowed to apply for the €600 income subsidy targeting self-employed and temporary workers, agriculture workers, domestic workers, and seasonal workers in the tourism sector according to the COVID-19 Cura Italia decree (Moroz, Shrestha, and Testaverde 2020). Ireland's €350 weekly Pandemic Unemployment Payment targeted individuals who lost their jobs as a result of the COVID-19 crisis regardless of their migration status, including irregular migrants. The Russian government enforced temporary halts on evictions of any individual, even undocumented migrants.

therefore be complemented by addressing de facto barriers to migrants' use of key services. To ensure that migrants have access to and use services that can help them protect themselves and others, the involvement of local organizations and the use of communications material in languages understood by migrants could be considered (Testaverde and Pavilon 2022).

Building responsive, resilient, adaptive, and effective migration management systems in host countries is also key to maximizing the welfare of migrants and host communities. The COVID-19 pandemic experience has shown that migration systems should also be adaptive and responsive to shocks, meaning that they should be flexible enough to respond rapidly and effectively to crisis and adapt to new economic circumstances after a global, regional, or national shock (pandemic, economic crisis, or war). A lack of rapid response can result in inefficiencies and high welfare costs; the evidence from COVID-19 and other economic shocks has shown that migrants tend to be more affected by crisis and their negative socioeconomic consequences (refer to annex 3B). Adapting and responding to shocks might entail, for instance, appropriately easing visa regulations temporarily to facilitate access to formal jobs and protection benefits designed in response to the crisis.

Establishing mechanisms to allow and ease migrants' access to health care and social welfare programs during crises can also help reduce or limit risks for all. One way to achieve this objective is by automatically covering migrants in new programs introduced during crisis periods. An alternative approach is to waive eligibility requirements and restrictions that prevent migrants from accessing standard social welfare programs in case of unexpected shocks. Such restrictions, for example, include the minimum stay requirement that limits migrants who have recently arrived in a country from accessing social welfare and other services (Testaverde and Pavilon 2022). Similar waivers could be considered for undocumented migrants, who often have limited access to health care and social welfare. Ensuring that these initiatives are automatically triggered in response to shocks could help countries react quickly and limit the negative repercussions that crises may have on both migrants and local communities.

Annex 3A: Assessing Migrants' Impact on Native-Born Workers' Welfare: A Calibration Exercise

On the basis of simple models of factor complementarity, economists have long been optimistic about the net positive welfare impact of immigration for native-born individuals (Borjas 1994). They have also been aware of factor price adjustment effects of immigration (Borjas 2003b) and of the possible consequences for welfare states (Razin and Sadka 2000). However, once one simultaneously accounts for labor market frictions and redistributive fiscal policies, the net effect of immigration on the welfare of native-born workers is harder to calculate. The analysis hereby updates the results of Battisti et al. (2018) by adding additional countries, enriching the baseline specification, and using more recent data.

The model by Battisti et al. (2018) is based on a search and matching frictions general equilibrium model that includes skill heterogeneity, wage bargaining, and a welfare state that taxes labor income to provide unemployment benefits and engages in redistributive policies. The model is calibrated separately for 24 countries to evaluate the effects of different migration scenarios on the welfare of different sections of the native-born population. The effect of immigration on labor market outcomes and welfare is likely to hinge on four important features of immigrants and host countries. First, it depends on how the skill composition of the immigrant labor force differs from that of native-born individuals. By the complementarity channel, additional supply of a certain type of worker negatively affects other workers of the same type (substitutes) and positively affects workers of different types (complements). For example, a new inflow of low-skilled immigrants reduces the wages of low-skilled native-born workers and increases those of high-skilled native-born workers. In about one-third of the surveyed countries, the share of those who are tertiary educated is larger for immigrants than for native-born people. In several countries, including France, Germany, and the United Kingdom, however, that share is substantially smaller for immigrants than for native-born individuals.

The second key fact relates to the relative wage levels of immigrants and native-born workers. Wage gaps may reflect differences in labor productivity, but they may also relate to differences in the outside option of native-born individuals relative to migrants. These two determinants of wage gaps have different implications for the labor market effects of immigrants.

The third fact relates to unemployment risk. In most countries both low- and high-skilled immigrants are much more likely to be unemployed than native-born workers of the same skill level. All countries in the sample provide some unemployment insurance, albeit at different levels of generosity. Such systems lead to net redistribution from the group with a lower unemployment rate to the group with a higher unemployment rate. Fourth, the size of government (measured by the share of taxes or public expenditures in gross domestic product) has important implications for the welfare effect of immigrants and varies significantly across countries. Although scale effects of migration have been the subject of some research and much public debate, a specific analysis by Battisti et al. (2018) includes the welfare state in a general equilibrium model featuring skill heterogeneity and labor market frictions.

These features describe four different margins through which immigrants affect the welfare of the native-born population. In the model, immigration affects native-born persons' welfare through four channels. Two work through the labor market: the traditional complementarity channel affects wages through relative supply of skills, whereas a job creation channel arises because an increase in the share of immigrant workers affects the incentives for job creation by firms (Chassamboulli and Palivos 2014). Its impact on native-born employment depends crucially on differences between native-born individuals and immigrants regarding productivity and outside options. Redistribution also works through two channels: one through unemployment benefits and another through proportional taxes and lump-sum transfers. How these channels affect the welfare of those who are native born depends on the relative skill composition of immigrants, as well as on the design of labor market institutions and the public sector.

Annex 3B: Change in Employment Trends during the COVID-19 Pandemic

FIGURE 3B.1

Change in employment and unemployment at the onset of the COVID-19 pandemic

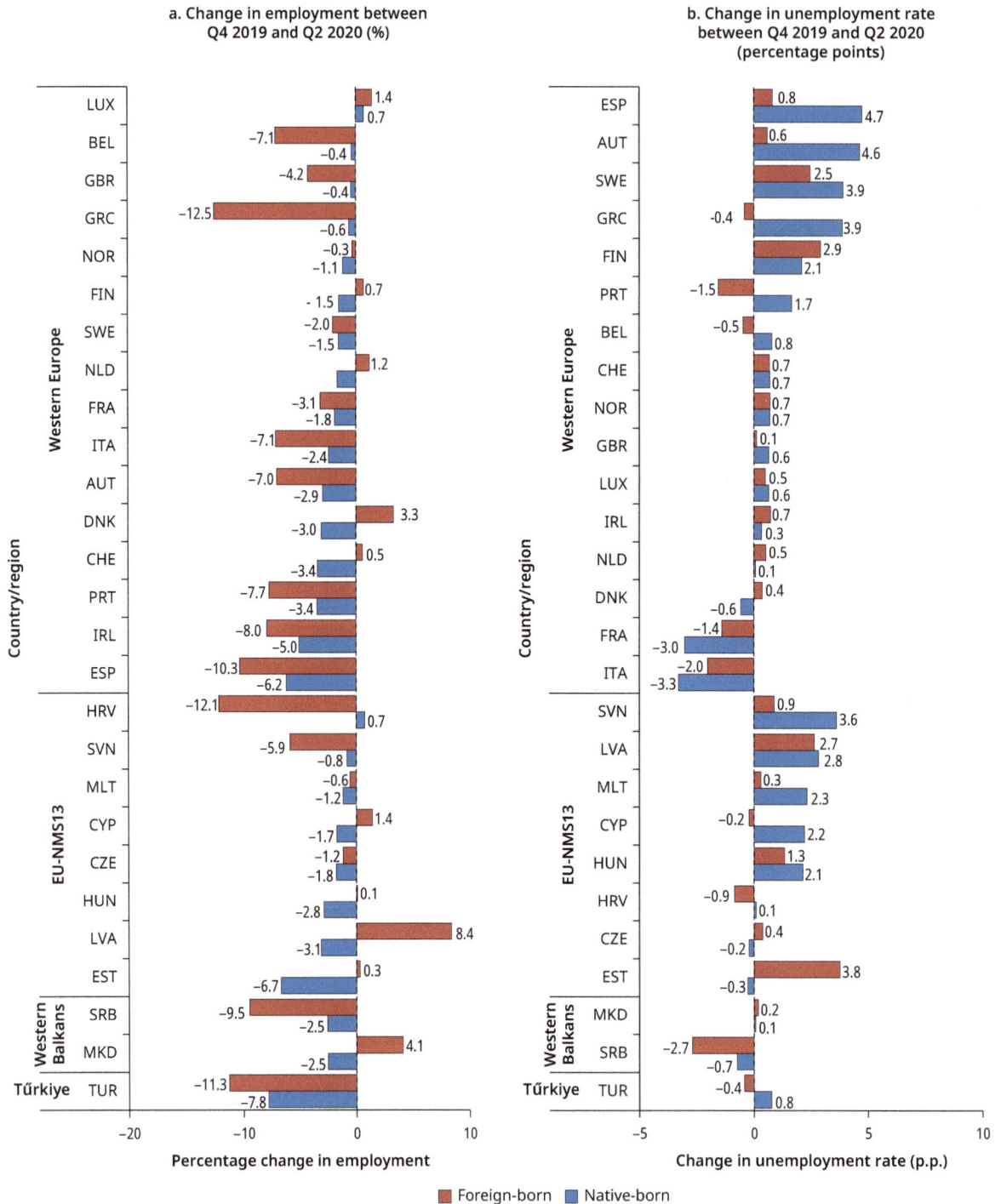

a. Change in employment between Q4 2019 and Q2 2020 (%)

Country/region		Foreign-born	Native-born
Western Europe	LUX	1.4	0.7
	BEL	−7.1	−0.4
	GBR	−4.2	−0.4
	GRC	−12.5	−0.6
	NOR	−0.3	−1.1
	FIN	0.7	−1.5
	SWE	−2.0	−1.5
	NLD	1.2	−1.5
	FRA	−3.1	−1.8
	ITA	−7.1	−2.4
	AUT	−7.0	−2.9
	DNK	3.3	−3.0
	CHE	0.5	−3.4
	PRT	−7.7	−3.4
	IRL	−8.0	−5.0
	ESP	−10.3	−6.2
EU-NMS13	HRV	−12.1	0.7
	SVN	−5.9	−0.8
	MLT	−0.6	−1.2
	CYP	1.4	−1.7
	CZE	−1.2	−1.8
	HUN	0.1	−2.8
	LVA	8.4	−3.1
	EST	0.3	−6.7
Western Balkans	SRB	−9.5	−2.5
	MKD	4.1	−2.5
Türkiye	TUR	−11.3	−7.8

Percentage change in employment (x-axis: −20, −10, 0, 10)

b. Change in unemployment rate between Q4 2019 and Q2 2020 (percentage points)

Country/region		Foreign-born	Native-born
Western Europe	ESP	0.8	4.7
	AUT	0.6	4.6
	SWE	2.5	3.9
	GRC	-0.4	3.9
	FIN	2.9	2.1
	PRT	−1.5	1.7
	BEL	−0.5	0.8
	CHE	0.7	0.7
	NOR	0.7	0.7
	GBR	0.1	0.6
	LUX	0.5	0.6
	IRL	0.7	0.3
	NLD	0.5	0.1
	DNK	-0.6	0.4
	FRA	−1.4	−3.0
	ITA	−2.0	−3.3
EU-NMS13	SVN	0.9	3.6
	LVA	2.7	2.8
	MLT	0.3	2.3
	CYP	−0.2	2.2
	HUN	1.3	2.1
	HRV	−0.9	0.1
	CZE	0.4	−0.2
	EST	3.8	−0.3
Western Balkans	MKD	0.2	0.1
	SRB	−2.7	−0.7
Türkiye	TUR	−0.4	0.8

Change in unemployment rate (p.p.) (x-axis: −5, 0, 5, 10)

■ Foreign-born ■ Native-born

Source: Eurostat (lfsq_egacob and lfsq_urgacob; https://ec.europa.eu/eurostat/web/main/data/database)
Note: For a list of country codes, go to https://www.iso.org/obp/ui/#search. EU-NMS13 = new member states joining the European Union in 2004, 2007, and 2013; Q2 = second quarter; Q4 = fourth quarter.

FIGURE 3B.2

Change in employment growth rates

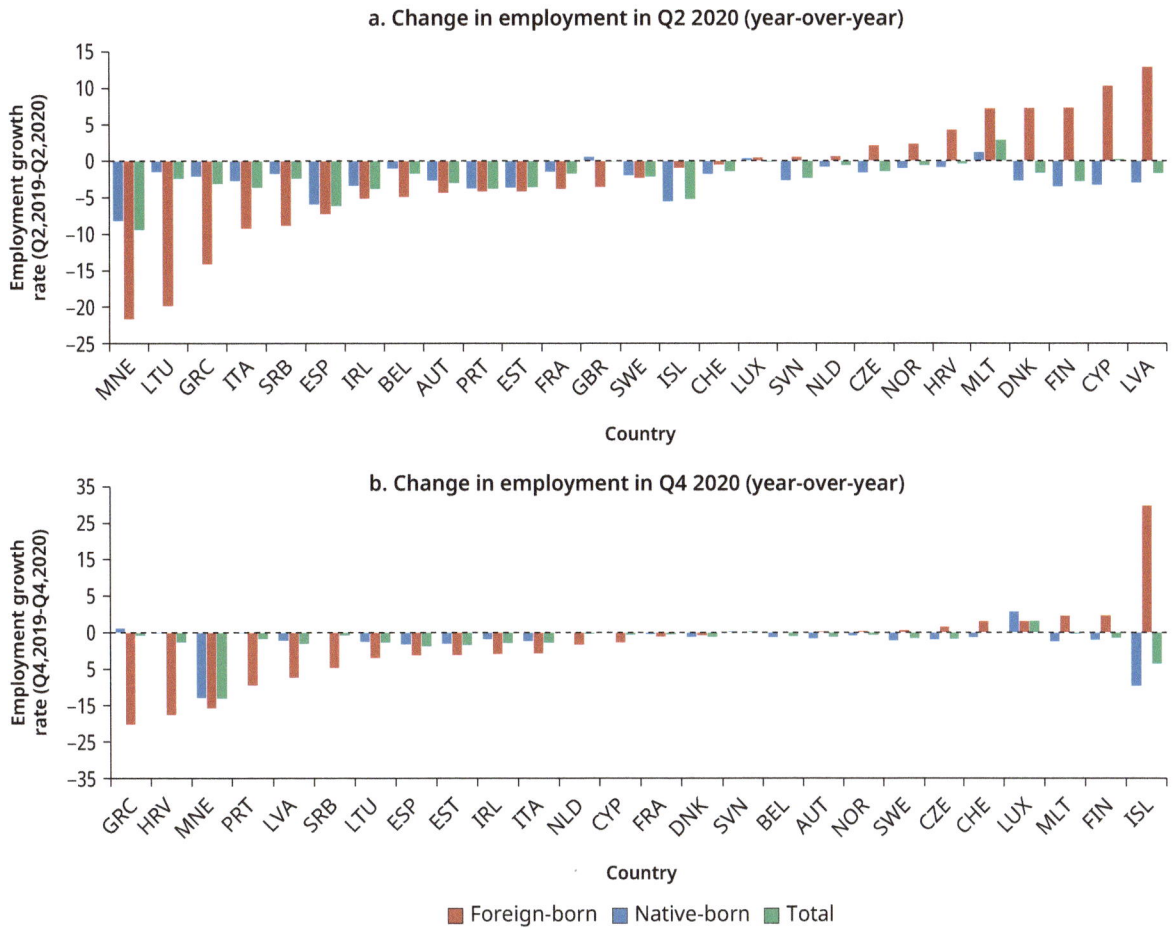

a. Change in employment in Q2 2020 (year-over-year)

b. Change in employment in Q4 2020 (year-over-year)

■ Foreign-born ■ Native-born ■ Total

Source: Eurostat (lfsq_egacob and lfsq_urgacob; https://ec.europa.eu/eurostat/web/main/data/database).
Note: For a list of country codes, go to https://www.iso.org/obp/ui/#search. Q2 = second quarter; Q4 = fourth quarter.

Notes

1. Higher shares of immigrant students have been shown to have larger negative impacts for low-ability native-born students in Italy (Frattini and Meschi 2019). The duration of stay of immigrant children in the host country also matters. In the Netherlands, the presence of recently arrived immigrants had a small negative impact on some native-born students' learning, whereas immigrant children who had been in the country for longer had no impact (Bossavie 2020).

2. The findings were based on whether respondents answered that migration was a "good thing," a "bad thing," or "it depends" for three domains: (1) immigrants living in this country, (2) an immigrant becoming your neighbor, and (3) an immigrant marrying one of your close relatives.

3. Higher values of the index correspond to occupations with a higher socioeconomic status, values above zero indicate occupations that are more prestigious than the national average, and vice versa for values below zero. If immigrants and native-born individuals within each country had the same distribution of occupational status, then the graph would show a straight line at 0.

4. For more details about occupational downgrade among high-skilled migrants and its drivers, see chapter 4 or Borjas (2015) and Friedberg (2000).

5. Residential segregation may originate from migrants' preference to locate in areas with a higher proportion of individuals from their own country, as shown in Denmark (Damm 2009). This phenomenon may be reinforced by native-born individuals' flight from areas with a high concentration of immigrants (Batut et al. 2022; Beckhusen et al. 2013).

6. The Migrant Integration Policy Index summarizes to which extent policies in different countries are more or less conducive to socioeconomic integration of migrants in destination countries. The overall index covers different domains of integration, including labor market participation, access to education and recognition of academic qualifications, access to social protection and social insurance benefits, family reunification, political participation, access to citizenship and permanent residency, and antidiscrimination, and it particularly focuses on measures favoring the integration of youth and women as well as non-EU third-country nationals.

7. In the case of Greece, the improvement can probably be imputed to easing regulations related to refugees' labor market access.

8. A comprehensive review of country-specific eligibility criteria and welfare entitlements for migrants in the European Union is provided by Lafleur and Vintila (2020). See also Fanjul and Dempster (2020).

9. For example, spending on social protection benefits in Greece decreased from 28% of GDP in 2012 to 25.2% of GDP in 2019. Since then the government has enacted several budgetary increases, raising the spending to 26.8% of GDP in 2021 (Eurostat social protection expenditures database spr_exp_sum).

10. In such systems, prospective migrants are scored on the basis of a set of criteria, such as skills, language, or demographics, and those who accrue enough points are allowed entry on a path that typically leads to naturalization.

11. The issue of occupational downgrade is discussed in more detail in chapter 4.

12. Signatories of the agreement are Armenia, Belarus, Kazakhstan, the Kyrgyz Republic, and the Russian Federation.

References

Accetturo, A., F. Manaresi, S. Mocetti, and E. Olivieri. 2014. "Don't Stand So Close to Me: The Urban Impact of Immigration." *Regional Science and Urban Economics* 45: 45–56.

Ajzenman, N., C. Giray Aksoy, and S. Guriev. 2022. "Exposure to Transit Migration: Public Attitudes and Entrepreneurship." *Journal of Development Economics* 158: 102899.

Aleksynska, M., and A. Tritah. 2015. "The Heterogeneity of Immigrants, Host Countries' Income, and Productivity: A Channel Accounting Approach." *Economic Inquiry* 53 (1): 150–72. https://doi.org/10.1111/ecin.12141.

Alesina, A. F., J. D. Harnoss, and H. Rapoport. 2016. "Birthplace Diversity and Economic Prosperity." *Journal of Economic Growth* 21 (2): 101–38. https://doi.org/10.1007/s10887-016-9127-6.

Alesina, A. F., A. Miano, and S. Stantcheva. 2023. "Immigration and Redistribution." *Review of Economic Studies* 90 (1): 1–39.

Angrist, J. D., and A. D. Kugler. 2003. "Protective or Counter-Productive? Labour Market Institutions and the Effect of Immigration on EU Natives." *Economic Journal* 113 (488): F302–31.

Avato, J., J. Koettl, and R. Sabates-Wheeler. 2010. "Social Security Regimes, Global Estimates, and Good Practices: The Status of Social Protection for International Migrants." *World Development* 38 (4): 455–66.

Bailey, M., D. M. Johnston, M. Koenen, T. Kuchler, D. Russel, and J. Stroebel. 2022. "The Social Integration of International Migrants: Evidence from the Networks of Syrians in Germany." Working Paper 29925, National Bureau of Economic Research, Cambridge, MA.

Ballatore, R. M., M. Fort, and A. Ichino. 2018. "Tower of Babel in the Classroom: Immigrants and Natives in Italian Schools." *Journal of Labor Economics* 36 (4): 885–921.

Baptista, I., E. Marlier, S. Spasova, R. Peña-Casas, B. Fronteddu, D. Ghailani, S. Sabato, and P. Regazzoni. 2021. *Social Protection and Inclusion Policy Responses to the COVID-19 Crisis: An Analysis of Policies in 35 Countries.* Luxembourg: European Social Policy Network, European Union.

Barbone, L., M. Bontch-Osmolovsky, and S. Zaidi. 2009. "The Foreign-Born Population in the European Union and Its Contribution to National Tax and Benefit Systems: Some Insights from Recent Household Survey

Data." Policy Research Working Paper 4899, World Bank, Washington, DC. https://doi.org/10.1596/1813 -9450-4899.

Barrett, A. 2009. "EU Enlargement and Ireland's Labour Market." Discussion Paper 4260, Institute for the Study of Labor, Bonn.

Basso, G., T. Boeri, A. Caiumi, and M. Paccagnella. 2020. "The New Hazardous Jobs and Worker Reallocation." Discussion Paper No. DP15100, Centre for Economic Policy Research, Institute of Labor Economics, Bonn. https://ssrn.com/abstract=3661444.

Battisti, M., G. Felbermayr, G. Peri, and P. Poutvaara. 2018. "Immigration, Search and Redistribution: A Quantitative Assessment of Native Welfare." *Journal of the European Economic Association* 16 (4): 1137–88. https://doi.org/10.1093/jeea/jvx035.

Battisti, M., and P. Poutvaara. 2021. "Immigration, Search, and Redistribution: Updated Cross-Country Evidence of Effects of Migration." Background paper, *The Journey Ahead: Supporting Successful Migration in Europe and Central Asia*, World Bank, Washington, DC.

Batut, C., and S. Schneider-Strawczynski. 2022. "Rival Guests or Defiant Hosts? The Local Economic Impact of Hosting Refugees." *Journal of Economic Geography* 22 (2): 327–50.

Beckhusen, J., R. J. Florax, J. Poot, and B.S. Waldorf. 2013. "Attracting Global Talent and Then What? Overeducated Immigrants in the United States." *Journal of Regional Science* 53 (5): 834–54.

Bell, B., F. Fasani, and S. Machin. 2013. "Crime and Immigration: Evidence from Large Immigrant Waves." *Review of Economics and Statistics* 95 (4): 1278–90.

Berntsen, L., and N. Skowronek. 2021. "State-of-the-Art Research Overview of the Impact of COVID-19 on Migrant Workers in the EU and the Netherlands." Nijmegen Sociology of Law Working Paper 2021/01, Institute for Sociology of Law, Radboud University Nijmegen. https://hdl.handle.net/2066/233185.

Bianchi, M., P. Buonanno, and P. Pinotti. 2012. "Do Immigrants Cause Crime?" *Journal of the European Economic Association* 10 (6): 1318–47.

Bilgili, Ö., T. Huddleston, and A. Joki. 2015. *The Dynamics between Integration Policies and Outcomes: A Synthesis of the Literature.* Barcelona Centre for International Affairs, Barcelona.

Blanchard, O., and A. Landier. 2002. "The Perverse Effects of Partial Labour Market Reform: Fixed-Term Contracts in France." *Economic Journal* 112 (480): F214–F244.

Blanchflower, D. G., and C. Shadforth. 2009. "Fear, Unemployment, and Migration." *Economic Journal* 119 (535): F136–82.

Boeri, T. 2010. "Immigration to the Land of Redistribution." *Economica* 77 (308): 651–87.

Borjas, G. J. 1994. "The Economic Benefits from Immigration." Working Paper 4955, National Bureau of Economic Research, Cambridge, MA. https://www.nber.org/system/files/working_papers/w4955/w4955.pdf.

Borjas, G.J. 2003a. "The Impact of Foreign Students on Native Enrollment in Graduate Programs." Harvard University. https://citeseerx.ist.psu.edu/document?repid=rep1&type=pdf&doi= 0375fed0620a21f77ef517d2986c37f4d1b1d858.

Borjas, G.J. 2003b. "The Labor Demand Curve Is Downward Sloping: Reexamining the Impact of Immigration on the Labor Market." Harvard University. https://scholar.harvard.edu/files/gborjas/files/qje2003.pdf.

Borjas, G. J. 2015. "The Slowdown in the Economic Assimilation of Immigrants: Aging and Cohort Effects Revisited Again." *Journal of Human Capital* 9 (4): 483–517.

Borjas, G. J. 2019. "Immigration and Economic Growth." Working Paper 25836, National Bureau of Economic Research, Cambridge, MA. https://doi.org/10.3386/w25836.

Bossavie, L. 2020. "The Effect of Immigration on Natives' School Achievement: Does Length of Stay in the Host Country Matter?" *Journal of Human Resources* 55 (2): 733–66.

Bossavie, L., D. Garrote Sanchez, M. Makovec, and C. Ozden. 2021. "Occupational Hazards: Why Migrants Faced Greater Economic and Health Risks during the COVID-19 Pandemic." Policy Research Working Paper 9873, World Bank, Washington, DC. https://documents1.worldbank.org/curated/en/692831638797417505/pdf /Occupational-Hazards-Migrants-and-the-Economic-and-Health-Risks-of-COVID-19-in-Western-Europe.pdf.

Bossavie, L., D. Garrote Sanchez, M. Makovec, and C. Ozden. 2022. "Do Immigrants Shield the Locals? Exposure to COVID-Related Risks in the European Union." *Review of International Economics.* https://doi.org/10.1111 /roie.12609.

Boubtane, E., J.-C. Dumont, and C. Rault. 2016. "Immigration and Economic Growth in the OECD Countries, 1986–2006." *Oxford Economic Papers* 68 (2): 340–60. https://doi.org/10.1093/oep/gpw001.

Brücker, H., and E. J. Jahn. 2011. "Migration and Wage-Setting: Reassessing the Labor Market Effects of Migration." *Scandinavian Journal of Economics* 113 (2): 286–317.

Budria, S., A. Colino, and C. M. de Ibarreta. 2019. "The Impact of Host Language Proficiency on Employment Outcomes among Immigrants in Spain." *Empirica* 46 (4): 625–52. https://doi.org/10.1007/s10663-018-9414-x.

Bursztyn, L., T. Chaney, T. Hassan, and A. Rao. 2024. "The Immigrant Next Door." *American Economic Review* 114 (2): 348–84. https://doi.org/10.1257/aer.20220376.

Carrasco, R., J. F. Jimeno, and A. C. Ortega. 2008. "The Effect of Immigration on the Labor Market Performance of Native-Born Workers: Some Evidence for Spain." *Journal of Population Economics* 21 (3): 627–48.

Chander, P., and S. M. Thangavelu. 2004. "Technology Adoption, Education, and Immigration Policy." *Journal of Development Economics* 75 (1): 79–94. https://doi.org/10.1016/j.jdeveco.2003.07.006.

Chojnicki, X. 2013. "The Fiscal Impact of Immigration in France: A Generational Accounting Approach." *World Economy* 36 (8): 1065–90. https://doi.org/10.1111/twec.12057.

Citizens Information. 2021. "Regularisation Scheme for Long-Term Undocumented Migrants." Dublin: Citizens Information. https://www.citizensinformation.ie/en/moving_country/moving_to_ireland/rights_of _residence_in_ireland/permission_to_remain_for_undocumented_noneea_nationals_in_ireland.html.

d'Albis, H., E. Boubtane, and D. Coulibaly. 2015. "Immigration Policy and Macroeconomic Performance in France." Etudes et Documents 5, Center for the Study and Research on International Development, Clermont-Ferrand University, Clermont-Ferrand, France. https://shs.hal.science/halshs-01135389 /document.

Damm, A. P. 2009. "Ethnic Enclaves and Immigrant Labor Market Outcomes: Quasi-Experimental Evidence." *Journal of Labor Economics* 27 (2): 281–314. https://doi.org/10.1086/599336.

D'Amuri, F., and G. Peri. 2014. "Immigration, Jobs, and Employment Protection: Evidence from Europe before and during the Great Recession." *Journal of the European Economic Association* 12 (2): 432–64. https://doi .org/10.1111/jeea.12040.

De Giorgi, G., M. Pellizzari, and C. Naghib. 2022. "Labor Market Outcomes of Migrants: Life-Cycle Perspectives from Swiss Micro-Data." Background paper, *The Journey Ahead: Supporting Successful Migration in Europe and Central Asia*, World Bank, Washington, DC.

De Giorgi, G., M. Prado, and B. Severgnini. 2022. "Migrants in the Danish Labor Market over the Life Cycle and across Generations." Background paper, *The Journey Ahead: Supporting Successful Migration in Europe and Central Asia*, World Bank, Washington, DC.

Denisenko, M., and V. Mukomel. 2020. "Labour Migration during the Corona Crisis." *Econs.online*, September 2, 2020. https://econs.online/en/articles/economics/labour-migration-during-the-corona-crisis/.

Devillanova, C., F. Fasani, and T. Frattini. 2018. "Employment of Undocumented Immigrants and the Prospect of Legal Status: Evidence from an Amnesty Program." *ILR Review* 71 (4): 853–81.

Docquier, F., R. Turati, J. Valette, and C. Vasilakis. 2018. "Birthplace Diversity and Economic Growth: Evidence from the US States in the Post–World War II Period." Discussion Paper 11802, Institute of Labor Economics, Bonn.

Dolado, J., A. Goria, and A. Ichino. 1994. "Immigration, Human Capital, and Growth in the Host Country: Evidence from Pooled Country Data." *Journal of Population Economics* 7: 193–215. https://doi.org/10.1007 /BF00173619.

Dražanová, L., and J. Gonnot. 2023. "Attitudes toward Immigration in Europe: Cross-Regional Differences." *Open Research Europe* 3: 66.

Dustmann, C. 1999. "Temporary Migration, Human Capital, and Language Fluency of Migrants." *Scandinavian Journal of Economics* 101 (2): 297–314.

Dustmann, C., and F. Fabbri. 2003. "Language Proficiency and Labour Market Performance of Immigrants in the UK." *Economic Journal* 113 (489): 695–717.

Dustmann, C., F. Fabbri, and I. Preston. 2005. "The Impact of Immigration on the British Labour Market." *Economic Journal* 115 (507): F324–41.

Dustmann, C., and T. Frattini. 2014. "The Fiscal Effects of Immigration to the United Kingdom." *Economic Journal* 124 (580): F593–643. https://doi.org/10.1111/ecoj.12181.

Dustmann, C., T. Frattini, and I. P. Preston. 2013. "The Effect of Immigration along the Distribution of Wages." *Review of Economic Studies* 80 (1): 145–73. https://doi.org/10.1093/restud/rds019.

Dustmann, C., A. Glitz, and T. Frattini. 2008. "The Labour Market Impact of Immigration." *Oxford Review of Economic Policy* 24 (3): 477–94.

Dustmann, C., A. Glitz, and T. Vogel. 2010. "Employment, Wages, and the Economic Cycle: Differences between Immigrants and Natives." *European Economic Review* 54 (1): 1–17. https://doi.org/10.1016/j.euroecorev .2009.04.004.

Dustmann, C., and A. van Soest. 2001 "Language Fluency and Earnings: Estimation with Misclassified Language Indicators." *Review of Economics and Statistics* 83 (4): 663–74.

Edo, A. 2015. "The Impact of Immigration on Native Wages and Employment." *BE Journal of Economic Analysis & Policy* 15 (3): 1151–96.

Edo, A. 2016. "How Do Rigid Labor Markets Absorb Immigration? Evidence from France." *IZA Journal of Migration* 5 (1): 7.

Edo, A. 2019. "The Impact of Immigration on the Labor Market." *Journal of Economic Surveys* 33 (3): 922–48.

Edo, A., and F. Toubal. 2015. "Selective Immigration Policies and Wages Inequality." *Review of International Economics* 23 (1): 160–87.

Esipova, N., J. Fleming, and J. Ray. 2017. "New Index Shows Least-, Most-Accepting Countries for Migrants." *Gallup*, August 23, 2017. http://www.gallup.com/poll/216377/new-indexshows-least-accepting-countries -migrants.aspx?g_source=mn2-us.

ESS Data Portal. 2020. *ESS Round 10: Democracy, Digital Social Contacts.* London: ESS ERIC. https://ess.sikt.no /en/?tab=overview.

European Commission, Directorate-General for Migration and Home Affairs. 2021. *Integration of Immigrants in the European Union.* Luxembourg: Publications Office of the European Union. https://doi.org /10.2837/672792.

Fanjul, G., and H. Dempster. 2020. "Regularizing Migrant Workers in Response to COVID-19." *Center for Global Development* (blog), July 28, 2020. https://www.cgdev.org/blog/regularizing-migrant-workers -response-covid-19.

Farré, L., L. González, and F. Ortega. 2011. "Immigration, Family Responsibilities and the Labor Supply of Skilled Native Women." *BE Journal of Economic Analysis & Policy* 11 (1). https://doi.org/10.2202 /1935-1682.2875.

Farré, L., F. Ortega, and R. Tanaka. 2018. "Immigration and the Public–Private School Choice." *Labour Economics* 51: 184–201.

Fasani, F. 2018. "Immigrant Crime and Legal Status: Evidence from Repeated Amnesty Programs." *Journal of Economic Geography* 18 (4): 887–914.

Fasani, F., and J. Mazza. 2020a. "Being on the Frontline? Immigrant Workers in Europe and the COVID-19 Pandemic." Discussion Paper 13963, Institute of Labor Economics, Bonn. https://www.iza.org/publications /dp/13963/being-on-the-frontline-immigrant-workers-in-europe-and-the-covid-19-pandemic.

Fasani, F., and J. Mazza. 2020b. "Immigrant Key Workers: Their Contribution to Europe's COVID-19 Response." Policy Paper 155, Institute of Labor Economics, Bonn. https://www.iza.org/publications/pp/155/ immigrant-key-workers-their-contribution-to-europes-covid-19-response.

Felbermayr, G. J., S. Hiller, and D. Sala. 2010. "Does Immigration Boost Per Capita Income?" *Economics Letters* 107 (2): 177–9.

Finotelli, C., and Rinken, S. 2023. "A Pragmatic Bet: The Evolution of Spain's Immigration System." *Migration Information Source.* https://www.migrationpolicy.org/article/spain-immigration-system-evolution.

Fiorio, C., T. Frattini, A. Riganti, and M. Christl. 2024. "Migration and Public Finances in the EU." *International Tax and Public Finance* 31 (3): 635–84. https://doi.org/10.1007/s10797-023-09787-9.

Foged, M., and G. Peri. 2016. "Immigrants' Effect on Native Workers: New Analysis on Longitudinal Data." American Economic Journal: Applied Economics 8 (2): 1–34.

Foged, M., L. Hasager, G. Peri, J. N. Arendt, and I. Bolvig. 2022. "Intergenerational Spillover Effects of Language Training for Refugees." Working Paper 30341, National Bureau of Economic Research, Cambridge, MA.

Foged, M., and G. Peri. 2016. "Immigrants' Effect on Native Workers: New Analysis on Longitudinal Data." *American Economic Journal: Applied Economics* 8 (2): 1–34. https://doi.org/10.1257/app.20150114.

Frattini, T., and E. Meschi. 2019. "The Effect of Immigrant Peers in Vocational Schools." *European Economic Review* 113: 1–22.

Frattini, T., and P. Ciampa. 2020. *Fourth Migration Observatory Report: Immigrant Integration in Europe.* Turin: Centro Studi Luca d'Agliano.

Freier, L. F. 2020. *COVID-19 and Rethinking the Need for Legal Pathways to Mobility: Taking Human Security Seriously.* Geneva: International Organization for Migration. https://publications.iom.int/system/files/pdf/rethinking-the-need-for-legal.pdf.

Friedberg, R. M. 2000. "You Can't Take It with You? Immigrant Assimilation and the Portability of Human Capital." *Journal of Labor Economics* 18 (2): 221–51.

Ghio, D., M. Bratti, and S. Bignami. 2023. "Linguistic Barriers to Immigrants' Labor Market Integration in Italy." *International Migration Review* 57 (1): 357–94.

Giuntella, O., C. Nicodemo, and C. Vargas-Silva. 2018. "The Effects of Immigration on NHS Waiting Times." *Journal of Health Economics* 58: 123–43.

Glitz, A. 2012. "The Labor Market Impact of Immigration: A Quasi-Experiment Exploiting Immigrant Location Rules in Germany." *Journal of Labor Economics* 30 (1): 175–213.

Goubin, S., A. Ruelens, and I. Nicaise. 2022. *Trends in Attitudes towards Migration in Europe. A Comparative Analysis.* Leuven, Belgium: HIVA—Research Institute for Work and Society.

Grigorieff, A., C. Roth, and D. Ubfal. 2020. "Does Information Change Attitudes toward Immigrants?" *Demography* 57 (3): 1117–43.

Haaland, I., and C. Roth. 2020. "Labor Market Concerns and Support for Immigration." *Journal of Public Economics* 191: 104256.

Hansen, M. F., M. L. Schultz-Nielsen, and T. Tranaes. 2017. "The Fiscal Impact of Immigration to Welfare States of the Scandinavian Type." *Journal of Population Economics* 30: 925–52. https://doi.org/10.1007/s00148-017-0636-1.

Hopkins, D. J., J. Sides, and J. Citrin. 2019. "The Muted Consequences of Correct Information about Immigration." *Journal of Politics* 81 (1).

Huddleston, T. 2020. "Global Links between Indicators of Integration Policies and Outcomes: A Roadmap to Improve Integration Policies and Outcomes for Egyptian Immigrants." Research Paper no. 5, UCD Clinton Institute, Dublin.

Hunt, J., and M. Gauthier-Loiselle. 2010. "How Much Does Immigration Boost Innovation?" *American Economic Journal: Macroeconomics* 2 (2): 31–56. https://doi.org/10.1257/mac.2.2.31.

Immigration Lawyers Spain. n.d. "Reforma Ley de Extranjería en España 2022." https://www.immigrationspain.es/reforma-ley-extranjeria/.

IOM (International Organization for Migration). 2020a. *COVID-19 Analytical Snapshot #28: Impacts on Immigration Policies.* Geneva: IOM. https://www.iom.int/sites/default/files/documents/covid-19_analytical_snapshot_28_-_impacts_on_immigration_policies.pdf.

IOM (International Organization for Migration). 2020b. *COVID-19 Analytical Snapshot #70: Migrant Health Impacts.* Geneva: IOM. https://www.iom.int/sites/g/files/tmzbdl486/files/documents/covid-19_analytical_snapshot_70_-_migrant_health_impacts.pdf.

Isphording, I. E. 2015. "What Drives the Language Proficiency of Immigrants?" *IZA World of Labor* 2015: 177.

Jaumotte, F., K. Koloskova, and S. C. Saxena. 2016. "Impact of Migration on Income Levels in Advanced Economies." Spillover Note 2016/008, International Monetary Fund, Washington, DC.

Jensen, P., and A. W. Rasmussen. 2011. "The Effect of Immigrant Concentration in Schools on Native and Immigrant Children's Reading and Math Skills." *Economics of Education Review* 30 (6): 1503–15.

Jørgensen, F., and M. Osmundsen. 2022. "Correcting Citizens' Misperceptions about Non-Western Immigrants: Corrective Information, Interpretations, and Policy Opinions." *Journal of Experimental Political Science* 9 (1): 64–73.

Jürges, H., A. M. Makles, A. Naghavi, and K. Schneider. 2022. "Melting Pot Kindergarten: The Effect of Linguistic Diversity in Early Education." *Labour Economics* 75: 102119.

Kende, J., O. Sarrasin, A. Manatschal, K. Phalet, and E. G. T. Green. 2022. "Policies and Prejudice: Integration Policies Moderate the Link between Immigrant Presence and Anti-Immigrant Prejudice." *Journal of Personality and Social Psychology* 123 (2): 337–52. https://doi.org/10.1037/pspi0000376.

Kuosmanen, I., and H. Pesola. 2022. "Labor Market Outcomes of Migrants in Finland." Background paper, *The Journey Ahead: Supporting Successful Migration in Europe and Central Asia*, World Bank, Washington, DC.

Lafleur, J. M., and D. Vintila, eds. 2020. *Migration and Social Protection in Europe and Beyond (Volume 1): Comparing Access to Welfare Entitlements*. Cham, Switzerland: Springer.

Lang, J. 2022. "Employment Effects of Language Training for Unemployed Immigrants." *Journal of Population Economics* 35 (2): 719–54.

Levada-Center. 2017. "Attitudes toward Migrants." Press release, May 29, 2017. https://www.levada.ru/en/2017/05/29/attitudes-toward-migrants/.

Lochmann, A., H. Rapoport, and B. Speciale. 2019. "The Effect of Language Training on Immigrants' Economic Integration: Empirical Evidence from France." *European Economic Review* 113: 265–96.

Lodigiani, E. 2008. "Diaspora Externalities and Technology Diffusion." *Économie Internationale* 3 (115): 43–64. https://doi.org/10.3917/ecoi.115.0043.

Mastrobuoni, G., and P. Pinotti. 2015. "Legal Status and the Criminal Activity of Immigrants." *American Economic Journal: Applied Economics* 7 (2): 175–206.

Matusz, P., and E. Aivaliotou. 2020. *Circular and Temporary Migration in Poland during COVID-19: ADMIGOV Deliverable 3.2*. Wrocław, Poland: University of Wrocław. https://admigov.eu/upload/Deliverable_32_Matusz_Temporary_and_Circular_Migration_Poland.pdf.

Mazzilli, C. 2021. "Regularising Migrants: Portugal's Missed Chance." *Social Europe*, December 6. https://socialeurope.eu/regularising-migrants-portugals-missed-chance.

Mitaritonna, C., G. Orefice, and G. Peri. 2017. "Immigrants and Firms' Outcomes: Evidence from France." *European Economic Review* 96: 62–82.

Moroz, H., M. Shrestha, and M. Testaverde. 2020. "Potential Responses to the COVID-19 Outbreak in Support of Migrant Workers." Living Paper Version 10, World Bank Group, Washington, DC. https://documents1.worldbank.org/curated/en/428451587390154689/pdf/Potential-Responses-to-the-COVID-19-Outbreak-in-Support-of-Migrant-Workers-June-19-2020.pdf.

Muysken, J., and T. H. W. Ziesemer. 2011. "The Effect of Net Immigration on Economic Growth in an Ageing Economy: Transitory and Permanent Shocks." Working Paper 2011-055, United Nations University, Maastricht Economic and Social Research Institute on Innovation and Technology, Maastricht.

Nielson, J. 2004. "Trade Agreements and Recognition." In *Quality and Recognition in Higher Education: The Cross Border Challenge*, edited by K. Larsen and K. Momii, 155–203. Paris: OECD.

Nunziata, L. 2015. "Immigration and Crime: Evidence from Victimization Data." *Journal of Population Economics* 28: 697–736.

OECD (Organisation for Economic Co-operation and Development). 2013. "The Fiscal Impact of Immigration in OECD Countries." In *International Migration Outlook 2013*, 125–89. Paris: OECD. https://www.oecd.org/els/mig/IMO-2013-chap3-fiscal-impact-of-immigration.pdf.

OECD (Organisation for Economic Co-operation and Development). 2021. *International Migration Outlook 2021*. Paris: OECD. https://doi.org/10.1787/29f23e9d-en.

Ohinata, A., and J. C. Van Ours. 2013. "How Immigrant Children Affect the Academic Achievement of Native Dutch Children." *Economic Journal* 123 (570): F308–31.

Open Society Foundation. 2020. *Towards an EU Toolbox for Migrant Workers: Labour Mobility and Regularization in Germany, Italy and Spain in 2020*. Brussels: Open Society European Policy Institute. https://www.opensocietyfoundations.org/publications/towards-an-eu-toolbox-for-migrant-workers.

Orefice, G. 2010. "Skilled Migration and Economic Performances: Evidence from OECD Countries." Discussion Paper 2010-15, Institut de Recherches Economiques et Sociales, Université Catholique de Louvain, Louvain-la-Neuve, Belgium.

Orrenius, P. M., and M. Zavodny. 2009. "Do Immigrants Work in Riskier Jobs?" *Demography* 46: 535–51.

Orrenius, P. M., and M. Zavodny. 2010. "Mexican Immigrant Employment Outcomes over the Business Cycle." *American Economic Review* 100 (2): 316–20. https://doi.org/10.1257/aer.100.2.316.

Orrenius, P.M., and M. Zavodny. 2013. "Immigrants in Risky Occupations." In *International Handbook on the Economics of Migration*, edited by A.F. Constant and K.F. Zimmerman, 214–26. Cheltenham, UK: Edward Elgar.

Ortega, F., and G. Peri. 2009. "The Causes and Effects of International Migrations: Evidence from OECD Countries 1980–2005." Working Paper 14833, National Bureau of Economic Research, Cambridge, MA. https://www.nber.org/papers/w14833.

Ortega, F., and G. Peri. 2014. "The Aggregate Effects of Trade and Migration: Evidence from OECD Countries." In *The Socio-Economic Impact of Migration Flows: Effects Trade, Remittances, Output, and the Labour Market*, edited by A. Artal-Tur, G. Peri, and F. Requena-Silvente, 19–52. Cham, Switzerland: Springer. https://doi.org/10.1007/978-3-319-04078-3_2.

Ottaviano, G. I. P., and G. Peri. 2012. "Rethinking the Effect of Immigration on Wages." *Journal of the European Economic Association* 10 (1): 152–97.

Ottaviano, G. I. P., G. Peri, and G. C. Wright. 2018. "Immigration, Trade, and Productivity in Services: Evidence from U.K. Firms." *Journal of International Economics* 112: 88–108. https://doi.org/10.1016/j.jinteco.2018.02.007.

Docquier, F., Ç. Ozden, and G. Peri. 2014. "The Labour Market Effects of Immigration and Emigration in OECD Countries." *Economic Journal* 124 (579): 1106–1145. https://doi.org/10.1111/ecoj.12077.

Palumbo, L. 2020. "The Italian Plan for Regularisation: Real Progress for Migrants' Rights?" *MPC Blog*, June 8, 2020. https://blogs.eui.eu/migrationpolicycentre/italian-plan-regularisation-real-progress-migrants-rights/.

Pecoraro, M., A. Manatschal, E. Green, and P. Wanner. 2022. "How Effective Are Integration Policy Reforms? The Case of Asylum—Related Migrants." *International Migration* 60 (6): 95–110.

Peri, G. 2012. "The Effect of Immigration on Productivity: Evidence from US States." *Review of Economics and Statistics* 94 (1): 348–58.

Peri, G., and C. Sparber. 2009. "Task Specialization, Immigration, and Wages." *American Economic Journal: Applied Economics* 1 (3): 135–69. https://doi.org/10.1257/app.1.3.135.

Pinotti, P. 2017. "Clicking on Heaven's Door: The Effect of Immigrant Legalization on Crime." *American Economic Review* 107 (1): 138–68.

Razin, A., and E. Sadka. 2000. "Unskilled Migration: A Burden or a Boon for the Welfare State?" *Scandinavian Journal of Economics* 102 (3): 463–79.

Rowthorn, R. 2008. "The Fiscal Impact of Immigration on the Advanced Economies." *Oxford Review of Economic Policy* 24 (3): 560–80. https://doi.org/10.1093/oxrep/grn025.

Rutledge, Z., and T. Kane. 2018. "Immigration and Economic Performance in the US: Evidence from the 50 States." Presented at the Agricultural and Applied Economics Association's Annual Meeting, Washington, DC, August 5-7, 2018.

Sá, F. 2015. "Immigration and House Prices in the UK." *Economic Journal* 125 (587): 1393–424.

Schneeweis, N. 2015. "Immigrant Concentration in Schools: Consequences for Native and Migrant Students." *Labour Economics* 35: 63–76.

Schuettler, K. 2017. "Public Perceptions of Migration: The Fear of the Other Is More Nuanced than We Think." *World Bank Blogs* (blog), December 16, 2017.

Sides, J., and J. Citrin. 2007. "European Opinion about Immigration: The Role of Identities, Interests and Information." *British Journal of Political Science* 37 (3): 477–504.

Signorelli, S. 2024. "Do Skilled Migrants Compete with Native Workers? Analysis of a Selective Immigration Policy." *Journal of Human Resources*, forthcoming.

Sparber, C., and M. Zavodny. 2022. "Immigration, Working Conditions, and Compensating Differentials." *ILR Review* 75 (4): 1054–81.

Sumption, M., and C. Vargas-Silva. 2019. "Love Is Not All You Need: Income Requirement for Visa Sponsorship of Foreign Family Members." *Journal of Economics, Race, and Policy* 2: 62–76.

Tanaka, R., L. Farré, and F. Ortega. 2018. "Immigration, Assimilation, and the Future of Public Education." *European Journal of Political Economy* 52: 141–65.

Terry, S., T. Chaney, K. Burchardi, L. Tarquinio, and T. Hassan. 2020. "Immigration, Innovation, and Growth." Discussion Paper 14719, Centre for Economic Policy Research, London. https://cepr.org/publications /dp14719.

Testaverde, M., and J. Pavilon. 2022. *Building Resilient Migration Systems in the Mediterranean Region: Lessons from COVID-19.* Washington, DC: World Bank.

Tonello, M. 2016. "Peer Effects of Non-Native Students on Natives' Educational Outcomes: Mechanisms and Evidence." *Empirical Economics* 51 (1): 383–414.

Trax, M., S. Brunow, and J. Suedekum. 2015. "Cultural Diversity and Plant-Level Productivity." *Regional Science and Urban Economics* 53: 85–96. https://doi.org/10.1016/j.regsciurbeco.2015.05.004.

Tumen, S. 2019. "Refugees and 'Native Flight' from Public to Private Schools." *Economics Letters* 181: 154–9.

Vandenbussche, J., P. Aghion, and C. Meghir. 2006. "Growth, Distance to Frontier, and Composition of Human Capital." *Journal of Economic Growth* 11 (2): 97–127. https://doi.org/10.1007/s10887-006-9002-y.

Vargas-Silva, C. 2016. "EU Migration to and from the UK after Brexit." *Intereconomics* 51: 251–5. https://doi .org/10.1007/s10272-016-0613-z.

Varshaver, E., N. Ivanova, and A. Rocheva. 2020. *Migrants in Russia during the COVID-19 Pandemic: Survey Results.* Moscow: Russian Academy of National Economy and Public Administration. https://doi.org/10.2139/ssrn .3672397.

World Bank. 2017. *Migration and Mobility.* Europe and Central Asia Economic Update (October). Washington, DC: World Bank. https://doi.org/10.1596/978-1-4648-1219-4.

World Bank. 2018. *Moving for Prosperity: Global Migration and Labor Markets.* Washington, DC: World Bank.

World Bank. 2019. *Migration and Brain Drain.* Europe and Central Asia Economic Update (Fall). Washington, DC: World Bank. https://doi.org/10.1596/978-1-4648-1506-5.

World Bank. 2023. *World Development Report 2023: Migrants, Refugees, and Societies.* Washington, DC: World Bank.

Zorlu, A., and J. Hartog. 2005. "The Effect of Immigration on Wages in Three European Countries." *Journal of Population Economics* 18 (1): 113–51.

From Brain Drain to Brain Gain
Leveraging Emigration of High-Skilled Workers in Origin Countries

Chapter Highlights

- In most countries of origin, workers who emigrate have higher education levels than those who do not.

- The emigration of high-skilled workers is widespread in some of the smaller middle-income Europe and Central Asia (ECA) countries; about one-third of those with tertiary education from some countries in the Western Balkans live abroad.

- High-skilled emigration reduces human capital in countries of origin in the short run, which, under certain conditions, can generate labor shortages in essential sectors of activity, such as health, and affect productivity in home economies.

- In aging economies, high-skilled emigration can accelerate the decline in the working-age population and further shrink the fiscal base.

- Emigrants often come from the most disadvantaged areas in sending countries, potentially exacerbating the phenomenon of lagging regions.

- Despite high levels of educational attainment in countries of origin, high-skilled migrants from ECA often face occupational downgrade abroad.

- In the medium to long term, high-skilled emigration can incentivize investment in human capital in sending countries as a response to greater internal and external demand for skilled professionals.

- In a few ECA countries, the increase in the supply of high-skilled graduates in response to migration opportunities was sufficient to compensate for the outflow of workers, but not in others.

- Sending countries can benefit from their high-skilled diaspora in multiple ways, including remittances, knowledge transfers, and increased foreign direct investment and trade.

- High-skilled emigration can also raise productivity and create jobs in countries of origin through return migration: high-skilled return migrants are often more productive and engage more frequently in entrepreneurial activities compared with nonmigrants.

- In contrast with Western European countries, Central EU and Western Balkan countries of origin have been struggling to attract their qualified emigrants back.

- The net effects of high-skilled emigration for countries of origin depend on whether the costs from losing highly qualified workers outweigh the benefits from the remittances, knowledge spillovers, and productivity gains generated by these workers.

Main Policy Recommendations

- Origin countries that want to reduce high-skilled emigration must address its root causes through policies supporting the creation of domestic employment and labor market functioning, together with strengthening home institutions and public services.

- Given the strength of the push and pull factors behind high-skilled migration, well-managed labor mobility is critical to enhancing its potential benefits while reducing potential costs for migrants, origin countries, and destination countries.

- Establishing functioning skills monitoring systems in countries of origin is essential to help anticipate skills shortages in response to increased external demand.

- Expanding capacity and relaxing potential rigidities in the rapid expansion of the supply of high-skilled graduates is also crucial to help prevent or mitigate skill shortages associated with emigration.

- If educational systems cannot expand the skill supply in a timely manner, opening domestic labor markets to non-ECA countries in occupations where skill shortages are anticipated can help in importing needed skills. Such measures, however, must be considered within the broader political and social context of each individual country.

- Global skill partnerships between sending and receiving countries, in which the latter provide technical and financial resources for the training of prospective migrants, can help better distribute the costs and benefits of high-skilled migration between origin and destination countries.

- Reforms in public education financing schemes in countries of origin, combined with bilateral agreements with destination countries, can also support a more equitable distribution of the costs and benefits of high-skilled migration.

- Strengthening ongoing efforts to certify foreign credentials across ECA can help reduce the brain waste associated with migrants' occupational downgrade.

- Programs to establish and engage diaspora networks, foster knowledge exchange, and support investment back home can help origin countries better leverage their high-skilled migrants.

- A first and low-cost step toward increasing the chances that high-skilled migrants will return is to remove the regulatory, bureaucratic, and informational barriers that inhibit return migration.

- The portability of social benefits across borders can also help alleviate bureaucratic constraints to return migration and incentivize returns from among the high-skilled diaspora.

- Financial incentives can be effective at increasing permanent return among high-skilled migrants, if they are large enough while being fiscally neutral.

- To support productive return of high-skilled migrants, reintegration plans need to be established, followed by a comprehensive set of at-scale interventions tailored to the identified needs of returnees.

- Policy interventions at the return stage must be informed by systematic impact evaluations to assess their effectiveness, ideally before scale-up.

Introduction

High-skilled migration is on the rise and widespread in Europe and Central Asia (ECA), especially from smaller middle-income countries. High-skilled emigration from ECA countries has been rising even more rapidly than overall migration. The number of high-skilled migrants in the European Union (EU), the main destination of high-skilled migrants from ECA, more than tripled over the 2004–18 period, increasing from about 4 million to 13 million. The share of high-skilled emigrants among total migrants increased from

21 percent in 2004 to 30 percent in 2019. In some countries in ECA—particularly smaller ones, such as those in the Western Balkans—the incidence of high-skilled emigration compared with the size of the working-age population is quite large. In Albania and Bosnia and Herzegovina, for example, it is estimated that close to 30 and 45 percent, respectively, of the working-age population with a tertiary degree lives abroad.

This chapter highlights that the impacts of high-skilled emigration on countries of origin are complex and multichanneled, generating both costs and benefits over different time horizons. They are also highly context dependent and heavily influenced by the emigration experience of origin countries and their demographic structure. As shown in the "Patterns, Trends, and Heterogeneity in High-Skilled Emigration in Europe and Central Asia" section of this chapter, emigration from ECA countries is heterogeneous in terms of magnitude, skill intensity, and occupational content. Policy parameters, as shown in this chapter, also play an important role in the way high-skilled emigration affects labor markets and broader welfare outcomes in countries of origin. Depending on these parameters, skilled emigration produces both costs and benefits, which vary in the short, medium, and long run.

A leading concern in countries of origin is that high-skilled emigration, often referred to as "brain drain," may create shortages in essential occupations, increase fiscal pressures, and affect job creation and growth. Mechanically, high-skilled emigration reduces the stock of human capital in origin countries in the short run, especially if emigrants are positively selected (more skilled, on average, than the origin country population who does not emigrate), which is the case in most ECA countries. Although the emigration of high-skilled migrants also comes with a range of benefits, as discussed in this chapter, it can be problematic if the departure of high-skilled workers results in domestic labor shortages, especially in critical sectors and occupations for which internal demand is high (World Bank 2023). One example is the case of health professionals such as doctors or nurses and information technology (IT) professionals. The departure of such workers could also negatively affect the productivity, innovation, and growth of the broader economy in the short run. In ECA countries with an already aging population and low fertility rates, such as those in the Central EU and the Western Balkans, the departures also exacerbate population aging and labor force shortages and can worsen the gap between prospering and lagging regions. This also raises related concerns about the sustainability of pension systems. From a fiscal standpoint, outflows of high-skilled labor also shrink the fiscal base, especially when emigration is concentrated among higher-paid workers.

As shown in this chapter, high-skilled migration also generates benefits for countries of origin, primarily through remittances, knowledge transfers, investment in human capital, and return migration. As discussed in the "Medium- and Long-Term Impacts on Origin Countries" section, in the medium run, emigration can help alleviate unemployment pressures in sending regions that are struggling to create more and better jobs, especially for youth. It may also lead to a reallocation of labor to more productive sectors. Furthermore, high-skilled emigration opportunities can increase the stock of human capital in the medium to long term, a phenomenon referred to as "brain gain." A key mechanism through which this can occur is by incentivizing investments in tertiary education in response to rising returns to higher skill levels driven by foreign demand. In addition, if high-skilled migrants return, countries of origin can benefit from the human and financial capital gained by the migrants while abroad. The initial brain drain can thus, under certain conditions, turn into a net increase in human capital in countries of origin in the longer term. Using the case of medical doctors, the chapter shows that brain gain has been observed in some countries of origin in ECA but not in others. This suggests that local context and policy parameters are key to maximizing the benefits of brain circulation and turning brain drain into brain gain. As the chapter shows, the presence of high-skilled workers abroad can also produce a range of positive spillovers on countries of origin through remittance flows, knowledge transfers, and international networks and a reduction in transaction and trade costs. The extent to which countries of origin benefit from such spillovers is shaped by policies and programs in place to better leverage high-skilled mobility.

The chapter proposes policies that can be implemented by origin countries, some of them in collaboration with destination countries, to reduce the costs and enhance the benefits of high-skilled emigration. Building on the evidence provided in the "Patterns, Trends, and Heterogeneity in High-Skilled Emigration in Europe and Central Asia," "Short-Term Impacts of High-Skilled Emigration on Origin Countries," and "Medium- and Long-Term Impacts on Origin Countries" sections, the "Policy Recommendations" section discusses educational and skills-training policies that can ensure a fairer distribution of the costs and benefits of high-skilled emigration between origin and destination countries. It also examines options to enhance the benefits of the high-skilled migration experience for all actors, including migrants. Finally, it discusses policy options to increase the return flows of high-skilled migrants and to take better advantage of the human and financial capital that return with high-skilled migrants, and their migration experience more broadly. Although some of these policies can be implemented unilaterally by countries of origin, others require close coordination with destination countries, or even at the regional level with other countries of origin.

Patterns, Trends, and Heterogeneity in High-Skilled Emigration in Europe and Central Asia

Rising Skill Level of Emigrants from ECA Countries

The skill level of emigrants from ECA countries has been rising. The share of high-skilled emigrants among total migrants within the European Union increased from 21 percent in 2004 to 30 percent in 2019 (refer to figure 4.1). Migrants from EU-15 countries (that is, countries that were European Union members before 2004) to other EU countries have traditionally had higher educational attainment relative to the overall population of the EU-15. This pattern has become more pronounced over time because the share of migrants with tertiary education from the EU-15 has risen more rapidly than the corresponding share in the overall EU population. In recent years, almost one-half of migrants from the EU-15 to other EU countries have had tertiary degrees. Compared with migrants from the EU-15, migrants from new member states in the Central EU have

FIGURE 4.1

Share of migrants (ages 25–64 years) with tertiary education, European Union, by region of origin

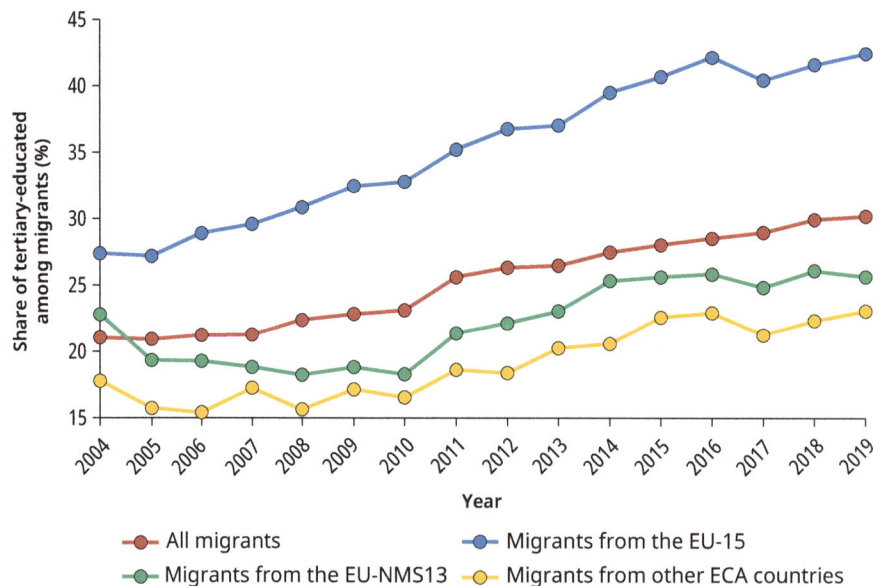

Sources: Original calculations based on the EU Labour Force Survey (database), Eurostat (https://ec .europa.eu/eurostat/statistics-explained/index.php/EU_labour_force_survey); Russia Longitudinal Monitoring Survey (https://rlms-hse.cpc.unc.edu/); and Turkish Household Labor Force Surveys (https:// webapps.ilo.org/surveyLib/index.php/catalog/LFS/?page=1&country%5B%5D=218).
Note: EU-15 = European Union members before 2004; EU-NMS13 = new member states joining the European Union in 2004, 2007, and 2013.

lower overall educational attainment, reflecting the lower human capital at origin. In addition, the share of migrants with tertiary education has increased less rapidly among migrants from the 13 new member states joining the European Union in 2004, 2007, and 2013 (EU-NMS13) and from the rest of the world than it has among migrants from the EU-15.

The share of migrants in occupations requiring nonroutine tasks is rising more quickly in the European Union than among the overall population. Reflecting technological change, the share of workers engaged in nonroutine cognitive tasks in the European Union has increased, although at a moderate pace. The share has grown more rapidly in the EU-15 than in the EU-NMS13 (refer to figure 4.2). Meanwhile, the share of individuals engaged in such activities has risen more quickly among migrants from the EU-15 than among the overall EU population, reflecting a large increase in the share of high-skilled migrants from the EU-15. In addition, the share of

FIGURE 4.2

Workers (ages 25–64 years) employed in nonroutine cognitive jobs, European Union

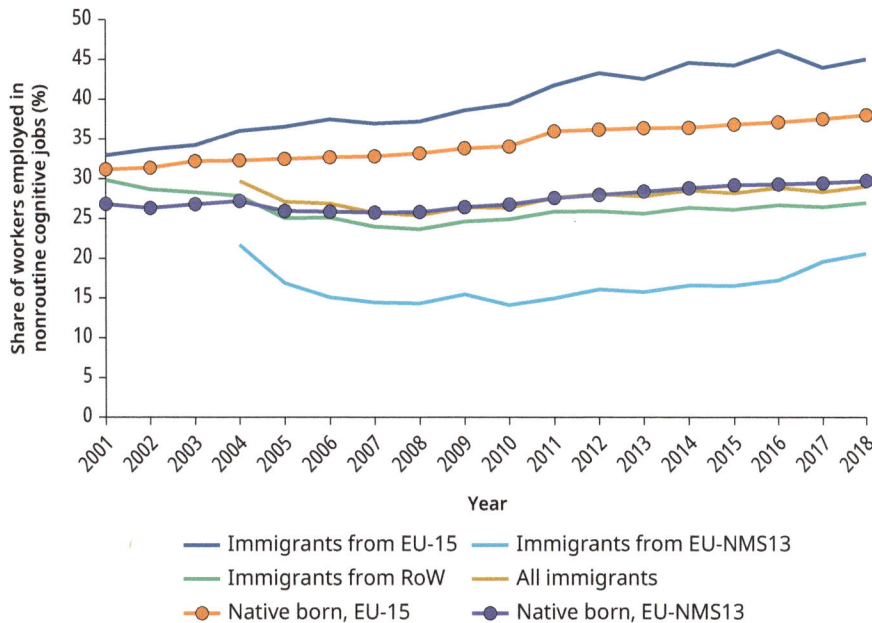

Source: EU Labour Force Survey (database), Eurostat (https://ec.europa.eu/eurostat/statistics-explained/index.php/EU_labour_force_survey).
Note: Nonroutine jobs are those that involve activities that are not repetitive or based on rules and may require flexibility and task switching. Cognitive jobs are those that involve problem solving and analysis and are associated with higher educational attainment. Nonroutine cognitive jobs include public relations and analytical, medical, and technical positions. EU-15 = European Union members before 2004; EU-NMS13 = new member states joining the European Union in 2004, 2007, and 2013; RoW = rest of the world.

migrants from the EU-NMS13 and the rest of the world who are engaged in nonroutine cognitive tasks has risen at a more moderate pace, although still more rapidly relative to the share among the overall population.

Disparities in High-Skilled Emigration across Country, Region, and Sector Activity

The skill content of emigrants varies across countries. Not surprisingly, skill content is closely linked to levels of economic development in countries of origin (refer to figure 4.3). High-skilled emigration predominates in high-income countries in Western Europe, such as Belgium, France, the Netherlands, and Spain, as well as in Scandinavian countries, where more than half of the working-age population emigrating holds a tertiary degree. In contrast, the share of tertiary-educated emigrants is below 10 percent in some poorer origin countries in Central Asia, the Caucasus, and the

FIGURE 4.3

Economic development and skill content of emigration

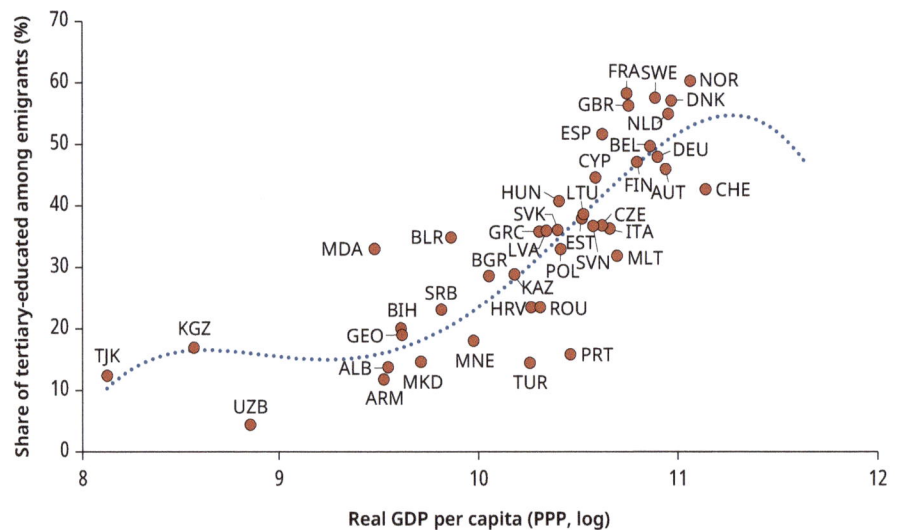

Sources: UN Department of Economic and Social Affairs International Migrant Stock 2020 (https://www .un.org/development/desa/pd/content/international-migrant-stock); Organisation for Economic Co-operation and Development Database on Immigrants in OECD and Non-OECD Countries 2015 (https://www.oecd.org/els/mig/dioc.htm); Russia Labor Force Survey 2017, Armenia Labor Force Survey 2018, and Kyrgyz Integrated Household Survey 2018 (for information on Labor Force Surveys, see https://webapps.ilo.org/surveyLib/index.php/catalog/LFS/?page=1&ps=15&repo=LFS); Listening to the Citizens of Tajikistan 2017 (https://www.worldbank.org/en/country/tajikistan/brief/listening2tajikistan); and Listening to the Citizens of Uzbekistan 2018 (https://www.worldbank.org/en/country/uzbekistan /brief/l2cu#1).
Note: Purchasing power parity is used to compare the value of a country's currency to another country's currency by looking at the price of a basket of goods and services in each country. For a list of country codes, go to https://www.iso.org/obp/ui/#search. GDP = gross domestic product; Log = logarithmic scale; PPP = purchasing power parity.

Western Balkans. In the Central EU economies, the skill intensity of emigration is more moderate, with 20–35 percent of emigrants having some tertiary education.

Globally, emigration has been shown to increase with the level of development until a certain point at which it starts to decrease (Clemens 2014; Dao et al. 2018). A similar pattern is observed for high-skilled emigration from ECA countries (refer to figure 4.4, panel a). High-skilled emigration initially increases as countries move from a low-income level (Central Asian economies) to a middle-income level. Middle-income and middle- to high-income countries have the highest incidence of high-skilled emigration per the working-age population. Once higher- to middle-income levels are reached, however, the incidence of high-skilled emigration among those who are working age declines overall, despite higher levels of educational attainment in richer countries. Differences in the incidence of high-skilled emigration among the population of origin countries are partly

FIGURE 4.4

Economic development and emigration

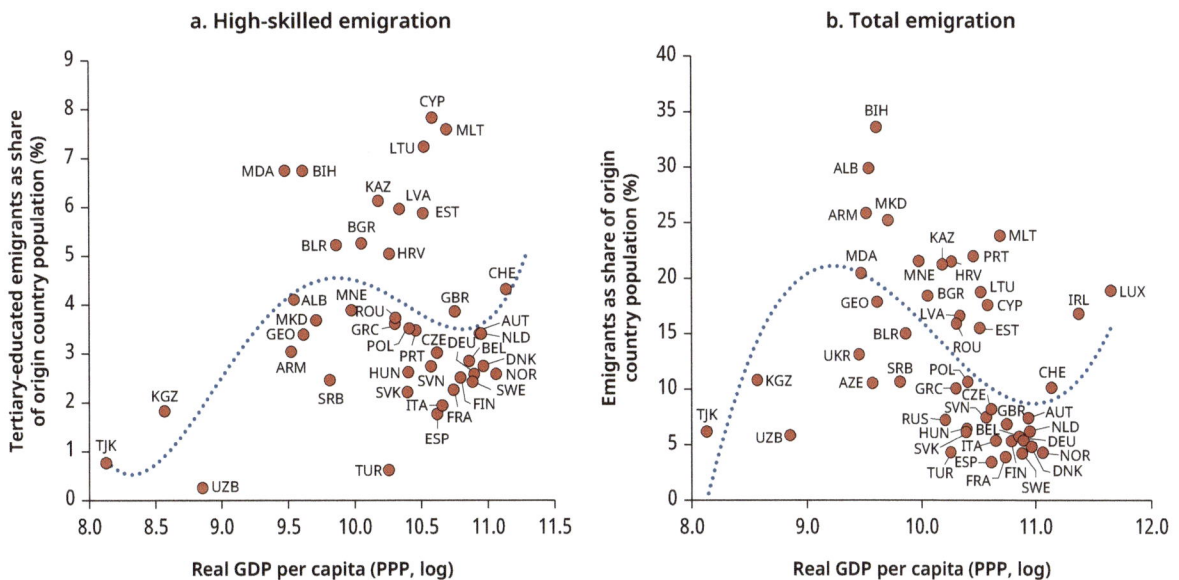

a. High-skilled emigration

b. Total emigration

Sources: UN Department of Economic and Social Affairs International Migrant Stock 2020 (https://www.un.org/development/desa/pd /content/international-migrant-stock); Organisation for Economic Co-operation and Development Database on Immigrants in OECD and Non-OECD Countries 2015 (https://www.oecd.org/els/mig/dioc.htm); Russia Labor Force Survey 2017, Armenia Labor Force Survey 2018, and Kyrgyz Integrated Household Survey 2018 (for information on Labor Force Surveys, see https://webapps.ilo.org/surveyLib/index.php /catalog/LFS/?page=1&ps=15&repo=LFS); Listening to the Citizens of Tajikistan 2017 (https://www.worldbank.org/en/country/tajikistan /brief/listening2tajikistan); and Listening to the Citizens of Uzbekistan 2018 (https://www.worldbank.org/en/country/uzbekistan/brief /l2cu#1).

Note: High-skilled emigrants are defined as individuals with tertiary education who live abroad. Purchasing power parity is used to compare the value of a country's currency to another country's currency by looking at the price of a basket of goods and services in each country. For a list of country codes, go to https://www.iso.org/obp/ui/#search. GDP = gross domestic product; Log = logarithmic scale; PPP = purchasing power parity.

driven by a decline in overall emigration rates as ECA countries further develop toward high-income levels (refer to panel b of figure 4.4). This is likely driven by a reduction in push and pull factors to migrate as origin countries reach high-income status.

The high skill content of emigrants also reflects the profile of workers who choose to or can emigrate. Workers who emigrate often have a different skill profile from those who do not. They may be, on average, more highly educated than workers who do not emigrate (positive selection) or, in some cases, less educated (negative selection). The sign of selection into emigration is determined by the relative wage structure and skill premium at origin and at destination (Docquier, Lohest, and Marfouk 2007; Docquier and Rapoport 2012; World Bank 2018). Figure 4.5 displays the share of emigrants from ECA countries who have attained some tertiary education,

FIGURE 4.5

Share of workers with tertiary education, by emigration status

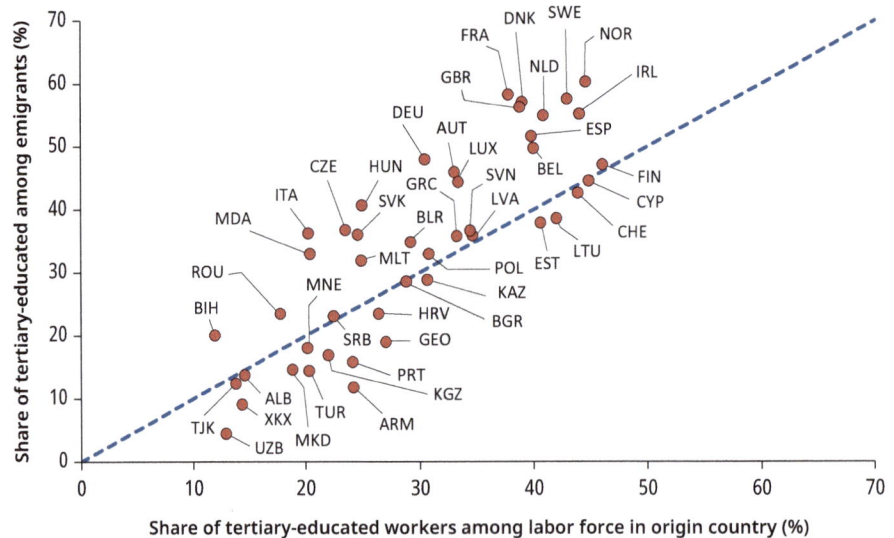

Sources: UN Department of Economic and Social Affairs International Migrant Stock 2020 (https://www .un.org/development/desa/pd/content/international-migrant-stock); Organisation for Economic Co-operation and Development Database on Immigrants in OECD and Non-OECD Countries 2015 (https://www.oecd.org/els/mig/dioc.htm); Russia Labor Force Survey 2017, Armenia Labor Force Survey 2018, and Kyrgyz Integrated Household Survey 2018 (for information on Labor Force Surveys, see https://webapps.ilo.org/surveyLib/index.php/catalog/LFS/?page=1&ps=15&repo=LFS); Listening to the Citizens of Tajikistan 2017 (https://www.worldbank.org/en/country/tajikistan/brief/listening2tajikistan); and Listening to the Citizens of Uzbekistan 2018 (https://www.worldbank.org/en/country/uzbekistan /brief/l2cu#1).

Note: The dashed 45-degree line represents parity in the share of emigrants and stayers with tertiary education in each country of origin. In countries above the line, the share of emigrants with tertiary education is higher than that of stayers; in countries below the line, the share of emigrants with tertiary education is lower than that of stayers. For a list of country codes, go to https://www.iso.org/obp /ui/#search. Kosovo has no ISO 3166 code and has been given a user-assigned code XKX. This designation is without prejudice to positions on status and is in line with United Nations Security Council Resolution 1244/1999 and the International Court of Justice Opinion on the Kosovo declaration of independence.

together with the share of tertiary-educated nonmigrants, by country of origin. As shown in the figure, most countries of origin in ECA are above the 45-degree line. This indicates that in most countries, emigrants are on average more educated than the population that does not emigrate. Positive selection in emigration is especially pronounced in Scandinavian countries, as well as in France and Italy, which are far above the 45-degree line. In comparison, a few countries in ECA, such as some in the Caucasus, Central Asia, and the Western Balkans, exhibit negative selection in emigration, in addition to lower levels of human capital among the working-age population overall.

Emigration from the Central EU countries and the Western Balkans is more pronounced in high-skilled sectors such as health or IT, which are considered critical occupations. Emigration from EU-NMS13 countries after the EU enlargement has been more pronounced in some sectors than in others (refer to figure 4.6). The increase in emigration has been especially large in the health care and social sectors: the share of workers from the Central EU working in those sectors employed abroad (as opposed to their origin countries) more than tripled between 2008 and 2018.[1] By 2014, outflows of doctors from the EU-NMS13 and the southern EU-15 had reached, respectively, 0.7 percent and 1.5 percent of the total stock of physicians in these regions. In Estonia and Romania, the annual emigration of health professionals, including doctors, averaged 3.9 percent and 2.5 percent, respectively, during the same period. High emigration rates in the health care sector have also been observed in the Western Balkans (OECD 2022): in 2017–18, more than 2,700 home-trained Serbian doctors and 1,500 home-trained North Macedonian doctors were identified in Organisation for Economic Co-operation and Development (OECD) countries, representing an emigration rate of about 8 percent and 22 percent, respectively (OECD 2022). Emigration also rose significantly among high-skilled workers from the IT sector: the share of IT sector workers from the Central EU employed in other EU countries more than doubled from 2008 to 2018, representing 15 percent of the total stock of information and communications technology (ICT) workers in origin countries in 2018.

Characteristics and Occupational Patterns of High-Skilled Emigrants

High-skilled emigration is driven by large wage disparities in high-skilled occupations across the region. Even within the European Union, where wage differentials for high-skilled workers have been declining, average wage differentials between Western and Central EU countries remain large, especially among workers with tertiary education (refer to figure 4.7). This acts as a key determinant of skilled migration from the Central to the

FIGURE 4.6

Share of workers from 13 new member state countries who are employed in the other 28 EU countries, by sector of activity

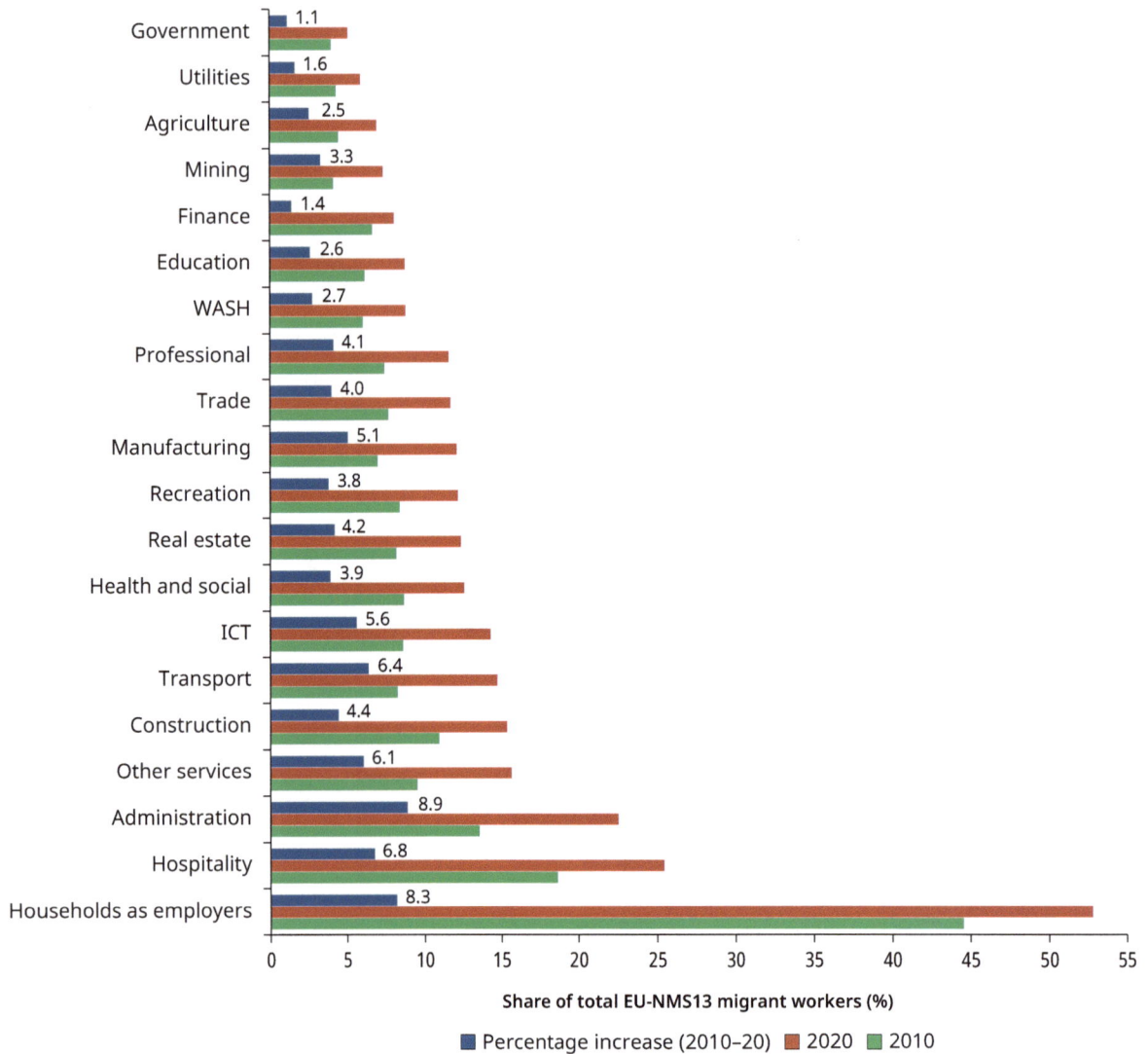

Sector	Percentage increase (2010–20)
Government	1.1
Utilities	1.6
Agriculture	2.5
Mining	3.3
Finance	1.4
Education	2.6
WASH	2.7
Professional	4.1
Trade	4.0
Manufacturing	5.1
Recreation	3.8
Real estate	4.2
Health and social	3.9
ICT	5.6
Transport	6.4
Construction	4.4
Other services	6.1
Administration	8.9
Hospitality	6.8
Households as employers	8.3

Share of total EU-NMS13 migrant workers (%)

■ Percentage increase (2010–20)　■ 2020　■ 2010

Source: Original calculations based on EU Labour Force Survey, Eurostat (https://ec.europa.eu/eurostat/statistics-explained/index.php/EU_labour_force_survey).
Note: The share of emigrants is the number of EU-NMS13 emigrants in other EU countries working in a specific NACE one-digit sector divided by the total number of people born in EU-NMS13 countries working in that same sector (both in their home EU-NMS13 countries or abroad in other EU countries). EU = European Union; EU-NMS13 = new member states joining the European Union in 2004, 2007, and 2013; ICT = information and communications technology; NACE = Nomenclature des Activités Économiques dans la Communauté Européenne; WASH = water, sanitation, and hygiene.

Western EU. A young graduate from Bulgaria or Romania working in Austria or the Netherlands, for example, can expect to earn about 6.5 times the wage that they would back home, and in Denmark the wage would be almost 8 times greater. Part of these large gaps is mitigated by the higher costs of living in receiving countries. Still, in purchasing power standards, young

FIGURE 4.7

Full-time gross monthly earnings of tertiary-educated workers, European Union

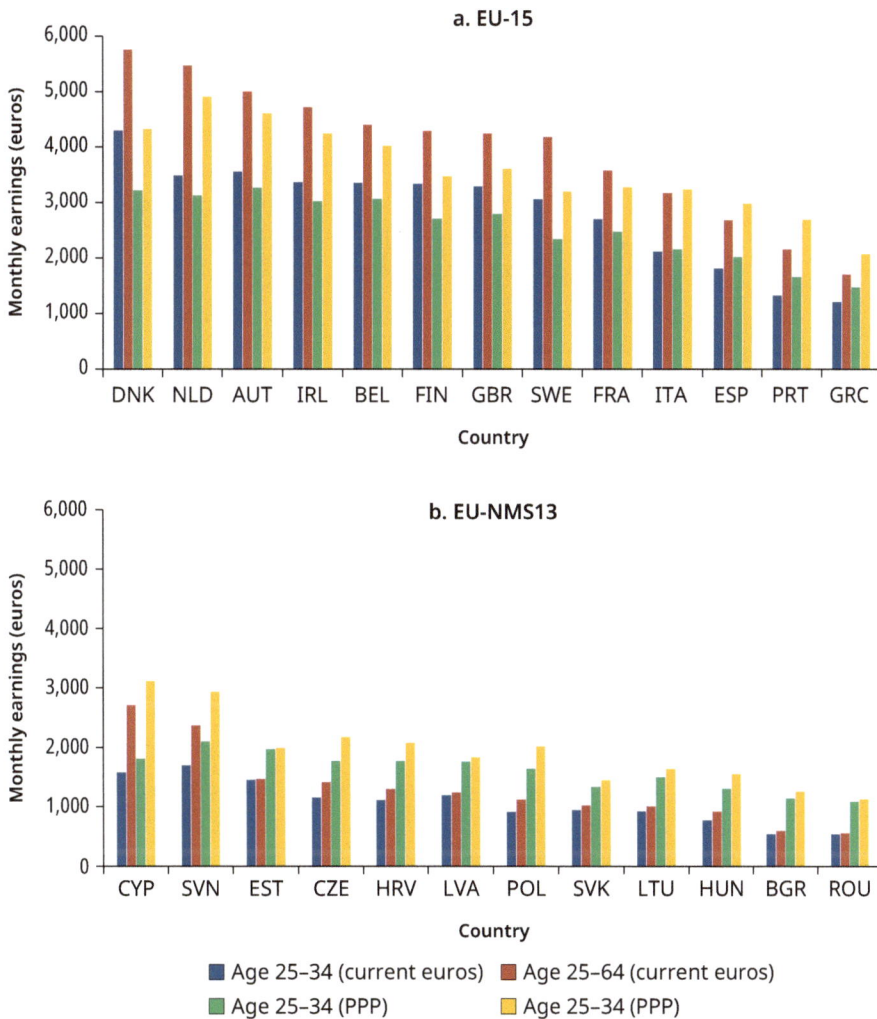

a. EU-15

b. EU-NMS13

■ Age 25–34 (current euros) ■ Age 25–64 (current euros)
■ Age 25–34 (PPP) ■ Age 25–34 (PPP)

Source: Bossavie et al. 2022.
Note: Wages are expressed in current euros or euros adjusted by purchasing power standards (which consider differences in price levels across countries). Purchasing power parity is used to compare the value of a country's currency to another country's currency by looking at the price of a basket of goods and services in each country. For a list of country codes, go to https://www.iso.org/obp/ui/#search. EU-15 = European Union members before 2004; EU-NMS13 = new member states joining the European Union in 2004, 2007, and 2013; PPP = purchasing power parity.

graduates from Bulgaria or Romania can expect to earn up to three times the wages in Austria or the Netherlands as they would earn in their countries of origin. Not only can high-skilled workers earn higher wages by moving to another ECA country, but they can also increase their likelihood of finding employment: unemployment rates are significantly higher in ECA origin countries than in the main destination countries. In the Western Balkans, the average unemployment rate is at around 16 percent, ranging from 9 percent in Serbia to as much as 26 percent in Kosovo, which is more than double the EU average (OECD 2022). Because high-skilled workers are typically more mobile across countries than low-skilled migrants, they are more likely to benefit from better-alternative job opportunities abroad, also thanks to the free movement of labor in the European Union.

High-skilled migration flows are largely directed to the European Union. As with overall migration, the concentration of highly educated migrants is largely in EU-15 countries (97 percent of all skilled migrants in the European Union). Disparities in skill content across EU regions and countries of destination are also large: in most regions of the Nordic countries and the United Kingdom, for example, more than half of migrants from the European Union have a tertiary education degree. In Italy, in contrast, a minority of immigrants have attained some tertiary education. In countries such as France and Spain, the prevalence of high-skilled migrants varies quite substantially by region. In terms of the share of the total adult population (ages 25–64), high-skilled migrants represent more than 15 percent of that population in some urban areas in Ireland, Switzerland, and the southeastern United Kingdom, surpassing 10 percent in the metropolitan areas of Luxembourg, Paris, Stockholm, and Vienna.

In contrast to low-skilled emigration, women represent a large and increasing share of high-skilled migrants. Women now constitute most high-skilled migrants within ECA (refer to figure 4.8). The share of high-skilled female emigrants has been on the rise in recent years, especially from the EU-NMS13 to EU countries, but also to the Russian Federation and Türkiye. Although this partly reflects rising female labor force participation in origin countries, women are overrepresented among high-skilled migrants from ECA relative to the share of women in the high-skilled active population in origin countries. In contrast to the broad gender parity among migrants from the EU-15, women are now overrepresented among migrants from the EU-NMS13, especially among those who are highly educated. Additionally, the share of women among EU-NMS13 migrants with tertiary education has been rising, whereas among migrants from the EU-15, it has remained constant. Finally, more than half of high-skilled migrants from the Western Balkans to EU countries are women (OECD 2022).

Compared with the overall working-age population, highly educated migrants are concentrated among younger age groups. Like all migrants, high-skilled migrants to the European Union tend to be clustered in the 25–44 age group (Bossavie et al. 2022; World Bank 2018). This is particularly true for high-skilled migrants coming from EU-NMS13 countries, among whom 70 percent are within that age range, compared with only 54 percent of native-born workers. In contrast, high-skilled

FIGURE 4.8

Share of women among international migrants ages 25–64, Europe and Central Asia

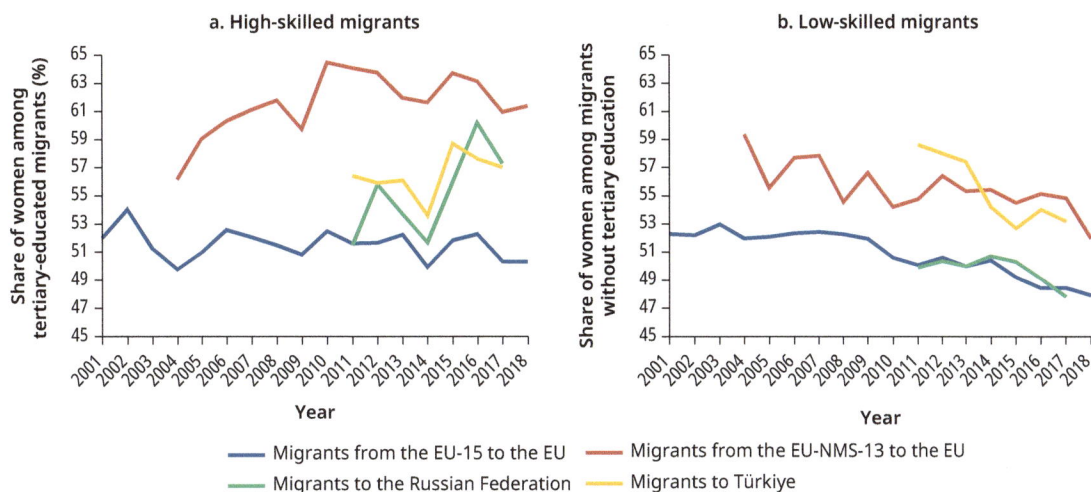

Sources: Original calculations based on the European Union Labour Force Survey (database), Eurostat (https://ec.europa.eu/eurostat /statistics-explained/index.php/EU_labour_force_survey); Russia Longitudinal Monitoring Survey (https://rlms-hse.cpc.unc.edu, http://www.hse.ru/org/hse/rlms) and Turkish Household Labor Force Surveys (https://webapps.ilo.org/surveyLib/index.php/catalog /LFS/?page=1&country%5B%5D=218).
Note: High-skilled migrants are defined as foreign-born individuals with some tertiary education. Low-skilled migrants are defined as foreign-born individuals without tertiary education. EU-NMS13 = new member states joining the European Union in 2004, 2007, and 2013; EU-15 = European Union members before 2004.

migrants from EU-15 countries have an age distribution more like that of native-born workers. The age distribution of high-skilled emigrants is important to keep in mind when assessing the impacts of emigration on countries of origin, especially in the context of the overall aging observed in the labor market.

High-skilled migrants from ECA are concentrated in occupations requiring more quantitative or analytical skills. Workers who migrate from ECA countries to the European Union work in different occupations than native-born workers in receiving countries (Bossavie et al. 2022). As shown in figure 4.9, native-born male workers in the European Union are more likely to have jobs requiring communication skills (for example, sales, legal and finance professionals, teachers, and administrative workers), whereas high-skilled migrants concentrate in occupations requiring more quantitative or analytical skills. Those include ICT professionals, software developers, engineers, and medical doctors. Software and application development is the leading occupation of high-skilled migrants from the EU-NMS13 to the European Union (refer to figure 4.9, panel b). High-skilled female migrant workers have a different occupational profile than high-skilled male migrant workers (refer to figure 4.9, panels b and d). Their occupational profile also differs strongly from that of native-born women: they primarily concentrate in personal care, household services, sales, and the medical profession, whereas teaching is the most common occupation among high-skilled native-born women (refer to figure 4.9, panels c and d).

High-skilled migrants, especially from non-EU countries, often face occupational downgrade. *Occupational downgrade* refers to being employed in a lower-skilled occupation than one's formal level of educational attainment would predict. By region of origin, occupational downgrade particularly affects highly educated migrants from the EU-NMS13. Immigrants from the EU-NMS13 have, on average, 1.3 more years of

FIGURE 4.9

Top occupations of individuals (ages 25–64) with tertiary education, European Union

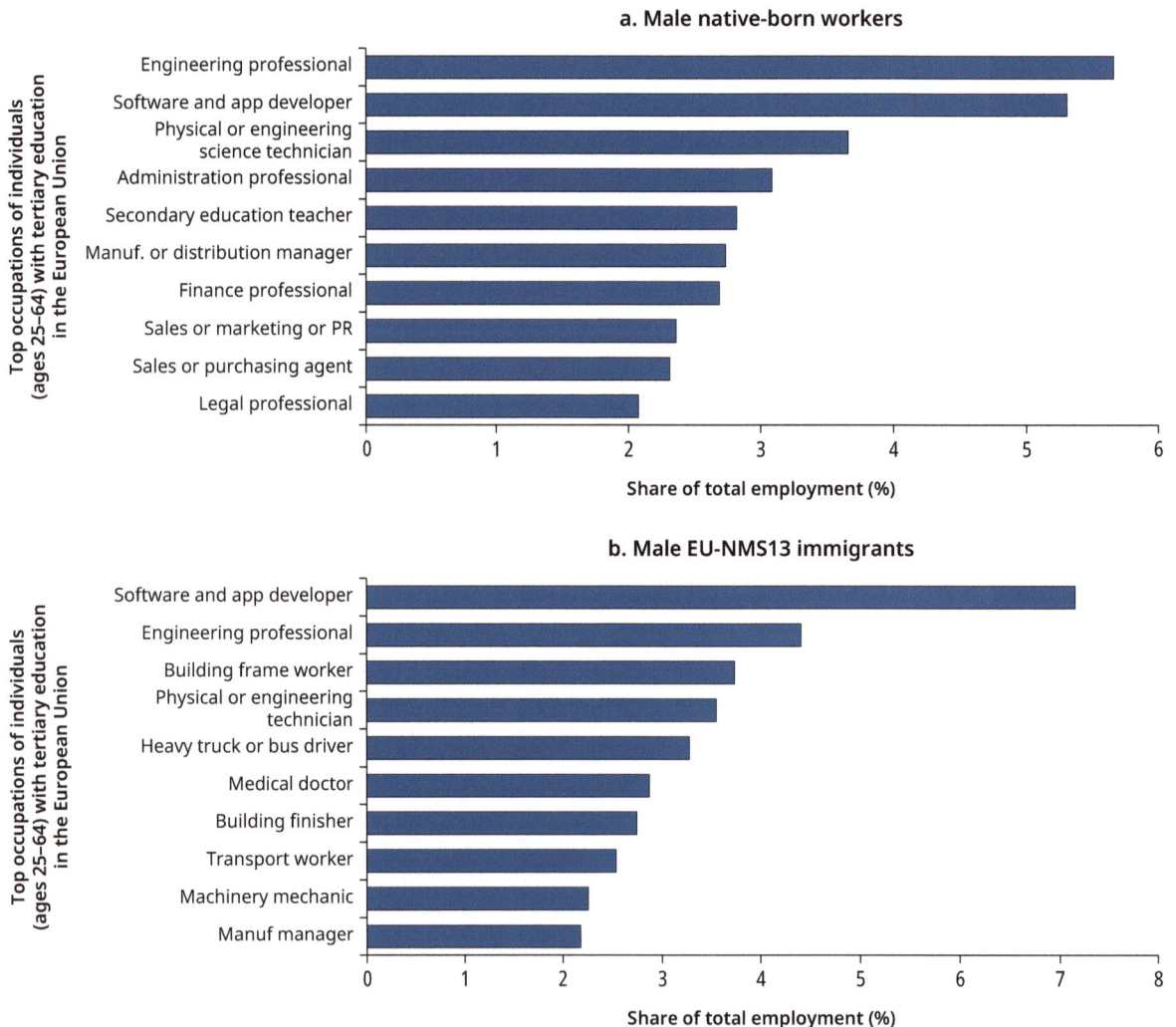

a. Male native-born workers

b. Male EU-NMS13 immigrants

Continued

Figure 4.9

Top occupations of individuals (ages 25–64) with tertiary education, European Union *(Continued)*

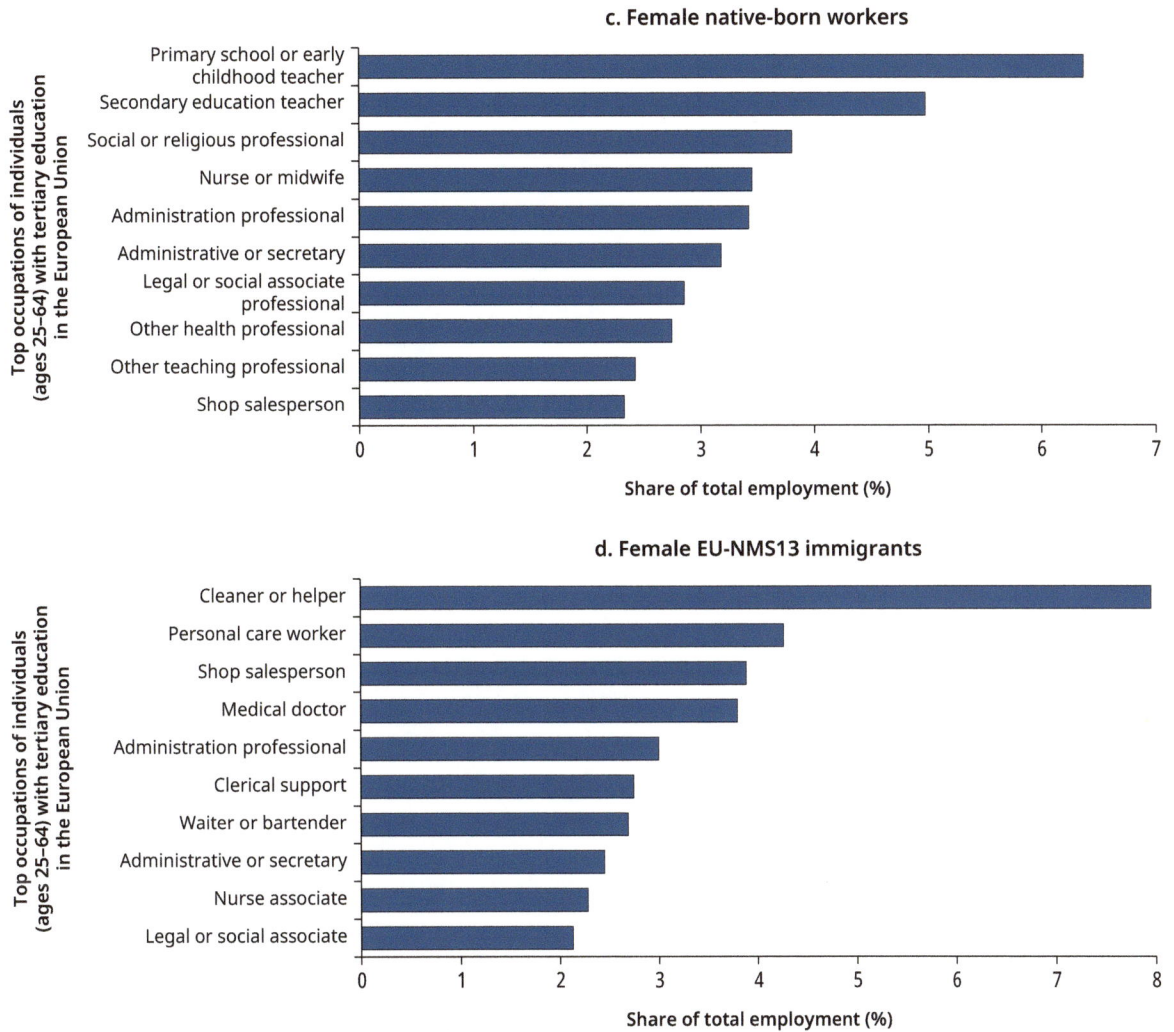

c. Female native-born workers

d. Female EU-NMS13 immigrants

Source: Bossavie et al. 2022, based on the European Union Labour Force Survey.
Note: EU-NMS13 = new member states joining the European Union in 2004, 2007, and 2013; Manuf. = manufacturing; PR = public relations.

schooling than do native-born workers in the same occupation, whereas the gap is only 0.3 years (about 3.5 months) for tertiary-educated EU-15 migrants (refer to figure 4.10). Overqualification among high-skilled migrants from non-EU ECA countries, such as in the Western Balkans, is also widespread: more than half of the migrants from Albania (56 percent) and Kosovo (61 percent) were overqualified in 2015–16 compared with about one-third of highly skilled migrants in OECD countries overall. This rate of overqualification among migrants from Kosovo, Montenegro, North Macedonia, and Serbia has also risen in recent years (OECD 2022).

FIGURE 4.10

Number of years of education relative to occupational mean, European Union, by migrants' region of origin

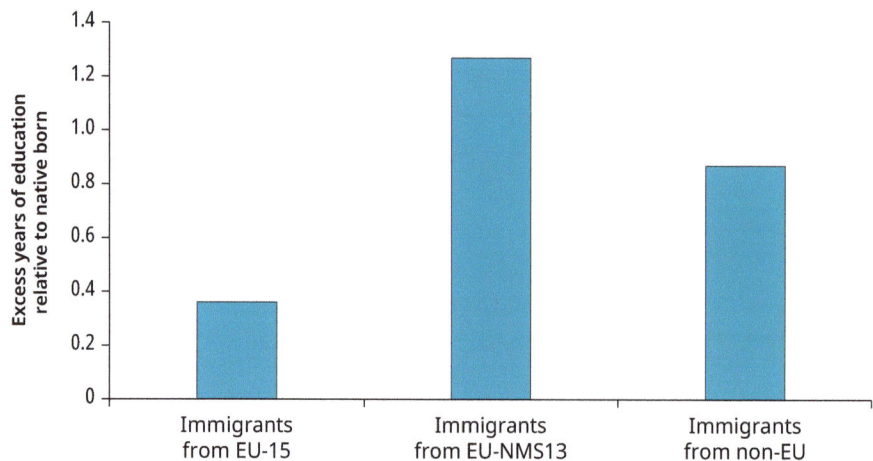

Source: Original calculations based on data from the European Union Labour Force Survey 2018 (database), Eurostat (https://ec.europa.eu/eurostat/statistics-explained/index.php/EU_labour_force _survey).
Note: The figure compares the excess education of tertiary-educated migrants versus tertiary-educated native-born workers. *Excess education* refers to a person's years of education compared with the average years of education of workers in the same occupation (using ISCO-08 three-digit level). EU-15 = European Union members before 2004; EU-NMS13 = new member states joining the European Union in 2004, 2007, and 2013; ISCO = International Standard Classification of Occupations.

Occupational downgrade is observed for both female and male migrants from ECA countries. Occupational downgrade among high-skilled female migrants to the European Union is striking because the top two occupations of tertiary-educated female migrants from the EU-NMS13 are cleaners-helpers and personal care workers (refer to figure 4.9, panel d). Among qualified EU-NMS13 female migrant workers, five of the top 10 jobs require medium to low skill levels. According to the 2018 EU Labour Force Survey, five of the top 10 occupations in which highly educated male EU-NMS13 migrants work can be categorized as low skill (building frame workers, heavy truck or bus drivers, building finishers, transportation or storage workers, and machinery mechanics) compared with none of the top 10 occupations for high-skilled male native-born workers.

The occupational downgrade of high-skilled migrants is linked to imperfect transferability of skills combined with informational barriers (Borjas 2015; Friedberg 2000). Migrants' skills and human capital are often imperfectly transferred when they seek work in destination countries' labor markets. This can occur because of language barriers, which can, for example, prevent migrants from accessing occupations with high communications content in destination countries. It can take place because the value of an educational degree obtained in the country of origin may not match standards in destination countries. Even if it does, informational barriers may exist, because employers are likely to have limited information or knowledge about the validity of academic or occupational qualifications acquired abroad, reducing the perceived domestic value of those credentials. The imperfect recognition of foreign credentials is a key factor behind the informational barriers that contribute to occupational downgrade of qualified migrants in host countries (Chiswick and Miller 2009). For these reasons, migrants tend to select occupations that differ vertically (that is, they require a lower level of education) or horizontally (that is, they require the same education level but entail distinct types of tasks) from those of native-born workers.

This brain waste comes at a cost for both sending and receiving countries. At the destination, the untapped use of migrants' skills can reduce productivity and tax revenues. For migrants and sending countries, occupational downgrade lowers earnings potential and migrants' subsequent capacity to send remittances back to their origin country. Furthermore, not using certain higher skills during the migration episode can also hinder migrants' ability to use those skills upon return to their home country.

Short-Term Impacts of High-Skilled Emigration on Origin Countries

Human Capital and Labor Market Impacts

High-skilled emigration is widespread in some of the smaller middle-income ECA countries. In smaller countries in the Western Balkans, such as Bosnia and Herzegovina, for example, it is estimated that close to 45 percent of the working-age population with a tertiary degree lives abroad (refer to figure 4.11). Another smaller country in the Western Balkans, Albania, also exhibits very high rates of high-skilled emigration: close to 30 percent of the tertiary-educated working-age population is estimated to live abroad. In Moldova, the incidence of high-skilled emigration is of a similar magnitude. The very high incidence of emigration among high-skilled workers is a source of concern among origin-country policy makers, especially in countries with an aging population. In contrast, in Central Asian countries such as Tajikistan and Uzbekistan, less than 5 percent of the high-skilled population is estimated to live abroad.

FIGURE 4.11

Share of the working-age population with tertiary education living abroad, by country of origin

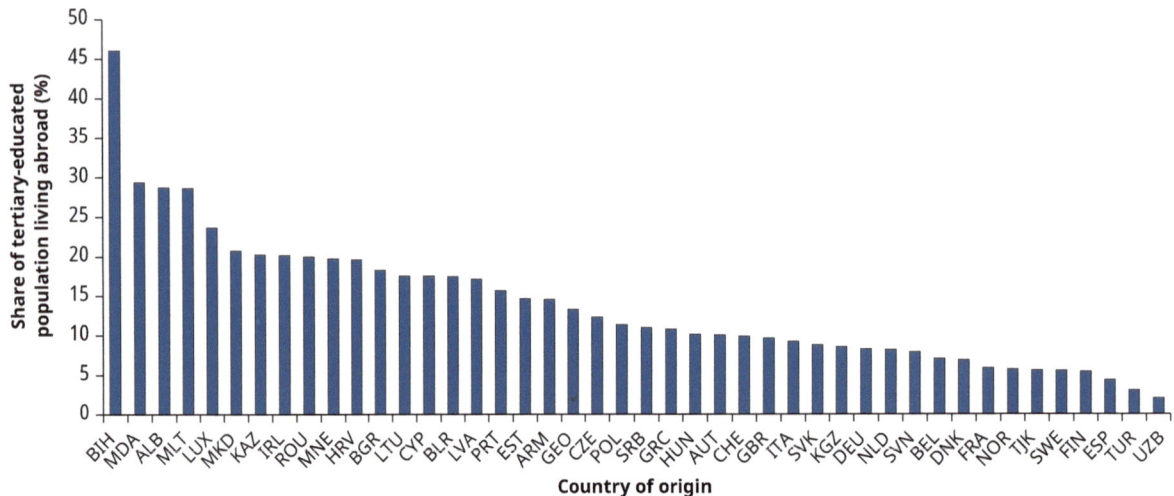

Source: Original calculations based on UN Department of Economic and Social Affairs (https://www.un.org/development/desa/pd/content/international-migrant-stock).

Note: For a list of country codes, go to https://www.iso.org/obp/ui/#search.

In the short run, high-skilled migration can reduce human capital in countries of origin, especially if emigrants are more skilled than nonmigrants. High-skilled migration affects the quantity and quality of labor and human capital available in the country of origin in the short run. The short-term human capital impacts of emigration are more severe if migrants are more skilled than the rest of the population in the origin country. This is the case in most ECA countries of origin. The impacts are more pronounced when emigration is widespread among the working-age population, as in the case of smaller origin countries in the Western Balkans and Central EU (Bossavie and Özden 2023).

Human capital growth and convergence is slower in countries that experience high emigration rates. Educational attainment among the adult population in the European Union has progressively increased since the European Union's enlargement in 2004, and among the EU-NMS13, there has been a process of catching up to the EU-15. This convergence is more visible in the younger population ages 30–34 years (refer to figure 4.12). However, the top migrant-sending regions among the EU-NMS13 have been slower to improve. They have not reached the EU-15 average and have experienced larger gaps relative to the average among populations in the EU-NMS13. Because of this, migration in NMS-sending regions, which usually involves more highly educated populations, seems to slow the convergence in human capital across these regions.

FIGURE 4.12

Changes in the share of tertiary-educated individuals (ages 30–34) in high-versus low-emigration regions of the European Union

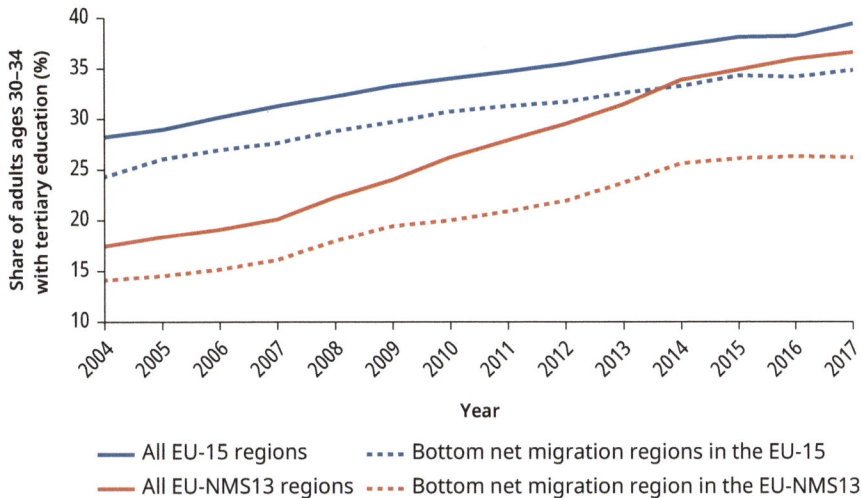

Source: Bossavie et al. 2022. Elaboration based on data from Education and Training database, Eurostat (https://ec.europa.eu/eurostat/web/education-and-training/overview).
Note: Bottom net migration regions are the bottom 30 percent of total EU-15 and EU-NMS13 NUTS-2 subdivisions with the lowest net inflows of international migrants, calculated as international arrivals minus international departures during the period 2004–18. EU-15 = European Union members before 2004; EU-NMS13 = new member states joining the European Union in 2004, 2007, and 2013; NUTS-2 = Nomenclature of Territorial Units for Statistics level 2.

Without the right policies in place, the departure of high-skilled workers can contribute to labor shortages in countries of origin, including in critical occupations. High-skilled emigrants represent a large share of the total stock of workers in some specific sectors of origin countries, particularly IT and health. As shown in figure 4.13, emigration has been a negative contributor to employment in the health sector among the EU-NMS13. In addition, ICT professionals from the EU-NMS13 who worked in other EU countries represented about 15 percent of the total stock of ICT workers in origin countries. In the health sector, this proportion was close to 20 percent. Emigration of high-skilled professionals can lead to labor shortages in critical occupations, such as medical doctors. This can be especially challenging for countries of origin that experience an increase in the demand for medical services associated with population aging. In the Western Balkans, an analysis of LinkedIn data carried out by LinkedIn and the World Bank suggests that net migration of LinkedIn members during the period 2015–19 was associated with the loss of business and tech skills. The analysis of LinkedIn data also showed a loss of industry-specific skills, such as ICT, engineering, and medical skills (https://linkedindata.worldbank.org/data). A series of reports from the European Training Foundation also point to high

FIGURE 4.13

Changes in employment due to nonmigrants and emigrants, new EU member states, 2008–18

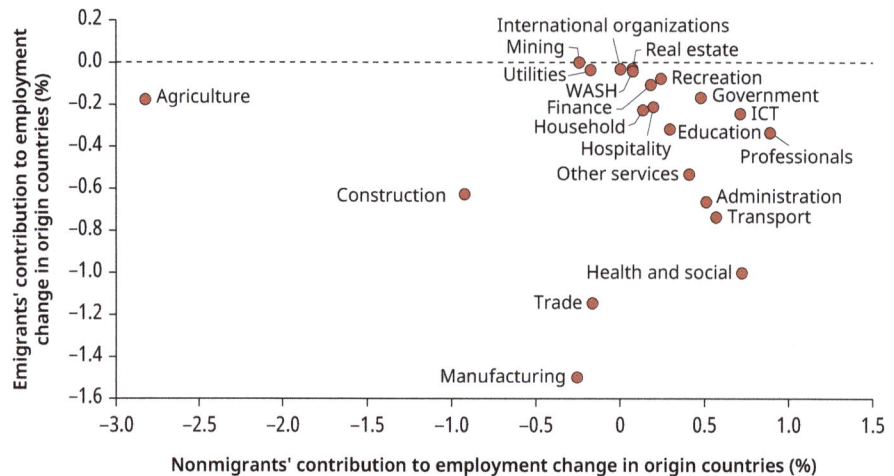

Source: European Union Labour Force Surveys (database), Eurostat (https://ec.europa.eu/eurostat /statistics-explained/index.php/EU_labour_force_survey).
Note: Statistics on the *x* axis are calculated as the change in employment in each sector of activity in the EU-NMS13 between 2008 and 2018, divided by the change in total employment in the EU-NMS13 over the same period. Statistics on the *y* axis are calculated as the change in employment in each sector of activity of migrants from the EU-NMS13 in other EU countries between 2008 and 2018, divided by the change in total employment in the EU-NMS13 over the same period. EU-NMS13 = new member states joining the European Union in 2004, 2007, and 2013; Household = households as employers; ICT = information and communications technology; NUTS-2 = Nomenclature of Territorial Units for Statistics level 2; WASH = water, sanitation, and hygiene.

labor demand and shortages in the ICT sector in the Western Balkans and Central EU (for example, ETF 2021; OECD 2022).

A few studies of ECA countries suggest that high-skilled emigration may negatively affect capital growth, productivity, and innovation in countries of origin. At the theoretical level, it has been shown that the emigration of high-skilled workers may have repercussions on productivity in countries of origin through various channels. First, in the presence of skill complementarities or externalities between high-skilled workers in a firm, the emigration of high-skilled workers may negatively affect productivity among those who stay (Docquier, Lohest, and Marfouk 2007). Second, although it allows innovators at home to access valuable knowledge accumulated abroad, the emigration of high-skilled migrants can also have negative impacts on the rest of the economy by weakening local knowledge networks (Agrawal et al. 2011). In the ECA context, high-skilled emigration has been reported to have negative impacts on firm productivity and total factor productivity in some Central EU countries (Giesing and Laurentsyeva 2018). Third, because of the imperfect substitutability between low-skilled and high-skilled labor, skill-selective emigration can lead to slower capital growth and technological downgrading (Bhagwati and Rodriguez 1975; Docquier and

Rapoport 2012; Haque and Kim 1995; Miyagiwa 1991). Finally, entrepreneurship and innovation may be negatively affected by the departure of young, high-skilled workers: some studies find negative effects of youth emigration on entrepreneurship and innovation in Italy (Anelli et al. 2019).

Because high-skilled migrants mostly come from lower-income regions within ECA, human capital loss and skills shortages may increase gaps between lagging and leading regions. As shown in the "Patterns, Trends, and Heterogeneity in High-Skilled Emigration in Europe and Central Asia" section, high-skilled emigration disproportionately comes from the less economically developed regions of ECA origin countries. This may lead to a vicious circle in which poor economic conditions in some regions lead to emigration, which further degrades economic conditions in those regions. In Romania, beyond the positive trends at the national level, regional analysis shows larger increases in the number of doctors per capita (as well as in the number in other skilled professions, such as engineers) in counties with less net migration outflows, whereas some of the lagging regions with higher outmigration did not see meaningful gains in the supply of doctors (refer to figure 4.14). Available evidence for ECA, however, mostly looks at the association between high-skilled emigration and labor shortages. Much more evidence is needed to establish a causal link.

FIGURE 4.14

Changes in the number of medical doctors per capita in high- and low-emigration regions, Romania, 2002–11

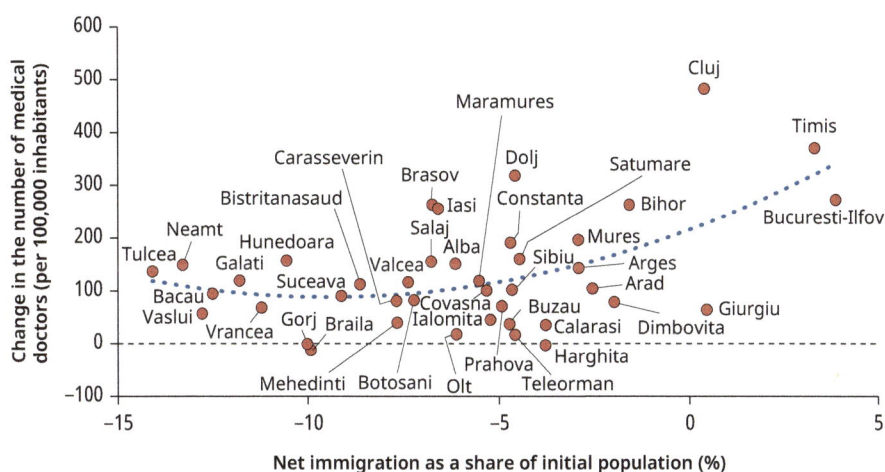

Sources: Ten percent samples of the 2002 and 2011 censuses from Minnesota Population Center Integrated Public Use Microdata Series 2019 (https://www.ipums.org/projects/ipums-international/d020 .v7.2).
Note: Net immigration is defined as the number of immigrants (arrivals) minus the number of emigrants (departures) from 2002 to 2011 in each region. Regions listed are the Nomenclature of Territorial Units for Statistics level 3 regions of Romania.

Fiscal Impacts

The departure of high-skilled workers shrinks the fiscal base with potentially negative impacts on public finances. Tax revenues may be reduced because of the lower economic activity resulting from labor outflows (Gibson and McKenzie 2012). Remittances, however, can raise consumption taxes, thereby exerting a mitigating impact. On the expenditure side, the older population left behind puts pressure on pension and health spending (Clements et al. 2015). Fiscal losses become larger if emigrants are concentrated among prime-age, highly educated, and high-earning workers (Desai et al. 2009). In the EU-NMS13, net immigration has been associated with higher social spending on pensions and health care during periods of weaker economic growth (Atoyan et al. 2016). The reduction of the fiscal base is especially a problem in education because nonmigrants must subsidize those who leave.

Medium- and Long-Term Impacts on Origin Countries

Human Capital Impacts

In the medium to long term, countries of origin can experience net gains in human capital if certain conditions are fulfilled. In addition to the immediate short-term drain on human capital associated with emigration, the departure of skilled workers can also lead, eventually, to what has been referred to as brain gain in migrant-sending countries. Brain gain occurs through two main channels: one is by increasing the returns to education and investments in human capital in the origin country, because of the high wage premium associated with the demand for high-skilled employment abroad, and the other is through the return of high-skilled migrants who have accumulated additional human, financial, and social capital while in another country. For instance, the direct effect of the emigration of doctors, which reduces the stock of doctors in ECA sending countries, may be offset by the greater incentives to graduate in medicine because of higher earnings potential in destination countries and the option value of returning from abroad with enhanced skills.

Cross-country studies including ECA countries have reported a net positive association between emigration and human capital accumulation in origin countries, if emigration rates remain moderate. A positive relationship between skilled emigration and skill formation, after accounting for initial human capital levels, has been reported by cross-country studies (Beine, Docquier, and Oden-Defoort 2011; Beine, Docquier, and Rapoport 2008; Docquier, Lohest, and Marfouk 2007). These studies show, however, that this finding holds if emigration rates remain below 20 or 30 percent, depending on countries' characteristics. A similar positive association has been reported for samples of ECA countries. Among sending countries in the Central EU, return migration, combined with the education incentive channel, has been shown to turn the drain on human capital into a gain (Beine, Docquier, and Rapoport 2001, 2008; Docquier and Rapoport 2012; Mayr and Peri 2009): a 0–20 percent increase in emigration rates, in the long run, has been estimated to increase average schooling by about one year in origin countries in the Central EU (Mayr and Peri 2009). Support for the brain gain hypothesis has also been found in a panel regression estimation for the 10 countries that joined the European Union in the 1980s and 2004 (Farchy 2009). In Romania, temporary emigration was found to have positive long-run effects on skill levels at home (Ambrosini et al. 2015).

Human Capital Investments in Origin Countries in Response to Migration Opportunities

The main mechanism behind human capital gains for countries of origin is the increase in educational investments that takes place in response to emigration opportunities. Recent empirical studies of brain gain outside ECA offer evidence that high-skilled emigration can have net positive effects on the supply of high-skilled labor in origin countries by incentivizing investment in human capital through increased emigration opportunities. Two recent studies of nurses in the Philippines and IT workers in India find that the incentive effect of potential migration on human capital acquisition far outweighs the observed migration (Abarcar and Theoharides 2021; Khanna and Morales 2017). In both cases, the increase in the supply of graduates in response to emigration opportunities has compensated for the departure of high-skilled workers severalfold.

Two main conditions, however, need to be satisfied for a net gain in human capital (brain gain) to materialize. First, migrants' countries of origin must be able to increase educational institutions' capacity to meet the increased demand. Second, there needs to be a large enough number of newly educated individuals who do not emigrate and end up being employed in the country of origin or who return after working abroad.

As high-skilled emigration rose, countries of origin in ECA did register an increase in the number of graduates in essential occupations such as doctors. Overall, the stock of doctors in all subregions of ECA has risen over the past 15 years, despite the incidence of the emigration of doctors in some countries of origin in the subregion. In fact, the supply of new graduates has increased more rapidly in ECA origin countries that experienced higher emigration rates. Although the size of the cohort of new graduates in medicine was close to constant in the northern EU-15 countries between 2004 and 2016, the number of new graduates in medicine showed an upward trend in the EU-NMS13, especially during the first five or six years after EU accession (refer to figure 4.15). In the 10 new member states that completed formal EU accession in 2004 (Cyprus, Czechia, Estonia, Hungary, Latvia, Lithuania, Malta, Poland, Slovak Republic, and Slovenia), the size of the cohort of graduates in medicine accelerated in 2009. In the three member states that entered the European Union in 2007 (Bulgaria and Romania) and 2013 (Croatia), graduate flows accelerated beginning in 2013.

In a few ECA origin countries, the increase in the number of new medical graduates was large enough to compensate for emigration in high-skilled occupations, but not in others. In Romania, the increase in medical graduates in response to emigration was high enough that the emigration of high-skilled doctors did not hamper the catching-up process with other countries. The number of graduates in medicine increased after Romania's EU accession in 2007 and accelerated for six years after that, a period in line with the length of time it takes to complete medical school programs (refer to figure 4.16). In fact, the ratio of doctors vis-à-vis the EU average increased from 66 percent in 2000 to 82 percent in 2018. Although other factors might be at play, the fact that most of the increase in medical graduates in Romania stems from programs in English and French is

FIGURE 4.15

New graduates in medicine, member states entering the European Union in 2004, 2007, and 2013

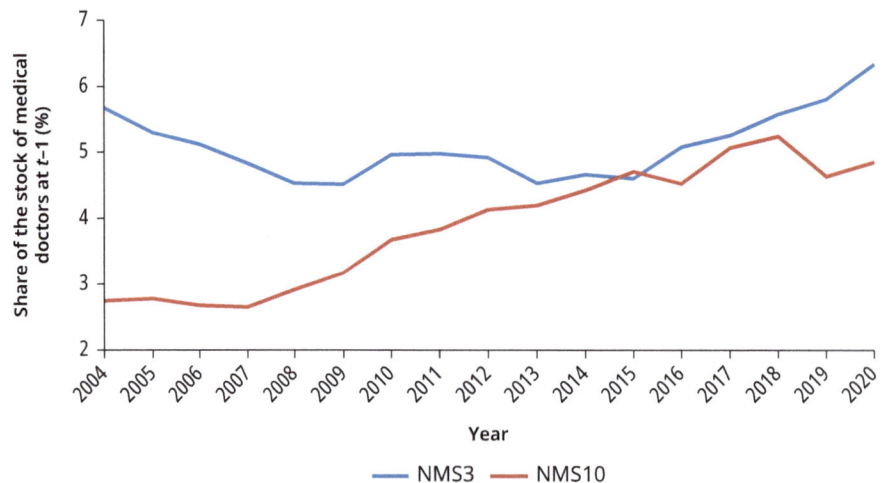

Source: European Commission Regulated Professions Database (https://ec.europa.eu/growth/tools -databases/regprof/index.cfm?action=homepage).
Note: On the *y* axis, *t*–1 refers to the year immediately before the one reported on the *x* axis. The blue line shows the trends for the share of doctors after EU accession in NMS10 countries, and the red line shows the trend for NMS3 countries. EU = European Union; NMS10 = new member states that completed formal EU accession in 2004 (Cyprus, Czechia, Estonia, Hungary, Latvia, Lithuania, Malta, Poland, Slovak Republic, and Slovenia); NMS3 = new member states that completed formal EU accession in 2007 (Bulgaria and Romania) and 2013 (Croatia).

consistent with increased investment in education in response to higher demand for internationally transferable skills. Other migrant-sending countries, such as Czechia and Slovenia, also witnessed a rapid rise in the number of graduates in medicine that more than compensated for the emigration of doctors. In other countries, however, the change in the number of high-skilled graduates did not compensate for the emigration of high-skilled workers. In Estonia, Hungary, and Latvia, for example, the additional supply of new graduates was not sufficient to make up for the departure of human resources (refer to figure 4.17 for a comparison of Hungary and Romania).

The heterogeneity of experiences among ECA countries suggests that policies and local contexts are key in determining whether origin countries' supply of high-skilled workers increases in the face of migration opportunities. One determinant of the net gains in human capital from high-skilled emigration is the ability of the educational

FIGURE 4.16

Supply of medical students and stock of medical doctors, Romania, 2000–20

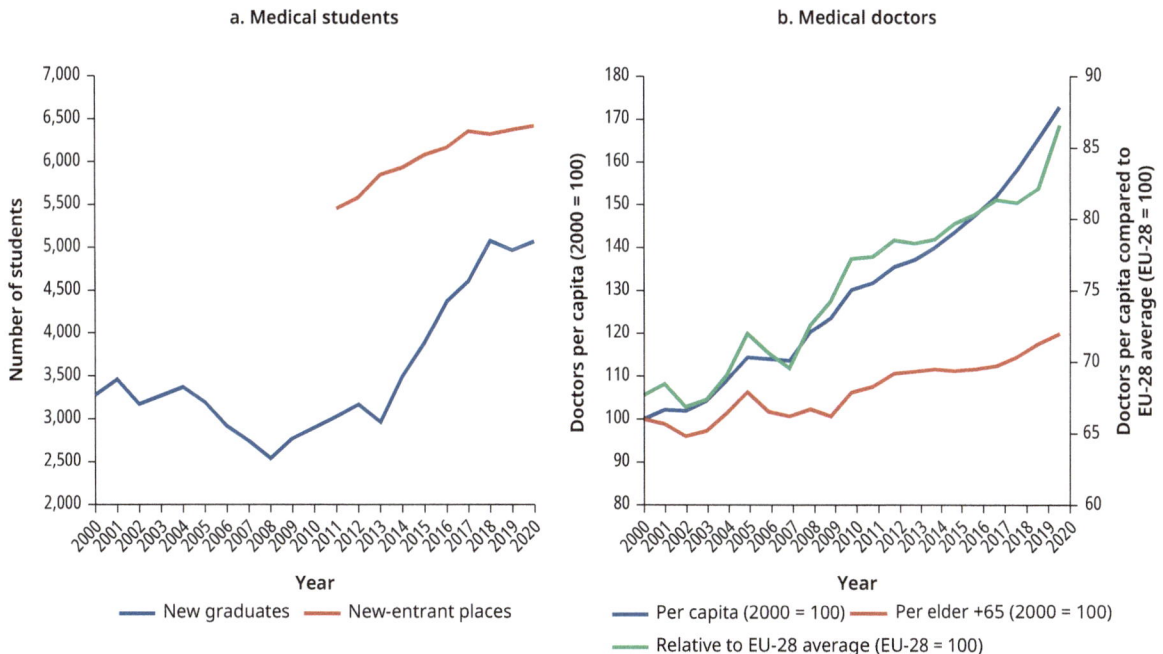

Sources: Health graduates: Eurostat (https://appsso.eurostat.ec.europa.eu/nui/show.do?dataset=hlth_rs_grd&lang=en); stock of doctors: health personnel by NUTS-2 regions, Eurostat (https://ec.europa.eu/eurostat/en/web/products-datasets/-/HLTH_RS_PRSRG); new-entrant places: Ungureanu and Socha-Dietrich 2019; population: Eurostat Population database, reference years 2013, 2018, population on January 1, by age group, and sex (https://ec.europa.eu/eurostat/web/population/overview).

Note: New-entrant places refers to the number of students who start studying medicine. On the left-hand y axis of panel b, the number of doctors per capita per year is reported relative to the number of doctors per capita in 2000, where the reference value in 2000 is 100 (2000 = 100). On the right-hand y axis of panel b, the number of doctors per capita in Romania per year is reported relative to the average number of doctors per capita in the EU-28 in the same year, where the reference value for the EU-28 average is normalized to 100 (EU-28 = 100). NUTS-2 = Nomenclature of Territorial Units for Statistics level 2.

FIGURE 4.17

Changes in the stock of medical doctors, Hungary and Romania, 2000–17

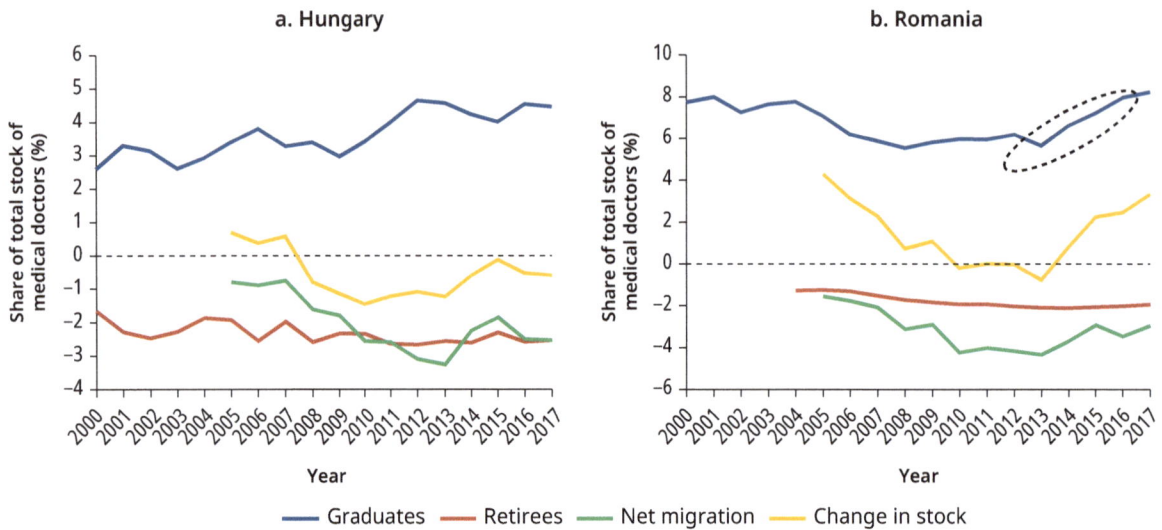

Source: Bossavie et al. 2022, based on Regulated Professions Database, European Commission (https://ec.europa.eu/growth/tools
-databases/regprof/index.cfm?action=homepage).
Note: Net migration is defined as the difference between immigration flows (arrivals) and emigration flows (departures) in each European
region. The dashed oval in panel b highlights the increase in the number of new graduates as a share of the total stock of doctors six years
after Romania's accession to the European Union.

system to respond quickly by increasing the supply of high-skilled
graduates. This is not always possible. For example, one distinct feature
of the educational system for high-skilled health professionals such as
doctors is that the number of places in education institutions in these
fields of study is often capped (the so-called *numerus clausus*). In
addition, for the educational system to be able to rapidly respond, it
needs not only to be flexible but also to receive timely and precise
information on the demand for high-skilled professionals domestically
and abroad. Such careful monitoring of demand for high-skilled workers
is only available in a handful of countries.

Even with an increase in the domestic supply of skilled workers, it may be
difficult for countries of origin to perceive high-skilled emigration as brain
gain because of other ongoing demographic trends. One key example is the
increase in the supply of medical graduates in response to migration
opportunities, in the context of an aging population. Even if the total stock
of doctors has increased in ECA origin countries, descriptive evidence
suggests that the increased supply has not caught up with the larger
demand, which stems from population aging and the related increased
demand for health care services. The number of doctors measured against
the size of the older population (those age 65 and older) can approximate
these demand pressures. The share of doctors in the EU-15 has dropped by

3.7 percent since 2011, from 1,982 doctors per 100,000 elderly population to 1,909 doctors (refer to figure 4.18, panel a). This shortage may represent a pull factor that attracts doctors and other health care professionals from elsewhere in Europe. In the EU-NMS13, the ratio of doctors per 100,000 elderly population has fallen even more, by more than 13 percent since the 2004 EU accession and by 8 percent since 2011. Thus, although the stock of doctors in the EU-NMS13 has risen despite the migration outflow to

FIGURE 4.18

Stock of medical doctors over time, Europe and Central Asia

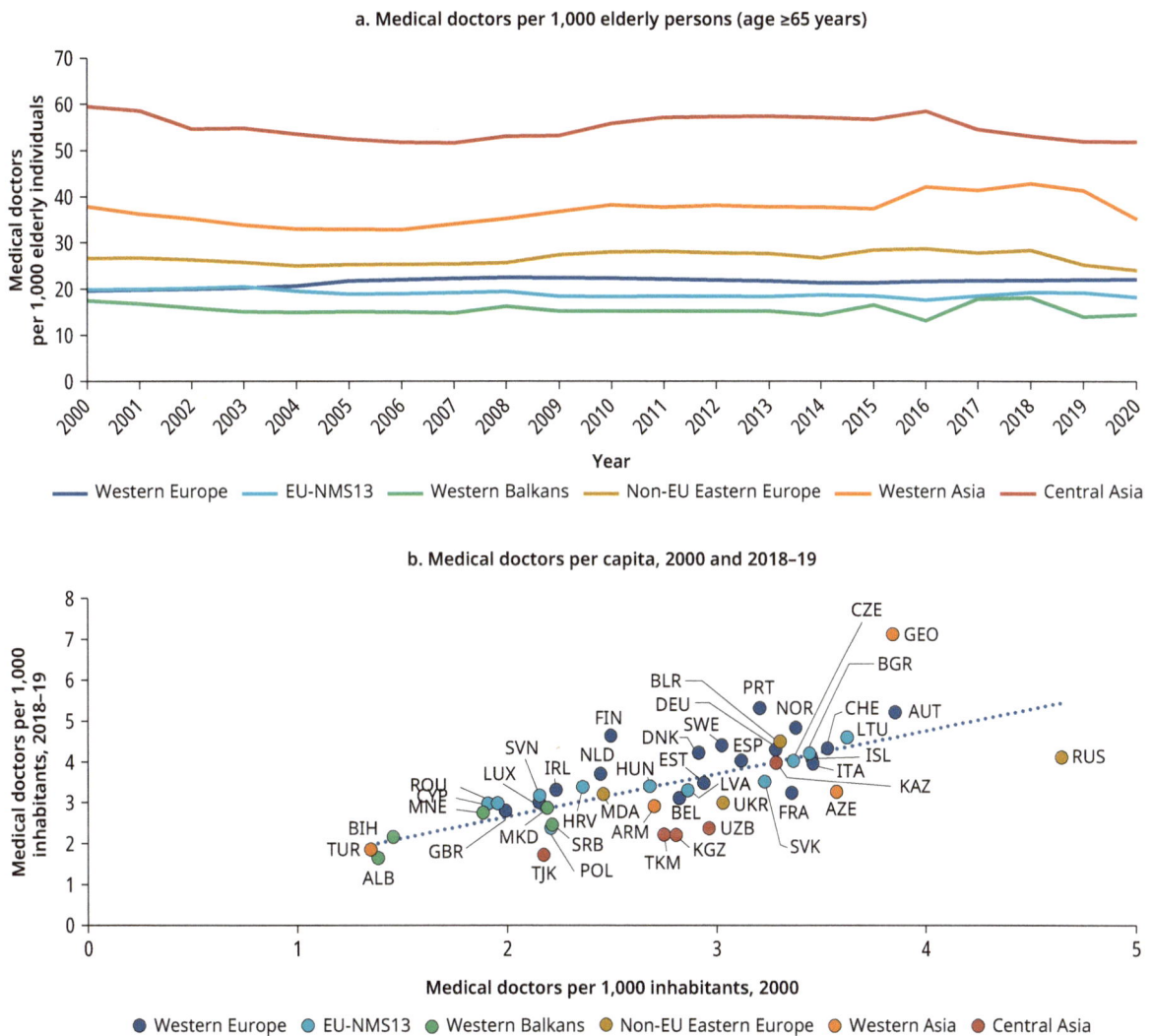

a. Medical doctors per 1,000 elderly persons (age ≥65 years)

b. Medical doctors per capita, 2000 and 2018–19

Sources: World Development Indicators database, World Bank (https://databank.worldbank.org/source/world-development-indicators); World Health Organization (https://www.who.int/data/gho/data/indicators).

Note: EU-NMS13 = new member states joining the European Union in 2004, 2007, and 2013; Western Europe = Austria, Belgium, Denmark, Finland, France, Germany, Greece, Iceland, Ireland, Italy, Liechtenstein, Luxembourg, Netherlands, Norway, Portugal, Spain, Sweden, Switzerland, and United Kingdom; Non-EU Eastern Europe = Belarus, Moldova, Russian Federation, and Ukraine; Western Asia = Armenia, Azerbaijan, Georgia, and Türkiye.

higher-income European countries, the expansion in supply has not kept up with the aging of the population and the consequent increase in the demand for health care services. As shown in figure 4.18, panel b, disparities in the number of doctors per capita have increased in ECA: net emigration countries such as Albania and Latvia or Central Asia have lower ratios than in 2000.

Human Capital Gains through Return Migration

Origin countries can also benefit from high-skilled migration through the return of their high-skilled migrant workers. When high-skilled emigration is only temporary, returning migrants can bring back productive skills that benefit the home economy (Borjas and Bratsberg 1996; Dustmann, Fadlon, and Weiss 2011; Dustmann and Weiss 2007). This can create a positive effect even with initial emigration (Dos Santos and Postel-Vinay 2003).

In addition to increasing the productivity of return migrants, temporary migration may increase the human capital and productivity of nonmigrants through knowledge transfers. Return migration can have an expansionary effect through knowledge diffusion that in turn narrows the technological gap between the host and source countries (Dos Santos and Postel-Vinay 2003). Evidence of such knowledge spillovers is scarce, although recent evidence shows that return migration from Germany to the former Yugoslavia after the end of the Balkan war led to significant productivity and export gains in workers' home countries (Bahar et al. 2022). Emerging evidence for outside ECA also shows that more return migration increases knowledge diffusion and human capital in the sending country (Choudhury 2016). However, more evidence specific to the ECA context is required to generalize those findings.

Most studies for ECA find that, compared with nonmigrants, high-skilled migrants experience wage gains upon their return, suggesting that the migration experience increases productivity in home labor markets. Among those who return to their home countries, migrants from the EU-NMS13 earn higher wages when they have a salaried job and are more likely to become self-employed than nonmigrants, generating new activities and potentially creating more jobs (Piracha and Vadean, 2010). Several studies find that returning migrants in ECA earn a positive wage premium.[2] Results show substantive income premiums for return migrants, ranging from 40 percent in Hungary (Co, Gang, and Yun 2000), to 10–45 percent in a selected group of EU new member states including Romania (Martin and Radu 2010), to almost 100 percent in Albania (de Coulon and Piracha 2005). Data from the EU Labour Force Survey ad hoc module for 2014 (https://ec.europa.eu/eurostat/data/database?node_code=lfso_14) show that in 2014 Romanian return migrants were 15 percent more likely to be in the top three percentiles of income, controlling for observable characteristics such as age, marital status, gender, education level, and NUTS-2 region of residence. Figure 4.19 shows that in most countries from the EU-NMS13, return migrants who are wage workers are more likely than nonmigrants to be among the top earners, even after controlling for systematic differences in observable characteristics. Such gains may originate from actual productivity increases due to human capital accumulation abroad and from the signaling effects to employers in origin countries of having worked abroad (Reinhold and Thom 2013). A related, albeit scarcer, literature examines whether migrants who return to their country of origin improve their labor market outcomes in addition to experiencing wage gains. In Albania, high-skilled returning migrants have been found to experience upward occupational mobility compared with nonmigrants (Carletto and Kilic 2011).

The human capital benefits of the migration experience for high-skilled migrants and countries of origin depend on multiple factors that are affected by policies in both sending and origin countries. These factors include migrants' educational level, whether the work experience and human capital gained at destination countries are in demand in the home

FIGURE 4.19

Difference in the share of returnees and nonmigrants in the top three earnings deciles, EU-NMS13

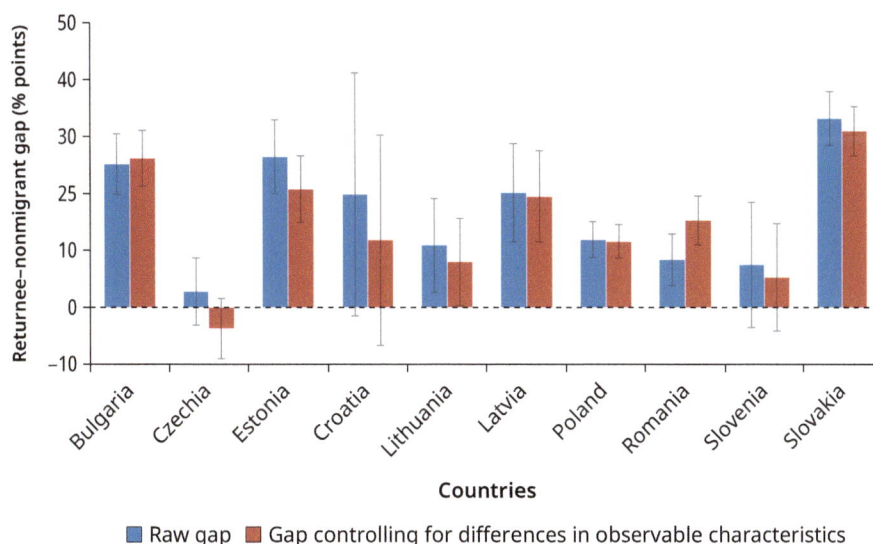

Raw gap   Gap controlling for differences in observable characteristics

Source: Bossavie et al. 2022, based on EU Labour Force Survey, Ad Hoc Module, "2014 Labor Market Situation of Migrants and Their Immediate Descendants," Eurostat (https://ec.europa.eu/eurostat/data /database?node_code=lfso_14).
Note: Returnees are defined as working-age individuals who lived abroad in the past. Raw (unconditional) gaps are based on differences in means of returnees compared with stayers with no controls. The gaps with controls are the beta coefficients of a Logit regression where a binary variable for being in the top three income deciles nationwide (outcome variable) is regressed on a binary variable for being a return migrant (explanatory variable), controlling for age, gender, education, and region of resettlement. Error bars represent 95 percent confidence intervals. For a list of country codes, go to https://www.iso.org/obp/ui/#search.

labor market, and whether the duration of stay abroad was long enough for human capital accumulation (Bossavie and Özden 2023). One emerging consensus from the empirical literature, which includes ECA countries, is that higher-skilled temporary migrants experience greater human capital, productivity, and wage gains from the migration experience than low-skilled migrants (Ambrosini et al. 2015; Gibson, McKenzie, and Stillman 2011; McCormick and Wahba 2001; Wahba 2015).[3] The duration of the stay abroad has also been shown to matter in the context of return migration to Romania (Shima 2010). Migrants who stay abroad longer have more time to accumulate human capital, but the value of the skills gained depreciates if they are not used. Human capital gains also depend on whether there is a match in the home labor market for the human capital gained by returning migrants (Dustmann, Fadlon, and Weiss 2011; Mayr and Peri 2009). If the human capital accumulated while abroad is not in demand, skill waste can take place, along with inactivity, as found for migrants returning to Poland (Coniglio and Brzozowski 2018). Finally, temporary migrants' destination countries may matter in whether there are benefits of return migration for migrants and their home economy (Dustmann, Fadlon, and Weiss 2011), as shown in Albania (Carletto and Kilic 2011).

The human capital benefits of migration for countries of origin also depend on who returns among workers who went abroad. Migrants who choose to return to their country of origin may either be more skilled and successful than those who choose to stay abroad (positive selection in return migration) or vice versa (negative selection in return migration).[4] A few studies have examined this question for ECA countries and report mixed findings. In the case of immigrants to the Netherlands, a U-shaped relationship between return intensity and migrants' income abroad is observed. Returns are more common among very low-income migrants and high-income migrants than among middle-income ones (Bijwaard, Schluter, and Wahba 2014). In the case of immigrants in Germany, higher wages have been shown to lead to more and faster returns (Dustmann 2003). From the perspective of sending countries, return migrants to the EU-NMS13 are negatively selected on education compared with current migrants and nonmigrants in almost all countries, except for Croatia and Slovenia (refer to figure 4.20), where return migrants are more likely than nonmigrants and current migrants to have some tertiary education.

High-skilled migration to the European Union exhibits a high degree of circularity overall, but countries in the EU-NMS13 and the Western Balkans struggle to attract their qualified emigrants back. High-skilled emigrants within the European Union are significantly more likely than low-skilled migrants to return to their home country within five years (refer to figure 4.21). There is, however, a great deal of heterogeneity depending on

FIGURE 4.20

Share of the working-age population (ages 25–64) with tertiary education, by migration status

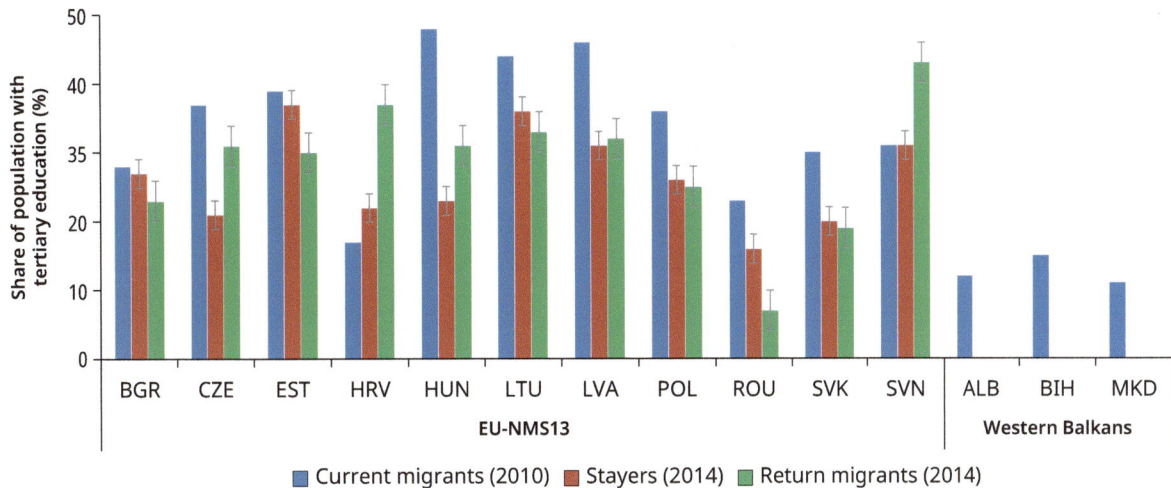

Sources: EU Labour Force Survey (database), Eurostat (https://ec.europa.eu/eurostat/statistics-explained/index.php/EU_labour_force _survey); Organisation for Economic Co-operation and Development Database on Immigrants in OECD and Non-OECD Countries (https://www.oecd.org/els/mig/dioc.htm).
Note: Current migrants are defined as working-age individuals who are currently absent from their household for work abroad the time of the survey. Return migrants are defined as working-age individuals who have returned to their household from abroad during the past five years. Stayers are defined as individuals who are neither current migrants nor return migrants. Error bars represent 95 percent confidence intervals. For a list of country codes, go to https://www.iso.org/obp/ui/#search. EU-NMS13 = new member states joining the European Union in 2004, 2007, and 2013.

the high-skilled migrants' region of origin. Among high-skilled migrants from the EU-15 who were abroad in 2010, 40 percent had returned to their home country five years later. In contrast, countries of the EU-NMS13 face significantly more difficulties in attracting back their migrants, and it is estimated that after five years, only 12 percent of their high-skilled migrants return home. One possible explanation is the persistence of economic challenges and push factors that led skilled migrants to move out of the country in the first place. Return rates are particularly low among high-skilled migrants from the EU-NMS13 who moved to non-EU OECD countries, such as Australia, Canada, and the United States. In the Western Balkans, recent analyses of net migration flow by educational attainment in the period 2010–19 reveal some differences across countries of origin (Leitner 2021). The results indicate a net outflow of highly skilled migrants with little evidence of return to Albania, Bosnia and Herzegovina, and Kosovo, whereas Montenegro, North Macedonia, and Serbia experienced positive net migration among those with the highest skill levels, especially among the younger cohorts. The findings indicate that return migration in the form of students returning home after acquiring university education abroad is taking place in Montenegro, North Macedonia, and Serbia (Leitner 2021).

FIGURE 4.21

Estimated share of international migrants to the European Union who return home, by educational attainment and region of origin

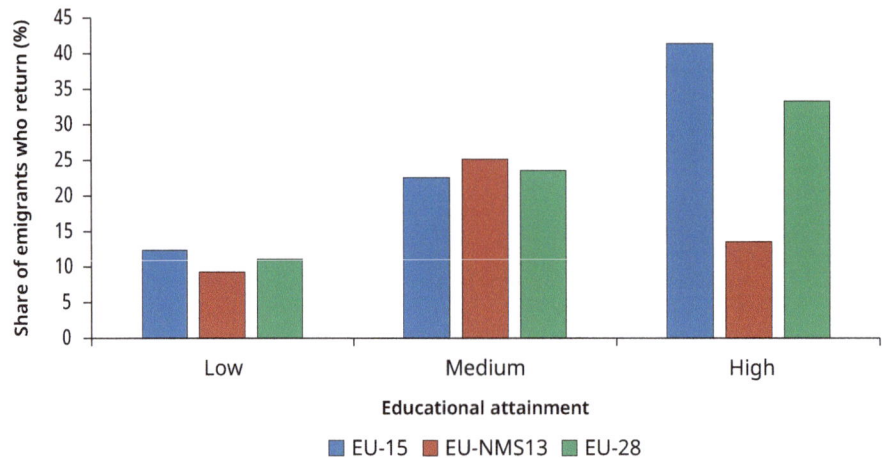

Sources: Adapted from Bossavie et al. 2022. Estimates based on data from the Centre d'Etudes Prospectives et d'Informations Internationales GeoDist Database (http://www.cepii.fr/CEPII/en/bdd _modele/presentation.asp?id=6); Organisation for Economic Co-operation and Development Database on Immigrants in OECD and Non-OECD Countries, reference years 2010 and 2011 (https://www.oecd.org /els/mig/dioc.htm); and EU Union Labour Force Survey, Ad Hoc Module, "2014 Labor Market Situation of Migrants and Their Immediate Descendants," Eurostat (https://ec.europa.eu/eurostat/data /database?node_code=lfso_14).

Note: Return rates are estimated by dividing by the number of returnees in 2014 by the stock of migrants in 2010, multiplied by the elasticity of returnees to migrants derived from a gravity-type equation that controls for a set of geographic and social ties between the sending and receiving countries (distance, contiguity, share of common ethnic groups). Low educational attainment refers to those with less than upper-secondary education; medium educational attainment, to those with upper-secondary education; and high educational attainment, to those with tertiary education. Returnee rates are estimated by dividing the number of returnees in 2014 by the stock of migrants in 2010 and multiplying by the elasticity of returnees to migrants (the percentage change in returnees for a 1 percent change in the number of migrants), which is derived from a gravity-type equation that controls for a set of geographical and social ties between the sending and receiving countries, including distance, contiguity, and share of common ethnic groups. EU-15 = European Union members before 2004; EU-NMS13 = new member states joining the European Union in 2004, 2007, and 2013.

Labor Market Impacts

High-skilled emigration can alleviate unemployment pressures in sending regions with scant job opportunities, especially among the tertiary-educated youth. By design, high-skilled emigration reduces pressures on origin countries' labor markets by providing employment opportunities outside the domestic labor market. This can particularly benefit the youth population, for whom the transition from the educational system to the labor market can be problematic, especially in contexts in which domestic labor demand is lagging. Descriptive evidence in the EU reported in figure 4.22 is consistent with this phenomenon: before the 2008–09 global financial crisis, migration from high- to low-unemployment areas coincided with a substantial decline in unemployment in the top migrant-sending countries.

FIGURE 4.22

Relationship between emigration and unemployment, EU origin countries

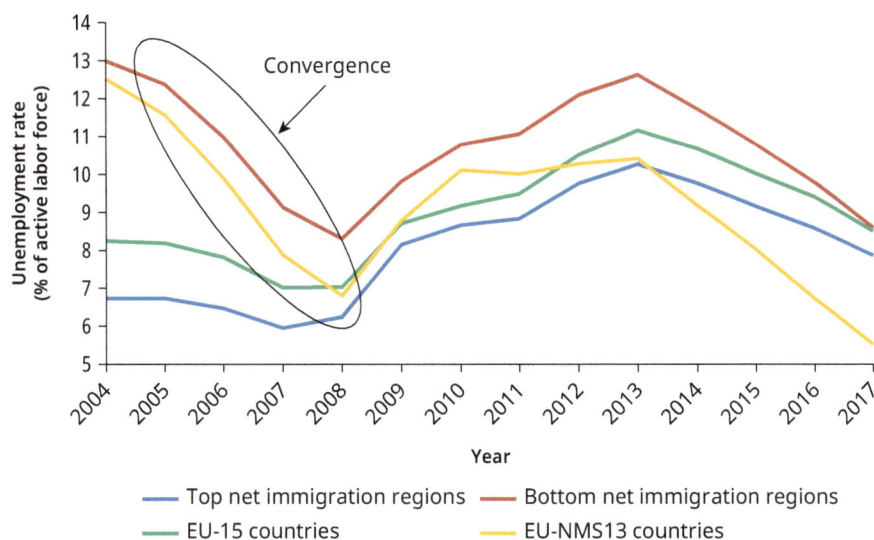

Sources: Bossavie et al. 2022, based on data from the EU Union Labour Force Survey (database), Eurostat (https://ec.europa.eu/eurostat/statistics-explained/index.php/EU_labour_force_survey); Eurostat Population database (https://ec.europa.eu/eurostat/web/population/overview).
Note: Top net immigration and emigration areas are the top 30 percent of NUTS-2 country administrative subdivisions with the highest migrant inflows minus outflows and outflows minus inflows, respectively, during 2004–17. EU-15 = European Union members before 2004; EU-NMS13 = new member states joining the European Union in 2004, 2007, and 2013; NUTS-2 = Nomenclature of Territorial Units for Statistics level 2.

Similarly, the period that followed the EU enlargement was accompanied by a much steeper decline in unemployment in top migrant-sending countries in the European Union than in top receiving countries, especially among the EU-NMS13. Although this evidence should be interpreted as descriptive and may also have been driven by other economic factors associated with EU enlargement, it is compatible with the hypothesis that high-skilled emigration helps alleviate pressures in home labor markets.[5]

The effects of emigration on wages in origin countries' labor markets are small. In Lithuania and Poland (Dustmann, Frattini, and Rosso 2015; Elsner 2013), emigration was found to have a positive effect on wages of workers in the home country who have skills like those of the workers who emigrated, because of reduced competition. Also, emigration has been found to have negative effects on the wages of less-educated native-born workers who have skills that complement those of high-skilled emigrants (Docquier, Ozden, and Peri 2014; Dustmann, Frattini, and Rosso 2015). It is important to note, however, that across the board, the magnitude of these impacts is small; in addition, the other two opposite forces at play in equilibrium wages—aging of the native-born population and upskilling—have more than compensated for any negative effects of emigration on the wages of native-born workers in migrant-sending countries (Docquier et al. 2019).[6]

Spillovers from the Diaspora of High-Skilled Workers to Origin Countries

The most direct and tangible impact of the diaspora of highly skilled workers on countries of origin is through remittances sent back home. High-skilled migrants typically send remittances back home, especially if they moved abroad without the rest of their household with the intention of returning home (Bossavie and Özden 2023). Although remittances have immediate impacts on the welfare of household members left behind, they can also produce a range of indirect effects in countries of origin. These effects include increased investments in education and health by households left behind, an easing of financial constraints, and increased entrepreneurship. Remittances can help countries of origin and households mitigate the impacts of negative shocks because they are not affected by business fluctuations in countries of origin and have been shown to increase during economic downturns.[7] At the macro level, they can support macroeconomic stability by producing a more stable source of foreign exchange compared with more volatile financial flows such as foreign direct investment (FDI) or official development assistance.

The presence of high-skilled migrants abroad can help increase the transfer of knowledge and technology to and support trade with and financial investments in countries of origin. Evidence suggests that emigrants, especially those who are highly skilled, keep a wide range of professional ties to their native countries (Docquier and Lodigiani 2010; Saxenian 2002; Wescott and Brinkerhoff 2006). As such, skilled migrants can help ease information imperfections by reducing information asymmetries and creating trust among parties (Kerr 2008). Evidence for knowledge and technology diffusion linked to emigration has been reported for ECA in the context of migration from the former Yugoslavia to Germany (Bahar et al. 2022). The reduction in information asymmetries and transaction costs can also benefit trade. Empirically, a growing literature, although not specific to ECA, has reported a strong positive relationship between the size of the migrant community and trade with countries of origin (Genc et al. 2012; Gould 1994; Head and Ries 1998). The reduction in transaction costs enabled by the diaspora can also help raise international investments in countries of origin. Skilled migration has been shown to be associated with future increases in FDI inflows due to the formation of business networks (Kugler and Rapoport 2007).

The relationship between FDI and migration has been reported to be stronger for migrants with tertiary education than for less-educated migrants (Javorcik et al. 2011). Although most of the evidence on migration and FDI is from contexts outside ECA, similar impacts from diasporas are expected in ECA given the existence of informational barriers and transaction costs associated with FDI, especially for countries outside the European Union.

Beyond economic impacts, diasporas can also affect institutions and governance in migrant-sending countries. Diaspora networks can have an effect that is not purely economic but is also cultural, through migrants' transfers of behavioral and cultural norms to their home communities, which have been referred to as "social remittances" (Rapoport 2019). While abroad, migrants absorb added information and are exposed to new attitudes, preferences, and practices that can spill over to their home communities through contacts with relatives, friends, and other members of social networks. These social remittances include political values, fertility norms, religious attitudes, and practices. It has been shown, for example, that migrants to more democratic societies can affect social, economic, and political institutions in their home country (Docquier et al. 2016; Spilimbergo 2009). In Moldova, for instance, the emigration wave that started in the aftermath of the 1998 crisis in Russia has been argued to have affected electoral outcomes and political preferences during the following decade, eventually contributing to the fall of the last Communist government in Europe (Barsbai et al. 2017). In contrast, cross-country studies that include ECA countries have suggested that emigration may have a determinantal effect on institutional quality in countries of origin, especially on corruption (Abdih et al. 2012).

Policy Recommendations

This section builds on the evidence gathered in previous sections to propose policy solutions to increase the benefits and reduce the costs of high-skilled emigration for sending countries. It first examines policies that can help reduce incentives to emigrate among the high-skilled population, such as addressing bottlenecks in domestic labor markets and broader improvements in institutions, governance, or public services. It then proposes policies, particularly within the realm of education financing, skills monitoring, and bilateral agreements, to better distribute the costs of high-skilled migration between origin and destination countries. Finally, it focuses on policies to increase the benefits of the high-skilled migration experience for migrants themselves, origin countries, and destination countries.

Reducing the Strength of Push Factors to Emigrating

Despite the gains that high-skilled emigration can generate for countries of origin, those that would like to reduce it must address its root causes. This willingness to reduce emigration flows may be strong in countries that experience high emigration rates among their high-skilled population, as observed in smaller origin countries in the Western Balkans. As highlighted in previous sections, high-skilled migration flows within ECA are mainly driven by disparities in economic opportunities and broader living standards—including access to public services—and governance. Although some of these conditions are structural and can only be altered in the medium to long term, some policies can be implemented in the short term to reduce bottlenecks in domestic labor markets, the business environment, and access to public services.

Addressing bottlenecks in domestic labor markets can increase the attractiveness of home economies, reducing the push and pull factors to emigrate. Overall, policies that can help make the domestic labor market more attractive and efficient—especially for the youth who have a higher propensity to emigrate—can help reduce the strength of push and pull factors. Such policies and programs include traditional labor market policies, such as support to entrepreneurship; active labor market policies, including wage subsidy programs, training, and labor market intermediation; and changes in labor regulations that may discourage employment. These supply-side measures can be complemented by broader demand-side policies that affect the labor market and employment creation, such as measures to improve the broader business and macroeconomic environment, or the tax and benefit system.[8]

Strengthening home institutions, public services, and governance may also reduce incentives to emigrate. Countries addressing corruption in both public and private spheres and investing in improving the quality of governance and public institutions might be able to reduce, directly or indirectly, the extent of brain drain (Bernini et al. 2024). In addition, the provision of quality public services, primarily through greater investment in health and education services, may also increase incentives for highly skilled workers and their families to remain in their home country. In the short run, policies to increase access to services can include targeted housing subsidies during the first years of these workers' career (especially young couples) and increasing the quantity and quality of childcare services. In addition to reducing incentives to emigrate, improvements in local labor market conditions, governance, and access to public services may also incentivize the return of high-skilled migrants.

Reducing the Costs of High-Skilled Emigration for Sending Countries

Reform in graduate education financing, together with cost-sharing arrangements between origin and destination countries, can help mitigate fiscal losses associated with graduates' emigration. Several education financing options have been proposed to help better distribute the cost of education of high-skilled migrant workers among origin countries, destination countries, and migrants. Such measures include the introduction of a graduate tax, according to which graduates would be required to pay part of their taxes to the origin country where they received their education, regardless of their current residence (Poutvaara 2008). As an alternative, income-contingent loans (ICLs), which would be collected from migrant graduates, could also support that objective.[9] By making ICL loan repayments feasible and tax deductible in destination countries, such programs would imply that destination countries would refund some of the education expenditures of the sending countries on the human capital that has been lost (Poutvaara 2004). The implementation of such ICL schemes or graduate taxes would require formal education cost-sharing arrangements between sending and receiving countries, for example, in the context of the European Union's unique labor market. As an alternative, in the absence of bilateral agreements allowing the repayment of ICLs in receiving countries, ICLs should involve regular annuity payments if beneficiaries are residing abroad (Chapman and Higgins 2013). Such potential reforms in education financing, however, should be very carefully considered against their potential effects on incentives to invest in education and broader human capital development in countries of origin.

Establishing or strengthening skills monitoring systems, together with tracking emigration flows, is essential to ensuring a timely response to external and internal demand for high-skilled workers. Better emigration and skills management must start with the collection of data on emigrants' skills and educational profile at the time of departure and by putting in place adequate skills monitoring systems to track the demand and supply of skills and anticipate shortages, especially in critical occupations. Such skills monitoring systems are being implemented in Czechia and Sweden, where a comprehensive labor market information system produces data on skills and jobs in demand in different regions and industries, allowing the detection of potential shortages of skilled workers. Such initiatives, however, remain rare in middle-income countries where high-skilled emigration is widespread. Among countries in the Western Balkans, for example, only the State Statistical Office of North Macedonia publishes information on annual emigration flows (OECD 2022). Even among origin countries that record emigration flows, the skills and occupational profiles of emigrants are typically not available. In North Macedonia, the Ministry of

Education and Science has sought to establish a Skills Observatory, and the Ministry of Labor and Social Policy runs econometric models for skills forecasting. However, the potential of the two initiatives remains to be fully realized, because skills needs and mismatches have not been thoroughly analyzed in the context of migration (OECD 2022).

Once skill needs have been identified, addressing constraints to the supply expansion of high-skilled graduates is crucial. Improvements in the quantity and quality of the provision of skills are essential to preventing labor shortages and harnessing the incentivizing effects of migration on human capital accumulation. Domestic educational systems need to be flexible enough to rapidly respond to increased demand for skilled labor, either domestically or externally. Efforts to respond to skill demand can be made at both the intensive margin (by enhancing the capacity of schools and universities) and the extensive margin (by establishing new education centers). Rigid training systems for certain occupations—such as highly regulated systems based on narrow entry criteria or a small, fixed number of places in medical education—are not necessarily aligned with the needs created by changes in internal or international demand for these occupations. In contrast, education systems without quota systems or with quotas that may be readily adjusted to account for shifts in demand are likely to be able to respond more quickly to prevent potential shortages associated with emigration.

If educational systems cannot expand skill supply in a timely manner, opening domestic labor markets to non-ECA countries in select occupations where skill shortages are anticipated can help in importing needed skills. Immigration in response to emigration is already a rising phenomenon in parts of EU-NMS13, especially among citizens of non-EU Eastern European countries. Poland, which has traditionally been a migrant-sending country, is increasingly turning into an immigration hub within the European Union, to compensate for the emigration of its high-skilled workers (Bossavie et al. 2023). One way to boost immigration is by promoting bilateral labor agreements and by easing the hiring of foreign workers among companies in sectors with rising labor demand. The economic benefits of relying on immigration flows to address domestic labor shortages, however, must be considered within the broader sociopolitical environment of each country, weighted against potential political backlash.

Enhancing the Benefits of the Migration Experience for High-Skilled Migrants, Origin Countries, and Destination Countries

Strengthening ongoing efforts to certify foreign credentials across ECA can enhance the mobility of high-skilled workers and increase the benefits of the migration experience for all actors. To reduce occupational downgrade, countries of origin need to adjust education and training curricula to international standards. This can help ensure that the quality of education and productivity levels of graduates in each occupation are comparable to those in destination countries. Once this is achieved, extending skills recognition systems through close collaboration between origin and destination countries can also help reassure employers about the productivity of foreign graduates. Institutionalized cooperation between vocational education and training schools and universities in countries of origin and public employment agencies in destination countries is also key to extending skills recognition systems (OECD 2022).

Multilateral migration arrangements can serve as an institutional base to enhance the benefits of high-skilled migrants for all parties involved. Such multilateral arrangements and partnerships can offer a way to combine migration opportunities with long-term investments in key areas such as labor market assessments, education, migrant reintegration, and diaspora engagement. They also imply a shift in focus from recruitment to investing and building skills in countries of both origin and destination. The new EU Pact on Migration and Asylum (European Commission 2020), announced by the European Commission in September 2020, includes new tools for the management of labor migration at the EU level, including Talent Partnerships. These partnerships were established to create better job opportunities at home and legal routes to the European Union, starting first in the European Union's neighborhood and the Western Balkans. The partnerships will combine mobility schemes for workers and students with related capacity-building support in migrant origin countries. Similar partnership models have also been piloted at a bilateral level through mobility skills partnerships.

Global skill partnerships (GSPs) between sending and receiving countries are promising instruments to address human capital and financial losses in the former while ensuring better skills matches in the latter. GSPs can address the potential loss of essential human capital in countries of origin while preparing potential migrants for work in the host country (Clemens 2015). Under these bilateral arrangements, the country of origin agrees to train people in the skills needed in both origin and destination countries. Some trainees choose to stay and increase human capital in the origin country, and others migrate to the destination country for some time. In exchange for receiving migrants with specifically needed skills, the destination country provides technology and finance for the training. In Europe, this approach has already been implemented by Germany, through the German Agency for International Cooperation, with pilots in Kosovo. Other destination countries such as Austria and Switzerland have already invested in similar partnering with training centers in the Western Balkans to improve vocational and educational training for potential future migrants. For example, the Austrian Development Agency and the Austrian Federal Economic Chamber have been working together with the Serbian Federal Economic Chamber and other project partners to implement the Austrian dual-training apprenticeship system.

GSPs need to satisfy several conditions to be successfully implemented, stay sustainable, and operate at scale. First, investing in human capital expansion in both origin and destination countries should be the paramount goal, leading to long-term economic development and growth in all countries across the income spectrum. Second, extensive cooperation and collaboration between origin and destination countries formalized by enforceable bilateral or multilateral agreements are essential because GSPs involve long-term investments in both training and labor market access. Third, well-managed and systematic international social protection and labor market intermediation systems are key. Furthermore, strong institutional capacity is needed for recruitment and training provision, labor market intermediation, and diaspora engagement. In many cases, private agencies play a role in recruitment and training, which also requires capacity for oversight from education and technical and vocational education and training authorities.

To better leverage their highly skilled migrants, countries of origin can establish or strengthen strategic frameworks and institutional structures for diaspora engagement. To guide and support the implementation of diaspora programs, strategic frameworks for encouraging skills and knowledge transfers can be adopted by countries of origin. Such strategies aim to create institutional structures and implement policies or programs to attract diaspora professionals for short- and long-term engagements. Such strategies have started to be developed in some countries of origin, such as those in the Western Balkans, although implementation is still underway (OECD 2022). One example is the Albanian National Diaspora Strategy for the period 2021–25, which lays out an action plan to promote the inclusion and contribution of the diaspora in the country's socioeconomic and political development (World Bank 2023).

Developing or strengthening platforms to connect with the diaspora is a first step toward leveraging it. These platforms can provide matching and network services that connect diaspora members from different destination countries with the private and public sectors in countries of origin, and also with each other. Such initiatives can include diaspora registries, interactive portals, diaspora forums, and fellowship programs. In Albania, for example, the National Diaspora Agency has established a network of hundreds of thousands of contacts through outreach by using diplomatic networks, newsletters, social networks, and cultural events (World Bank 2023). Diaspora forums can also help strengthen connection, dialogue, and close collaborative ties with a country's diaspora. Such forums bring together prominent diaspora members, government officials, members of academia, civil society, private entities, and international organizations, with the aim of networking and establishing cooperation opportunities in various fields. They have been implemented, for example, in Georgia (https://gda.ge/pages/economic-forum-of-the-georgian-diaspora). More evidence, however, is needed to assess which of these programs are most effective in expanding diaspora outreach and in sustaining engagement over time.

Diaspora programs can help enhance knowledge spillovers to the home country. Once linkages with the diaspora are in place, collaboration between researchers and individuals or institutions in countries of origin and abroad can generate knowledge spillovers to origin countries. This collaboration can be facilitated by establishing scientific networks, knowledge funds, or fellowship programs, potentially accompanied by financial incentives. One example of such programs is the Polish Scientists Abroad Network, which developed a scientific community that allowed Poland to expand its network and exchange ideas on a global scale. Serbia also has put significant effort into engaging with its diaspora members in education and science. The Serbian Science and Diaspora Collaboration Program established in 2019 provides financial incentives for the collaboration between local research and development agencies and the diaspora, knowledge exchange, and visits to host institutions. In addition, as part of the reforms envisioned under the Serbia Accelerating Innovation and Growth Entrepreneurship project, the Serbian Diaspora Facility was established to finance technical assistance and provide grants to scientists, researchers, and entrepreneurs from the Serbian diaspora to transfer their knowledge and skills back to the country. Some countries have sought other ways to integrate the scientific diaspora into domestic research activities. The Croatian Unity through Knowledge Fund, for example, is a dedicated grant facility for joint research projects between the Croatian diaspora and local research institutions in Croatia. Funding is awarded to research initiatives that have the potential to strengthen the Croatian economy or contribute to the development of the country's research infrastructure.

Other diaspora programs can help support investment and business creation in countries of origin. Origin countries can mobilize the diaspora to encourage foreign companies to engage in business at home. To do so, countries of origin can connect diaspora members with opportunities at home by leveraging memorandum of understanding agreements with government and nongovernment agencies (including consulates and embassies), as is done in Albania. Some diaspora programs can also be specifically targeted to entrepreneurs. Programs providing financial incentives for the diaspora to establish businesses in their home country have been implemented in Armenia and Romania. The latter has attracted more than 1,000 Romanian migrants to develop businesses in Romania (Croitoru 2021). Other types of diaspora programs include temporary return programs for highly skilled individuals to share their expertise with experts in their home country. Another successful example of diaspora engagement programs with highly skilled emigrants that had a notable impact on the local economy was the Diaspora Invest Project in Bosnia and Herzegovina (World Bank 2023). The program was implemented between 2017 and 2022 and offered grants and technical assistance to incentivize diaspora members who are entrepreneurs to open or expand businesses in Bosnia and Herzegovina. In four years, the project provided US$2 million in grants to 164 firms. This resulted in total investments by diaspora members of US$22 million; created 1,571 jobs; and increased sales in supported businesses by 70 percent (World Bank 2023). About 75 percent of these additional sales took place in the export market, primarily in the former destination countries of diaspora members, highlighting the influence of emigrants' expertise and network.

Increasing the Benefits of the Migration Experience through Return Migration

Three main types of policy can help increase the benefits of high-skilled labor mobility through return migration. The first two types aim to increase the incidence of return migration among high-skilled migrants by (1) removing existing regulatory, bureaucratic, and informational barriers that inhibit return migration and (2) changing the financial and nonfinancial incentives to return to the home country. Finally, the third type of policy is intended to make return migrants more productive and enhance the benefits of return migration for the home economy.[10]

A first step toward increasing returns among high-skilled migrants is to remove regulatory, bureaucratic, and informational barriers that inhibit return migration. Several regulatory and bureaucratic barriers can make it difficult and costly for migrants to return to their home country. An example of such barriers relates to citizenship or residency rights. Migrants from countries without dual citizenship may have had to give up their home country citizenship to gain citizenship abroad, which can create difficulties if they want to permanently return. Additionally, they may face the disincentive of closing the option of migrating again by means of giving up their newly acquired foreign citizenship. Using cross-sectional data on migrants in Germany and Spain, it has been shown that migrants from countries that offer dual citizenship send more remittances and express higher intent to return (Leblang 2017). Although dual citizenship makes it easier for migrants to return, many migrants marry citizens of other countries. Another constraint they face in this case is a limit to the ability of their noncitizen spouse and children to live, work, and attend school in the migrant's country of origin. These regulatory and bureaucratic bottlenecks, however, can be addressed quickly and at low cost through regulation changes. To address these issues, origin countries can give permanent residence status to foreign spouses and children to facilitate return migration, as is done in Malaysia (Lowell 2001). In the context of ECA, a recent comprehensive program made up of 50 measures to remove personal, professional, and administrative barriers was implemented in Spain.

Greater portability of social benefits, particularly retirement benefits, can also help alleviate bureaucratic constraints to return migration and may increase returns. Two key issues related to the portability of social benefits for high-skilled migrants can be identified (McKenzie and Yang 2015). The first is that migrants who work in multiple countries may not accrue enough years of work to become fully vested in the contributory pension systems of either their home or their destination country. The second is whether migrants retain eligibility to receive pension payments if they return to their home country. EU countries have many bilateral agreements, but coverage is limited for migrants who move from a non-EU ECA country to the European Union (Avato, Koettl, and Sabates-Wheeler 2010). Although pension portability can directly improve the well-being of return migrants, literature quantifying this finding or examining the impact of pension portability on the rate of return migration is lacking.

Policies relaxing informational barriers on employment opportunities and changes in conditions in the home country may also help increase returns. In addition to regulatory and bureaucratic barriers, informational barriers may prevent some migrants from returning. These barriers include a general lack of information regarding specific job opportunities or about changes in labor market conditions in the home country. Several ECA countries have attempted to reduce job search frictions by making it easier for domestic firms to locate emigrant workers interested in returning and vice versa. Job fairs, such as the ones implemented by Bulgaria or by Moldova in Italy (TFMI 2012), can help initiate direct contact between emigrants and leading companies in the home country. Offering returning migrants dedicated websites and a return migrant handbook with information on programs to help them find work and deal with the logistics of resettlement, such as in Poland, may also support return migration (TFMI 2012). Rigorous evaluations, however, have yet to be conducted to assess the effectiveness of such measures.

Increasing the Incentives to Return

Education programs encouraging brain circulation with return conditions can help countries of origin benefit from migrants' human capital accumulation. One way for countries of origin to take advantage of high-skilled emigration is to implement mobility programs for high-skilled migrants with return conditions after a certain amount of time spent in the destination country. These measures aim to encourage mobility and human capital accumulation abroad while ensuring that the country of origin ultimately benefits from the migration experience by making returns mandatory. Such programs have been implemented in several origin countries, including Kazakhstan, where the government-funded Bolashak program supports talented Kazakh students to study abroad and requires them to return to Kazakhstan and work in their respective fields for at least five years.

Financial incentive packages for the permanent return of high-skilled migrants can be effective in some contexts, if incentives are sufficiently large. Such programs include tax exemptions and benefits, interest-free or low-interest loans, temporary salary supplements to facilitate career entry, assistance with housing, schooling for children, and employment opportunities for spouses (Jonkers 2008; Lowell 2001; TFMI 2012). In Malaysia, the Returning Expert Program provides a flat tax of 15 percent on employment income for five years, the ability to import two cars tax-free, and permanent residence status to a foreign spouse and children within six months. An evaluation of this program showed that it increased the return probability for applicants with a preexisting job offer back in the home country by 40 percent and generated modest fiscal gains for the country of origin (Del Carpio et al. 2016).[11] In the ECA context, the number of such programs has grown substantially in the past two decades, although they are mostly low scale, with the exception of the Spanish return migrant program (Plan de Retorno a España). Portugal and the Slovak Republic implemented programs providing fiscal incentives to return migrants, but the magnitude of the incentives provided has been argued to be too small to have a meaningful impact on returns when compared with the large earnings gains of high-skilled migrants abroad. Even if high-skilled migrants return, narrative evidence suggests that beneficiaries of such programs use the benefits only temporarily and tend to leave the country again once the benefits expire.

Supporting the Reintegration of High-Skilled Migrants in Home Labor Markets

Policies aimed at supporting the reintegration and return of highly skilled migrants may also help increase the benefits of skilled migration. Despite the positive wage premiums available to them in the labor market, returnees still face challenges. Once high-skilled migrants have decided to return to their home country, a second policy challenge for the origin country is to promote reintegration programs that help smooth returning migrants' transition into the domestic labor market and support returnees in starting up businesses. This is important, because migrants tend to have weaker domestic networks upon return than those who stay in the country and, given the higher rates of self-employment and entrepreneurship among returnees, may be negatively affected by administrative and institutional barriers to setting up businesses.

Reintegration plans and interventions for return migrants can be strengthened by offering a comprehensive set of services tailored to their needs, return circumstances, and future migration intentions. Reintegration programs for return migrants have existed for several years in many countries in ECA. However, a government strategy and a centralized reintegration mechanism are often lacking. As a result, those programs typically have very limited resources and outreach. Returnees could benefit from larger-scale support delivering a comprehensive array of services to eligible and interested return migrants. These services could be provided through one-stop shops for returnees and could include assistance in planning the return; helping to define a professional plan; and finding employment, lodging, and financial help for those moving back. Such support measures for returnees, however, require an upgrade and better integration of migration management systems (databases, services, and systems). Information about available resources and the procedures to obtain them through different public administrations, employment offers, and facilitation of networks of returnees could also be provided. One other key element of reintegration programs for returnees is the active participation of interested firms in connecting labor supply and demand, as included in Spain's comprehensive Plan de Retorno a España (refer to box 4.1).

Certifying skills acquired abroad may help migrants take greater advantage of their migration experience at home and in future migration episodes. Through their work experience abroad, migrants acquire skills and experience that can be valuable in origin countries' labor markets but also in another migration experience. Those skills can be destination specific, but they may also be transferable to other destination countries and potentially generate higher earnings the next time around. In Armenia, for example, more than half of returned migrants reported acquiring new skills during their experience abroad; however, almost none of these new skills were certified or documented. Within Western Europe, the Bologna Process aims to formalize recognition of higher education qualifications,

BOX 4.1 *El Plan de Retorno a España:* An Example of a Comprehensive Program for Return Migrants

In 2019, the Spanish government published the *Plan de Retorno a España* (Plan to Return to Spain), made up of 50 measures to remove personal, professional, and administrative barriers to returning to Spain, including assistance to plan the return and define a professional plan (SGIE 2019). Furthermore, the Spanish State Employment Service elaborated a plan to address the problem of high youth unemployment; one of the plan's measures is to create a program to incentivize the return of the diaspora of young people and support mobility (SEPE 2019). It includes support for self-employment and finding employment and financial help for moving back to Spain and finding lodging. It also helps returnees with one-stop shops that include information about resources available from different public administrations and their procedures, employment offers, and networks of returnees. One key element is the active participation of interested firms in the process, to connect labor supply and demand. Although the actual return of young emigrants is largely linked to employment opportunities in Spain, these measures can smooth the transition and reduce bureaucratic and information barriers while keeping stronger links with the diaspora.

but many migrants from ECA origin countries still experience difficulties obtaining overseas qualifications that are recognized in their home countries. Outside ECA, a few programs have been implemented to facilitate the recognition of qualifications and skills gained abroad, such as Argentina's Red de Argentinos Investigadores y Científicos en el Exterior (Network of Argentine Researchers and Scientists Abroad) program, which offers the translation and accreditation of qualifications formally earned abroad.

Although policy interventions to support productive return migration are being tested and implemented, systematic impact evaluations are essential in assessing their effectiveness before scale-up. Overall, global evidence on the effectiveness of policies targeted at incentivizing returns and improving the outcomes of returnees remains quite scarce. Rigorous impact evaluations are especially lacking (McKenzie and Yang 2015). Despite the incidence of self-employment among low-skilled return migrants, the effectiveness of programs facilitating entrepreneurship among returnees is also poorly documented. Similarly, for returnees who seek wage employment, it has yet to be determined whether programs aimed at reducing job search frictions are effective and under what conditions. The implementation of small-scale programs targeted to returning migrants should be systematically accompanied by rigorous impact evaluations

beyond simple follow-up quantitative and qualitative surveys
and process evaluations. One example of such rigorous impact evaluations
is the one assessing the impacts of the Returning Expert Program in
Malaysia (Del Carpio et al. 2016).

More detailed data collection on return migrants through national
household surveys or ad hoc migration surveys is needed to inform policies
for high-skilled returnees. Available nationally representative household
surveys rarely provide detailed information about the migration journey of
past international migrants, their human capital accumulation, labor
market experience, or the motivations behind the decision to migrate and
return (voluntary-involuntary or planned-unplanned). This lack of
information hampers the ability to better understand the impact of
migration and to design adequate programs that support migrants
throughout their journey, including after returning to their home country.
To address this data gap, either more detailed modules on past migration
episodes could be included in nationally representative household surveys
or comprehensive ad hoc surveys could be developed, targeted at the
population of return migrants. Nationally representative household surveys
need to collect detailed information on past migration abroad to identify
return migrants and link the details of their past migration experiences to
labor market outcomes back home. Although such datasets remain rare,
examples include the Egyptian Labor Market Survey outside ECA and the
Albania Living Standard Measurement Survey in ECA,[12] which was
implemented more than a decade ago. Comprehensive ad hoc migration
surveys also remain quite rare in ECA and globally. Recent exceptions
include the 2019 World Bank Return Migrant Survey for Bangladesh, which
collected very detailed information about the past and current employment
outcomes of a representative sample of those returning to Bangladesh.
In ECA, the recent 2023 Kyrgyz Migration Survey, also carried out by the
World Bank, collected detailed information on the past and current
migration episodes and labor market outcomes of a representative sample
of the Kyrgyz Republic's working-age population. Evidence-based policies
targeting return migrants would benefit from implementing similar surveys
in other countries of origin in the region.

Although more demanding, linking microdata between origin and
destination countries is another promising avenue to connect returnees
with their migration experience and inform policies for more productive
high-skilled return migration. Scandinavian countries are at the forefront of
these efforts. Finnish and Swedish population registers have, for example,
been linked to better understand emigrant and returnee selection, using
birth date, gender, municipality of residence, and year of migration to
match more than 85 percent of Finns who migrated to Sweden after 1970

and who lived there in 1990 (Rooth and Saarela 2007). Such efforts to merge administrative data across national borders also extend to historical data, although such mergers are constrained by the availability of variables without which they are infeasible.

Notes

1. This share is calculated as the number of Central EU workers employed in the health care and social sectors abroad over the total number of Central EU workers employed in those sectors, both in their home countries and abroad.
2. Studies vary in terms of rigidity, particularly in terms of how they account for the double selection that happens among return migrants at both the departure and the return stages (Wahba 2015).
3. In some ECA countries, such as Albania (Carletto and Kilic 2011) and Estonia (Masso, Eamets, and Mõtsmees 2014), migrants returning from low-skilled occupations abroad do not experience significant occupational mobility upon return.
4. Borjas and Bratsberg (1996) propose a theoretical framework to account for the selection of returnees among a host country's immigrant population. They argue that selection depends on the relative skill levels in the two locations, with the skill level of return migrants lying between that of nonmigrants and migrants who stay abroad permanently. Thus, when emigrants are positively selected from the origin country's population, returnees will be negatively selected among all migrants. When emigrants are negatively selected, return migrants will be positively selected.
5. The distinct nature of intra-EU migration flows might limit the generalization of these results to other non-EU ECA countries. Descriptive evidence of the supportive effect of migration in alleviating excess labor supply in other ECA countries is more scarce. For example, during the last two decades unemployment rates in the Western Balkans have significantly dropped, coinciding with high emigration rates.
6. While evidence of the impact of emigration on wages is concentrated among OECD ECA countries, there is a lack of rigorous studies for non-OECD ECA countries.
7. See chapter 5 for a more detailed discussion of the impacts of remittance on origin countries.
8. For example, rigid employment protection legislation in countries of origin, as opposed to more flexible employment protection regulation in destination countries, has been shown to imply larger bilateral flows at the macro level (Bossavie et al. 2022).
9. Unlike regular student loans, whereby students repay the loan in fixed annuity amounts over a predetermined time horizon until the debt is extinguished, students taking out income-contingent loans begin repaying the loans only once their income exceeds a certain threshold, and the repayment amount is adjusted proportionally depending on the labor incomes of the beneficiaries (Chapman 2006).
10. See McKenzie and Yang (2015) for a detailed discussion.
11. However, no effect was reported for high-skilled emigrants without a job offer back home.
12. The dataset for Egypt is available at https://www.erfdataportal.com/index.php/catalog/157. The dataset for Albania is available at https://microdata.worldbank.org/index.php/catalog/1970.

References

Abarcar, P., and C. Theoharides. 2021. "Medical Worker Migration and Origin-Country Human Capital: Evidence from U.S. Visa Policy." *Review of Economics and Statistics* 106 (1): 20–35. https://doi.org /10.1162/rest_a_01131.

Abdih, Y., R. Chami, J. Dagher, and P. Montiel. 2012. "Remittances and Institutions: Are Remittances a Curse?" *World Development* 40 (4): 657–66. https://doi.org/10.1016/j.worlddev.2011.09.014.

Agrawal, A., D. Kapur, J. McHale, and A. Oettl. 2011. "Brain Drain or Brain Bank? The Impact of Skilled Emigration on Poor-Country Innovation." *Journal of Urban Economics* 69 (1): 43–55. https://doi.org /10.1016/j.jue.2010.06.003.

Ambrosini, J. W., K. Mayr, G. Peri, and D. Radu. 2015. "The Selection of Migrants and Returnees in Romania: Evidence and Long-Run Implications." *Economics of Transition* 23 (4): 753–93. https://doi.org/10.1111 /ecot.12077.

Anelli, M., G. Basso, G. Ippedico, and G. Peri. 2019. "Youth Drain, Entrepreneurship and Innovation." Working Paper 26055, National Bureau of Economic Research, Cambridge, MA. https://doi.org/10.3386/w26055.

Atoyan, R., L. Christiansen, A. Dizioli, C. Ebeke, N. Ilahi, A. Ilyina, G. Mehrez, H. Qu, F. Raei, A. Rhee, and D. Zakharova. 2016. "Emigration and Its Economic Impact on Eastern Europe." Staff Discussion Note 16/07, International Monetary Fund, Washington, DC. https://www.imf.org/external/pubs/ft/sdn/2016 /sdn1607.pdf.

Avato, J., J. Koettl, and R. Sabates-Wheeler. 2010. "Social Security Regimes, Global Estimates, and Good Practices: The Status of Social Protection for International Migrants." *World Development* 38 (4): 455–66.

Bahar, D., A. Hauptmann, C. Özgüzel, and H. Rapoport. 2022. "Migration and Knowledge Diffusion: The Effect of Returning Refugees on Export Performance in the Former Yugoslavia." *Review of Economics and Statistics* 106 (2): 287–304. https://doi.org/10.1162/rest_a_01165.

Barsbai, T., H. Rapoport, A. Steinmayr, and C. Trebesch. 2017. "The Effect of Labor Migration on the Diffusion of Democracy: Evidence from a Former Soviet Republic." *American Economic Journal: Applied Economics* 9 (3): 36–69. https://doi.org/10.1257/app.20150517.

Beine, M., F. Docquier, and C. Oden-Defoort. 2011. "A Panel Data Analysis of the Brain Gain." *World Development* 39 (4): 523–32.

Beine, M., F. Docquier, and H. Rapoport. 2001. "Brain Drain and Economic Growth: Theory and Evidence." *Journal of Development Economics* 64 (1): 275–89. https://doi.org/10.1016/S0304-3878(00)00133-4.

Beine, M., F. Docquier, and H. Rapoport. 2008. "Brain Drain and Human Capital Formation in Developing Countries: Winners and Losers." *Economic Journal* 118 (528): 631–52. https://doi.org/10.1111/j.1468 -0297.2008.02135.x.

Bernini, A., L. Bossavie, D. Garrote-Sánchez, and M. Makovec. 2024. "Corruption as a Push and Pull Factor of Migration Flows: Evidence from European Countries." *Empirica* 51 (1): 263–81.

Bhagwati, J., and C. Rodriguez. 1975. "Welfare-Theoretical Analyses of the Brain Drain." *Journal of Development Economics* 2 (3): 195–221. https://doi.org/10.1016/0304-3878(75)90002-4.

Bijwaard, G. E., C. Schluter, and J. Wahba. 2014. "The Impact of Labor Market Dynamics on the Return Migration of Immigrants." *Review of Economics and Statistics* 96 (3): 483–94. https://doi.org/10.1162/REST _a_00389.

Borjas, G. J. 2015. "The Slowdown in the Economic Assimilation of Immigrants: Aging and Cohort Effects Revisited Again." *Journal of Human Capital* 9 (4): 483–517.

Borjas, G. J., and B. Bratsberg. 1996. "Who Leaves? The Outmigration of the Foreign-Born." *Review of Economics and Statistics* 78 (1): 165–76.

Bossavie, L., D. Garrote-Sánchez, M. Makovec, and Ç. Özden. 2022. *Skilled Migration: A Sign of Europe's Divide or Integration?* Washington, DC: World Bank. https://doi.org/10.1596/978-1-4648-1732-8.

Bossavie, L., and Ç. Özden. 2023. "Impacts of Temporary Migration on Development in Origin Countries." *World Bank Research Observer* 36 (2): 249–94. https://doi.org/wbro/lkad003.

Carletto, C., and T. Kilic. 2011. "Moving Up the Ladder? The Impact of Migration Experience on Occupational Mobility in Albania." *Journal of Development Studies* 47 (6): 846–69. https://doi.org/10.1080 /00220388.2010.509926.

Chapman, B. 2006. "Income Contingent Loans for Higher Education: International Reforms." In *Handbook of the Economics of Education*, edited by E. Hanushek and F. Welch, 1435–503. Vol. 2 of *Handbooks in Economics*. Amsterdam: North-Holland. https://doi.org/10.1016/S1574-0692(06)02025-3.

Chapman, B., and T. Higgins. 2013. "The Costs of Unpaid Higher Education Contribution Scheme Debts of Graduates Working Abroad." *Australian Economic Review* 46 (3): 286–99.

Chiswick, B. R., and P. W. Miller. 2009. "The International Transferability of Immigrants' Human Capital." *Economics of Education Review* 28 (2): 162–9. https://doi.org/10.1016/j.econedurev.2008.07.002.

Choudhury, P. 2016. "Return Migration and Geography of Innovation in MNEs: A Natural Experiment of Knowledge Production by Local Workers Reporting to Return Migrants." *Journal of Economic Geography* 16 (3): 585–610. https://doi.org/10.1093/jeg/lbv025.

Clemens, M. A. 2014. "Does Development Reduce Migration?" Discussion Paper 8592, Institute for the Study of Labor, Bonn. https://docs.iza.org/dp8592.pdf.

Clemens, M. A. 2015. "Global Skill Partnerships: A Proposal for Technical Training in a Mobile World." *IZA Journal of Labor Policy* 4: 2. https://doi.org/10.1186/s40173-014-0028-z.

Clements, B., K. Dybczak, V. Gaspar, S. Gupta, and M. Soto. 2015. "The Fiscal Consequences of Shrinking Populations." Staff Discussion Note 15/21, International Monetary Fund, Washington, DC. https://www.imf.org/external/pubs/ft/sdn/2015/sdn1521.pdf.

Co, C. Y., I. N. Gang, and M.-S. Yun. 2000. "Returns to Returning." *Journal of Population Economics* 13: 57–79. https://doi.org/10.1007/s001480050123.

Coniglio, N. D., and J. Brzozowski. 2018. "Migration and Development at Home: Bitter or Sweet Return? Evidence from Poland." *European Urban and Regional Studies* 25 (1): 85–105. https://doi.org/10.1177/0969776416681625.

Croitoru, A. 2021. "Diaspora Start-Ups Programs and Creative Industries: Evidence from Romania." *Transylvanian Review of Administrative Sciences* 17 (63): 5–29. https://doi.org/10.24193/tras.63E.1.

Dao, T. H., F. Docquier, C. Parsons, and G. Peri. 2018. "Migration and Development: Dissecting the Anatomy of the Mobility Transition." *Journal of Development Economics* 132: 88–101. https://doi.org/10.1016/j.jdeveco.2017.12.003.

de Coulon, A., and M. Piracha. 2005. "Self-Selection and the Performance of Return Migrants: The Source Country Perspective." *Journal of Population Economics* 18: 779–807. https://doi.org/10.1007/s00148-005-0004-4.

Del Carpio, X. V., C. Ozden, M. Testaverde, and M. C. Wagner. 2016. "Global Migration of Talent and Tax Incentives: Evidence from Malaysia's Returning Expert Program." Policy Research Working Paper 7875, World Bank, Washington, DC. http://hdl.handle.net/10986/25675.

Desai, M. A., D. Kapur, J. McHale, and K. Rogers. 2009. "The Fiscal Impact of High-Skilled Emigration: Flows of Indians to the US." *Journal of Development Economics* 88 (1): 32–44. https://doi.org/10.1016/j.jdeveco.2008.01.008.

Docquier, F., Z. L. Kone, A. Mattoo, and C. Ozden. 2019. "Labor Market Effects of Demographic Shifts and Migration in OECD Countries." *European Economic Review* 113: 297–324.

Docquier, F., and E. Lodigiani. 2010. "Skilled Migration and Business Networks." *Open Economies Review* 21: 565–88. https://doi.org/10.1007/s11079-008-9102-8.

Docquier, F., E. Lodigiani, H. Rapoport, and M. Schiff. 2016. "Emigration and Democracy." *Journal of Development Economics* 120: 209–23.

Docquier, F., O. Lohest, and A. Marfouk. 2007. "Brain Drain in Developing Countries." *World Bank Economic Review* 21 (2): 193–218. https://doi.org/10.1093/wber/lhm008.

Docquier, F., Ç. Ozden, and G. Peri. 2014. "The Labour Market Effects of Immigration and Emigration in OECD Countries." *Economic Journal* 124 (579): 1106–45. https://doi.org/10.1111/ecoj.12077.

Docquier, F., and H. Rapoport. 2009. "Documenting the Brain Drain of 'La Crème de la Crème': Three Case-Studies on International Migration at the Upper Tail of the Education Distribution." *Jahrbücher für Nationalökonomie und Statistik* 229 (6): 679–705. https://doi.org/10.1515/jbnst-2009-0603.

Docquier, F., and H. Rapoport. 2012. "Globalization, Brain Drain, and Development." *Journal of Economic Literature* 50 (3): 681–730. https://doi.org/10.1257/jel.50.3.681.

Dos Santos, M. D., and F. Postel-Vinay. 2003. "Migration as a Source of Growth: The Perspective of a Developing Country." *Journal of Population Economics* 16: 161–75. https://doi.org/10.1007/s001480100117.

Dumont, J.-C., and G. Spielvogel. 2008. "Return Migration: A New Perspective." In *International Migration Outlook 2008*, edited by Organisation for Economic Co-operation and Development, 163–212. Paris: Organisation for Economic Co-operation and Development. https://doi.org/10.1787/migr_outlook -2008-7-en.

Dustmann, C. 2003. "Return Migration, Wage Differentials, and the Optimal Migration Duration." *European Economic Review* 47 (2): 353–69. https://doi.org/10.1016/S0014-2921(01)00184-2.

Dustmann, C., I. Fadlon, and Y. Weiss. 2011. "Return Migration, Human Capital Accumulation and the Brain Drain." *Journal of Development Economics* 95 (1): 58–67. https://doi.org/10.1016/j.jdeveco.2010.04.006.

Dustmann, C., T. Frattini, and A. C. Rosso. 2015. "The Effect of Emigration from Poland on Polish Wages." *Scandinavian Journal of Economics* 117 (2): 522–64. https://doi.org/10.1111/sjoe.12102.

Dustmann, C., and Y. Weiss. 2007. "Return Migration: Theory and Empirical Evidence from the UK." *British Journal of Industrial Relations* 45 (2): 236–56. https://doi.org/10.1111/j.1467-8543.2007.00613.x.

Elsner, B. 2013. "Emigration and Wages: The EU Enlargement Experiment." *Journal of International Economics* 91 (1): 154–63. https://doi.org/10.1016/j.jinteco.2013.06.002.

ETF (European Training Foundation). 2021. "How Migration, Human Capital and the Labour Market Interact in Albania." Turin: ETF. http://www.etf.europa.eu/sites/default/files/2021-09/migration_albania.pdf.

European Commission. 2020. "Communication from the Commission to the European Parliament, the Council, the European Economic and Social Committee and the Committee of the Regions on a New Pact on Migration and Asylum." Document 52020DC0609. *Eur-Lex*, September 23, 2020. https://eur-lex .europa.eu/legal-content/EN/TXT/?uri=COM%3A2020%3A609%3AFIN.

Farchy, E. 2009. "The Impact of EU Accession on Human Capital Formation: Can Migration Fuel a Brain Gain?" Policy Research Working Paper 4845, World Bank, Washington, DC. https://doi.org/10.1596/1813 -9450-4845.

Friedberg, R. M. 2000. "You Can't Take It with You? Immigrant Assimilation and the Portability of Human Capital." *Journal of Labor Economics* 18 (2): 221–51.

GDA.GE. n.d. "Economic Forum of the Georgian Diaspora." https://gda.ge/pages/economic-forum-of-the -georgian-diaspora.

Genc, M., M. Gheasi, P. Nijkamp, and J. Poot. 2012. "The Impact of Immigration on International Trade: A Meta-Analysis." In *Migration Impact Assessment*, edited by P. Nijkamp, J. Poot, and M. Sahin, 301–37. Cheltenham, UK: Edward Elgar. https://doi.org/10.4337/9780857934581.00019.

Gibson, J., and D. McKenzie. 2012. "The Economic Consequences of 'Brain Drain' of the Best and Brightest: Microeconomic Evidence from Five Countries." *Economic Journal* 122 (560): 339–75. https://doi.org /10.1111/j.1468-0297.2012.02498.x.

Gibson, J., D. McKenzie, and S. Stillman. 2011. "The Impacts of International Migration on Remaining Household Members: Omnibus Results from a Migration Lottery Program." *Review of Economics and Statistics* 93 (4): 1297–318. https://doi.org/10.1162/REST_a_00129.

Giesing, Y., and N. Laurentsyeva. 2018. "Firms Left Behind: Emigration and Firm Productivity." Working Paper 6815, CESIfo, Munich. https://www.cesifo.org/en/publications/2017/working-paper/firms-left -behind-emigration-and-firm-productivity.

Gould, D. M. 1994. "Immigrant Links to the Home Country: Empirical Implications for US Bilateral Trade Flows." *Review of Economics and Statistics* 76 (2): 302–16. https://doi.org/10.2307/2109884.

Haque, N. U., and S.-J. Kim. 1995. "'Human Capital Flight': Impact of Migration on Income and Growth." *Staff Papers* 42 (3): 577–607. https://doi.org/10.5089/9781451973396.024.

Head, K., and J. Ries. 1998. "Immigration and Trade Creation: Econometric Evidence from Canada." *Canadian Journal of Economics* 31 (1): 47–62. https://doi.org/10.2307/136376.

Javorcik, B. S., Ç. Özden, M. Spatareanu, and C. Neagu. 2011. "Migrant Networks and Foreign Direct Investment." *Journal of Development Economics* 94 (2): 231–41.

Jonkers, K. 2008. *A Comparative Study of Return Migration Policies Targeting the Highly Skilled in Four Major Sending Countries.* Analytical Report MIREM-AR 2008/05. Fiesole, Italy: European University Institute, Robert Schuman Centre for Advanced Studies. https://hdl.handle.net/1814/9454.

Kerr, W. R. 2008. "Ethnic Scientific Communities and International Technology Diffusion." *Review of Economics and Statistics* 90 (3): 518–37. https://doi.org/10.1162/rest.90.3.518.

Khanna, G., and N. Morales. 2017. "The IT Boom and Other Unintended Consequences of Chasing the American Dream." *Center for Global Development Working Paper*, 460.

Kugler, M., and H. Rapoport. 2007. "International Labor and Capital Flows: Complements or Substitutes?" *Economics Letters* 94 (2): 155–62. https://doi.org/10.1016/j.econlet.2006.06.023.

Leblang, D. 2017. "Harnessing the Diaspora: Dual Citizenship, Migrant Remittances and Return." *Comparative Political Studies* 50 (1): 75–101. https://doi.org/10.1177/0010414015606736.

Leitner, S. M. 2021. "Net Migration and Its Skill Composition in the Western Balkan Countries between 2010 and 2019: Results from a Cohort Approach Analysis." Policy Notes and Reports 47, Vienna Institute for International Economic Studies, Vienna.

Lowell, B. L. 2001. "Policy Responses to the International Mobility of Skilled Labour." International Migration Paper 45, International Labour Organization, Geneva. https://www.ilo.org/wcmsp5/groups/public/---ed_protect/---protrav/---migrant/documents/publication/wcms_201774.pdf.

Masso, J., R. Eamets, and P. Mõtsmees. 2014. "Temporary Migrants and Occupational Mobility: Evidence from the Case of Estonia." *International Journal of Manpower* 35 (6): 753–75. https://doi.org/10.1108/IJM-06-2013-0138.

Mayr, K., and G. Peri. 2009. "Brain Drain and Brain Return: Theory and Application to Eastern-Western Europe." *BE Journal of Economic Analysis & Policy* 9 (1): 1–52. https://doi.org/10.2202/1935-1682.2271.

McCormick, B., and J. Wahba. 2001. "Overseas Work Experience, Savings and Entrepreneurship amongst Return Migrants to LDCs." *Scottish Journal of Political Economy* 48 (2): 164–78. https://doi.org/10.1111/1467-9485.00192.

McKenzie, D., and D. Yang. 2015. "Evidence on Policies to Increase the Development Impacts of International Migration." *World Bank Research Observer* 30 (2): 155–92. https://doi.org/10.1093/wbro/lkv001.

Miyagiwa, K. 1991. "Scale Economies in Education and the Brain Drain Problem." *International Economic Review* 32 (3): 743–59. https://doi.org/10.2307/2527117.

OECD (Organisation for Economic Co-operation and Development). 2022. *Labour Migration in the Western Balkans: Mapping Patterns, Addressing Challenges and Reaping Benefits*. Paris: OECD. https://www.oecd.org/south-east-europe/programme/Labour-Migration-report.pdf.

Piracha, M., and F. Vadean. 2010. "Return Migration and Occupational Choice: Evidence from Albania." *World Development* 38 (8): 1141–55.

Poutvaara, P. 2004. "Educating Europe: Should Public Education Be Financed with Graduate Taxes or Income-Contingent Loans?" *CESifo Economic Studies* 50 (4): 663–84.

Poutvaara, P. 2008. "Public and Private Education in an Integrated Europe: Studying to Migrate and Teaching to Stay?" *Scandinavian Journal of Economics* 110 (3): 591–608. https://doi.org/10.1111/j.1467-9442.2008.00552.x.

Rapoport, H. 2019. "Diaspora Externalities." *IZA Journal of Development and Migration* 10 (2): 43–55.

Reinhold, S., and K. Thom. 2013. "Migration Experience and Earnings in the Mexican Labor Market." *Journal of Human Resources* 48 (3): 768–820. https://doi.org/10.3368/jhr.48.3.768.

Rooth, D.-O., and J. Saarela. 2007. "Selection in Migration and Return Migration: Evidence from Micro Data." *Economics Letters* 94 (1): 90–5. https://doi.org/10.1016/j.econlet.2006.08.006.

Saxenian, A. 2002. "Brain Circulation: How High-Skill Immigration Makes Everyone Better Off." *Brookings Review* 20 (1): 28–31.

SEPE (Spanish State Employment Service). 2019. *Plan de Choque por el Empleo Joven 2019–2021*. Madrid: Ministerio de Trabajo, Migraciones y Seguridad Social. https://sepe.es/SiteSepe/contenidos/que_es_el_sepe/publicaciones/pdf/pdf_empleo/Plan-de-Choque-Empleo-Joven-2019-2021.pdf.

Shima, I. 2010. "Return Migration and Labour Market Outcomes of the Returnees. Does the Return Really Pay Off? The Case-Study of Romania and Bulgaria." Research Report 2009/10-07, Research Centre International Economics, Vienna. http://hdl.handle.net/10419/121213.

Spilimbergo, A. 2009. "Democracy and Foreign Education." *American Economic Review* 99 (1): 528–43. https://doi.org/10.1257/aer.99.1.528.

TFMI (Transatlantic Forum on Migration and Integration). 2012. *Welcome Home? Challenges and Chances of Return Migration*. Washington, DC: German Marshall Fund of the United States and Robert Bosch Foundation.

Ungureanu, M., and K. Socha-Dietrich. 2019. "Romania: A Growing International Medical Education Hub." In *Recent Trends in International Migration of Doctors, Nurses and Medical Students*, 11–27. Paris: Organisation for Economic Co-operation and Development. https://doi.org/10.1787/5571ef48-en.

Wahba, J. 2015. "Selection, Selection, Selection: The Impact of Return Migration." *Journal of Population Economics* 28: 535–63. https://doi.org/10.1007/s00148-015-0541-4.

Wescott, C. G., and J. M. Brinkerhoff, eds. 2006. *Converting Migration Drains into Gains: Harnessing the Resources of Overseas Professionals*. Manila: Asian Development Bank. http://hdl.handle.net/11540/238.

World Bank. 2018. *Moving for Prosperity: Global Migration and Labor Markets*. Washington, DC: World Bank.

World Bank. 2023. *Leveraging Migration for Albania's Development*. Washington, DC: World Bank.

Low-Skilled Migration
Harnessing Development Impacts for Migrants and Origin Countries

Chapter Highlights

- The migration experience of low-skilled individuals in Europe and Central Asia is diverse and multifaceted; it can be permanent, temporary (one time), or circular (repeated migration to the same destination).

- Low-skilled migration from Central Asia and the Caucasus to the Russian Federation is typically temporary and seasonal, whereas among countries in the European Union, it is more often permanent.

- Low-skilled migration is concentrated among the poorest households and regions in countries of origin; as such, it is a major source of poverty reduction, mainly through remittances.

- Low-skilled migration affects development in origin countries through other, more indirect, channels, including human capital investments, entrepreneurship, and labor market impacts in home economies.

- In destination countries, it helps fill labor shortages, especially in occupations in which the native-born population is unwilling to engage at prevailing wages.

- If not well managed, low-skilled migration can involve inefficiencies and vulnerabilities at each stage of the migration life cycle: predeparture, during migration, and after return.

- Despite the importance of migration for many lower-income countries, migration systems in countries of origin are still maturing.

- Low-skilled migrants are often ill prepared for work abroad, have imperfect information about employment opportunities in destination countries, and often migrate through informal arrangements, all of which contribute to vulnerability.

- They are highly exposed to negative shocks in destination countries because of a high concentration of migrants in one or a few destinations and in a handful of sectors that are exposed to demand shocks.

- Low-skilled migrants, especially if migration is temporary or seasonal, have limited access to social protection programs and services to cope with shocks.

- Migrants who unexpectedly return to their home country often face vulnerability; for returnees who had planned their return, there is scope to better leverage their migration experience in home labor markets.

Policy Recommendations

- Promoting formal migration through managed low-skilled migration systems is critical to increase access to migration; protect low-skilled migrants; and enhance migration's benefits for migrants, origin countries, and destination countries.

- Publicly provided intermediation through government-to-government agreements can help formalize low-skilled migration and reduce vulnerability but requires strong administrative capacity, especially if implemented at a large scale.

- Institutional arrangements with destination countries—bilateral labor agreements, seasonal worker programs, migration regulatory agencies— must be further developed and strengthened to promote a rights-based approach to low-skilled migration.

- Strengthening the role of public institutions and regulatory frameworks in providing information about migration opportunities can reduce information asymmetries and contribute to more equitable access to migration opportunities.

- Strengthened cooperation between origin and destination countries, through demand monitoring and data-sharing arrangements, is a prerequisite to ensuring a better match of low-skilled migrants to jobs abroad.

- Predeparture training programs and upskilling for labor migrants based on demand identified by destination countries can help increase preparedness and productivity while they are abroad.

- Global Skill Partnership programs designed according to a set of key principles can facilitate a better match between the skills of low-skilled migrants and demand from destination countries.

- To reduce the volatility of low-skilled migration flows, origin countries can attempt to diversify migrants' destinations and sectors of activity through migrants' upskilling and training and by developing new institutional arrangements with destination countries.

- A more productive use of remittances can be facilitated by formalizing remittance flows through reduced transaction costs and greater financial inclusion in origin countries.

- Financial literacy programs to enhance migrants' knowledge of savings and investment opportunities is another possible step toward more productive use of remittances.

- In the long run, the development of social protection programs tailored to the needs of labor migrants, such as portable unemployment benefits, savings accounts, and social protection schemes, can help mitigate adverse impacts of shocks at destination.

- More productive reintegration of return migrants into home labor markets could be achieved through stronger linkages with existing active labor market policies and a strenghtening of those programs, support of entrepreneurship, and closer cooperation with receiving countries.

- In the case of an unexpected return to the home country, temporary social protection support for forced returnees can help alleviate vulnerability upon return and smooth transitions into home countries' labor markets.

- The impact of policy interventions to improve the efficiency of low-skilled migration and reduce vulnerabilities should be systematically evaluated, ideally before scale-up, to broaden the evidence base for cost-effective interventions.

Introduction

In lower-income countries in Central Asia, the Caucasus, and to some extent the Western Balkans, much of the population that emigrates does not have a tertiary education degree. Several lower-income countries in Europe and Central Asia (ECA) are among the top receivers of remittances globally, especially in Central Asia: in the Kyrgyz Republic and Tajikistan, remittances sent home by low-skilled labor migrants represent up to 33 percent and 30 percent of total gross domestic product (GDP), respectively, ranking them the second and third highest levels globally in terms of remittances-to-GDP ratio. The contribution of remittances sent by international migrants to GDP is also quite large in some smaller countries in the Western Balkans and Eastern Europe, such as Bosnia and Herzegovina and Moldova. Given its magnitude and the large wage gains experienced by low-skilled workers abroad, low-skilled emigration plays a significant role in the development path of lower-income countries in ECA.

This chapter shows that low-skilled emigration can generate tremendous benefits for migrants and their families, as well as for origin and destination countries. The most obvious impact of low-skilled emigration is an increase in the wages of low-skilled migrant workers and the subsequent increase in household income and welfare, enabling poorer households to escape poverty. Beyond these direct welfare impacts, low-skilled emigration can also generate a broad range of indirect impacts on the households and communities left behind. These impacts include larger investments from migrant households in children, human capital, labor market participation and activities, financial literacy, and women's empowerment. At the macroeconomic level, low-skilled emigration generates large income flows to origin countries that can also play a countercyclical role and act as an income stabilizer at the aggregate level. Beyond the beneficial impacts of remittances on sending countries' economies, low-skilled emigration can also help absorb a growing labor force and alleviate pressure on domestic labor markets in contexts in which job creation has not been able to keep up with the growing entry of youth into the labor market. In destination countries, low-skilled migration can help fill labor shortages in occupations or sectors in which the domestic labor supply is low (refer to chapter 3 for more details).

Low-skilled migration in ECA, however, has yet to reach its full development potential; if not well managed, it involves inefficiencies and vulnerabilities, most of which are borne by migrants and their households. This chapter shows that low-skilled migration within ECA currently involves significant risks and vulnerabilities, most of which are borne by migrants and their families but also by the country of origin more broadly. In the case of temporary migration, those risks and vulnerabilities are present at all stages of the migration life cycle, including before departure, during migration, and after return. The COVID-19 pandemic, and more recently the economic spillovers of Russia's invasion of Ukraine, exposed both the limitations of current migration systems and the vulnerabilities of low-skilled migrants in Central Asia and the Caucasus to shocks. Although some of the challenges faced during the pandemic were specific to the COVID-19 context, many migrants' vulnerabilities already existed before the pandemic and will persist in the absence of policy measures.

This chapter examines the diverse facets of low-skilled migration in ECA and its benefits and costs for all parties involved, and it proposes policy options to enhance gains while reducing migration's risks. The remainder of the chapter is organized as follows. The "Multiple Facets of Low-Skilled Migration and Its Linkages to Countries' Development Paths" section discusses the patterns and features of low-skilled migration from ECA countries and highlights its diverse nature and linkages to origin countries' development path. It also introduces the migration life cycle framework for low-skilled migration used throughout the chapter. The "Low-Skilled Migration Fosters Development in Origin Countries" section highlights the development impacts of low-skilled migration at the macro and micro levels for migrants themselves, their families, and the home economy. The "The Barriers, Vulnerabilities, and Costs Faced by Low-Skilled Migrants along Their Journey" section discusses the vulnerabilities, risks, and costs borne by low-skilled migrants before, during, and after their journey, as well as aggregate risks when low-skilled migration is concentrated in few sectors or countries. The "Policy Recommendations" section presents the impacts of recent negative shocks on low-skilled migration from ECA and how these shocks highlighted existing inefficiencies and vulnerabilities associated with low-skilled migration. The "Policy Recommendations" section provides policy recommendations to reduce the vulnerabilities associated with low-skilled migration while maximizing its benefits.

Multiple Facets of Low-Skilled Migration and Its Linkages to Countries' Development Paths

Economic Development as the Main Push Factor of Low-Skilled Emigration

Migration from most countries of origin remains low skilled. Figure 5.1 displays the share of both emigrants (on the y-axis) and stayers (on the x-axis) from ECA countries who are low skilled. The 45-degree line indicates perfect parity between the two. Except for eight Western European countries, low-skilled migrants (those with less than tertiary education) still represent most emigrants in all other ECA countries. The share of low-skilled individuals among total emigrants is especially large in the Caucasus, Central Asia, and the Western Balkans. In Uzbekistan, for example, more than 95 percent of migrants are lower skilled.[1] Similarly, close to 90 percent of migrants from Armenia, Kosovo, and Tajikistan did not receive tertiary education. In most Western Balkan countries and in Georgia, the share of low-skilled individuals among migrants is slightly lower but remains quite high at around 80 percent for most countries. In Eastern European countries, the share of low-skilled migrants is between 60 percent and 80 percent. The low skill level of emigrants partly reflects the lower levels of educational attainment in the broader working-age population of countries of origin: as shown in figure 5.1,

FIGURE 5.1

Share of low-skilled individuals, by emigration status

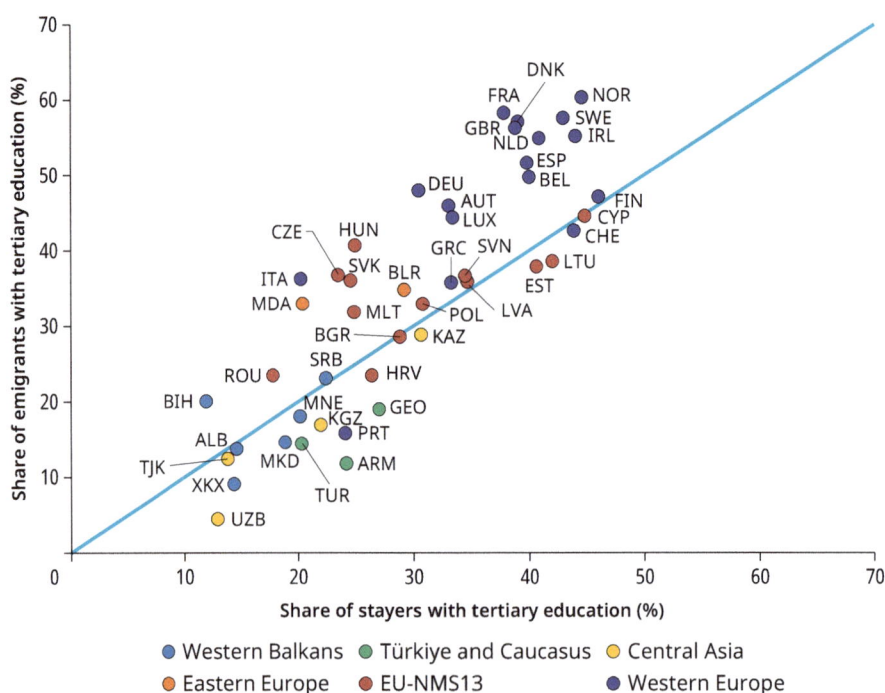

Sources: Database on Immigrants in OECD and Non-OECD Countries 2015, Organisation for Economic Co-operation and Development (https://www.oecd.org/els/mig/dioc.htm); Russia Labor Force Survey 2017, Armenia Labor Force Survey 2018, and Kyrgyz Republic Integrated Household Survey 2018 (for information on Labor Force Surveys, see https://webapps.ilo.org/surveyLib/index.php/catalog/LFS /?page=1&ps=15&repo=LFS); Listening to the Citizens of Tajikistan 2017 (https://www.worldbank.org/en /country/tajikistan/brief/listening2tajikistan); and Listening to the Citizens of Uzbekistan 2018 (https://www.worldbank.org/en/country/uzbekistan/brief/l2cu#1).
Note: The 45-degree line indicates parity in the share of emigrants and stayers with tertiary education. In countries above the 45-degree line, the share of tertiary-educated emigrants is higher than the share of tertiary-educated nonmigrants. In countries below the 45-degree line, the share of tertiary-educated emigrants is lower than the share of tertiary-educated nonmigrants. EU-NMS13 = new member states joining the European Union in 2004, 2007, and 2013.

most countries are in the vicinity of the 45-degree line, which indicates that the average skill level of emigrants is close to that of the nonmigrant population. Evidence from individual countries' survey data indicate that emigration from ECA countries is more frequent among working-age individuals with a vocational diploma or upper-secondary education than among individuals with tertiary education or primary education at most.

Low-skilled emigration is linked to origin countries' development paths. As for high-skilled migration (refer to chapter 4 for more details), the relationship between economic development and low-skilled emigration from ECA countries follows an inverted-U shape (refer to figure 5.2, panel a). The incidence of low-skilled emigration (as well as the incidence of total emigration) in the working-age population remains low for the poorest Central Asian countries in ECA (the Kyrgyz Republic, Tajikistan, and Uzbekistan) but increases sharply when middle-income levels are reached. Middle-income countries from the Caucasus (Armenia, Georgia) and the Western Balkans (Albania, Bosnia and Herzegovina, Montenegro, North Macedonia) exhibit the highest incidence of low-skilled emigration in their total population. At high levels of income, the incidence of low-skilled emigration drops, likely reflecting higher domestic wages for low-skill jobs, hence lower returns to low-skilled emigration. Relative to high-skilled emigration (refer to figure 5.2, panel b), low-skilled emigration falls more rapidly than high-skilled emigration at high levels of economic development.

Poor domestic labor market conditions are a critical push factor for low-skilled migration. Emigration from Central Asia, the Caucasus, and the Western Balkans is mainly driven by higher poverty rates, weaker labor market conditions, and larger wage differentials in the sending regions relative to the main destination countries. In general, many countries in the Caucasus and the Western Balkans have exhibited very high rates of youth unemployment over the past decades—reaching as high as 43% in Georgia in 2009 (30% as of 2022) and 68% in North Macedonia in 2003 (32% as of 2022). Additionally, higher-wage jobs have not been created rapidly enough to accommodate the rising number of youth in Central Asian countries. The search for better employment opportunities is by far the most reported motive for migrating abroad in these regions (Honorati, Kerschbaumer, and Yi 2019; Seitz 2019). Low-skilled migrants from these countries have been shown to have poorer employment outcomes before departure compared with nonmigrants: in the Kyrgyz Republic, Tajikistan, and Uzbekistan, more than half of temporary migrants were not employed before moving abroad, a much higher rate than for nonmigrants. In Armenia, 70 percent of temporary migrants and about 60 percent of permanent migrants were either unemployed or inactive in the labor market before leaving the country (Miluka et al. 2010). In Albania, evidence also shows rural households use migration as a pathway out of having to work in agriculture (Miluka et al. 2010).

FIGURE 5.2

Economic development and emigration, by skill level

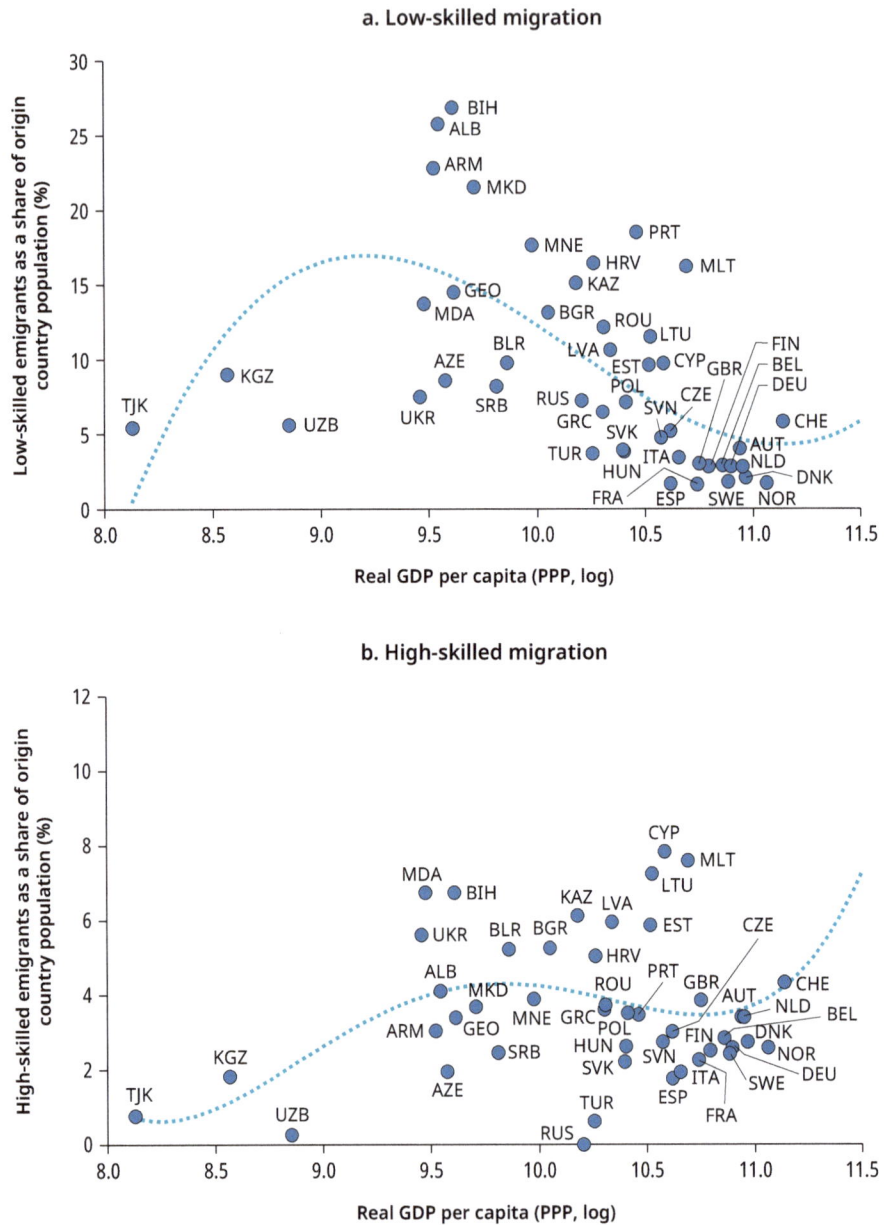

a. Low-skilled migration

b. High-skilled migration

Sources: UN Department of Economic and Social Affairs International Migrant Stock 2020; Database on Immigrants in OECD and Non-OECD Countries 2015, Organisation for Economic Co-operation and Development (https://www.oecd.org/els/mig/dioc.htm); Russia Labor Force Survey 2017, Armenia Labor Force Survey 2018, and Kyrgyz Integrated Household Survey 2018 (for information on Labor Force Surveys, see https://webapps.ilo.org/surveyLib/index.php/catalog/LFS/?page=1&ps=15&repo=LFS); Listening to the Citizens of Tajikistan 2017 (https://www.worldbank.org/en/country/tajikistan/brief/listening2tajikistan); and Listening to the Citizens of Uzbekistan 2018 (https://www.worldbank.org/en/country/uzbekistan/brief/l2cu#1).

Note: High-skilled emigrants are defined as tertiary-educated individuals living abroad. Low-skilled emigrants are defined as individuals without tertiary education living abroad. The dotted light-blue line represents the estimated nonlinear relationship between emigration and level of economic development in origin countries. GDP = gross domestic product; PPP = purchasing power parity; log = logarithm.

There are marked differences in emigration between regions of origin countries, reflecting heterogeneity in economic development. In the Caucasus, Central Asia, and the Western Balkans, low-skilled emigration is very unevenly distributed across regions. Emigrants disproportionately come from the poorest rural and peri-urban areas in sending countries. During the 2019–21 period, about 21 percent of households in the poorest quintile of Central Asian districts reported a member abroad, whereas those in the typical top quintile districts reported almost none (Seitz 2019). In Uzbekistan, the incidence of labor migration is higher in rural regions, from households facing difficulties in paying for utilities and from larger households (Honorati 2021). Similar patterns are observed in Armenia and the Kyrgyz Republic (Bossavie and Garrote-Sánchez 2022; Honorati, Kerschbaumer, and Yi 2019). Figure 5.3 illustrates the negative relationship between economic conditions in origin regions and emigration rates in the Kyrgyz Republic and Romania.

At the household level, emigrants disproportionately come from poor or vulnerable households. Emigration from Central Asian countries and

FIGURE 5.3

Relationship between regional economic conditions and emigration, Romania and Kyrgyz Republic

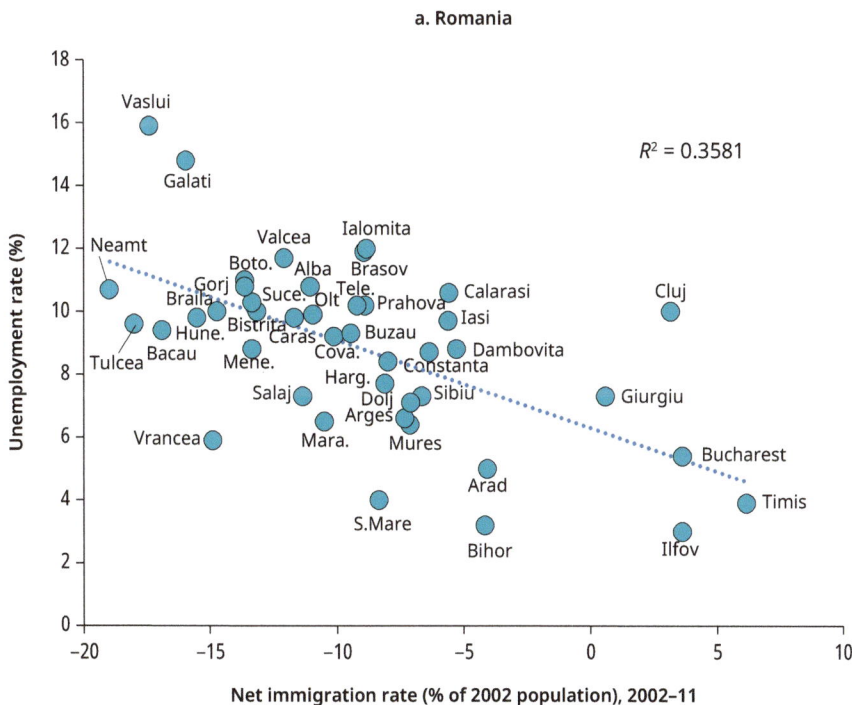

a. Romania

$R^2 = 0.3581$

Net immigration rate (% of 2002 population), 2002–11

Unemployment rate (%)

Continued

Figure 5.3

Relationship between regional economic conditions and emigration, Romania and Kyrgyz Republic *(Continued)*

b. Kyrgyz Republic

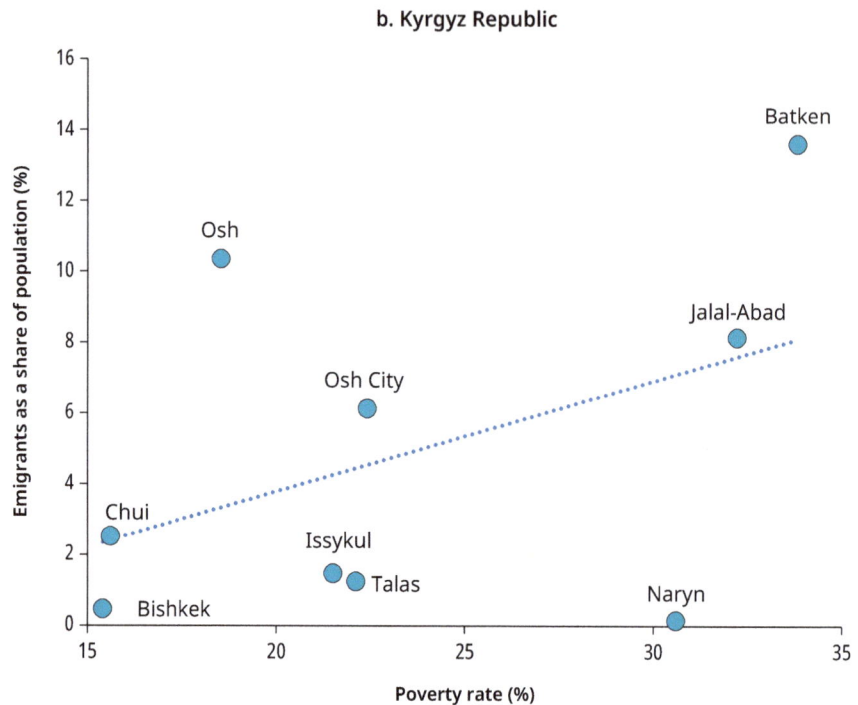

Sources: Romania: Samples of the 2002 and 2011 censuses from Minnesota Population Center Integrated Public Use Microdata Series 2019 (https://www.ipums.org/projects/ipums-international/d020. v7.2) and Eurostat (https://ec.europa.eu/eurostat/data/database); Kyrgyz Republic: Kyrgyz Integrated Household Survey 2018 (https://stat.gov.kg/en/).

Note: The unemployment rate is defined as the number of individuals ages 15–64 looking for employment, divided by the population ages 15–64 who is economically active. The poverty rate is defined as the percentage of households below the national poverty line. Net immigration is defined as the cumulative migration inflows (arrivals) minus the cumulative migration outflows (departures) from 2002 to 2011. The blue dotted line in each panel represents the estimated linear relationship between the x-axis variable and y-axis variable, estimated by ordinary least square.

Albania is disproportionately concentrated among the poorest households (refer to figure 5.4). In addition to stronger push factors, this emigration is also explained by the relatively low costs of migrating to Russia, the main destination of migrants from Central Asia, compared with other international destinations. In Albania, the Kyrgyz Republic, and Uzbekistan, one observes a clear negative relationship between household wealth and having a member who is currently working abroad. In Albania, about 15 percent of households in the bottom two quintiles have a member working abroad, compared with fewer than 5 percent in the top quintile. In Uzbekistan, 25 percent of households in the poorest quintile report having a member working abroad compared with the national average of 16 percent of households (Honorati and Carraro 2019). In contrast,

FIGURE 5.4
Share of households with a member currently abroad, by expenditure quintile

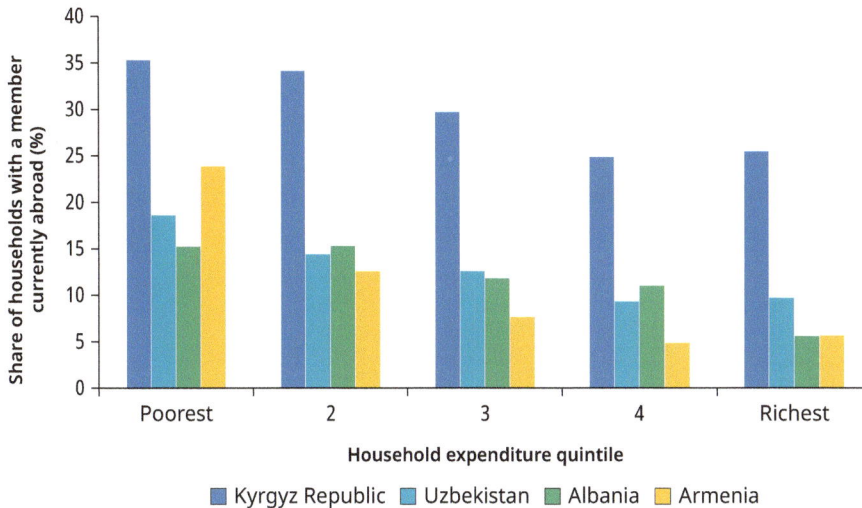

Sources: Albania: Demographic and Health Survey, 2018 (INSTAT, IPH, and ICF 2018); Armenia: Integrated Living Condition Survey (https://armstat.am/en/?nid=205); Kyrgyz Republic: Listening to the Citizens of the Kyrgyz Republic baseline survey (https://www.worldbank.org/en/country/kyrgyzrepublic/brief/l2kgz); Uzbekistan: Listening to the Citizens of Uzbekistan baseline survey (https://www.worldbank.org/en/country/uzbekistan/brief/l2cu#1).
Note: The richest and poorest quintiles consist of the top 20 percent of households with the highest and lowest levels, respectively, of expenditure per capita nationwide.

in Armenia, emigration is more equally distributed across income quintiles: migrants are overrepresented among the poorest consumption quintiles and the two richest ones. This may reflect greater high-skilled migration opportunities than for workers from Albania and Central Asia. In addition to absolute welfare levels, low-skilled emigration has also been shown to be associated with vulnerability to economic shocks. In Uzbekistan, for instance, there is a strong relationship between household negative shocks and emigration (Seitz 2019).

In corridors in which migration costs are higher, extreme poverty may, however, impede low-skilled migration. High migration costs, when combined with credit constraints, may deter low-skilled migration among poorer households facing liquidity constraints (Ahmed and Bossavie 2022; Clemens 2020). In Kosovo, for example, although poorer households tend to migrate more than wealthier households, those who are extremely poor have weaker access to international migration and tend to receive fewer remittances from abroad (Möllers and Meyer 2014). In the case of migration from Albania to Greece or Italy, household poverty has been shown to be a constraining factor in international migration (Zezza, Carletto, and Davis 2005). Similarly, in Armenia and Uzbekistan, the relationship between skill level and propensity to migrate is an inverted-U shape (refer to figure 5.5): the incidence of emigration is lowest among individuals with low levels of education (at most, primary education), is highest for individuals with intermediate levels of education (some secondary schooling), and declines for individuals who have attained some tertiary education.[2] Because educational attainment is highly correlated with household income, low rates of migration among lower-educated individuals may reflect liquidity and credit constraint to cover migration costs. In contrast, in Albania, where household income levels tend to be higher, a linear and negative relationship between levels of educational attainment and emigration is observed.

FIGURE 5.5

Educational attainment of the working-age population (ages 25–64), by country of origin and emigration status

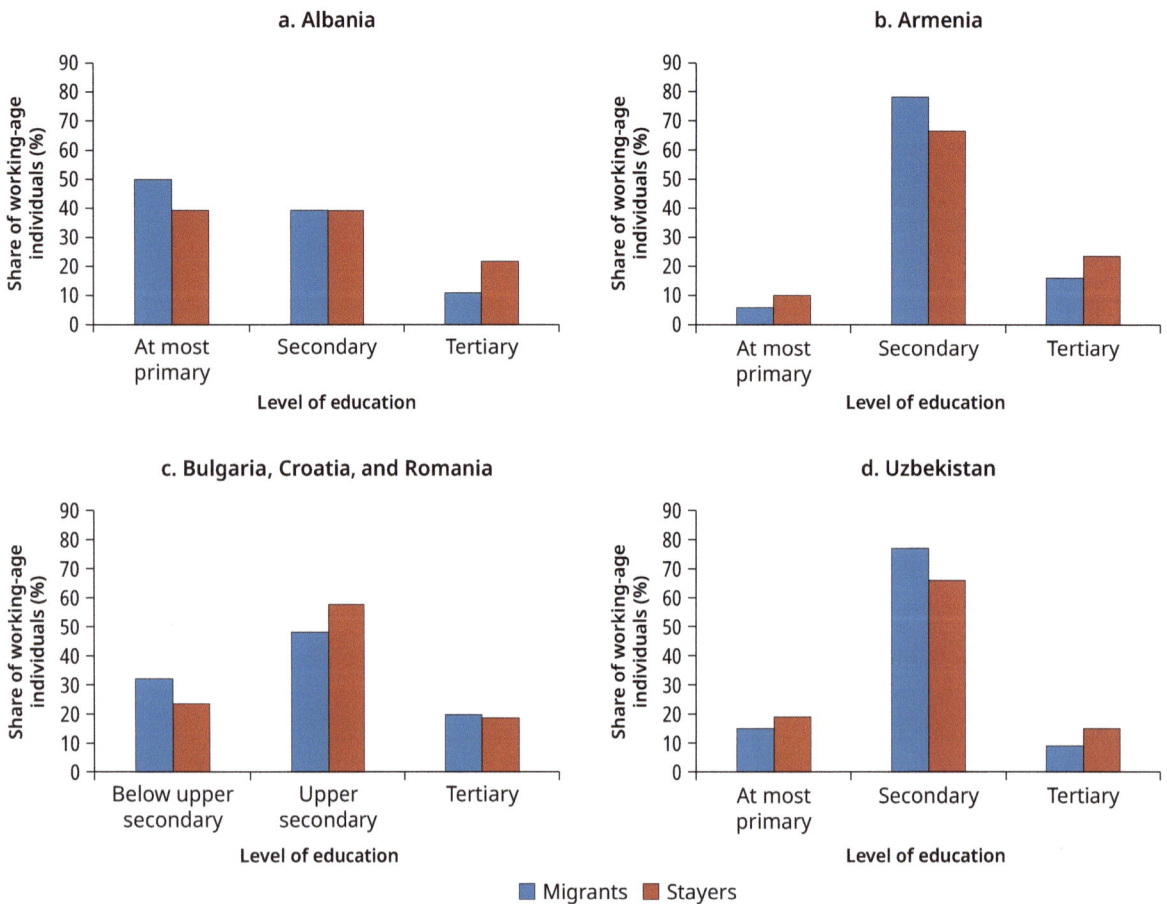

a. Albania

b. Armenia

c. Bulgaria, Croatia, and Romania

d. Uzbekistan

■ Migrants ■ Stayers

Sources: Uzbekistan: Listening to the Citizens of Uzbekistan (https://www.worldbank.org/en/country/uzbekistan/brief/l2cu#1); Albania: Demographic and Health Survey 2017–2018 (INSTAT, IPH, and ICF 2018); Armenia: Integrated Living Condition Survey (https://armstat.am /en/?nid=205); Bulgaria, Croatia, and Romania: European Union Labor Force Survey (https://ec.europa.eu/eurostat/web/microdata /european-union-labour-force-survey).

Note: Statistics for Bulgaria, Croatia, and Romania are grouped together because data are unavailable for each individual country.

Noneconomic factors also contribute to low-skilled migration and destination choice, mostly through their impact on migration costs. Physical and cultural distances are also important determinants of mobility costs, especially for low-skilled migrants. Short physical distances impose lower transportation costs and can enable most low-skilled migrants with tight budget constraints who would not be able to migrate to faraway destinations to move to neighboring countries (World Bank 2019b). Cultural adaptation and settlement are also costly, so existing personal and social networks shape migration flows. In addition to providing more favorable labor market conditions, Russia has been an attractive destination for low-skilled migrants from the Caucasus and Central Asia because of several cultural and historical factors, such as shared history, shared language, familiarity with Russian culture, visa-free regimes, solid migrant networks, and low transportation costs. In Armenia and Georgia, largely unresolved conflicts—that is, the Karabakh War (1988, 1994), the War in Abkhazia (1992, 1993, 2008), and the War in Ossetia (1991, 1992)—combined with political instability because of crime and corruption have also acted as important noneconomic push factors to migrate. Political instability, especially after independence in the 1990s, has also been a push factor for international labor migration in the former Soviet republics. Weaker social protection and welfare systems in countries of origin may also play a role in low-skilled emigration (Bossavie et al. 2022).

Patterns and Heterogeneity in Low-Skilled Migration from ECA Countries

As for high-skilled migration, Western Europe is the main destination of low-skilled migrants in ECA, primarily coming from the Western Balkans, Western Europe, and other countries of the European Union. Low-skilled migration within the European Union dates back from its creation, which involved free labor mobility but was boosted by the subsequent and more recent EU enlargements to the Central EU economies, which led to large increases in low-skilled migration from the Central EU, primarily to Germany, Greece, Italy, and Spain. Low-skilled migration since the 1990s from Albania to Greece and Italy, a major corridor of low-skilled migration within ECA, is historically rooted. It was initiated by bilateral agreements for agricultural employment in Greece and Italy after the collapse of the communist regime in Albania and the transition from a centralized to an open economy. Low-skilled migration from other Western Balkan countries such as Bosnia and Herzegovina, Kosovo, North Macedonia, and Serbia is primarily to Germany (OECD 2022). It was boosted by the Western Balkan Regulation introduced in 2016 (Center for Global Development 2021) to create legal channels for citizens from that region to migrate to Germany, especially for low-skilled workers in the construction sector.

In contrast with high-skilled migration, Russia is the second main destination of low-skilled migrants within ECA. Low-skilled migrants to Russia primarily come from the lower-income former Soviet republics of Central Asia (the Kyrgyz Republic, Tajikistan, and Uzbekistan) and the Caucasus (Armenia, Azerbaijan, and Georgia). Low-skilled migration from those lower-income countries is deeply rooted historically and dates to the 1990s after the collapse of the Soviet Union, and even before that. Labor migration between those countries is regulated by several multilateral and bilateral agreements aimed at forming a common labor market. Russia has bilateral treaties with Armenia, the Kyrgyz Republic, Moldova, Tajikistan, Ukraine, and Uzbekistan. All treaty countries are obligated to recognize the education, work experience, entitlement to compensation for damages, and social security contributions of migrant workers. Every year, the Russian government defines how many work permits can be issued and how they will be distributed among the constituent components of Russia, depending on the labor market situation and the opinions of labor unions. Quotas are divided by region, profession, and field of employment.

Low-skilled migration from Central Asia and the Caucasus to Russia is often temporary and of short duration. Migration spells for these low-skilled migration corridors are of a short duration, on average, when compared with high-skilled migration in ECA or low-skilled migration for other migration corridors. About half of temporary migrants from the Kyrgyz Republic stay in the destination country for less than six months, and the median duration of stay abroad is about nine months (refer to figure 5.6). Although migrants from Albania, Armenia, and Uzbekistan stay at their destination somewhat longer, half still return to their origin country within less than a year. This contrasts with other low-skilled migration corridors, such as from South Asia to the Persian Gulf, where duration of stay abroad is at least a few years (Ahmed and Bossavie 2022).

Low-skilled migration in these corridors is often seasonal and circular. In addition to staying abroad for short periods of time, low-skilled temporary migrants from Central Asia and the Caucasus to Russia often repeat migration over time. More than half of temporary migrants from the Kyrgyz Republic and Uzbekistan have migrated to Russia more than once (refer to figure 5.7). In comparison, low-skilled migrants from South Asia to the Gulf Cooperation Council countries or East Asia typically migrate only once (Ahmed and Bossavie 2022). The multiplicity of migration episodes observed for these ECA corridors can be explained by their relatively low monetary costs of migration compared with other corridors, combined with the seasonal nature of the economic activities carried out at destination, mainly in tourism and construction. Indeed, low-skilled migration from Central Asia and the Caucasus to Russia also exhibits strong seasonal patterns: departures spike in the spring, and returns typically take place in late fall or winter.

FIGURE 5.6

Duration of stay abroad in the most recent migration episode, by migrants' country of origin

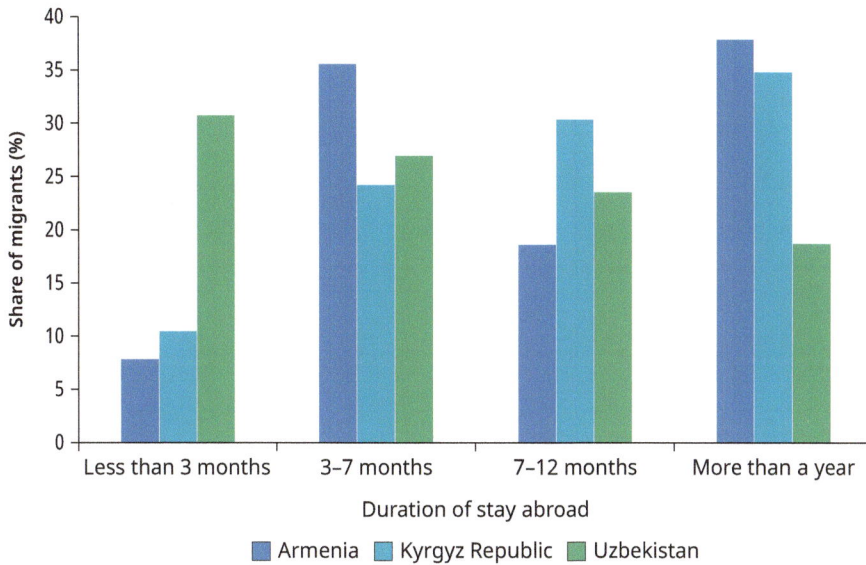

Sources: Armenia: Integrated Living Condition Survey (https://armstat.am/en/?nid=205); Kyrgyz Republic: Listening to the Citizens of the Kyrgyz Republic survey (https://www.worldbank.org/en/country /kyrgyzrepublic/brief/l2kgz#:~:text=Listening%20to%20the%20Kyrgyz%20Republic%20(L2KGZ)%20is%20 a%20monthly%20panel,regions%20of%20the%20Kyrgyz%20Republic.); Uzbekistan: Listening to the Citizens of Uzbekistan survey (https://www.worldbank.org/en/country/uzbekistan/brief/l2cu).

FIGURE 5.7

Circularity of migration from Central Asia to the Russian Federation

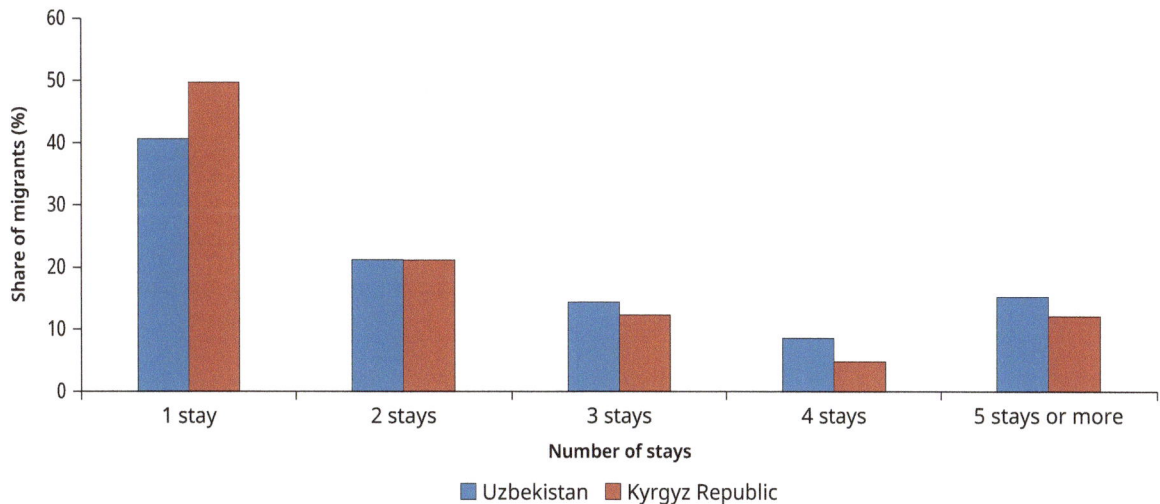

a. Number of migration episodes abroad among past international migrants

Continued

Figure 5.7
Circularity of migration from Central Asia to the Russian Federation *(Continued)*

b. Stock of temporary migrants from Kyrgyz Republic abroad, by quarter

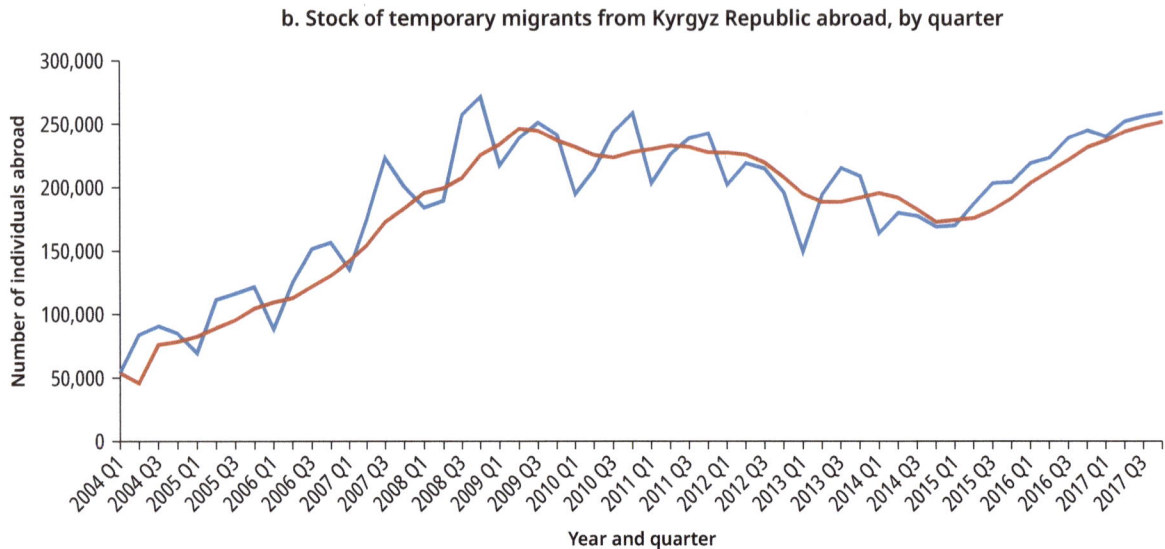

Sources: Panel a: Listening to the Citizens of Kyrgyz Republic (https://www.worldbank.org/en/country/kyrgyzrepublic/brief
/l2kgz#:~:text=Listening%20to%20the%20Kyrgyz%20Republic%20(L2KGZ)%20is%20a%20monthly%20panel,regions%20of%20the%20
Kyrgyz%20Republic) and Uzbekistan surveys (https://www.worldbank.org/en/country/uzbekistan/brief/l2cu); panel b: Quarterly Kyrgyz
Integrated Household Survey (https://stat.gov.kg/en/).
Note: In panel b, the blue line represents the actual number of individuals from the Kyrgyz Republic who are currently abroad (not
seasonally adjusted). The smoothed red line represents the 4-month moving average (seasonally adjusted) of the number of individuals
abroad. Q = quarter.

Low-skilled migration from ECA countries to the European Union, in
contrast, is more often permanent. Low-skilled migration to the European
Union tends to be more permanent than high-skilled migration: low-skilled
migrants from other Western European countries and from the EU-NMS13
have a lower propensity to return than their high-skilled counterparts (refer
to figure 5.8). The difference in the propensity to return is especially stark
for low-skilled migrants from the higher-income EU-15 countries: whereas
about 40 percent of high-skilled migrants from the EU-15 are estimated to
return to their home country after five years, only 12 percent of low-skilled
migrants from EU-15 countries return within that time frame. Return
rates are estimated to be even lower among low-skilled migrants from
the EU-NMS13, although return rates for high-skilled migrants from
this region are also low.

Temporary low-skilled migration is largely male, whereas permanent
low-skilled migration is more gender balanced. Although high-skilled
migration from ECA is increasingly female, as discussed in chapter 4,
low-skilled migration from Central Asian countries, Albania, and Armenia
remains largely male. These gender patterns are even more pronounced
when considering temporary migration, in which migrants typically move

FIGURE 5.8

Incidence of return among migrants to the European Union, by level of educational attainment and region of origin

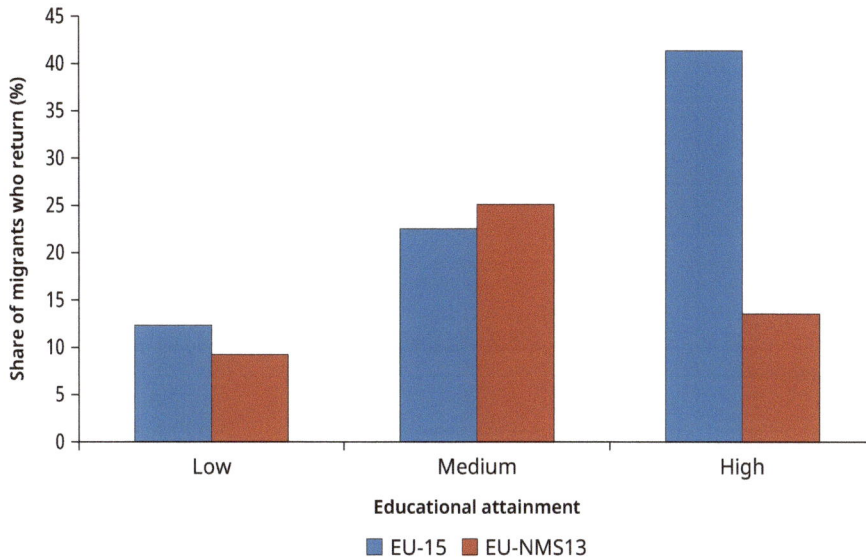

Sources: Original estimates based on EU Labour Force Survey 2014 module (https://ec.europa.eu /eurostat/web/microdata/european-union-labour-force-survey); Database on Immigrants in OECD and Non-OECD Countries 2010, Organisation for Economic Co-operation and Development (https://www .oecd.org/els/mig/dioc.htm); and Centre d'Études Prospectives et d'Informations Internationales bilateral database (http://www.cepii.fr/CEPII/en/bdd_modele/bdd_modele_item.asp?id=37).
Note: Returnee rates are estimated by dividing by the number of returnees in 2014 by the stock of migrants in 2010, multiplied by the elasticity of returnees to migrants derived from a gravity-type equation that controls for a set of geographic and social ties between the sending and receiving countries (distance, contiguity, share of common ethnic groups). Low education is defined as having, at most, primary schooling. Medium education is defined as having completed primary but not tertiary education. High education is defined as having some tertiary education. EU-NMS13 = new member states joining the European Union in 2004, 2007, and 2013.

without the rest of their families. For example, more than 90 percent of temporary migrants in Albania and Armenia, close to 90 percent in Tajikistan and Uzbekistan, and nearly 80 percent in the Kyrgyz Republic are male. These gender patterns are driven by low levels of female labor force participation in the origin countries, the fact that temporary migrants typically migrate without family in a context in which women remain the primary caregivers in origin countries, and the associated negative perceptions of female migrants. In contrast, more permanent low-skilled migration, primarily to the European Union, is more gender balanced: among low-skilled permanent migrants to the European Union, mostly from the EU-NMS13 and the Western Balkans, the gender balance is close to parity. This can be partly explained by entire families moving together in the case of permanent migration, as opposed to seasonal or temporary migration. Low-skilled migration from Georgia and Moldova is also more gender balanced.

Low-skilled migrants are younger than higher-skilled migrants. Globally, migrants tend to be younger than the working-age population in the origin country (World Bank 2018). The pattern is even more pronounced among low-skilled migrants in ECA, where low-skilled migrants are younger than the average working-age population in the country of origin and younger than their high-skilled counterparts. Temporary emigrants from Albania and Uzbekistan are concentrated in the 18–35 age group compared with the working-age population that does not emigrate (refer to figure 5.9). This partly reflects the fact that low-skilled emigrants complete their

FIGURE 5.9

Age profile of the working-age population, by country of origin and migration status

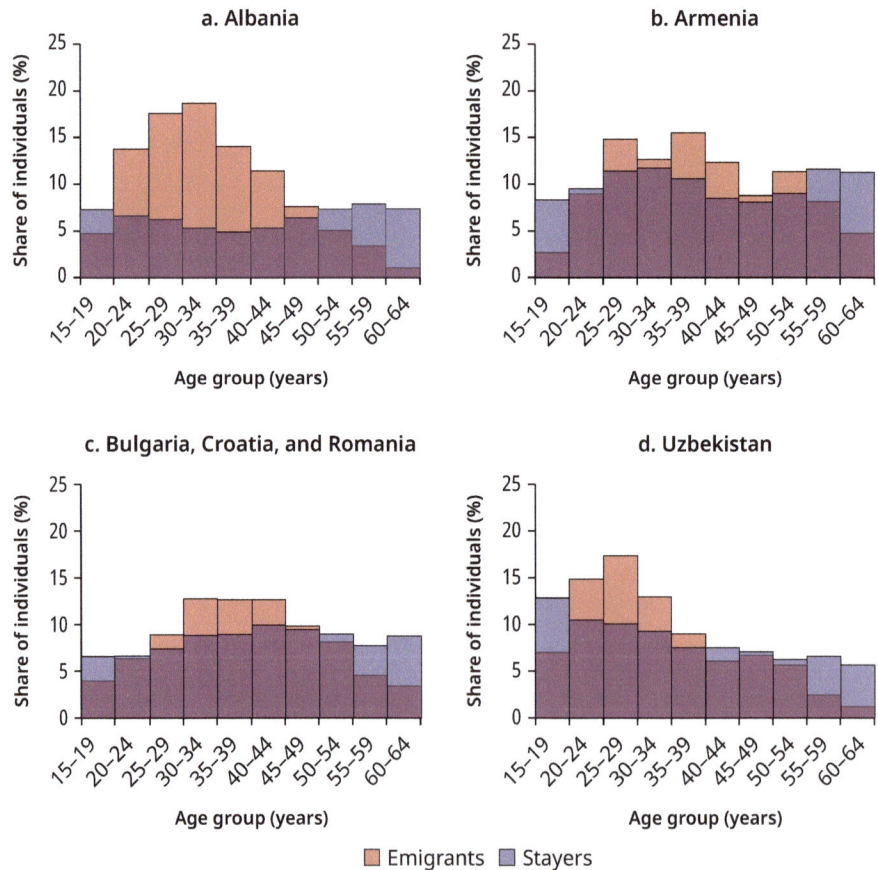

a. Albania

b. Armenia

c. Bulgaria, Croatia, and Romania

d. Uzbekistan

■ Emigrants ■ Stayers

Sources: Listening to the Citizens surveys for Kyrgyz Republic (https://www.worldbank.org/en/country /kyrgyzrepublic/brief/l2kgz#:~:text=Listening%20to%20the%20Kyrgyz%20Republic%20(L2KGZ)%20is%20 a%20monthly%20panel,regions%20of%20the%20Kyrgyz%20Republic) and Uzbekistan (https://www .worldbank.org/en/country/uzbekistan/brief/l2cu), 2018; Albania: Demographic and Health Survey, 2019 (https://microdata.worldbank.org/index.php/catalog/3404); Armenia: Integrated Household Survey, 2019 (https://armstat.am/en/?nid=205); Bulgaria, Croatia, and Romania: EU Labour Force Survey (https://ec.europa.eu/eurostat/web/microdata/european-union-labour-force-survey).
Note: Purple shading represents overlap between the two groups depicted in each panel.

education at an earlier age, together with the low cost of migrating at a younger age (World Bank 2018). Although international labor migration enables an accommodation of growing youth populations that cannot be absorbed by domestic markets, such as in Central Asia, the concentration of low-skilled migration among youth also raises the question of whether low-skilled migration opportunities disincentivize investment in education among the young population in origin countries (Bossavie and Özden 2023; McKenzie and Rapoport 2011), as discussed in the "Low-Skilled Migration Fosters Development in Origin Countries" section of the chapter. In Armenia, Bulgaria, Croatia, and Romania, the age distribution of migrants is closer to that of the working-age population, but emigrants are still more likely than the nonmigrant population to be in the 18–35 age group.

Development Impacts of Low-Skilled Migration in Origin Countries

Direct Welfare Impacts through Large Income Gains

Low-skilled migrants directly benefit from international labor mobility through higher earnings abroad. Low-skilled workers experience large wage gains abroad compared with what they can earn in their country of origin, which is the main motive for migrating in the first place. Working migrants from Armenia and the Kyrgyz Republic, for example, can expect to double their earnings compared with what they would earn back home (refer to figure 5.10, panels a and b): low-skilled minimum wage migrant workers from Montenegro, North Macedonia, and Serbia can also expect to double their wages by moving to EU destinations such as France or Germany, and low-skilled migrants from Albania can earn up to three times more (OECD 2022). There is, however, important variation in the place premium depending on migrants' educational attainment. In Armenia, wage gains abroad are highest among workers with intermediary levels of education (some secondary education), compared with workers with, at most, primary or some tertiary education. In the Kyrgyz Republic, workers with a low or middle level of education experience larger wage gains than tertiary-educated workers. Similar patterns are observed among migrants from Romania going to Spain, where the place wage premium is largest among low-skilled migrants (refer to figure 5.10, panel c).

In the context of low-skilled temporary migration, higher wages earned abroad translate to remittances to households left behind. The large wage gains of low-skilled migrants abroad enable large welfare gains at the

FIGURE 5.10

Wages earned by international migrants relative to stayers, by migration corridor and level of education

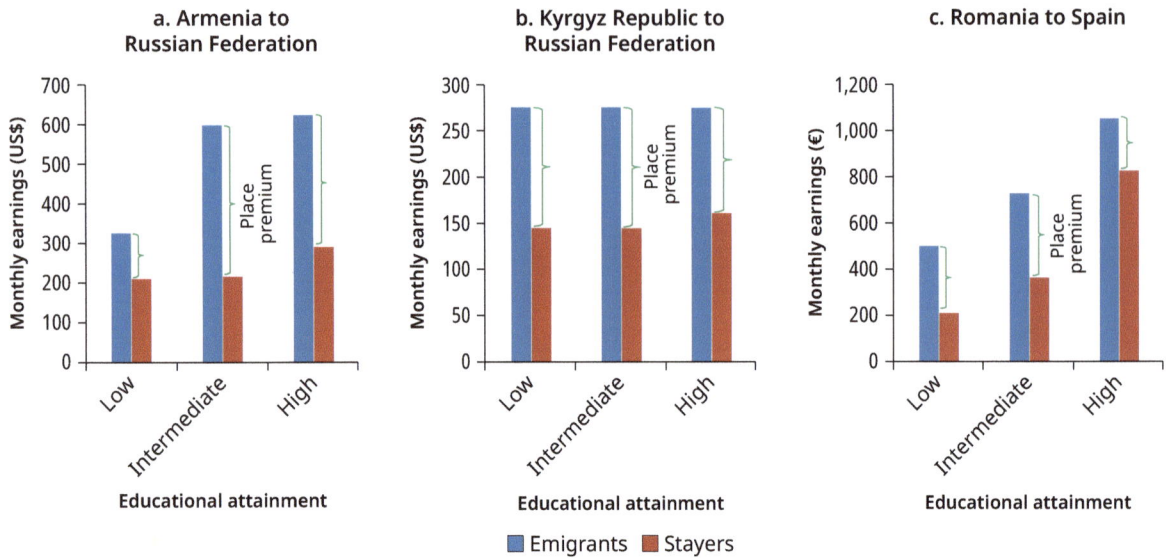

a. Armenia to Russian Federation

b. Kyrgyz Republic to Russian Federation

c. Romania to Spain

■ Emigrants ■ Stayers

Sources: Armenia: Labor Force Survey 2017 (https://armstat.am/en/?nid=212); Russian Federation: Russia Longitudinal Monitoring Survey 2017 (https://rlms-hse.cpc.unc.edu/); Kyrgyz Republic: Kyrgyz Integrated Household Survey 2018 (https://stat.gov.kg/en/); Romania: EU Statistics on Income and Living Conditions (database), Eurostat (https://ec.europa.eu/eurostat/web/microdata/european-union-statistics -on-income-and-living-conditions); Database on Immigrants in OECD and Non-OECD Countries, Organisation for Economic Co-operation and Development (https://www.oecd.org/els/mig/dioc.htm).
Note: "Place premium" represents the average earnings differential between workers employed in the country of origin and workers from that same country of origin employed in the destination country. Wages in panels a and b are in current US dollars. Wages in panel c are in euros and deflated by the price levels in each country based on Eurostat statistics (prc_ppp_ind). Low educational attainment = less than upper-secondary education; intermediate educational attainment = upper-secondary education; high educational attainment = tertiary education.

household level through migrants' remittances to families left behind. Improving the welfare and consumption of family members left behind is a key motive for migrants sending remittances back home (Faini 1994; Funkhouser 1995; Lucas and Stark 1985; Rapoport and Docquier 2006). Low-skilled temporary migrants often migrate without the rest of their households and as a result have been shown to send more remittances home than higher-skilled migrants (Adams 2009; Dustmann and Mestres 2010; Niimi, Ozden, and Schiff 2010). In the Kyrgyz Republic, for example, 94 percent of households with a member working abroad report receiving remittances. Figures are also more than 90 percent in other Central Asian countries as well as in Armenia (Honorati, Kerschbaumer, and Yi 2019).

Remittances generated by low-skilled emigrants are a key contributor to national income in many countries of origin, where remittance levels are often very high in relative terms. Many low- and middle-income countries in ECA are among the top recipients of remittances worldwide in relative terms, particularly in Central Asia (refer to figure 5.11).

FIGURE 5.11

Remittances received as a percentage of gross domestic product, top 50 countries globally

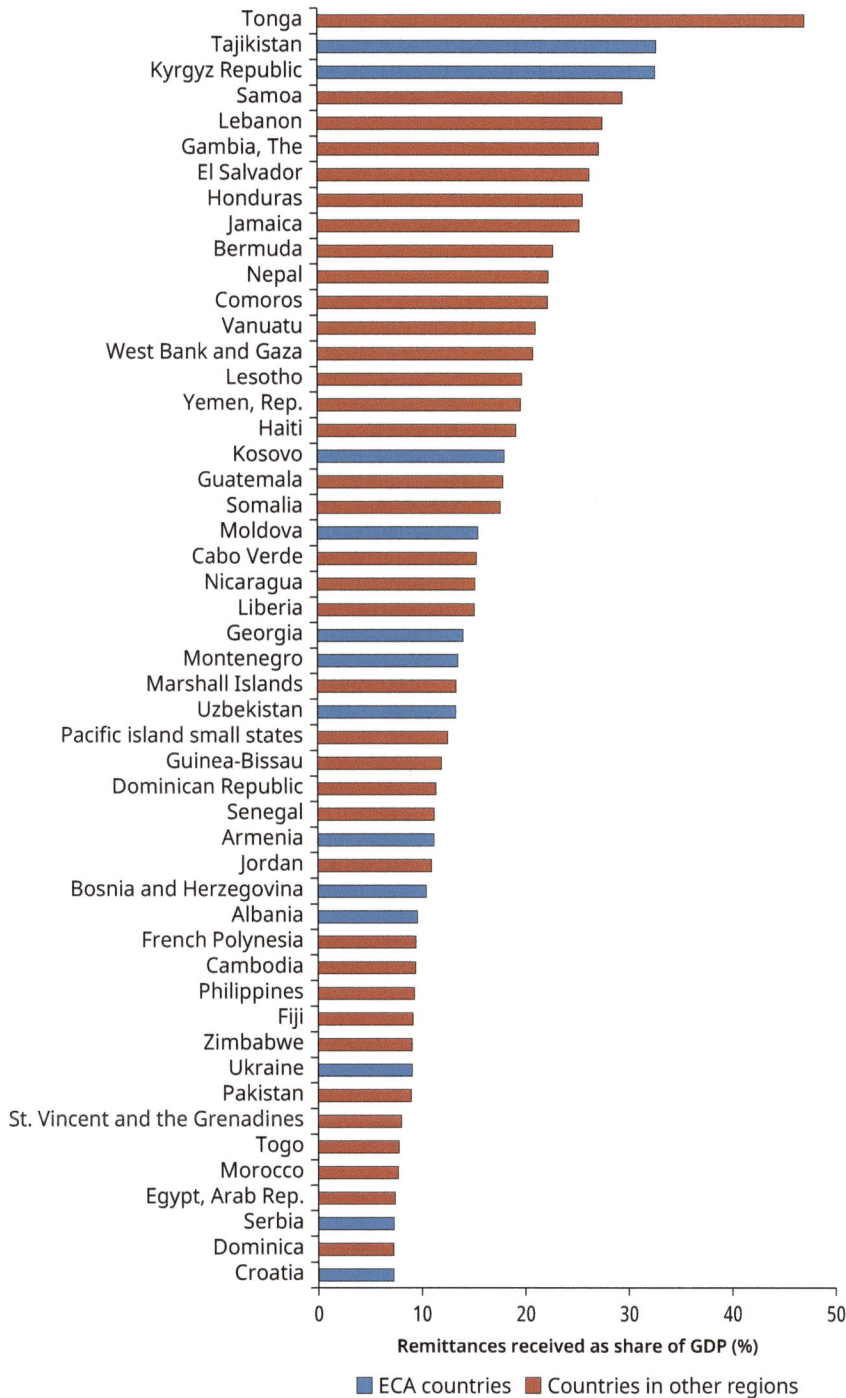

Source: World Development Indicators (database), World Bank (https://databank.worldbank.org/source /world-development-indicators). Data are for 2021.
Note: GDP = gross domestic product.

Among the top three receivers of remittances as a share of GDP, two are in Central Asia (the Kyrgyz Republic and Tajikistan), where remittances represent more than 30 percent of total GDP. Remittances constitute a major source of national income for countries in the Caucasus (Armenia, Georgia), Eastern Europe (Moldova), and the Western Balkans (Bosnia and Herzegovina, Kosovo, Montenegro). In all these ECA migrant-sending countries, remittances received from abroad exceed 10 percent of GDP.

At the micro level, remittances represent a very large share of household income in lower-income ECA countries. Remittance recipients are typically migrants' families, close relatives, or community members. As per the incidence of emigration, there is an overall negative relationship between household income level and receipt of remittances from abroad. In the Kyrgyz Republic and Uzbekistan, for example, more than 20 percent of those in the poorest quintile receive some remittance income compared with 7 percent and 1 percent of those in the top two quintiles. In Tajikistan, about 36 percent of those in the poorest quintile received remittances each month, tapering to about 27 percent for those in the top quintile. Remittances from abroad represent a very large share of the total income of migrant households in low- and middle-income ECA countries. In the Kyrgyz Republic, for example, remittances received from abroad account for more than half (58 percent) of the total income of households with an international migrant, more than labor earnings and other sources of income combined (Bossavie and Garrote-Sánchez 2022). Similarly, in Armenia, about 46 percent of migrant households' income before the COVID-19 pandemic came from remittances, higher than income from employment (37 percent) and pensions (10 percent).

In low- and middle-income countries, remittances are mostly spent on immediate consumption, substantially increasing household income. Depending on the income level of the remittance-receiving household, funds are spent differently. Poor families tend to spend remittances on consumption, whereas wealthier households are more likely to spend them on productive and investment goods such as health and education (World Bank 2018). In Central Asian countries, which exhibit some of the highest rates of poverty in ECA, remittances are mostly channeled to food purchases and housing improvements with little additional spending on investment and education (Dubashov, Kruse, and Ismailakhunova 2017). Likewise, in Uzbekistan, food expenditures are the main use of remittances, together with buying or improving housing. In Armenia, although food and clothes consumption remain the main use of remittances, their usage is more diversified than in Central Asia, with remittance income more often being spent on heating, debt payment, and medical needs (Honorati, Kerschbaumer, and Yi 2019).

As a result, remittances are a key contributor to poverty reduction. Using cross-country data that include ECA countries, it was estimated that a 10 percent increase per capita in international remittances led to a 3.5 percent decline in the share of people living in poverty (Adams and Page 2005). It has also been shown that the greater the share of low-skilled migrants in a country's migrant population, the greater the flow of remittances (Adams 2011). In line with these cross-country findings, remittances have been associated with a significant decline in poverty across low- and middle-income countries in the region. It is estimated that in the absence of remittances, the poverty rate in the Kyrgyz Republic would rise from 22.4 percent (in 2018) to 30.6 percent (Bossavie and Garrote-Sánchez 2022). Among migrant households, the share of poor families was estimated to drop from 50.2 percent to only 6.7 percent once remittances are considered (refer to figure 5.12). In Uzbekistan, the poverty rate (measured at US$3.20/day purchasing power parity) would rise from 9.6 percent to 16.8 percent in the absence of remittances (Seitz 2019). Similarly, the poverty rate for migrant households in Armenia would almost double (from 30 percent to 57.2 percent), and overall poverty in the country would increase

FIGURE 5.12

Estimated poverty rates, with and without remittances received from abroad

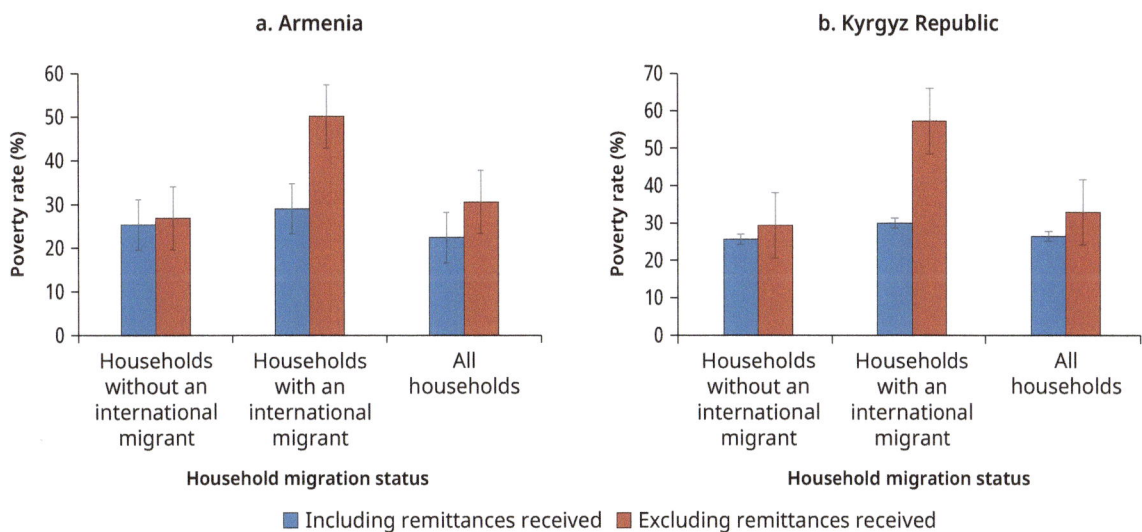

Sources: Kyrgyz Republic: Kyrgyz Integrated Household Survey 2018 (https://stat.gov.kg/en/); Armenia: 2019 Integrated Living Condition Survey (https://armstat.am/en/?nid=205).
Note: The poverty rate is defined as the percentage of households below the national poverty line. The vertical lines with brackets represent the 95 percent confidence intervals with upper and lower limit of estimated poverty rates.

from 26.4 percent to 32.9 percent.[3] In Kosovo, depending on the poverty line chosen, up to 41 percent of households with an international migrant are no longer poor, and around 40 percent of vulnerable households are lifted above the vulnerability threshold because of access to remittances (Möllers and Meyer 2014). Welfare impacts on those in extreme poverty, however, may be more muted, primarily because of their limited access to international migration and remittances (Seitz 2019).

Remittances may also indirectly enhance the welfare of nonrecipient households. The welfare benefits of remittances may extend beyond their direct recipients. It has been shown that if the flow of remittances exceeds a certain critical amount, the remaining residents benefit from migration even if they do not receive any of the remittances themselves (Djajić 1986). Households that receive remittances increase their spending, which boosts local economic activity and the incomes of other households in the community. Spending from remittances can, for example, support domestic employment creation in nontradable sectors, such as construction (Chami et al. 2018). In Albania, international migrants have been shown to invest in businesses and housing, fueling urban job creation and internal migration (Chami et al. 2018; Gedeshi and de Zwager 2012). Outside ECA, positive spillover effects on nonremittance recipients have been reported in the Philippines, where both temporary and permanent emigration is observed (Yang and Martinez 2006).

Remittances can play a countercyclical role and have an income-smoothing effect at the macro level. Remittances are directly received by households and therefore much less influenced by the political, economic, or geographic characteristics of the home country than are official development assistance, export revenue, and FDI. Flows can be procyclical (moving in the same direction as the home country's business cycle), countercyclical (moving in the opposite direction), or acyclical (not correlated with the home country's output; Frankel 2010; Lueth and Ruiz-Arranz 2007; World Bank 2015). In the context of ECA, remittances from Russia to the Caucasus and Central Asia have been shown to play a countercyclical role and to help stabilize outputs in recipient countries (Poghosyan 2023). In contexts in which low-skilled migration is heavily concentrated in one single destination, however, such as migration from Central Asia and the Caucasus to Russia, it can also expose sending countries to negative shocks in the destination country.

At the micro level, remittances can improve household welfare through an income-stabilizing effect. Unlike capital flows, which tend to be highly cyclical, remittances are relatively stable and often consumption smoothing, acting as insurance during economic crises or after natural disasters (Bettin and Zazzaro 2018; De et al. 2019; Ratha 2003; Yang and

Choi 2007). The countercyclical pattern also points to the key role of migration as a household economic diversification strategy to hedge against income risks such as loss of employment by or underemployment of some of their members. In Uzbekistan, for example, current migrants are more likely to send remittance payments when household members report worsening economic conditions at home (Seitz 2019).

The magnitude of remittances received by smaller, lower-income countries in ECA, however, has raised questions about undesirable effects in sending countries. There are concerns that the massive inflow of foreign currency could be associated with a real exchange rate appreciation and loss of international competitiveness, which, in turn, could lead to a decline in the production of manufactured and other tradable goods (Dutch disease). Increased domestic income from remittances can indeed push up domestic prices and migration flows, increasing wages and eventually diminishing the competitiveness of the other sectors. Another implication of Dutch disease would be that it moves labor away from other sectors, such as manufacturing, into foreign labor markets. Such a phenomenon has been evidenced in the case of small economies in ECA that are highly reliant on remittances, such as the Kyrgyz Republic, where a loss in competitiveness through real exchange appreciation, an increase in the size of the nontradable sector, and a fast growth of real wages have been reported (Dubashov, Kruse, and Ismailakhunova 2017).

At the micro level, the high reliance on remittances among poor households in ECA exposes them to shocks affecting international migration. In recent years, migrant households have become more reliant on remittance income; in 2008, just more than one-third of total income in migrant households was from remittances (World Bank 2015). For example, highly remittance-dependent migrant households in the Kyrgyz Republic can be pushed into debt when migrant household members lose their job and stop sending remittances home (Thieme 2014).

Beyond the direct impact of remittances on consumption, low-skilled migration may affect human development in sending countries through multiple channels. The first channel through which low-skilled migration affects human development in sending countries is through remittances received and used, for example, to invest in children's human capital among households left behind. Second, by raising household income, remittances may also affect incentives to work among household members left behind. Third, the absence of an adult family member may influence family dynamics and therefore outcomes such as children's development, gender dynamics, and bargaining power among migrant households (and potentially nonmigrant households in origin countries). Fourth, return migrants, by bringing back human and financial capital as well as social norms from destination countries, can also impact development back in the origin country. Finally, low-skilled emigration, if of sufficient scale, can produce general equilibrium effects on labor markets in sending countries. These various channels and their effects on human development outcomes are discussed in the next section.

Indirect Impacts on Human Capital

Evidence on the impact of remittances on educational attainment in countries of origin is mixed for ECA. Low-skilled emigration can affect educational attainment back home through multiple and conflicting channels (refer to box 5.1). For this reason, impact estimates reported for ECA are context specific and heterogeneous, depending on which transmission channel prevails in the specific context studied. In addition to the multiple channels at play, mixed results may also be driven by the methodological difficulties in isolating the causal effects of emigration on children's outcomes back in their home country (Bossavie and Özden 2023).

Although high-skilled temporary migration has been shown to raise productivity back home through return migration and human capital accumulation, evidence for low-skilled migration is more mixed. One emerging consensus from the literature is that higher-skilled temporary migrants experience greater human capital, productivity, and wage gains from the migration experience (Bossavie and Özden 2023). In Albania, for example, high-skilled returnees experience upward mobility in the labor market upon return, whereas low-skilled migrants do not (Carletto and Kilic 2011; de Coulon and Piracha 2005). Part of the explanation may be that low-skilled migrants in the Albanian context engage largely in seasonal short-term migration spells in the agricultural sector in Greece, which may limit opportunities for human capital accumulation. In Romania, the wage premium earned by returnees also turns out to increase with their skill level (Ambrosini et al. 2015). More studies looking at the causal link between low-skilled migration and labor productivity back home are, however, needed to generalize those findings to low- and middle-income countries in ECA.

Labor Market Impacts

Low-skilled emigration helps alleviate pressures on domestic labor markets in sending countries with a youth bulge and limited domestic employment opportunities. Some low- and middle-income regions in ECA, such as in Central Asia, are still experiencing an increase in their youth population,

BOX 5.1 Impacts of Low-Skilled Migration on Educational Attainment in Origin Countries: Theory and Evidence

The impact of low-skilled emigration and remittances on educational attainment back in the home country is complex and multichanneled. Low-skilled migration can affect human capital investment in multiple ways. First, temporary migration may positively affect investment in education by relaxing liquidity constraints to invest in education through remittances received. On the one hand, the additional household income from remittances received may also reduce the necessity to engage in child labor, therefore freeing up time for school attendance (Acosta 2011; Jaupart 2019). This income effect can improve educational outcomes among children left behind. On the other hand, the absence of an adult household member may increase the necessity for young members to participate in household or market work, disrupting family life in a manner that hinders children's academic progress (Amuedo-Dorantes, Georges, and Pozo 2010). Finally, low-skilled emigration opportunities may also affect incentives to invest in education at home: as low-skilled emigration opportunities increase the relative returns to lower skill levels, they may reduce incentives to invest in education (McKenzie and Rapoport 2011). Given these multiple and conflicting effects, the net effects of low-skilled emigration on human capital in the origin country are ambiguous and context dependent (Bossavie and Özden 2023). Given the multiple channels at play, the effect of low-skilled emigration and children's human capital and development is a priori ambiguous.

Estimated impacts for Europe and Central Asia are mixed, heterogeneous, and context specific. Positive effects of parental migration on children's educational attainment have been reported in the context of Tajikistan, especially for boys of all ages (Jaupart 2019). The simultaneous decline in the number of hours worked by young boys suggests that the effects are driven by the improved economic situation of migrant households and the reduced need for child labor. In the Kyrgyz Republic, however, migrant households do not spend more on education than nonmigrant households, and having an international migrant has a small negative effect on the likelihood of having children ages 14–18 enrolled in education (Akmoldoev and Budaichieva 2012; Kroeger and Anderson 2014). In the Kyrgyz Republic, Tajikistan, and Uzbekistan, descriptive evidence suggests that youth in high-migration regions tend to forgo professional education in their origin country in the presence of low-skilled migration opportunities (Abdulloev, Epstein, and Gang 2020). In Armenia, it has been reported that remittance-receiving households spend less on the education of their children (Grigorian and Melkonyan 2011). In Albania and Moldova, parental migration has been reported to result in poorer school performance, decreased attendance, and declining graduation rates (Giannelli and Mangiavacchi 2010; Salah 2008). Available evidence, however, is mostly descriptive and suggestive, and more rigorous studies are needed to establish a causal link between low-skilled migration opportunities and investment in human capital in countries of origin.

resulting in a large inflow of youth into the labor market every year. However, the youth bulge has put pressure on domestic labor markets because labor demand in sending countries has struggled to keep up with an increasingly young labor force. In this context, emigration has played a key role in alleviating pressure on domestic labor markets by providing employment opportunities to a significant share of the growing population in sending countries, especially among youth, who are overrepresented among low-skilled labor migrants (refer to the "Multiple Facets of Low-Skilled Migration and Its Linkages to Countries' Development Paths" section). Because low-skilled workers tend to be abundant in those contexts in comparison with high-skilled migrants, policy makers tend to be less concerned about larger impacts on the productivity of the broader economy.

Well-managed low-skilled migration can help fill labor shortages in destination countries, especially in occupations and sectors in which the native-born population is less willing to engage. Those labor shortages typically exist in sectors and occupations characterized by low pay and difficult working conditions in which the native-born population is unwilling to engage. This is, for example, the case with the agricultural and construction sectors, to which a large share of low-skilled migrants, especially temporary or seasonal ones, are directed. For example, EU destination countries such as Greece have relied extensively on low-skilled migrant labor from lower-income countries in ECA, such as Albania, since the 1990s. Similarly, the construction sector in Russia, characterized by low wages and hazardous working conditions, has heavily relied on low-skilled migration from Central Asian countries and the Caucasus.

In countries of origin in which the working-age population is shrinking, however, lower-skilled emigration may exacerbate labor shortages, especially in lagging regions. In Eastern European economies with an aging population, such as Romania, labor shortages seem to have taken place between 2002 and 2011 in certain sectors such as hospitality. Also, although the supply of low- and mid-level workers in other sectors such as construction was not systematically reduced across Romania, certain regions with some of the largest emigration rates (for example, Hunedoara, Vrancea) experienced significant drops in the number of blue-collar workers per capita (refer to figure 5.13). Overall, although emigration might have increased vacancies per worker (and per unemployed) in specific counties and sectors, particularly those requiring lower skills, strong evidence of improved local labor market conditions because of emigration, especially in lagging subregions, is not observed.

FIGURE 5.13

Net migration and labor supply, construction sector, Romanian counties

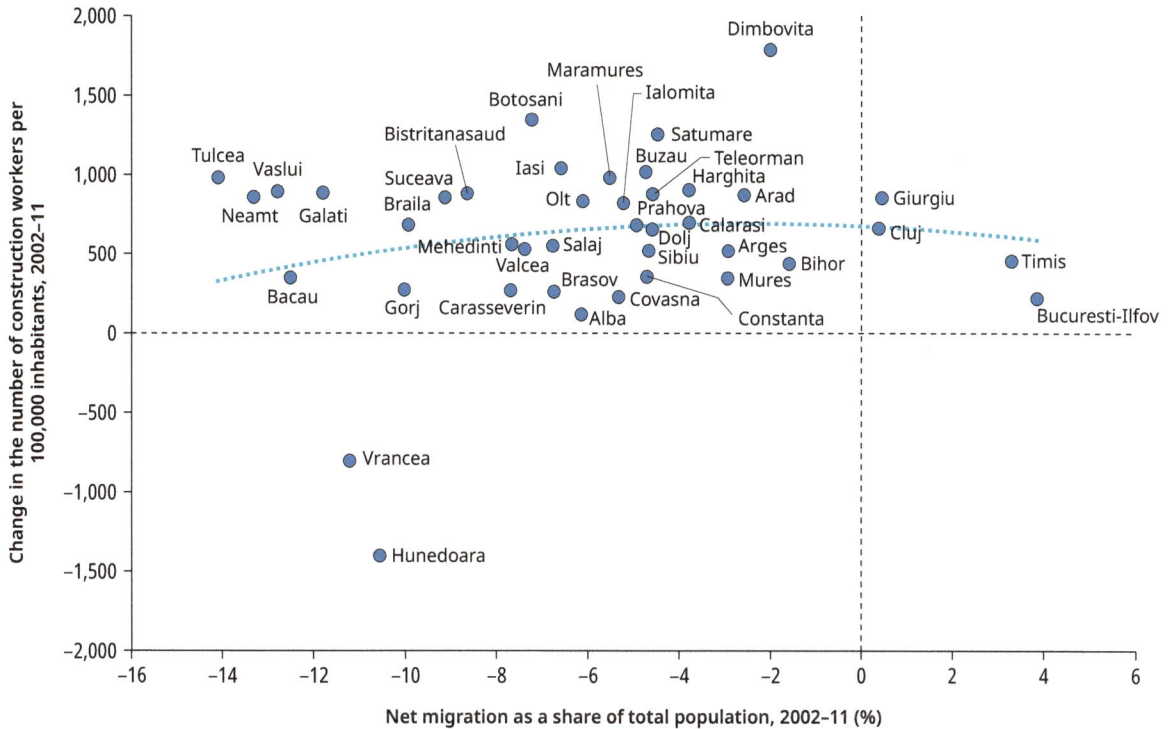

Sources: 2002 and 2011 Romania censuses, Minnesota Population Center Integrated Public Use Microdata Series (https://pop.umn.edu /projects/ipums-i) 2019.
Note: Net migration is defined as the cumulative number of immigrants (arrivals) minus the cumulative number of emigrants (departures) from 2002 to 2011 as a percentage of the initial population in each region. The blue dotted line represents the estimated nonlinear between the x-axis and y-axis variables.

Low-skilled emigration and remittances can also affect the economic activities of household members left behind in countries of origin. Overall, available evidence for ECA has reported a negative and gender-specific association between low-skilled emigration and the economic participation of female household members left behind. The most likely mechanism is a decrease in the incentives to work and higher reservation wages due to remittances received (income effect). However, more rigorous causal studies are needed to establish a causal link and generalize those findings (refer to box 5.2 for a more detailed discussion). Low-skilled emigration may also affect the type of economic activities carried out by members left behind in their countries of origin. Such effects seem to vary over time, depending on whether the migration episode is ongoing or has already ended. The migration of a household member has been shown to increase

BOX 5.2 Theory and Evidence on the Impacts of Temporary Migration on the Economic Activities of Household Members Left Behind

The departure of one economically active household member has a theoretically ambiguous effect on the labor supply of members left behind. Temporary migration by a household member can affect the economic activities of members left behind through two main channels, with opposite effects on labor supply. First, an income effect may increase total household income through remittances. According to the standard neoclassical model of optimal labor leisure allocation (Killingsworth 1983), the increase in household disposable income due to remittances can raise the reservation wage of adult family members left behind (Acosta, Lartey, and Mandelman 2009; Adams 2011). Presumably, the income effect may disproportionately affect females, given their weaker attachment to the labor market in low- and middle-income countries in the region. Second, the receipt of remittances is contemporaneous with the absence of working-age migrant household members, which may induce changes in the labor supply of remaining members to compensate for the forgone income or to defray migration-related expenses (Amuedo-Dorantes and Pozo 2006). These two channels presumably have opposite effects. As a result, temporary migration's effect on the labor supply of remaining household members is theoretically ambiguous.

A negative association between emigration and labor force participation of household members left behind has been reported in some origin countries in Europe and Central Asia (ECA), mostly for females. Figure B5.2.1 shows that the employment of both males and females is lower in households that have an international migrant in Albania, Armenia, and Uzbekistan, whereas employment rates in nonmigrant and migrant households are similar in the Kyrgyz Republic. In Armenia, members of households receiving remittances from abroad have been shown to work fewer hours (Grigorian and Melkonyan 2011). In the Kyrgyz Republic and Uzbekistan, a negative association between outmigration and labor supply of both males and females at the intensive and extensive margins has been reported (Bossavie and Garrote-Sánchez 2022; Justino and Shemyakina 2012; Seitz 2019). A negative and significant relationship between migration and the labor force participation of females left behind has been also reported in Georgia, Kosovo, and North Macedonia (Atoyan and Rahman 2017; Berulava 2019; Petreski 2019; Rudi 2014).

This descriptive evidence, however, cannot be interpreted as causal, and more evidence is needed to establish a causal link. The overall negative association between low-skilled emigration and the economic activity of members left behind may be driven by compositional change due to the departure from the household of an economically active adult member. Throughout the available literature, rigorous evidence on the causal effects of emigration on the labor force participation and employment of members left behind in ECA appears to be available only for Albania and Tajikistan (Mendola and Carletto 2012; Murakami, Yamada, and Sioson 2021). In Albania, negative impacts on labor market activities have been reported for females but not males. In Tajikistan, a recent causal analysis shows that sending

Continued

BOX 5.2 Theory and Evidence on the Impacts of Temporary Migration on the Economic Activities of Household Members Left Behind *(Continued)*

migrants abroad reduces the labor supply of the left-behind members by 5.4 percentage points and receiving remittances reduces it by 10.2 percentage points (Murakami, Yamada, and Sioson 2021). These findings suggest that the reservation wage effect of having a migrant member and receiving remittances surpasses other positive effects they might have in the Tajik context.

FIGURE B5.2.1

Employment rate of adults ages 15–64 in households with or without a member currently abroad

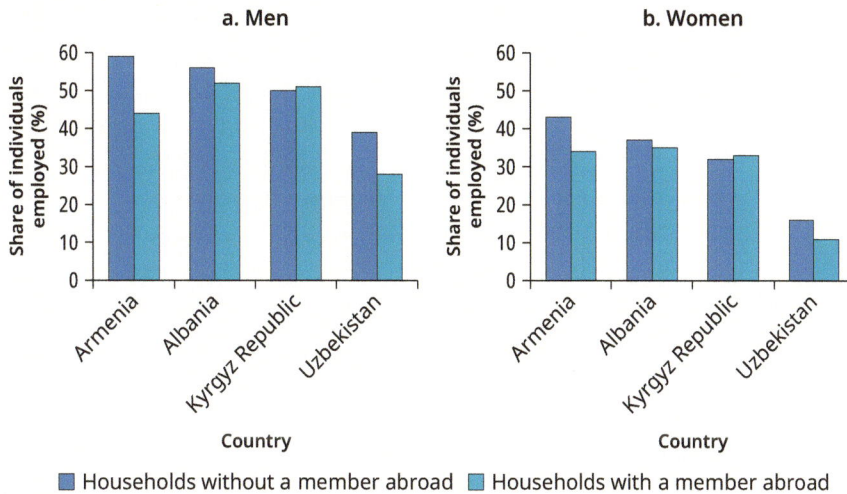

Sources: Armenia: 2018 Labor Force Survey (https://armstat.am/en/?nid=212); Albania: Demographic and Health Survey 2017–2018 (INSTAT, IPH, and ICF 2018); Uzbekistan: Listening to the Citizens of Uzbekistan (L2CU) survey (https://www.worldbank.org/en/country/uzbekistan/brief /l2cu); the Kyrgyz Republic: Listening to the Citizens of the Kyrgyz Republic survey (https://www .worldbank.org/en/country/kyrgyzrepublic/brief/l2kgz#:~:text=Listening%20to%20the%20 Kyrgyz%20Republic%20(L2KGZ)%20is%20a%20monthly%20panel,regions%20of%20the%20 Kyrgyz%20Republic).

the choice of female household members to be unpaid family workers during the migration episode of a male member in Albania and the Kyrgyz Republic (Karymshakov and Sulaimanova 2017; Mendola and Carletto 2012). In contrast, once the migration episodes end, women in households with a return migrant are more likely to engage in entrepreneurship, as evidenced in Albania (Mendola and Carletto 2012; Saurav 2017).[4] More broadly, evidence from some ECA countries, such as Albania, suggests that rural households use low-skilled migration as a pathway out of agricultural work (Miluka et al. 2010).

Low-skilled emigration has been associated with increased investment and entrepreneurship in some countries of origin, mainly through the return of entrepreneurial migrants. Seeking self-employment and entrepreneurship opportunities after returning to the origin country has been argued to be among the main drivers of temporary migration: in the presence of credit constraints at home, temporary migration allows individuals to accumulate savings faster and to engage in self-employment activities when they return (Bossavie et al. 2021; Djajić 2010; Dustmann and Kirchkamp 2002; Rapoport 2002). Evidence from several ECA countries shows that return migrants are more likely to become entrepreneurs than nonmigrants. After accounting for selection in emigration and return migration in Albania, return migrants are more likely to become entrepreneurs upon return (Piracha and Vadean 2010). In Moldova, low-skilled workers who achieve their migration objectives are more likely to become entrepreneurs upon return as opposed to being wage employed (Pogorevici 2019). Self-employment activities started by return migrants have also been shown to be more successful and to generate more jobs for the local economy in Albania (Kilic et al. 2009; Piracha and Vadean 2010). In some contexts, such as in the Kyrgyz Republic, however, self-employment after the return of migrants has been shown to be a temporary choice before finding wage employment (Bruck et al. 2018).

The ability of temporary migrants to start businesses at home (after they return) depends on their migration experience. Employment outcomes after return are linked to the parameters and outcomes of the migration episode, including migration costs, wages abroad, and duration of stay (Bossavie et al. 2021; Dustmann and Görlach 2016). Savings and duration of stay have indeed been shown to be positively associated with self-employment after return in Albania (Kilic et al. 2009; Piracha and Vadean 2010). Entrepreneurship after the return has also been linked to the reasons for returning. In Albania, the fact that migration was planned as temporary ex ante as opposed to resulting from an unexpected return has been shown to increase the likelihood of becoming an entrepreneur after return (Gubert and Nordman 2011; Piracha and Vadean 2010). Similarly, in Moldova, those who have a disappointing migration experience or who migrate illegally are less likely to become entrepreneurs upon return (Borodak and Piracha 2011). Intentions to remigrate are also negatively associated with the likelihood of becoming an entrepreneur after returning to Albania (Piracha and Vadean 2010).

Barriers, Vulnerabilities, and Costs Faced by Low-Skilled Migrants along Their Journey

Before Departure

Predeparture circumstances have repercussions on low-skilled migrants' vulnerability and outcomes throughout the migration life cycle. Although the migration life cycle can be divided into stages for policy discussion, as discussed in chapter 1, all stages are interdependent. Outcomes and policy parameters at one stage of the migration life cycle—for example, before departure—have dynamic repercussions on the entire migration experience and even after return to the home country (Bossavie et al. 2021). For instance, the vulnerability and outcomes of migrants while abroad are affected by predeparture policies in place in origin countries.

Formal sources of information about migration opportunities remain underdeveloped in most countries of origin of low-skilled migrants in ECA. Structured regulation of information about low-skilled migration is currently lacking in most countries of origin. Government entities typically play a marginal role in advertising low-skilled migration opportunities. In some countries, private agencies specializing in supporting domestic workers' access to low-skilled migration opportunities are in place. However, their scale of operation and the number of prospective migrants they serve is still very limited compared with the total flow of low-skilled migrants who go abroad every year. In some cases, public employment agencies also advertise migration opportunities abroad, but the number of positions is also small compared with migration flows, and offices tend to be concentrated in urban areas.

Social networks remain a key source of information about migration processes, costs, and benefits. According to results from a recent survey in the Kyrgyz Republic carried out by the Word Bank (the Kyrgyz Migration Survey), close to four of five prospective Kyrgyz migrants obtain the necessary information about the migration process through their network of relatives and friends, especially those living abroad. Similarly, two-thirds of Kyrgyz migrants choose their country of destination on the basis of the presence of a relative or friend. In non-ECA contexts, the reliance on social networks for migration information has been shown to lead to biased information about migration opportunities and their associated economic and personal costs abroad (Bah and Batista 2020; Bossavie et al. 2021; McKenzie, Gibson, and Stillman 2013; Seshan and Zubrickas 2017; Shrestha 2020). In the ECA context, the Kyrgyz Migration Survey shows that working-age individuals in the Kyrgyz Republic systematically overestimate wages to be earned abroad by more than 30 percent (refer to figure 5.14). The reliance on social

FIGURE 5.14

Distribution of monthly wages expected before departure by migrants from Kyrgyz Republic compared with actual wages earned abroad

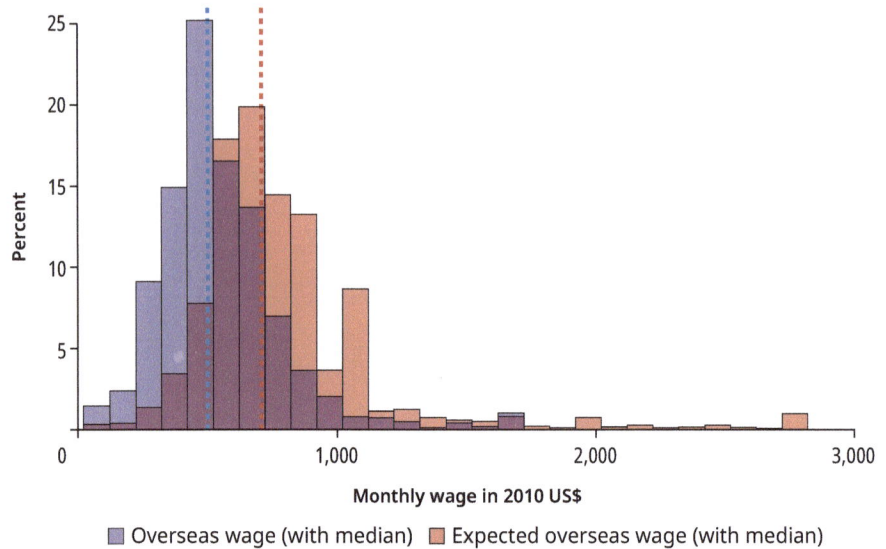

Monthly wage in 2010 US$

■ Overseas wage (with median)　■ Expected overseas wage (with median)

Source: Kyrgyz Migration Survey 2022/23, World Bank.
Note: Purple shading represents overlap between the histogram for overseas wages and the histogram for expected overseas wages. Vertical dashed lines represent median values.

networks for migration opportunities may also contribute to the concentration of migrants in specific occupations in destination countries (Beaman 2012; Patel and Vella 2013).

Low-skilled migrants typically lack prior experience and adequate skills for the most in-demand jobs in destination countries. Mismatches between demand at destination and the skill of prospective migrants are partly due to occupational mobility upon migration. For migrants from the Kyrgyz Republic, the Kyrgyz Migration Survey shows that most migrants were employed in a different occupation and sector before departure compared with during the migration episode and that only 2 percent of migrants took skills training before departure. A large portion of male migrants from Central Asia have an agricultural background but are hired as construction workers in Russia. In other sectors, this lack of training often results in an occupational downgrade (Bossavie and Garrote-Sánchez 2022). Likewise in the Caucasus countries, such as in Armenia, for example, nearly all migrants (98 percent) leave for their destination country without any specific training to prepare them for living abroad (ETF 2013).

Beyond technical skills, low-skilled migrants often lack overall preparedness before going abroad. As evidenced in the "Multiple Facets of Low-Skilled Migration and Its Linkages to Countries' Development Paths" section, low-skilled prospective migrants from ECA typically come from rural and more disadvantaged backgrounds. As a result, they often lack a full and accurate understanding of migration opportunities because of limited access to information. In many instances, migrants are unaware of their full labor rights and benefits, given the specificities of legislation in destination countries. Given their typically low educational attainment, they often have been shown to have limited levels of financial literacy, which is critical to managing savings abroad and taking better advantage of their migration experience.

Informal migration and employment arrangements at destination also contribute to vulnerability. Many low-skilled migrants, especially temporary migrants, leave without securing an employment contract with an employer abroad, and in some cases work without one once at destination: most temporary migrants from Armenia and the Kyrgyz Republic did not have a contract with a Russian employer before migrating to Russia. In Central Asia, the widespread provisions for visa-free travel and the geographical proximity between countries in the region stimulate spontaneous, temporary, and circular migration, which often takes place through informal arrangements. Although they may arrive in the host country legally, migrants are often employed informally, without an employment contract. That leaves them without social protection and the state without tax revenue from their work.

Undocumented migration further increases vulnerability. Part of low-skilled migration flows within ECA are not only informal but also undocumented. In 2022, around 330,000 irregular border crossings were detected at the European Union's external border, according to preliminary calculations. This is the highest number since 2016 and an increase of 64 percent from the previous year. In 2022, close to half of these irregular entries took place through the Western Balkans: in that year, 145,600 irregular border crossings were reported on the Western Balkans route, an increase of 136 percent from 2021. In Russia, it was estimated that about 2 million long-term migrants in the country were undocumented (Chudinovskin 2021).

During Migration

Low-skilled migration from Central Asia, the Caucasus, and the Western Balkans is highly concentrated in one or two destinations. Four-fifths of Georgian, Kyrgyz, and Tajik emigrants and two-thirds of Armenian emigrants live in a single destination in ECA—namely, Russia. In the Kyrgyz Republic, the remaining 15 percent of migrants settle in Kazakhstan, whose economic cycles are also closely aligned with those of Russia. In the Western Balkans, 87 percent of low-skilled emigration from Albania goes to either Greece or Italy (Cinque and Poggi 2024). The concentration of low-skilled migration in one single destination is even more pronounced among temporary migrants: about 95 percent of temporary migrants from Armenia and the Kyrgyz Republic go and work in Russia. In Albania, 70 percent of return migrants who had migrated temporarily went to Greece. Migration from Kazakhstan and Uzbekistan is slightly more diversified, although still highly concentrated, with 64 percent of Kazaks and 58 percent of Uzbeks living in Russia. In contrast, low-skilled emigration from the Central EU is more diversified in terms of destination countries within ECA.

This lack of diversification exposes low-skilled migrants and countries of origin to economic shocks in the destination country. The demand for labor in Russia, one of the two main destinations of low-skilled migrants in ECA, is highly tied to its economic fluctuations. There is a very strong and statistically significant correlation (.76) between GDP growth in Russia and the number of yearly visas offered for foreign employment, which exhibits significant fluctuations over time (refer to figure 5.15). As a result,

FIGURE 5.15

Macroeconomic fluctuations in the Russian Federation and demand for foreign labor

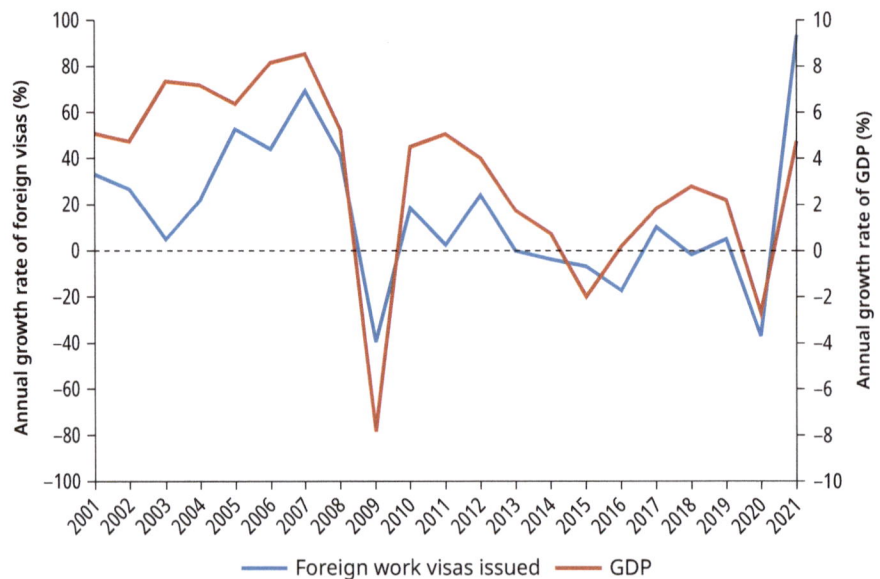

Sources: World Economic Outlook database, World Bank (https://www.imf.org/en/Publications/SPROLLs /world-economic-outlook-databases#sort=%40imfdate%20descending); International Monetary Fund; and Russian Federal Migration Service (http://archive.government.ru/eng/power/247/).
Note: The blue line plots the annual growth rate in migration visas issued by Russia from 2001 to 2021. The red line plots the annual growth rate of GDP in Russia over the same period. Migration visas include both work permits and licenses issued in Russia for working purposes. GDP = gross domestic product.

low-skilled migrants, their families, and their sending economies, especially if emigration is widespread, are highly exposed to economic fluctuations in Russia. Low-skilled migrants from Central Asia also work in Kazakhstan, whose economic cycles are highly aligned with those of Russia, reinforcing exposure to economic volatility.

Low-skilled migrants are concentrated in a few sectors of activity where demand is volatile, further exposing them to shocks. Globally, migrant workers have been shown to be concentrated in occupations more sensitive to business cycle fluctuations (Dustmann, Glitz, and Vogel 2010; Orrenius and Zavodny 2010). Likewise, low-skilled temporary or seasonal migrants from the Caucasus and Central Asia are heavily concentrated in specific sectors of activity in destination countries, especially in the construction and tourism sectors, which are both procyclical. More than three-quarters of Armenian temporary migrants in Russia work in the construction sector and, to a smaller extent, the tourism sector. About half of Kyrgyz male migrants work in construction and half of female migrants work in the hospitality sector. Longer-term low-skilled migrants from ECA to the European Union are more evenly distributed across employment sectors but are still more likely to be employed in the construction or tourism sectors. Low-skilled immigrants from ECA are also disproportionately concentrated in the accommodation and food service sectors: more than 10 percent of low-skilled migrants from ECA are employed in the sector, compared with only about 5 percent of native-born workers and high-skilled migrants from ECA.

Low-skilled migrants' exposure to shocks is exacerbated by their contractual arrangements, because they often hold temporary employment contracts. Low-skilled migrant workers in the European Union are much more likely to hold temporary employment contracts than native-born workers in receiving countries or high-skilled migrants (Fasani and Mazza 2020). These contractual arrangements further expose low-skilled migrants to negative shocks: given the lower firing costs associated with temporary contracts, fixed-term workers are typically the first to be laid off when negative shocks hit firms or sectors (Blanchard and Landier 2002; Boeri and Garibaldi 2007). This has been shown specifically for migrant workers in the context of the COVID-19 pandemic (Fasani and Mazza 2023).

Low-skilled migrants with informal employment arrangements have little to no access to social protection to mitigate the impact of shocks. Informal employment arrangements are common among low-skilled migrants, preventing them from accessing formal social protection systems in their destination country. Low-skilled migrants from ECA are more often informally employed than both high-skilled migrants and native-born workers in destination countries. For example, more than two-thirds of

Kyrgyz emigrants in Russia and Kazakhstan had a verbal contract or other informal arrangement with their employer as opposed to any written contract as required by national labor laws. These types of agreements, which are more prevalent among migrants with low education levels, limit the labor protection of workers, which is particularly harmful when large negative shocks hit the economy. In 2018, only a minority of emigrants from the Kyrgyz Republic benefited from social security (13 percent) or paid leave (18 percent) or had furlough mechanisms of mandatory temporary leave instead of layoffs (12 percent). This contrasts with a close to universal access to these employment benefits in the Kyrgyz Republic (93 percent, 89 percent, and 87 percent, respectively). These vulnerabilities have been brought to light by two recent shocks, which exposed both the insufficiencies of current migration systems and the need for policy reforms to reduce low-skilled migrants' vulnerability to shocks and mitigate their impacts (refer to box 5.3 and annex 5A for more details).

BOX 5.3 Vulnerability or Resilience of Low-Skilled Migration: Lessons from Two Recent Shocks

Low-skilled migration in Europe and Central Asia (ECA) has been successively hit by the COVID-19 pandemic and spillovers from Russia's invasion of Ukraine, revealing its high exposure to shocks and current migration systems' shortcomings. Both shocks heavily affected labor migration from the perspective of origin and destination countries. These two shocks, however, somewhat differed in nature: whereas COVID-19 affected both origin and destination countries in a simultaneous and similar way, Russia's invasion of Ukraine disproportionately affected the economic situation of one of the main destinations of low-skilled migrants in ECA, Russia. Examining the impacts of each of these two shocks thus allows us to gain somewhat different insights into the exposure of low-skilled migration to negative shocks and their impacts on migrants, their families, and the home economy (refer to annex 5A for more details).

COVID-19 brought to light several inefficiencies and vulnerabilities associated with low-skilled migration, most of which already existed before the pandemic. Although a subset of the challenges faced by low-skilled migrants in ECA during COVID-19 were specific to the pandemic, most of these already existed before it and were brought to light by it. COVID-19 exposed the vulnerabilities faced by low-skilled migrants at all stages of the migration life cycle (Bossavie and

Continued

BOX 5.3 Vulnerability or Resilience of Low-Skilled Migration: Lessons from Two Recent Shocks *(Continued)*

Garrote-Sánchez 2022). For example, it revealed migrants' high vulnerability to job loss in destination countries, often driven by informal migration and employment arrangements, together with no or limited access to social protection programs and employment benefits, especially among temporary or seasonal migrants. The pandemic has also exposed the need for support among migrants who unexpectedly returned home, who have been shown to often be placed in vulnerable situations (refer to annex 5A for more details). More broadly, it highlighted the lack of maturity of low-skilled migration systems, especially in protecting migrants against shocks.

The spillovers from Russia's invasion of Ukraine revealed the exposure of low-skilled migrants and home economies to shocks affecting one single destination. First, they affected the demand for migrant labor from Central Asia and the Caucasus, resulting in a drop in new migration outflows and a sharp increase in unplanned returns, at least in the short run. Second, they affected the employment outcomes of migrants already at their destination, resulting in job and income loss. Finally, they affected remittances and the gains from the migration experience through large fluctuations in the destination country currency. These impacts were most pronounced for origin countries such as the Kyrgyz Republic, where close to 95 percent of migrants go to Russia, revealing the high exposure of migrants and the home economy to shocks in Russia. In contrast, in origin countries where migration flows are more diversified, such as Uzbekistan, the response of migration flows and remittances to the economic situation in Russia was smaller.

The vulnerabilities and inefficiencies identified during these shocks can be used as an opportunity to strengthen migration systems. These two successive large shocks brought attention to the need to develop or strengthen programs or policies that reduce migrants' vulnerability to shocks and mitigate the impacts of future shocks that may affect labor migration and remittances. These programs or policies include, for example, development of stronger social protection systems for migrants, the need to diversify destination countries through new bilateral agreements and upskilling, and support for the reintegration of return migrants, especially those who unexpectedly return to their home country before completion of their migration plans.

Seasonal and circular migrants are especially vulnerable and fall through the cracks of traditional social protection systems. Social protection for these workers, if received at all, is typically limited to some work injury compensation or health benefits, and it almost never includes unemployment assistance (Moroz, Shrestha, and Testaverde 2020). EU destination countries such as Greece and Spain offer seasonal workers unemployment benefits, but those are linked to the trajectory of previous contributions, so seasonal migrant workers are eligible for less. Seasonal migrants in France and Germany contribute to social security, including unemployment and retirement programs, while not being able to meet the minimum periods to access the services and having limited access to social protection as a result. This creates disincentives to making financial contributions for these services (Brickenstein 2015). Regarding unemployment benefits, resident requirements are very stringent in France, and seasonal workers are excluded entirely from unemployment assistance. In Italy, non-EU seasonal workers are excluded (Testaverde and Pavilon 2022). A job loss outbreak for these categories of migrants therefore means loss of income for consumption, remittances home, and repayment of loans often taken out to finance migration. Job loss may even result in loss of housing because accommodations are often provided by employers.

Low-skilled temporary migrants also have limited access to social protection programs back in their home country. In Armenia, migrant households are less likely to be eligible for the main cash transfer program in the country (Family Benefit Program) because the targeting formula used to determine eligibility assigns a lower score for every member absent from the household. In addition, Armenian migrants are not eligible for unemployment benefits and other earnings-related social insurance benefits in the origin country. Furthermore, Armenian international temporary migrants are often not covered by health insurance, increasing their vulnerability to health shocks such as evidenced during the COVID-19 pandemic (Honorati, Kerschbaumer, and Yi 2019).

In addition to increasing vulnerability, informal migration arrangements may also significantly worsen migration outcomes. Studies outside ECA have evidenced a strong and positive association between legal arrangements for temporary migration and a range of migration outcomes. In the context of temporary migration from the Arab Republic of Egypt to the Persian Gulf, it has been shown that undocumented low-skilled migrants experience a large wage penalty abroad compared with documented migrants (El Mallakh and Wahba 2021). Undocumented migrants also experience significantly lower savings abroad, shorter migration duration, lower incidence of remitting, and lower ranked occupations abroad, but also lower earnings after returning to their home country. Although the contrast between documented and undocumented migrants is stark, further studies in ECA are needed to generalize those findings.

Remittances to ECA countries are often sent through informal channels, which may limit their productive use and associated development impacts. Large shares of remittances in ECA are still sent through informal channels, mostly because of a lack of trust, high transaction costs, low banking among receivers, and a related lack of information and financial education (World Bank 2018). Remittances sent through informal channels not only increase the risks and make the flows more difficult to monitor, but they also limit the investment options of the receivers, because they are not able to save and borrow money in the formal financial system (OECD 2022).

After Return

Many low-skilled migrants from ECA ultimately return home, either temporarily or permanently, where they can also be exposed to risks, vulnerabilities, and inefficiencies. In the context of low-skilled migration from ECA, returns are often an integral part of the migration life cycle because low-skilled migration is often seasonal or temporary. In this context, the vulnerabilities and risks faced by low-skilled migrants can extend to the return stage. These vulnerabilities and risks are shaped by the migration experience abroad, the circumstances of return, and the related intentions to remigrate in the short run (Bossavie and Özden 2023). The return stage is also critical for sending countries and temporary migrants to reap the full benefits of the migration experience, beyond remittances sent during the migration episode.

Challenges faced by migrants and countries of origin at the return stage depend on the circumstances of a migrant's return. The return of low-skilled migrants to their home countries in ECA can be either planned or unplanned. It can be planned, for example, if low-skilled migrants seek seasonal employment abroad for one part of the year before returning to the sending country for the rest of the year. The return may also be planned in the case of longer-term temporary migration, when low-skilled migrants plan to go abroad for a given period to accumulate human and financial capital before returning to their home country. Finally, a migrant's return home may not have been planned at all. Migrants may originally have planned to stay permanently abroad but ultimately return or return earlier than they had originally planned. These unanticipated returns can be voluntary because of a change in circumstances in the home or destination country, for example, in the case of a large economic shock such as COVID-19, or forced because of low-skilled migration regulations in destination countries.

Low-skilled migrants who unexpectedly return experience more acute vulnerabilities and risks. Unexpected or forced returns are especially common in the context of low-skilled temporary migration, because low-skilled migrants are greatly exposed to shocks in destination countries. Temporary migrants who unexpectedly return have paid upfront costs to go abroad (sometimes by taking loans), cannot stay abroad and earn as much income as expected, and face potential unemployment at home. Unexpected returns are especially problematic in the context of large negative shocks inducing large return flows, such as the COVID-19 pandemic, given the limited absorbing capacity of labor markets in sending countries. In the Kyrgyz Republic, for example, families with a member who unexpectedly returned from abroad during the COVID-19 pandemic were significantly more likely to report using strategies such as cutting food spending to cope with the unexpected loss of income (Bossavie and Garrote-Sánchez 2022).

In the case of voluntary returns, there is scope to enhance the benefits of the migration experience for returnees and the country of origin. Evidence for some sending countries of low-skilled migrants in ECA—for example, in Central Asia—shows that low-skilled return migrants are more likely to be employed after return compared with before their departure (Bossavie and Bartl 2024). They are also more likely to be employed than nonmigrants. However, the same evidence shows that, overall, the benefits of the migration experience for productivity and wages after return, as measured by the earnings of returnees relative to nonmigrants, are lower for low-skilled migrants than for high-skilled migrants. This suggests that low-skilled return migrants who find employment in wage jobs back home are not able to take much advantage of their migration experience abroad, limiting the benefits of low-skilled return migration for sending countries. This may be partly driven by the fact that low-skilled return migrants are often employed in occupations back home that are very different from those in which they were employed in their destination country, as evidenced, for example, in Central Asia (Bossavie and Garrote-Sánchez 2022). In the context of seasonal or repeated migration, a key policy issue is being able to take advantage of previous migration experiences to increase the benefits and reduce the vulnerabilities encountered in the next migration episode. Another important challenge is how to incentivize economic activities among temporary returnees and take advantage of the migration experience in home labor markets.

Policy Recommendations

Strengthening Migration Systems and Institutional Frameworks

Strengthening institutional frameworks and systems for formal migration is the building block of more productive and resilient low-skilled migration. Despite the importance of low-skilled emigration for development, migration systems are still maturing in many origin countries. Reducing vulnerabilities and enhancing the benefits of low-skilled migration start with a general strengthening of migration systems and frameworks. Recent shocks such as the COVID-19 pandemic highlight the need to strengthen institutions, frameworks, and safe and legal migration from sending countries. Despite the large outflows of low-skilled migrants from low- and middle-income ECA countries and the large potential development impacts in those countries, there has been a lack of coherent, long-term migration policy in many sending countries beyond managing remittances.

Coordination between destination and sending countries is essential to strenghtening migration systems. By its very nature, migration involves a multiplicity of actors, including government entities in countries of destination and origin, private entities at origin such as recruitment agencies, employers at the destination, migrants themselves and their households, and, in some cases, other migrant-sending countries in the region. Migrants would highly benefit from further dialogue with the main receiving countries to increase their rights and enhance formal labor migration through regular formal contracts. Putting in place and implementing such arrangements may even require regional collaboration to ensure uniformity and avoid a race to the bottom (whereby sending countries compete by loosening regulations and migrant protection with the intention of making their migrant labor more attractive to foreign employers).

Multilateral and regional collaboration can be supported by several types of arrangements. The less binding type of multilateral arrangement is through the creation of regional forums and dialogue to foster knowledge exchange, strengthen technical capacity, and facilitate cooperation on migration policy among countries in the region. One example of such an initiative is the Migration and Remittance Peer-Assisted Learning Network project, carried out between 2009 and 2012 among Commonwealth of Independent States countries (refer to box 5.4).

Another, more binding form of multilateral collaboration is through the creation of regional economic unions that incorporate binding rules regarding low-skilled migration policies. One example of such an initiative is the Eurasian Economic Union (EaEU), which provides a unique platform to tackle

BOX 5.4 The Migration and Remittance Peer-Assisted Learning Network Project: An Example of a Regional Policy Platform to Foster Dialogue and Cooperation on Migration Policy in Europe and Central Asia

The Migration and Remittance Peer-Assisted Learning Network (MiRPAL) is one example of a regional migration initiative that brought together migration experts and practitioners from sending and receiving countries in Europe and Central Asia. The initiative was created in 2009 as the first cross-country policy forum and the first step in establishing the dialogue on migration policy in nine sending and receiving Commonwealth of Independent States countries (Armenia, Belarus, Kazakhstan, the Kyrgyz Republic, Moldova, the Russian Federation, Tajikistan, Ukraine, and Uzbekistan). The objective of the initiative was threefold: 1. demonstrate how a managed and regulated migration process can contribute to economic and social development, 2. offer advice to countries on how to manage the migration process in their counties, and 3. build and share knowledge on migration that could be applied to other parts of the world. The initiative provided technical assistance in developing country-specific action plans to improve migration management systems and serve as a road map for migration policies, institutions, and projects for governments and donors.

The initiative, organized with technical assistance from multilateral agencies such as the Department for International Development and the World Bank, led to a series of conferences and knowledge exchange events between the governments of sending and receiving countries. The knowledge exchanges and technical assistance provided as part of the project helped establish country-specific migration strategies and action plans that were approved by origin-country governments, for example, in the Kyrgyz Republic and Tajikistan. In Tajikistan, a new government migration service was established that specifically addresses labor migration issues. In Russia, MiRPAL's advocacy and knowledge-sharing work helped raise the visibility of migration in the public and policy discourses, and a new law on permits for migrants was adopted to tackle the issue of illegal migration. The law makes the issuance of work permits easier and more transparent.

the issue of migrants' rights between Central Asia and Russia multilaterally (refer to box 5.5). Beyond the Eurasian Economic Union, the Global Compact for Safe, Orderly, and Regular Migration, implemented under the auspices of the United Nations in 2018, presents a framework for comprehensive international cooperation on migrants and human mobility, contributing to the global governance and coordination of international migration policies. Origin countries that are not yet part of this treaty may benefit from signing it, following 164 other countries that have already signed, in parallel with bilateral agreements reached with main destination countries.

BOX 5.5 Eurasian Economic Union

The Eurasian Economic Union (EaEU) has promoted legal migration for some of the low-skilled migration corridors in Europe and Central Asia, primarily to the Russian Federation. The EaEU founding treaty approved in 2015 establishes the free movement of labor across member states—currently Armenia, Belarus, Kazakhstan, the Kyrgyz Republic, and Russia (Eurasian Economic Commission 2015). Migrants from member states also benefit from the recognition of foreign credentials, as well as de jure equal rights to social security benefits and emergency medical services, as do citizens of the host member state (Madiyev 2021). However, the EaEU enforcement mechanisms for migrants' rights remain weak, leading to gaps between de jure and de facto protection of legal rights and access to social services. The EaEU treaty also leaves room for countries to restrict migrants' access to the host labor market in cases "determined by this Treaty and the legislation of the Member States aimed at ensuring their national security (including in economic sectors of strategic importance) and public order" (Eurasian Economic Commission 2015, Article 97.2). The entry into force of the Eurasian Economic Union comes with an increasingly securitized migration rhetoric and policy in Kazakhstan and Russia. In Russia, the government approved a new regulation according to which migrants are forced to leave the country within five days after two administrative law violations (including traffic fines) or one migration law violation and can be banned from reentering the country for up to 10 years (Schenk 2018). In this context, challenges remain to enforce the protection of low-skilled migrants' rights in the main destination countries, and further collaboration and cooperation with governments are needed.

Bilateral labor agreements (BLAs) between origin and destination countries have been shown to be effective instruments to promote safe, legal, and productive migration. BLAs are essentially legal agreements between sending and receiving countries to ensure that migration takes place in accordance with agreed-on principles and procedures. They can have different objectives, but they often focus on promoting regular migration and protecting migrant rights and are often implemented in the context of temporary migration. These agreements, for example, fix the maximum quotas of manpower that can migrate temporarily between origin and destination each year and regulate important conditions that affect labor migrants' contract durations, renewal policies, minimum wages, and migration costs. They ensure continued access to foreign labor markets and opportunities to promote the protection and welfare of their workers for sending countries. Among receiving countries, they help achieve a flow of labor that meets the needs of employers and industrial sectors while allowing that flow to be managed and regulated.

BLAs can also increase the magnitude of migration flows from origin to destination countries where labor imbalances are identified. BLAs practically ensure the continued access of low-skilled migrants from selected origin countries to foreign labor markets and opportunities while helping to achieve a managed and regulated flow of labor that meets the needs of employers and industrial sectors in destination countries. By doing so, BLAs can drastically increase managed and regulated migration flows between sending and origin countries. One example of such a scheme in ECA is the Western Balkan Regulation, which opened Germany's labor market to nationals from the Western Balkans (box 5.6).

The design and implementation of some of the existing BLAs, however, need to be strengthened to achieve these objectives, especially to better protect labor migrants. There is often a lack of transparency in the bilateral negotiation process surrounding many of the agreements, which makes it difficult to work with destination countries on issues affecting migrants while in their jurisdiction. The general and sometimes vague objectives set out in some bilateral instruments also make it difficult to follow up on state obligations, and the secrecy of negotiations prevents legislatures and people from holding their governments accountable. In addition, BLAs can overlook fundamental issues in the protection of the rights of migrant workers and members of their families. In destination countries, there is

BOX 5.6 The Western Balkan Regulation between the Western Balkans and Germany

This policy allows citizens of Albania, Bosnia and Herzegovina, Kosovo, Montenegro, North Macedonia, and Serbia to enter Germany for employment without any formal qualification requirements, if they have a binding job offer. German employers must prove that they cannot find local workers for the positions and that the employment conditions meet a certain minimum standard.[a] Since the introduction of the Western Balkan Regulation, Germany has experienced an increase in legal migration as well as a significant drop in asylum applications. Although no causal impact can be established, it is highly plausible to assume that the regulation played a central role. About half of the contracts submitted for preapproval under the regulation in the years immediately following its introduction (2016–17) were for unskilled or low-skilled immigrants, which indicates that this may have opened up a channel for migration for a category of migrants who had limited options. Existing qualitative and quantitative evaluations of the first few years of the program overall show positive effects on labor market outcomes of migrants and on overall satisfaction with the migration experience (Bither and Ziebarth 2018; Brücker et al. 2020).

a. Nearly 60 percent of migrants from Uzbekistan have vocational education, 30 percent have upper-secondary education, 6 percent have secondary general education or below, and only about 4 percent have tertiary education.

also often no trace of government action to implement agreed-on provisions of the memoranda of understanding, such as strengthened workplace inspection procedures and increased awareness of workers' rights on the part of employers. Furthermore, a lack of implementation mechanisms and monitoring and evaluation practices often hinders the proper enforcement of BLAs. For example, practical enforcement of migrants' rights as part of the EaEU treaties remains weak. The implementation process of the Western Balkan Regulation suffered from a lack of coordination and a clear mandate. There were also bottlenecks in the application process, which created long wait times for visas to be approved. Furthermore, a lack of communication strategy for the economies of origin opened the door to misinformation and created uncertainty about the policy (OECD 2022).

Government to government (G2G) programs can guarantee formal labor migration and the protection of migrants' rights but require high administrative capacity. G2G programs use public intermediation to regulate the migrant recruitment process. They have been shown to promote formal migration channels and can greatly increase the benefits of migration for migrants, the home economy, and destination countries. G2G agreements for low-skilled migration have been shown to have multiple benefits: they can drastically reduce migration costs, improve information provision, and significantly enhance workers' protection and welfare at the destination. Such programs can also enhance access to migration opportunities among households that lack migration networks and provide avenues into new markets, both new destinations and new types of professions. They have, however, been of limited scale so far because of their high administrative and enforcement capacity requirements. Scaling them up requires significant investments in the sending country's administrative capacity, which can be a binding constraint for their further expansion.

Global Skill Partnerships (GSPs) can also be an effective policy tool to ensure legal, safe, and productive migration. In the context of GSP programs, also discussed in chapter 4, all actors—and, above all, the migrants themselves—benefit from fully legal migration pathways and guaranteed employment opportunities that facilitate greater migrant integration. This, in turn, is key to improving migrant productivity at destination and increases the benefits of emigration for the country of origin via remittances, human capital accumulation, and business networks and FDI. In this process, job-matching mechanisms included in GSP programs can help to ensure strong and productive worker-firm matches.

For circular migration, seasonal worker programs can be effective in formalizing flows, enhancing benefits for origin and destination countries, and protecting circular migrants. To reduce vulnerability and enhance the benefits of seasonal migration, seasonal employment programs in ECA could be further developed and strengthened. Several destination countries in the European Union implement seasonal worker programs, which have been harmonized at the EU level through the 2014 Seasonal Workers Directive (European Parliament and Council of the European Union 2014). However, many of these programs currently provide insufficient protection to seasonal workers, and their design could be altered to enhance the benefits of seasonal migration for all actors (Hooper and Le Coz 2020). In the other main destination countries of low-skilled migrants, such as Russia, these programs are not well developed. One example of good practice outside ECA is New Zealand's Recognized Seasonal Employer program, implemented with countries of origin in the Pacific Islands (box 5.7).[5]

Recent shocks revealed the need for countries of origin to diversify destinations to reduce the volatility of migration flows and remittances. Origin countries' governments can explore institutional frameworks such as BLAs, G2G arrangements, Global Skill Partnerships, and memoranda of understanding with new destinations with a potential labor demand given their demographic or labor market trends (for example, in Europe, the Republic of Korea, Malaysia, or the Persian Gulf). Outside ECA, the Philippines, a country with a long tradition of emigration and with a well-developed migration system, has diversified the number of destination countries over the years by being very active in negotiating new BLAs and by building a qualified workforce with credible credentials (Testaverde et al. 2017). In Armenia, the recent ratification of the EU Comprehensive

BOX 5.7 Example of Good Practices for Seasonal Migration Programs: The Recognized Seasonal Employer Program

The Recognized Seasonal Employer program sets a quota of seasonal migrants who can work in specific sectors in New Zealand each year, and it ensures that seasonal migrants receive the same minimum wage and worker rights as native-born workers through safeguard mechanisms built into the temporary migration programs. They are also offered formal employment contracts and access to social protection and other services in the destination country for the seasonal work period. To ensure compliance with the program's rules, destination country governments actively monitor employers' practices by conducting check-ins with both employers and employees (Doan, Dornan, and Edwards 2023). Such programs have been shown to produce large positive effects on migrant household income, consumption, savings, durable goods ownership, subjective standards of living, and even child schooling in countries of origin (Gibson and MacKenzie 2014).

and Enhanced Partnership Agreement (European Union 2018) can serve as a pivot to expand bilateral labor arrangements with EU member countries.

Migration can also be diversified in terms of occupations. Although the Eurasian Economic Union allows Central Asian migrants in Kazakhstan and Russia to work in all sectors, further cooperation might be needed with these countries to fully recognize foreign credentials. This, combined with the provision of information to migrants on the types of job opportunities available in destination countries and the provision of training to prospective migrants based on the demand for identified skills, can expand the employment opportunities available across sectors and professions.

Entering these newer markets and sectors would require diversifying the skill profile of prospective migrants. Destinations that offer higher wages and better protections for workers require additional skills, even for jobs in labor-intensive sectors such as agriculture. These skills include language knowledge and noncognitive skills such as teamwork and collaboration. For larger markets, such as Japan and Hong Kong SAR, China, where the demand for caregivers (childcare and care of elderly individuals) is growing, the supply of such professionals will have to increase, as will the supply of skills development services to train aspiring migrants to become caregivers. Line agencies responsible for managing labor migration may also need the capacity to take proactive measures, such as identifying potential demands for different types of workers from new and existing markets. This information will be critical for reorienting the skills development architecture and gaining a detailed understanding of the scope for foreign labor offered by those markets.

Registration systems for migrants are another key element of safe and more productive low-skilled migration. Detailed data on migrants are essential to providing services to this population, informing policy makers, and monitoring safe migration. Existing migration management in low- and middle-income countries in ECA, however, often lacks a centralized data system and intersectoral collaboration throughout the migration cycle—from migration plans and preparations, to support and protection during the migration experience, to the reintegration of return migrants. As a first step, countries of origin can centralize information from different governmental bodies—which requires interagency cooperation and data sharing—and create a unified registry of migrants. This registry could cover all prospective migrants, current migrants, and returnees, either at reception centers or at different points of exit or entry into the country. It can be a starting point for collecting data on the skills and labor market situation of prospective migrants so they can be referred to appropriate training or premigration programs. The registry can also serve as a building block to facilitate the reintegration of returnees and to create monitoring systems (IOM 2018). Such a unified registry of emigrants has recently been established in Uzbekistan, where return migrants can also register to benefit from support to entrepreneurship.

To complement administrative data, household surveys collecting detailed information on representative samples of current and past migrants can help better understand low-skilled migration and formulate evidence-based policies. This can be achieved by including detailed migration modules in nationally representative household surveys in sending countries. Compared with what is collected, those modules should gather much more granular information on household members currently abroad and on past migration experience. For example, many nationally representative household surveys in the Western Balkans, a region where the incidence of low-skilled emigration is one of the highest, do not collect any information on emigration beyond remittances received by the household. An alternative is to carry out stand-alone ad hoc migration surveys that oversample migrant households in sending countries and ask detailed questions on constraints, vulnerabilities, and outcomes before, during, and after migrating. A recent example of such surveys is the 2023 Kyrgyz Migration Survey implemented by the World Bank.

Institutional frameworks and migration systems must be complemented by policies and programs at each stage of the migration life cycle that address vulnerability and inefficiencies. The remainder of this section presents policies that can be implemented (predecision, predeparture, during migration, and after return) to increase both the resilience and the productivity of low-skilled migration from the ECA region. Although the division of the life cycle into these four stages categorizes low-skilled migration policies, it is critical to keep in mind that all these stages are interlinked. As a result, policies implemented at one stage of the migration life cycle will affect outcomes and vulnerabilities in other stages. This understanding is essential when designing and implementing policies to increase the returns and reduce the risks of low-skilled migration for migrants, their families, and their countries of origin.

Predeparture Policies

Strengthening the role of public institutions and regulatory frameworks in providing information about migration opportunities can help reduce information asymmetries and ensure more equitable access to migration. The role of public agencies as regulators—providing clearance for foreign job opportunities and formal employment contracts—and as intermediaries to complement private employment agencies in remote areas has proved successful in contexts outside ECA. For example, the G2G program between Bangladesh and Malaysia increased access to migration opportunities for those without social networks abroad (Mobarak, Sharif, and Shrestha 2023). Sending country governments could consider expanding the migration information services provided by public agencies and potentially partnering with private migration agencies to ensure the diffusion of migration-related information and opportunities to more remote areas, where most migrants come from. Low-skilled migration policy may also benefit from more centralized information management and diffusion regarding migration opportunities.

Improved labor market intermediation could be supported by a greater role of the public sector, together with quality insurance mechanisms for private recruitment agencies. G2G programs have been shown to be effective in matching prospective migrants to employers abroad in contexts outside ECA (Mobarak, Sharif, and Shrestha 2023). However, one potential issue of G2G programs is their scalability, because of the administrative capacity they require. In many countries of origin, private recruitment agencies and intermediaries still play a crucial role in matching prospective migrants to employers abroad. To prevent abuse and ensure quality intermediation, introducing a government rating program has been shown to cause recruitment agencies to invest in improving their reputation and better screening employers (Fernando and Singh forthcoming). The protection of migrants through the recruitment process by private agencies could also be guaranteed by developing regulatory frameworks in accordance with the Private Employment Agencies Convention, 1997 (No. 181; International Labour Organization 1997), of which some of the low- and middle-income sending countries in ECA are not yet signatories.

Interventions to support migrants' legal and financial literacy and overall preparedness can reduce vulnerability and enhance the benefits of the migration experience. Premigration orientation courses for prospective migrants can provide essential information on their legal rights—in particular, with respect to their labor contracts, financial literacy and planning targets for savings, access to services at destination, and foreign language and soft skills that enhance the migration experience. They can also include information on health and safety and travel procedures. One of the most comprehensive such programs is the Pre-Departure Education Program that the government of the Philippines runs for prospective migrants, which lasts four to six days. Although there has been little evaluation of such programs, the existing evidence suggests an overall positive impact (McKenzie and Yang 2015). For example, financial literacy programs for migrants and their household members have been shown to be effective in increasing financial knowledge, savings, and information about remittance-sending methods (Doi, McKenzie, and Zia 2014; Gibson, McKenzie, and Zia 2014).

Predeparture skills training programs could be modified and expanded to increase the returns to the migration experience for all actors. Training efforts for low-skilled migrants need to be expanded, as evidenced by the currently low share of migrants taking up training before migrating abroad in many countries of origin. Only a very small proportion of temporary migrants from Armenia and the Kyrgyz Republic report having taken any type of technical skills training before departure. The need for such training is enhanced by the fact that low-skilled migrants from Central Asia and the Caucasus often take up work in destination countries that differs from their occupation before migrating (Bossavie and Garrote-Sánchez 2022; Honorati, Kerschbaumer, and Yi 2019).

Monitoring and information systems on skills in demand by destination countries can help inform the design of training programs for migrants. Sending countries have a central role to play, in coordination with employment agencies, in providing up-to-date information about vacant jobs in growing sectors in destination countries. Accurate and up-to-date information, however, can only be generated through close coordination with destination countries where skills monitoring systems need to be in place. Sophisticated skills gap monitoring systems have been implemented in several destination countries outside ECA, such as Korea and Malaysia. These are used to determine the needs for migrant labor, which is then communicated to authorities in sending countries, typically in the context of G2G agreements to ensure prospective migrants are trained accordingly in origin countries (Cho et al. 2018; Mobarak, Sharif, and Shrestha 2023).

Coordination between origin and destination countries on skilling for migrant workers can be supported by Global Skill Partnership programs. One of the main objectives of these programs, discussed in more detail in chapter 4, is to ensure a better match between the skills brought by migrants, including low-skilled migrants, and demand from destination countries. The origin country benefits from investment in skills development and training for nonmigrant workers and increased incomes for citizens who emigrate. For the destination country, the costs of providing the technology and finance for training are recouped by the economic benefits brought through immigration. This is achieved by ensuring that the training follows the legal and technical requirements of the destination country. Coordination between origin and destination needs to primarily take place for the following components—harmonization of the training curriculum, recognition of certificates and degrees, apprenticeship opportunities, and public job-matching services. Germany has been active in this space, for example, with a pilot of the Kosovo–Germany skills partnership.

Given the increasing demand for skilled migrants, investments in tertiary education by countries of origin can also support diversification efforts and increase returns from the migration experience. As discussed in more detail in chapter 4, demand for high-skilled migrants is increasing in the main destination countries in ECA, especially in the European Union. The current chapter has also highlighted the need for diversification of migration flows for origin countries, which tend to be very highly concentrated in very few sectors and low-skilled occupations. Given these patterns, large investment in tertiary education could not only benefit productivity and growth in ECA origin countries but also raise the benefits of emigration for origin countries by increasing flows and monetary gains associated with the migration experience while reducing risks and vulnerability associated with a lack of diversification.

Policies and Programs while at Destination

Recent shocks highlighted the need to build social protection systems to mitigate the impact of negative shocks on labor migrants. Increasing formal employment channels will improve access to social protection systems, but specific arrangements need to be implemented beyond the legal status of employment, because currently even migrants with a legal contract have barely any social protection. Sending country governments could coordinate with destination countries—for example, within existing institutional frameworks such as the Eurasian Economic Union—to create systems to which migrant workers contribute, giving them access to unemployment benefits and health care on par with those of nationals from the country of residency. The portability of social rights is a feature developed in other economic unions such as the European Union—where migrants have access to health care, social welfare, or pensions, as does any citizen of the host country. Migrants from countries in the Eurasian Economic Union would greatly benefit from a similar framework as well, especially regarding the portability of pensions, which has been shown not only to enhance migrants' welfare but also to incentivize migrants to return home (Avato, Koettl, and Sabates-Wheeler 2010).

While formalizing low-skilled migration, there is a need to increase protection among migrants with informal employment arrangements. To help mitigate sudden job loss risks during migration, origin countries could work together with the private sector to develop an insurance product that could cover job loss risks during migration, especially against exogenous shocks (for example, unemployment insurance). In parallel, low-skilled emigrants could benefit from an increasing role for and capacity of consular sections (including the deployment of labor attachés in the main receiving countries) to provide more efficient and accessible legal counseling to any emigrant in need. Finally, welfare funds, facilitated by migrant registration systems, can ensure migrants can be reached by support systems needed while in the destination country.

Formalizing remittances through reductions in transfer costs can help channel remittances toward more productive use in countries of origin. Although remittances are private funds and individual receivers decide how to use them according to their own needs, several measures can encourage productive use. The first is by implementing measures to formalize remittance flows. An important part of this process is to reduce transfer costs. In the Western Balkans, for example, those costs remain above the target of Sustainable Development Goals (OECD 2022). As expected, several studies have shown that lowering transfer fees increases both the number of times migrants remit and the amount remitted in each transaction (Ambler et al. 2014; Aycinena et al. 2010). Origin countries in ECA could consider exempting remittance flows from fees to promote their transfer through financial systems.

Policies promoting greater financial inclusion among migrant households can also support this objective. Besides the high costs of sending and receiving remittances, formalizing these flows also requires that receivers have access to the financial sector. Studies have shown that having access to a formal bank account can significantly increase migrants' savings (Chin, Karkoviata, and Wilcox 2011). Formal banking is relatively low in the Western Balkans and Central Asia, which constrains the economic contribution of remittances to the overall economy. Financial inclusion among remittance receivers may be lower than the average in the population, especially because remittance receivers are often in rural areas. According to a report published by the Bank of Albania (2020), only 7.5 percent of families who receive remittances have a bank account. Electronic payment solutions to facilitate and formalize remittance transfers can create pathways to the formal financial sector for users. This approach has been tested in different contexts globally where the use of mobile phones for payments is common (OECD 2022). In the context of the broader strategy to digitalize payments for social protection and other programs, the governments of some sending countries, such as Armenia, could consider facilitating an expansion in the use of digital payment networks to support the safe transmission of remittances (Honorati, Kerschbaumer, and Yi 2019). Other countries of origin, such as those in the Western Balkans, have recently seen growth in the use of financial technology services and infrastructure in terms of internet and mobile broadband (Odorović et al. 2020).

Financial literacy programs to enhance migrants' knowledge of savings and investment opportunities are another step toward more productive use of remittances. To ensure a more productive use of remittances, households also need to have sufficient information about and understanding of the available options for investments and savings. Financial literacy programs could enhance migrant households' understanding of the available options for investments and savings. Financial instruments and training for remittance recipients have been used in many contexts to create an enabling environment for remittance investments. An example is the pilot program Greenback 2.0, which the World Bank has implemented in four Western Balkan economies. In contexts outside of ECA, financial literacy programs for migrants and their household members have been shown to be effective in increasing financial knowledge, savings, and knowledge of remittance-sending methods (Doi, McKenzie, and Zia 2014; Gibson, McKenzie, and Zia 2014). The results of these studies also highlight that it is important to train not only migrants but all their family members to maximize the positive impacts on financial awareness.

Postreturn Policies

Developing comprehensive reintegration plans and strategies for return migration in countries of origin is the foundation of more productive return migration. Reintegration programs for return migrants have existed for several years in several ECA countries, but they often lack a general government strategy and a centralized reintegration mechanism and suffer from very limited resources and outreach. They are often restricted to specific groups of return migrants, for example, those with negative migration experiences. There is, therefore, a need to develop comprehensive reintegration strategies that consider the diversity of return migration experiences. This includes whether the return was planned or unplanned, whether migrants intend to stay permanently in the origin country, and whether they aspire to find wage jobs or start entrepreneurship, among others.

Registration systems for return migrants are a first step toward delivering tailored interventions for that population. Because they have been away from their home country, return migrants often fall through the cracks of standard registries. In addition, dedicated comprehensive registries of return remain quite rare in the ECA region. In Uzbekistan, return migrants can now register in the unified database of labor emigrants kept since 2021, but registration is voluntary and mostly linked to entrepreneurship support programs rather than being systematic. In Georgia, the 2021–30 migration strategy (State Commission on Migration Issues 2020) advocates the improvement of data collection and a consolidated process of registering return migrants, but such initiatives have not yet been implemented. Addressing this important gap thus starts with establishing a consolidated process of registering return migrants and collecting data on this population at the time of return. This registration process could be carried out in one-stop shops at any of the different points of reentry (airports, borders).

To populate this registry, rapid needs assessments could be conducted upon return and combined with information provision on services available to returnees. Within the broader framework of returnee reintegration, authorities could create a rapid needs and plans assessment form for use during returnees' registration process. The information collected would include educational attainment, technical skills, and past work experience in origin and destination countries, as well as the conditions of returns, intentions to stay in the origin country, and labor market aspirations back home. Such registries could then be linked to national registries or existing employment registries so that return migrants can be directed to tailored employment and social protection interventions to support their needs. On the basis of returnees' identified needs and interests, representatives could provide an overview of the services returnees can access, including relevant contact details of service providers. This information can help returnees navigate the bureaucratic system. Migration services could reach out to return migrants to link them to job opportunities through, for example, mediation and job-matching measures, as well as to ensure access to essential services such as health care, shelter, and education.

For low-skilled returnees who aspire to wage employment, better linkages with existing active labor market policies (ALMPs) should be established. Reintegration programs specifically targeted to low-skilled migrants exist in some ECA countries but are currently low scale. Origin countries such as Georgia have been implementing such programs, but awareness among return migrants is currently very low: only 150 individuals benefited from the program in 2019 out of a total of 8,630 returnees that year. Better linkages of return migrants to ALMPs, building on information on experience abroad collected as part of the return migrant registry, can help support reintegration into home labor markets. Although there have been recent legislative and institutional improvements, the variety and reach of ALMPs in many sending countries of low-skilled migrants in ECA remain limited. To better cover return migrants, the endowment to ALMPs could be increased, and eligibility criteria could be relaxed. Training programs especially could be better linked to employers' demand for skills in the origin country.[6] In addition to links to existing ALMPs, origin countries ought to establish programs with receiving countries to support the reintegration of returnees by, for example, providing training in line with the aspirations returnees had while employed abroad (as seen in Korea's employment permit system, a low-skilled labor migration system) and creating retraining courses that enable returnees to use skills acquired abroad.

Legal and formal pathways for low-skilled migration may also increase the benefits of return migration for migrants and home economies. Emerging evidence outside ECA indicates that temporary low-skilled migrants benefit from migrating legally through higher earnings not only during the migration but also after returning to the home country. In the context of temporary migration from Egypt, not only do illegal migrants experience a 19 percent wage penalty abroad relative to legal migrants, but they also experience a large wage penalty after return to the home country, relative to legal return migrants and nonmigrants (El-Mallakh and Wahba 2021). This suggests that the benefits of legal low-skilled migration may extend way beyond the migration episode in the case of temporary migration and have implications for workers' entire life cycle and lifetime earnings.

Given the higher propensity of becoming self-employed among low-skilled returnees, support of entrepreneurship may enhance the benefits of return migration. Programs of this sort can include an array of services delivered through a one-stop-shop framework. Those may include in-kind assistance, financial literacy, support to develop a business plan, and access to banking and microcredit as well as other financial instruments to make productive use of savings.[7] To improve the success rate of entrepreneurial activities, support programs have started to include analyses of skills gaps in local labor markets to ensure that returnees have the skills required and that the entrepreneurial endeavor produces goods or services in high demand in the region of residence.[8] The effectiveness of such entrepreneurship support to returnees, however, remains to be rigorously evaluated because almost no evidence is currently available on their impacts (McKenzie and Yang 2015). In addition to such programs, removing administrative and institutional barriers to setting up and running a business can smooth the transition of return migrants to the labor market.

In case of unexpected returns, short-term social protection support to returnees could help alleviate temporary hardship. The COVID-19 pandemic showed that migrants who unexpectedly return are often in a vulnerable situation: they earned wages abroad for a shorter period than anticipated while typically not having planned their reintegration into home labor markets. Shorter-term interventions to support the emergency needs of migrants forced to return could include cash transfer support. Such interventions have been implemented in the context of the COVID-19 pandemic to meet the urgent needs of return migrants and their families placed in vulnerable situations. Other possible short-term interventions for returnees who unexpectedly return include public work programs. Such emergency public work programs were implemented, for example, in Armenia for circular migrants in the context of the COVID-19 pandemic (Honorati, Kerschbaumer, and Yi 2019).

Annex 5A. Vulnerability or Resilience of Low-Skilled Migration to Shocks: Lessons from COVID-19 and the Spillovers from Russia's Invasion of Ukraine

Since 2020, low-skilled migration from European and Central Asian countries has been hit by two large, successive negative shocks—the COVID-19 pandemic and the spillovers from Russia's invasion of Ukraine. Although both shocks presumably had a negative impact on migration flows from origin countries, the former affected both origin and destination countries to a similar extent, whereas the latter has disproportionately affected the economic situation in Russia. This annex examines the impacts of these two shocks on low-skilled migration from sending countries and their consequences on households in countries of origin. It shows that both shocks have in most cases exacerbated and brought to light vulnerabilities and inefficiencies that existed before them. The challenging context brought by those shocks can thus be used as an opportunity to strengthen the migration system by developing policies and programs that can equip origin countries with the tools necessary to support migrants—through a coherent and comprehensive labor migration policy—and to be better prepared for future shocks that may affect labor migration and remittances.

Low-Skilled Migration and the COVID-19 Pandemic

In the short run, COVID-19 led to a large drop in demand for migrant labor in most sectors and destinations, revealing the exposure of low-skilled migration to shocks. Labor demand in the main destinations of low-skilled migrants in Europe and Central Asia (ECA) sharply dropped after the outset of the pandemic, at least in the short run. For example, in 2020, Russia—one of the main destinations of low-skilled migrants—granted fewer than half the number of work authorizations issued in 2019 (Bossavie and Garrote Sánchez 2022).

This sharp decline pointed to a drastic limitation of labor migration as a poverty alleviation tool in low-skilled migrants' sending countries, placing further pressure on their domestic labor market. COVID-19 has affected not only the demand for low-skilled labor in destination countries but also the sectoral composition of labor demand in the short and potentially longer terms, with uncertainty about the strength of the future recovery of occupations with a traditionally high demand for migrants, such as tourism and hospitality, whereas other sectors have rapidly grown in the new context, such as delivery services. Prolonged travel restrictions may also have induced additional technological change in certain sectors that heavily rely on migrant labor, reducing future demand (Clemens, Lewis, and Postel 2018).

The COVID-19 pandemic resulted in a temporary decline in the stock of low-skilled migrants, especially those migrating from Central Asia to Russia. As a result of both mobility restrictions and decreased demand for foreign labor in Russia, the stock of low-skilled migrants from Central Asia, such as Uzbekistan and Tajikistan, immediately dropped in the months after the outbreak of the pandemic. This was mostly driven by a drop in new outflows of migrants going abroad in a given month compared to the same month in the previous year. (refer to figure 5A.1). The drop in new outflows of migrants from the two countries persisted until the end of 2020 but began increasing in early 2021 when some mobility restrictions were relaxed.

Households with members forced to cancel or postpone their migration plans were often placed in vulnerable situations, with simultaneous limited employment opportunities at home. Evidence from Central Asia shows that intentions to migrate dropped in the months directly after the COVID-19 outbreak, and many migrants canceled their migration plans with negative welfare implications for their households. Lower-income households had significantly larger employment losses. Surveys carried out in some Central Asian countries during COVID-19 show that households with a member unable to migrate were twice as likely to report employment losses during the pandemic as those who did not have intentions to migrate (Bossavie and Garrote-Sánchez 2022). They were also more likely to report wage-income losses and the need to use drastic coping mechanisms, such as cutting food spending, because of lack of income.

The net impacts of negative shocks affecting both origin and destination countries, such as the COVID-19 pandemic, on remittances are a priori

FIGURE 5A.1

International migration from Uzbekistan before and after the outbreak of the COVID-19 pandemic

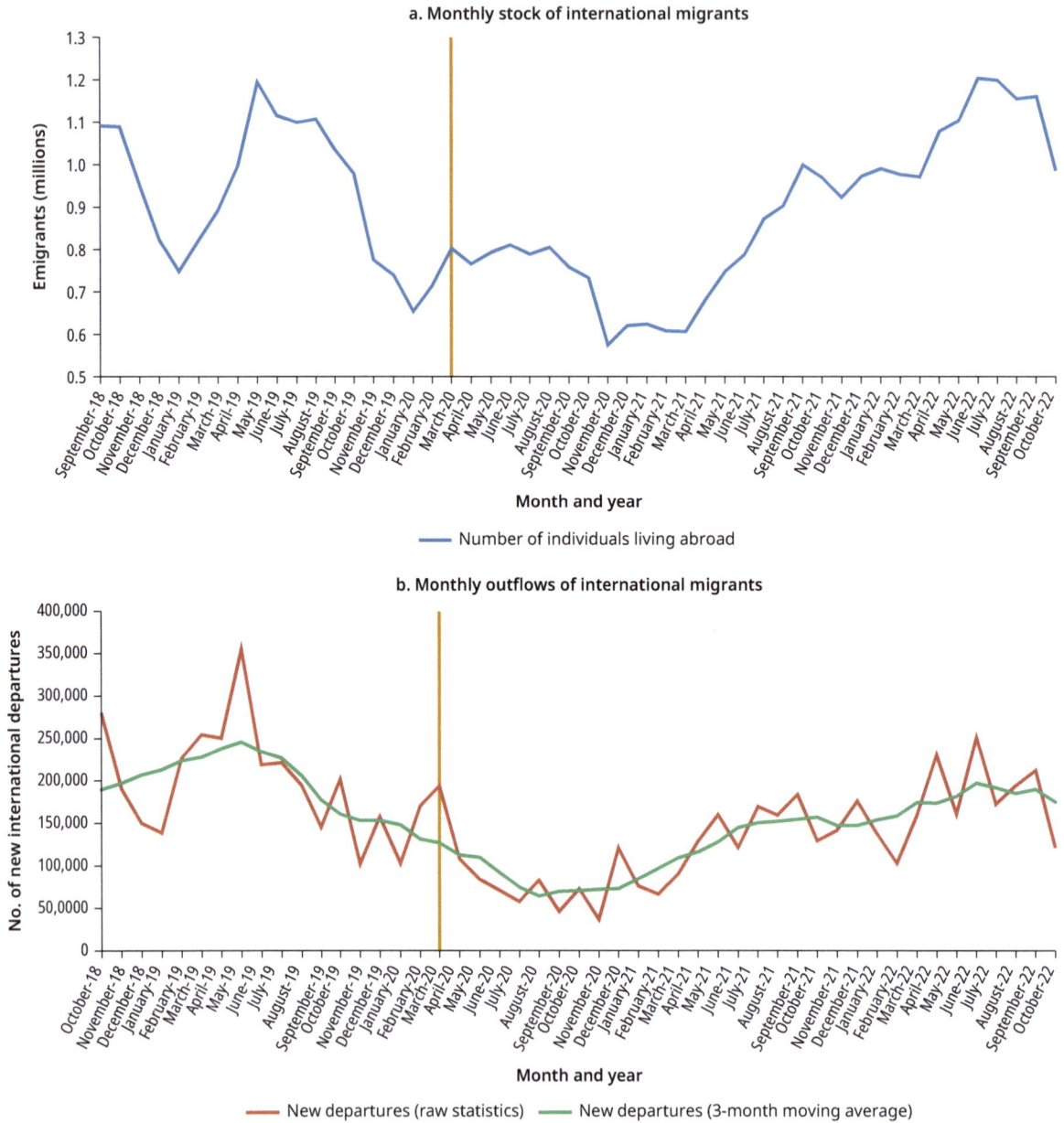

a. Monthly stock of international migrants

Number of individuals living abroad

b. Monthly outflows of international migrants

New departures (raw statistics)   New departures (3-month moving average)

Source: Listening to the Citizens of Uzbekistan monthly follow-up surveys (https://www.worldbank.org/en/country/uzbekistan/brief/l2cu).
Note: In panel a, the blue line plots the estimated monthly number of new departures from Uzbekistan from January 2019 to October 2022. In panel b, the green line plots the three-month moving average of monthly new departures from Uzbekistan from January 2019 to October 2022. The vertical orange line at March 2020 represents the start of the COVID-19 pandemic.

ambiguous. Remittances are affected by the number of emigrants but also by their ability to remit, based on their savings and earnings (Clemens and McKenzie 2018). Given the drop in migrant labor demand in destination countries, total remittances are expected to decline, simply because of a decline in the number of migrants abroad (extensive margin effect). Regarding the number of remittances sent per migrant abroad (intensive margin), impacts are ambiguous. On the one hand, migrant labor income is expected to be negatively affected by shocks, resulting in a decline in the number of remittances sent per migrant. On the other hand, migrants have been shown to remit more when the needs of relatives and friends in the country of origin are higher globally (Gupta 2006). In the ECA region, a similar pattern has been reported, for example, in Uzbekistan (Seitz 2019). Because the home economy and households left behind were also affected by the pandemic, the total remittance amount sent per migrant may thus increase to help household members left behind cope with the ongoing negative impacts of the crisis.

Remittances sent by temporary migrants to their home countries dropped sharply right after the pandemic's outbreak. This drop was driven by both a decline in the stock of migrants and a drop in the amount remitted per migrant. The initial drop in the number of remittances sent can be attributed to income loss at the destination and, in some cases, employment loss, the negative shock to their employment, and income at their destination. Remittances to Central Asia saw their largest drops in recent history, with a year-on-year fall of more than 50 percent in April 2020.

The widespread reduction in remittances during the first months of the pandemic had persisting adverse impacts on the welfare of migrant households. At the household level, surveys show a widespread reduction in remittances in the first months of the pandemic, prompting a severe negative impact on the welfare of migrant households. In Russia, for example, 79 percent of migrants who had previously sent remittances had stopped sending any money by the end of April 2020 (Ryazantsev et al. 2020). This trend is very similar to the drop in remittances observed at the macro level during that month. In the Kyrgyz Republic, the National Statistical Committee survey in October 2020 shows that 16 percent of Kyrgyz households experienced a reduction in remittances received. At the regional level, a higher drop in remittances also correlated with higher overall income losses, highlighting the role of remittances as a key source of income. In Central Asia, households experiencing a loss in remittances after the pandemic were more likely to resort to coping strategies such as cutting food spending (Bossavie and Garrote-Sánchez 2022). The pandemic, therefore, highlighted the heavy reliance on remittances among poor households in sending countries and the strong welfare impacts of any disruption in remittances due to shocks in destination countries.

Remittances, however, increased rapidly after this initial drop, highlighting the resilience of low-skilled migration and remittances to shocks in the medium term. Remittances returned to normal levels by summer 2020, and the cumulative flows by October 2020 were only 2.3 percent lower than in the same month in 2019. Considering the continuing reduction in the number of Central Asian emigrants to Russia until the third quarter of 2020 and the still-dire labor market situation in receiving countries, the rebound in remittances suggests a higher elasticity of foreign earnings to remittances of emigrants, perhaps financed by previous savings, in an increased effort to support the larger needs of household members in Central Asia. Low-skilled emigration and remittances, however, continued recovering by early 2021, highlighting the resilience of low-skilled migration to shocks (refer to figure 5A.2).

The pandemic had countervailing effects on return migration, with international mobility restrictions limiting return flows and low employment opportunities in host countries incentivizing them. Many migrants who wanted to return home could not do so because of border closures and cancelled international flights. According to the Listening to

FIGURE 5A.2

Percentage change in the total amount of international remittances sent back to origin countries before and during the COVID-19 pandemic

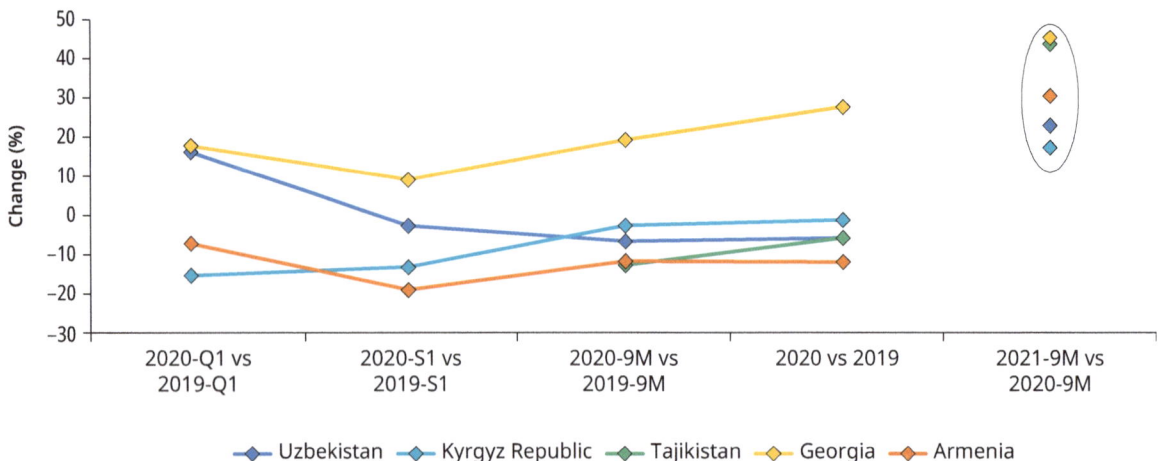

Sources: National Central Banks and World Bank Migrant Remittance Inflows (https://databank.worldbank.org/source/world-development -indicators), accessed October 2020.
Note: 9M = the first nine months of the year; Q1 = first quarter; S1 = first and second quarters.

the Citizens of the Kyrgyz Republic survey of 2021 (https://www
.worldbank.org/en/country/kyrgyzrepublic/brief
/l2kgz#:~:text=Listening%20to%20the%20Kyrgyz%20Republic%20
(L2KGZ)%20is%20a%20monthly%20panel,regions%20of%20the%20
Kyrgyz%20Republic), the upward trend in the share of return migrants
arriving, as observed in previous years, came to a halt in 2020. This was
due, in part, to the almost nonexistent migrant return in the first three
months of the pandemic (April–June 2020). More strikingly, 8 percent of
the Kyrgyz households in the National Statistical Committee Household
Survey of 2020 reported having a member abroad who was unable to
return home, the equivalent of 128,000 households (and at minimum
that number of current emigrants).

Labor migrants not employed abroad were more likely to return. Labor
market outcomes in destination countries have been shown to affect
migrant return decisions (Bijwaard, Schluter, and Wahba 2014). In the
context of the COVID-19 pandemic, evidence from the Kyrgyz Republic
and Uzbekistan shows that low-skilled workers who were abroad during
the COVID-19 pandemic were more likely to return to their home
countries the following month. Furthermore, low-skilled migrants from
Uzbekistan not employed in the destination country in the previous
month were more likely to return.

Forced returnees and their households were often in a vulnerable situation
upon the migrants' return. Among migrants from Central Asia who returned
from Russia after the COVID-19 outbreak, only 40 percent were working by
early June 2020 (Denisenko and Mukomel 2023). The Kyrgyz National
Statistics Committee COVID-19 survey (Mukomel and Benisenko 2023) also
shows a higher degree of economic and health vulnerability among
households with members who were either forced to return from abroad or
were stranded and could not return. Although fewer than 20 percent of
nonmigrant households reported having members who had lost their jobs
during the pandemic, the rate reached 33 percent for households with a
migrant who was stranded and 54 percent for households with a member
who had to return to the Kyrgyz Republic. Households with recent
returnees were more likely than nonmigrant families to see a reduction in
both wage income and remittances since the start of the pandemic. Given
the larger negative shock faced by families with return migrants, they were
also significantly more likely to report using strategies such as cutting food
spending.

Spillovers from Russia's Invasion of Ukraine

Remittances from Russia dropped directly after the outbreak of conflict with Ukraine but increased a few months later. Remittances from Russia to the Kyrgyz Republic significantly dropped in the short term, specifically in the two months after the outbreak of the conflict (refer to figure 5A.3, panel a). This short-term drop in remittances was mainly driven by a decline in the propensity to remit among migrants and in the amount remitted, although the total stock of migrants in Russia immediately remained unchanged. The amount of remittances per migrant declined right after the outbreak of the conflict (refer to figure 5A.3, panel b).

The initial drop in remittances was driven by a decline in the propensity to remit and in the amount remitted per migrant, exacerbated by a depreciation of the Russian ruble. The outbreak of conflict was followed by a declining propensity to remit. In the months after the initial conflict, the share of Uzbek households receiving any remittance transfers fell from 7.8 percent in January to 2.7 percent in March (–65 percent), from 33 percent to 23 percent in Tajikistan (–31 percent), and from 17.5 percent to 14.8 percent in the Kyrgyz Republic (–16 percent). Among migrants who sent remittances, the amount remitted also declined. The depreciation of the Russian ruble contributed to a decline in the remittance amount received in local currency (refer to figure 5A.3, panel c). Exchange rates fluctuated considerably immediately after the conflict began. In February and March 2022, the ruble fell, at one point, by 32 percent against the Kyrgyz som and 42 percent against both the Tajik somoni and the Uzbek som. After adjusting for inflation and exchange rates, the value of a typical remittance transfer fell by 15 percent in the Kyrgyz Republic, by 18 percent in Uzbekistan, and by as much as 57 percent in Tajikistan in March compared with January.

The depreciation of the Russian ruble was an explanatory factor only in the decline of the number of remittances sent by migrants, because the average amount remitted by migrants in Russian rubles also declined right after the conflict broke out before strongly increasing a few months later (refer to figure 5A.3). One likely explanation for these fluctuations in remittances sent in rubles is that migrants postponed transferring remittances in the period when the Russian ruble strongly depreciated. Indeed, as the Russian ruble started to reappreciate after a few months, total remittances and average remittances increased sharply, driven by both an increase in the amount sent per migrant in Russian rubles and by an appreciation of the exchange rate. This pattern highlights the exposure of low-skilled migrants to fluctuations in exchange rates between the destination and origin country currencies. These fluctuations affect not only the number of remittances received in local currency but also migrants' remitting behavior by, for example, postponing transfers when the destination country currency depreciates.

FIGURE 5A.3

International remittances sent to the Kyrgyz Republic, before and after Russia's invasion of Ukraine

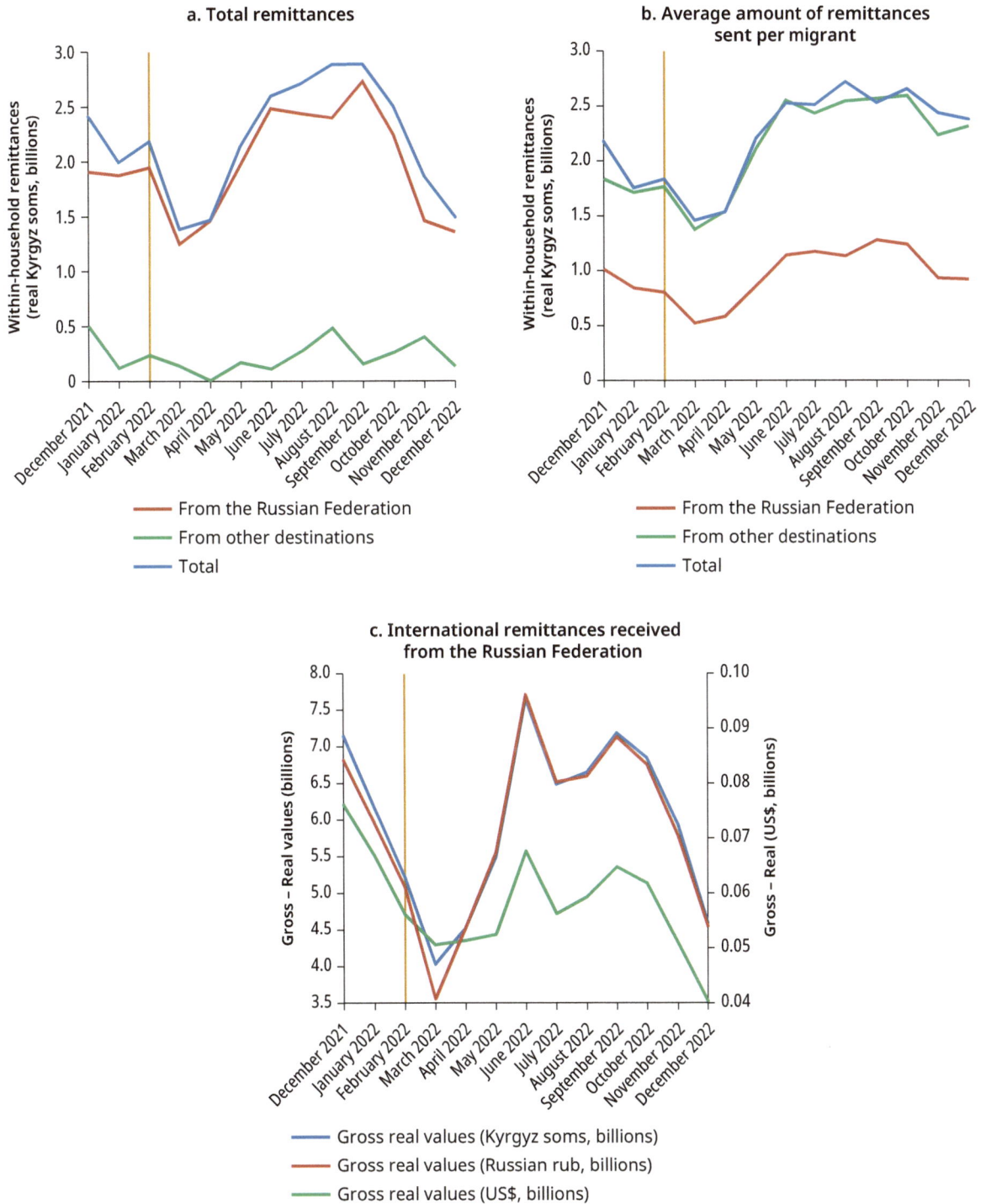

a. Total remittances

b. Average amount of remittances sent per migrant

c. International remittances received from the Russian Federation

Source: Listening to the Citizens of the Kyrgyz Republic monthly panel surveys (https://www.worldbank.org/en/country/kyrgyzrepublic /brief/l2kgz#:~:text=Listening%20to%20the%20Kyrgyz%20Republic%20(L2KGZ)%20is%20a%20monthly%20panel,regions%20of%20the%20 Kyrgyz%20Republic).
Note: The vertical orange line represents the start of Russia's invasion of Ukraine in February 2022.

In contrast, the stock of migrants in Russia began to decline a few months after the conflict started. Although the stock of migrants from Central Asia to Russia did not drop immediately after the start of the conflict, the total stock of migrants from the Kyrgyz Republic significantly declined in the following months (refer to figure 5A.4, panel a). In line with this finding, there was a sharp drop in new intentions to migrate right after the conflict

FIGURE 5A.4

Migration from the Kyrgyz Republic before and after Russia's invasion of Ukraine

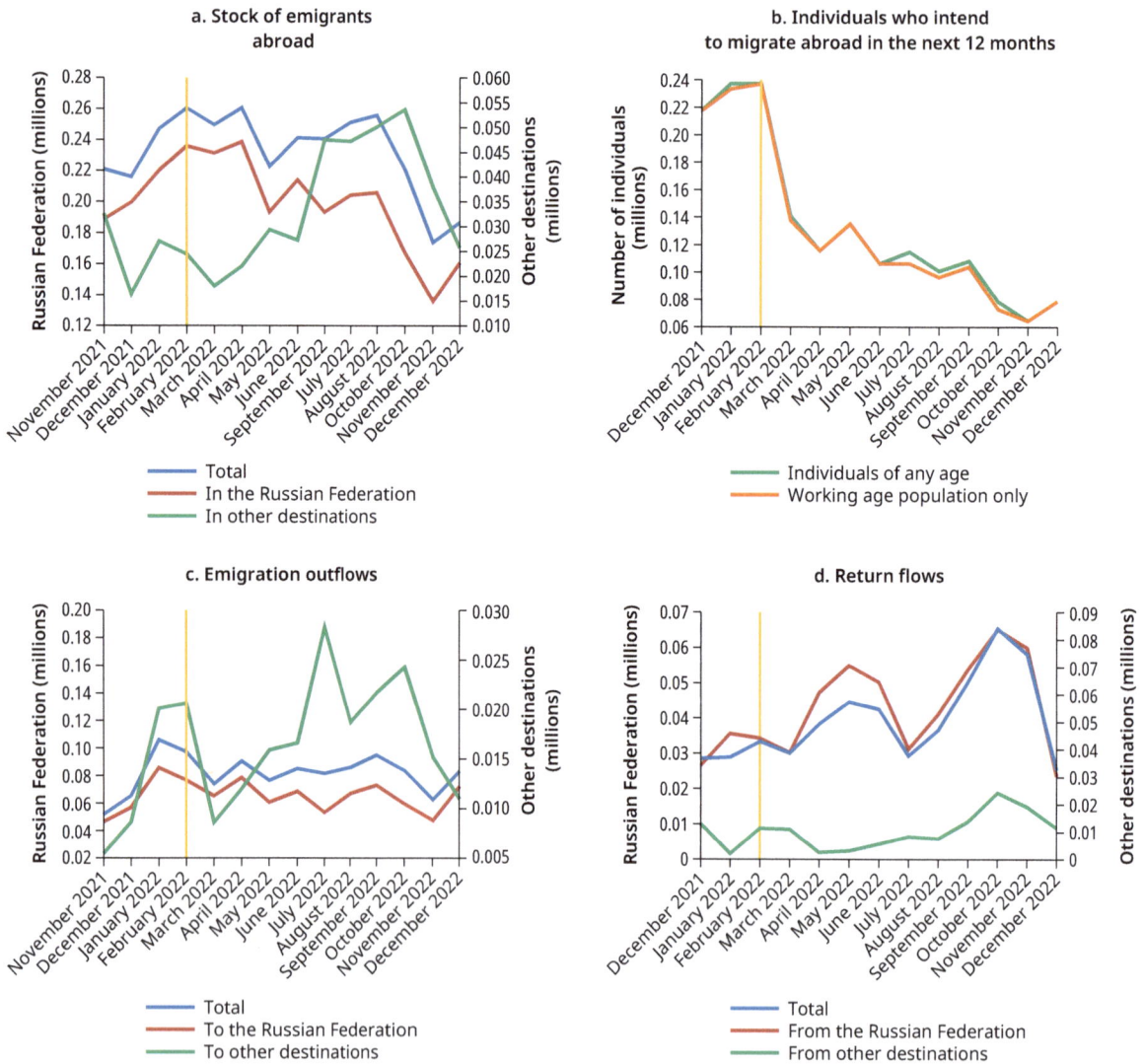

Source: Listening to the Citizens of the Kyrgyz Republic monthly panel surveys (https://www.worldbank.org/en/country/kyrgyzrepublic/brief/l2kgz#:~:text=Listening%20to%20the%20Kyrgyz%20Republic%20(L2KGZ)%20is%20a%20monthly%20panel,regions%20of%20the%20Kyrgyz%20Republic).
Note: The vertical yellow line represents the start of Russia's invasion of Ukraine in February 2022.

broke out (refer to figure 5A.4, panel b). In the Kyrgyz Republic, the share of households with a member considering migration fell from 13 percent to 8 percent, and in Tajikistan, the share fell from 12 percent to 6 percent. In Uzbekistan, there were nearly no respondents who expected that any member would be soon going abroad in the months after the conflict broke out.

The initial decline in the stock of migrants in Russia was the result of a drop in new departures and increased returns. The shift in migration intentions that took place directly after the conflict broke out was followed by an actual drop in new departures to Russia (refer to figure 5A.4, panel c). Similarly, returns from Russia increased in the months following the outbreak of the conflict, whereas those from other destinations declined. In addition, returns from Russia spiked in the months after the conflict broke out, whereas they declined in other destinations (refer to figure 5A.4, panel d). These trends suggest that the decline in outbound migration to Russia, combined with increased returns, was one of the most meaningful channels of the crisis for households that typically rely on migration and remittances.

The decline in the stock of migrants in Russia was accompanied by an increase in migration flows to new destinations for migrants from the Kyrgyz Republic. In addition to a decline in emigration, the composition of preferred destinations for outbound migration also shifted. The percentage of migrants reporting Russia as their favorite destination in Central Asia fell from about 68 percent of migrants to only 51 percent in March. The decline in the stock of Kyrgyz migrants in Russia was also accompanied by an increase in the stock of migrants to other destinations, suggesting some reallocation of new migration flows away from Russia to new destinations.

Notes

1. Nearly 60 percent of migrants from Uzbekistan have vocational education, 30 percent have upper-secondary education, 6 percent have secondary general education or below, and only about 4 percent have tertiary education.
2. A similar relationship has been evidenced in the Kyrgyz Republic (Bossavie and Garrote-Sánchez 2022). This inverted-U–shaped relationship may be explained by lower returns to migrating for high-skilled individuals in the presence of barriers to work in professional occupations and limited demand for high-skilled labor in the traditional destinations of migrants from Central Asia. Although educational attainment is also correlated with household income and could also reflect the inability to finance migration costs at very low income levels, the inverted-U shape is robust to controlling for household wealth.

3. Counterfactual scenarios that consider the potential earnings of migrants had they stayed in Armenia lessen the poverty reduction capacity of remittances by around 30 percent but remain highly significant (World Bank 2019).

4. Similar findings have been reported by Binzel and Assaad (2011) in the Egyptian context. Here, they found that during the migration episode, women's paid labor supply decreased while unpaid work typically increased, presumably driven by the household's need to replace the migrant's labor. In contrast, once the migration episode ended, women were less likely to be in unpaid work and more likely to be in self-employment. This suggests that the impacts of temporary migration on the labor supply and occupational choices of household members left behind are dynamic and vary throughout the migration life cycle.

5. A similar program also exists between Australia and the Pacific Islands.

6. In Sri Lanka, for example, the Skills Passport program, introduced by the Tertiary and Vocational Educational Commission of the Ministry of Skills Development, Employment and Labor Relations, the Employers' Federation of Ceylon, and the International Labour Organization, was designed to support the successful reintegration of workers returning to Sri Lanka by providing relevant skills and networks with companies.

7. One of the most comprehensive programs of this sort, outside Europe and Central Asia, is the Overseas Foreign Worker reintegration program in the Philippines, a one-stop center that provides a package of services to return migrants, including expedited access to credit for creating a business and capacity development training.

8. The International Organisation for Migration in Switzerland has published statistics on the success rates of certain business projects in different countries to increase potential returnees' information on home labor markets.

References

Abdulloev, I., G. S. Epstein, and I. N. Gang. 2020. "Migration and Forsaken Schooling in Kyrgyzstan, Tajikistan, and Uzbekistan." *IZA Journal of Development and Migration* 11 (1): 4. https://doi.org/10.2478/izajodm-2020-0004.

Acosta, P. 2011. "School Attendance, Child Labour, and Remittances from International Migration in El Salvador." *Journal of Development Studies* 47 (6): 913–36. https://doi.org/10.1080/00220388.2011.563298.

Acosta, P. A., E. K. K. Lartey, and F. S. Mandelman. 2009. "Remittances and the Dutch Disease." *Journal of International Economics* 79 (1): 102–16.

Adams, R. H., Jr. 2011. "Evaluating the Economic Impact of International Remittances on Developing Countries Using Household Surveys: A Literature Review." *Journal of Development Studies* 47 (6): 809–28. https://doi.org/10.1080/00220388.2011.563299.

Adams, R. H., Jr. 2009. "The Determinants of International Remittances in Developing Countries." *World Development* 37 (1): 93–103.

Adams, R. H., Jr., and J. Page. 2005. "Do International Migration and Remittances Reduce Poverty in Developing Countries?" *World Development* 33 (10): 1645–69.

Ahmed, S. A., and L. Bossavie. 2022. *Toward Safer and More Productive Migration for South Asia*. Washington, DC: World Bank. http://documents.worldbank.org/curated/en/903161585816440273/Toward-Safer-and-More-Productive-Migration-for-South-Asia.

Akmoldoev, K., and A. Budaichieva. 2012. "The Impact of Remittances on Kyrgyzstan Economy." *Реформа* 4: 57–63.

Ambler, K., D. Aycinena, and D. Yang. 2014. "Remittance Responses to Temporary Discounts: A Field Experiment among Central American Migrants." Working Paper 20522, National Bureau of Economic Research, Cambridge, MA.

Ambrosini, J. W., K. Mayr, G. Peri, and D. Radu. 2015. "The Selection of Migrants and Returnees in Romania: Evidence and Long-Run Implications." *Economics of Transition* 23 (4): 753–93. https://doi.org/10.1111/ecot.12077.

Amuedo-Dorantes, C., A. Georges, and S. Pozo. 2010. "Migration, Remittances, and Children's Schooling in Haiti." *Annals of the American Academy of Political and Social Science* 630 (1): 224–44.

Amuedo-Dorantes, C., and S. Pozo. 2006. "Migration, Remittances, and Male and Female Employment Patterns." *American Economic Review* 96 (2): 222–6. https://doi.org/10.1257/000282806777211946.

Atoyan, R. V., and J. Rahman. 2017. "Western Balkans: Increasing Women's Role in the Economy." IMF Working Paper WP/17/194, International Monetary Fund, Washington, DC. https://doi.org/10.5089/9781484315569.001.

Avato, J., J. Koettl, and R. Sabates-Wheeler. 2010. "Social Security Regimes, Global Estimates, and Good Practices: The Status of Social Protection for International Migrants." *World Development* 38 (4): 455–66.

Aycinena, D., C. Martinez, and D. Yang. 2010. "The Impact of Remittance Fees on Remittance Flows: Evidence from a Field Experiment among Salvadoran Migrants." Working Paper, University of Michigan, Ann Arbor.

Bah, T. L., and C. Batista. 2020. "Why Do People Migrate Irregularly? Evidence from a Lab-in-the-Field Experiment in West Africa." Working Paper 435, Helen Kellogg Institute for International Studies, University of Notre Dame, Notre Dame, IN. https://kellogg.nd.edu/why-do-people-migrate-irregularly-evidence-lab-field-experiment-west-africa.

Bank of Albania. 2020. "Economic Review 2020 H2." Tirana: Bank of Albania.

Beaman, L. A. 2012. "Social Networks and the Dynamics of Labour Market Outcomes: Evidence from Refugees Resettled in the U.S." *Review of Economic Studies* 79 (1): 128–61. https://doi.org/10.1093/restud/rdr017.

Berulava, G. 2019. "Migration and Labor Supply in Georgia: An Empirical Study." *Eurasian Economic Review* 9 (3): 395–419. https://doi.org/10.1007/s40822-018-0106-4.

Bettin, G., and A. Zazzaro. 2018. "The Impact of Natural Disasters on Remittances to Low- and Middle-Income Countries." *Journal of Development Studies* 54 (3): 481–500. https://doi.org/10.1080/00220388.2017.1303672.

Bijwaard, G. E., C. Schluter, and J. Wahba. 2014. "The Impact of Labor Market Dynamics on the Return Migration of Immigrants." *Review of Economics and Statistics* 96 (3): 483–94. https://doi.org/10.1162/REST_a_00389.

Binzel, C., and R. Assaad. 2011. "Egyptian Men Working Abroad: Labour Supply Responses by the Women Left Behind." *Labour Economics* 18 (Supplement 1): S98–114. https://doi.org/10.1016/j.labeco.2011.03.002.

Bither, J., and A. Ziebarth. 2018. *Creating Legal Pathways to Reduce Irregular Migration? What We Can Learn from Germany's "Western Balkan Regulation."* Migration Strategy Group on International Cooperation and Development. Washington, DC: German Marshall Fund; Gütersloh, Germany: Bertelsmann Stiftung; Stuttgart: Robert Bosch Stiftung.

Blanchard, O., and A. Landier. 2002. "The Perverse Effects of Partial Labour Market Reform: Fixed-Term Contracts in France." *Economic Journal* 112 (480): F214–44.

Boeri, T., and P. Garibaldi. 2007. "Two Tier Reforms of Employment Protection: A Honeymoon Effect?" *Economic Journal* 117 (521): F357–85.

Borodak, D., and M. Piracha. 2011. "Occupational Choice of Return Migrants in Moldova." *Eastern European Economics* 49 (4): 24–46.

Bossavie, L., and E. Bartl. 2024. "Temporary Migration from the Kyrgyz Republic: Challenges, Opportunities, and Policy Solutions." Washington, DC: World Bank.

Bossavie, L., and D. Garrote-Sánchez. 2022. *Safe and Productive Migration from the Kyrgyz Republic.* Washington, DC: World Bank. https://doi.org/10.1596/978-1-4648-1905-6.

Bossavie, L., D. Garrote-Sánchez, M. Makovec, and Ç. Özden. 2022. *Skilled Migration: A Sign of Europe's Divide or Integration?* Washington, DC: World Bank. https://doi.org/10.1596/978-1-4648-1732-8.

Bossavie, L., J. S. Görlach, C. Özden, and H. Wang. 2021. "Temporary Migration for Long-Term Investment." Policy Research Working Paper 9740, World Bank, Washington, DC. https://doi.org/10.1596/1813-9450-9740.

Bossavie, L., and C. Özden. 2023. "Impacts of Temporary Migration on Development in Origin Countries." *World Bank Research Observer* 38 (2): 249–94.

Brickenstein, C. 2015. "Social Protection of Foreign Seasonal Workers: From State to Best Practice." *Comparative Migration Studies* 3: 2. https://doi.org/10.1007/s40878-015-0004-9.

Brück T., C. Mahé, and W. Naudé. 2018. "Return Migration and Self-Employment: Evidence from Kyrgyzstan." IZA Discussion Paper 11332. Bonn: IZA Institute of Labor Economics.

Brücker, H., M. Falkenhain, T. Fendel, M. Promberger, and M. Raab. 2020. "Strong Demand and Sound Labour Market Integration: Labour Migration to Germany Based on the Western Balkans Regulation." Brief Report 16, Institute for Employment Research, Nuremberg. https://doku.iab.de/kurzber/2020/kb1620_englisch.pdf.

Carletto, G., and T. Kilic. 2011. "Moving Up the Ladder? The Impact of Migration Experience on Occupational Mobility in Albania." *Journal of Development Studies* 47 (6): 846–69. https://doi.org/10.1080/00220388.2010.509926.

Center for Global Development. 2021. "Migration Pathways: Western Balkan Regulation." Washington, DC: Center for Global Development. https://gsp.cgdev.org/wp-content/uploads/2021/07/CGD-Legal-Pathways-Database_Western-Balkan-Regulation-1.pdf.

Chami, R., E. Ernst, C. Fullenkamp, and A. Oeking. 2018. "Are Remittances Good for Labor Markets in LICs, MICs and Fragile States? Evidence from Cross-Country Data." IMF Working Paper WP/18/102, International Monetary Fund, Washington, DC.

Chin, A., L. Karkoviata, and N. Wilcox. 2011. "Impact of Bank Accounts on Migrant Savings and Remittances: Evidence from a Field Experiment." http://www.uh.edu/~achin/research/ckw_banking_june2011.pdf.

Cho, Y., A. Denisova, S. Yi, and U. Khadka. 2018. "Bilateral Arrangement of Temporary Labor Migration: Lessons from Korea's Employment Permit System." Policy Brief, World Bank, Washington, DC. http://documents.worldbank.org/curated/en/645571537423013613/Bilateral-Arrangement-of-Temporary-Labor-Migration-Lessons-from-Korea-s-Employment-Permit-System-Policy-Brief.

Chudinovskin, O. 2021. "Estimating Irregular Migration in the Russian Federation." Paper presented at the International Organization for Migration Second International Forum on Migration Statistics, Cairo, January 19–21.

Cinque, A., and C. Poggi. 2024. "How Does Fertility Affect Female Employment? Evidence from Albania." *Journal of Development Studies*: 1–19. https://doi.org/10.1080/00220388.2024.2322969.

Clemens, M. A. 2020. "The Emigration Life Cycle: How Development Shapes Emigration from Poor Countries." Discussion Paper 13614, Institute of Labor Economics, Bonn.

Clemens, M. A., E. G. Lewis, and H. M. Postel. 2018. "Immigration Restrictions as Active Labor Market Policy: Evidence from the Mexican Bracero Exclusion." *American Economic Review* 108 (6): 1468–87. https://doi.org/10.1257/aer.20170765.

Clemens, M. A., and D. McKenzie. 2018. "Why Don't Remittances Appear to Affect Growth?" *Economic Journal* 128 (612): F179–209. https://doi.org/10.1111/ecoj.12463.

De, S., E. Islamaj, M. A. Kose, and S. R. Yousefi. 2019. "Remittances over the Business Cycle: Theory and Evidence." *Economic Notes: Review of Banking, Finance and Monetary Economics* 48 (3): 12143.

de Coulon, A., and M. Piracha. 2005. "Self-Selection and the Performance of Return Migrants: The Source Country Perspective." *Journal of Population Economics* 18: 779–807. https://doi.org/10.1007/s00148-005-0004-4.

Denisenko, M. B., and V. I. Mukomel. 2023. "Foreign Workers in Russia: Employers' Opinions." [In Russian.] *Sotsiologicheskie Issledovaniia* 1 (9441): 26–37. https://www.socis.isras.ru/files/File/2023/1/Denisenko.pdf.

Djajić, S. 1986. "International Migration, Remittances and Welfare in a Dependent Economy." *Journal of Development Economics* 21 (2): 229–34.

Djajić, S. 2010. "Investment Opportunities in the Source Country and Temporary Migration." *Canadian Journal of Economics/Revue canadienne d'économique* 43 (2): 663–82.

Doan, D., M. Dornan, and R. Edwards. 2023. *The Gains and Pains of Working Away from Home: The Case of Pacific Temporary Migrant Workers in Australia and New Zealand.* Canberra: Australian National University; Washington, DC: World Bank.

Doi, Y., D. McKenzie, and B. Zia. 2014. "Who You Train Matters: Identifying Combined Effects of Financial Education on Migrant Households." *Journal of Development Economics* 109: 39–55. https://doi.org/10.1016/j.jdeveco.2014.03.009.

Dubashov, B., A. Kruse, and S. Ismailakhunova. 2017. *Kyrgyz Republic Economic Update No. 6, Fall/Winter 2017: A Robust Recovery with Underlying Weaknesses.* Washington, DC: World Bank. https://doi.org/10.1596/29261.

Dustmann, C., A. Glitz, and T. Vogel. 2010. "Employment, Wages, and the Economic Cycle: Differences between Immigrants and Natives." *European Economic Review* 54 (1): 1–17. https://doi.org/10.1016/j.euroecorev.2009 .04.004.

Dustmann, C., and J. S. Görlach. 2016. "The Economics of Temporary Migrations." *Journal of Economic Literature* 54 (1): 98–136. https://doi.org/10.1257/jel.54.1.98.

Dustmann, C., and O. Kirchkamp. 2002. "The Optimal Migration Duration and Activity Choice after Re-Migration." *Journal of Development Economics* 67 (2): 351–72.

Dustmann, C., and J. Mestres. 2010. "Remittances and Temporary Migration." *Journal of Development Economics* 92 (1): 62–70.

El-Mallakh, N., and J. Wahba. 2021. "Return Migrants and the Wage Premium: Does the Legal Status of Migrants Matter?" *Journal of Population Economics* 35: 1631–85.

ETF (European Training Foundation). 2013. *Migration and Skills in Armenia and Georgia: Comparative Report.* Turin: ETF. https://www.etf.europa.eu/sites/default/files/m/B711838175EB762EC1257B4D0042FF65 _Migration&skills_Armenia&Georgia.pdf.

Eurasian Economic Commission. 2015. *The Treaty on the Eurasian Economic Union (EAEU).* Moscow: Eurasian Economic Commission. https://docs.eaeunion.org/docs/en-us/0017353/itia_05062014_doc.pdf.

European Parliament and Council of the European Union. 2014. "Directive 2014/36/EU of the European Parliament and of the Council of 26 February 2014 on the Conditions of Entry and Stay of Third-Country Nationals for the Purpose of Employment as Seasonal Workers." *EUR-Lex,* March 28, 2014. https://eur-lex .europa.eu/legal-content/en/TXT/?uri=celex%3A32014L0036.

European Union. 2018. "Comprehensive and Enhanced Partnership Agreement between the European Union and the European Atomic Energy Community and Their Member States, of the One Part, and the Republic of Armenia, of the Other Part." *EUR-Lex,* January 26, 2018. http://data.europa.eu/eli/agree_internation /2018/104/oj.

Faini, R. 1994. "Export Supply, Capacity and Relative Prices." *Journal of Development Economics* 45 (1): 81–100. https://doi.org/10.1016/0304-3878(94)90060-4.

Fasani, F., and J. Mazza. 2020. "Immigrant Key Workers: Their Contribution to Europe's COVID-19 Response." Policy Paper 155, Institute of Labor Economics, Bonn. https://www.iza.org/publications/pp/155/immigrant -key-workers-their-contribution-to-europes-covid-19-response.

Fasani, F., and J. Mazza. 2023. "Being on the Frontline? Immigrant Workers in Europe and the COVID-19 Pandemic." *ILR Review* 76 (5): 890–918.

Fernando, N. A., and N. Singh. forthcoming. "Regulation by Reputation? Intermediaries, Labor Abuses and International Migration." *Review of Economics and Statistics.*

Frankel, J. 2010. "Are Bilateral Remittances Countercyclical?" Faculty Working Paper 185, Center for International Development, Harvard Kennedy School, Cambridge, MA. https://www.hks.harvard.edu/sites /default/files/centers/cid/files/publications/faculty-working-papers/185.pdf.

Funkhouser, E. 1995. "Remittances from International Migration: A Comparison of El Salvador and Nicaragua." *Review of Economics and Statistics* 77 (1): 137–46. https://doi.org/10.2307/2109999.

Gedeshi, I., and N. de Zwager. 2012. "Effects of the Global Crisis on Migration and Remittances in Albania." In *Migration and Remittances during the Global Financial Crisis and Beyond,* edited by I. Sirkeci, J. H. Cohen, and D. Ratha, 237–54. Washington, DC: World Bank.

Giannelli, G. C., and L. Mangiavacchi. 2010. "Children's Schooling and Parental Migration: Empirical Evidence of the 'Left Behind' Generation in Albania." Discussion Paper 4888, Institute for the Study of Labor, Bonn. https://docs.iza.org/dp4888.pdf.

Gibson, J., and D. McKenzie. 2014. "The Development Impact of a Best Practice Seasonal Worker Policy." *Review of Economics and Statistics* 96 (2): 229–43.

Gibson, J., D. McKenzie, and B. Zia. 2014. "The Impact of Financial Literacy Training for Migrants." *World Bank Economic Review* 28 (1): 130–61. https://doi.org/10.1093/wber/lhs034.

Grigorian, D. A., and T. A. Melkonyan. 2011. "Destined to Receive: The Impact of Remittances on Household Decisions in Armenia." *Review of Development Economics* 15 (1): 139–53. https://doi.org/10.1111/j.1467-9361 .2010.00598.x.

Gubert, F., and C. J. Nordman. 2011. "Return Migration and Small Enterprise Development in the Maghreb." In *Diaspora for Development in Africa*, edited by S. Plaza and D. Ratha, 103–26. Washington, DC: World Bank. https://www.cbd.int/financial/charity/africa-diasporas.pdf.

Gupta, P. 2006. "Macroeconomic Determinants of Remittances: Evidence from India." *Economic and Political Weekly* 41 (26): 2769–75.

Honorati, M. 2021. *International Migration from Uzbekistan*. Washington, DC: World Bank. https://documents .worldbank.org/curated/en/402861625844540309/International-Migration-from-Uzbekistan.

Honorati, M., and L. Carraro. 2019. *Uzbekistan: Social Assistance Targeting Assessment*. Washington, DC: World Bank. https://documents1.worldbank.org/curated/en/756191577683400252/pdf/Uzbekistan -Social-Assistance-Targeting-Assessment.pdf.

Honorati, M., F. P. Kerschbaumer, and S. Yi. 2019. *Armenia: Better Understanding International Labor Mobility*. Washington, DC: World Bank. https://documents.worldbank.org/curated/en/598211564662844457/Armenia -Better-Understanding-International-Labor-Mobility.

Hooper, K., and C. Le Coz. 2020. "Seasonal Worker Programmes in Europe: Promising Practices and Ongoing Challenges." Brussels: Migration Policy Institute Europe. https://www.migrationpolicy.org/sites/default /files/publications/MPIE-Seasonal-Workers-Policy-Brief-Final.pdf.

International Labour Organization. 1997. "Private Employment Agencies Convention (No. 181)." *NORMLEX*. https://normlex.ilo.org/dyn/normlex/en/f?p=NORMLEXPUB:12100:0::NO:12100:P12100_INSTRUMENT _ID:312326:NO.

INSTAT (Institute of Statistics), IPH (Institute of Public Health), and ICF. 2018. "Albania Demographic and Health Survey 2017–2018." Tirana, Albania: INSTAT, IPH, and ICF. http://dhsprogram.com/pubs/pdf/FR348/FR348.pdf.

IOM (International Organisation for Migration). 2018. "Supporting Safe, Orderly and Dignified Migration through Assisted Voluntary Return and Reintegration." Global Compact Thematic Paper, Assisted Voluntary Return and Reintegration, IOM, Geneva. https://www.iom.int/sites/g/files/tmzbdl486/files/our _work/ODG/GCM/IOM-Thematic-Paper-Assisted-Voluntary-Return-and-Reintegration.pdf.

Jaupart, P. 2019. "No Country for Young Men: International Migration and Left-Behind Children in Tajikistan." *Economics of Transition and Institutional Change* 27 (3): 579–614. https://doi.org/10.1111/ecot.12187.

Justino, P., and O. N. Shemyakina. 2012. "Remittances and Labour Supply in Post-Conflict Tajikistan." *IZA Journal of Labor & Development* 1 (8): 1–28. https://doi.org/10.1186/2193-9020-1-8.

Karymshakov, K., and B. Sulaimanova. 2017. "Migration Impact on Left-Behind Women's Labour Participation and Time-Use Evidence from Kyrgyzstan." Working Paper 2017/119, United Nations University World Institute for Development Economics Research, Helsinki. https://www.wider.unu.edu/sites/default/files /wp2017-119.pdf.

Kilic, T., G. Carletto, B. Davis, and A. Zezza. 2009. "Investing Back Home: Return Migration and Business Ownership in Albania." *Economics of Transition* 17 (3): 587–623.

Killingsworth, M. R. 1983. "Effects of Immigration into the United States on the U.S. Labor Market: Analytical and Policy Issues." In *U.S. Immigration and Refugee Policy: Global and Domestic Issues*, edited by M. M. Kritz, 249–68. Lexington, MA: Lexington Books.

Kroeger, A., and K. H. Anderson. 2014. "Remittances and the Human Capital of Children: New Evidence from Kyrgyzstan during Revolution and Financial Crisis, 2005–2009." *Journal of Comparative Economics* 42 (3): 770–85. https://doi.org/10.1016/j.jce.2013.06.001.

Lafleur, J. M., and D. Vintila, eds. 2020. *Migration and Social Protection in Europe and Beyond (Volume 1): Comparing Access to Welfare Entitlements*. Cham, Switzerland: Springer.

Lucas, R. E., and O. Stark. 1985. "Motivations to Remit: Evidence from Botswana." *Journal of Political Economy* 93 (5): 901–18.

Lueth, E., and M. Ruiz-Arranz. 2007. "Are Workers' Remittances a Hedge against Macroeconomic Shocks? The Case of Sri Lanka." Working Paper 07/22, International Monetary Fund, Washington, DC. https://www .imf.org/external/pubs/ft/wp/2007/wp0722.pdf.

Madiyev, O. 2021. "The Eurasian Economic Union: Repaving Central Asia's Road to Russia?" *Migration Information Source*, February 3, 2021. https://www.migrationpolicy.org/article/eurasian-economic -union-central-asia-russia.

McKenzie, D., J. Gibson, and S. Stillman. 2013. "A Land of Milk and Honey with Streets Paved with Gold: Do Emigrants Have Over-Optimistic Expectations about Incomes Abroad?" *Journal of Development Economics* 102: 116–27. https://doi.org/10.1016/j.jdeveco.2012.01.001.

McKenzie, D., and H. Rapoport. 2011. "Can Migration Reduce Educational Attainment? Evidence from Mexico." *Journal of Population Economics* 24: 1331–58. https://doi.org/10.1007/s00148-010-0316-x.

McKenzie, D., and D. Yang. 2015. "Evidence on Policies to Increase the Development Impacts of International Migration." *World Bank Research Observer* 30 (2): 155–92. https://doi.org/10.1093/wbro/lkv001.

Mendola, M., and G. Carletto. 2012. "Migration and Gender Differences in the Home Labour Market: Evidence from Albania." *Labour Economics* 19 (6): 870–80. https://doi.org/10.1016/j.labeco.2012.08.009.

Miluka, J., G. Carletto, B. Davis, and A. Zezza. 2010. "The Vanishing Farms? The Impact of International Migration on Albanian Family Farming." *Journal of Development Studies* 46 (1): 140–61. https://doi.org/10.1080/00220380903197978.

Mobarak, A. M., I. Sharif, and M. Shrestha. 2023. "Returns to International Migration: Evidence from a Bangladesh-Malaysia Visa Lottery." *American Economic Journal: Applied Economics* 15 (4): 353–88.

Möllers, J., and W. Meyer. 2014. "The Effects of Migration on Poverty and Inequality in Rural Kosovo." *IZA Journal of Labor & Development* 3: 16. https://doi.org/10.1186/2193-9020-3-16.

Moroz, H., M. Shrestha, and M. Testaverde. 2020. "Potential Responses to the COVID-19 Outbreak in Support of Migrant Workers." Living Paper Version 10, World Bank, Washington, DC. https://documents1.worldbank.org/curated/en/428451587390154689/pdf/Potential-Responses-to-the-COVID-19-Outbreak-in-Support-of-Migrant-Workers-June-19-2020.pdf.

Mukomel, V. I., and M. B. Denisenko. 2023. "Foreign Workers in Russia: Employers' Opinions." *Sociologičeskie issledovaniâ* 1: 26–37.

Murakami, E., E. Yamada, and E. P. Sioson. 2021. "The Impact of Migration and Remittances on Labor Supply in Tajikistan." *Journal of Asian Economics* 73: 101268. https://doi.org/10.1016/j.asieco.2020.101268.

National Statistical Committee. 2020. "The Impact of the COVID-19 Pandemic on Households." Bishkek: Government of the Kyrgyz Republic, National Statistical Committee.

Niimi, Y., C. Ozden, and M. Schiff. 2010. "Remittances and the Brain Drain: Skilled Migrants Do Remit Less." *Annals of Economics and Statistics* 97/98: 123–41. https://doi.org/10.2307/41219112.

Odorović, A., G. McKain, K. Garvey, E. Schizas, B. Z. Zhang, P. Rowan, and T. Ziegler. 2020. *FinTech Innovation in the Western Balkans: Policy and Regulatory Implications and Potential Interventions*. Rochester, NY: Social Science Research Network. https://doi.org/10.2139/ssrn.3619214.

OECD (Organisation for Economic Co-operation and Development). 2022. *Labour Migration in the Western Balkans: Mapping Patterns, Addressing Challenges and Reaping Benefits*. Paris: OECD. https://www.oecd.org/south-east-europe/programme/Labour-Migration-report.pdf.

Orrenius, P. M., and M. Zavodny. 2010. "Mexican Immigrant Employment Outcomes over the Business Cycle." *American Economic Review* 100 (2): 316–20. https://doi.org/10.1257/aer.100.2.316.

Patel, K., and F. Vella. 2013. "Immigrant Networks and Their Implications for Occupational Choice and Wages." *Review of Economics and Statistics* 95 (4): 1249–77. https://doi.org/10.1162/REST_a_00327.

Petreski, M. 2019. "Remittances and Labour Supply Revisited: New Evidence from the Macedonian Behavioural Tax and Benefit Microsimulation Model." *Migration Letters* 16 (2): 219–34. https://doi.org/10.33182//ml.v16i2.537.

Piracha, M., and F. Vadean. 2010. "Return Migration and Occupational Choice: Evidence from Albania." *World Development* 38 (8): 1141–55. https://doi.org/10.1016/j.worlddev.2009.12.015.

Poghosyan, T. 2023. "Remittances in Russia and Caucasus and Central Asia: The Gravity Model." *Review of Development Economics* 27 (2): 1224–41. https://doi.org/10.1111/rode.12976.

Pogorevici, C. 2019. "Entrepreneurship in the Republic of Moldova. Challenges and Recommendations." Working Paper, University of Pennsylvania, Wharton School, Philadelphia. https://repository.upenn.edu/handle/20.500.14332/47013.

Rapoport, H. 2002. "Migration, Credit Constraints and Self-Employment: A Simple Model of Occupational Choice, Inequality and Growth." *Economics Bulletin* 15 (7): 1–5.

Rapoport, H., and F. Docquier. 2006. "The Economics of Migrants' Remittances." In *Handbook of the Economics of Giving, Altruism and Reciprocity*, edited by S.-C. Kolm and J. M. Ythier, 1135–98. New York: Elsevier.

Ratha, D. 2003. "Workers' Remittances: An Important and Stable Source of External Development Finance." In *Global Development Finance 2003*, 157–75. Washington, DC: World Bank. https://documents1.worldbank .org/curated/en/698051468128113998/310436360_20050014094932/additional/multiopage.pdf.

Rudi, J. 2014. "Remittances and Labor Supply: The Case of Kosovo." Unpublished working paper, September 2014, PDF. https://bqk-kos.org/repository/docs/2014/Jeta%20Rudi-%20Remittances%20and%20 Labor%20Supply%20The%20Case%20of%20Kosovo%20.pdf.

Ryazantsev, S., Z. Vazirov, M. Khramova, and A. Smirnov. 2020. "The Impact of the COVID-19 Pandemic on the Position of Labor Migrants from Central Asia in Russia." *Central Asia and the Caucasus* 21 (3): 58–70.

Salah, M. A. 2008. "The Impacts of Migration on Children in Moldova." Working Paper, United Nations Children's Fund, Division of Policy and Practice, New York.

Saurav, A. 2017. "Impact of Spousal Migration on Entrepreneurial Activity of Left-Behind Female Spouse: Evidence from Romania." PhD diss., George Washington University, Washington, DC.

Schenk, C. 2018. "Labour Migration in the Eurasian Economic Union." In *Migration and the Ukraine Crisis: A Two-Country Perspective*, edited by A. Pikulicka-Wilczewska and G. Uehling. London: E-International Relations.

Seitz, W. H. 2019. "International Migration and Household Well-Being: Evidence from Uzbekistan." Policy Research Working Paper 8910, World Bank, Washington, DC. https://documents1.worldbank.org/curated /en/615721561125387061/pdf/International-Migration-and-Household-Well-Being-Evidence-from -Uzbekistan.pdf.

Seshan, G., and R. Zubrickas. 2017. "Asymmetric Information about Migrant Earnings and Remittance Flows." *World Bank Economic Review* 31 (1): 24–43. https://doi.org/10.1093/wber/lhv032.

Shrestha, M. 2020. "'Get Rich or Die Tryin': Perceived Earnings, Perceived Mortality Rates, and Migration Decisions of Potential Work Migrants from Nepal." *World Bank Economic Review* 34 (1): 1–27. https://doi .org/10.1093/wber/lhz023.

State Commission on Migration Issues. 2020. *Migration Strategy of Georgia 2021–2030*. Tbilisi: State Commission on Migration Issues. https://migration.commission.ge/files/ms30_eng_web2.pdf.

Testaverde, M., H. Moroz, C. H. Hollweg, and A. Schmillen. 2017. *Migrating to Opportunity: Overcoming Barriers to Labor Mobility in Southeast Asia*. Washington, DC: World Bank. http://hdl.handle.net/10986/28342.

Testaverde, M., and J. Pavilon. 2022. *Building Resilient Migration Systems in the Mediterranean Region: Lessons from COVID-19*. Washington, DC: World Bank. http://hdl.handle.net/10986/37534.

Thieme, S. 2014. "Coming Home? Patterns and Characteristics of Return Migration in Kyrgyzstan." *International Migration* 52 (5): 127–43. https://doi.org/10.5167/uzh-77847.

United Nations. 2018. "Global Compact for Safe, Orderly and Regular Migration." UN General Assembly Resolution A/RES/73/195, 73rd Sess., 60th and 61st Meetings. https://www.un.org/en/development/desa /population/migration/generalassembly/docs/globalcompact/A_RES_73_195.pdf.

World Bank. 2015. *Labor Migration and Welfare in the Kyrgyz Republic (2008–2013)*. Report 99771-KG. Washington, DC: World Bank. https://hdl.handle.net/10986/22960.

World Bank. 2016. *Systematic Country Diagnostic for Eight Small Pacific Island Countries: Priorities for Ending Poverty and Boosting Shared Prosperity*. Washington, DC: World Bank. https://openknowledge.worldbank .org/handle/10986/23952.

World Bank. 2018. *Moving for Prosperity: Global Migration and Labor Markets*. Washington, DC: World Bank. https://doi.org/10.1596/978-1-4648-1281-1.

World Bank. 2019b. *Migration and Brain Drain*. Europe and Central Asia Economic Update (Fall). Washington, DC: World Bank. https://doi.org/10.1596/978-1-4648-1506-5.

Yang, D., and H. Choi. 2007. "Are Remittances Insurance? Evidence from Rainfall Shocks in the Philippines." *World Bank Economic Review* 21 (2): 219–48. https://doi.org/10.1093/wber/lhm003.

Yang, D., and C. Martinez. 2006. "Remittances and Poverty in Migrants' Home Areas: Evidence from the Philippines." In *International Migration, Remittances and the Brain Drain*, edited by C. Ozden and N. Schiff, 81–121. Washington, DC: World Bank.

Zezza, A., G. Carletto, and B. Davis. 2005. "Moving Away from Poverty: A Spatial Analysis of Poverty and Migration in Albania." *Journal of Southern Europe and the Balkans Online* 7 (2): 175–93.

www.ingramcontent.com/pod-product-compliance
Lightning Source LLC
Chambersburg PA
CBHW041239020426
42333CB00002B/16